# Post-Traditional Public Administration Theory

This book describes what is argued to be the most effective way of doing public administration thinking. Its aim is to encourage governments to govern fundamentally better in terms of policy and administration.

A better understanding of context and identities, imaginization, epistemic pluralism, anti-administration, and the context of economics are examples of what is critical for high effectiveness.

The pieces included in this book have been handpicked from the vast academic collection that David John Farmer has authored over the last 30 years and which were published in the *Journal of Administrative Theory and Praxis* and the *Journal of Public Administration Education*. Collectively, these chapters are intended to help governments use post-traditional public administration theory in order to achieve better praxis.

**David John Farmer** is Professor Emeritus of Philosophy and Public Affairs at the School of Government and Public Affairs, Virginia Commonwealth University, USA. He has worked as a budget, an administrative, and an economic analyst. He has provided management consulting services to some twenty U.S. city governments and others. He was Special Assistant to the N.Y.P.D. Police Commissioner and a Division Director in the U.S. Department of Justice.

# Post-Traditional Public Administration Theory
For Better Governmental Praxis

**David John Farmer**

LONDON AND NEW YORK

First published 2021
by Routledge
2 Park Square, Milton Park, Abingdon, Oxon, OX14 4RN

and by Routledge
52 Vanderbilt Avenue, New York, NY 10017

*Routledge is an imprint of the Taylor & Francis Group, an informa business*

Chapters 1–12, 14–33 © 2021 Public Administration Theory Network

Chapter 13 © 2021 Network of Schools of Public Policy, Affairs, and Administration

All rights reserved. No part of this book may be reprinted or reproduced or utilised in any form or by any electronic, mechanical, or other means, now known or hereafter invented, including photocopying and recording, or in any information storage or retrieval system, without permission in writing from the publishers.

*Trademark notice*: Product or corporate names may be trademarks or registered trademarks, and are used only for identification and explanation without intent to infringe.

*British Library Cataloguing-in-Publication Data*
A catalogue record for this book is available from the British Library

ISBN13: 978-0-367-68305-4 (hbk)
ISBN13: 978-1-003-13682-8 (ebk)

Typeset in Times LT Std
by codeMantra

**Publisher's Note**
The publisher accepts responsibility for any inconsistencies that may have arisen during the conversion of this book from journal articles to book chapters, namely the inclusion of journal terminology.

**Disclaimer**
Every effort has been made to contact copyright holders for their permission to reprint material in this book. The publishers would be grateful to hear from any copyright holder who is not here acknowledged and will undertake to rectify any errors or omissions in future editions of this book.

# Contents

*Citation Information* vii

Introduction 1

1 Contemplating Bureaucracies: A Tale of Identities – Essay 4 4

2 In the Pink? 17

3 Contemplating Cops: A Tale of Identities – Essay 1 25

4 Contemplating Cops: A Tale of Identities – Essay 2 40

5 Contemplating Bureaucracies: A Tale of Identities – Essay 3 52

6 Imagine! Preface to the Post-Traditional 65

7 Theorizing in Perspective: Epistemic Pluralism 72

8 The Allure of Rhetoric and the Truancy of Poetry 83

9 Because My Master Bathes Me 111

10 Mapping Anti-Administration: Introduction to the Symposium 139

11 Dogs of War: Fighting Back 157

12 Public Administration in a World of Economics 173

13 Coping With The Super-Abstract: Teaching About the Implications of Postmodernism for Public Administration 185

14 A Conversation Between Song Jinzhou and David John Farmer 197

15 The Ladder of Organization-Think: Beyond Flatland 213

# CONTENTS

16  ~~Red Queen~~                                                                      236

17  Power Speaking v. Speaking to Power: A Discourse War?                              247

18  Fractured Governmentality: A Night in the Emergency Room (E.R.)                    250

19  Froglets or Fairy Tales?                                                           256

20  Tonto and the Lone Ranger: Concepts Reveal, Concepts Mask                          259

21  Expanding the Ethical Sphere                                                       267

22  Medusa: Helene Cixous and the Writing of Laughter                                  273

23  Somatic Writing: Attending to Our Bodies                                           287

24  Silence                                                                            305

25  Power of Refusal: Introduction to the Symposium                                    312

26  Anti-Admin: With Help from Herbert Marcuse                                         322

27  Love and Un-Engineering                                                            327

28  The Devil's Rope                                                                   339

29  Frigginomics Begins in Kindergarten: The Social Construction of "Normal"
    Citizens and Their Dreams                                                          345

30  Wal-Mart®: Neo-Feudal (K)Night?                                                    357

31  Change the Course, Neurons!                                                        371

32  The Spirit of Our Age: PA-think as Uncovering                                      382

33  A Dancing Star: Arguments From Imagination                                         391

    *Index*                                                                            405

# Citation Information

The following chapters, except Chapter 13, were originally published in the *Administrative Theory & Praxis*. Chapter 13 was originally published in the *Journal of Public Administration Education*. When citing this material, please use the original journal information and page numbering for each article, as follows:

## Chapter 1
*Contemplating Bureaucracies: A Tale of Identities – Essay 4*
David John Farmer
*Administrative Theory & Praxis,* volume 40, issue 1 (2018) pp. 83–95

## Chapter 2
*In the Pink?*
David John Farmer
*Administrative Theory & Praxis,* volume 25, issue 3 (2003) pp. 419–426

## Chapter 3
*Contemplating Cops: A Tale of Identities – Essay 1*
David John Farmer
*Administrative Theory & Praxis,* volume 39, issue 2 (2017) pp. 142–156

## Chapter 4
*Contemplating Cops: A Tale of Identities – Essay 2*
David John Farmer
*Administrative Theory & Praxis,* volume 39, issue 3 (2017) pp. 240–251

## Chapter 5
*Contemplating Bureaucracies: A Tale of Identities – Essay 3*
David John Farmer
*Administrative Theory & Praxis,* volume 39, issue 4 (2017) pp. 331–343

## Chapter 6
*Imagine! Preface to the Post-Traditional*
David John Farmer
*Administrative Theory & Praxis,* volume 28, issue 2 (2006) pp. 169–175

**Chapter 7**
*Theorizing in Perspective: Epistemic Pluralism*
David John Farmer
*Administrative Theory & Praxis,* volume 34, issue 2 (2012) pp. 180–190

**Chapter 8**
*The Allure of Rhetoric and the Truancy of Poetry*
David John Farmer
*Administrative Theory & Praxis,* volume 25, issue 1 (2003) pp. 9–36

**Chapter 9**
*Because My Master Bathes Me*
David John Farmer
*Administrative Theory & Praxis,* volume 25, issue 2 (2003) pp. 205–232

**Chapter 10**
*Mapping Anti-Administration: Introduction to the Symposium*
David John Farmer
*Administrative Theory & Praxis,* volume 23, issue 4 (2001) pp. 475–492

**Chapter 11**
*Dogs of War: Fighting Back*
David John Farmer
*Administrative Theory & Praxis,* volume 37, issue 4 (2015) pp. 252–267

**Chapter 12**
*Public Administration in a World of Economics*
David John Farmer
*Administrative Theory & Praxis,* volume 32, issue 3 (2010) pp. 373–384

**Chapter 13**
*Coping With The Super-Abstract: Teaching About the Implications of Postmodernism for Public Administration*
David John Farmer
*Journal of Public Administration Education,* volume 1, issue 2 (1995) pp. 90–101

**Chapter 14**
*A Conversation Between Song Jinzhou and David John Farmer*
David John Farmer
*Administrative Theory & Praxis,* volume 31, issue 2 (2009) pp. 266–281

**Chapter 15**
*The Ladder of Organization-Think: Beyond Flatland*
David John Farmer
*Administrative Theory & Praxis,* volume 22, issue 1 (2000) pp. 66–88

## Chapter 16
*Red Queen*
David John Farmer
*Administrative Theory & Praxis*, volume 29, issue 3 (2007) pp. 359–369

## Chapter 17
*Power Speaking v. Speaking to Power: A Discourse War?*
David John Farmer
*Administrative Theory & Praxis*, volume 21, issue 2 (1999) pp. 240–242

## Chapter 18
*Fractured Governmentality: A Night in the Emergency Room (E.R.)*
David John Farmer
*Administrative Theory & Praxis*, volume 23, issue 2 (2001) pp. 293–298

## Chapter 19
*Froglets or Fairy Tales?*
David John Farmer
*Administrative Theory & Praxis*, volume 21, issue 1 (1999) pp. 154–156

## Chapter 20
*Tonto and the Lone Ranger: Concepts Reveal, Concepts Mask*
David John Farmer
*Administrative Theory & Praxis*, volume 23, issue 3 (2001) pp. 459–466

## Chapter 21
*Expanding the Ethical Sphere*
David John Farmer
*Administrative Theory & Praxis*, volume 25, issue 1 (2003) pp. 137–142

## Chapter 22
*Medusa: Helene Cixous and the Writing of Laughter*
David John Farmer
*Administrative Theory & Praxis*, volume 23, issue 4 (2001) pp. 559–572

## Chapter 23
*Somatic Writing: Attending to Our Bodies*
David John Farmer
*Administrative Theory & Praxis*, volume 23, issue 2 (2001) pp. 187–204

## Chapter 24
*Silence*
David John Farmer
*Administrative Theory & Praxis*, volume 26, issue 3 (2004) pp. 438–444

**Chapter 25**
*Power of Refusal: Introduction to the Symposium*
David John Farmer
*Administrative Theory & Praxis,* volume 25, issue 2 (2003) pp. 173–182

**Chapter 26**
*Anti-Admin: With Help from Herbert Marcuse*
David John Farmer
*Administrative Theory & Praxis,* volume 21, issue 4 (1999) pp. 497–501

**Chapter 27**
*Love and Un-Engineering*
David John Farmer
*Administrative Theory & Praxis,* volume 24, issue 2 (2002) pp. 369–380

**Chapter 28**
*The Devil's Rope*
David John Farmer
*Administrative Theory & Praxis,* volume 24, issue 4 (2002) pp. 781–786

**Chapter 29**
*Frigginomics Begins in Kindergarten: The Social Construction of "Normal" Citizens and Their Dreams*
David John Farmer
*Administrative Theory & Praxis,* volume 27, issue 4 (2005) pp. 707–718

**Chapter 30**
*Wal-Mart®: Neo-Feudal (K)Night?*
David John Farmer
*Administrative Theory & Praxis,* volume 28, issue 1 (2006) pp. 148–161

**Chapter 31**
*Change the Course, Neurons!*
David John Farmer
*Administrative Theory & Praxis,* volume 29, issue 1 (2007) pp. 182–192

**Chapter 32**
*The Spirit of Our Age: PA-think as Uncovering*
David John Farmer
*Administrative Theory & Praxis,* volume 28, issue 3 (2006) pp. 465–473

**Chapter 33**
*A Dancing Star: Arguments From Imagination*
David John Farmer
*Administrative Theory & Praxis,* volume 27, issue 2 (2005) pp. 413–425

For any permission-related enquiries please visit:
http://www.tandfonline.com/page/help/permissions

# Introduction

Post-traditional Public Administration (P.A.) is worth contemplating because it can help in devising ways to nudge government to govern fundamentally better in terms of policy and administration. The following articles – chosen from among the 40 or so articles I have written over the years for the *Journal of Administrative Theory & Praxis* – are intended to help. Additionally, there is one article from the *Journal of Public Administration Education*.

Chapter 1. I suggest contemplation both about the theory and praxis of P.A. and government ("praxis" being practice as distinguished from theory), and about the nature and context of the reader's own reflection and praxis related to P.A. and government. This contemplation can be considered as impacting the reader's own identity and thus the reader's way of thinking. For example, identities include factors such as job history (e.g., being a detective in Montana for ten years v. being a police chief in three departments), educational background (e.g., having a doctorate in history v. a bachelor's degree), and even being a child long before or long after certain inventions that have changed lives radically – credit cards (1950), laptop (1982), mobile phone (1947), robot (1921), television (1925), etc. Both analysis (of P.A. and Govt.) and self-analysis (by the reader) can be helpful, even in an occupation that can be misunderstood as limited to the mechanical and the traditional.

Chapters 1 and 2. Encountering or Re-encountering the Post-traditional hopefully can encourage the reader to think what can be learned about the post-traditional from her own theoretical and praxis identities and experiences. It is neither necessary nor desirable to suppose that governance and bureaucracy should be described in terms of (in opposition to, as a supplement to) traditional thinking. If you like a more difficult claim, you could speak in the same way that Jean Francois Lyotard speaks of the postmodern as preceding the modern. To make a more helpful analogy when exploring physics, it is neither necessary nor desirable to start with alchemy. Reflecting on her own theoretical experiences when reading the two articles, the reader should not be limited to her own reflections. For example, the reader may wish to stress opportunities for post-traditional P.A. thinking beyond those offered a few years ago. The reader might (or might not) agree that a problem with both democratic and non-democratic governments is that the focus is too much on the present. For one thing, the reader's contemplation of the future might look to the radical developments expected for Artificial and Decision Intelligence, perhaps developing a new global underclass.

> Artificial intelligence is already here … It is the quiet backbone of our financial systems, the power grid, and the retail supply chain … In the United States, Google, Amazon, Apple, IBM, Microsoft and Facebook are hamstrung by the relentless short-term demands of capitalistic society, while in China, Baidu, Alibaba and Tencent are fueling the government's authoritarian ambitions (Webb, 2019, pp. 2 & 4).

The reader may suppose that the future should look to the relative disadvantages of entities like surveillance capitalism: do you doubt that corporations obtain even more data from customers' cell phones – and they will acquire even more? "Are we all going to be working for a smart machine, or will we have smart people around the machine?" (Zuboff, 2019, p. 3): "It was the best of times, it was the worst of times" (Dickens, 1839/1040, p. 1). It is a positive environment; it is a negative environment.

Chapters 3, 4, 5. Encountering or Re-encountering Traditional Praxis, the reader should also analyze her own theoretical and praxis experiences. But aren't there parts of Post-traditional P.A. thinking that are obviously useful. For instance, I advocated epistemic pluralism for P.A. I illustrated what I advocated could be learned about P.A. from 11 perspectives – from a traditional, a business, an economic, a political, a critical theory, a post-structural, a psychoanalytic, a neuroscience, a feminist, an ethical, and a data perspective. I also explained how what is learned by the 11 perspectives could be synthesized for different purposes – for P.A. planning, for P.A. managing, for what underlies P.A., for the P.A. field, for imaginative creativity, and for P.A. as a whole. Again, the reader should not be limited in her thinking. For example, some might favor what is often called transdisciplinarity – or in the importance of this or that perspective. For instance, economics has such a connection with (say) mathematics, but the reader might wonder if that adds more authority rather than insight. However, some readers may wish to utilize and apply thinking from Jean Piaget and others (see Wikipedia on *Transdisciplinarity*), viewing transdisciplinarity as more complex and abstract than multidisciplinarity, pluridisciplinarity, cross-disciplinarity, and interdisciplinarity. When working on contemplating cops and contemplating bureaucracies, often the theoretical approaches are profoundly limiting – e.g., supposing that administration is a science even if it is basically limited to one culture.

Chapters 6–32. The reader should continue contemplation on the nature and context of Post-traditional P.A. approaches, and on the relevance of the reader's own thinking and the context of that thinking. The section also includes supplementary chapters, where the reader might be challenged to notice their immediate connection with the post-traditional. Dear reader, please enjoy!

I remain a supporter (surprise!) of Post-traditional P.A., even though my academic titles (part of context) moved away toward Political Science and Public Administration and then to Philosophy and Public Affairs. I also authored a book arguing that government should be nudged to govern fundamentally better in terms of policy. The book's title is *Beyond Public Administration: Contemplating and Nudging Government-in-Context*. It claims that the scope of government should include the public sector but also the impacting context of significant parts of the private sector. The powerfully constricting contextual feature is the mal trinity of infiltration, exfiltration, and post-truth. And the book offers a four-stage plan to start addressing the mal-trinity. Infiltration into government includes the entry and access by big money, big corporations, and billionaires. The middle- and lower- income classes are being exfiltrated as a result of free market theory and corporate and big money involvement in government – and by government involvement with big business. Post-truth thoughts, beliefs, and actions shape public understandings. As President Kennedy remarked

> For the great enemy of the truth is very often not the lie – deliberate, contrived and dishonest – but the myth, persistent, persuasive and unrealistic ... Mythology distracts us everywhere – in government as in business, in politics and in economics (Kennedy, 1962).

### Chapter 33. Continuing Reflection

A Dancing Star: Arguments From Imagination. (Published online 2014) (2005)

And for readers who want to reflect even more about Post-traditional P.A., here are two books on the topic.

Farmer, David John (2005). *To Kill the King: Post-Traditional Governance and Bureaucracy.* M.E. Sharpe: Armonk, New York.

Farmer, David John (2010). *Public Administration in Perspective: Theory and Practice Through Multiple Lenses.* M.E. Sharpe: Armonk, New York.

For readers wanting to reflect more also about Post-modernism, the following book is also available:

Farmer, David John (1995). *The Language of Public Administration: Bureaucracy, Modernity, and Postmodernity.* The University of Alabama Press: Tuscaloosa and London.

## References

Dickens, C. (1859). A Tale of Two Cities. Chapman and Hill; London, England.
Kennedy, J. (1962). Commencement Address at Yale University, June 11, New Haven, Connecticut.
Webb, A. (2019). The Big Nine: How the Tech Titans and Their Thinking Machines Could Warp Humanity. Public Affairs; New York, New York.
Zuboff, S. (2019). The Age of Surveillance Capitalism: The Fight for a Human Future at the New Frontier of Human Power. Hacette of Book Group. New York, New York.

# Contemplating Bureaucracies: A Tale of Identities – Essay 4

## David John Farmer

"It was the best of times, it was the worst of times, it was the age of wisdom, it was the age of foolishness" (Dickens, 1859/1940, p. 1), it was the age of wave-particle duality, the age of the uncertainty principle (Ford, 2011, p. 2), it was the epoch of the post-traditional, it was the epoch of the business entrepreneur as hero. This fourth essay aims for the creation of an ever-upgrading post-traditional consciousness that can revitalize governance and bureaucracy. To the reader, it recommends prefacing contemplating bureaucracies by contemplating the post-traditional. This essay discusses, in turn, the traditional and the post-traditional in terms of my identity as a professor, and offers suggestions for the reader to contemplate the post-traditional. It follows Essay 3, which contemplated traditional American and traditional foreign kinds of bureaucratic practice. Contemplating Cops (in Essays 1 and 2) preceded this continued contemplation of bureaucracies.

I have participated in traditional public administration as a user and in post-traditional public administration as a contributor. These terms, "user" and "contributor," overlap somewhat. The using has to include interpreting the traditional for others, including bureaucracies, and contributing has to utilize the giant steps that others have made. I have done so when my identity as a professor has shifted to some extent. For instance, the university adjusted my title post-1991 to "public administration" and post-2011 to "philosophy and public affairs." Also, there have been other shifts in many universities, where there now seem to be many more well-paid administrators eager to gain ever more customer-students.

Readers may wish to consider how useful—or not—post-traditional public administration is for contemplating the usual public bureaucracies. Those who are professors may wish to evaluate their own work identities within their university bureaucracies. For instance, to what extent is your perspective facilitated or diminished by the heavy reliance on disciplinary specialization—running against the idea, for instance, of epistemic pluralism. Especially before attaining tenure, work identity at universities is frequently unfortunately restrictive in terms of disciplinary boundaries. An academic paper outside of the boundary may not even be counted, and the old saying (I don't know if it is true) is that "a dean can count but s/he cannot read." (After the long wait for the final promotion, there may be even less eagerness to step outside the well-trodden zone.) However, and as noted in Essay 2, I usually taught one course per semester out of my title area, e.g., political theory (usually ancient and medieval) and economics. And I recall the way that one of my deans, who was an economist, would speak to me in a friendly way about "our science." Yes, a university identity is freeing; but could it be even more free? Maybe readers might wish to examine the impact of their contexts on their university identities.

This essay is divided into three sections: "Traditional," "Post-Traditional," and "Contemplating the Post-Traditional."

## TRADITIONAL

Traditional or modern(ist) or mainstream public administration achieved, in my view, both good (and bad) results. The impetus to public administration practice has also been sometimes positive but also constricted. As I wrote of modernist public administration in *The Language of Public Administration*

> Modernist Public Administration is valuable, yet limiting. The public administration literature grows larger and stronger, but it is limited as an explanatory and catalytic force in resolving the problems of bureaucracy .... As a matter of history, public administration has gone from an early optimism about reform and about establishing a science to (or perhaps through) a period of concern about an identity crisis, a crisis about the nature of public administration. (Farmer, 1995, p. 34)

Variations are indeed available in traditional public administration, no less than in post-traditional, views. For one example of the traditional, a loose liaison can be, and has been, made in many academic programs between public administration and public policy and/or political science. But such marriages are not always straightforward. The situation is yet more complex in two respects. First, compelling arguments exist denying that public administration (or political science or public policy) is a science: a student would have to understand epistemology to know why. Second, some "disciplines" are even narrower than public administration. In terms of subject, some limit the subjects to particular program areas, e.g., police policy and administration. Public administration has no such "one-policy-program" limitation: yet it is constricted by limits (noticed at the beginning of Essay 3) like that of the signature dichotomy and constricted macro practicality (noticed later).

The history of traditional American public administration can be described in terms of a profusion on the surface of pre-paradigms (pre-paradigms because they are not scientific paradigms), and these can be (and have been) ordered—to give, at a minimum, the impression of orderly progress. Relying on Stillman (1991) and others, I (2010, pp. 20–23) have described examples of such orderings in terms of periods:

1. Before World War II
2. Human relations
3. Post–World War II challenge to POSDCORB (planning, organizing, staffing, directing, coordinating, reporting, budgeting)

4. Heterodoxy
5. Oppositional emphasis in 1960s and 1970s
6. New Public Management
7. Pluralist or disconnect

Other "prettified" versions of ordering are also noted (e.g., McCurdy, 1972):

1. Administrative reform movement (1870–1926)
2. Orthodox period: administrative science movement (1906–1952)
3. Politics period (1935–1967)
4. Human relations and behavioral science (1933–present)
5. Program effectiveness (1964–present)

"Ideas about public administration that jelled into an identifiable field of study have, by and large, reflected the particular contours of state developments in the United States," claims Stillman (1991, p. 105).

I was a user of traditional public administration when I worked for the Saskatchewan (1960–1961) and the Ontario governments (1962–1965), for Public Administration Service (1965–1970), for The Jacobs Company (1970–1971), for the New York City Police Department (1971–1974), for the National Institute of Justice (1974–1980), and for Virginia Commonwealth University (1980–1991). See the descriptions in the earlier essays. Clearly, my identity—during all these periods—embraced traditional public administration. But eventually there came a recognition of limitations.

Let me explain. Later study (referenced in Essay 2) at the University of Virginia (UVA) for my Ph.D. in philosophy took place when I was chair of the Department of Administration of Justice and Public Safety at Virginia Commonwealth University (1983–1991), adding to my Ph.D. in economics from the University of London. This study of philosophy awakened me—with a jolt—to the inadequacy of traditional public administration. The jolt was accidental in the sense that it arose as a side-effect in my mind: and I am not suggesting that any of the philosophy professors had any interest or knowledge of public administration. The chief joys experienced at UVA's Corcoran Department of Philosophy included studying the ancient Greeks and writing a master's thesis on "Aristotle: Persistence of Matter." Chief joys also included studying modern philosophers (the "usual suspects") and writing a dissertation and a book on *Time and McTaggart's Paradox*. The jolt came when, for one of my last classes, I enrolled for an evening seminar with Richard Rorty, a distinguished philosopher located from 1982 to 1988 in the English Department at UVA. Incidentally, I read his *Philosophy and the Mirror of Nature*. But what staggered me about this class on the later Freud was focusing on the works of the French postmodernists—like Jacques Derrida, Michel Foucault, Jean Baudrillard, Gilles Deleuze, and Félix Guattari. So began that direction in my reading. And, when I shifted to VCU's Graduate Department of Public Administration on an affiliate basis in 1986 and on a full-time basis in 1991, I began to write my 1995 book titled *The Language of Public Administration: Bureaucracy, Modernity, and Postmodernity*. It analyzes the public administration dialect of modernity—discussing the limits of particularism, of scientism, of technologism, of enterprise, and of hermeneutics. Then it analyzes the dialect of postmodernity—of imagination, of deconstruction, of deterritorialization, and of alterity. The book's epilogue comments that the aim in studying "the postmodern and modern frameworks [was] to struggle away from a unidimensional and distorted understanding of public bureaucracy and public administration" (Farmer, 1995, p. 146).

## POST-TRADITIONAL

Post-traditional public administration theory seeks imaginization, and it includes not only the postmodern but also other elements like epistemic pluralism, critical theory, ethics, philosophy, neuroscience, and economics – transforming the traditional, the mainstream. This section notes my activity as a contributor. The post-traditional (like the traditional) does underscore that it is important to recognize that our identity and context shape what we know and what "knowing" means. It is no less important to appreciate what they shape us not to know.

### Imaginization

Post-traditional public administration theory aims for contemplation/imaginization of bureaucracies and all that constitutes the identity and context of governance bureaucracies. This requires radical and challenging changes. Don't worry that this sounds impractical; the 9/11 National Commission on Terrorist Attacks upon the United States recommended that "it is therefore crucial to find a way of routinizing, even bureaucratizing, the exercise of imagination" (9/11 Commission, 2004, p. 344). As explained in *To Kill the King*, "Imagine imagination pervading all of governance for all major aims, as much as for government outwitting terrorism. Imagine that an adequate sense of imagination is more than merely connecting dots. What would be required for such a reign of imagination? I suggest that this rule of imagination requires post-traditional governance and bureaucracy" (Farmer, 2005, p. xi). It also quotes another claim by the 9/11 National Commission (2004, p. 344): that "imagination is not a gift usually associated with bureaucracies."

I explain post-traditional imaginization as including thinking as play, justice as seeking, and practice as art (Farmer, 2005) – and six chapters are devoted to discussing each. Such activities are intended to refer both to bureaucracy and also to the context of bureaucracy and the identity of bureaucrats and others. For instance, part of the context of governance is not only the state of the public sector but also of the private sector, and shortly we will again comment on the aggressive or warlike character of what I and others would call the religion of the free market that is part of the private sector context. This religion of free enterprise is what is added, as an extension of the Dickensian quote in the first sentence, as "the epoch of the business entrepreneur as hero." The first aim of these three elements of imaginization, as is explained in the book's preface, is a new consciousness. The second is that the subjects transcend current disciplinary constraints.

I have advocated this major aim of imaginization throughout my contributions toward the post-traditional. Consider the discussions of imaginization in Farmer (1995, chap. 10) and Farmer (2010, chap, 17), The first of these chapters begins:

> *Imaginization. To imaginize. Imaginization* suggests a divergence from Weber's notion of the primary characteristic of modernity, a divergence from rationalization. The departure does not mean that reason should be banished.... What it is intended to suggest is that modernity's

autonomous spheres implode and as the aesthetic, the scientific, and the normative lose their exclusive internal logics, *imaginization* should be a dominating part of the new thinking and action dynamic.... . *Imaginization* would have a parallel pervasive and catalytic effect on society in postmodernity. (Farmer, 1995, p. 158)

The second of the chapters begins:

What can we learn about imaginative creativity? What should we learn about imaginative creativity in public administration from synthesizing, in its complexity, the implications of its multiple perspectives? *Imagine*. Public administration should adopt a strategy to seek and to use imaginative creativity, both extraordinary and ordinary, in both theorizing and practice. Two levels of creativity are distinguished in creativity studies in neuroscience and elsewhere. Extraordinary creativity can be understood as the imaginative activity that is required for the equivalent of paradigm shifting. Ordinary creativity can be described as the imaginative activity that is required for problem solving capable of resolving puzzles within an orthodox framework. (Farmer, 2010, p. 211)

The post-traditional should indeed include postmodern understandings (such as those offered by Jacques Derrida about deconstruction and Michel Foucault about the relationship of truth and power). It should also benefit from epistemic pluralism that includes not only the postmodern but also non-postmodern insights from disciplines like critical theory, psychoanalysis, and philosophy.

The non-work elements of identity can be expected to influence a reader's reaction to the significance of imaginization in the public workplace. I imagine that even a few clerical or routine workers – say, at a post office or a prison – have overcome unconscious inhibitions against valuing imaginization: and others have not. Similarly, even a few professors can have such unconscious inhibitions: and others do not. That person when a child might, or might not, have been prompted toward the imaginative through parental encouragement or through love of playing in one's spare time (say) jazz or Beethoven. Of the several childhood sources of my pro attitude toward imaginization, one surely could have been the inclusion of chess-playing in my childhood: a player since the age of ten, I won school championships and later was president of the L.S.E. chess club and a player for the University of London. While an entirely rational game, playing at an advanced level typically requires the involvement of the imagination – and, speaking at a much higher level of playing, Kasparov (2007, p. 60) explained that "In chess, we have a name for the sort of imagination required to break out of the usual patterns and startle our opponents; we call it fantasy" – although I prefer a better word. About the same age, astronomy and star gazing – along with reading about archaeology - consumed a lot of my spare time. My father, working for the research and development section of an airplane company, was also a positive factor encouraging imaginative perspectives: I loved seeing the Bristol Brabazon fly, a huge airplane that used (I was told) a specially-built one and three-quarter mile runway for its maiden flight. I can see that studying Latin (as it embraces the distant past) and taking long walks several times per week into the countryside (as it embraces nature) can incline a person to the pro side. I can see that playing rugby, although it was a necessity where I went to secondary school, could be on the con side. But it need not start until later. Shouldn't we advocate that our graduate students in Public Administration should take a Quantum Physics 101 class – to learn how inconsistent its exhilarating central ideas are to what counts as common sense?

Or should we advocate the utility of hobbies in neuroscience or psychology – as stimulants for valuing the imaginative?

The post-traditional, like most topics, including the traditional, does not arrive complete and inviting no additions and subtractions; so adjustments would be natural over the years, and they should be hoped for in the future. In *To Kill the King* (Farmer, 2005, pp. 49–53), for example, I described three periods—what I called my pale white, green, and pink periods. "In my white period I was a technicist and I celebrated traditional theories .... I was also impressed by the power of commonsense rules of thumb" (Farmer, 2005, p. 49). In the green period, I did feel "a need for thinking to probe deeper under the surface about society and governance, and to shift toward a more philosophical perspective" (Farmer, 2005, p. 53). My pink period was when I focused on post-traditional governance and bureaucracy, the sub-title of my 2005 book. Looking back at Farmer (1995), later I reported writing too much in deference to technicism and use-value. Rather than three periods, I later thought it would be better to speak in terms of two periods—accepting that there are varieties in each period. As here, they could be called traditional and post-traditional. But I have little doubt that the imaginization will identify additional help and insights as capability and policy needs develop and change—the capability of using Big Data or perhaps the policy need of "policing" the Internet, and so on. For instance, I remember writing only one paper about the relevance of Big Data.

Talking about contributing to post-traditional public administration, the next sub-section indicates the extent and character of my public administration theorizing over the years in terms of three books, some sixty articles, and some forty presentations. In doing this I enjoyed support from many members of the Public Administration Theory Network (PATNet) and other organizations. I was pleased when *ATP* republished my article "The Allure of Rhetoric and the Truancy of Poetry" (Farmer, 2003b,) in *A Virtual Issue Celebrating 35 Years of Administrative Theory and Praxis: Ground-Breaking Research from the Archives of ATP*. On a much lesser level, earlier I was given a Distinguished Scholar Award by my university's College of Humanities and Sciences (1999).

## Contributing Books, Papers, and Presentations

Three of my seven books were intended to contribute to public administration theorizing. The first, as just described, was *The Language of Public Administration*. It was also subsequently translated and published in Korean and in Chinese. The second was *To Kill the King: Post-Traditional Governance and Bureaucracy* (Farmer, 2005). To repeat, it advocated thoughts on how traditional public administration theory could be developed to the level of the post-traditional. The third was *Public Administration in Perspective: Theory and Practice Through Multiple Perspectives* (Farmer, 2010). This book describes and analyzes epistemic pluralism. It shows how public administration could be upgraded by data from eleven perspectives—from the perspectives of traditional public administration, of business, of economics, of politics, of critical theory, of poststructuralism, of neuroscience, of psychoanalysis, of feminism, of ethics, and of a data perspective. It explains how these inputs could be synthesized.

More than sixty of my eighty-five or so peer-reviewed academic papers have analyzed different aspects of liberating public administration theory away from its traditional shackles. The titles of some of these papers are listed in the references – e.g., Farmer (2001a;

2001b; 2002; 2003a; 2008a; 2012; 2015a). More may be found on the Internet at www.people.vcu.edu/~dfarmer/pubs.htm or at David John Farmer Wiki, by clicking references 2. Some ideas were constant during the twenty or so years during which these papers and books were written; for example, the idea borrowed and developed from Wittgenstein and others to the effect that "the limits of my language mean the limits of my world" (Wittgenstein, 1922, #5.6). But I don't suppose—not for a second—that none of my ideas changed and developed; and that nothing new was added. For example, my appreciation and understanding of the practical significance of neuroscience came later in articles, such as "Toward Epistemic Pluralism and Neuroscience" (Farmer & Farmer, 2012), "Neuro-Gov: Neuroscience as Catalyst" (Farmer, 2008b), "Change the Course, Neurons" (Farmer, 2006), and my book *Public Administration in Perspective* (Farmer, 2010, pp. 115–127).

The shackles of traditional public administration have been described in various writings, e.g., some in Out of the Fly-Bottle: A Post-Script on Post-Traditional Public Administration (Farmer, 2016, pp. 90–102). The sample of such shackles can be re-visited (as illustrated in the next three paragraphs) in terms of misjudgments. But there are others, e.g., misjudgment (as just noted) in failing to recognize the implications of Wittgenstein's and Derrida's claims about the constraining nature of language.

Misjudgment failing to recognize the relatively greater importance of the macro is but one of the constraints in traditional public administration. This is the case in public administration teaching in many universities because most students are not high-level bureaucrats. It privileges obvious practicality in terms of results, to what existing practitioners—again, the majority of whom are lower and mid-level practitioners—recognize as practical. In *Public Administration in Perspective* (Farmer, 2010, pp. 230–233), this emphasis on micro practicality is discussed in more detail—by contrasting unexamined and examined experience, by distinguishing common sense and good sense. Yes, public administration rightly recognizes (and so do I) the learning benefit in lived experience. But there are negative side-effects from mislearning, as is indicated in the extensive literature on different kinds of experienced realities, such as what Ursula Franklin (1990) describes as vernacular, constructed (reconstructed), and projected realities.

Recall another misjudgment–the shackle of the signature dichotomy in public administration promoted by Woodrow Wilson and others. Faced with a problematic bureaucracy, it is understakable that a politician like President Wilson would want to keep his subordinate and ill-organized bureaucrats out of political science; an unkind person might think that it is reasonable for a gentleman to want better "butlers" of all kinds. The identity of American public administration practice (as well as traditional theory) suffers from the constraint of the wall between public administration and public policy, wanting only neutral public administration. One might object to the dominant role in public policy of business and money.

Such a neutral public administration identity can indeed be a shackle. My neutral identity, when it was traditional, constricted me from recognizing the kind of thoughts that I advocated in "Dogs of War: Fighting Back," an article which "argues that public administration should focus on fighting back against the *American business model* (ABM), which currently limits the world of the public sector and public administration" (Farmer, 2015b, p. 252). Noting Justice Lewis Powell's twenty-five action points for the American Chamber of Commerce, my argument was that the ABM was more than a mere model; in fact, it was part of an anti-government fighting plan. Returning to the post-traditional emphasis on governance (rather than the narrower notion of government), should not public administration become involved in the private-enterprise context of government and fight back? This "Dogs of War" article—citing economists like Chang (2014), who argues that economics is too important to be left only to professional economists—recommends that post-traditional public administration thinkers should also become engaged in economics. Opening a door in the boundary wall dividing public administration and public policy surely could help in recognizing the character of the claims about the virtues of that hypothetical item called the "free market."

A main outlet (and resource) in my public administration thinking has been the Public Administration Theory Network—and, to mention it for the second time, its excellent journal. I was (and still am) a member of the editorial boards of the following public administration journals:

*Administrative Theory and Praxis,*
*Administration and Society,*
*Public Voices,*
*Employee Responsibilities and Rights,* and
*Public Administration Quarterly.*

I was a reviewer for each of these five journals and for others, like *International Journal of Organization Theory and Behavior* (IJOTB). I have also been published in the *Chinese Journal of Public Administration, the International Journal of Public Administration, Journal of Management History, American Behavioral Scientist, Journal of Organizational Change Management*, and *Journal of Public Administration Education*.

By contrast, my book *Crime Control: The Use and Misuse of Police Resources* (1984), the seven or so articles and fifteen or so professional presentations (see Essay 2 on contemplating cops) on police management were in the spirit of traditional public administration. Yes, police administrative and policymaking reforms were recommended. But there was no postmodern or other elements of post-traditional public administration "reform" proposed in my police book, academic articles, and presentations.

Let us return to a description of the contribution to post-traditional public administration theory. Some forty presentations were also made at annual conferences of the Public Administration Theory Network and at other conferences like those on teaching public administration of the American Society for Public Administration, of the American Political Science Association, of the City University of Hong Kong. of the Lomonosov Moscow State University, of the American Association of Public Policy Analysis and Management, of the Virginia Political Scientists, of the International Conference of the International Association of Business Disciplines, and of the Society for the Psychoanalysis of Society and Culture. This does not include talks about police (in the period 1980–1991), about philosophy, and about economics.

## CONTEMPLATING THE POST-TRADITIONAL

Contemplating the post-traditional is what is recommended as a preface for contemplating bureaucracies. The traditional method of explaining the post-traditional would be to describe the key concepts and to note how they can upgrade public administration practice. This is available to the reader from a reading of the three books noted earlier, *The Language of Public Administration, To Kill the King,* and *Public Administration in Perspective.* Such a reader might choose (or not choose) to read first each of the prefaces and chapters.

Information in the three books can be helpful in analyzing the validity and relevance of the post-traditional claims. For instance, recall the earlier claim from the first book (Farmer, 1995, p. ix) that traditional public administration is hampered by its limited self-conception and constructed mind-set. Consider such a claim in light of discussion in the chapters on psychoanalysis and neuroscience in the third book. The first chapter explains how "common sense planning—for the discipline, for theorizing, and for practice—is socially constructed and limited by unconscious facts; the point is that unanalyzed common sense may or may not be harmful to such planning" (Farmer, 1995, pp. 106–107). The third book discusses how neuroscience changes understandings about how and why the self thinks, feels and behaves—the self at the center of public administration managing. It gives reasons for supposing that it is a no-brainer for public administration (concerned with getting things done through people) should embrace the brain. "[N]euroscience makes it clear that it is false to think that humans are thinking beings who have emotions. Rather we are emotional beings who have thoughts. Barring brain injury or malformation, a non-emotional human moment is a fiction" (Farmer, 2010, pp. 122–124).

Rather than this traditional reading approach, another possibility is for the reader to start applying, and trying out, post-traditional thinking. This alternative could be especially helpful if the reader's identity and context includes commitment to traditional public administration's notions about practice. The choice of concepts could include the following that occur in my books and articles:

Thinking as play (Book, 2005)
Unconscious (Book, 1995)
Ethics as seeking (Book, 2005)
Deconstruction (Books, 1995 and 2010)
Practice as art (Book, 2005)
Arborescence (Book, 1995)
Epistemic pluralism (Book, 2010)
Critical theory (Book, 2010)
Dogs of war (Article, 2015)
Neuro-Gov. (Article, 2008)
Un-engineering (Article, 2002)
Power (Article, 2003)
Anti-administration (Article, 2001)
Postmodernism (Article, 2001)
The practicality of poetry (Article, 2015)
Economics (Article, 2014)
The allure of rhetoric (Article, 2003)

Consider the following five examples of this method of trying out, and applying, post-traditional concepts. As a first example, contemplate (seriously)—while sitting in a library or while running on a treadmill or wandering through a park—the last paragraph of *The Language of Public Administration.* This paragraph—offering an argument for a form of epistemic pluralism—promises that:

> the study and practice of public administration can become a more aware (more self-aware) thinking activity. To do so, it would seem helpful for theorists to become more aware by reaching further into other areas—further into philosophy, deeper into social theory, more agilely into economics, for example. That effort is always useful. Nevertheless, the main need is the awareness that could come from loosening the grip of the unconscious mind-sets. (Farmer, 1995, p. 248)

Does this claim, if it is true, relate to your identity and context? What could you do about it?

Second, and also related to the claim that we all have unconscious mind-sets, play thoughtfully and contemplate your mind-set about the structure of knowledge and about the territorialization of knowledge disciplines. Focus on the tree/rhizome distinction drawn by Gilles Deleuze and Félix Guattari, as described in *The Language of Public Administration.* The latter indicates that the

> arborescent description reflects the fact that knowledge in the Western tradition is conceptualized in the form of a tree .... Knowledge is divided in a hierarchical character into branches and sub-branches. There is an essential rootedness of knowledge, and there is a unity of knowledge .... Deleuze and Guattari contrast this model with the rhizomatic .... A rhizome in botany is a root-like and typically horizontal stem that grows along or under the ground and sends out roots below and stems above .... The rhizome decenters information into divergent languages; it destroys roots and binaries; it produces multiplicities of differences. (Farmer, 1995, p. 220)

What led you to believe that knowledge is like a tree, and what difference would there be if you switched to a rhizome belief?

As a third example, try thinking playfully about deconstruction—and starting to apply deconstruction in your workplace. If you have already done it, try to do it again—once per day for a week. The suggestion reflects the idea that all disciplines tend to be artificial and victims of their narratives and sub-narratives, heavily impacted by the reader's (or recipient's) identity. Deconstruction can be considered to mean "essentially good reading of a text." As explained in *Public Administration in Perspective* (Farmer, 2010, p. 95), text is used to include not only narratives and meanings but also meanings implicit in administrative and other situations, events and even lives. Deconstruction has been compared to x-raying a painting to reveal underlying pictures.

As a fourth example, try starting to apply, and to try out, Dwight Waldo's idea that "administrative thought must establish a working relationship with every major province in the realm of human learning." Why would he say such a thing about what we call epistemic pluralism, and (for those who work in the public sector) how could it be applied in your workplace?

As a fifth example, try starting to think playfully about what was described as the relevance of post-traditional public administration theory in the "Symposium on David Farmer's Public Administration Theory" [*International Journal of Organization Theory and Behavior, 19*(1): Spring 2016*]* and in the "Review Symposium: *To Kill the King* by David John Farmer" [*Public Administration Quarterly, 33*(3): 2009]. The papers in the 2016 symposium were:

B. Cunningham, & A. Wachhaus. Symposium
A. Wachhaus. What Is Newark?

Barth, T. Applying Farmer's Lenses: Two Illustrations

R. Huff, C. Cors, J. Song, and Y. Pang. Of Rhizomes and Pointillism: David John Farmer's Influence, Method and Art in the Field

C. Shults. Advancing the Practice of Performance Measurement in Public Organizations: Observations from the Tennessee Municipal Benchmarking Project,

R. A. Schneider. Heroes, Superheroes, and Policy Outcomes: An Alternative View of Leadership of Public Organizations.

R. Schmukler. The Practicality of Poetic Contemplation: A Reflection on David Farmer as Methodologist.

O. White. David Farmer's Body of Work: A Retrospective View.

The papers in the 2009 symposium were:

R. Cunningham. Introduction

O. C. McSwite. Socrates Redux: A Roundabout Exegesis of David Farmer's *To Kill the King*

T. Catlaw. Kill the King, Love Your Neighbor.

H. L. Schachter. Is Art the Weapon to Kill the King?

A. Kouzman, M. Witt, and K. Thorne. "Killing the King" in Public Administration: From Critical Epistemology to Fractured Ontology and Limited Agency, A Review Essay

The economist Ha-Joon Chang argues that "work is the defining condition of mankind" (Chang, 2014, p. 251). He adds that work shapes and "forms" us; it affects our physical, intellectual and psychological human being. Chang claims that liking one's jobs can lead often to a greater sense of self-fulfillment (Chang, 2014, p. 253). On the other hand, earlier I have indicated the obvious-enough view that identity and context is not confined only to work. I agree—as noted in the earlier essays—that Chang's description of identity (and mine in this chapter) could be expanded to reflect the claim that identity and context shape all hermeneutic claims and understandings, consciously or unconsciously. However, some readers also do it: but I recommend that all readers (including university professors) consider examining their own identities and contexts and note how they shape their understandings.

## EPILOGUE

"Let's create a post-traditional consciousness that can revitalize governance and bureaucracy." So begins the publisher's spiel on the back of one of the books, *To Kill the King: Post-Traditional Governance and Bureaucracy* (Farmer, 2005). I agree with it whole-heartedly.

It was the age of wave-particle duality
It was the age of the uncertainty principle (Ford, 2011, p. 2)
It was the epoch of belief
It was the epoch of incredulity
It was the season of Light (Dickens, 1859/1940)
It was the season of "we have that covered"
It was the spring of hope, of revitalizing the post-traditional

## REFERENCES

9/11 Commission. (2004). *Final report of the National Commission on Terrorist Attacks Upon the United States*. New York, NY: W. W. Norton. Retrieved from https://www.gpo.gov/fdsys/pkg/GPO-911REPORT/pdf/GPO-911REPORT.pdf

Chang, H. (2014). *Economics: The user's guide*. New York, NY: Bloomsbury Press.

Dickens, C. (1859/1940). *A tale of two cities*. London, UK: Chapman & Hall.

Farmer, D. (1984). *Crime Control: The Use and Misuse of Police Resources*. New York, NY: Plenum Publishing Corporation.

Farmer, D. J. (1995). *The language of public administration: Bureaucracy, modernity, and postmodernity*. Tuscaloosa, AL: University of Alabama Press. Retrieved from https://muse.jhu.edu/book/36750

Farmer, D. J. (2001a). Medusa: Hélène Cixous and the writing of laughter. *Administrative Theory and Praxis*, 23(4), 559–572. doi:10.1080/10841806.2001.11643545.

Farmer, D. J. (2001b). The discourses of anti-administration. In J. S. Jun (Ed.), *Rethinking administrative theory: The challenge of the new century* (pp. 271–289). Westport, CT: Praeger; http://www.abc-clio.com/ABC-CLIO Corporate/product.aspx?pc=D7267C. Retrieved from https://www.questia.com/read/117800043/rethinking-administrative-theory-the-challenge-of

Farmer, D. J. (2002). Love and un-engineering. *Administrative Theory and Praxis*, 24(2), 368–380. doi:10.1080/10841806.2002.11029358.

Farmer, D. J. (2003a). Because my master bathes me. *Administrative Theory and Praxis*, 25(2), 205–232. doi:10.1080/10841806.2003.11029402.

Farmer, D. J. (2003b). The allure of rhetoric and the truancy of poetry. *Administrative Theory and Praxis*, 25(1), 9–36. doi:10.1080/10841806.2003.11029394.

Farmer, D. J. (2005). *To kill the king: Post-traditional governance and bureaucracy*. Armonk, NY: M.E. Sharpe. doi:10.4324/9781315698670.

Farmer, D. J. (2006). Change the course, neurons! *Administrative Theory and Praxis*, 29(1), 182–192. doi:10.1080/10841806.2007.11029566.

Farmer, D. J. (2008a). Epistemic pluralism and neuroscience. *Administrative Theory and Praxis*, 30(3), 285–295. doi:10.1080/10841806.2008.11029643.

Farmer, D. J. (2008b). Neuro-Gov: Neuroscience as catalyst. In C. Senior & M. Butler (Eds.), *Social cognitive neuroscience of organizations* (Annals of the New York Academy of Sciences, 1118, 74–89). Boston, MA: Blackwell/New York Academy of Sciences. doi:10.1196/annals.1412.002.

Farmer, D. J. (2010). *Public administration in perspective: Theory and practice through multiple lenses*. Armonk, NY: M.E. Sharpe.

Farmer, D. J. (2012). Theorizing in perspective: Epistemic pluralism. *Administrative Theory and Praxis*, 34(2), 180–190. doi:10.2753/atp1084-1806340201.

Farmer, D. J. (2015a). Practical leadership in public administration: The practicality of poetry. *Public Voices*, 14(2), 9–18. doi:10.22140/pv.4.

Farmer, D. J. (2015b). Dogs of war: Fighting back. *Administrative Theory and Praxis*, 37(4), 252–267. doi:10.1080/10841806.2015.1083826.

Farmer, D. J. (2016). Out of the fly-bottle? A post-script on post-traditional public administration. *International Journal of Organization Theory and Behavior*, 10(1), 90–102. Retrieved from http://pracademics.com/attachments/article/1251/Symp%20Article%207_Farmer.pdf

Farmer, D. J., & Farmer, R. L. (2012). Toward epistemic pluralism and neuroscience. In A. Porshakova (Ed.), *Public administration in the twenty-first century: Traditions and implications* (pp. 87–91). Moscow, Russia: Lomonosov Moscow State University.

Ford, K. (2011). *101 Quantum Questions: What you need to know about the world you can't see*. Cambridge, MA: Harvard University Press.

Franklin, U. (1990). *The real world of technology*. Toronto, Canada: Anansi.

Kasparov, G. (2007). *How life imitates chess: Making the right moves, from the board to the boardroom*. New York, NY: Bloomsbury.

McCurdy, H. E. (1972). *Public administration: A bibliography*. Washington, DC: American University.

Stillman, R. J. (1991). *Preface to public administration: A search for themes and direction.* New York, NY: St. Martin's Press.
Wittgenstein, L. (1922). *Tractatus Logico-Philosophicus.* London, UK: Kegan Paul.

# In the Pink?

## David John Farmer

> Art is made to disturb. Science reassures. (Georges Braque)
>
> Art is an action against death. It is a denial of death. (Jacques Lipchitz)
>
> Art washes away from the soul the dust of everyday life. (Pablo Picasso)

I have gone through at least three different attitudes about the relationship of my own PA thinking to traditional PA theory—a white, a green, and now a pink period. Not only are they historical stages, but also I choose to see them as quasi-evolutionary. The pink period in me sees PA theorizing-as-it-should-be (not the traditional version) as an artistic or poetic activity, where the intended benefits-for-PA are limited to space clearing for PA practice to turn more resolutely toward the truly human. By truly human, I mean where each and every individual is treated in her fullest human dimensions (psycho, socio, bio, spiritual and other dimensions)—treated as if each person were a poet. The pink period in me sees traditional PA theory, in terms of the aim of fostering the fully human, not only as basically irrelevant but also as distracting or harmful. This stage declares my independence. Forget traditional PA theory—and forget the attitudes and practice that engender it! At least, that's how it seems to me now.

The poetic imagination is too much of a stranger in traditional PA theory, even in the context of discovery it seems to me—similar to the way I imagine that such poetry as is involved in theoretical chemistry or physics is alien to alchemy. The poetic imagination, as I understand it (2003), is part of what Aristotle called contemplation. It includes what that involves, e.g. being thoroughly open to surprises in seeking what is truly human. At a minimum, the poetic imagination has the utility of not being chained to optimism about the prospects for—and to what seems useful for—making gold out of the baser metals of public administration experience. For instance, which traditional PA conference will be the first to adopt as its theme "PA and Agnatology?" Alien sounding for traditional PA, agnatology is the study of the cultural production of ignorance. An April 2003 conference at Pennsylvania State University examined how ignorance is produced and maintained in different settings, e.g., about cigarettes, birth control—and the effects of disciplinarity on agnatogenesis. An idea is that, while epistemology (what it is to know) is overtheorized, how or why we don't know is undertheorized. Hosts of other items are alien to the spirit of traditional PA, it seems to me. Which conference is likely to adopt as a conference theme "PA and Indifference." I have in mind the book by Hertzfeld on *The Social Production of Indifference: Exploring the Symbolic Roots of Western Bureaucracy* (1992). In the pink, I want to resist the allure of PA as alchemy.

Pink period contemplation could include (would not have to!) a PA shift toward the aesthetic, in the context of justification no less than in that of discovery. Recall that the aesthetic imagination has long played a minor role in justifying propositions, e.g., Ockham's Razor; in the context of discovery, imaginative insights routinely are part of the game in vigorous disciplines, e.g., Archimedes in his bath tub. Later I try to explain any such shift in the context of justification toward poetic imagination when talking, after Foucault, about creating PA theory as if it were a piece of pottery. A shift toward the poetic in the context of justification does not exclude the rational, it should be added.

My choice of colors has no significant meaning. I have chosen "white" because long ago when I started doing public management consulting work my employer would have had a corporate heart attack if I had not turned up in a white shirt. In those years, it would have been quite logical for me each night to have retired to bed in a three-piece suit. I have chosen "green" because that was the color of the cover of my book on "The Language of Public Administration." I have chosen "pink" in recognition of the phrase "in the pink." Absent poetic imagination, can a PA theorist expect to be in the pink? I think not.

## WHITE PERIOD

In my pale white period (my efficiency or surface period), I was a technicist, and I celebrated traditional PA theories—the administrative-traditional and the economic-traditional. On the administrative-traditional side, I was genuinely impressed with the capability of commonsense systems analysis and commonsense rules-of-thumb to ameliorate serious surface-level hurts in administrative agencies, typically for short periods. "NASA's Failings Go Far Beyond Foam Hitting Shuttle, Panel Says" is the title of a lead story in the *New York Times* (June 7, 2003, p. 1)—and we go on to read that the administrative study shows failings as including a "flawed institutional culture that plays down problems...." Valuable, albeit upsetting, stuff! Turn from the relatively large to the small. Of course, there are brilliant managers; and there are others. Serious surface-level hurts can occur when managers violate, say, even the elementary "rules" of POSDCORBing. That's more the rule than the exception, I sometimes suppose. I remember how the Model Cities director of Reading, Pennsylvania—a fun man—did not know about span of control. He didn't know that it hurt his agency to require every single subordinate to report directly to him. Some managers—literally—didn't know that it helps to plan, as another example. I remember how cities did not know how to cooperate in order to quell riots. Coming out of my work for the National Advisory Commission on Civil Disorders, I wrote a booklet (1968) about inter-city and intra-city coordination. I was one of those who whispered in the ears of mayors and police chiefs—care-laden ears—controlling riots in the late sixties or so. A banner headline in a Durham, North Carolina, newspaper (late in the sixties) blazoned a quote from me, "You should learn to walk before you try to run." A banner headline! No wonder the ears were care-laden!

> When NASA first started sending up astronauts, they quickly discovered that ballpoint pens would not work in 0 gravity. To combat this problem, NASA scientists spent a decade and $12 billion developing a pen that writes in zero gravity, upside down, underwater, on almost any surface including glass and at temperatures ranging from below freezing to over 300 centigrade. The Russians used a pencil. (J. Twigg, personal communication, March 1, 2003)

I am still impressed by the fact that every single agency I have ever encountered inflicts surface level hurts by violation of common sense. Too many fire and police agencies still have rotating shifts, in violation of commonsense when looked at by an outsider, for instance; managers still fall foul of fascistic tendencies, in spite of common sense when looked at by an outsider; the list is long and obvious. I am impressed by the cleverness of some administrative reports, just as I used to be impressed by my own—so shiny, so watertight—although I do agree that madness has its own watertight logic. So I still recognize society's need to worry about short-term balms to heal surface-level hurts. I recognize that getting into the modern age is not a trivial move, and I notice the example Bernard Lewis (2002, p. 47) offers of the enthusiastic reception given in some quarters of eighteenth century Islamic society to efficiency in bureaucratic administration. Yes, pale white period commonsense attitudes can ameliorate the human condition wonderfully. But I came to doubt whether PA administrative-traditional rises to the level of the theory that humans need to be human in the world.

On the economic-traditional side, my original interest in economics—nothing to do with business—was fired by my belief that economic theory can help in changing the world for the better. John Maynard Keynes has always been a hero for me, for instance. I never was a believer in neo-liberal Economics, or economic fundamentalism. For me, the self-regulating, beneficent, perfect market—the market as a god—lives in the world of the model, a prisoner, as it were, of its own constraints. I never could rejoice in what is called the 1980's Washington Consensus, the belief in fiscal austerity, privatization and market liberalization that Joseph Stiglitz (2003) describes the International Monetary Fund as inflicting on the world. I do not buy what economists sometimes (great rhetoric?) call a minimalist view of government's role in generating economic success and well-being. I do not buy that economic systems can be understood without considering institutions (e.g., for a view of radical institutionalism, see Dugger, 1989). Foolishly perhaps, I used to suppose that neo-classical economics was dead, and I did not realize that its resurrection would triumph for so long.

Yet, even as I celebrated the administrative-traditional surface tending, I had a prejudice that economic theory can help the PA thinker and practitioner to see longer-term features or constraints acting on the surface of the PA situation. I never did suppose that Niskanen or Migue and Belanger (and the other modelers described in a useful seed-catalogue like Mueller, 2003) saw beneath the surface "the truth, the whole truth, and nothing but the truth"—nor was what they saw untrue. What they achieved was re-describing, describing from another and—for me—more interesting point of view or framework. PA could now be seen in the context of the "glorious" Mozart-like panorama of economic theory. I taught Public Choice Economics for several years, and I believed that it offered powerful insights for change—especially where (to employ Matthew Witt's apposite terms) "vigor," not rigor, is the principal concern. I enjoyed creating (1984) what I called a Conditional Model—not a complex affair—about the trade-offs of public and private interests. This brings up a point. Modeling is very commonsensical; but lumping it in with traditional administrative theory doesn't completely work, because models exist—in a way that admin theory usually doesn't—in a sort of realm of Platonic forms. Model building (creating is different from reading somebody else's) can be hard on the brain; but it's safe, as long as the audience remembers that the economic theorist lives in the world of the model and that the so-called real world (ugly name, ugly mixture of blessings and warts) is touched only where it touches. Still, I recognize that economics as a tool is valuable (albeit mixed in value) for PA, just as I think it is hard to understand our contemporary world—or contemporary PA—in ignorance of economics. I think a PA theorist would want to have a considered view of the role of government in its economic context (e.g., what was right or wrong about the East Asian view that governments should shape markets)? Yet, same comment as before! Economics-inspired insights do not rise to the level of a PA theory that humanity deserves in our context. Economic man, as I like to write, is an anemic substitute for a full-blooded human.

## GREEN PERIOD

In my green or under-the-surface (under the coverlet) period, I felt a need for PA thinking to snorkel deeper under the surface, to encompass new understandings about society and PA, and to shift toward a more philosophical perspective. It seemed odd to me to aim toward mere efficiency, for instance, in a context where we have (in the phrase used by Greg Palast, 2003) the "best democracy money can buy." It seemed odd to me to think of government only in narrow traditional terms, when Palast (for one) finds it necessary to encompass the "governing" foibles of private enterprise as well as public. Yet, in this green period, I saw what I did as subordinate to the spirit of traditional PA thinking—in the sense that, despite what I said about scientism and so on, I wrote too much in deference to technicism and use-value-for-PA. Even when I wrote (1995) about a world (the postmodern world) that lies beyond the traditional modernist world, I was pursuing traditional PA story lines. One story line harbored the traditional PA assumption that—for a PA story to be told and to be publishable—a better alternative that is more useful-for-PA must be proffered, and use-for-PA is the criterion. Maybe a non-linear or other less familiar pattern was then not a practical option—neither for the audience nor for me. I was motivated by the thought that it was important that traditional thinkers and practitioners have the opportunity to see that their world-view is too limited.

> The heaviest element yet known to science was recently discovered by investigators at a major U.S. research university. The new element, tentatively named administratium, has no protons or electrons and thus has an atomic number of 0. However, it does have one neutron, 125 assistant neutrons, 75 (deputy) neutrons, and 111 assistant (deputy) neutrons, which gives it an atomic mass of 312. These 312 particles are held together by a force... called morons. Since it has no electrons, administratium is inert. However, it can be detected chemically as it impedes every reaction it comes into contact with... Administratium has a normal half-life of 3 years; (it) does not decay but undergoes a reorganization in which a portion of the assistant neutrons and (deputy) neutrons exchange places... (A)dministratium occurs naturally in the atmosphere. It tends to concentrate at certain points such as government agencies, large corporations, and universities... (DeBuwitz, 1988, p. 1—ignorant or cute story? bad or good taste? from a physics teacher.)

When I first wrote about anti-administration, I was thinking of a catchword for "the" PA postmodern perspective—thinking what a pomo PA would be like that included imaginization, deconstruction, deterritorialization, and a new view of alterity. It had taken me a long time to achieve whatever understanding I had of postmodernism; but that didn't prepare me for what O.C. McSwite calls—and I call—the shallowness of the PA response to postmodernism. The word "pomo" has had its half-day, although virtually all the constituent ideas are very much alive. But, as if it were an angel dancing on the end of a needle, PA talk hopped on the surface of the word—often willfully innocent of the substance. My own "mistake" was to cast postmodernism as a useful-for-PA notion. It is not that the ideas are not useful (of course, they are); the point is that that is not the point. When it came to play (1998), I don't think I started by inclining to the ironic by calling it "Play with a Purpose." However, I am impressed by traditional PA's unwillingness to snorkel deeper under the surface, and to encompass (the best, such as it is, I have written about this is "The Devil's Rope," 2003) new understandings about society and PA. I am impressed by the unwillingness in traditional PA to see the PA situation in macro terms, and I have surely worn out my welcome by repeating that a central problem of bureaucracy is the unintended pleasure-pain that entire bureaucratic systems (and the entire set of systems) inflict on humans. Again, I don't see technicist-inspired doodling rising to the level of PA theory that humankind deserves in our emerging context—that is, that is deserved if all are to be self-actualized.

## PINK PERIOD

In my present pink period, I want to focus on PA theorizing as art or poetry, accepting the irrelevance of traditional PA Theory and of associated practitioner micro concerns. As I have explained before (2003), I am using poetry and art in the most catholic of senses, the widest sense of "poetry" that is intended by Michael Oakeshott. I do not stand against the aims of my pale white and my green periods. On the former, I am happy when problems at the surface are handled. On the latter, there is a strong useful-for-PA element (correction, a "revolutionary" useful-for-PA element) in exploring PA in relation to speaking-from-power and speaking-to-power. The same is true of what I wrote last year about love as a more "useful" regulative ideal for public employee motivation than "efficiency." But my aim now is to see my writing (work, play) as non-technicist, directed toward useful-for-PA no more than as a space-making activity. My paper (2003) on "The Allure of Rhetoric and the Truancy of Poetry" is in the pink, as I see it.

The pink period cannot be constrained by the traditional disciplinary boundaries of PA, I want to stress, any more than it could in the green period. PA's traditional boundaries constrain and distort what can be said, limiting thinkers to dealing with what are considered—artificially—to be "PA things." Even on a utilitarian basis, the traditional boundaries of PA are too constrained. For example, can traditional PA Theory mount an intellectual defense against economic fundamentalism? Can the mouse of traditional PA Theory mount an intellectual defense against the eagle of economic fundamentalism? It is not just that church mice aspire to such heights as fellowship in a National Academy of PA, while Nobel prizes are awarded in economics. It is also a matter of the relative strength of symbolic systems, and symbols are outside the traditional PA and the traditional economics folds.

Poetry and scholarship are not mutually exclusive categories, I think. Weren't Isaac Newton and Albert Einstein poets? Could they have made the scholarly contributions they did if they had not been poets? Isn't Keynes' *General Theory of Employment, Interest and Money* a poem? Aren't Friedrich Nietzsche's scholarly *Thus Spoke Zarathustra* and Sigmund Freud's scholarly *Interpretation of Dreams* poetry?

Back to the role of poetic imagination in the context of justification! In my view, both PA theory and PA practice should be more like an art, where the theorist and the practitioner carry out their activities as if each were creating a piece of pottery. Not the same art and not the same piece of pottery—to each her own pot! The poetic imagination can be confined to the context of discovery; or, it can be extended to the context of justification. Recall that, when speaking about Ancient Greek ethics, Michel Foucault speaks of a person leading (and justifying) an "ethical" life as if she or he were a work of art, as if he or she were a pot. I am thinking in a parallel way for PA theory and PA practice. In both cases (i.e., confined to discovery or extended to the context of justification), the incidental use-for-PA of PA theory should be limited to clearing a space for humans to be treated more like humans, as I have said—and for humans to be more human. The poetry of PA theory and practice is to move away from the world of mere things—to the world of the symbols that relate to what it is to be purely human. In this, I see the world of traditional PA theory to be basically irrelevant and, insofar as it distracts and gives the impression of "real" progress (PA hyperreality at work!), harmful. The pink stage in me declares my independence.

> To the extent that the bureaucracy is efficient, it is also inhuman. (Herzfeld, 1992, p. 45, writing about Weber)
>
> Financial management is arguably the most important, if not prominent, management system within government operations. (The Government Performance Project, ch. 10, p. 9. – cute story? good taste? from a teaching institution.)

In a PA forum (even here), a "forget it" claim has a strange ring, although I am sure that others in PAT-Net have preceded me in this shift and in similar moves. I leave them to speak for themselves. I don't think it would have a strange ring in a theoretical science forum—where the idea of science for science's sake (truth for truth's sake) is a well-worn cliche. Perhaps the social sciences need more self-assurance. Yet, even here, remember the economic modelers and recall the steps taken in social science toward such a move. For instance, recently I (2003) quoted Leo Strauss talking about the superior hermeneutic value of literature for social science understandings—compared against the insights available from standard social science studies. I know that others in parallel fields have often pointed to the relative importance for social science of the literary (e.g., the September 2003 organization theory conference in Venice). The importance of the literary is also exemplified in some PA writings (e.g., in Patterson, 2003).

I am hoping that others in the PAT-Net community will continue to help me in playing with the implications of this move toward the widest sense of art. I expect to backslide, e.g., to succumb to the temptation of offering this or that oh-so-useful suggestion or yet another presentation on the sandy soil of locations like ASPA. As for theorizing, the pink stage calls me to shift more firmly toward poetry. As for traditional PA theory, I think of it as having what for the contemporary physical scientist must be all the-allure-of-alchemy. Forget it! Let's color, in the pink!

## REFERENCES

DeBuvitz, W. (1988). *New chemical element discovered*. Retrieved from http://lhup.edu/~dsimanek/administ.htm

Dugger, W. M. (1989). *Radical institutionalism: Contemporary voices*. Westport, CT: Greenwood Press.

Farmer, D. J. (1998). Public administration discourse as play with a purpose. In D. J. Farmer (Ed.), *Papers on the art of anti-administration* (pp. 37-56). Burke, VA: Chatelaine Press.

Farmer, D. J. (2002). The devil's rope. *Administrative Theory & Praxis, 25*, 781-786.

Farmer, D. J. (2003). The allure of rhetoric and the truancy of poetry. *Administrative Theory & Praxis, 25*, 9-36.

Hertzfeld, M. (1992). *The social production of indifference: Exploring the symbolic roots of western bureaucracy*. New York: Berg.

Government Performance Project. (2003). *Paths to performance in state and local government: A final assessment from the Maxwell School of Citizenship and Public Affairs*. Retrieved from http://www.maxwell.syr.edu/gpp/

Lewis, B. (2002). *What went wrong? The clash between Islam and modernity in the Middle East*. New York: Oxford University Press.

Muller, D. (2003). *Public choice economics 3*. New York: Cambridge University Press.

Palast, G. (2003). *The best democracy money can buy: The truth about corporate cons, globalization, and high-finance fraudsters*. New York: Penguin.

Patterson, P. M. (2003). Interpretation, contradiction and refusal: The best lack all conviction? *Administrative Theory & Praxis, 25*, 233-242.

Stiglitz, J. E. (2003). *Globalization and its discontents*. New York: W. W. Norton.

# Contemplating Cops: A Tale of Identities – Essay 1

## David John Farmer

"It was the best of times, it was the worst of times, it was the age of wisdom, it was the age of foolishness" (Dickens, 1859/1940, p. 1), it was the epoch of traditional police policy and administration, it was the epoch of intermittent openness about identity and context—and is it still? How could public administration, cops and noncops, and other thinkers learn from contemplating differing identities and contexts in police management?

The first two essays in this series focus on three different police management work identities, and the last two essays center on three different public administration identities—on the contrast between the traditional and the opportunity for openness and for (as sketched in Essay 4) the post-traditional. Essay 1 reflects on my work identity as special assistant to the New York City Police Department (NYPD) police commissioner, with emphasis on the complexity of openness. Essay 2 considers the other police-related identities. The readers may wish to attempt contemplation of openness by conjoining nonwork identity components—the unconscious, the economic, and others. Contemplation is rarely comprehensive; it rarely covers everything.

I continued my thinking about police policy and administration, affected by three differing work aspects of my identity and context. A door opened for my contemplation about police policy and administration when I became special assistant to the police commissioner of the NYPD (1971–1974). Another opened when I was appointed director of the Police Division in the U.S. Department of Justice's National Institute of Law Enforcement and Criminal Justice (1974–1980). Yet another door opened later, as I became a faculty member of the Department of Administration of Justice and Public Safety at Virginia Commonwealth University—becoming department chair (1982–1991). Let us look at openness in the mainly closed context of the NYPD.

## NYPD: NEW YORK'S FINEST

Do police policy and practice suffer from undue lack of openness? A door opened (as just noted), admitting me and a few others in the early seventies (1971–1974), when I joined the

NYPD as a special assistant to the police commissioner. "6 Civilian Specialists Join Police as Murphy's Aides" was the headline of a front-page story in *The New York Times*, October 5, 1971 (Fosburgh, 1971). The story described me as "a management consultant from Chicago, specializing in law enforcement problems." It quoted Police Commissioner (P.C.) Patrick V. Murphy. "Mr. Murphy said the work of the six assistants 'will be critical to the success of the many changes I have undertaken and will undertake in the future. It is my impression that police departments have traditionally failed to be as open as they should be.'" He continued, "This lack of openness has resulted in the department's failure to take advantage of many outside civilian resources and expertise that could help us deal with many everyday problems. I am happy to break with that tradition."

Police policy and administration can profit from greater access to broader perspectives, and this can be facilitated by adjustments in police identity. For one example discussed later, NYPD and similar departments should be appropriately open to nonpolice skills helpful to cope with police problems. For another example, it will be suggested that NYPD commanders—and similar commanders in other departments—should become more open to triggers encouraging commanders to assume more responsibility for the activities of subordinates. For yet another example, it is proposed that adjustments should be welcomed in the meaning of, as it will be explained, the police badge.

## ENTERING HEADQUARTERS

"Don't grow a badge!" After introducing himself and saying that he knew that I was visiting the police commissioner, then-current Chief of Personnel Sydney Cooper called out this advice to me when I entered the headquarters of the NYPD. That was on October 4, 1971, many years ago. On that date, police headquarters was an Edwardian baroque-style behemoth—at 240 Centre Street in Manhattan's Little Italy—headquarters from 1909 until 1973, when we moved to the present—and less architecturally interesting—police headquarters building at 1 Police Plaza, near City Hall and the Brooklyn Bridge. I was going up one side of the ultra-wide stairs just inside the main door left of the guard kiosk, and Sydney, with aides, was walking down the other side. Chief Cooper (1920–1994) told me later that he had conducted supplementary investigations of all the applicants for special assistant, including me, as part of Police Commissioner Murphy's selection process.

"Don't grow a badge!" What does that mean? I believed that a badge is a mark or symbol of sworn police identity, with legal and subtextual obligations and privileges regarding behavior—including implications for some thinking and some interrelationships. These implications included relationships with the public served and with other officers—and even with non–police officers, as will be mentioned later. The badge holder was obligated to keep his/her mouth shut about the job, especially when items were dicey. The holder evokes sympathy because danger and even death can occur. The story is longer in that the sign of identity is said to relate to medieval knights. It would not be unique in referring to the medieval: academe (the third identity in our present tale) has the identity image of the hood and gown, which developed in the twelfth and thirteenth centuries. I would learn later that the story is even more complicated—in that there were various ethnic and religious social associations of police officers. For instance, the largest ethnic association was Irish, and another was German (which I joined, even though I was not of German origin: the um-pa-pa music and big beer glasses were attractive!). However, I didn't then on the stairs have time (nor did I want such time) to calculate what was ultimately a question about, at least, identity and context options. At the time, I understood Chief Cooper appearing—on initial contact—to be friendly and probably helpful. I agree that when my wife and I saw him in post-NYPD years, I should have asked him what he meant: but I didn't think of it. A first and most probable meaning is that Sydney is advising that "Come up with ideas that are out of the traditional, and be comfortable having your own identity."

"Don't grow a badge!" A second possibility consistent with Chief Cooper's own fuller work identity, I now suppose, is that he might have been saying that "In your work for the NYPD, don't be limited by the motivation of got-your-back for what police officers do and want." He might have been making the important claim that the general pattern of NYPD officers is that too many exhibited what Chief Cooper (and eventually the Knapp Commission) would describe as corrupt got-your-back behavior. The Knapp Commission identified (as did Chief Cooper) two classes of corrupted police officer—"grass eaters" (e.g., seeking smallish $10 or $20 gratuities) and "meat eaters," and where grass eating was often used to "prove" loyalty to the brotherhood of the badge, the brotherhood of silence. The plainclothes police officers were often given as an example of where the incidence of meat eating was exceptionally high. Sydney was a relentless corruption fighter when he was police borough commander of the Bronx and when chief of the Internal Affairs Division and beyond. Sydney was celebrated (and despised—as was the police commissioner, sadly) for making significant contributions to such activities as the Knapp Commission (Commission to Investigate Alleged Police Corruption, established by Mayor John V. Lindsey in April 1970 and issuing its final report in December 1972). The commission eventually made recommendations such as that commanders should be held responsible for their subordinates' actions, that undercover informants should be placed in all precincts, and so on. Armstrong (2012), chief counsel of the Knapp Commission, described the work of the Knapp Commission—including Sydney Cooper's significant contribution.

"Don't grow a badge!" A third and less likely meaning of Sydney's shout-out is that people (especially those in privileged sectors of society) are likely to overlook or to deny police malpractice and suboptimal police practice as they are being protecting, fueled by such subtexts as their desire for personal security and shock at societal violence—and also fueled by sub-subtexts (which Chief Cooper would reject) that demand honor to be due to first-responders regardless of their exploitative and corrupt behavior at the expense of really helping. I would not have supposed Sydney to be saying that got-your-back feelings should ignore the genuine needs of senior managers—and thus of the officers on the street. I set out to learn about the ways they worked and then tried to help. Every day I learned more from the many officers who talked with me and on my visits to the field. For example, I spent three whole days in my second week sitting next to Chief Inspector Michael Codd (highest-ranking officer of the uniformed department and later police commissioner himself) watching him work and talking with him. Then, with the commissioner's approval, I took a desk near his office. I was assigned a lieutenant and a sergeant to work for me; they facilitated my getting out to the precincts and to the streets. Later I would join the chief of detectives, Louis Cottell, and had a desk next to his office for months. Even later, I joined the chief of operations, Hugo Masini, and the then-P.C.

Donald Cawley, and he appointed me director of management operations, and he asked me to manage some 1,200 police employees. More of this later.

"Don't grow a badge!" Whatever the precise meaning, I appreciate that Chief Cooper's advice relates to complexity and forms of lack of openness. Consider the complexity of our changing narrative identities. Consider your own—parent, young person/old person, television watcher, and others. Consider discussion of the philosophy and sociology of narrative identities: Is it timelessly true that "I am me," that "you are s/he?" Is the Kantian option of being a "rational person" rational? Think whether identities are voluntary or both voluntary/involuntary, whether they have subtexts or even sub-subtexts, and so forth. Doesn't a job or a skill or a profession or a vocation give a kind of identity, shaping thinking and behavior? Doesn't a police badge contribute to identity of rank? For Sydney, one badge of his life was his police badge (adjusted as he was promoted from rank to rank) and one achievement of his life was to clean others' dirty badges. How many identities do you have, dear reader? If the reader were in, say, my place as listener to Chief Cooper, what would the context be? What would be the context for an inhabitant of New York's silk-stocking district, or a low-paid worker living in the 1970s horrors of the South Bronx, or a homeless person living in the 1970s Bowery? One of my identities was described by *The New York Times* (quoted above) as management consultant from Chicago specializing in law enforcement problems. Well, the forty or so management consulting assignments included more than merely law enforcement problems. But it did include law enforcement services to cities (e.g., Tacoma, Milwaukee, Cedar Rapids, Durham, and Atlanta) and a study about intra– and inter–police agency planning for riot control (mentioned later) for the Kerner Commission—and I had written a book that was titled *Civil Disorder Control* (Farmer, 1968). My badge (my flag, my business card, my … ) was to help public organizations and public policy, including law enforcement. It was to help—in my own way—managers and departments and others to move forward positively, to cope.

## THE P.C.'S OFFICE

So I arrived at the office of P.C. Patrick V. Murphy. It was a second visit; the first was my interview with him for the job. He explained that we would be free to work as we thought best. Then a photographer took a picture of the commissioner with his newly minted special assistants, and we went to the P.C.'s press conference. My contacts would continue with him until a decade after we both left the NYPD. The last time was when he visited me and Virginia Commonwealth University in 1984.

Justifiably, Pat Murphy (1920–2011) was one of the most respected figures in American policing. He started as a NYPD police officer in 1945, rising to the rank of deputy inspector. He was the former head of the police departments of Syracuse (1963–1964), Washington, D.C. (1967–1969), Detroit (1969–1970)—and now police commissioner of the city of New York (1970–1973). Later he would be president of the Police Foundation (1973–1985). Since the 1968 disorders in Washington, D.C., he was well recognized for encouraging police restraint—and he continued to do so throughout his career. For example, consider the importance of the following sample of ideas from his important 1977 book *Commissioner;* there are other examples.

On the view of many political establishments, he wrote that police departments are seen as organizations "with the sole mission of bending to the whims of the power structure" (Murphy

& Plate, 1977, p. 68). This is always open to the standard bureaucratic reply "We have that covered."

On his view of police chief training, he wrote, "There is no police chief school to prepare one for the job. There is the F.B.I. Academy in Washington, which I graduated from in 1957, but it was really of little help" (Murphy & Plate, 1977, p. 56). And we may ask, why not? Looking at police and other issues from a macro perspective would surely help. Again, a variation of the standard bureaucratic reply can be used: "We now have that covered."

On the claim that police departments enforce laws equally, he wrote that this "of course is nonsense. To make such a silly statement is to suggest that higher levels of American policing are ignorant of the larger problems they are supposed to be managing, or are covering up" (Murphy & Plate, 1977, p. 53). What are the identity and context options that would encourage such "silly statements"?

On race relations, he wrote, "In the occupational army school of policing, minority communities suffer the most repressive policies. Indeed, in a great many departments there is a built-in policy duality at the patrol level, with one set of policies (usually sophisticated, suburban-style) for the white neighborhoods and another (usually heavy-handed inner-city) for the non-white" (Murphy & Plate, 1977, p. 69). This was a live issue in the seventies (e.g., with the Black Liberation Army), and it is currently (with a different organization).

On prosecutors and judges, he wrote, "In the last fifty years policing in America has improved more than judging or prosecuting. The police world has been more willing to change, and to do so expeditiously, than prosecutors and judges" (Murphy & Plate, 1977, p. 71)

On looking for ideas from other police departments, he wrote that his "very idea of looking to other police forces for ideas about policing and management was instantly hilarious within the NYPD. 'Doesn't the P.C. know that this is the greatest police force in the world? He can't learn anything from those cow-town departments' " (1977, p. 49). That was a subtextual view at least of the NYPD badge wearer. I remember once making a presentation to an NYPD meeting about my visit to study the Kansas City Preventive Patrol Experiment. I was irritated when one robbery squad commander remarked to me during a break, "Who has ever heard of Kansas City?" Yes, Kansas City is not New York City, but why could a squad commander be that stupid? Nor was such a feeling confined to the NYPD. I recall visiting the Chicago Police Department, and Chicago's first deputy superintendent launched into a tirade of complaint about Commissioner Murphy attempting to study what the Chicago Police Department is doing.

What did I achieve in my work as special assistant to the police commissioner? When it came to April 27, 1973 and when he had resigned and was about to leave the NYPD, the police commissioner sent me a letter. The letter read as follows:

Dear David:

This is to express my thanks for all the assistance you have provided me since October 1971 as my special assistant.

Your contribution to the Department has been substantial. You have conceived, initiated and implemented such management innovations as the Manpower Allocation Review System (MARS), the Management Objectives Program, and the Master Plan System. You have contributed to increasing management and operational effectiveness in such areas as investigations, and you have directed research and analysis in areas including organization, manpower allocation, management practices, operating practices and administrative procedures. Your advice on matters of Department policy and management has been extremely helpful. Your services to me and to the Department have been of the highest professional level and extremely effective. They are appreciated.

Sincerely,

Pat

What Murphy describes as management innovations (starting with MARS) will be described in the following description of coping by the chief inspector, the chief of patrol, the chief of detectives, and then the chief of operations.

## COPING: CHIEF INSPECTOR

I worked with the Chief Inspector Michael Codd, the top uniformed officer in the NYPD, and developed the Manpower Allocation Review System (MARS). As mentioned, I spent the first three days of the next week with him, and then accepted a desk in his staff area. Chief Codd (1916–1985) had joined the police force in 1941 and he was appointed as senior uniformed officer by P.C. Murphy in 1970. He became police commissioner himself from January 1974 to January 1978, a different world when the police force was reduced by 6,000 officers—a bitter time for the NYPD.

Chief Codd was celebrated for what has been called his "gentlemanly" behavior. He spoke with a deep and resonant voice, and he was always calm and dignified in his behavior—beautiful at funerals and any solemn events where he represented the NYPD. At a later time, he was often called Chief Straight Arrow, although I never heard that title when we collaborated. I believe that his demeanor must have helped during the force reduction period. He was indeed an inspiring figure. On the other hand, he was criticized for his conservatism. I always remember speaking to him when I returned from visiting the guarded control center at headquarters. I had been struck by the fact that the main function of the center seemed to be to monitor the news and television programs, and so I asked him if it would be a good idea to reassign the 18 police officers and to close down the unit. He replied to me in his deep voice, "Dave, an organization like the NYPD always needs some pizzazz." Much later, when Michael Codd was to become police commissioner, I remember asking Chief of Operations Hugo Masini why he—Hugo—was so anxious to make changes when he knew that he was leaving the NYPD so soon—and Hugo's reply alleged that, "Well, Codd is so conservative that any improvement we make before he takes the job, he will keep."

I did appreciate Chief Codd, and he included me as an invitee to certain personal events—lunches and even a touching family wake. The lunches, I should add, were in Little Italy, because that is where police headquarters was located. There were only certain restaurants that we could frequent, and I was warned which ones to avoid because of mob associations. Chief Codd would only go to even fewer restaurants, as he had to have a restaurant that would make sure that he received any urgent telephone calls from the office. None of the lunches with Chief Codd included Umberto's Clam House. But I did like the Clam House, which subsequently moved. So it was a shock on April 8, 1972 (at least to me and probably to Pete the Greek and Crazy Joe's two other guards) when Crazy Joey Gallo, a Brooklyn mob boss, was assassinated in Umberto's Clam House at 129 Mulberry Street amid an exchange of twenty or more bullets. Crazy Joe was deceived that there was an effective agreement among gangsters that Little Italy was off-limits to settling scores.

It was during this period that I developed and sold the idea of the Manpower Allocation Review System to Chief Codd and Commissioner Murphy. I was living at the Young Women's Christian Association hostel on 8th Avenue in Midtown. In those days, BTW, Midtown was a kind of sin-city—with prostitutes three deep on some sidewalks, and the remarkable upgrading of Midtown occurred later, thanks to the nonpolice work of the city of New York. (It suggests how crime control is, as we know, not entirely a police function.) I remember how, one evening in that miserable YWCA room, it occurred to me that Manpower Allocation Review System spelled MARS—and that had mythological fighting associations. It has taken forty more years for me to criticize myself for the sexism in the title. The word "manpower" does not recognize the larger part that women would come to play in street policing. A fewer number of women had police opportunities in the seventies, like Muggable Mary (who played a dramatic role in plainclothes) and Lt. Julie Tucker (commanding officer of the Rape Analysis and Investigations Unit). But "manpower" is a tad sexist for me for today. And I never did think of an alternative like Policepower Allocation Review System (PARS).

The plan of the MARS program was for the senior leaders of the police department to think with the component unit leaders about options for the component units. So a schedule of MARS defense meetings—like budget meetings, as it were—took place in the police commissioner's conference room. For instance, the Aviation Unit at that time had five helicopters (excluding one that had crashed recently). How many helicopters and how many officers and pilots should that unit have? Options included define objectives, greater use of helicopters and personnel, or reduction. As another example, should the Mounted Unit have more or less horses and more or less riders? Options included elimination, reduction, or redefinition. Here are some additional examples: Stakeout Unit—reduction, transfer to detective bureau, or elimination; Taxi Safety Squad—elimination, or reduction and modification of mission; and Motorcycle District—redesignate the motorcycle district as the highway patrol district and eliminate the use of motorcycles, or implement one-man radio patrol for selected low and medium hazard posts. One can see that this is a useful thing for the top brass and those in charge of specific units to offer and evaluate whatever arguments they wished, especially because there is no simple and satisfactory numerical system of answering such questions—as I will explain in the next paragraph.

My thoughts on measuring police productivity were re-explained in the first issue of the NYPD publication *Overview: A Police Publication on Organization, Administration and Operations* (vol. 1, no. 1, 1973). It was put together by the Office of Programs and Policies, and the police commissioner explained that he hoped that this would become a "stimulating exchange of ideas and information." I explained in my article the well-known problem that "police productivity is difficult to define and even more difficult to measure." Arrest activity is often taken as a prime indicator of productivity, and the Detective Bureau had especially placed undue reliance on arrest statistics. The article denies that, on a given day, the detective or patrol officer who makes one arrest is necessarily more productive than one who does not. It all depends on circumstances. The article gives examples of these circumstances in this two-officer case. "Was the single arrest an easy one? Did the arrest result from the officer's own mishandling of a situation? Was it a difficult arrest, involving the frustration of a major crime? Did the officer who made no arrests do other useful things like prevent crimes, undertake significant community relations work, or continue significant investigative activity?" (Farmer, 1973, p. 18). And so on.

The Management by Objectives Program was also summarized in the same article. It described the substitution of directed (or responsive) and anti-crime patrol for preventive patrol, an overused technique. It also indicated the move away from undirected management by setting goals for management. The article gave four examples from the New York experience—"the setting of goals for field commanders, setting of goals for headquarters commanders, the encouragement of participatory management, and the strengthening of accountability (Farmer, 1973, p. 19). Examples of the second are the master plans, discussed below, for the Patrol Bureau and for the Detective Bureau.

Not everything was, or would be, at the level of the grand plans I mentioned. The plans could not have evolved adequately without informal learning about the city and about police problems. I mentioned earlier the lunches with Chief Codd and others. The most enjoyable and also useful was the day-to-day contact and informality with this or that commander—including what can be called corridor-talk. I did that without supposing that I was growing the equivalent of a badge. But my personal involvement at the human level had an effect—on me and on the commanders involved. For example, the senior commander of one unit and I used to talk in the corridor many days, and when his mother was dying. I had great empathy for his sorrow, and I cannot imagine that that had no effect on me or his work. Empathy is a necessary part of how to develop plans.

## COPING: CHIEF OF PATROL

It was gratifying to work on a Master Plan System for the Patrol Bureau, because the alternatives were either an inadequate emphasis on change or an unintegrated set of changes. A master plan also has the advantage of emphasizing change rather than business as usual. It emphasizes impetus from the commanders, rather than (say) C.Y.A.

The chief of patrol was Donald Cawley (1929–1990). Chief Cawley had joined the NYPD in 1951, and worked his way up to his appointment by P.C. Murphy as chief of patrol. When P.C. Murphy resigned, Don Cawley himself became the police commissioner. But the tenure was short (May 1973–January 1974). The reason seemed to be that a new mayor assumed office. The New York practice, as I understood it then, is that the incumbent police commissioner submits his resignation as a courtesy to the next mayor, who can then reappoint him or somebody else. At the time, it disturbed me that Donald Cawley was advised not to submit his courtesy resignation; as otherwise he might have been reappointed. Nevertheless, Don Cawley was a progressive and energetic chief of patrol and police commissioner. I remember visiting him at the Chemical Bank after he had ceased being police commissioner and where he worked after leaving NYPD, and I was saddened that he was not police commissioner.

The Patrol Bureau Master Plan System was completed and promulgated in 1972. As the plan explained, it set out to upgrade patrol services in the coming twenty-four months in "ten major areas—the allocation of manpower, field operations, management practices, organization, personnel, patrol function, utilization of civilians, administrative procedures, equipment, and in the area of other departmental programs impacting on the patrol service" (Master Plan

System, p. 5). As noted (p. 6), a high priority is given to a directed patrol program, rather than unstructured random patrol. The chief then sent me the following May 19, 1972 memorandum:

Dear David,

The magnificent job you accomplished in creating and nurturing the Master Plan has been astounding. I fully appreciate the time, the effort, and yes, the anguish that the task entailed. In retrospect, if I had foreseen the tremendous pressures that were generated, I might have faltered. I am glad that I did not, because you came through nobly. Your leadership and drive has been an inspiration to me. You are a man of considerable talent. Please accept my sincere personal thanks and the thanks of the Department for a great contribution.

Sincerely,

Don

The master plan required—not surprisingly—the approval of the chief of patrol. Later, the chief sent me another note written on a photograph. The note read as follows. "Dave, Without your help much of what has already been discussed would otherwise be on the drawing board. Thanks, Don." And when he became police commissioner, P.C. Cawley soon developed and promulgated a master plan for the entire department. Very gratifying, indeed!

An effective master plan must recognize that it is not only people who have identities; it is also things and places. Such identities affect the extent of openness. (Yes, timing is also a causal element. For example, it is unsurprising that an impetus toward militarization of the NYPD could be encouraged by the reaction to the 1972 Munich Olympic Games massacre.) For an example about places, consider that at that time the Patrol Bureau contained seventy-one precincts, and the command structure grouped these precincts into divisions (each commanded by an inspector). The divisions were then divided into five borough commands. An important point about a Patrol Bureau master plan is that not all precincts are the same, and that not all patrol officers are the same. But they do have a lot in common. A master plan should, and did, recognize this. As an example, contrast the 41st in the Bronx and the 123rd precinct on the south of Staten Island. The nickname of the first was Fort Apache, and it was a different world from the 123rd district where I lived. I remember my first visit to Fort Apache in 1972. After talking with the precinct commander, I was taken out by a police lieutenant and an officer that evening to see the local sights. The one that has stayed deeply in my mind is the sight of a car on fire. When I asked what it was, the lieutenant replied, "Oh, that is a patrol car." The condition of the 41st in the early seventies is described in Police Captain Tom Walker's book *Fort Apache: New York's Most Violent Precinct* (1981). It was also depicted in a Paul Newman movie *Fort Apache, the Bronx* (1981). And we drove on, but the image of the burning patrol car in the 41st precinct stayed long and deep in my mind. The story about the 123rd precinct that stays in my mind was told to me by a police lieutenant, also called Pat Murphy, who lived in south Staten Island and who later (long after I was no longer there) became the chief of operations. He told me (maybe he was just repeating a cute story) of someone who lived in the 41st and who was transferred to the 123rd precinct. The person allegedly reported being frightened in the 123rd: it was then too much (for him) countryside, sparsely inhabited. And this is an identity issue to be considered when developing a master plan for a huge organization like the NYPD Patrol Bureau.

## COPING: THE DETECTIVE BUREAU

It was an even greater pleasure to work with the chief of detectives, Louis Cottell, and, when he was ill, with his substitute, James B. Meehan. Louis Cottell—a long-time member of the force, having joined in 1942—was appointed chief of detectives in May 1972, and I relocated to a desk next to his office. Louis was P.C. Murphy's second appointment to the chief's position. The first had been the more flamboyant and cigar-chomping Albert Seedman from 1971 to 1972. Louis was a calm and thoughtful person, and I met and talked with him frequently. At one point, he sent me the following message written on a photograph: "To Dave. A good mind and respected advisor. Louis."

Jim Meehan later became chief of the New York City Transit Police (1979–1987), a sizable force (2,800 in 1975) that was independent until 1995, when it became part of the NYPD. I visited Jim only once in his Transit days. But in his earlier capacity as a commander in New York's Finest, I would often go with him on field visits. He used to joke that we ate lunch together only in the best restaurants—like a stand-up place on Bleecker Street. I was with him when we visited a lock-up where the police had just arrested a cop killer. There were some thirty enraged cops. And I was impressed when Chief Meehan used a commanding voice to rule out the possibility of improper police behavior against the arrestee.

The Master Plan System—the Comprehensive Command Review Program—was developed and implemented for the Detective Bureau. It developed plans for functions, organization, manpower allocation, operational procedures, administrative procedures, personnel, and supporting services and equipment.

The most satisfying part of association with the Detective Bureau was the larger opportunity to be of direct help to the chief of detectives. Here is an example, and it relates to the large number of detectives—some 900—then working against the Black Liberation Army (BLA). It wasn't like a detective movie, where Detective Singleton handles the whole thing with nothing more than his brain and detective skill. There was an independent central core of detectives (more than 200), and then each of the major boroughs had set up independent units to cope with the BLA. Composed largely of former Black Panthers, the Black Liberation Army was understood as being in a violent struggle—as they said—for the liberation and self-determination of Afro-American people in the United States; the police saw them as cop-killers. The leaders included Eldridge Cleaver and Joanne Deborah Chesimard (also known as Assata Shaker). The BLA was begun in 1970 and ended in 1981 or so—long after I had left the NYPD. But it can be considered to have "started" in May 1971, before my entrance to the NYPD—with the brutal murder of two on-duty patrolmen, Joseph Piagentini and Waverly Jones. And the story went around that one had been deliberately shot in the testicles. Between 1970 and 1976, there were some seventy incidents involving the BLA, and the Fraternal Order of Police claimed that there were thirteen police deaths. The murder of NYPD officers had a profound effect on the department. For example, the department started two-car patrols—not just two officers in a single patrol car, but one two-officer car following another two-officer patrol car. So there was pressure to resolve the problem, unsurprisingly.

There was a meeting of the detective borough commanders with the chief of detectives and with me. The meeting had two parts. The first was that one of the borough commanders played a message intercepted from Joanne Chesimard, aka Assata Shaker. She would go on to alleged actions including a shoot-out with New Jersey police in May 1973, conviction for murder and other offenses in 1977, imprisonment for life and what she described as torture, escape from prison on November 1979, escape to Cuba, listing on the FBI's most wanted terrorist list in May 2013, plus offers of rewards totaling $2,000,000. I heard her voice again on the Internet a couple of years ago (anybody can find it on the Internet), and I was certain that it was the same as the voice I heard many years before. In the chief of detectives's meeting, her recording sounded intelligent, and I had an unpleasant concern at that time that "my" people might not be as smart as "their" people. Even if it is understandable to object to such reaction, it is dichotomous thinking to object that "because X is rotten (if s/he is) and also unacceptable, X must also be stupid." But that was not the place for that conversation. The second part of the 1972 meeting was like a vintage movie. The chief of detectives walked around the room and shouted at the borough commanders—with a strong New York accent—"If some of youse guys don't get results quick, some of youse guys are going to lose your jobs!" He said it twice. So the meeting ended.

After the meeting was over, I walked back into the chief's office, "Louis, I see that you were upset in our meeting about the BLA. I wonder if there is anything I can do for you." He replied, "Yes, Dave, go and visit each of the units, and see what they are doing about the BLA." "Sure!" I replied. "And he added, "And don't take any cops with you." I visited each of the commanders during the next week, and each gave me a presentation about what they were doing about the BLA. What struck me the hardest was that each unit had no clue what the other units were doing and had done, and it surprised me that they were pursuing different sets of criminals—more than twenty-eight different BLA. people. I returned to the chief of detectives, and I gave him my recommendations. I advised that he centralize all the units working on the BLA; I gave him my reasons for this; and I made my recommendations about the kind of commander he should appoint. Louis Cottell accepted and implemented my recommendations. He chose to consolidate under a new commander, Deputy Chief Harold Schryver, a twenty-seven-year NYPD veteran. The new system appeared to work, and at last it was announced that all six of the BLA leaders had been arrested. (I wondered what had happened to the twenty-two others.) A few years later, I encountered Deputy Chief Harold Schryver on a boat party on the Hudson. We chatted, and one of the things he said was, "It's odd that few or no people will ever know how much you contributed to our success with the BLA people." Thanks from him and Louis was enough.

As an example of a nonuseful but much more pleasant activity, there was November 14, 1972, from 10 PM until November 15 at 6 AM. As the certificate signed by Mayor John V. Lindsay attests, I was then night mayor for the city of New York. I turned up at City Hall. I told the police officer at the door who I was, and asked him to look after me, I then went to one of the volunteers who were taking calls from citizens. I was impressed with her ability. One caller asked, "What should I do with a squirrel who has come into my garage?" I would never have thought of the right answer, which was, "Leave the garage door open, and go away for an hour." I was assigned the empty office of Bess Myerson, head of consumer affairs and 1945's Miss America. I watched the television for a while, and then I went to sleep on her couch. My job was to alert the mayor by telephone if any crisis arose. Night mayors were forbidden to go out of City Hall, because some in the past had interfered with firefighting activities. Nothing whatsoever happened during my tenure—zero. And at 6 AM, I exited City Hall.

## COPING: CHIEF OF OPERATIONS

Hugo J. Masini (1925–2013) was appointed chief of operations by the new police commissioner, Donald Cawley, in May 1973. He was the chief uniformed officer, now with a new title for what previously (when held by Chief Codd) was called chief inspector. I joined him in the same month, with a desk near his office.

I was also given an additional title of director of operations management, and, as mentioned earlier, allocated some 1,200 officers to manage. Some were operational and others were planning. On the operational side, as an example, one was the smallish unit that used to monitor and facilitate the making of movies in New York City. The city administration had a great interest in fostering the making of movies in the city, and I recollect being told that about eighty such movies were then made annually. I never met the unit members. But I did receive a telephone call from its head officer, who asked me if I wanted a police car for official business. I replied in the negative, because I already had one for that purpose (BTW, "Park it anywhere, but don't use Broadway," I had been told when I first obtained it). On the planning side, I inherited two sizeable planning units from Don Cawley when he was elevated from chief of patrol to P.C. Each was commanded by a deputy inspector, and both units together occupied an entire precinct building in Brooklyn—appropriately made nonaccessible to the public. I decided to replace one of the deputy inspectors—no problem, but I don't think he ever forgave me.

BTW, when I was asked (in addition to being special assistant to the police commissioner) to be director of operations and management for the chief of operations, accidentally in my reply I left out the word "and"—and both the chief of operations and the police commissioner "loved"—as the chief put it—the title of director of operations management.

A pleasurable project was participating in making a presentation at a rape reduction workshop with the Denver Anti-Crime Council. I worked on this project with Lt. Julie Tucker, mentioned earlier in this chapter as commander of the Rape Analysis and Investigations Unit. That was also my first time on television—about the workshop topic.

Another part of the work was learning even more about the imitation badge that I could have, according to Sydney Cooper, grown. I learned detail and the power that context gives to the badge. On detail, for instance, I learned that it was considered important to give preferential treatment to fire officers. Chief Masini mentioned how important it was for police officers to proffer such preferential treatment to "brother" fire fighters, because (as he said) they are … brothers. He was unimpressed by my response that that seemed unethical; "No, it is not," he replied. On power, I was often reminded how powerful a grip the badge had for its holders, not only because of its utility in the field but also because of family relatives. For instance, my secretary at this stage was a female police officer, and she gave me a gift of a book she had written (King & Thurman, 1975), my secretary adding a note that it was given to "a nice person and one of the nicest bosses I have had the pleasure of working with." Thanks, Irene. Her husband had been a cop; her father was a retired police captain and a member of the force for thirty-one years; her sister Carolyn was a detective: her sister's husband was a cop. The badge in such circumstances (and they were not that uncommon) was a family matter.

As I was nearing the end of my stay in New York, I reflected on my work at the NYPD. As special assistant to the police commissioner, my work and my identity had been shaped by working as a management consultant for two Chicago companies—Public Administration Service (1965–1970) and The Jacobs Company (1970–1971)—and by employment as a management analyst and economist by governments in Canada and in Australia. This and other identity ingredients—like my education at various universities—will be noted elsewhere. I had provided management consulting services to some forty state and local governments (e.g., states such as Pennsylvania and cities including Los Angeles, Atlanta, Reading, Salt Lake, New Hope, and Milwaukee). Some of the consulting services had been to police departments—e.g., including advising the mayor and police chief of Durham, North Carolina, during a riot. It left me comfortable working rapidly doing the consulting assignment as I thought fit, while fitting in with the principal people in the agency. On the structure of policing in the country, I had agreed with the President's Commission on Law Enforcement and Administration of Justice that "America is essentially a nation of small police forces, each acting independently within the limits of its jurisdiction" (1967, p. 117) and I applauded—and recommended—police coordination and pooling in my work for the commission and in my book on civil disorder control (Farmer, 1968). I had explained the need for interlocal cooperation and intralocal coordination for riot control planning.

I recall eventually becoming a tad disquieted by the limits of the scope for improvements available for me within the NYPD. Consider the limits of action feasible in practice on corruption and on the structure of policing. I remember a meeting with the police commissioner and senior commanders about the Knapp Commission and the likely impact on the NYPD; the likelihood of low-level police being identified as corrupt was greater than identifying more sophisticated nonpolice offenders. I remember the P.C. asking a soulful question, "What are they doing out there?" I did not have an intelligent or informed enough answer when he turned and asked, "What do you think, Dave?" I think that I must have adapted to the NYPD context—perhaps even starting to grow a bit of a fake badge. I remember a deputy inspector early after my arrival telling me that in meetings he found himself forgetting that I was not a cop. I also remember that—as was the police custom at that time—it was normal to swear freely, and apparently I started to do that in serious meetings—and it took effort after I left to cut that out. I also remember on several occasions, someone would say, "Shush, there is a woman in the next room"—because it was not acceptable to swear in the hearing of a "good" woman. Being used to cursing, except before women and very senior commanders, was as natural as getting used to downtown New York. In the first months, I was conscious of smells from the streets in the area of headquarters; later, my nose/brain learned not to smell them.

## ISSUES ON OPENNESS

Let us return to the promise—in this essay's second and third paragraphs—to look at openness in the mainly closed context of the NYPD. Here are examples of desirable openness from the police department. Yet more openness should be available from other participants in the criminal justice system and politicians—perhaps also the public.

On a first issue about greater police openness, the NYPD and similar departments should be appropriately open to nonpolice skills that might be helpful to cope with police problems. Even the largest police department in the United States (i.e., New York's Finest) needs input from other police departments and from nonpolice sources such as not only me but also (say) the Department of Justice or (say) the Kerner Commission (the National Advisory Commission on Civil Disorders). The "badge" did not then have adequate understanding of inter-agency and intra-agency civil disorder control. For instance, the police commissioner hired me for skills that he thought that the NYPD did not have, and he summarized that identity—as noted earlier—as being "a management consultant." There will be other skill sets; later there could be such skill sets relating, say, to big data and automation needs. The degree of openness is more complicated, however. For example, rank is critical in a police agency (as Murphy and others have noted), and so, designating someone as special assistant to the police commissioner is different than merely hiring an outsider. It is a safe expectation that such openness will fluctuate in the NYPD from one P.C. to another (e.g., from Murphy to Codd, etc.).

On a second issue, the NYPD commanders—and similar commanders in other departments—should become more open to triggers and mechanisms encouraging commanders to assume more responsibility for the activities of subordinates. It is not being suggested that commanders are never in charge: when they walk into a precinct, for instance, the subordinates stand to paramilitary attention. But the reference is to moving from a C.Y.A. management approach to management implied in part by the Knapp Commission (as noted earlier, and to repeat one example) when it recommended that commanders should be held responsible for their subordinates' actions. The triggers and mechanisms intended to facilitate such effective management include the Manpower Allocation Review System (MARS) and master plans for its patrol and detective and other bureaus. Once again, this would be influenced by the identity of the police commissioner and the changing contexts.

As a third example, adjustments should be welcomed in the meaning of the police badge. Shouldn't more of those with a badge, and those without, be willing to recognize that the NYPD—like most (if not all) police departments—is a mixture of good and bad. On the good (plus some bad) side, Deputy Chief Harold Schryver contributed to the eventual defeat of the armed elements of the BLA. On the bad (plus some good) side, the shadow on the badge remained. This was evidenced by the Mollen Commission (The City of New York Commission to Investigate Allegations of Police Corruption and the Anti-Corruption Procedures of the Police Department), set up by Mayor David N. Dinkins in June 1992 and reporting two years later. *The New York Times* (Raab, 1993) summarized the findings by saying that the NYPD "had failed at every level to uproot corruption and had instead tolerated a culture that fostered misconduct and concealed lawlessness by police officers." The Mollen Commission reported: "Today's corruption is not the corruption of Knapp Commission days. Corruption was largely a corruption of accommodation of police officers, giving and taking bribes, buying and selling protection.... Today's corruption is characterized by brutality, theft, abuses of authority and active police criminality." In contemporary terms, this might be illustrated in terms of even greater acceptance of body cameras—or even changes that would lead to less need for such cameras. *Good police policy* and bad; *bad police policy* and good; nobody's perfect—surely no agency should be too good to learn from others.

Yet more openness should be available from the perspectives of others. Examples of such perspectives are those of participants in the criminal justice system and politicians—perhaps also the public. On the former, consider the later claim by P.C. Patrick Murphy about the criminal justice system. Murphy wrote that the "main problem of the criminal justice system in the United States is, simply, that it is not a system" (Murphy & Plate, 1977, p. 82). On the matter of politicians, it seems hard to expect easy changes in the difficulties created by politicians wishing special treatment by the police. For instance, the situation in the seventies was that a significant number of police promotions and careers (above the rank of captain, where examinations were not used) were facilitated by what were called "rabbis" (e.g., a "rabbi" in one case of a deputy chief being a cardinal). Don't we all, cops and noncops, cope with the identities and contexts that we recognize—consciously and unconsciously.

On such lack of openness, consider the utility of the celebrated rebuttal (or cover) statements, both then and now. "What does s/he know?" "That was years ago!" "Things have changed." "We have that covered." "We have that covered now!" "We have the greatest police forces (country, universities) in the world."

## REFERENCES

Armstrong, M. F. (2012). *They wished they were honest: The Knapp commission and New York City police corruption*. New York, NY: Columbia University Press.

Dickens, C. (1859/1940). *A tale of two cities*. London, UK: Chapman & Hall.

Farmer, D. J. (1968). *Civil disorder control: A planning program of municipal coordination and cooperation*. Chicago, IL: Public Administration Service.

Farmer, D. J. (1973). *Police productivity. Overview: A police publication on organization, administration and operations*. New York, NY: New York Police Department.

Fosburgh L. (1971, October 5). 6 Civilian Specialists Join Police as Murphy's Aides. *The New York Times*. Retrieved from http://www.nytimes.com/1971/10/05/archives/6-civ-ilian-specialists-join-police-as-murphys-aides-murphy-selects.html

King, I., & Thurman, C. (1975). *She's a cop, isn't she?* New York, NY: Dial Press.

Murphy, P. V., & Plate, T. (1977). *Commissioner: A view from the top of American law enforcement*. New York, NY: Simon & Schuster.

President's Commission on Law Enforcement and Administration of Justice. (1967). *The challenge of crime in a free society*. Washington, DC: GPO. Retrieved from https://www.ncjrs.gov/pdffiles1/nij/42.pdf

Raab, S. (1993, December 29). New York's police allow corruption, Mollen panel says. *The New York Times*. Retrieved from http://www.nytimes.com/1993/12/29/nyregion/new-york-s-police-allow-corruption-mollen-panel-says.html.

Walker, T. (2007). *Fort Apache: New York's most violent precinct*. Bloomington, IN: Rooftop.

# Contemplating Cops: A Tale of Identities – Essay 2

David John Farmer

"It was the epoch of belief, it was the epoch of incredulity, it was the season of Light, it was the season of Darkness" (Dickens, 1859/1940, p. 1), it was an age of the emergence of some traditional research relating to police policy and administration, it was the age of continuing police support for the police badge. Again, the first two essays focus on three different police policy and management work identities, and the third and fourth essays center on three different public administration identities. Essay 1 discusses my work identity and contemplation as special assistant to the NYPD police commissioner. Essay 2 describes my identity and context when I was director of the Police Division in the National Institute (within the U.S. Department of Justice) and professor and chair (within Virginia Commonwealth University's Department of Administration of Justice and Public Safety). In the first identity, I was a federal government employee specializing in fostering police research; in the second. I was (until 1991) a university professor specializing in police studies. How can public administration and other thinkers learn from such recognition of the relevance of identities and contexts? I leave it to the reader to evaluate and assess the significance of your own identity and contexts.

The issue of increasing openness is raised not only by police employee identity but also by the work identities encouraged in the federal government and university context. Recall the discussion in Essay 1 of the reluctance of many police officers to understand why the police commissioner wanted to know about how other U.S. police departments handled this or that police matter: after all, for them, New York is the finest. It is useful to think of police thinking in terms of at least four levels. First is the category of micro-level perspectives of lower-ranking cops and non-cops, including both those on the street and those with insider jobs. Second is the category of macro perspectives at the senior command level, including those that should be expected from a police commissioner, a chief inspector, a chief of patrol, a chief of detectives, and a chief of operations. Third is the category of perspectives at the national level, perspectives about police but also extending to perspectives about the criminal justice system. An earlier example was the President's Commission on Law Enforcement and Administration of Justice. This resulted in the Law Enforcement Assistance Administration (LEAA), which I joined in 1974. Fourth is the category of perspectives at the world level both for the police and for the criminal justice system, and beyond to problems like the prevalence of guns. (Why not?) Police Commissioner Murphy was right when he observed that policing needed a perspective from the world level.

An identity encouraged in the United States government, requiring opening, tends not to privilege the world level on this list of four levels. For its own reasons, most of the National Institute's research was limited to the United States. *The Justice Assistance News*, describing an exception noted later, quoted me (as director of the Police Division) as saying that "much police research and literature tends to be parochial, focusing solely on experiences in this country. Cross-national studies offer the advantages of identifying police activities that have evolved culturally and arbitrarily, thus suggesting opportunities for improvement. Countries can learn from one another, despite cultural variations" (Police Research from an International Perspective, 1980, p. 11). Other opportunities for opening will be noticed.

An identity encouraged in universities teaching about policing inclines toward a lack of emphasis on the second, third and fourth levels just noted – perspectives from the macro, the national and the world levels. A problem is a priority in teaching administration of justice in such a way that it appears "practical" to practitioners—appealing to the practical for low-ranking police and for students who want to be police officers. A consideration is that the police world of the bottom level is not simply the same as the world of the senior police commanders; the former—not some of the latter—might not welcome study of the Knapp or Mollen Commission. So a bureaucratic university, judging on the basis of students' satisfaction as consumers, is not likely to want to challenge the sense of practicality of enrolled students The fact is that it is rare to have senior commanders in classes. This problem of lack of openness is multidirectional. It is not at all confined to universities; it is also a lack of openness from police, and also from society.

My work identities for contemplating cops were progressive but traditional. Why did my identity and context not include—until later—utilization of the postmodern and other elements of the post-traditional? As Shakespeare (As You Like It, II, vii, 139) observes, "And one man in his time plays many (interrelated) parts. His acts being seven ages – (with the sub-texts of the acts being interrelated with one another and with society, and of the seven ages being interrelated)."

## THE FEDERAL GOVERNMENT

Should the federal government, and others, be more open in contemplating cops and in helping cops to cope? Another door opened when I left the NYPD. It admitted me as director of the Police Division in the seventies (1974–1980) when I joined the National Institute of Law Enforcement and Criminal Justice (renamed National Institute of Justice in 1978). The National Institute was part of the U.S. Department of Justice, through the Law Enforcement Assistance Administration (until its title changed in 1982 and rechanged in 1984 to Office of Justice Programs). A major identity for me at the National Institute was as a federal employee helping police to cope. But the identity and context—self-understanding of the equivalent to the police badge, if you like—altered. A primary emphasis shifted to researchers and research institutions, and not merely police institutions wanting research monies.

As the National Institute's director of the Police Division, my main function was to recommend grant awards for police research. In other words, it was to take all the advice and help and administrative steps that seemed desirable (and what the Institute required) to recommend the expenditure of research grants that would supply what I considered to be useful perspectives to help police in the United States to cope. The police research budget was approximately $3 million to spend in the first year. Using the Consumer Price Index (if you believe such claims), that is said to be $15,358,766 in today's dollars.

The director of the National Institute itself, responsible for the institute's organization and management, was appointed by the president of the United States. The director when I was hired was Gerald Caplan (1973–1977), appointed by President Richard Nixon. Geoffrey Alprin (also a lawyer) was a close advisor of the director. Other directors during my term of employment were Blair Ewing (1977–1979) and Harry Bratt (1979–1981). I had a small staff of some five people. Only one had been a police officer; only one was a minority member; only two were female; and all, except my secretary, were university graduates.

There was a sense that the seventies presented an opportunity for significantly more open and rational police policy and practice. This opportunity for an "open door" (open both "inward" into policing and "outward" from policing) followed the "police science" of four (or so) studies and five (or so) events. The four studies are described in the next and later paragraphs—about preventive patrol, response time, detective investigations, and forensics. The preceding events were the 159 or so riots in the Long Hot Summer of 1967 and the subsequent Kerner Commission (1968), which urged that "our nation is moving toward two societies, one black, one white—separate and unequal"; the establishment of the National Institute of Justice under the Omnibus Crime Control and Safe Streets Act of 1968; the creation of the Police Foundation in 1970 and the funding of the NYPD for hiring the special assistants in 1971; and the start of the Police Executive Research Forum (PERF) in 1976.

When it came to the mid-seventies, some of us found it helpful to talk about a possible revolution in policing. One of my articles had this title (the Research "Revolution," 1978—with the word "Revolution" in quotes). But other articles made a similar point (e.g., Farmer, 1975a, 1975b, 1976, 1979, 1980) in specialist journals like *Police Magazine, National Sheriff, Police Chief*, and other publications. (I also gave talks making the same claim—at Bramshill, the British police academy, and elsewhere.) The Research "Revolution" article—and others—conceded that police research has revealed much that is trivial and already well-known. But "it has also yielded results that nothing less than a revolution in operating practices is mandated for police agencies over the next several decades" (Farmer, 1978, p. 5). The Police Foundation website still speaks of the era of "The Early Years" (the seventies and eighties) as "a new paradigm for police science." Later eras are described by the website as the community policing and technical assistance era (1990s and 2000s), the technology, data, and accountability era in policing (1990s and beyond), and recent history (2000 and beyond). Perhaps it would have been better to use nonrevolutionary language; we could have spoken of the "open door."

Let's look more closely at the four studies—and follow-up studies—that demonstrated an opening door. The possibility of a door being open was triggered significantly by the Kansas City Response Time Study, the Kansas City Preventive Patrol Study, the RAND Study of Criminal Investigations, and the Forensic Science Foundation Crime Laboratory Proficiency Study. Each of the four studies provides important information. "But when the study findings are considered together, the insights are magnified; the whole is greater than the sum of the parts" (Farmer, 1978, p. 5).

The Kansas City Response Time study, started in 1972 and funded by the Police Foundation, opened the door to the possibilities of the organization and management of police utilizing a differential response strategy. The dominant theme of the main activity of traditional policing was (is) patrol—not only for cars on patrol for order maintenance and for crime prevention but also to be in the best position to respond rapidly. By contrast, a differential response strategy attempts to tailor the response to the character and timing of the situation. The Kansas City Response Time Study (Bieck, 1977, 1979, 1980) analyzed the relationship of response time to the outcomes of on-scene criminal apprehension, witness availability, citizen satisfaction, the frequency of citizen injuries, and so forth. The study did not rely on officer self-reporting. Citizen mobilization was the forgotten element in response time. As the study indicated, because of "the time citizens take to report crime, police response time will have negligible impact on crime outcomes" (Bieck, 1980, p. 4)—and if procedures can be developed to discriminate accurately between emergency and nonemergency calls, "more productive response-related outcomes can be achieved" (Bieck, 1980, p. 4). The Kansas City study was eventually replicated by the Police Executive Research Forum in Jacksonville-Duvall, San Diego, and Peoria. Work was also done on differential police strategies in the city of Birmingham, Alabama, funded by the Police Executive Research Forum. Four response categories were tried by sworn officers—immediate, expedited, routine, and appointment. The city of Wilmington examined an example of a split-force strategy, funded by the National Institute. This separated the police cars into two separate groups—entirely call-for-service and entirely preventive patrol (Cahn & Tien, 1980).

The Kansas City Preventive Patrol Experiment, starting in 1972, examined fifteen beats. In five "proactive" beats, the number of patrol cars was increased three times; in five other beats, the number of cars was kept the same; and in yet another five "reactive" beats, preventive patrol was eliminated. The experiment was continued for a year. The study did not assume that police patrol is of no value. But the experiment did conclude that the three "experimental patrol conditions appeared not to affect crime, service delivery, and citizen feelings in ways the public and the police often assume they do" (Kelling et al., 1974, p. 2). Some have interpreted this experiment as concluding, in the words of Police Chief Joseph McNamara, that "routine patrol in marked police cars has little value in preventing crime or making citizens feel safe" (Farmer, 1981, p. 26); others have criticized the methodology of the experiment (e.g., Larson, 1975).

The RAND study of the criminal investigation process, starting in 1973 and funded by the National Institute, undertook an evaluation of investigative organization and practices (Greenwood & Petersilia, 1975). It consisted of a national survey of all municipal and county police agencies that employed more than 150 officers or served a jurisdiction with a 1970 population in excess of 100,000. Additionally, interviews and observations were conducted in more than twenty-five departments selected to represent different investigative styles. The study reported that more than half of all serious reported crimes receive only superficial attention from investigators; an investigator's time is mainly consumed by cases that experience indicates will not be solved; the investigator spends more time on post-arrest processing than on the pre-arrest phase; the single most important determinant of whether a case will be solved is the information the victim supplies to the immediately responding patrol officer; and in many departments, investigators do not thoroughly document the key evidentiary facts. The RAND study concluded that "investigative activities play only a minor role in contributing to overall arrest rates and much of an investigator's time is consumed with administrative paperwork or attempting to locate and interview witnesses in cases that empirical evidence show[s] have a small likelihood of ever being solved" (Greenwood, 1979, p. 12). In other words, LOL, most TV detective shows are utterly misguided.

A proficiency study, funded by the National Institute, was conducted in 1978 by the Forensic Sciences Foundation. It studied a sample of (some 205) crime laboratories. Participating laboratories were sent common forensic items. The numbers of identification errors were high: 71.2 percent for blood and 67.8 percent for hair (Peterson, 1978). In other words, LOL, TV is wrong again.

The size of grants for police research, in the years when I was at the National Institute, was about $400,000 for big studies and $100,000 for small ones. There were many studies—beyond the four just discussed—that were useful in the seventies. This was the start of the vast amount of research that has been nourished by subsequent administrators—and encouraged as more and more police officers have obtained university degrees. Here are two administrators who created useful studies: Gary Hayes was the first president of PERF, and I recall him using a typewriter in my office (yes, we had typewriters in those days!) to fill out forms needed for the establishment of his new organization. I was in contact with him and with ex–police commissioner Patrick V. Murphy, then president of the Police Foundation. Here are two scholars who were among those who were significantly available for reflective conversation: Dr. Eleanor Ostrom, future Nobel Prize winner in economics, and Dr. Al Reiss, research director for the Kerner Commission in 1967 and then a sociologist at Yale. Here are two National Institute employees: Dr. Richard Barnes, mathematician and director of crime prevention, and Bob Burkhart, later institute director. Bother were engaging thinkers. And then there were the various police officials who contacted me. For example, I remember the first time I met Chief Roy Clinton McLaren, who had been the second author in the later editions of O. W. Wilson's much-respected textbook *Police Administration*. I was giving a talk in Chief McLaren's location of Arlington, Virginia, and I was criticizing the textbook *Police Administration* for not including the word "corruption" or any ideas about police corruption—not one word. I was taken aback at the end of my talk to be told that Chief McLaren was in the audience. The next day he visited me in my office, and in a very friendly way told me that he was working on the fourth edition—and could I help him by telling him what I recommended that he should add about police corruption.

## ISSUES ON OPENNESS

Here are three examples of issues of openness relating to federal government police research. Two supplementary issues about identity are also noted.

On the first of three openness issues, federally-funded research should aim not only to help American policing to cope, but it also should encourage more police self-understanding. They could aim for (as suggested in the second paragraph of this essay) more adequate police understanding of the macro, the national and world levels – as well as the micro.

Research is rarely perfect (except yours and mine LOL); but still it certainly can be very useful at all the levels for, say, assisting in making sure that police enforce laws equally. Recall, as an example, a story of an imperfection from the past, which can be dismissed easily enough because it is from the past. I was shocked – when we were told later – that neither the country nor the very helpful President's Commission on Law Enforcement and Administration of Justice had known how many police departments the U.S. really had. The President's Commission reported that the U.S. had 40,000 police departments. Chapter 4 of the Commission's report The Challenge of Crime in a Free Society (1967, p. 91) started by saying "The police – some 420,000 people working for approximately 40,000 separate agencies that spend more than $2½ billion a year – are the part of the criminal justice system that is in direct contact both with crime and … " That was false: the correct number of police departments was alleged to be more like 17,500. But, the report was useful.

More macro, national and world openness might be expected eventually to lead to a broader approach to police policy-making. With another story from the past, note that the National Institute and other American police research in the 1970s was focused on efficiency and effectiveness – and heavy use was made of the four studies discussed earlier. It could not have been 'sensible' to do otherwise. But I have described the service that Herman Goldstein did for police by stressing that the police reform movement had centered too much on means rather than ends (Farmer, 1981, p. 57). I quoted Herman writing that "the whole reform movement in policing has been short-sighted in focusing almost exclusively on improving the police establishment without having given adequate attention to some serious underlying problems that grow out of the basic arrangements for policing in our society" (Goldstein, 1977, p. 7).

On a second example of an issue about increasing openness (others may suggest other examples), this country has too many very small police departments. I wish that the number of such agencies could be reduced. Could the 17,500 police agencies have been profitably reduced to, say, less than a thousand? Of course, such a change is difficult: of course, it would be beneficial, if you agree with a minority of cops like Police Commissioner Pat Murphy in his claims like "small departments are less immune to political interference than larger police departments" (Murphy & Plate, 1977, p. 72) and "small departments blunder in their homicide investigations all the time" (Murphy & Plate, 1977, p. 73). I had also analyzed (Farmer, 1968) the lack of coordination between police departments when it came to civil disorder control.

On the third of three issues about increasing the openness of research itself, recall the claim at the beginning of this essay to the effect that most of the National Institute's research was located within the United States. The March 1980 issue of the *Justice Assistance News* carried a story about an exception; the story was titled "Police Research from an International Perspective." It described me (with a photo) as having "formulated the idea for the project several years ago." The project featured was about detective work and was being carried out by Holland (Department of Justice), Great Britain (Home Office), Canada (Solicitor-General's Office), Sweden (National Police Board), Australia (Institute of Criminology and Victoria Police Commissioner's Office), and the United States (PERF).

Here is the first of two supplementary issues about openness relating to changes in my attitude toward my work identity as director of the Police Division with the National Institute. Recall that some elements of identity are tied in with work and paychecks. I wanted to think out of the box. I wondered whether other disciplines could be, or had to be, involved. I was very fond of the people at the National Institute, but I was increasingly made a little uncomfortable by the narrowness of ideas I was obtaining at the institute. I found that I gained more pleasure from teaching evening classes on police-related subjects at American

University. To be very personal (and isn't that a participating determinant of identity?), I was married during my time at the National Institute (in 1978 to a person who was a practicing psychotherapist and who later became a professor of social work), and that opened up new avenues of intellectual pleasure. For example, I became hyper- interested (as she was) in Sigmund Freud—even went with my wife to visit his apartment in Vienna and his house in London. I do not mean that this is (or is not) "the" solution to law enforcement problems. But it is an example of a branch of understanding that spills over into other knowledge fiefdoms. I wanted a work environment that provided a greater expectation of new and different understandings.

On the second of two supplementary issues about openness relating to my work identity as the institute's director of the Police Division, we did have different elements of the criminal justice "system" (insofar as it is a system) represented in the different organizational units of the National Institute—the divisions of corrections, courts, and so on. But I was the director of the Police Division, and my work identity did not encourage "poaching." My identity, my interest, my work area was the police.

## UNIVERSITY POLICE SCHOLARSHIP

Should university disciplinary specialties be more open? When the door opened in 1980, I became a faculty member in the Department of Administration of Justice and Public Safety (AJPS) in the School of Community and Public Affairs at Virginia Commonwealth University (VCU). VCU was—and is—located in Richmond, Virginia. In 1982, and following what was called a national search, I became department chair—and I remained so until 1991, when my wish was granted to be reassigned to a different department and to a different specialty—public administration. At the end of that period, the name of the Department of Administration of Justice and Public Safety was changed to Criminal Justice (CJ); the School of Community and Public Affairs was happily merged as a component of the College of Humanities and Sciences; and stand by for countermoves later. Yes, universities involve elaborate bureaucracies and bureaucratic moves—and this has consequences for contemplating cops.

The School of Community and Public Affairs itself consisted of divisions (programs) not only for AJPS but also for public administration, urban studies, rehabilitation counseling, parks and recreation, and so on. Our AJPS department had some 450 undergraduate students and some 100 master's students. On the faculty, we had the knowledgeable "usual suspects"— including three ex–police chiefs (Jim Hooker, David Geary, and Phil Ash), a lawyer and ex-FBI agent (Jim Hague), a corrections scholar (Paul Keve) who had headed two state correctional systems, public safety researchers (Mike McDonald and Bob Breitenbach), criminal justice researchers (Alan Barrett, Donna Towberman, and Jan Thomas), my secretary, Gloria Evans—and a partridge in a pear tree. As time went on, I changed our faculty meetings so that we spent only a short time on administration; the majority of the time was spent on substantive comments on research and thoughts from faculty members. Having informal conversations with the faculty and with some students was enjoyable. For instance, having frequent conversations with Paul Keve was helpful in thinking about prisons—as did reading his books, such as *Prisons and the American Conscience: History of U.S. Federal Corrections* (Keve, 1991). I told Paul once that "when I grow up, I want to be like you."

Virginia Commonwealth University, when I joined in 1980, was much smaller that it was in 2015, when I became an emeritus professor. My impression is that it is harder for a university—like a police department—not to be more bureaucratic when—a matter of context—it is significantly larger. But there are surely other factors: identities of people and the growth of technology and the triumph of the business outlook in university management—and increasing administrative salaries and the galloping number of administrators. When I became department chair in 1982, I telephoned the university's president, Dr. Edward Ackell, and requested a meeting. I spent an hour or more with him about what I had in mind, and he told me about his days at medical school in New York and how he felt about this and that. Whenever he saw me on the street, he would indulge in a friendly pat on the back. In those early days, the provost, Wayne Hall—while celebrated for his brevity—was willing to chat. (A story about his brevity is that he was asked to give a welcome speech. He walked up to the microphone, said "Welcome," and then sat down.) Certainly VCU seems to have changed as the years continued.

I taught; I communicated; I served. I taught four AJPS classes per semester before becoming chair: after becoming chair, I started to teach two graduate classes within the areas of police policy and practice—twice the usual number, because I enjoyed it. As the years went on, one of the two classes was a doctoral or a master's or an honors class in public administration. I communicated by making multiple presentations—and I listened—throughout the eighties at various professional criminal justice meetings; for example, at the Academy of Criminal Justice Sciences, the Virginia Association of Criminal Justice Educators, the American Society of Criminology, the Association of Criminal Justice Sciences, and others. Also, I communicated by publishing articles and book chapters, mainly on police management and systems issues. As mentioned earlier, there was also a book on *Crime Control: The Use and Misuse of Police Resources* (Farmer, 1984). "Out of Hugger-Mugger" (using an antiquated phrase) was a sentiment describing how police resources should be employed more rationally—in accordance with research findings. That phrase was used in a book chapter titled "Out of Hugger-Mugger: The Case of Police Field Services" (Farmer, 1980) and in a presentation titled "Hugger-Mugger Revisited: More About Resources Allocation" made in San Antonio, Texas, in 1983 to the Academy of Criminal Justice Sciences.

I served on committees, a typical university task. Inside the university, I served on promotion and tenure and other committees, and each week, as chairs, we had an administrative meeting with the dean. For five years, I was a member of the University Graduate Council, and also a member of the subcommittee on programs and courses; I also was a member of the University Faculty Senate. Outside the university, I was a member of a couple of community boards—for Human Resources Incorporated and Jump Street Drug and Rehabilitation programs. I was also a community service associate for Virginia Secretary of Public Safety Robert L. Suthard (1990–1992)—the incumbent being a former superintendent of the state police (1984–1990). It was a little more advanced than in the sixties, when I was a member in Illinois of the Park Forest South (later renamed "University Park") Police Board. I talked with Secretary Bob, often over lunch, about whatever was on his mind.

My first dean of the School of Community and Public Affairs was a scholar named Laurin Henry; his associate dean was Alvin Schexnider. We had many friendly and helpful conversations. When the school started a doctoral degree, he asked me to co-teach a course with him about public administration: that was a pleasure, and I continued to teach in the program by myself when Laurin retired. I also raised the issue of how to expand my understanding, and he was very supportive and encouraging when I enrolled in the graduate program of philosophy at the University of Virginia. Well, it was only 70 miles away, and the only thing that worried me was that I tended to be conscious when I started driving and when I arrived in Charlottesville—but I drove the part in the middle with what is called *highway hypnosis*. A few times, Laurin would take me with him to a meeting somewhere and to chat on the way: once by way of his sheep farm in Bath County, Virginia, near the underground bunker where Congress planned to hide in the event of atomic war, and once to Washington so that on the way we could see the house where Booth hid after assassinating President Lincoln. Eventually, Laurin retired, and moved to Charlottesville.

## ISSUES ON OPENNESS

University police research can be in a good position to contribute to upgrading police self-understanding at the four levels noted in the second paragraph – not only the micro but especially the macro, the national and the world levels. The following five issues could be interpreted in that way.

On the first of five examples of issues about the lack of openness in helping cops to police, the preface to my 1984 book *Crime Control: The Use and Misuse of Police Resources* (Farmer, 1984, p. ix) begins by asking, "How can crime be controlled more effectively? The widespread public urge for an easy answer to this difficult question reflects not only the seriousness of the problem but also a general reluctance to treat the matter as seriously as it deserves." The book criticizes a societal context that privileges simplistic answers and dualistic thinking. It explains that

> public policymaking and debate about crime control remains shackled by dualistic thinking and by the child-like impulse for simplistic answers. The dualistic character of the thinking, assuming only a dichotomous world of "right versus wrong" and "we versus they," is reflected in the nature of our perennial debates over gun control and capital punishment. The urge for the "one-liner" solution in the character of the remedies commonly touted for the crime problem—"Lock them up and throw away the key" and "Abolish unemployment" and "Eliminate the insanity defense." As long as we are constrained by a proclivity toward such instant solutions, we will remain impotent in addressing the crime control problem. (Farmer, 1984, pp. ix & x).

Yes, the lack of openness is inward from the person (the cop or the member of the public) who thinks in this dichotomous way. It is also outward from the university if the university teaching ends up with graduates who think in this dualistic way. It is also a limitation from society that supposes that there must be a quick-fix for the crime problem. This point about society was made where *Crime Control* indicated "The error of the Great Society programs, of which crime control was one, was an underlying thesis that the quick-fix is possible. 'America can control crime, if it will,' concluded the President's Commission on Law Enforcement and Administration of Justice" (Farmer, 1984, p. 4).

On the second of five issues about the lack of openness that limits the ability of cops to cope, there is a problem when confining police education to police science—when confining criminal justice to a separate branch of study. In later years, I have written about epistemic pluralism in relation to subjects like public administration and economics. But when I reread earlier materials, I notice that—without realizing it—I always have tended in that direction. Consider, for police education purposes, the benefits of using political science or economics. (You may wish to substitute any other "foreign" discipline, like English literature.) If political science is worth its salt, political science should figure significantly in police science or criminal justice education. My *Crime Control* book (1984) contains a chapter on politics and policing (pp. 85–119). For example, it wrote about "pervasive politics" and "controlling political intrusion," and quoted the fourth edition of Wilson and McLaren (1977)—the edition mentioned earlier—as commenting that many "police officials ... believe that a forthright discussion of police and politics is somehow on the forbidden list of thoughts that must remain in verbal form only." In 1991, when I switched to public administration, the School of Community and Public Affairs did break up—and public administration was connected with political science. So I began to teach an undergraduate course on ancient and medieval political philosophy, and I did so for twenty years. I like to think that such a course—studying Plato's *Republic*, Aristotle's *Nicomachean Ethics*, and St. Augustine's *City of God*—could help both students and cops to begin thinking more perceptively about coping. If economics is worth its salt, the study of economics has relevance to criminal justice and police policy. Consider the use of privately owned prisons; does that have no connection with economics? Consider the way that society is shaped by some economists' belief in, for instance, the idea of the free market? Consider the way that business ethics shapes social thinking. Consider the claim by the distinguished economist Ha-Joon Chang (in *23 Things They Don't Tell You About Capitalism*; 2010) that there is no such thing as the free market, and yet people celebrate it. Writes Chang (in *Economics: The User's Guide*, 2014, p. 327), "Economics is a political argument. It is not—and never can be—a science; there are no objective truths in economics that can be established independently of political, and frequently moral, judgements. Therefore, when faced with an economic argument, you must ask the age-old question 'Cui bono?' (Who benefits?), first made famous by the Roman statesman and orator Marcus Tullius Cicero."

On the third of five issues about the lack of openness, there is that caused by the isolation of philosophy from a "practical" subject like police practice and policy. I was awarded a doctorate in philosophy from the University of Virginia, and I concede that something like my dissertation on the nature of time would appear to have nothing to do with the world of the practical. But that appearance would be false. The practical relevance is clearer when one considers such philosophical topics as epistemology and ethics. On epistemology, there is utility in considering questions like whether police science is indeed a science, whether political science is a science, whether economics is indeed the queen of the social sciences, and so forth. On ethics, there is utility in considering meta-ethical questions like what is the nature of ethics or applied ethics, such as whether it is ethical to sentence someone—like a neighbor of mine, a lawyer who stole $600,000—to 160 years in prison.

The fourth of five issues about lack of openness concerns the inequalities in law enforcement. Recall that Police Commissioner Patrick V. Murphy described the claim that police departments enforce all laws equally as "nonsense" and "silly" (Murphy & Plate, 1977, p. 53). Wouldn't the BLA, discussed in Essay 1, have agreed with the Police Commissioner? Openness to the inequality of law enforcement treatment is more than a "mere" police or bureaucratic matter. Let me comment by referring to Governor L. Douglas Wilder, the first

African-American state governor in U.S. history, and learning from his book *Son of Virginia* (Wilder, 2015) – the governor signing the book and referring to me on the title page as his "colleague, friend and consultant." I was shocked to read that Doug's grandmother and grandfather were slaves (I thought it would have been great-grandparents or whatever); that information brought it for me to a direct human level. Whenever I am near the graves of my own grandfather George and grandmother Eva, my mother Gladys and other ancestors, I sense my love for them. I told Douglas one day that I don't know much about slavery but, if my grandparents had been slaves, I would never, never have forgiven their oppressors. He replied, "You know more than most people." And his book starts by talking of this Virginia governor's opposition to the Virginia state song *Take Me Back to Old Virginny*. The second stanza sings of the slave, when dead, reuniting in paradise with his slave owners. Wow! Equal law enforcement is critical.

The fifth issue that concerns the lack of openness also has a pro and con. Recall the pro argument—earlier in this essay—which claims that a problem is the priority in teaching administration of justice in such a way that it appears practical to practitioners—appealing to what appears practical to lower-ranking police and other students. Recall the con argument—in Essay 1—that involves the closed-minded rebuttal (or cover) statements, both then and now. "That was years ago!" "We have that covered now!" "We have the greatest police force (government, university, etc.) in the world (or state, or immediate area)."

## EPILOGUE

To the extent that it is shut, should not the door be opened fully between police (or criminal justice) studies, on the one hand, and public administration, on the other? Cannot they learn from each other? But, isn't the extent to which police studies can learn from public administration limited by the extent the door is closed between public administration and public policy?

## REFERENCES

Anonymous. (1980). *Police research from an international perspective: Law Enforcement Assistance Administration. Journal Assistance News.* Washington, DC: GPO.
Bieck, W. (1977). *Response time analysis (Summary Vol. 1. Methodology. Vol. 2, Analysis).* Kansas City, MO: Kansas City Police Department.
Bieck, W. (1979). *Response time analysis (Vol. 3. Part 2. 0 Crime analysis).* Kansas City, MO: Kansas City Police Department.
Bieck, W. (1980). *Response time analysis (Vol. 4. Non-crime call analysis).* Kansas City, MO: Kansas City Police Department.
Cahn, M., & Tien, J. (1980). *Alternative approach in police patrol: The Wilmington split-force experiment.* Cambridge, MA: Public System Evaluation.
Chang, H. (2010). *23 things they don't tell you about capitalism.* New York, NY: Bloomsbury Press.
Chang, H. (2014). *Economics: The user's guide.* New York, NY: Bloomsbury Press.
Dickens, C. (1859/1940). *A tale of two cities.* London, UK: Chapman & Hall.
Farmer, D. J. (1968). *Civil disorder control: A planning program of municipal coordination and cooperation.* Chicago, IL: Public Administration Service.

Farmer, D. J. (1975a). Police research programs. *Police Chief*, *8*(2), 31–43.

Farmer, D. J. (1975b). Strengthening patrol operations. *National Sheriff*, *24*(3), 23–35.

Farmer, D. J. (1976). Fact versus fact: A selective view of police research in the United States. *The Police Journal*, *49*(2), 17–31. doi:10.1177/0032258X7604900205.

Farmer, D. J. (1978). The research revolution. *Police Magazine*, *3*(4), 14–23.

Farmer, D. J. (1979). The future of local law enforcement: The federal role. In J. T. O'Brien & M. Marcus (Eds.), *Crime and justice in America* (pp. 18–33). Elmsford, NY: Pergamon Press.

Farmer, D. J. (1980). Out of hugger-mugger: The case of police field services. In R. Clarke & M. Hough (Eds.), *Police effectiveness* (pp. 17–34). Scarborough, England: Gower Publishing.

Farmer, D. J. (1981). Thinking about research: The contribution of social science research to contemporary policing. *Police Studies*, *3*(4), 22–40.

Farmer, D. J. (1984). *Crime control: The use and misuse of police resources*. New York, NY: Plenum Press. Retrieved from http://www.springer.com/us/book/9781468447835

Goldstein, H. (1977). *Policing a free society*. Cambridge, MA: Ballinger.

Greenwood, P. W. (1979). *The RAND criminal investigation study: Its findings and impacts to date*. Santa Monica, CA: RAND.

Greenwood, P. W., & Petersilia, J. (1975). *The criminal investigation process. Vol. 1: Summary and policy implications*. Santa Monica, CA: RAND.

Kelling, G. L., et al. (1974). *The Kansas City Preventive Patrol Experiment: A technical report*. Washington, DC: Police Foundation.

Kerner Commission. (1968). *Report of the National Advisory Commission on Civil Disorders*. Washington, DC: GPO.

Keve, P. W. (1991). *Prisons and the American conscience: A history of U.S. federal corrections*. Carbondale & Edwardsville, IL: Southern Illinois University Press.

Larson, R. (1975). What happened to patrol operations in Kansas City? A review of the Kansas City Preventive Patrol Experiment. *Journal of Criminal Justice*, *3*(4), 267–297.

Murphy, P. V., & Plate, T. (1977). *Commissioner: A View from the top of American law enforcement*. New York, NY: Simon & Schuster.

Peterson, J. (1978). *Crime laboratory proficiency study*. Washington, DC: GPO.

President's Commission on Law Enforcement and Administration of Justice. (1967). *The challenge of crime in a free society*. Washington, DC: GPO.

Wilder, D. L. (2015). *Son of America: A life in America's political arena*. Guilford, CT: Rowman & Littlefield.

Wilson, O., & McLaren, R. (1977). *Police Administration*. New York, NY: McGraw Hill.

# Contemplating Bureaucracies: A Tale of Identities – Essay 3

### David John Farmer

It "was the spring of hope, it was the winter of despair, we had everything before us, we had nothing before us" (Dickens, 1859/1940, p. 1), it was an age of traditional public administration practice, it was an age of limited interest in foreign practice. This third essay—third in a series of four—discusses (in section 1) traditional American public administration practice in terms of tales of my work identities and context as a management consultant and public manager. It describes (in section 2) foreign public administration practice in terms of tales of my work identity as a budget analyst, administrative analyst, economist, and chief of methods research in two Canadian provincial governments and the Australian federal government. The fourth essay comments on traditional and post-traditional theorizing in terms including the work identity of professor. Let's turn from contemplating cops (in Essays 1 and 2) to a somewhat similar subject—contemplating bureaucracies.

This essay suggests that greater openness could be—and should be—obtained by opening doors (or eliminating walls, if you prefer). Can contemplating bureaucracies be facilitated by practical experience in more than one country? Can mislearning occur by limiting practice to one country, or one location within any one country? Can such contemplation be helped by experiencing practice within different policy environments? Could mislearning be experienced by ignoring differences between policy environments? Indeed, it can be suggested that contemplating bureaucracies might well benefit from opening the door between public administration practices in differing countries—and locations within countries. Beyond that, this facilitative need could well include opening the door wider between policy and administration.

Section 1: Traditional public administration practice (and traditional public administration theory which contributes to shaping practice) includes widely recognizable features of its identity—of its equivalent of a public administration badge, if you wish. One such feature of traditional American public administration practice (and traditional public administration theory), for example, is the discipline's signature dichotomy that was a legacy of Woodrow Wilson (1856–1924) and his *The Study of Administration* (1887)—and of others like Frank Goodnow (1859–1939) and Leonard White (1891–1958). Helping to shape the identity of a public administration specialist, the signature dichotomy is the separation of politics and administration and the development (at least at first) of an administrative "science" emphasizing efficiency.

Yes, there are other significant dichotomies beyond this so-called signature dichotomy of public administration practice and theory. One example is the separation between a public administration that remains within its own disciplinary cul-de-sac and a public administration that uses epistemic pluralism to take advantage of other disciplinary perspectives (Farmer, 2010); another example is a failure to recognize the need to contemplate public administration thinking within the context of the warring antagonism of private, against public, enterprise (Farmer, 2015).

Section 2: Foreign public administration practice raises questions for American public administration theory and practice. Recall the distinguished public administration thinker Frederick Mosher, writing about the American bias of public administration, noting that public administration was established "for the most part as an American invention, indigenous, sui generis" (Mosher, 1975, pp. 7–8). Yet celebrated public administration scholar Robert Dahl had noted that public administration's claim to be "scientific" depends on developing "a body of generalized principles independent of their national setting" (Dahl, 1947, pp. 8). For him, a U.S. public administration and an administrative science are incompatible, if only because the latter requires more than a one-nation perspective. Even university professorial practices and identities are limited by a one-nation perspective; as a single example, the practice of giving grades in each class differs from the English practice of combining lectures without grading but with anonymous examiners evaluating final examinations. Even without "science," public administration practice is also limited by a one-nation perspective.

This account concerns a period when I was excited by traditional public administration thinking and this account is confined to work identity. An explanation and a caution might be helpful. I was delighted – after I had written *The Language of Public Administration* (Farmer, 1995) – to be invited by Orion White to have lunch with Dwight Waldo. I had enjoyed Dwight's writings. We found him standing outside the restaurant with my book in his hand, and he asked me to sign it (I replied that I should be asking him to sign his *The Administrative State* for me). I was even more delighted when later he wrote to me saying that my 1995 book was the most "erudite" public administration book for the past fifty years. Soon he wrote me another letter – on August 8, 1997 – explaining that he didn't mean to imply that he was thinking of his own *The Administrative State* that was written fifty years ago. And this next sentence astonished me. Dwight wrote, "I was thinking, rather, that you had to be compared to Weber!" This brings me to the caution. Max Weber (1864–1920), a public administration traditional hero, described the effects on humans of modern society functioning like an "iron cage." My caution is that work identity is a good starter: but public administration theorists have to go on to the remainder of the identities. Consider modern identity from society as an iron cage, for example. As Charles Taylor explained, the "claim that an instrumental society, one in which, say, a utilitarian value outlook is entrenched in the institutions of a commercial, capitalist, and finally a bureaucratic mode of existence, tends to empty life of its richness, depth, or meaning. The experiential charge takes various forms: there is no more room for heroism, or aristocratic virtues, or high purposes in life, or things worth dying for…" (Taylor, 1989, p. 500). Let us return, in this essay, to work identity.

## AMERICAN PUBLIC ADMINISTRATION: PRACTICE

I started to think about the practice of American public administration when I was a management consultant working in Chicago for Public Administration Service (November 1965–January 1970) and then for the Jacobs Company, part of the Planning Research Corporation (January 1970–October 1971). This thinking about American public administration practice was continued when I was a public manager as director of operations management in the New York City Police Department (May 1973–1974); one can have two identities, and the major one during the period (when I was special assistant to the police commissioner) was *management consultant specializing in law enforcement.* This thinking continued as public manager when director of the Police Division in the National Institute of the U.S. Department of Justice (1974–1980), and as chair of the Department of Administration of Justice and Public Safety at Virginia Commonwealth University (1982–1991).

### Management Consultant

#### *Public Administration Service*

By the date I arrived at the headquarters building (November 1965), Public Administration Service (PAS) had long been located at 1313 East 60th Street—a grand-looking road built for the 1893 Chicago World's Fair. That address (known simply as 1313) had become a celebrated symbol of support (pro and con, famous and infamous) for the American public service. The building 1313 was opened well before World War II, and it was built on land donated by the University of Chicago and supported by a grant from the Spelman Foundation. It was established in accordance with the pro–public service vision of two advocates for the public service professions—Charles E. Merriam (Chicago political science professor and city alderman) and Louis Brownlow (once chairman of the Public Administration Clearing House). Within a few years, it had become the "nerve center for American public administration" (Kurtz, 2010). By the time I arrived, it consisted of twenty-one nonprofit institutions, including Public Administration Service, American Public Works Association, American Public Welfare Association, American Society of Planning Officials, American Society of Public Administration, National Legislative Conference, National Association of State Budget Officers, and National Association of Attorneys General. In the late eighties and beyond, there was an exodus to Washington, D.C. Long after I had left, this migration to D.C. included Public Administration Service.

I remember being first told about the fame and right-wing ill-fame of 1313 in 1966 when doing consulting work in Atlanta, Georgia—in a bar with the PAS regional representative, who was, like many others at PAS, an ex–city manager. The right-wing opposition that emerged in the fifties used the epithet "Terrible, Terrible 1313." I imagine that it was a bubble hooked into anti-government or pro-business sentiment stretching back to 1917 (and into the nineteenth century). I remember being amused but not impressed. At that time, I did not recognize how important the "religion of the free market" would become for American public administration. My identity did not allow me in the 1960s to think in such terms: I was a neutral management consultant. I was quite happy to be told the famous, but indifferent to the infamous, side of 1313.

Public Administration Service was incorporated on June 27, 1933. Its first director had been Donald Crawford Stone (living from 1903 to 1995); later he had been an assistant budget director in the Roosevelt and Truman White Houses. During my employment with PAS, the executive director was Herman G. Pope (1907–1973). Longer than the four years I spent there, Herman Pope was PAS director for 34 years. The associate director who "managed" the management consultants was G. M. (Mike) Morris (1918–2010); and significant headquarters representatives were Theodore Sitkoff (who later became executive director), Thomas R. Jacobs, and Joseph Molkup. Jacque K. Boyer, director of the headquarters division, was the one who helped me focus on police after ex–police chief George Eastman departed for greener pastures as a faculty member at Kent State,

However, the verb "managed" in the last paragraph's phrase "managed the management consultants" should be interpreted narrowly, because—after being told the client and the assignment—management consulting was essentially a lone wolf's (or lone wolves' job.) On arriving in Chicago on my first day, for example, I was introduced to the principal people still in the office and had nice chats, given the address of my first client, a copy of the agreement with the client, and invited to ask any questions that occurred to me. Next day, I set off by car with my family and some belongings from Chicago to Helena, Montana. It was a drive of some 1,444 miles—and that was in November 1965. I met the superintendent of public instruction at the State Capitol, and was introduced to her principal directors. I was then free to do whatever seemed desirable to develop my report on a *Recommended Records Management Program*, including talking and socializing with the superintendent and her directors as it seemed desirable. The report was reviewed and contained a cover letter from Mike Morris. Then, in January 1966, I was free to drive to my next assignment about their position classification and pay plan in Tacoma, Washington. That was some 601 miles away. Then, in April 1966, I was free to drive to my next assignment in the city of Atlanta, Georgia. That was a drive of some 2,648 miles.

For some two years, we traveled from consulting job to job. There were pluses and increasing minuses on a personal basis: I am currently a tad surprised that we agreed to such a mobile arrangement in the first place. Toward the end of the second year, we arranged with the associate director, Mike Morris, to change the agreement to air travel—and we bought a house in a Chicago suburb, Park Forest South (later renamed University Park). And, as an incidental experience, I became a member of the village's own police board; it was also a slightly disagreeable experience when the chairman (an ex-chief) didn't like to hear from me that he was wrong to arrange for extra money for the village by using the cops to prioritize giving tickets to out-of-town motorists. The remaining two years of my employment by PAS still involved most of my time at non-Chicago locations; but there was some time in the Chicago office. Two instances I remember. One was in August 1968 and the violence associated with the Democratic Convention—alleged as linked to Chicago Mayor Richard Daley. I remember next day driving with a colleague to the convention hall: and we were both impressed (surely should not have been) at the peace and quiet that prevailed. The second, and more stressing, instance was April 4, 1968, when Martin Luther King Jr. was assassinated by James Earl Ray. We all left the office very early in the mid-day, a few of us driven by Mike Morris. Most car lights were turned on (a signal for honoring Dr. King, I was told) as we passed East 60th Street.

All my management consulting services when working for PAS were within the constraints of traditional public administration. They were limited, for example, within the signature dichotomy, and they were utterly devoted to obvious practicality (with a big P). The services centered on such subjects as recommendations about organization and methods, human resources such as salaries and classifications, police administration (in the latter part of my employment), and other items within the sphere of how to manage programs and to get clear bureaucratic results. The client public agencies that I worked for over the four or so years included the state of Montana; city of Tacoma, Washington; city of Atlanta, Georgia; New York State Conference of Mayors; Milwaukee city and county, Wisconsin; Kansas City, Missouri; city of Moberly, Missouri; city of Cedar Rapids, Iowa; city of Joliet, Illinois; Plymouth Township, Pennsylvania; Georgia Institute of Technology, Atlanta, Georgia: Evanston Public Library, Evanston, Illinois; city of Independence, Missouri; Maryland State Department of Education; the state of Illinois; Grand Rapids, Michigan; city of Denver, Colorado; and Sterling Heights, Michigan. Most locations had partially different elements within their sense of social identity: I was told of Moberly's social identity including affection for General Omar Bradley, Independence's identity including positive feelings for President Harry Truman, Montana's for Senator Mike Mansfield, and so on.

It was pleasing to see American government through the eyes of the bureaucracy. Bosses were very open with me—in all but a few jurisdictions. And I learned much that (from their point of view) was off the record and that was not at all politically correct in terms of action or speech. To give two examples among many, I still remember the policing in Atlanta—watching the police investigate a murder in a very poor area (shall we say, not in the manner of Sherlock Holmes), as well as the police chief taking me to an Atlanta Braves ball game and offering me uncensored views on society. For the second example, I will long remember being with the mayor of Durham, North Carolina, and others during a riot in his city. The riot was scheduled to start at 7 PM one evening. Just before 7 PM, the mayor and his police chief came to me with a worry that the rioters might be able to intercept our messages—and should we change to a different band? I advised the mayor that it would be best to leave the situation unchanged, as the riot was so near. Then we went out in the mayor's car. And I remember the car window being broken by a rioter's stone; the driver, a police captain, saying that they must have been aiming at his cap, and us shouting in unison at him to take off his cap. Then the mayor contacted the governor, who called out the National Guard.

It was no less pleasing to be a member of Public Administration Service. I liked the other consultants and the job. But I felt the need to move on to another learning opportunity, and one reason was that the salary was higher—and the new opportunity was also in Chicago. This is the letter that PAS associate director Mike wrote to me on December 31, 1969:

Dear David.
With your departure from PAS soon to occur, I want to tell you that you will be missed. During your 4 years at PAS, you have performed an imposing range and variety of assignments. All of your assignments have been carried out with industry and competence. Your relationships with client representatives have been excellent as have your relationships with your co-workers. I am sure that all of your colleagues at PAS join me in wishing you well.

Sincerely Yours,
Mike

## The Jacobs Company

For the first part of my employment there, the Jacobs Company was located downtown in Chicago; for my last six months, the office was moved to another downtown location on the river opposite the site where the 108-story Sears Tower was being built, the tallest building in the world from 1973 (when it was completed) to 1998. The construction had started in 1970; I was happy to look down on the very short tallest building—because we were on our ninth floor.

By contrast with PAS, the Jacobs Company was a for-profit corporation. Like PAS, it specialized in providing management consulting services to governments. The owner, Tom Jacobs, had once worked with Chicago's Mayor Richard J. Daley—and the story was that the company was always waiting for "the" call from the city (i.e., from the mayor): I don't know if it ever came. The director of the management consultants was Edward Gregory, and he was later outranked by a recently retired major general. I enjoyed both of them, although the major general did complain in a friendly way that he wished I and another person would not always talk to him giving military examples—as if we thought he could understand nothing else. I came to the Jacobs Company in January 1970, and, after it had had some financial difficulties and laid off some of the consultants (not me), I left in October 1971. I was lucky at that time to be offered jobs in the same month by the World Bank and by the NYPD—and I chose the latter.

My management consulting work for the Jacobs Company was mainly for cities in the Model Cities Program. It was conducted, therefore, for the federal government's Department of Housing and Urban Development: HUD was the client. And I visited HUD often enough. (BTW, I remember one morning flying from Chicago to Washington, D.C., to find that the federal government was closed that day because of snow. I liked joking—foolishly—that, if I could fly 697 miles, couldn't they drive 20 or 30 miles to work?) Cities to which I was assigned to provide management consultation included Salt Lake City, Utah; Reading, Pennsylvania; Laredo, Texas; and Los Angeles, California. For example, I provided "Technical Assistance in Public Administration to the Salt Lake Model Cities Program" in June 1970. With the name changed, that was the title for the consulting service provided to all of the cities. Working with different kinds of clients at the different locations was pleasurable (e.g., with a LDS stake leader in Salt Lake City, and with a war veteran, Mayor Victor Robert Hewlett Yarnell, in Reading).

The Model Cities Program was a November 1966 part of President Lyndon Johnson's Great Society and War on Poverty. And more than 150 U.S. cities were designated as model cities. The program was terminated in 1974, having spent about $3 billion. Bureaucratic difficulties were noted as contributing to the termination. However, more significant were the urban riots—and also the shift to the political right.

Public Manager

Although the content of this section was discussed in Essays 1 and 2 on Contemplating Cops, the fact of the following public manager work would be mischaracterized if it were not mentioned in this Contemplating Bureaucracies essay. This section includes public manager work in the NYPD as director of operations management, in the U. S. Department of Justice as director of the Police Division in the National Institute, and as chairman of the VCU Department of Administration and Justice,

### NYPD

Being director of operations management did involve having 1,200 subordinates. But being special assistant to the police commissioner and management consultant did constitute the bigger part of my work.

### U.S. Department of Justice

Being director of the Police Division in the National Institute of Justice involved the direction, coordination, and control (as the federal job description puts it) of police research funding and of my five or so subordinates.

### University Program Chair

Being chair, Department of Administration of Justice and Public Safety, involved administering some twelve professors and some two secretarial staff, and overseeing some 450 undergraduate students and 100 or so graduate students who were majoring in administration of justice and public safety. Again, this is a kind of public administration—no joke intended.

## FOREIGN PUBLIC ADMINISTRATION: PRACTICE

The adjective "foreign" in the description "foreign public administration" is satisfactory but odd. It is satisfactory in that other countries are indeed foreign from the perspective of the United States; clearly, they are different countries. Consider the United States versus three foreign countries—Canada, Australia, and the United Kingdom. The "foreign" description is satisfactory in that the political context of these three countries does differ from that in the United States—for example, in that they have parliamentary systems, while the United States does not; their election processes are brief (e.g., five weeks in the United Kingdom) rather than up to two years in the United States; and the United Kingdom and Saskatchewan had elected democratic socialist governments. Even at the entirely civil service level, there is said to be more movement between departments than in the United States. It is odd, however, if public administration is regarded as an essentially American discipline, beginning as a legacy of Woodrow Wilson. Do we really think that the Canadians, the Australians, and the British—or the ancient Egyptians, the ancient Chinese, and the ancient Romans, who had massive bureaucracies—had no systematic thoughts about how to administer? Budgeting and personnel administration, for instance, are not completely different in such differing contemporary contexts. Wouldn't it be odd if there were nothing that could be learned from the foreigner? Wouldn't it be more desirable to think that more can—and should—be learned from differing identities and differing contexts?

My identity with the Budget Bureau of the province of Saskatchewan was as a budget analyst and as an administrative analyst (April 1960–August 1961). With my brief tenure with the Treasury Department of the federal government of Australia, my identity was federal employee (September 1961–December1961). I had three identities—linked with economics—with the Ontario government in Canada. I was employed as an economist with the Provincial Civil

Service Commission (June 1962–May 1963); I was an organization and methods analyst with the Organization and Methods Services in the Ontario Treasury Department (June 1963–May 1964) and my next identity was as chief of methods research in the Department of Economics and Development of the Ontario government (June 1964–May 1965).

## Budget Bureau, Saskatchewan

When I joined in April 1960, the Budget Bureau (established some twenty-four years earlier) had achieved a significant reputation in advising on the machinery of the provincial government and on management processes. It attracted many talented people from other parts of Canada and elsewhere. For the previous decade, the bureau's director had been Donald Tansley (1925–2007). And in 1960, its deputy director was Wes Bolstead (1930–2008). For evidence of these claims of significant reputation, see articles such as Pasolli (2009), titled "Bureaucratizing the Atlantic Revolution: The 'Saskatchewan Mafia' in the New Brunswick Civil Service, 1960–1970." Pasolli's article describes how seven budget bureau ex-employees—including Don Tansley—had moved to New Brunswick when the Saskatchewan government changed in 1964. The description "mafia" in the title of Pasolli's article has no "real" connection whatsoever to the criminal mafia. It is intended, in a way that appealed in Canada-speak, to reflect competence and getting results, I remember with pleasure, shortly after my arrival, Don Tansley having two of us relatively new bureau members ride with him when he went to a meeting in Saskatoon—to relate to one another, and so forth. I remember that the road between these two major cities was still partially unpaved.

I was in the Budget Bureau when Thomas Clement "Tommy" Douglas was still premier of Saskatchewan. The Saskatchewan government under Premier Tommy Douglas (living from 1904 to 1986) did provide a different political context, and—to express it in contemporary terms, and if he were alive today—perhaps he would have been a good friend of Bernie Sanders. Tommy Douglas was the seventh premier of Saskatchewan (from June 1944 to November 1961). He was a leader in Saskatchewan of the Co-operative Commonwealth Federation Party (which later changed its name to the New Democratic Party). Premier Douglas led the Saskatchewan provincial government as the first democratic socialist—or socialist democratic—government in North America. It was the same Saskatchewan that introduced the single-payer Medicare system in 1962, and Douglas worked with Canadian Prime Ministers Lester Pearson and John Diefenbaker to introduce the health system later at the federal level. A former Baptist minister born in Scotland, Douglas had had a difficult medical illness when he was ten years old—and it significantly influenced his positive attitude toward healthcare reform. I met Tommy Douglas only once. I was in a queue in the cafeteria at the Provincial Legislative Building, and Premier Douglas lined up behind me. I asked him to go ahead of me. He chortled, declined, and told me to stay ahead of him—an able politician!

The first of my three tasks in the Budget Bureau was to write a book on the stated functions of the different parts of the government's administrative structure—as an educational exercise. This involved visiting and talking with administrators, and also meeting with the Queen's Printer. The latter was the title given to the Saskatchewan official in charge of provincial government printing. I remember him well not only because he published my first so-called book but also because the Queen's Printer had a habit (which I enjoyed) of overusing the phrase "what we call"—once pointing to a hole on the side of a page and saying that "This is where we have *what we call* a hole." The second task was to be a budget analyst for the upcoming budget. I was assigned a quarter of the government's budget—and I was asked to analyze certain questions, and to develop and answer additional questions. These analyses were ended when a supervising budgeteer walked in and called out, "The Treasury Board has just decided that all lines are to be increased by one half percent." I also remember, when we were taking part in checking the budget numbers (on the UK model, all Canadian budgets were secret until they were delivered to the respective legislatures), suddenly the same seasoned budgeteer looked up at the ceiling light and said "Shhh! Is there someone up there listening?" (After it was investigated, it was decided that there was not.) The third task was to conduct an assigned organization and methods study for one of the governmental departments. I remember being received by the deputy-minister (that department's chief civil servant, as opposed to the minister, who is always a politician) with the greeting, "Ah, here is the young administrative analyst."

This was my first government job. Why was I considered for it? Maybe it was, at least in part, my immediate past. Among my earlier jobs in Canada were two simultaneous jobs— teaching full-time at the Estevan High School (July 1959–March 1960) and part-time as a reporter (soon only reporter) for a weekly newspaper, *The Estevan Mercury* (July 1959– March 1960). The first job produced more salary, and the second produced more fun—as I came to write the entire front page. I started to learn that there were some corruption and other peculiarities in the government of the small city of Estevan; one prominent local official made money out of renting airport property, the police had no emergency response telephone number that was open after office hours, and the like. Kindly, the editor, Sterling King, gave me a free hand. I spent a lot of time talking with local officials, including socializing with the elected representative Kim Thorsen of the Saskatchewan legislative assembly—and Kim was even younger than I was. A crisis was reached that resulted, in part, from my learning when teaching the history of Canada to the ninth grade—I learned about a sad chapter from the 1810s to 1830s called the "Family Compact." The Family Compact is a disparaging epithet about a small group who exercised governing and economic power in Upper Canada (modern Ontario); it had its equivalent in the Chateau Clique in Lower Canada. The boiling point came when I wrote a newspaper story describing the Estevan city government in terms of a "family compact." The school superintendent told me that the school board was upset, wasn't interested in the fact that the principal spoke well of my work, and had decided that I would be fired if I did not stop working for the local newspaper, because they were receiving undisclosed pressure from prominent locals about my writings. So I resigned from both the newspaper and the school, and I told my friend who was a member of the Legislative Assembly. Based on our many conversations, he recommended that I make application to the Budget Bureau. Accordingly, I was interviewed.

### Treasury Department, Australian Federal Government

The day after I arrived in Sydney, I visited the employment office of the Australian government. As I had been told, I produced my passport and was informed that—because I had a university degree—I could start work tomorrow as a government employee in a Sydney office of the Treasury Department. I would then be investigated and (if approved) contacted in about a week and transferred to the capital, Canberra, and then—without any commitment on my part—I would be considered over the next few months for promotion within the Treasury Department. Next day, I arrived at the designated office, met some nice people, and did the little that they asked me to do. A week later, I was told that I would be driven to the airport next day and be flown to Canberra. This happened, and I started next day at the federal government's Treasury Department headquarters in the capital city of Canberra. Meanwhile, my promotion was considered, and eventually approved. I make no claim that I did much of significance for the government.

## Ontario Government

Back in Canada, I was hired to work in different capacities in the Ontario provincial government. By contrast with Saskatchewan, this province was run by a conservative party. The seventeenth premier was the Progressive Conservative John Parmenter Robarts, serving as premier from November 1961 to March 1971. Initially he was opposed to Canadian Medicare; but later he endorsed it completely. He was also opposed (as were many others) to the separation from Canada of Québec, a province with a French inheritance. (Feelings were high at that date. I remember once talking with a French Canadian in Ottawa, and being shocked when he said, "Yes, you understand us French Canadians because you are not a Canadian.")

I worked as an economist for the Ontario Civil Service Commission (June 1962–May 1963). I became an organization and methods analyst for the Ontario Treasury Department's Organization and Methods Services (June 1963–May 1964). Later, I was appointed chief of methods research for the Ontario Department of Economics and Development (June 1964–October 1965). There is an economics association between these three jobs.

### Ontario Civil Service Commission

The commission had taken an increased interest in the fringe benefits of civil servants, and I was hired to develop information on fringe benefits. I reported to Elsie Etchen, who gave me considerable freedom in doing my work: The Civil Service Commission had never before—I was told—had an employee assigned to this topic. Perhaps it helped in my rapid hiring that I had a bachelor's degree in economics from the London School of Economics and Political Science. I pursued economics further by also enrolling for a master's degree at the University of Toronto, which is a leading Canadian university. It is true that the fringe benefit topic was too narrow to hold me for long.

### Ontario Treasury Department's Organization and Methods Services

Most of my time in this division was spent providing analytical assistance to the Ontario Department of Economics and Development. Very limited assistance was provided by me to any other client departments in the Ontario Government.

Here is an example of work I did for the Department of Economics and Development. It is from a report as part of a service provided on September 15, 1963, and the report was titled

"The Function of the Economist in the Government of Ontario." It contained the following explanation:

> This is a working paper on the function of the economist in the government, with special reference to the Department of Economics and Development. The paper is designed to serve as a basis for a discussion with Mr. S. W. Clarkson, Deputy-Minister of the Department of Economics and Development. It contains no recommendations, and its entirely tentative views are offered merely as "trial balloons." Use has been made of the Glassco Commission's Report. (O and M General Report 025, p. iv)

The report contained three sections and two appendices. The sections were (1) The work of the professional economist; (2) The clients' requirements; and (3) The role of the Department of Economics and Development in the field of economics. The appendices were titled (1) Definitions of economic analysis, economic intelligence and specific investigation, and (2) Aspects of the working environment.

I also found it stimulating to complete the University of Toronto's master's degree in economics. My dissertation (recall that, unlike in the United States, a master's thesis is called a dissertation in Canada—and vice-versa for a doctorate) was titled "The Origins of the English National Health Service." Following the introduction, the dissertation was divided into three chapters, each with two subparts:

Nineteenth-Century Roots

    The New Environmental Health services

    The Rise of Scientific Medicine

Twentieth-Century Beginnings

    The Growth of the Personal Health Services

    Inter-war Dissatisfactions

The Impetus

    The War

    The Labor Government

I imagine that the choice of topic was influenced by the progress being made in Canada in introducing a healthcare system, following Tommy Douglas's initiative. But it probably mainly reflected a positive attitude toward the British initiative in establishing its National Health Service in July 5, 1948, permitting the minister of health to exclaim, "After tomorrow, the weak will be entitled to clamor" (*The Times*, 1948, p. 4).

## Ontario Department of Economics and Development

Anne Cameron was the director of administration and my boss in the Department of Economics and Development. On October 18, 1965, she wrote me a memorandum summarizing what I had done in the department. Anne explained my job as: "Chief of Methods Research was established with [his] appointment. The Unit originally consisted of a Chief, a Systems and Procedures Officer and a secretary. At the high point before [he] left, the Unit included seven people." On my work qualities, Anne stated that I "displayed an above average degree of effort and persistence. [He] has a nice balance of aggressive and modest personality characteristics. [He] takes a well organized, energetic creative approach to problems. [He] possesses marked analytical abilities as well as excellent communicatory abilities. [His] work results with the Department of Economics and Development have been excellent,"

I very much also appreciated the high quality of Anne's administrative work, and it angered me that some men—behind her back—often enough referred to her as the Black Widow. Shame on the sexism!

Some months of this work were spent helping the chief economist of the Ontario government, Hugh Ian McDonald. He was, earlier in 1962, an assistant professor of economics at the University of Toronto (although I did not know him there), and he was appointed chief economist only in 1965 and immediately assigned to our department. We worked closely together in adjusting the structure and activity of the economics units—in order that he could gain the programmatic results he wanted. In a letter dated October 29, 1965, Ian wrote the following to me:

> Dear David:
> Before you depart, I would like to tell you how much I have appreciated the generous assistance which you have provided to me during the last few months. Although I often had occasion to be grateful for your co-operation, I have been particularly conscious of your contribution in the past few weeks, as I have prepared to carry out the reorganization. It is not customary for civil servants to find monuments erected to themselves but I shall consider that you have made a lasting impact on the important work which we are undertaking here and I thank you for that. With my very best wishes in your new career and new surroundings.
> 
> Yours sincerely,
> Ian

Ian was kind enough, a little earlier, to have offered me the job of special assistant to the chief economist. But I had decided that I wanted to move to PAS. Later in 1974 (and until 1984) Ian McDonald was appointed president of York University.

Facilitating so many job moves was also the economic context of the time. The economist Ha-Joon Chang describes the period 1945–1973 as the Golden Age of Capitalism. His view is that, in that period, capitalism "performed well on all fronts: growth, employment and stability" (Chang, 2010, p. 59).

## EPILOGUE

I have found that there is real benefit in stimulating the imagination by playing with other thinking and practices about governance and people and cultures. But it is always difficult to see the foreign, because the misconceptions of the nonforeign always intrude; and that is one reason why involvement in the practice of foreign bureaucracy is helpful. As I left Australia and sailed to Italy and beyond, I was thrilled by the cultural variety—with visits to Indonesia, India, through the Suez Canal, Egypt, and a Mediterranean hurricane. For each of the past thirty-five years, wife Rosemary and I have benefited by spending at least three or four weeks each year in another country. This included taking language coursework at the Sorbonne, University of Paris (Summer 1989), at the Centro Linguistico Dante Alighieri, Scuola per Stranieri (Summer 1990), and at the Universidad Complutense de Madrid (Summer 1991). Also, I was once a visiting professor at the City University of Hong Kong. Actually working in a foreign bureaucracy (not merely attending a conference or visiting a bar or sitting on a beach or learning a few words in a foreign language) is a powerful way to recognize how odd it is to think that clever people could suppose that there could be only one culture with a public administration discipline, with public administration–relevant information.

Contemplating bureaucracies could be facilitated, as suggested in the second paragraph, if practice involvement were experienced by more public administration (and other) specialists in more than a single country. This parallels the aim of enriching the contemplation of bureaucracies with multi-disciplinary perspectives (Farmer, 2010), as noted earlier. To the extent that it is not fully open, a plan should be developed to open the door wider between American public administration practice and foreign public administration practice. Even more promising would be a better practice view—in more than one country—of both administration and policy. Why cannot the doors be opened wider?

## REFERENCES

Chang, H.-J. (2010). *Economics: The user's guide*. New York, NY: Bloomsbury Press.

Dahl, R. A. (1947). The science of public administration: Three problems. *Public Administration Review, 7*(1), 1–11. doi:10.2307/972349.

Dickens, C. (1859/1940). *A tale of two cities*. London, UK: Chapman & Hall.

Farmer, D. J. (1995). *The language of public administration: Bureaucracy, modernity, and postmodernity*. Tuscaloosa, AL: The University of Alabama Press.

Farmer, D. J. (2010). *Public administration in perspective: Theory and practice through multiple lenses*. Armonk, NY: M.E. Sharpe. doi:10.4324/9781315701455.

Farmer, D. J. (2015). Dogs of war: Fighting back. *Administrative Theory and Praxis, 37*(4), 252–267. doi:10.1080/10841806.2015.1083826.

Kurtz, K. (2010, March). 1313: A Famous (or Infamous) Landmark of Public Administration. *The Thicket at State Legislatures*. Denver, CO: National Conference of State Legislatures.

Mosher, F. C. (Ed.). (1975). *American public administration: Past present, future*. Tuscaloosa, AL: University of Alabama Press.

Pasolli, L. (2009). Bureaucratizing the Atlantic revolution: The "Saskatchewan mafia" in the New Brunswick civil service, 1960–1970. *Acadiensis, 38*(1), 126–150. Retrieved from https://journals.lib.unb.ca/index.php/acadiensis/article/view/12473/13396

Taylor, C. (1989). *Sources of the Self: The Making of the Modern Identity*. Cambridge, MA: Harvard University Press.

# IMAGINE! PREFACE TO THE POST-TRADITIONAL

David John Farmer

This symposium is about theorizing a fresh consciousness. It's about a radically imaginative field(s) of study and action that will provide quantum and macro improvement in terms of post-traditional governance and bureaucracy.

This preface: (a) offers a nutshell description of post-traditional governance and bureaucracy; (b) identifies the symposiasts; (c) sketches how the symposiasts' contributions relate to more specifics about post-traditional governance and bureaucracy; and (d) indicates a partial history of the idea of the post-traditional, avant la lettre.

## IN A NUTSHELL, WHAT'S POST-TRADITIONAL GOVERNANCE AND BUREAUCRACY?

The post-traditional is a consciousness (on scope) that extends throughout governance, public and private and non-profit and all other forms of institutionalization, visible and invisible. It is consciousness where (on method) radical imagination is primary in thought, justice and action. On one view (Farmer, 2005), I imagine this consciousness in terms of three intertwined and interacting notions—thinking as play, justice as seeking, and action as art. Central are *playing, seeking, artistry*. They are central for the radically imaginative, the quality of government that the 9/11 Commission noted as essential for practical results. Imagination is not merely what is perky. This fresh consciousness is not imagined to be a unified or single vision.

The post-traditional is *beyond* postmodernism. It is *beyond* critical theory. How can that be? Hegel's system suggests one way, synthesis that yields full understanding only at the end of all the syntheses. However, the word *beyond* can be replaced, for example, with *before* or *beside* or *underneath* or *separate from*. Relating to this, the post-traditional is not the same (a nicer word?) as something else like critical theory or postmodernism. Yet there are affinities to these and to other isms like feminism, critical legal theory, post-colonial theory, etc.

The post-traditional regards traditional Public Administration (PA) as unduly constrained in scope and method. *Post-traditional*, especially when it comes to resolving non-trivial and macro problems, is *the* practical (praaac-tical) option.

## WHO ARE THE CONTRIBUTORS TO THIS SYMPOSIUM?

Heartfelt thanks to the others who are contributors; their articles are first class. In poor man's Madison Avenue style, here are questions to "advertise" each paper.

- **O. C. McSwite**—what about the social bond? Is it something that should be left to the "king"?
- **Thomas Catlaw**—what about the death of the practitioner? A big funeral? How can such symbolism be explained to a literalist?
- **Catherine Horiuchi**—what is this thing called consciousness? Isn't consciousness where "there" is?
- **Matt Witt**—how can we understand the non-linearity of the post-traditional? Should we try to accommodate non-linearity in linear thinking?
- **Margaret Vickers**—what about an individual human's grief? Isn't that a good example that illuminates the idea of the person-in-herself in-her-difference?
- **Kym Thorne** and **Alexander Kouzmin**—what about rampant hyper-capitalism?
- **Swan Hua Xu**—why have we missed the significance of Zhuangzi and Taoism?
- **Self**—should we re-introduce the post-traditional, perhaps with a different practical example? What about lobbying and fixing for a fee, usually corporate?

## MORE SPECIFICS ABOUT POST-TRADITIONAL GOVERNANCE AND BUREAUCRACY: HOW DO THE SYMPOSIUM PAPERS RELATE?

The post-traditional does involve a flexible scope beyond present disciplinary borders, although it does not propose an unrealistic and humongous super-subject. For topic and turf, for example, tailored approaches have been described, taking intellectual resources from where they are relevant. I have long argued for the idea of a genuinely macro PA. I do object to a macro-light PA. But now I'm becoming clearer that macro PA itself is too narrow in scope. Without a scope that extends to private enterprise and not-for-profit, macro PA implodes. Without appropriate attention to societal consciousness, it's next to hopeless. That's why I have switched to the $20 word "governance." Narrow social science-y specialties are inter-related. For one example, isn't a central issue for governance the fundamental character of the economy? Isn't economics co-constitutive of subjects like politics, policy-making and PA? Kym Thorne and Alexander Kouzmin use economics as an exemplar to discuss what they describe as invisibility in contemporary hegemony.

The post-traditional does not privilege linearity. For example, these symposium papers are arranged in random order—with the exception of the last paper. They can be read in any order. Matt Witt writes in this symposium about the non-linearity of post-traditionalism. The post-traditional is not confined to transcending traditional PA. It also seeks to bypass constrictive blinders in other fields and disciplines, for example, not only in traditional PA theory but also in traditional organization theory and even in the more elegant mainstream economic theory. This is reflected in such analyses as that of the death of the practitioner, both a scope and method issue. It's very distorting when disciplines like microeconomics focus so intently on the entrepreneur, and action subjects like PA focus so blindly on the mid-level practitioner. Thomas Catlaw extends this topic in his discussion of the death of the practitioner.

The post-traditional takes thinking and action outside of traditional patterns. The nature of the self is critical for post-traditional governance, for example, in thinking as playing, justice as seeking, and action as art. Long ago, Paul Roazen (1986, p. 3) wrote that, "Almost every college instructor in an introductory course in political science will point out that all political philosophies in the past have been based on theories of human nature. . . . And yet at present very few political theorists focus on this issue. Still, it is hard to imagine how any of the humanistic sciences are going to be able to develop very far without a systematic notion of human motivation." Another reason that the self is important is Helene Cixous' injunction to write myself (yourself). The person-in-herself in-her-difference is central for post-traditional governance and bureaucracy—and for day-to-day human happiness. Margaret Vickers extends this in her paper, with her example of grief.

The post-traditional extends beyond the study of mere things and systems of things. For example, there is societal consciousness as "a" causative agent, and the likelihood that there is a back and forth movement between surface and deeper features in the consciousness. Wouldn't the technological be an example—the idea that the social is co-determined not only by individuals, etc., but also by consciousness of the technical? We so slavishly celebrate the technical that (following the Newtonian scheme, seeing the World as machine) items like your body and my body are traditionally conceptualized as machines, not to mention the "machinery of government" or the mechanics of the market. Many thinkers have discussed this consciousness, for example, Cornelius Castoriadis, Jurgen Habermas, Jacques Lacan and Michel Foucault. As generations go on, we usually become even more aware of the relevance of changing consciousness. In this symposium, Catherine Horiuchi discusses the emerging consciousness.

Post-traditional interpretation of the depths of consciousness is of practical utility. There's benefit, albeit limited, in skating on the surface; but, if the thinker does, she or he can recognize that—in a sense—it's as if the surface were governed by the deep. Look at what's happening in our society. A vital source of the most critical and macro changes in governance and bureaucracy lies within features deep within society's consciousness. On the smaller scale, I give the examples of immigration and prisons (Farmer, 2005, pp. 168-176). On a larger scale, there are the examples of the cult of the leader (pp. 141-153), the invisible hand (pp. 154-162) and the form of the modern corporation (pp. 162-167). On the largest scale, there's a killing of the king, a king with many faces (pp. 131-140, 183-194). These depths are not equally deep, and they surely interact. Frank Knight, the founding dean of the orthodox Chicago school of economics, discussed the social bond in his own terms. O. C. McSwite in this symposium discusses the social bond in terms of Lacanian psychoanalytic theory, which speaks to a deeper level.

The post-traditional cannot be a merely Western phenomenon. Reflecting on non-Western insights (in other words, insights that are non-traditional in the West) can significantly enrich. Thinkers like Schopenhauer long enough ago recognized this, and it's a no-brainer that inter-cultural integration will become increasingly important. My chapter 12 speaks about Confucian insights (Farmer, 2005). In this symposium, Swan Hua Xu writes about the relevant ideas of Zhuangzi and Taoism.

The post-traditional has the capability of resolving non-trivial macro problems, where "resolving" is contrasted with applying a band-aid. In this symposium, my paper attempts to illustrate this by focusing on fixing-for-a-fee, usually corporate.

The post-traditional has other aspects. There are other significant aspects, for example, of thinking as playing, justice as seeking, and action as art. These aspects are left for another day.

## WHAT'S THE HISTORY OF THE POST-TRADITIONAL?

The post-traditional has been discussed before. There was another symposium, for example, in the *International Journal of Public Administration* (2005). Those papers were written by Cathy McGinn and Tricia Patterson, Richard Box, Robert Cunningham, Susan Fitzpatrick, Rupa Thadhani, and Louis Howe. The papers spoke of the post-traditional from perspectives that include feminism, critical theory, religion or spirituality, Zen, postcolonialism, and the links between power, knowledge and the discourse of technological virtue. The paper titles are included, below. In that symposium, I described the post-traditional in terms of two polar visions of the mechanics of governance. I (2005a, p. 904) discussed:

> A quintet of features relevant to democratic governance. Each of the visions can be best conceptualized as at the extreme poles of a range of kinds of consciousness of governance that can be seen as implicated in the culture wars, with the intermediate positions on the range populated by types that share in varying degrees characteristics from both of the extremes.

The post-traditional is not a new notion. To personalize it, I have discussed it for more than a decade, in parts and avant la lettre. For example, there's the reflexive interpretation, or reflexive language paradigm. I described it as "a process of playful and attuned dialogue with the underlying content of the language of public bureaucracy" (Farmer, 1995, p. 12). The book went on to claim that:

> Reflexive interpretation is an art that seeks to draw out and use the consequences of the hermeneutic, reflexive, and linguistic character of the way in which we should understand and create public administration phenomena. It is an art that examines the set of assumptions and social constructions that constitute the theoretical lens through which we see, and it speculates about an alternative set or sets of socially constructed assumptions (that form another lens) through which we could see.

That book also talked about play and about anti-administration. But there were subsequent developments, extensions. My thoughts developed about play (especially in a 1998 edited book) and about anti-administration (especially in a December 2001 symposium). At that time, I attempted to derive anti-administration not only from a postmodern, but also from a modern and a medieval, mind-set. Rather than postmodern, I suggested that anti-administration should be considered in post-ist terms.

> The term *post-ist* is a neologism that refers to our post-ist intellectual context, a condition that is variously characterized, in part or in whole, by descriptors such as post-positivist, post-industrial, post-patriarchal, post-structural, post-modern, post-Freudian, post-colonial, post-metaphysical, and other post-ist terms. (Farmer, 2001, p. 486)

I now describe anti-administration as part of thinking-as-playing-with-a-gadfly-purpose. (Farmer, 2005, pp. 28-31). Others may have different views. Another is to think of post-traditionalism as a child of anti-administration, and as the grandchild of the reflexive language paradigm. Yet another view is to think of reflexive interpretation and anti-administration as alternative versions of the post-traditional.

The post-traditional matured (festered) within PAT-Net. A heart-felt statement is where I acknowledge that "The most important event in my administrative life was in 1994 when I started to attend the meetings of the Public Administration Theory Network" (2005, p. 53). I should stress the sharing that resulted. I was happy to participate in a 1997 book, edited by Hugh Miller and Charles Fox, that included Adrian Carr, Ralph Hummel, Charles Goodsell, Chuck Fox and Hugh Miller, O. C. McSwite, and Gary Marshall. My 1998 edited book contained articles by O. C. McSwite, Janet Hutchinson, Camilla Stivers, Rosemary Farmer, John Larkin, Charles Goodsell, Hugh Miller and Chuck Fox, and Adrian Carr and Liza Zanetti. The 2001 anti-administration symposium included O. C. McSwite, Michael Spicer, Patricia Patterson, Richard Box, Robert Cunningham and Robert Schneider, Janet Hutchinson, and Debra Jacobs. I imagine that many others in PAT-Net would say similar things as I have about the post-traditional, with dissimilar words. Forget Heraclitus' "one step" river. I think that most, or many, in PAT-Net are steeped in this or that part of the same river, "sort of" the same river — even with its streams and side-twists, thick green bits and rocky rapids.

Meanwhile, traditional PA has continued with business as usual. It's *as if* traditional PA isn't satisfied to have all the limbs it should have — in terms of scope and methods and in terms of practical relevance. Body Integrity Identity Disorder (B.I.I.D.) is a psychological condition in which a person actively pursues an elective amputation. The symptoms include a feeling of incompleteness and a belief that an amputation will lead to wholeness; and repeated feelings of depression and suicidal thoughts, relieved only by an actual amputation (e.g., see Bayne & Levy, 2005). Traditional PA is not actively pursuing amputations. Yet it's *as if* it is in bliss to have been constituted in an amputated form.

## REFERENCES

Bayne, T., & Levy, N. (2005). Amuptee by choice: Body integrity identity disorder and the ethics of amputation. *Journal of Applied Psychology, 22,* 75-86.

Farmer, D. J. (2001). Mapping anti-administration: Introduction to the symposium. *Administrative Theory & Praxis, 23,* 475-492.

Farmer, D. J. (2005). *To kill the king: Post-traditional governance and bureaucracy.* Armonk, NY: M. E. Sharpe.

Farmer, D. J. (2005a). Quintet: Introduction to post-traditional theory. *International Journal of Public Administration, 28,* 903-908.

Farmer, D. J. (1995). *The language of public administration: Bureaucracy, modernity and postmodernity.* Tuscaloosa: University of Alabama Press.

Roazen, P. (1986). *Freud: Political and social thought.* New York: Da Capo.

# Theorizing in Perspective: Epistemic Pluralism

David John Farmer

## ABSTRACT

*This article examines the claim that public administration theorizing can upgrade its language game, even in the short run, by a grand strategy of epistemic pluralism that includes perspectives like neuroscience. It indicates why public administration should care about neuroscience, and how public administration can evaluate whether epistemic pluralism has important benefits. It comments on myths that tend to impede the upgrading.*

Epistemic pluralism is a strategy for transforming, even in the short run, the language game of public administration theorizing. Recommended is a grand strategy that includes perspectives as "foreign" as neuroscience. Such a grand strategy is both optimal and practical for public administration theorizing.

To explain, let us ask five questions. First, why start with Wittgenstein (1922/1961), and what is an example of a powerful public administration myth that encourages the disciplinary status quo? Second, what is epistemic pluralism? Third, what is neuroscience? Fourth, why should public administration care about such a remote and unfamiliar discipline as neuroscience? Fifth, how can public administration evaluate whether epistemic pluralism has significant benefits?

## WHY WITTGENSTEIN?

Public administration has its own set of language games, as do economics and philosophy and the rest of the disciplines, and epistemic pluralism is directed in the shorter run toward upgrading public administration's language game.

Wittgenstein is well known for pointing to the nature and the significance of a language game. On nature, he points out that language is an activity or a form of life, a game, and that people participate in a variety of language games; he notes that the words and the action (thinking, emoting, judging, and acting, we may add) constitute the language game. For instance, a language is at least *embedded*, as is public administration's set of language games. It is also a game which thus is played and is played with, and it interacts with other language games.

Michel Foucault, Maurice Merleau-Ponty, and Roland Barthes have all added to Wittgenstein's comments. Foucault (1980) writes about the activity of power and normalizing in shaping what counts as truth (little *t* truth). Merleau-Ponty (1962) writes of bodies as living organisms that *body forth* the possibilities in the world. Barthes writes of language as lending itself to myth. For him, myth is itself a communication system. He writes of "the language which myth gets hold of" (1972, p. 111), and he asserts that "myth is always a language-robbery" (p. 131). An example is the messaging that is effected in advertising and public relations and that is involved in creating modern mythology—and Barthes talks about items like soap powders and detergents. Such myth-making and myths are part of our public administration and other language games.

On the significance of language games, there is Wittgenstein's well-known claim that "the limits of my language mean the limits of my world" (1922/1961, p. 56). Although the meaning seems obvious, let us give three examples— starting with a technicist or practical example. I enjoy pronouncing the word *praaac-tical*. I also choose it because having to stay within the lines of obvious practicality rules out from its world even practical ways of thinking like "thinking as play." As I mention the three examples, I wonder if you would mind playing with the following questions. I would say yes to each. Do you have one or many language games? Is it the same for public administration? Do your language games relate to the intellectual, emotional, aesthetic, and biological? Are there levels of languages (and myths), with some being more powerful than others? If the limits of my language limit my world, do the limits of my world also limit my language? Are languages chosen mainly for unconscious reasons, including, for example, to maintain my comfortable life? Do you think that Wittgenstein means that you should do what it takes to understand your own language, being ready to tweak it? Well, I think so.

For the first of three examples of language games, turn to the mythic language limit that public administration–speak must be obviously practical, perhaps limiting the scope of practicality, for example, to what is perceived as practical. Mythic language tends to be open-ended, and we notice that what is considered practical by a GS-1 (relatively few in the federal government) is not what is considered practical by a department head. Or, is practical what is considered practical by our audiences—for example, by practical mid-level bureaucrats, constituting the highest level of virtually all our MPA students? My public administration language would thereby be limited to favor the tech-

---

This article was adapted from the author's previous writings and plenary address presented at the Public Administration Theory Network (PAT-Net) Conference hosted by Old Dominion University in Norfolk, Virginia, May 2011.

nicist. It would also be limited to the micro, and what works right away (i.e., like, metaphorically, what a public employee might do at work next Monday morning). This language game may (or may not) be covered by supplementary mythic pronouncements like (on the ASPA Web site) "advancing excellence in public service" or "promotes professionalism in public administration." Is this the same or another language game (with the biological features we will mention later) that can be described in terms of common sense?

How will a language of public administration so practical (or commonsensical) tend to result in limiting my world? How will it devalue the other (better: barely see the other)? For one thing, we can agree that it will devalue the long run and the macro. For another thing, it will not see as administrative issues what upgraded governmental administration seems to require. Here are two examples, and others can be identified. For instance, such a language might not attach importance to the relevance of lobbying for administrative programs (partly perhaps because its vision is limited to the middle-level manager) or the relevance for bureaucracy of the growing gap between very rich and poorer folks. The last item may appear less weird if one takes into account the argument by Pickett and Wilkinson (2010) that increasing wealth disparity increases certain bureaucratic needs and costs.

Recall the questions about whether you have a multiplicity of languages that somehow glob together to construct you and your world, socially or unconsciously or not. My public administration language must include other languages—for example, from my era, from where I live and work, from how I play. For the second of the three examples of language games, let us imagine it is true that your public administration language is shaped to incorporate the national myths described by Richard Hughes (2004, pp. 19–65, 126–189). These include the myth that the United States is the chosen nation, the myth of the United States being nature's nation (uniquely a natural phenomenon), the myth of the United States being always the innocent nation (not to mention the mythic dimensions of American capitalism). Wouldn't you tend to construct your public administration world on an exceptionalist basis? How far (if at all) does such myth-constricted language limit the world of American political science (as in APSA) or of public administration? Is this a reason why American public administration recognizes that public administration began with Woodrow Wilson?

For the third of three examples of language games, a number of public administration theorists (many in PAT-Net) have a variety of broader language games. For the sake of practicality both narrow and broad, my interest is in tweaking these language games with epistemic pluralism. I don't mean to imply that epistemic pluralism is a cure-all for public administration's language games. It has a catalytic effect, but more is required to give what I would consider desirable in public administration thinking, emoting, judging, and action limitations. The gods are cruel and deceitful, especially when it comes to killing the language that is king.

Are you happy with the umph on both the public administration theory side and the practice side when you compare with (say) the economic and business language games? I didn't say truth; I said *umph*—the kind of umph that mathematical economics and the cell phone business exude. I will just speak about the theory side, and ask whether it is too much to hope that public administration could upgrade its disciplinary game record when it comes to openness to new ideas. With the exception of public administration at its edge, public administration has exhibited what may be termed a ham-handedly dull reception to sets of new ideas like poststructuralism, postcolonialism, and the New Rhetoric. Don't forget that deconstruction, as another example of something very practical, was introduced to the United States by Jacques Derrida in a 1966 seminar at Johns Hopkins. Despite its influence in the 1980s and the early 1990s on social sciences like political science, it wasn't until the mid-1990s that deconstruction dipped its toe into public administration—and the water was a tad chilly. What in public administration language games is making the emotional parts of the games chilly?

I agree that public administration writers will have to take the lead in laying a foundation for changing the language, and I agree that epistemic pluralism is hard. It will be difficult even for the public administration discipline to change the traditional structure of its teaching to incorporate epistemic pluralism. The mythic bureaucratic response, it seems, will ever be "We are already doing that."

## WHAT IS EPISTEMIC PLURALISM?

Epistemic refers to knowing, and pluralism can refer to a minimal strategy of more than one way. Rather than a minimal strategy, I understand it here as a grand strategy that refers to a multiplicity of perspectives. It is a grand but realistic strategy that reflects the late Dwight Waldo's claim that administrative "thought must establish a working relationship with every major province in the realm of human learning" (1984, p. 203).

I repeat that I don't mean that a single or a minimal strategy is never to be preferred, just as it is not meant that nothing else is needed. Mainstream public administration and other mainstream disciplines have yielded some valuable results without utilizing any perspectives except their own. Again, public administration and most social disciplines have used one or a minimal number of different perspectives—for example, perspectives like the political, psychological, or economic. These individual perspectives have also produced enriching results. Yet, by itself and in isolation, a solitary way of looking can be misleading. Similarly, a minimal strategy of using perspectives can give only parts of puzzles, parts of the road map. A grand strategy, rather than a minimal strategy, of epistemic pluralism can yield a quantum gain in understandings.

It is a myth that epistemic pluralism is a form of relativism. Epistemic pluralism can yield better hypotheses for positivist exploration, or it can be used for hermeneutic purposes. Just because there are two or more perspectives does not mean that there is a relativist conclusion, any more than the existence of two roads to Chicago means that there are two Chicagos.

Let us repeat a quickie illustration. Imagine that Richard Clarke (2008, p. 2) is right that the homeland security function in the U.S. government suffers from the administrative problem of *bloat*. What could non–homeland security perspectives add to the study of bloat, a problem perhaps of managing, money, effectiveness, and planning?

Consider possible insights from five specialties. First, couldn't the business perspective tell us about the relevance of supply chain management. Second, couldn't the economic perspective tell us how corporate money warps the administration of policy and coshapes policies—buying, for instance, contracts and jobs and tax relief. Third, couldn't the poststructural (or the postmodern) inform us more fully how the hyperreal accentuates fear. The hyperreal refers to items or events that, rather than being merely real or unreal, are more real than real. Fourth, couldn't traditional public administration mention the existence of the catch-22 problem of homeland security administrators not feeling free to talk publicly about the impossibility of "full protection" (Kettl, 2004, p. 76)—a system under stress.

Fifth, the psychoanalytic perspective can offer supplementary help. Let us consider Carl Jung's compensation view of myth. As Walker puts it, Jung presents the "mythic world as a potential means of compensation for the sense of meaningless that plagues modern culture, proud of its rationality but at the same time a prey to doubts and existential anguish" (2002, pp. 22–23). As an example, recall Jung's description of the myth of UFOs in his "Flying Saucers: A Modern Myth of Things Seen in the Skies." In this work Jung (1970) talks about the UFO, among other things, as a collective projection that creates meaning, where flying saucers are the traditional symbol for wholeness—the mandala. To offer a simplified account of his meaning, it was a myth that was popular in the dawn of the nuclear age when the two halves of the world faced the fate that for the first time each could destroy the whole of humanity. In a parallel way, cannot the myth of absolute security reflect similar compensation?

Clearly, there are yet other perspectives. Equally clearly, it is simplistic to suppose that each perspective (e.g., the business, the economic, or any of the others) yields only a singular understanding.

The preference in my *Public Administration in Perspective* was to use 11 perspectives, and several understandings are recognized as emanating from the mainstream of each perspective. These perspectives were public administration from a traditional perspective and from the perspectives of business, economics, politics, critical theory, poststructuralism, psychoanalysis, neuroscience, feminism, ethics, and data (or philosophy of science). These perspectives were used to identify insights about five public administration elements that were used as vehicles, as it were, for examining implications for public administration theory and practice. The five vehicles were the different kinds of planning, the different kinds of management, the meaning and relevance of what underlies public administration (e.g., the social construction of relevant societal beliefs and attitudes), the scope of public administration, and the extent of imaginative creativity in public administration—considering not only the mid-level. As I mention below, the five sets of implications have to be synthesized on a hermeneutic basis.

## WHAT IS NEUROSCIENCE?

Neuroscience may well be "the" science of the twenty-first century. It has produced—and is creating—spectacular results.

As we all know, neuroscience is the variety of specialties that study the brain—the central and the peripheral nervous systems—and the relationships of these organs to such activities as remembering, thinking, behaving, judging, deciding, and feeling. (This seems a large part of what is involved in public administration.) The levels of analysis in neuroscience include the molecular, cellular, systems, behavioral, and cognitive; they extend to many other divisions.

Other social sciences are way ahead of public administration in using neuroscience. Neuroeconomics has existed on the margin of economics for more than a decade. And, true to form, political science trails after economics but before public administration. Sorry to reemphasize this (e.g., see Farmer, 2007, pp. 77–80).

It is important to recognize that the biology of the brain is shaped by its experience. Yes, our three pounds of brain is biological; but it is more than that. Not only biological but also social, psychological, spiritual, and other factors shape and reshape the functioning of the brain. Neuroplasticity refers to the brain's capability of adapting through rewiring the 100 billion or so neurons in the average brain—perhaps more than the stars in the sky. The brain is shaped and reshaped by its experiences. To illustrate this feature, it is also pleasing to repeat that as we read and as we write, neuroscientists claim, our own brains are changing.

## WHY SHOULD PUBLIC ADMINISTRATION CARE ABOUT NEUROSCIENCE?

Neuroscience can be helpful to public administration at both the macro and the micro levels, in both the shorter and longer runs. Ideology, aggression, creativity, morality, individual differences, and sense of identity are topics of relevance to public administration. There are huge and vibrant literatures on each of these topics in neuroscience. One example is a book titled *Hardwired Behavior: What Neuroscience Reveals About Morality* (Tancredi, 2005). Another example is *Brain and Culture: Neurobiology, Ideology, and Social Change* (Wexler, 2006).

Richard Restak (2006) claims that neuroscience will "revolutionize how we think about ourselves and our interactions with other people" (p. 1). The subtitle of his book is *How the Emerging Neurosociety Is Changing How We Live, Work, and Love*. I have quoted him and listed his seven brain-based developments providing new societal capabilities—for example, brain scans for certain jobs, tests to reveal private tendencies and thoughts, and chemical enhancers to stimulate wants.

For the public administration managing element, couldn't the literature of neuroscience be relevant when considering the nature of the administrative person? This literature describes the role and functioning (as indicated earlier) of such brain parts as the amygdalae and the thalamus in processing fear? For example, there is the somatic marker hypothesis. Couldn't public administration specialists revisit the functioning of fear in bureaucratic life, in view of the neurobiology of fear. For instance, doesn't this relate to issues like courage in bureaucracy, and even undue deference by some subordinate employees to their supervisors.

For what underlies the practice and study of public administration or any other discipline, aren't many administrative and other beliefs shaped within the brain? The mirror neuron system (functioning when we look one another in the eye and when we look at another person's actions) is implicated in inducing copying behavior between humans. Does this not suggest how public administration theory might find it useful if it is the case that the brain unconsciously shapes the idea that *familiar and commonsense information is probably true information*, especially when common sense is unanalyzed? Again, doesn't this have relevance not only for discouraging undesirable, but also encouraging desirable, behavior?

I agree with Bacon, Descartes, Kant, Hegel, and Comte and our contemporaries like the biologist E.O. Wilson that the fragmentation of knowledge distorts knowledge. In public administration, the distortion is as great as in any subject. I have written about the options of a larger restructuring of the social sciences, for example across the board, and of a narrower restructuring, for example in such terms as "neuro-governance" (Farmer, 2007). I applaud the attempts, largely vain and counterproductive, of the National Science Foundation—and before it of national agencies like the Social Science Research Council in the 1920s—to work toward the lost unity. An obvious problem, however, for a larger or even a narrower union is that complete victory is unlikely: the cats are out of the bag. I don't think it is really hopeful to seek such broadening of scope *primarily* organizationally or bureaucratically. However,

I do see epistemic pluralism as a feasible opportunity to avoid the organizational (or bureaucratic) solution. If that leads eventually to re-restructuring, that is fine. Meantime, a more attractive aim (helped by the catalytic power of neuroscience) is shorter-term—major language game tweaking or more, with powerful programmatic results.

## HOW CAN PUBLIC ADMINISTRATION EVALUATE WHETHER EPISTEMIC PLURALISM HAS SIGNIFICANT BENEFITS?

Try epistemic pluralism for the shorter run. Play with the possibilities. The shorter-run aim is an expansion, through epistemic pluralism, of public administration's language game. Theorists have to take the lead, or not.

Here are two possibilities. First, try reading about any non–public administration discipline that interests you, not excluding one with which you are unfamiliar—for example, mythology or evolutionary biology, or quantum mechanics. And jot down in your mind any ideas that are suggested about public administration. Or, attend any conference of that discipline. Let us imagine that you chose mythology. I think that you would opt not to limit yourself to approaching mythology from a traditional point of view, that is, perhaps like Ovid or Virgil, thinking of myth as emotionally and aesthetically pleasing but as intellectual nonsense. Instead I suggest you would include more up-to-date myth theory. Here is an example. You might notice the relevance of theorists of myth and ritual (e.g., see Segal, 1999, pp. 37–46), many stressing the primacy of ritual over myth. One of your jottings might comment on the parallel between bureaucratic and ritual procedures (aren't bureaucratic procedures rituals, and aren't rituals bureaucratic procedures, or some or all?), doing so by considering the duo of ritual and language in a pro- and anti-administrative way. Is there is a parallel or equivalence between procedure and ritual (visit any bureaucracy), and what else does that imply (if anything) for public administration?

A critical problem is lack of confidence in coping with outlying perspectives. Discussing philosophy or neuroscience or economics, there are inevitably difficulties for the nonspecialist. There is need for serious exploratory work. But there is no need for the perfection that perhaps the character Edward Casaubon aimed for in George Eliot's novel *Middlemarch: A Study of Provincial Life* (1874). One reason that Casaubon could not finish his *Key to All Mythologies*, according to his young cousin Will Ladislaw, is that Casaubon was unacquainted with German scholarship. It would be pleasing to be perfect; but it is less pleasing if the perfect is the enemy of the good.

Second, here is another (and unrelated) possibility. Try it, or not. All you need is a sheet of paper and a pencil. Down the left side of a sheet of paper, list perspectives with which you are familiar—or alternatively (say) 12 perspectives. If you wish, you can copy the 11 perspectives I use in *Public*

*Administration in Perspective: Theory and Practice Through Multiple Lenses* (2010). It is helpful to choose an additional perspective of your own, even, for example, myth theory. Typically disciplines contain more than one variety or branch: I recommend choosing whatever is mainstream. Across the top of the page, list one or two—or alternatively (say) six—subparts or elements of public administration. Again if you wish, you can choose the elements I chose—planning, managing, what lies underneath public administration, the scope of public administration, and imaginative creativity within public administration. Yet again, it is helpful to choose an additional element, a particular focus, for example, like big government, or outsourcing, or cost.

The object of the exercise would be to fill in the boxes with notes from each perspective for each of the elements. For instance, what is an implication of psychoanalysis for public administration planning? I claim it is that public administration planning should recognize the unconscious more than it does. What is an implication of psychoanalysis for public administration managing? My first choice is to ask for understanding of psychoanalytic organization theory. What is an implication for what underlies public administration? My choice is to ask whether there is an unconscious workplace. And so on. The goal is to interpret the perspective, as Paul Diesing (1991) explains for hermeneutics, to fit all the details into a consistent and coherent message that fits into the context (pp. 104–106). It is to interpret the relevance of the perspective for public administration, which might be different for the original aim of the perspective, for example, to influence a target set of non–public administration issues, rather than to help public administration.

Try it in different ways. A possibility is to ask students to start with such a set of boxes, and they can engage in group work to begin the process. Another possibility is to continue to amend the notes during the semester. Students (or others) can begin by imitating and borrowing from my book, but they are asked to develop their own candidate items—and develop their own justifications in sheets on each box. Sometimes students amaze me with what they can achieve; at other times, not so. The most interesting part is often when perspectives contradict one another. Imagine how insights from (say) the economics or politics or business perspective might compare and contrast with those from the critical theory, poststructural, psychoanalytic, ethical, feminist, and neuroscientific perspectives. Imagine what (say) neuroscience would (and will) contribute.

When that first exercise is completed, at least three others remain. The first is to summarize and synthesize the implications for each of the elements or subparts of public administration. The second is to synthesize what has been learned for public administration as a whole, using the insights for further reflection. (I spare students and myself from doing anything additional of a positivist nature, but that could be done—possibly—in terms of creating and testing the more interesting hypotheses that might emerge.) The third exercise is to reflect on—to contemplate one at a time—any substantive conclusions the students or you have reached.

This procedural description makes it seem that the exercises described are bureaucratic, ritualistic—as if creative imagination and reading and excitement were not required. Let me replay the last exercise to make the point at least for the high-key creative imagination being recommended. In contemplating a substantive conclusion, one alternative—or not—is to follow neuroscientist Nancy Andreasen's advice (2005) to reflect while walking on a treadmill and to start by practicing imagining. Riding the treadmill induces neurons to fire, and I have often fantasized about taking a class to the gym (maybe next semester). She also recommends pumping up the imagination by getting outside yourself. If you are like Einstein, imagine yourself riding on a photon; if you like cars, imagine yourself as a carburetor. The reflection can move to reflecting on your own lived and work experience, if you think it might be relevant. Does this synthesized point conflict or agree with my examined lived and work experience? In this case, is my examined commonsense vernacular (see Franklin, 1999) constructed, or projected reality? Is an alternative lived and work experience feasible? (I don't mean to suggest that the work and lived experience is always the complete loser; but neither is it a complete winner.) Then go on to contemplate the application; reflect on its being applied in X and then in Y—now or within 40 years. Then reflect on the proposition itself by itself. And so on. Alternatively, students as a start (or you) can write an analytical paper in a parallel fashion—or not—that discusses the implications for public administration of (say) three perspectives and that synthesizes the implications for public administration as a whole, pointing out examples of important implications excluded from this minimal approach.

## EPILOGUE

Epistemic pluralism promises to transform, even in the short run, the language game of theorizing. This article recommends a grand strategy of epistemic pluralism that includes perspectives as "remote" as neuroscience. Such a strategy is practical and optimal for public administration theorizing.

## REFERENCES

Andreasen, N.C. (2005). *The creative brain: The neuroscience of genius.* New York: Dana Press.

Barthes, R. (1972). *Mythologies.* New York: Farrar, Straus and Giroux.

Clarke, R. (2008). *Your government failed you: Breaking the cycle of national security disasters.* New York: Harper & Row.

Diesing, P. (1991). *How does social science work? Reflections on practice.* Pittsburgh: University of Pittsburgh Press.

Farmer, D.J. (2007). Neuro-gov: Neuroscience as catalyst. In C. Senior & M. Butler (Eds.), *The social cognitive neuroscience of organizations* (pp. 74–89). Boston: Blackwell.

Farmer, D.J. (2010). *Public administration in perspective: Theory and practice through multiple lenses.* Armonk, NY: M.E. Sharpe.

Foucault, M. (1980). *Power/knowledge: Selected interviews and other writings, 1972–1977.* Brighton, UK: Harvester Press.

Franklin, U. (1999). *The real world of technology.* Toronto: Anansi.

Hughes, R. (2004). *Myths America lives by.* Chicago: University of Illinois Press.

Jung, C. (1970). *Flying saucers: A modern myth of things seen in the skies.* Princeton: Princeton University Press.

Kettl, D.F. (2004). *System under stress: Homeland security and American politics.* Washington, DC: CQ Press.

Merleau-Ponty, M. (1962). *Phenomenology of perception.* London: Routledge & Kegan Paul.

Pickett, K., & Wilkinson, R. (2010). *The spirit level: Why greater equality makes societies stronger.* New York: Bloomsbury.

Restak, R. (2006). *The naked brain: How the emerging neurosociety is changing how we live, work, and love.* New York: Harmon.

Segal, R. (1999). *Theorizing about myth.* Amherst: University of Massachusetts Press.

Tancredi, L. (2005). *Hardwired behavior: What neuroscience reveals about morality.* New York: Cambridge University Press.

Waldo, D. (1984). *The administrative state: The study of the political theory of American public administration.* New York: Holmes & Meier.

Walker, S. (2002). *Jung and the Jungians on myth.* New York: Routledge.

Wexler, B. (2006). *Brain and culture: Neurobiology, ideology, and social change.* Cambridge: MIT Press.

Wittgenstein, L. (1922/1961). *Tractatus logico-philosophicus.* London: Routledge & Kegan Paul.

# THE ALLURE OF RHETORIC AND THE TRUANCY OF POETRY

David John Farmer

## ABSTRACT

*This paper offers suggestions for new directions in PA Theory—four allures of rhetorical analysis. First, it points toward New Rhetoric and rhetoric as more than the twirl on the top of the chocolate cake. Second, it suggests a five-step quick-and-dirty technique for getting into rhetorical analysis to help PA thinking. Third, it recommends greater ownership of our individual signatures. Fourth, it suggests changes in our group signature. It suggests that PA theory should include at its center a playful study of the symbolic, especially of mutuality as it relates to people aiming toward patterns of cooperative public action.*

Only on questioning did we hear the story of the symbols. When attending the October 2002 Southeastern Conference for Public Administration (SECOPA) in Columbia, South Carolina, I joined others in visiting the state legislature and heard a version of the flag controversy. Since 1962 the Confederate naval flag had hung from the dome of the state legislature, the docent explained. He added that the flag had been raised, on an anniversary of the Civil War, to symbolize respect for the masses of Confederate dead. He didn't mention whether the flag's raising had been to symbolize, as other South Carolinians see it, opposition to the civil rights movement and to the end of legalized segregation. The battle of symbols boiled, and still simmers. Since Summer 2000 a Confederate battle flag, said to be smaller, has flown atop a flagpole directly in front of the legislature. Indeed a barbed wrought-iron fence—a symbolic fence—surrounds it. A statue of George Washington symbolically stares at the flag. Meanwhile, on our visit my friends and I (must have been that time of year!) saw hundreds of moths infesting the capital steps—moths, traditionally symbols of fragility and (let's look it up in a book of myths!) what else. The political world is replete with swarms of symbols, sometimes beautiful and oft-times ugly but always powerful.

In South Carolina, symbols turn on political lights, themselves symbols. The State's Senate uses a sword, a copy of the original. The legislature's other house sports a mace, an original continuously in use except following the opening of the Revolutionary War when it was hidden in fear of the oncoming imperial power—and subsequently either lost or purloined for forty years. When these bodies are "in session," these symbols—the sword and the mace—are placed on special holders. Lo and behold! The acts of placing the sword and the mace automatically switch on clusters of electric lights at both right and left. When this was conceived, wasn't electric power seen as a prime symbol of human progress? Rural electrification, as you know, was a big idea. The symbolic power of the legislature combined with what was once seen as a symbol of progress—electric power. This poetry of power enlightens.

Let's pay more attention to the rhetoric of public administration (PA), especially understanding PA in terms of symbolic action. Rhetorical analysis, when rhetoric is properly understood, is a key to a better PA conversation. That the political world—like that in the South Carolina story—can be understood in terms of symbols and symbolic interaction is well recognized in the writings of Murray Edelman (1971) and others, and it has been well described in policy analysis by Deborah Stone (2001) and others. By contrast, PA is not widely understood in symbolic terms, one that can be analyzed through rhetorical analysis. PA has been described in such terms as language (Farmer, 1995), storytelling (King & Kensen, 2002; White, 2000), writing (Czarniawska, 2000), and so forth. Yet, PA remains mired in a mechanistic and rational—a hydraulic—view.

No less than in the political world, the public administration (PA) sphere abounds in the symbolic; rhetoric is a stock in trade of PA practice. Administrator is my name; rhetoric is my game. The Police Commissioner—to take a single example of a public administrator—shows himself as he visits one of his precincts. He displays himself attending a funeral for a slain officer. Publicly, he makes an award for bravery. He conducts a ceremony to promote an officer.

He visits the scene of a major crime. He is known to reprimand, or overlook, the action of a senior subordinate in accepting a free lunch. He announces that he is assigning more officers to high crime areas. He is televised in a spirited defense of an officer accused of brutality. He is saluted. Doors are swung open as he exits, and a flunky holds open the door of his chauffeur-driven car. The Commissioner is seen visiting a community organization in a church hall to discuss the police service.

The symbolic is the business of all engaged in administrative and policy actions, not just the police. My intuition is that there may be a direct relationship between height on the organizational ladder and the availability of opportunities for symbolic action. Higher officials get more chance to do all things, including the symbolic; nevertheless, symbolic action occurs at even the humblest level, even if there it takes merely the form of "binging" or "postal" behaviors symbolically directed against superiors or against the world in general. At the top of his hierarchy, the fire chief in full uniform is televised at the scene of a fire; a symbolic message is that he is "in control" and that the fire is as "under control" as it can be. The mid-level director holds "the Director's meeting" and all subordinates are expected to attend and to be on time—symbols of deference. At the lower end of the ladder, the meter maid and the garbage collector wear symbols in the form of uniforms, with add-on symbols like flags. Even things can be symbolic, like white on the chief's helmet or the red—the color of fire—on the fire truck. The practice of PA dwells significantly in the world of symbols, at least as much as it functions merely in terms of things and people.

There is a rhetoric of symbols, political or administrative. A symbol can tell a variety of stories, some meaning this to this group and that to other groups of readers. The South Columbia flag is an example. The meanings can be indeed overt or covert, conscious or unconscious. Where it is elevated so far above the other tables, for instance, the elevation of a head table at a conference luncheon can transmit an unconscious message of the greater worth of those at that head table—while the same message is provided consciously as members of the head table give awards to fellow-Brahmins at the same table. Beware the head table! The elevation is not just to make it easier for the peons to see. The flag behind the director's desk is not just to express the director's loyalty. The appointment of a high-level committee to study a particular problem is not just to study the particular problem.

Routine administrative actions exhibit subtle and complex rhetoric—as well as obvious symbolic meanings. The mere drawing of a traditional organization chart is symbolic of order of a particular kind. On the surface, the drawing merely describes relationships. A subtle meaning conveyed—subliminally, if one likes to put it that way—is that there are no uneven nodes of power in the agency. The boss, with teary eye and jutting jaw, telling agency members that they are members of a family—that the agency is a family—on the surface may be merely telling his employees that they should act like brothers and sisters. Subliminally perhaps, he is saying that he is their parent, attached with all that psychological baggage of loyalty etcetera. The complexity lies in the fact that symbols pile on symbols, rhetoric piles on rhetoric—just as metaphors pile on metaphors in language. The complexity also lies in the fact that symbolic stories, often enough, give mixed and flickering messages. The director, as he closes his door, tells his subordinates that he has an "open door" policy. The admiring director, as he stares at her breasts, tells his subordinate what a professional job she has done.

Let PA theorists turn more toward the allure of rhetoric analysis in order to improve the PA conversation—the kind that McClosky mentions and that, as discussed later, Oakeshott characterizes! Be encouraged by McClosky's struggle in a corner of a conservative discipline, Economics! In *The Rhetoric of Economics*, for instance, Deidre McClosky (1998) has demonstrated how rhetorical analysis can help achieve better economics results. I don't want to give the wrong impression. Mainstream economics opposes all talk of rhetoric. However, McClosky has continued to write helpfully about the rhetoric of economics (1990, 1994, 1997). As McClosky puts it (1998, p. 186), "A rhetorical criticism of economics can perhaps make economics more modest, tolerant, and self-aware, and improve one of the conversations of (sic) mankind." Rhetorical criticism of PA can encourage and enlighten what other insights are available from psychological and other studies.

The allure of rhetoric for me means the allure of examined rhetoric, the increased PA capability that results from analyzing and changing the rhetoric that is unavoidably embedded in the warp and woof of administration. One of the anonymous reviewers is right that some rhetoric can be malicious and dishonest. To speak of the desirability of rhetorical analysis is not to approve of rhetoric that is malicious, however—just as speaking of the desirability of psychotherapy is not to approve of clinical depression. The allure is compelling for the PA theorist because PA actions—all human actions—are ineluctably replete with rhetoric. Some of the rhetoric is good; some is malicious; some is mixed; and some is neither good nor malicious. Significantly, some is conscious; but most is unconscious, unexamined. On more philosophical days, I agree with Plato's Socrates that the unexamined life is not worth living. Shouldn't he agree with me that unexamined PA rhetoric is not worth thinking, not worth experiencing?

In supporting this appeal for a better PA conversation, the allure of rhetorical analysis for PA will be discussed in this paper in four, sometimes overlapping, respects. First, *decoration* is alluring, but I will emphasize that rhetoric is not at all confined to mere decoration. For one thing, there's the New Rhetoric. Second, I will recommend rhetorical analysis as a *technique* for upgrading PA thinking. By technique, I mean a procedure that can provide significant help, even on a fundamentally business-as-usual basis. On this basis, the allure of rhetorical analysis is better PA engineering and re-engineering.

However, I don't think that business-as-usual is a satisfactory stopping point for PA. Attention should be given to the rhetoric of PA as more than a mere technique. Consistent with un-engineering, rhetoric should provide a larger role for the poetic and the imaginative in the PA conversation. As a result, third, I will go on to the allure of rhetoric as *individual signature*. Rhetoric will be discussed here in such terms as habits of mind and style. Fourth, I will write of the allure of rhetoric as *group signature*. My suggestion will be a change in PA's group signature toward symbolic analysis and toward what—after Oakeshott—we can call the truancy of poetry. I will suggest a change toward a playful analysis that focuses especially on mutuality relevant to people aiming toward patterns of cooperative public action. Without embracing more closely the symbolic, PA theory will tend to remain a victim of its own and others' rhetoric.

## DECORATION AND BEYOND:
## RHETORIC AS MORE THAN A CHOCOLATE TWIRL

Rhetoric is often misunderstood as nothing more than a way to improve prose composition. It is often misconceived as limited to style as ornament, the chocolate twirls that decorate a cake's substance. I'm not opposed to mere felicity in either composition or style. Mere decoration does have its own allure: up with it, I will put. But, by "rhetoric," I don't mean "empty rhetoric"—or "sales talk selling sales talk" as Richards (1936/1965) put it. I am attracted by "rhetoric" in the sense of the New Rhetoric that has been developed during the past century.

The New Rhetoric of the twentieth and twenty-first centuries is more like Sociology, exploring how a society gives rise to what is written-and-said and how what is written-and-said helps shape a society. This New Rhetoric, as David Fogarty (1959, p. 4) attempts to summarize it, is the study of symbolic "ways of arriving at mutual understanding among people working toward patterns of cooperative action." Yes, there are disagreements within New Rhetoric, and some would rather speak of rhetorics—plural. But Fogarty's description of the New Rhetoric as focusing on the symbolic and on mutuality is apposite.

These emphases on the symbolic and on mutuality can be found in the writings of the principal architects of the New Rhetoric, like Kenneth Burke and (the New Rhetorician already mentioned) Ivor Richards. This is why Burke and Richards are interested in language. Burke writes of the New Rhetoric as "rooted in an essential function of language itself...the use of language as a symbolic means of inducing cooperation in beings that by nature respond to symbols" (Burke, 1969, p. 43). Richards writes of the New Rhetoric as involving (although not confined to mere word or one-way stuff) an understanding of the "fundamental laws of the use of language" (Richards, 1936/1965, p. 5).

The New Rhetoric is required to achieve mutual understanding, according to Burke and Richards. Both hold that New Rhetoric is needed and important because they think people are in conflict with other individuals and groups; at least, there is critical lack of congruence. There is a natural separation between people, where A wants to join with B while A wants to retain her identity as A even as she joins with B. A can "identify herself" with B—and vice-versa—to the extent that she is persuaded to do so. At the center of Burke's view of the

New Rhetoric is concern with overcoming the divisions between individuals and groups, primarily a matter of consciousness. Burke writes of New Rhetoric as "the conscious or unconscious use of verbal or nonverbal strategies to achieve identification among people," and he speaks of rhetoric "as aiming to induce cooperation and as transcending hierarchy and estrangement" (Burke, 1966, p. 24). As he writes, "The (New) Rhetoric must lead us through the Scramble, the Wrangle of the Market Place, the flurries and flare-ups of the Human Barnyard, the Give and Take, the wavering line of pressure and counterpressure, the Logomachy, the onus of ownership, the Wars of Nerves" (p. 71). Richards describes the symbolic and mutuality in similar terms. He writes of the "natural isolation and severance of minds" (p. 71). Richards emphasizes the need for mutual understanding to overcome individual and groups divisions. For Richards and on these lines, New Rhetoric is "a study of misunderstanding and its remedies" (1936/1965, p. 6).

New Rhetoricians use prior rhetorical thinking. Rhetoric's history is a strange story. Once rhetoric was at the center of education; now it is not. In ancient times, convincing others of the truth was understood as including rhetoric as persuasion. As Aristotle defined it, rhetoric is "the faculty of observing in any given case the available means of persuasion" (1355b). Yet there were differences in understanding the nature of rhetoric. Isocrates was an anti-foundationalist, for instance, and he held that rhetoric should be understood as having a strong civilizing and democratizing effect. This was the Isocrates whose teacher was Gorgias, the person repeatedly backhanded by Plato, that great anti-rhetoric rhetorician. In medieval times, rhetoric was important for religious purposes; and the art of discovering the available means of persuasion—in sermons and ceremonial and all else—is a "practical" religious concern. In the modern period, the thinking was that we no longer need the open hand of rhetoric. As the sixteenth century rhetorician Peter Ramus and others argued, all we needed was the closed hand of logic that speaks for itself. So the open hand came to be seen as fulfilling the role of the chocolate twirl, something redundant and (strange fantasy) avoidable in writing and speaking, in constructing and communicating meaning.

## RHETORIC'S ALLURE AS TECHNIQUE: A BUSINESS-AS-USUAL EXPLORATION

Whether New Rhetoric or old but not rhetoric-as-chocolate-twirl, rhetorical analysis can be done readily and profitably enough by PA thinkers willing to jump in. As promised, here's a quick-and-dirty five-step *technique* for a business-as-usual exploration of the relevance of rhetoric to PA. Elsewhere, this has been expressed as a three-step technique (in Farmer & Patterson, 2003). Do attempt this at home; it is not dangerous if done without supervision – and we can return later to the more interesting possibilities of the New Rhetoric. The steps are to:

1. start reading a dictionary of rhetorical terms;

2. notice the examples of rhetorical analysis in books on rhetoric in other disciplines;

3. pick out from the dictionary whatever terms seem likely candidates;

4. reflect on the chosen terms in relation to selected PA texts, and let the imagination play;

5. do the same for PA practice.

A sixth step takes the analyst into the third and fourth sections of my paper—giving attention to the rhetoric of PA as more than a mere technique. But others may not wish to cross that Rubicon to business-as-unusual. For now, we stay on this side of the Rubicon.

**Step 1—Consult a dictionary of rhetorical terms.**

This is McClosky's suggestion, and she recommends Richard Lanham's "Handlist of Rhetorical Terms" (1991). When I did this with a class, I used a simpler dictionary—Linda Woodson's "A Handbook of Modern Rhetorical Terms" (1979). Dictionaries have all the disadvantages of dictionaries; but in this case it's painless to jump in the shallow end.

**Step 2—Notice the examples of rhetorical analysis offered in books on rhetoric in other disciplines.**

For example, there are McClosky's (e.g., 1985) on economics and Stone's (e.g., 2001) on policy analysis. You might be entertained by McClosky's rhetorical analysis of statistical significance, for instance; or you might not. She claims (1985, pp. 112–138) that "statistical significance has ruined empirical work in economics," and that "econometrics confuses statistical and scientific significance." She has a long section that argues that "the rhetorical history of statistics is the source of the difficulty." She fingers R.A. Fisher, who is described as having had a public relations flair, a gift for naming things. She argues that, despite warnings in statistics books, it is hard *not* to confuse statistical significance with the significance of everyday usage, where the latter refers to practical importance.

Some additional examples of rhetorical analysis can be classed as negative in that they shock positivist practitioner sensibilities. For instance, McClosky also argues (1985, p.23 ff.) that "proofs (sic) of the law of demand are mostly literary." (Let's put aside the question of how many proofs constitute proof.) Many practicing economists would be offended by McClosky's claim about the law of demand. As she explains, the claim is an apparent "attack" on belief in the law of demand that is what she calls "the distinguishing mark of an economist" (McClosky, 1985, p. 25). Other examples of rhetorical analysis are positive. For example, McClosky speaks (1985, p. 13) of Gary Becker's metaphors, "from criminals as small businessman (sic) to the family as a little firm." As she adds, "Becker is an economic poet, which is what we expect of our theorists."

**Step 3—Pick out from the dictionary whatever rhetorical terms seem likely candidates.**

As the *Handlist* categorizes them, the candidates include concepts and ideas that relate to antitheses, descriptions, emotional appeals, allusions, metaphorical substitutions, repetitions, techniques of argument and illogical uses of language.

Caveat lector. New terms can be odd, e.g. "boomphilogia" (bombastic speech). However, such words are not intrinsically harmful.

**Step 4—Reflect on the chosen terms in relation to selected PA texts.**

At the PAT-Net conference, I took as an example the term "exordium."

An "exordium" is described (Woodson, 1979, p. 23) as, in "traditional argument, the opening in which a writer or speaker attracts the audience's attention, establishes his or her reliability, and creates a sense of good intentions." It's an anecdote or story that is at the beginning of a speech or article, attempting to persuade. The problem is that the exordium can have unintended rhetorical consequences to the extent that it imposes internal constraints on what follows.

A conference talk usually opens with an exordium. To the extent that it was designed to ask for your attention and to lend legitimacy to what I am saying, the stories about South Carolina's legislature at the beginning of this paper constituted an exordium. Books can have several exordia, and sometimes not even at the beginning. Herbert Simon's chapter 3 on "Fact and Value in Decision Making" starts with an exordium, for example. This is where Simon writes that "The necessary ideas are already accessible in the literature of philosophy. Hence, the conclusions reached by a particular school of modern philosophy—logical positivism—will be accepted as a starting point, and their implications for the theory of decisions examined" (Simon, 1976, p. 45). The bottom of that page lists a number of logical positivists, then not out of vogue. That exordium, although brief, is written with such an appeal to authority ("apomnemonysis," quotation of an approved authority, as it is called in rhetorical analysis) that the reader is almost brutalized into following along with the writer.

The examples I gave at the PAT-Net annual conference (repeated in Farmer & Patterson, 2003) considered "September 11th" as an exordium for an article, with the usual goal of introducing the writer as a reliable and agreeable interpreter of PA events. The listener was asked to imagine that this particular exordium wants to do this by appealing to the weakness of our PA theorizing to explain how a government can be both excellent and putrid at the same time—and possibly in the same respect. The example given was the NYPD. It is the same Department that rushes to the World Trade Center that is also the NYPD of the Amadou Diallo and Abner Louima incidents. Examples of the simultaneity of the bureaucratic good and the bureaucratic ugly are easy to collect.

The problem with this September 11th exordium, it was explained, was that exordiums have unintended consequences in limiting the rest of the story. As was mentioned, the "speaker wanted to talk about good and bad performance emanating from the same agency. But she is now entrapped in the language of good and evil, heroes and terrorists. The exordium encourages the speaker into the very splitting—the postulation of things as either utterly good or utterly bad—that she needs to avoid in order to made sense of the paradoxical behavior storied in the same exordium" (Farmer & Patterson, 2003). Sadly, an additional point is that September 11th is the unwritten exordium for any and all articles written at this time about American PA.

**Step 5—Having done it for texts, do the same for PA practice, i.e. reflect on the chosen term in relation to a PA practice or practices, and imagine.**

At the PAT-Net conference, I asked listeners to consider "synecdoche." As the *Handlist* explains, a synecdoche consists of "substitution of part for whole, genus for species, or vice-versa" (Lanham, 1991, p. 148). That same entry quotes Burke as writing, "The more I examine both the structure of poetry and the structure of human relations outside of poetry, the more I am convinced that this is the 'basic' figure of speech" (Lanham, 1991, p. 148). In this, Burke differs from Richards who regards the metaphor as central. Stone explains that the synecdoche is very common in politics, where, as she writes, "examples are offered up as 'typical instances' or 'prototypical cases' of a larger problem. These typical cases then define the entire problem" (Stone, 2001, p. 116).

I find it difficult to specify the core objectives of practice. I suggest that the ambiguity and tenacity of "the" core objective traditionally ascribed to business practice suggest that such a symbol should be understood as a synecdoche. Does the chosen symbol stand in a hierarchical or logical relationship to a set of sub-objectives? Or, does the core objective function less like a central organizing principle and more like a synecdoche—like a flag "standing for" a country. At first sight, there seems little difficulty in identifying the core objective of business practice. It's "the bottom line." But what does this core objective mean? Compare the differing understandings of the core objective of business held by Henry Ford, by Alfred Sloan and by Exxon. The social construction changes, and keeps changing. I can see that "the bottom line" is like a flag.

The core objective of PA practice, I take it, is to advance the public interest—the top line. But advancing the public interest seems to function as a synecdoche for a complex of shifting activities and objectives. The headlines in the *New York Times* often provide startling examples. Recently, I quoted the story that "Hundreds of patients released from state psychiatric hospitals in New York in recent years are being locked away on isolated floors of nursing homes, where they are barred from going outside on their own, have almost no contact with others and have little ability to contest their confinement..." (Levy, 2002a, p. 1). In the PAT-Net talk, I gave another example about the mental homes regulated by the New York State Department of Health (April 28, 2002, p.1). One Brooklyn mental home resident with schizophrenia, often left alone to suffer seizures, reportedly had been dead twelve hours before he was found. "His back, curled and stiff with rigor mortis, had to be broken to fit him into the body bag" (Levy, 2002b, p. 1). Breaking the body rather than the body bag was the procedure. My point is that identifying the objective of PA practice has to accommodate my (and your) own experiences in governments and also the New York administrators just mentioned. The objective is not *simply* to advance the public interest. I don't think it's simply input-output efficiency either, and I don't think it is simply getting the most out of assigned resources. I don't think it is simply serving the public, for example, and I don't think it is simply serving oneself or one's boss or one's boss-of-bosses. I don't think it's simply about acting on assigned items (which may or may not include solving problems), for example, and I don't think it's simply about "knowing how" in assigned areas. However, I wouldn't rule out any of these candidates, especially as transient objectives. Sometimes it is this or that; many times it is not. One day, it's not an objective but an act that serves as synecdoche for all an organization's acts, as when the Immigration and Naturalization Service (INS) in March 2002 renewed the student visas of Mohamed Atta and Marwan Alshehhi. Another day, it's an item, as when a glossy annual report stands for a glossy organization. On this, stories like those from officials in New York and elsewhere undermine our over-simplifications.

Such is what can be gained from a quick-and-dirty technique for conducting a rhetorical analysis in PA. I think it's worth trying. But this five-step technique is perhaps too much within the current rhetoric of PA theorizing. For one thing, it doesn't take seriously enough the extensive content of rhetoric, new or old. Happily, rhetoric's allure extends beyond technique.

## RHETORIC'S ALLURE AS PERSONAL SIGNATURE

The study of rhetoric can focus on appropriating my (and your) individual PA signature, when my (and your) rhetoric is understood as my habit of mind or my style. It can increase my self-consciousness about my individual signature—my habit of mind, my style. It can support a determination in PA theorizing really to "own" my own PA-theorizing-signature, and thus to involve more closely in PA thinking my own individual humanity. My personal signature is my symbolic marking, as when I sign my individual signature in a distinctive way. The description of rhetoric as "habit of mind" is taken from Barbara Czarniawska (2000, p. 51), and the descriptions of rhetoric as style is derived from Nelson Goodman (1978, p. 35).

I am speaking of my signature as symbolizing ownership, not merely personal investment, assent, or approval. Yet this is not to speak nonsense about "finding" my own signature, as if it were a natural form; I am talking about creating. Nor am I suggesting that I should aim for an unchanging signature. The point is greater appropriation or ownership. More in possession of my signature, I can speak from within my own life's experience and my own body in making decisions about choice of problems, of criteria and solutions, of permissible evidence and what Gellner calls "of hunches to be followed up and of those to be ignored, the choice of 'language game' or of 'form of life'" (Gellner, 1980, p. 414.). Gellner was here referring to Philosophy; he could have been writing about PA.

Parallel claims about self-consciousness and signature have been made in a cutting-edge movement in analytic philosophy and elsewhere. As suggested before (Farmer, 1999), the analytic philosopher Goodman is an example. The intellectual context of understanding philosophical style has been changing, as it is recognized that it is dubious to pretend that we have available a God's-eye view of the world, a view—as Nagel put it—from nowhere. Yet style in philosophizing continues to be much ignored, as in PA. In Stanley Cavell's phrase, style is allowed in "only in ornamental doses" (Lang, 1995, p. 21.) Goodman and others recognize that style and content are inter-embedded, inextricably interwoven. "Obviously, subject is what is said, style is how. A little less obviously, that formula is full of faults" (Goodman, 1978, p. 23). He is concerned to reject the received opinion that style consists merely of the artist's conscious choice among alternative means of expression. Referring to a work of art, Goodman can point out that a feature of style may be "a feature of what is said, of what is exemplified, or what is expressed" (Goodman, 1978, p. 32).

On the negative side of the art of appropriating our own signatures, there are the habits of mind or the styles of group signatures. I am making the assumption that the grip of the group aspect of signature permits enough freedom for an individual to appropriate her own signature. I agree that group habits of mind radically limit this freedom. It seems contrary to lived experience and too pessimistic to think that some dosage of this freedom is unavailable, however.

On the positive side of appropriating our own individual signatures, how can a person release her own individuality in her PA thinking? How can she express her own PA wisdom? Each person should have her own preferences about how to release herself in her writing, I agree, although I don't believe that any personal signature is as good as any other. The best, in my view, requires the kind of contemplation that Aristotle had in mind when he wrote of its role in achieving long lasting satisfaction, eudaimonia. Such contemplation is more than a mere smelling of roses, or a mere thoughtfulness. As represented in Aristotle's own life, it begins in a life that wonders; its end is the love of wisdom. I think it is a life that is nourished by imaginative play, by the poetic. I think it must extend to the kind of playing with symbols that is described in my fourth section.

A life of writing is a life of contemplation, or not. I think it should be. How a writer moves toward a more contemplative form of life in the writing of PA theory depends on individual context, capabilities, hopes and even age. I notice that some undergraduates, less set in their ways, are sometimes better at contemplative bursts than some doctoral students. For most PA theorists, I think that a turn toward contemplative writing can be encouraged by imaginative play with writing's forms, with somatic writing, and with seeking to privilege wisdom over information.

"Rashomon," it will be recalled, was the title of Akira Kurosawa's 1950 movie in which a single event was told and re-told from the perspectives of the several participants in that event. These Rashomon opportunities (a sort of technique) can be encouraged in imaginative play with writing's forms—with multiple genres, stories and forms. Such play should aim to create individual signatures by transcending group moulds—even if the transcending fails. It is writing and re-writing in different ways; doodling experimentally with a variety of genres, stories and forms. Multiple genres and stories can be encouraged by literature already available in PA. Barbara Czarniawski (2000) analyzes various literary genres that management uses (e.g. the genre of the detective story) and Jay White (1999) argues that the logic of PA research should be more like storytelling. Various genres can be used in telling the same story. Even within the same genre, the same PA story can be told in different ways. Playing with multiple storying is valuable and almost a commonplace in literature. Would that more PA theorists had the courage and the talent to write in such P-and-T-irrelevant forms as PA short stories or PA poems! Related to experimenting with different forms is anti-administration and word-smithing. The former aims to admit excluded and marginalized perspectives; the latter aims to seek a kind of personal autonomy—strange as it may seem—in the joys of reflecting on language. I don't think that this is the same as copy editing, as much as I admire editors. It is indulging in the sensuality of finding not the right, but the best, expressions. Some PA writers amaze me by their rare talent for this. Even the study of old rhetoric can help in developing these Rashomon opportunities.

Somatic writing is a form that, in the present state of PA, I think that most PA writers should take seriously in their playing with genres and stories. This is the "feminine writing" that Helene Cixous advocates. This writing is not reserved for women. Cixous's view is that some women are bad at feminine writing, and some men are good at it. Feminine writing, in her view, involves "a transformation of our relationship to our body (and to another body)" (Cixous, 1980, p. 97). It entails what can be called *writing with my body*. A good account can be found in Cixous' *The Laugh of Medusa*. To mis-summarize it as a slogan, I would describe feminine writing, like somatic writing, as writing from within my guts, from within my lived experience. Some have written from within their guts in PA (e.g. Vickers, 2001). The advantage of somatic writing is that it can assist not only in transcending group moulds but also in investing an individual's own distinctive humanity in the writing.

Up the slippery slope toward greater appropriation of one's own signature, Roshomon opportunities are also available from playing with advice that runs contrary to PA's "conventional wisdom." Wise literary critics like Harold Bloom can be helpful; so can other writers. Playing with such advice doesn't necessarily mean buying it. But it does mean being open to walking toward the edge of my style, the edge of my rhetorical limits. Haven't the edges of discourses, like the edges of cultures and group discourses, normally proven abnormally fertile for generating new insights? To put it another way, isn't Homi Bhahba (1994, pp. 1–2) right that we constitute ourselves in the in-between, typically between one signature and the other. Bhahba writes of the in-between spaces where strategies of selfhood are elaborated—the "in-between spaces provide the terrain of elaborating strategies of selfhood…—singular or communal—that initiate new signs of identity, and innovative site of collaboration and contestation…."

It is Harold Bloom (2000, p. 19) who asks, "Information is endlessly available to us; where shall wisdom be found?" I can imagine him advising PA theorists to search, not for information, but for wisdom. PA theorists seeking individual signatures that privilege *mere* wisdom, at the expense of the allures of information, in my view would be positive.

Let's turn to the allure of rhetoric for changes in our group signature.

## RHETORIC'S ALLURE FOR PA'S GROUP SIGNATURE

Shouldn't PA theory emphasize the play of symbolic analysis, especially of mutuality relevant to people aiming toward patterns of cooperative public action? This should not be all that PA does. As a start, however, I think that PA should include this analysis at the center of what it does. I think that it should, as long as the analysis is in the spirit of Oakeshott's truancy of poetry. The symbolic analysis should be willing to play hooky from instrumentalist concerns. It should be willing to emphasize the poetic in the sense of releasing the play of the imagination.

This change in PA group signature takes a leaf from rhetoric's book. The proposed emphasis draws on Daniel Fogarty's description, mentioned earlier, of the New Rhetoric as the study of symbolic "ways of arriving at mutual understanding among people working towards patterns of cooperative action" (Fogarty, 1959, p. 4). It does so also by thinking in terms of Kenneth Burke's description (1966, p. 3) of the human being. Burke writes of man (and woman) "as the symbol-using animal (symbol-using, symbol-misusing)...."

I will recap the idea of group signature and then the suggested change in PA's traditional group signature.

### Idea of a Group Signature

Group signatures, overlapping with individual signatures, designate the rhetorical style or habits of mind within which our group thinks and acts. Another way to think of the limits of group signature is that they are virtually indistinguishable from the limits described in Foucault's discourse theory. The limits of my rhetoric, the boundaries of the higgledy-piggledy set of discourses that envelops and constitutes me, empowers and constrains my thinking and acting. I think of the negative effects (like the positive effects) of these rhetorical limits as operating beyond our consciousness, e.g. when a person or the discipline does not recognize what it excludes or marginalizes. Accidents of the time period in which a person lives translate into rhetorical limits or fences. Didn't the rhetoric of the circumstances of his time and place and the rhetoric of the way in which his mother Monica and others brought him up, constrain St. Augustine to think in the religious way he did? Wasn't he predestined, as it were, to believe in the predestination he believed in? We do speak through the vocabularies of our disciplines. We are also familiar with the idea that our discipline speaks through us; our group signature speaks through us.

The existence of group rhetorical features, especially when the features limit, is easier to spot in some disciplines rather than in one's own. Would anyone disagree that the rhetoric of modern mainstream economics includes the mathematical, for example, and that this both empowers economic thinking and also restricts it? If anyone would disagree, probably it would be an economist—when it comes to the restricting. Would anyone disagree that the rhetoric of PA includes privileging the perceived needs of the middle-level practitioner, both empowering and limiting the knowledge to be provided to our audience of middle level practitioners? If anyone would disagree, it would probably be a fellow ASPA member or a student of PA. Moving between disciplines like philosophy and economics presents startling contrasts of rhetoric. Socrates is alive and still bustling in the one discipline, but no dead economist is ever so alive in economics.

The habit-of-mind manifested in the theorizing that I-buy-into can own my individual theorizing. Subscribing to a discipline, I can, as it were, lose my individual mind. The individual dog expresses a group, as well as an individual, signature when he signs that particular fire hydrant. Marking hydrants is the rhetorical structure of what it is, in today's time and circumstances, to be a dog.

The allure of rhetoric for group signature is that it can help us to change PA's traditional group signature.

## Changes in PA Group Signature

I am suggesting changes in PA's group signature—as you will recall—in the form of emphasizing the play of symbolic analysis, especially of mutuality. I will discuss these changes under three sub-headings—mutuality, symbolic focus, and PA's conversation. It is appropriate to start with mutuality, as mutuality is allocated a higher priority in the new group signature.

### *Mutuality*

Proposing a group signature that places special emphasis on the symbolic analysis of mutuality or mutual understanding, connected with people aiming towards patterns of cooperative public action, is a symbolic or "political" recommendation. It's a Nietzschean move, if you will; for Nietzsche, the function of style—and group style—includes the prioritization of values.

Others may suggest something else, or they may want to keep the old PA religion. There are pitfalls in my emphasizing mutuality. Proposing symbolic analysis of mutuality suggests an unnecessary assumption that we can readily obtain something like beneficence through harmony. It also suggests, falsely, that mutuality precludes the ideal of recognizing individuals in their wholeness. No, we should not be Pollyannaish and regard mutuality as a simple union of people. Mutuality should be understood on the lines that the New Rhetorician Kenneth Burke discussed—as a unity that recognizes each individual's individuality and each individual's differences. As you know, there is a large literature on this. Mutuality cannot mean that unity which, in Georg Hegel's celebrated image, is like the night wherein all the cows are black.

The world is changing in ways that suggest that PA should increase its concern with the symbols of mutuality or cooperation, however. There are three, among a number, of familiar movements that seem relevant to that concern. A first is that there is talk about an increasingly multi-cultural society, including the excluded and the marginalized, and the shrinking global village. The heart of Burke's idea of New Rhetoric—the need for A to join with B, while maintaining her identity as A—seems more pressing in such circumstances. The need for policed women, policed minorities, transsexuals with policed sexualities and others to join the mainstream pot, without being melted, seems material for the symbolic analysis of mutuality. Precisely how this first movement will, or should, work out is open to disagreement. Earlier, I wrote of Homi Bhabha's view of selfhood being created in the in-between spaces, and I agree with him. Giorgio Agamben appears to contradict Bhabha. Agamben tells us that the coming person is "whatever being." The demarcation of "whatever being" is not by a property such as being conservative or Italian. She is designated only by her being (Agamben, 1993, pp. 1–2). Bhabha and Agamben disagree on the forms of the results, but they both imply that the symbolic effects are profound.

A second familiar movement is the decline in hierarchy. To the extent that we have less support from the symbolization of hierarchy, surely we have a need for even more workable symbolizations of mutuality. Some have difficulty distinguishing between the notion of "as little hierarchy as possible" and "no hierarchy." Some see this too much in purely administrative terms; legitimately, some have trouble in thinking of the present Internal Revenue Service (IRS) having a shorter chain of fleas on the inferior fleas' backs. A drift towards more laterality is more easily understood if the shift in the steepness of hierarchy and subordination is seen in terms that are longer and that go beyond the internally bureaucratic. For example, look at hierarchy and subordination from the perspectives of, say, feminism or womanism. A third familiar movement, internal to PA from PA's perspective, is the extent that we are interested in genuine citizen involvement in bureaucratic institutions. Recently, a number of us participated in a dialogue about constructing civil space (Farmer, 2002). My feelings on this originated when I did consulting work for cities with Model Cities programs, an initiative that made an effort to facilitate citizen participation in decision-making in local institutions. Clearly, institutional re-arrangements by themselves were not enough. I came to realize only later that the nub of the problem was a matter of language, of consciousness, of symbolization. As we write, "Without re-symbolization, effective citizen participation is out of reach" (Farmer & Patterson, 2003). Those in institutions are institutionalized in their understanding and in their reasoning; the chains are visible. Those outside bureaucratic institutions are no less institutionalized, although the latter are entangled in their thinking in what (adapting Marx) we can call invisible chains.

*Symbolic Focus*

The suggested change in PA's group signature involves a symbolic turn. I will speak of a symbolic focus in general, and then give two examples.

As Deborah Stone explains and as you know, a symbol is anything that stands for something else, and a symbol's meaning depends on how people interpret and use it. A symbol can be "an object, a person, a place, a word, a song, an event, even a logo on a T-shirt" (Stone, 2001, p. 108). She could have added that a symbol can be small items like these, or large objects like economics-as-a-whole or even God. Symbols constitute forms of language, whether a sophisticated language (like English or Chinese) or some other code that concerns meaning. As Stone goes on to say, "Any good symbolic device...shapes our perceptions and suspends skepticism, at least temporarily.... They are means of influence and control" (Stone, 2001, p. 108). The New Rhetoricians, unsurprisingly, agree that the elements of language are fundamental in our symbolizing. The basic function of rhetoric, according to Kenneth Burke (1969, p. 41), is the "use of words by human agents to form attitudes or to induce actions in other human agents...."

There is a tradition—as I mentioned at the beginning of this paper—of understanding politics as symbolic action, and there are important examples in policy analysis. In his book on *Politics as Symbolic Action*, for instance, Murray Edelman complains that "Americans have been taught to look upon government as a mechanism that is responsive to their wants and upon these in turn as rational reflections of their interests and their moral upbringing and therefore as stable and continuing" (Edelman, 1971, p. 3). He wants the center of attention to be political symbolizing whereby people adapt their worlds to their behaviors and vice versa. In policy analysis, Deborah Stone's textbook has gone through three editions, and Dvora Yanow has published on the construction of race and ethnicity in policy analysis (2002) and earlier. Jay White reminds his readers of the long history of public policy analysis as involving storytelling; he quotes Martin Rein (1976), for instance. Stone doesn't use the term "rhetoric." Her book is about constructing worlds of political and policy analysis. She opposes the idea that politics is a rational thing or even a thing at all. There is an elegant comment on the relevance of the symbolic from Kenneth Burke, the New Rhetorician, in Edelman's book. Burke writes, "And however important to us is the tiny sliver of reality each of us has experienced firsthand, the whole overall 'picture' is but a construct of our symbolic systems. To meditate on this fact until one sees its full implications is much like peering over the edge of things into an ultimate abyss" (Burke, 1966, p. 5).

The importance of the symbolic is one of the features of Lacanian psychoanalytical theory that, within and outside the PA context, has fascinated Orion White and Cynthia McSwain. Jacques Lacan's account is not unique in describing humans as living in the world of the symbolic, the world of language. It differs from the description offered by New Rhetoricians like Richards, who writes of "a natural isolation and severance of minds." Yet, Lacan's account is rich in its psychoanalytic depiction of the dynamics and consequences of how from a tender age we live in the symbolic world of language. For Lacan, we live *alienated* in this symbolic world. One of the more significant impacts of Lacan's thinking has been in the psychoanalytical analysis of culture, which of course includes PA. The principal forum in the United States for this cultural analysis is the Association for the Psychoanalysis of Society and Culture, and heading the PA section of that association is Orion White and Cynthia McSwain. For excellent accounts of Lacanian theory and for a discussion of its relevance for PA, see McSwite's writings (1997, pp. 43–63; 2000, pp. 45–71) Orion White and Cynthia McSwain write of the difficulty we face in understanding Lacan's account. They comment that they want to highlight "how completely the subject resides within and has its fate set by the world of language." Consciousness "itself is located outside the individual in the symbolic process" (McSwite, 1997, pp. 55–56).

Two examples can indicate how this description relates to the suggested change in PA's traditional group signature, to changes in the rhetoric of the PA field. No symbol is an island. Symbols interact, interweave—and interject others. Symbolic action extends between symbols and parts of symbols, with complexity suggestive of organic chemistry. There are even symbols within symbols, e.g., symbols within the symbol that is PA as-a-whole. In this context, there seems no end to useful and diverse opportunities to play with symbols in PA. A cottage industry awaits, an industry with many different jobs. There are at least as many ways and methods to explore symbols as to study "things." Some prefer to focus on the symbolization connected with particular functions or events, for instance; others choose particular symbols and their interrelationships. Yet others may prefer to create symbols, a hard job for non-poets. There are enough examples in the literature of the value of symbol playing in all of these ways. I want to recommend for PA theory's group signature symbol playing that is little concerned with immediate value—and with our bitter foe, common sense. My first example concerns a large PA symbol—PA theory as-a-whole. My second concerns two symbols within PA.

*Example 1:* Let's start with a meandering moral tale that takes as its starting point a contrast—a dubious contrast—between apology and celebration that McClosky (1998, p. 4) raises in a different context. Is traditional PA theory as-a-whole an *apology* for, or a *celebration* of, the administratively engineered component of our current economic, political other societal systems? By mentioning "apology," I am asking if PA theory as-a whole provides a symbol of justification for this administratively engineered component. By "celebration," I am asking if the symbolic action of PA theory as-a-whole constitutes an affirmation of, a rejoicing about, a validation for the administrative engineered component. I don't know if traditional PA theory-as-a-whole is an apology. I think that it's a celebration. I think that it should be neither; I prefer un-engineering. Let's approach through a back door, considering the case of economic theory.

What is symbolized by mainstream economic theory as-a-whole? The more familiar story is that mainstream economic theory's group signature opposes economic engineering *tout court*. Many will insist on this to the point of apoplexy, and they are not wrong. Consider the symbols within the symbol of economic theory as-a-whole. Most people will agree that a signature metaphor is the invisible hand, surely both an apology for capitalism and a celebration of capitalism. The metaphor can be both to the extent that an apology can be a celebration, and a celebration can be an apology. The invisible hand is an obscure symbol, and this obscurity may account for much of its force – in the same way that Augustine thought that much of the rhetorical force of the Bible comes from its obscurity. We know that it is about self-interest. "It is not from the benevolence of the butcher, the brewer, or the baker, that we expect our dinner, but from their regard to their own interests" (Campbell & Skinner, 1976, pp. 26–27).

One view is to see this signature metaphor of the invisible hand as standing for the debatable claim that, if everyone in a society tries to work for the public good, that society will be worse off than if everyone worked for her own selfish interests. Another view is to see the invisible hand as a metaphor for the automatic pricing mechanism that tends toward a final equilibrium. Or, in a reverse direction, one can see the pricing system as a signature metaphor for the invisible hand. Look with a lantern into any part of Economics, any nook or cranny—micro or macro; there lurks the metaphor of supply and demand!

Unsurprisingly, the story of the symbols within economic theory is more complicated than this, because in any discipline metaphor piles upon metaphor. So the economics story houses other signature metaphors—the will for equilibrium, and the searching at the margin. My favorite "Dictionary of Economic Terms" (first published in 1901 and last revised in 1951) pipes up. "Equilibrium—a term widely used in theoretical and applied economics and derived from two Latin words meaning an equal balance. An analogy is, of course, from the physical sciences and, as used in economics, any quantity of state of affairs is said to be in equilibrium if there are no forces acting on it, on balance, tending to change it one way or the other" (Winton, 1951, pp. 32–33).

The traditional hands-off interpretation of the invisible hand cuts deeper. Shapiro (1993, p. 103) points out that there are two poles in treating the social, emphasizing harmony, and emphasizing disharmony. Smith's invisible hand—and the law of supply and demand that works toward equilibrium—is in the first category. Shapiro claims that Adam Smith's poetic language is on the side that assumes the existence of God as the universe's author—but an author who has left behind the mechanisms guaranteeing that the self and other are always congruent. He holds that the congruence is not a characteristic of the world but rather a metaphor, a trope, in the organization of Smithian economic thinking.

Here is a better reading of what is symbolized by economic theory's group signature. We can call the reading "deviant," but it is not outside the mainstream economic tradition. Economic theory as-a-whole is a symbol of celebration in that it "rejoices" that, properly engineered, general equilibrium is achieved—as if that is good. (I see this rejoicing reflected in an incidental and minor way in the Mozart-like elegance of economic modeling.) Economic theory as-a-whole is a symbol of apology to the extent that it "proves" how, properly engineered, market economic practice is optimal. This sounds strange. But the more familiar story misses the point. Economies tend to develop structural imperfections like monopolies and oligopolies (not to mention problems of instability and growth), and the invisible hand needs a hand from the economic engineer. Economic "maintenance" engineering is required. Even in Adam Smith's account, the invisible hand does not work optimally without "rivalrous competition" and obstacles to this kind of competition have to be disassembled. I agree that Adam Smith—and certainly many of his enthusiastic followers—slide over what he wrote; after all, Smith was opposing the interference of mercantilism, and followers have their own axes to grind. Mainstream economic's list of conditions for the optimal functioning of an economy is hyper-demanding. As Allen Buchanan indicates, for instance, one of the demanding conditions is that either transaction costs must be zero, or there must be perfect competition and no externalities (Buchanan, 1991, pp. 184–185). For discussion of ways in which the invisible hand needs an economic engineering hand, see Paul Samuelson's mainstream economics textbook.

Can do! The apology and the celebration is that economic theory as-a-whole is up to the task of providing whatever maintenance engineering is needed. Recall Shapiro's deep structure interpretation about God as author, just given. Granted that there are many traps in symbolic analysis, especially as we strive for "simple" clarity. A misleading one is my reference to Shapiro as cutting "deeper" calling something deeper is a rhetorical choice dependent on a frame of reference. Another is all the rhetoric that Shapiro himself employs, talking about God. My main point here is different, however; it is that Shapiro's story can re-interpreted. The deeper structure can be read as speaking again to the possibility of engineering to achieve an optimal equilibrium, both apologizing for what can be perfected by engineering and celebrating the results of what can be engineered. Shapiro's "divine" interpretation wasn't quite right in its story of God reconciling self and other without human assistance. God provided man (it's always man!) with a fully effective do-it-yourself economic repair kit.

Having illustrated with economics, I want to ask whether traditional PA theory as-a-whole is an apology or a celebration. Is PA theory's group signature an apology in the sense that traditional PA theory has the know-how to engineer and re-engineer—how to fix—any administrative imperfections? Is it an apology in the sense that the laity is assured that bureaucracy does not have any unfixable machinery? While neglect or stupidity might be a factor, is it an apology for whatever is bad in bureaucracy in the sense that PA theory as-a-whole is up to the job of making whatever repairs are needed? Or, is PA theory a celebration in a parallel way? I don't mean human engineering in the sense of social programming; nor in the sense of creating economic and political systems. I mean "maintenance engineering"—fixing parts that break, opening the possibility of a smoothly running engine. Much in PA, like Herbert Simon's *Administrative Behavior* mentioned earlier, seems to fall on both sides of the fence; other literature may be more firmly on only one side.

I think that traditional PA theory as-a-whole is a celebration to the extent that its principal vital function is to applaud present PA practice. This celebration takes various forms, including those suggested above for the apology and others like awarding degrees to practitioners for learning about practitioner topics. There is a curious difference between the celebration in the PA as opposed to the economic case, however. Traditional PA theory as-a-whole celebrates through subservience to here-and-now practice practitioners; mainstream economic theory as-a-whole genuflects less deeply to the local chamber of commerce. Relative to theory, PA here-and-now practice is so dominant that the dominance typically seems normal and necessary. Many traditional PA theorists do tend to act as if they "need" justification from the here-and-now practitioners. Like the rhetoric of economics that makes a hero of the entrepreneur, the rhetoric of PA theory is firmly grounded on the practitioner-we-have, the hero of the PA theory story. A difference is that the entrepreneur in economic theory offers the mixed blessings of being a stick figure, an artifact of the theory; microeconomic theory focuses on "the firm" rather than on particular "real-life" firms. The blessing is regrettable in that it makes economics reductionist. But it does have the limited side-benefit for economic's group signature of diminishing any urge to be loyal to current practitioners. What would economic theory have been like, if David Ricardo or John Maynard Keynes had felt obligated to please the businessmen that Adam Smith mentioned—to please the local butcher, the local brewer and the local baker? There are some anti-establishment issues in the heart of economic theory; the critique of monopolies is an example. The result of this dominator-submissive relationship of practice to theory in PA's traditional group signature is not trivial; it is a factor in waving off PA theory as-a-whole from (as I like to repeat) speaking-to-power issues.

*Example 2:* Some symbols or words do have rhetorical mass. Earlier I mentioned the words "God, terrorist, hero, evil." I could add symbols like "welfare," "America," "veterans," "hard work," "effectiveness," "things" and "practical." Discussion of a PA component symbol (or word or idea) should surely consider its rhetorical mass and its place within relevant systems of symbols. Rhetorical mass refers to the additional mass that is carried by certain symbols, greater seductive or persuasive power. I am tempted to say that rhetorical mass operates like "magic." As examples of rhetorical weight and their symbolic functioning (and non-functioning) within PA's group signature, consider in turn two symbols that concern PA—efficiency and love. Consider the unevenness in any struggle between them within PA.

"Efficiency" is a symbol with rhetorical mass in PA thinking. Public officials can be said to be motivated by an efficiency ethic, and others can argue that better descriptions are ideas like "effectiveness" or—as mentioned earlier—"advancing the public interest." The rhetorical mass of "efficiency" is reflected in its tenacity and in its resistance to rational argument. Negligible dents seem inflicted by argumentation that efficiency is inadequate as a central motivational ethic for PA practice. "Efficiency" does seem to have a mass that exceeds the weight of its rational support. Efficiency's magical rhetorical mass results from "efficiency" being part of a dominant system of logical symbols—the symbols that attend and support the capitalist ethic. A great motivational force, capitalism has been characterized as the rational pursuit of ever more wealth (Weber, 1958, p. 17). Because it rationally strives for more and more wealth, the logic of capitalism is to value economic efficiency. As

Baechler (1975, p. 113) explains, the "specific feature that belongs only to the capitalist system is the privileged position accorded to the search for economic efficiency."

The play of symbolic analysis is also relevant for ideas that we would like to introduce into PA thinking—for making changes in PA's group signature. Consider "love" and the associated symbol of "un-engineering," and consider the uphill struggle such concepts would have in replacing others like "efficiency." I have argued that love should become the regulative ideal for the motivation of actions in the public sector (see Farmer, 2002); the current symbol for PA motivation should be deposed. A regulative ideal is a vision or benchmark of what should be done, even though it might be "impossible" to achieve fully. Examples of such ideals in politics include Rousseau's "general will" and in morality precepts like "love your neighbor as yourself." Satisfactory regulative ideals, as I mentioned before, are visions at which people sometimes succeed and often fail.

Love, I have suggested, should involve a shift toward un-engineering. It involves at least two aspects—love for an ideal (like love for country, or love for the public interest) and love for each person as she is in herself, warts and all (like Anthony for Cleopatra, and vice-versa). Especially for each person as she is in herself, love includes the idea of being-with, a caring-for, a wanting-to-know-about each individual. It seems inconsistent with the extent of the present PA focus on the mere administration of "things." Care can be a manifestation of love; but I don't think that it's enough by itself. In my view, love involves a shift away from viewing administration as a matter of things about rule-making-for-groups and about rule-application-for-groups. It is away from the mechanical or hydraulic view of administration. It is indeed toward the un-engineering that I see as opposed to symbols like re-engineering. Reengineering, successor to Total Quality Management, can be described in a variety of ways. But all the approaches share a proclivity for techniques that are motivated inwards toward the needs and functioning of the organization. Even when they focus on outward relationships, their primary interest is inward.

Un-engineering, as I see it, embraces the death of the practitioner. The death of the practitioner is not his physical execution, any more than the death of the author is the actual death of the writer. It means transcending. Earlier I suggested that PA engineering traditionally and centrally has focused on the here-and-now practitioner, the PA practitioner as the hero of the PA story. There have been suggestions in the past not to focus so directly on the practitioner (e.g. Michael Harmon, 1981, on action theory). Un-engineering involves a more radical shift to the citizen as a whole, extending beyond the citizen's role as a client or customer of a particular agency. PA would focus on the human-in-her-individuality and in-her-difference as that person engages in acts of mutuality. It would center on a person who might come into contact with this or that bureaucracy only incidentally. To repeat the slogans—the perspective of the subordinate and the largest societal concerns like the bureaucratization of human life would be de-marginalized.

Talk about love is implicated in the logic of symbolic systems like that of patriarchy. Look at bell hooks' third book on love. Writes bell hooks, "In the patriarchal male imagination, the subject of love was relegated to the realm of the weak and was replaced by narratives of power and domination.... Love became solely women's work" (hooks, 2002, p. 77). Earlier, she writes that "Patriarchy has always seen love as women's work, degraded and devalued labor" (hooks, 2002, p. xviii). Implicated also are the surprises of other symbolic systems (see Adams, 2000). In a contest for PA recognition with motivational forces like "efficiency," love has to surmount not only the rhetorical weight of competitor symbols. Also it has to operate from within the limits of other symbolic systems. In any such competition, love is a rhetorical underdog. Group signature is changed easily only when the symbols are, as it were, in the right constellation.

**PA's Conversation**

Through rhetorical analysis, PA's group signature should seek to privilege—and as un-engineering should include—the symbol of the truancy of poetry. In changing its group signature, PA should look forward to improving its conversation—paralleling McCloskey's aim, discussed at the beginning, of improving the conversation in her field. Michael Oakeshott advances and applauds the ideas both of what he calls the conversation of mankind and the truancy of poetry. He describes the conversation as ongoing, with multiple voices and idioms. For him, the preeminent voice in this conversation is what he understands as poetry.

For Oakeshott, this ideal conversation began in the primeval forests and it flourishes most mightily when it is not dominated by the shouts of technique and the cries of the hunt for the Big T of truth. Writes Oakeshott (1991, p. 490): "As civilized human beings, we are the inheritors, neither of an inquiry about ourselves and the world, nor an accumulating body of information, but of a conversation, begun in the primal forests and extended and made more articulate in the course of centuries." I think it is a blemish to hint at "a" single conversation, although Oakeshott (1991, p. 491) qualifies the blemish by speaking of the conversation of mankind as "the meeting place of various modes of imagining; and in this conversation there is, therefore, no voice without an idiom of its own...." I doubt whether he intends an onward-and-upward progression in the conversation. But we can accept the main point he is trying to make, despite any such warts. As he writes, in this conversation "the participants are not engaged in an inquiry or a debate; there is no 'truth' to be discovered, no proposition to be proved, no conclusion sought... Thoughts of different species take wing and play around one another, responding to each other's movements and provoking one another to fresh exertion" (Oakeshott, 1991, p. 489).

Oakeshott's point is to emphasize poetry. Poetry in this context is understood in a catholic sense as involved in writing, painting, sculpting, composing music, acting, dancing, singing and—if he had thought of it—even PA writing, properly understood. For Oakeshott, this poetry emerges in contemplative imagining. Oakeshott tells us that the "voice of contemplation is the voice of poetry...and it has no other utterance" (Oakeshott, 1991, p. 516). The group signature of PA should be fashioned to move toward this kind of poetry in this kind of conversation. As Oakeshott (1991, p. 541) writes, "Poetry is a sort of truancy, a dream within the dream of life, a wild flower planted among our wheat."

## CONCLUSION

This paper has discussed new directions for PA Theory—four allures of rhetorical analysis. First, it has pointed toward New Rhetoric. Second, it suggested a quick-and-dirty technique. Third, it recommended greater ownership of my individual signature. Fourth, it suggested changes in our group signature. It suggests a playful study of the symbolic, especially of mutuality as it relates to people aiming toward patterns of cooperative public action.

Through the symbolic, let's seek a more robust PA conversation that privileges, in Oakeshott's sense, the truancy of poetry. Through rhetorical analysis, let's seek a post-hydraulic, playful conversation such as that characterized in the Novalis' poem (2000, p. 1) that looks forward to a context "when geometric diagrams and digits/ Are no longer the keys to living things" and when:

> When society is returned once more
> To unimprisoned life, and to the universe,
> And when light and darkness mate
> Once more and make something transparent,
> And people see in poems and fairy tales
> The true history of the world,
> Then our entire twisted nature will turn
> And ......

## ENDNOTES

1. This paper results from the original paper prepared for a talk at a plenary session at the May 2002 annual conference of the Public Administration Theory Network (PAT-Net) in Cleveland Ohio. The talk contained much, but not all, of the original paper. Another paper, derived from the original and directed toward practitioners, appeared in *Public Administration Review*. This paper is the original, as amended in October 2002.

2. Thanks for the important contributions of Tricia M. Patterson of Florida Atlantic University in the writing of this paper. She also contributed substantially and invaluably to the original paper and the plenary version.

## REFERENCES

Adams, C. J. (2000). *The sexual politics of meat: A feminist-vegetarian critical theory*. New York: Continuum Publishing Company.

Agamben, G. (1993). *The coming community (theory out of bounds, Vol. 1)*. (M. Hardt, Trans.). Minneapolis: University of Minnesota Press.

Baechler, J. (1975). *The origins of capitalism*. Oxford: Blackwell.

Bhabha, H. (1994). *The location of culture*. London: Routledge.

Bloom, H. (2000). *How to read and why*. New York: Schribner.

Buchanon, A. (1991). Efficiency arguments for and against the market. In J. Arthur & W. H. Shaw (Eds.), *Justice and economic distribution* (pp. 182-191). Englewood Cliffs, NJ: Prentice Hall.

Burke, K. (1966). *Language as symbolic action*. Berkeley: University of California Press.

Burke, K. (1969). *A rhetoric of motives*. Berkeley: University of California Press.

Campbell, R. H., & Skinner, A. S. (1976). *Adam Smith: An inquiry into the nature and the causes of the wealth of nations*. Oxford: Clarendon Press.

Czarniawska, B. (2000). *Writing management: Organization theory as a literary genre*. New York: Oxford University Press.

Cixous, H. (1980). The laugh of Medusa. In E. Marks & I. de Coutivron (Eds.), *New French feminisms: An anthology* (pp. 245-264). Amherst: University of Massachusetts Press.

Edelman, M. (1971). *Politics as symbolic action*. New York: Academic Press.

Farmer, D. J. (1995). *The language of public administration: Bureaucracy, modernity, and postmodernity*. Tuscaloosa: University of Alabama Press.

Farmer, D. J. (2002). Administrative love and un-engineering. *Administrative Theory & Praxis, 24*, 369-380.

Farmer, D. J., & Patterson, P. M. (2003). The reflective practitioner and the uses of rhetoric. *Public Administration Review, 63*, 65–71.

Fogarty, D. (1959). *Roots for a new rhetoric*. New York: Teachers College of Columbia University.

Gellner, E. (1980). Sociology. In B. Lang (Ed.), *Philosophical style: Am anthology about the writing and reading of philosophy* (pp. 413–457). Chicago: Nelson-Hall.

Goodman, N. (1978). *Ways of worldmaking*. Indianapolis, IN: Hackett.

Harmon, M. M. (1981). *Action theory for public administration*. Boston, MA: Little, Brown.

hooks, b. (2002). *Communion: The female search for love*. New York: HarperCollins.

King, C., & Kensen, S. (2002). Associational public space: Politics, administration, and storytelling. *Administration and Society, 34*, 87–129.

Lang, B. (1995). The style of method: Repression and representation in the genealogy pf philosophy. In C. Van Eck, J. McAllister & R. Van de Vall (Eds.), *The question of style in philosophy and the arts* (pp. 18–36). New York: Cambridge University Press.

Lanham, R. A. (1991). *A handlist if rhetorical terms*. Berkeley: University of California Press.

Levy, C. J. (2002a, October 6). Mentally ill and locked away in nursing homes in New York. *The New York Times*, 1.

Levy, C. J. (2002b, April 28). For mentally ill, death and misery. *The New York Times*, 1.

McClosky, D. N. (1998). *The rhetoric of economics* (2nd ed.). Madison: University of Wisconsin Press.

McClosky, D. N. (1990). *If you're so smart: The narrative of economic expertise*. Chicago: University of Chicago Press.

McClosky, D. N. (1994). *Knowledge and persuasion in economics*. Cambridge: Cambridge University Press.

McClosky, D. N. (1997). *The vices of economists: The virtues of the bourgoisie*. Amstedam: University of Amsterdam Press.

McSwite, O. C. (1997). Jacques Lacan and the theory of the human subject: How psychoanalysis can help public administration. *American Behavioral Scientist, 41*, 46–63.

Novalis. (2000). When geometric diagrams... (R. Bly, Trans.). In *The poets tree: A celebration of poetry*, (p. 1). Retrieved February 16, 2003 from http://www.geocities.com/Paris/Pavillion/1467/files/west_novalis.html

Oakeshott, M. J. (Ed.). (1991). The voice of poetry in the conversation of mankind. In *Rationalism in politics and other essays* (pp. 488–541). Indianapolis, IN: Liberty Fund.

Rein, M. (1976). *Social science and public policy.* New York: Penguin.

Richards, I. A. (1936/1965). *The philosophy of rhetoric.* New York: Oxford University Press.

Shapiro, M. J. (1993). *Reading Adam Smith: Desire, history and value.* Newbury Park, CA: Sage Publications.

Simon, H. A. (1976). *Administrative behavior: A study of decision-making processes in administrative organization* (3rd ed). New York: Free Press.

Stone, D. (2001). *Public paradox and political reason.* New York: HarperCollins Publishers.

Vickers, M. (2001). *Work and unseen chronic illness: Silent voices.* London: Routledge,

Weber, M. (1958). *The Protestant ethic and the spirit of capitalism* (T. Parsons, Ed.). New York: Schribner.

White, J. D. (2000). *Taking language seriously: The narrative foundation of public administration research.* Washington, D.C.: Georgetown University Press.

Winton, J. R. (1951). *Dictionary of economic terms.* London: Routledge & Kegan Paul.

Woodson, L. (1979). *A handbook of modern rhetorical terms.* Urbana, IL: National Council of Teachers of English.

Yanow, D. (2002). *Constructing "race" and "ethnicity" in America: Category-making in public policy and administration.* Armonk, NY: M. E. Sharpe.

# BECAUSE MY MASTER BATHES ME

David John Farmer

## ABSTRACT

*Shouldn't we do more to correct the power imbalance afflicting PA theory and practice? I suggest a corrective program incorporating a relevant theory of PA reform. Relevant are layers of phenomena now virtual strangers in traditional PA thinking. Relevant is Dominique Laporte's analysis of civilizing as a kind of bathing.*

Governmental buildings in Washington D.C., solid and immense, symbolize governmental administration *speaking from power.* The Department of Justice, the Department of State, the Department of Agriculture, the Department of the Interior, and the Department of Labor, for instance, together present a top-down vision of the enduring strength and the huge value of our governmental systems. The ponderous messages engraved high on their sides are Moses-like, *speaking-from-power* symbols that seem to demand reverence. The Pentagon has now been repaired; it's better than new. Office buildings in Manhattan stand spectacular and scrape the sky. The Empire State and the Chrysler together present a vision of the power and brilliance of our economic systems; our economic systems *speak from power.* They witness to our age of seduction, *speaking-from-power* that is wedded to wealth and the mystique of the entrepreneur. The destruction of the Twin Towers and the mass killing of people were heartbreaking. Soon the Towers will be replaced—and probably by a building even higher and more splendid. To be fair, even Washington's huge buildings appear cloth-coat-republican compared with top-down royal excesses like France's Versailles or Russia's Kremlin.

What we need, in my view, is an optimal program to correct the excessive imbalance within, and outside, PA theory and practice between speaking-from-power and speaking-to-power. The more powerful perspective, or direction, is speaking from power; and this privileged perspective disproportionately shapes and reflects our visioning and our living. The character of the Washington and New York buildings symbolize this perspective; the character of the buildings is a speaking-from-power-commercial for traditional systems and systems themselves. The less powerful perspective is *speaking-to-power*. The Washington and New York buildings contrast with the relative smallness, the relative fragility, the relative unimportance of the humans who swarm to work in, to do business in, to walk past, or to lie on the heating grates of these buildings. These humans, if they were to speak to such a governmental or corporate administration, would *speak to power*. The buildings present visions, perhaps manifestations of the unconscious, of the majesty of our systems that can give identity to citizens. They offer visions of how governmental systems empower the lives of the citizens that belong. They offer visions of the relative—repeat, relative—unimportance of the creative, living and present actions of the person-in-herself in-her-differences. They do not directly represent the *speaking-to-power* gnostic creativity of the human.

Embrace the Great Refusal! Refuse to limit PA thinking and practice to the one-dimensionality of privileging speaking-from-power, or system-affirming, arrangements! An optimal program for refusal needs an adequate theory of reform, theory being used here to mean "a particular way of conceptualizing something" (Sayer, 1984, p. 50). It should recognize that speaking-from-power and speaking-to-power manifest themselves at three dynamic layers, or levels, of relevant PA reality. It should appreciate how these layers of relevant reality shape choices about relationships to power. At each of the three levels, there is a top-down bias that robs PA of understandings and practices available from a speaking-to-power perspective. An optimal program for refusal should take corrective steps at each of the three levels, especially at the symbolic levels. Remember the symbolic in Washington's and New York's buildings! Before discussing the top-down bias and the corrective steps at each of the three layers, let's turn to the nature of these layers.

## THREE LAYERS

> The Roman, like the Englishman who follows in his footsteps, brought to every new shore on which he set his foot...only his cloacal obsession. He gazed about him in his toga and he said: It is meet to be here. Let us construct a water closet, sneers Professor MacHugh, a character in James Joyce's *Ulysses* that was set in 1904. (Joyce, 1997, p. 181)

The three layers are dynamic levels of relevant PA reality, parallel to the way that the superego, ego and id are layers of psychic reality. By "relevant," I mean what is relevant to an optimal program for PA refusal. By "PA reality," I mean phenomena encountered in such a PA reform. The layers are "dynamic" in that they shape choice of speaking-from-power and speaking-to-power perspectives. Each layer provides both energies and constraints—impetus and direction—that shape thinking and practice at its own and at the other levels; they are not merely passive. The layers also can be understood as presenting different levels for thinking about power relationships.

The three layers are equally real, albeit not equally important. In speaking about reality, I'm sensitive to the quagmire quality of philosophical conversations about the real (e.g. see Farmer, 1990, pp. 29–34). Let's avoid these conversations by saying—in a prissy manner—that all three layers are equally real, insofar as any one layer is real. In the same manner, let's agree that there is a range of layers, and that others may want to identify a different number of them. Like any other set of categories, this explanatory scheme is open to deconstruction. For my money, the less familiar of these real layers are the more important for an optimal program for PA refusal.

I call the layers or levels: a) the transparent, b) the disciplinary symbolic, and c) the cloacal symbolic. Let's start first with the transparent level, the familiar. Then proceed to the two layers that are virtual strangers in traditional PA theory, the last layer encompassing the dynamic symbolism of the toilet—the water closet—to which the above quote from James Joyce refers.

**Transparent**

The transparent layer or level refers to the *non-symbolic elements in both PA and the PA context*. It points to what can be seen on the surface of PA thinking and practice. It points to what we can see—readily, I imagine—on the surface of the PA context.

It might be better to name the transparent layer the "surface layer;" but I think not. Recognizing top-down material in one's own field is often not *transparent* to the specialist who anxiously wants to believe in her scientific objectivity. Recognizing top-down material is often not transparent in the PA context, e.g. appreciating the economic motivations implicated in administrative choices. Choice of "surface layer" does avoid the verbal difficulty (that what is transparent often enough can be opaque), and it does have the advantage of suggesting that top-down material is on the surface of any textbook or action for any reader to notice. However, I'm hesitant about a surface v. non-surface dichotomy. For one thing, I'm reluctant to concede the surface entirely to the non-symbolic. For another, choice of "surface layer" can give the impression that the surface content is "caused" by material at the sub-surface layers. In a sense, it is. But I imagine a dynamic, a back-and-forth, relationship, similar to the interacting relationships in Marxism, as I understand it, between the contents of the superstructure and the substructure.

## Disciplinary Symbolic

The disciplinary symbolic layer refers to *symbols and symbolizations that, first, are relevant to choice of a speaking-from-power or a speaking-to-power perspective and, second, are within the discipline or field of PA thinking and practice.*

This symbolic layer is a category not only for PA but also for all disciplines or fields, like Economics, Sociology, and so on. I recognize that all these disciplines or fields interact, e.g., when advances in the physics of electricity and light are associated with impressionist and other interests in art. However, interest in this paper is confined to PA, and I will talk as if the disciplinary symbolic were populated by only one field—PA.

The disciplinary symbolic is captured in PA's language. Language is understood as discourse as the latter term is used in Michel Foucault's discourse theory. Language has a narrow sense—a matter of syntax and grammar and the literary rest. Language, as I mean it here, has the broad sense of encompassing a discipline's (or a field's) sense of an acceptable way of looking at the world and an acceptable way of doing things. The sense is broad in that language is not even limited to speaking and writing—just as Foucauldian discourse is not even limited to speech (e.g. Patterson, 2000, on silence as part of discourse.). Traditional PA does have established parameters for its discourse, a set language for looking at things. These parameters have definite benefits; but, when analyses are confined too much within them, they are disabling. (For a discussion of discourse theory and PA, see Box, 2002; Farmer 1999; Kensen, 2000, McSwite, 2000; Patterson, 2000a) A large mistake is to regard as common sense the acceptance of language at its face value, as if language could contain no hidden and distorting pushes and pulls.

## Cloacal Symbolic

The cloacal symbolic layer refers to *societal symbolizations that, first, are relevant to what-is-counted-as-civilized and, second, are not specifically PA symbols—unlike those at the disciplinary symbolic level. It is especially related to the action of the sewer, to what is counted as excrement.* "Cloacae: sewers" explains James Joyce (1997, p. 181), and "cloacal" is the adjective. "Civilization is the spoils: the cloaca maxima," Jacques Lacan is quoted as saying (Laporte, 1993, p. 56). At the cloacal symbolic layer and below (above) both the surface and the disciplinary symbolic, the top-down character of PA is absorbed from the "civilizing" action of society.

> Without a master, one cannot be cleaned.
> (Dominique Laporte, 1993, p. 1)

Recognize civilized humans as bathed, as cleaned, by a master! This claim is made by Dominique Laporte in her essay with a title and a subject that—in the particular configuration of our top-down world—seems to require an explanation or (worse) an apology. In terms of explanation, Slavoj Zizek comments on the book, "Far from being a theoretical joke about the unmentionable 'that,' Laporte's *History of Shit* confronts the most fundamental issues of what it means to be human" (Laporte, 1993, p. 166). In terms of the wish for apology, Laporte (1993, p. 77) herself notes, "The bourgeois never reconciles himself to his 'remnant of earth' and will go to great lengths to conceal it, to sneak it past even the words that name it."

There is a connection, Laporte suggests, between a hierarchy of power and "civilizing" fecal cleanliness; and between the "civilizing" action of a hierarchy of power and what-counts-as-truth—and that includes what-counts-as-PA-truth. But the civilizing bathing is not just a cleaning of physical fecal matter. Also it is a cleaning of what counts-as-true, what-counts-as-true-in-language. Laporte begins with two royal events that occurred in 1539. In that year, on "the day of the Immaculate Virgin impregnated by the Word," (1993, p. 1) King Francois took a step in the cleaning of the French language. His bathing edict was that henceforth all courts would issue edicts in "no other than the maternal French" (p. 2). The Latin excrement would be eliminated. Later that year, he imposed sweeping requirements on citizens concerning the disposal of merde (it's difficult to write the word in plain English for a journal, as opposed to a wall) and other remnants of earth. But Laporte goes further in her claim that one *requires* a master in order to be "cleaned." Of language as the conveyor of what-counts-as-true, Laporte (p. 7) observes that "If language is beautiful, it must be because a master bathes it—a master who cleans shit holes, sweeps offal, and expurgates city and speech to confer upon them order and beauty."

That whole chunks of human aspirations and experiences are lost by this bathing, and chunks are gained, is clear in Laporte's study. That a civilized society loses much, and gains much, from confining thinking to thinking-from-power is highlighted. Speaking-from-power brings the benefits of what-counts-as-civilization; this is what is gained. What is lost is what-is-also-human *but* what-does-not-count-as-civilization. The three requirements of civilization, according to Sigmund Freud, are cleanliness, order and beauty (Freud, 1961, chaps. 3 and 4), and what-counts-as-cleanliness-order-and-beauty is what is gained from a hierarchical, a speaking-from-power, perspective. So Freud can speak of the decline of the olfactory sense and the rise to a paramount status of the visual sense, as humans stand erect and show their genitals (one or the other sense being necessary for sexual excitement and the founding of families); that, for him, *counts* as civilizing. For Freud, although I do not agree, the process is "natural."

Yet the "civilizing" process is what-counts-as-civilizing, and it is hard for a person within a particular version of a civilizing process to give the time of day to what is not counted-from-within-her-particular-version as civilized. The cloacal obsession of the Roman and the English societies was part of how they socially constructed what is civilized. Talking about shit openly (fertilizer is a different matter) is marginalized or excluded, as it does not match the modern—or the Roman—social construction of what is civilized. It does not match what the powerful determine is civilized. This is in contrast to what-counts-as-civilization expressed in O'Donnovan's *Irish Annales* of the soon-to-be-king Aedh. To make a symbolic point, Aedh knowingly drank from priestly sewage. Explains Laporte, the "legitimacy of power has its foundations in the shit of the clergy. The mouth of power swallows the shit of God himself... The shit of the State drowns in its subjects, yet never stops purifying them" (Laporte, 1993, p. 110). During Laporte's description, you and I experience genuine repugnance and disgust at Aedh's version of what-counts-as-civilization; but the repugnance and disgust is also genuinely socially constructed.

What is suppressed by speaking-from-power can often be—in another version of what-counts-as-civilization—sublimely beautiful, orderly and clean. In my view, the struggle for human liberty against various forms of tyranny is a clear example. The best side of the history of Western civilization, I often imagine, is mainly what the powerful considered the merde-side. But we must refuse to romanticize speaking-to-power. Like Hitler's ideas composed when he was speaking-to-power and before he became a speaker-from-power, *Mein Kampf* is smelly reading. So, in my view, are the dissident ideas of speakers-to-power like militiamen and white supremacists. Further, even when not disgusting, ideas from the perspective of speaking-to-power can be as pathetic as ideas derived from the speaking-from-power perspective. Consider Michel Foucault's comments (wishful thinking about what we will later call citizen-ing!) on the Iranian revolution, e.g., announcing that the revolution would demonstrate "an art of not being governed" (see Eritron, 1991, pp. 281–295). If Foucault is counted as speaking-to-power, these comments constituted at best a fumble on the speaking-to-power side. One critic describes Foucault's remarks as more than this—as "a symptom of something troubling in the kind of left-wing thinking that mixes postmodernism, simplistic third worldism and illiberal inclinations" (Cohen, 2002, p. 18).

A reader of a draft of this paper suggested that I should avoid describing the civilizing process as "cleansing," because that word evoked the feeling of ethnic cleansing. That was welcome advice. But it did underscore that there can be unspeakable harshness, crudity and depravity in what-is-counted-as-civilizing. Civilizing sounds entirely soothing when the bathing is described in Freud's words (cleanliness, order and beauty); but I don't know of a civilization without a bitter underside. Consider the civilization (the honor of God) that Thomas More defended against Luther and also—until Thomas' execution—against King Henry. This "Man for All Seasons" (Paul Schofield acted St. Thomas brilliantly in the 1966 movie, based on Robert Bolt's play with the same title) had an urge to eliminate and an unspeakable cloacal pen. This Man for All Seasons writes, "Since (Luther) has already written that he has a prior right to bespatter and besmirch the royal crown with shit, we will not have the posterior right to proclaim the beshitted tongue of this practitioner of posteriorics most fit to lick with his anterior the very posterior of a pissing she-mule until he shall have learned..." (quoted in McGrath, 2002, p. 82). It is a pen that reminds me of the downside of the bathing process.

## TRANSPARENT LEVEL

> Domination is transfigured into
> Administration. (Marcuse, 1991, p. 32)

Righting a wrong in the short run: such speaking-to-power at the transparent level of PA and of the PA context is to be applauded. It should be edifying for the powers-that-be to be told what is wrong and what is right. It is edifying to contemplate sublime historical moments where truth is told to overwhelming power, like the young demonstrator blocking a tank in Tiannamen Square or like Aung San Suu Kyi defying the tyrants who act-from-power in Burma. Nothing that I am writing is intended to belittle the importance of speaking at the transparent level against injustice, against overwhelming power. Yet, as we can illustrate with recent talk about America's new gilded age, the symbols are inevitably part of the issue. I think that exclusive interest in the transparent layer is of marginal value, if the interest does not include a new consciousness that extends to the symbolic layers.

This section focuses on the transparent level, as the sub-title implies. The next two sections discuss in turn the other two layers. Each section discusses, for its respective level, PA's top-down tilt and available corrective action. So here, before turning to righting wrongs, I should speak about the top-down tilt in traditional PA at the transparent level.

## Top-down Bias

Despite the exceptions, there is a steep *net* top-down tilt at the transparent level in the content of mainstream PA's theory and practice. Speaking-from-power is manifested in the particular choice of questions and of prescriptions. Top-down is standard in traditional PA in such respects as (first) the hierarchical role of the very idea of administration, in (second) the emphasis on values like leadership, and in (third) the way that administrative topics are discussed.

First, the very idea of administration has a hierarchical relationship to programs in most mainstream PA thinking. Traditionally, to administer is to direct program activities; administrators are in charge of administering subordinate program specialists, and that is one reason they are usually paid a higher salary. Administrators direct, coordinate and control subordinate program specialists. Second, leadership as a value and as an activity features prominently at the transparent level in PA. If there were no top-down tilt, for instance, the choice of questions in PA would include less about seeking and nurturing leaders—executive managers rather than mere managers. Third, hierarchy is assumed in the way that administrative functions—like budgeting, reporting and staffing—are traditionally discussed. Don't budgeteers rightly assume a process of approval up the chain? The steepness of the hierarchy assumed, as I have mentioned before, is exemplified in the language of the typical job description. Directing, coordinating and controlling *all* the personnel and activities of the assigned unit is a job description worthy of, say, King Francois. But this is only part of the story. The steepness at the transparent layer represented by this PA example, I will note later, is paralleled by steepness in speaking-from-power at the disciplinary symbolic and cloacal symbolic layers.

I'm sure that economic theory is steeply top-down (Farmer, 2003). But I'm not convinced that, on a net basis, PA thinking is less so. Consider dissidents, for one thing. Recalling the smaller size of PA, it is true that the proportional number of dissident PA thinkers in organizations like the Public Administration Theory Network (PAT-Net) is substantial. Yet, Economics has more dissidents and more reform approaches. See the *Biographical Dictionary of Dissenting Economists* (Arestis & Sawyer, 2001), by no means the only such publication (e.g., see Prychitko, 1998). This dictionary lists more than 100 prominent economists outside the mainstream, i.e. outside the neo-classical tradition when that is broadly defined. It includes Radical Economists, Marxists, Post-Keynsians, Behaviorists, Kaleckians and Institutionalists. Many would be readily recognized, e.g., Thomas Balogh, Kenneth Boulding, Meghnad Desai, Maurice Dobb, John Galbraith, Robert

Heilbroner, Alfred Hirschman, Nicholas Kaldor, Michel Kelechi, Rosa Luxemburg, Wesley Mitchell, Gunnar Myrdal, Karl Polanyi, Joan Robinson, Amartya Sen, Piero Sraffa, Lorie Tarshis, and Thorstein Veblen.

Whatever the comparison with other fields, isn't it unfortunate that PA thinking is not blessed with more—and more varied—dissidents? It is especially unfortunate to the extent that dissidence in PA is understood, not as a sign of disciplinary vigor, but as something undesirable and simply impractical.

Not all PA theory and practice at the transparent level reflects a speaking-from-power perspective. Nowadays, matrix organizations are widely used and discussed; toward the "beginning" of American PA, Frederick Taylor wrote about functional management. Frederick Thayer's book *End to Hierarchy and Competition* (1981) is an example from theory. From practice, we all know of relatively egalitarian small groups e.g., in management analysis or computer groups—bands of brothers and sisters. For another thing, neither speaking-from-power nor speaking-to-power exists independently of the other; neither is monolithic. A text from a particular perspective can contain a sub-text that takes a different perspective, for example. But the point is the relative imbalance between the speaking-from-power and speaking-to-power perspectives.

**Corrective Steps: Righting Wrongs in the Short Run**

Speaking-to-power at the transparent level should aim to rectify perceived injustices, and it should aim to resist and to push back any tilt against speaking-to-power. Yet this pursuit of rectification will achieve little if it does not embrace a new PA consciousness that includes attention to the symbolic layers, as suggested earlier. Complete rectification requires a shift toward the new consciousness described in the disciplinary symbolic section. Critical injustice issues that seem utterly transparent have symbolic tails—relevant constraints and opportunities originating from, say, disciplinary or other language. Even for short run results, PA speaking-to-power fixing should go deeper than the transparent level.

To the extent feasible, however, perceived injustices within PA should be rectified at the transparent level. They should be corrected also at the transparent level of the PA context, as the following examples illustrate. Celebrate humans as smart fixers!

Krugman speaks to power, at the transparent level, when he writes of the present period in U.S. history as a new "gilded age" where the New Deal has been undone and where America is not—like he thought it once was—"a middle class society." "As the rich get richer, they can buy a lot besides goods and services. Money buys political influence; it also buys intellectual influence" (Krugman, 2002, p. 76). Politics has shifted in favor of the wealthy, in his view. He quotes Kevin Phillips' study of the increases in the inequality of wealth in the United States. "Either democracy must be renewed, with politics brought back to life, or wealth is likely to cement a new and less democratic regime—plutocracy by some other name" (Phillips, 2001, p. 422). The rhetoric of symbols drips from even this brief summary of the account, e.g. gilded age, middle class society, buy influence, inequality, back to life, regime, plutocracy.

Leveling as much as possible the tilt against speaking-to-power at the transparent level is indeed a reasonable shorter run aim. "Tilt" in this context refers to the degree of difficulty involved in speaking-to-power, where tilt invokes the symbol or idea of a non-level playing field. Those who favor privileging power would take the opposite position, perhaps believing that the tilt should be increased. I suppose that speaking-to-power and speaking-from-power exist side by side, and—with exceptions—a tilt against one may be a positive for the other. I also assume that in times of national stress the tilt will tend to go against speaking-to-power. Tilt changes are varied in terms of goodness/maliciousness of motive and in terms of mildness/violence of method.

At the transparent level, the so-called Lynne Cheney Report seemed to be a mild-mannered attempt to increase the tilt against speaking-to-power. But, the rhetoric of the symbolic was heavily invoked—even in the first two words of the title. The report was entitled *Defending Civilization: How Our Universities Are Failing America And What Can Be Done About It* (Martin & Neal, 2001), the first product of a Washington-based non-profit group's Defense of Civilization Fund. The report is named the "Lynne Cheney report" because, for one thing, it carries a quote on its cover from the current U.S. Vice-President's wife.

You might object that the methodology of the Lynne Cheney report is regrettable. The report strings together 115 "regrettable" quotes from an unscientific sample of people who made comments within earshot of a university. The quotes are from some professors, and also from a freelance writer, an unattributed person, a journalist, a speaker, a student, an Ivy League student, a chant, a sign, an unidentified person, a freshman, and more of the hodge-podge. Some of the quotes show a relevant attitude, e.g., "we will tumble from chauvinism into the abyss of recession and tribalism" Martin & Neal, 2001, p. 5). It's not clear what other quotes really show, e.g., "hate brings hate" [Sounds like something my grandmother might have said!]. More importantly, you might object to the report's interpretative weakness. Didn't all Americans—in and out of universities—feel sorrow at the sad events of

September 11th? But the report speaks of differences between the public and the universities in relation to "anger, patriotism, and support of military intervention" (p. 4). "Not so in academe. Even as many institutions enhanced security and many students exhibited American flags, professors across the country sponsored teach-ins that typically ranged from moral equivocation to explicit condemnation of America... Some even pointed accusatory fingers, not at the terrorists, but at America itself" (p. 1). The symbolism of "defending civilization" was discussed in the previous section—the bathing that Laporte describes.

## DISCIPLINARY SYMBOLIC LEVEL.

> After all, the cultivated person's first duty is to be always prepared to re-write the encyclopedia. (Umberto Eco, *Serendipities*, 1998, p. 21)

The top-down character of PA at the disciplinary symbolic layer can be illustrated by the poverty of PA's symbolism for "hierarchy" and for "PA itself"—examples of poverties at the disciplinary symbolic level that are significant for PA's corresponding poverties at the transparent level. Corrective actions at the disciplinary symbolic level should include upgrading traditional PA discourse as a more enabling vehicle for thinking and action. Re-symbolizations are needed, for one thing.

**Top-down Bias**

The disciplinary symbolic layer shapes, just as it reflects, what is included and what is excluded at the transparent and cloacal levels. It also reflects and shapes what is privileged and what is marginalized at those other levels. At the transparent level, PA is constrained by its symbolism for "hierarchy" in its understanding of hierarchy-within-organizations and hierarchy-within-society. At the transparent level, PA's symbolism for "PA itself" limits understanding of the larger societal picture. Let's look at these two examples.

*Hierarchy.* Poverty in the language of hierarchy at PA's disciplinary symbolic level narrows the capability at the transparent level for organizational analyses and interpretations except in speaking-from-power terms. There is a connection suggested between the language of hierarchy and the analysis of the larger meaning of, say, PA job specifications about "directing, coordinating and controlling." PA's language does not contain a rich set of symbols and concepts for "hierarchy." The claim may be made that there is basically the one word. The effect can be illustrated by contrasting English and Eskimo languages. Eskimos have many words for what we call "white;" and the same comparison can be drawn with Pacific Islanders and their many words for what we call "blue." We are funneled in a particular way in our talk about color. Returning to the PA example, it is not completely true in PA that a hierarchy is a hierarchy is a hierarchy, e.g. thinkers sometimes talk about participative management. But it can be recognized that there is a top-down connection between the example of the manager's job description given for the transparent level and the symbolic poverty of PA's wordage for "hierarchy." PA discussion at the transparent level is limited by PA's language of hierarchy, the discipline's way of thinking or symbolizing. That is why many theorists coin new words or symbols; but the new words always face an uphill struggle against the pressure of the "logic" of the symbolic systems already implicated in PA's language.

The constriction on PA's transparent thinking about hierarchy can be illustrated by the parallel example of the symbol "capitalism." The limitations of disciplinary symbolic or linguistic features are not confined to PA, it will be recognized. In Economics, the poverty of wordage for "capitalism" makes it hard for people to think about economic systems except in speaking-from-power terms. It makes it harder to think of alterations in the system of "free market capitalism"—a system-as-is that suits the interests of the power elite(s). Neologisms like "go-go-capitalism" and "hyper-capitalism" have fallen on barren ground. If capitalism is capitalism is capitalism and if the only alternative to capitalism is something like socialism, capitalism is privileged in many people's minds. That there are many varieties of capitalism is a truth that tends to be hidden. (A capitalist system that privileges private road transportation over public rail and other transportation is a different system from where the reverse situation prevails, for one instance. The difference between these two systems is not at all trivial, e.g., compare the effect of each on city life; but the choice is not between free enterprise and unfree enterprise.) The fact that there is more than one form of capitalism even within the United States—and there could be many others, without being socialism or communism—tends to be suppressed. The features of the language speak to us with power; they tend to shape and limit transparent economic—as well as PA—thinking.

***PA Itself.*** Poverty of symbolism for *PA itself* constrains PA's concern for the larger picture at the transparent level. Mainstream PA theory is symbolized variously by actions—written within PA's own language, understood in the wide sense—such as by its self-descriptions, by the kind of publications that appear in mainstream PA journals, by its history, by the kind of thinkers attracted to the subject, by the nature of PA practice, by the kind of training PA programs provide, etc. PA practice is symbolized by the kind of activities it undertakes and by the kind of people employed to do it, and so on. The character of PA's symbolism does set limits on the kind of talk that is branded as legitimate or illegitimate at the transparent level. It does set limits on PA's proclivity to speak to power.

Dear reader, please play with the symbol of PA's self-definition, and play with thoughts of how that linguistic symbol relates to thinking and acting at the transparent level. Mainstream PA has long had troubles in delineating itself, I must agree. For instance, discussions still occur on topics like the so-called politics-administration dichotomy or the so-called theory-practice divide. However, would your ideas on mainstream PA's self-definition wander far from a definition that was popular (not now) during PA's infancy and therefore during its formative stage—speaking of "getting things done through people?" Would your ideas on mainstream PA's self-definition stray far from a description that speaks about executing the will of "legitimate" political and other authorities? I think not.

Play with the idea that the PA definition you prefer sets symbolic limits on what is legitimate PA talk. First, for the "getting things done through people" version, your play may recognize that PA talk that is not primarily about "things" is symbolically illegitimate. Symbolically illegitimate is discussion that deals with larger societal issues that do not immediately and directly relate to getting things done. Symbolically illegitimate is talk about the symbolic.

Second, for the "executing the will of legitimate political and other authorities" version, your play may conclude that mainstream PA is a subject that expresses itself as dedicated to achieving whatever legitimate powers-that-be want done. In a sense, PA's raison d'etre is to facilitate speaking-from-power and acting-from power. It is for PA to be a tool for legitimate societal power. As your play proceeds, you may think that this would go some way toward explaining mainstream PA's reluctance at the transparent level to look at the larger picture, e.g., to prefer thoughts that do not involve fundamental changes in the existing structure of society.

Such play might lead you to suppose that this constricted symbolism at the disciplinary symbolic level makes understandable constrictions at the transparent level—where mainstream PA study is limited mainly to organizational production. PA theory is more like organizational theory in this respect, and—as I have mentioned before—Gibson Burrell (1997) speaks of organization theory's emphasis on the organization of production. *Organization of production*, meat and potatoes for traditional organization theory as well as for traditional PA, is contrasted (Burrell, 1997) with the *production of organization.* This symbolism reinforces society's cloacal desire (which I discuss next) for a discipline, even one it can disdain, that limits itself to "things" in the machinery of government to help achieve greater organizational production.

> *Ire Interrupts.* Anger interrupts the play, as I think about the *production of organization* and the recent systemic accounting scandals at Enron and elsewhere. I recall the extent to which PA's university programs limit themselves to preparing new entrants (and existing mid-level practitioners) for the bureaucratic machine, while shortchanging evaluation of the larger picture. How much self-serving effort did traditional professors of accounting spend on preparing new entrants for the accounting profession, without *confronting the powerful by alerting the public to the larger picture* about problems in accounting practices in contemporary business management? Professors of PA should aim to do better than professors of accounting.

## Corrective Steps: Disciplinary Symbolic Level

An aim of short-run PA speaking-to-power should be to upgrade traditional PA discourse as a more enabling vehicle for thinking and action, and this should include aiming for a consciousness that recognizes the ambiguities, contradictions and aporia of the human and PA context. Indeed, the past century experienced a linguistic turn in philosophy. Many philosophers as different as critical theorists, analytical philosophers and others came to recognize that language matters. They came to view the character of language as critical in shaping and limiting the possibility for thinking and acting. Yet traditional PA theory has not fully recognized the significance of Philosophy's linguistic turn.

PA speaking-to-power should use the toggle keystroke. Richard Lanham explains this "toggle" analogy when discussing one aim that postmodernists and others are trying to achieve with language. Toggle "in computerese (is) the keystroke that allows one to move from, say, looking at a stripped down version of a text on a screen to looking at a fully formatted version with all the ornaments in place" (Lanham, 1993, p. 120). Deidre McClosky goes on to quote Stanley Fish on modernist language-in-the-wide-sense. "Yes, (Stanley) Fish believes that modernism, whether rationalist or irrationalist, has some deliberative screws loose. We (those rejecting what she would consider the modernist pretensions about its language or discourse) propose to tighten them up. The conservatives want to carry screwily on" (McClosky, 2001, p. 123.) Conservative PA speaking-from-power falsely assumes that an uncritical approach to language is common sense. Speaking-to-power should aim to show that, on the contrary, the toggle keystroke is common sense.

PA speaking-to-power at the disciplinary symbolic level can lay bare assumptions, constraints and opportunities in the reigning PA discourse. For example, couldn't additional insights be gained by studying the symbolism of sovereignty and its relevance for the character of public management, budgeting, human resources and the other administrative functions? It's princely stuff! For PA, I have often suggested various approaches at the transparent level, e.g. emphasizing play, love, un-engineering, and so on. I had an understanding that symbolic features were involved. However, it was in preparing for the 2002 PAT-Net plenary in Cleveland that I came to a fuller and deeper recognition of the primacy of the symbolic in all these cases—and that in turn gave me a better understanding of what "postmodern" writers like Derrida and critical theorists like Marcuse have in mind. I don't want to repeat what I have written before on PA and symbolic and rhetorical analysis (in Farmer, 2003: Farmer & Patterson, 2003). Symbolic impediments to love as a motive within the bureaucracy, as compared against efficiency, are discussed in Farmer (2003). I could have sympathized with the idea that genuine play or un-engineering can thrive only at the fringes of mainstream PA's discourse, because traditional PA is so dominated (terrorized, smothered) by the logic of other symbolic systems like those relating to work and to the symbolic systems of sovereignty.

Meanwhile other conservative disciplines, like Economics, at their margins show signs of learning by self-examination of their rhetoric. PA theory can learn from such examples of speaking to the power of one's mainstream disciplinary discourse. Consider Rothschild (2001) speaking to the power of the Economics discipline. She provides additional insight into the invisible hand, a symbol that fascinates me (e.g., see Farmer, 2003). The invisible hand explanation that is now conventional is that, when each person pursues her own private interests, it is as if a beneficent "invisible hand" so arranged it that society is better off than if each person aimed for the public interest.

Surprise! Rothschild points out, rightly or wrongly, that Adam Smith might not have had in mind as beneficent an invisible hand as we suppose. The textual arguments do show that Smith did not attach as much weight to the invisible hand metaphor as do twentieth century and later commentators. But the interesting point she makes is that an eighteenth century thinker would tend to "see" an invisible hand in more ominous symbolic terms than we do—as the hand behind the back that carries a dagger. Smith was a close student and admirer of Shakespeare and Voltaire, and as a Scot he naturally enough had a close interest in *Macbeth*. Just before the murder of Banquo, Macbeth (Shakespeare, *Macbeth*, Act 3, Scene 2, 46–50) speaks of a bloody and invisible hand.

> Come, seeling night,
> Scarf up the tender eye of pitiful day,
> And with thy bloody and invisible hand
> Cancel and tear to pieces that great bond
> Which keeps me paled!

Smith was also an admirer of Voltaire's *Oedipe*. This is the play in which Oedipus is twice threatened by invisible hands. "Tremble, unfortunate King, an invisible hand suspends above your head." A significance of all this is that it should encourage the reader to think through the falsely comforting traps in the symbolic character of "the free market." That this is important is suggested by the state of international trade, where it has been said that one-third of the trade is not free but between branches of the same multi-national corporations (e.g., see Martin & Schumann, 1998, p. 112).

Resistance to PA's speaking to power would be lessened if PA could incorporate more of a symbolic repertoire from the humanities. But, is that too difficult? In other words, PA could expand its way of thinking if it sought symbols that at first sight do not fit, e.g., from philosophy, literature. Consider this prospectus for a conference:

> Conceiving management education solely as training in the management of an economy is to ignore the enormous power of administrators in determining the individual and social quality of life in the community—small or large—entrusted to them, in making their organizations pleasant or oppressive places in which to work, in fostering possible human happiness or at least reducing avoidable human suffering. If we believe that administrators are actually 'statespersons,' they should feel responsible not only for profit and turnover but also for the beauty of that part of the world which they have the fortune to govern. However, an administrator cannot be a 'statesperson' unless s/he has a profound humanistic culture, a thorough knowledge of history, of philosophy, of art, of the heritage of knowledge and sensibility that humankind has constructed in its history…, and which can be an inexhaustible source of inspiration and creativity. (Lombardi, 2002, p. 1)

This is part of the prospectus for a September 2003 conference on the *Role of Humanities in the Formation of New European Elites*. The conference, to be held in Venice, is promoted by Fondazione Giorgio Cini in cooperation with others. It is true that PA theorists, like organization theorists, have borrowed from the humanities. Yet, traditional PA's disciplinary symbolic system has been so impelled toward the technical by modernist rationalizing prejudices. The latter systems from the cloacal have been introjected within the guts of PA's disciplinary symbolic. Are the humanities effectively out of reach for traditional PA?

The approach of corrective action at the disciplinary symbolic layer—as at the transparent layer—should be directed toward a new consciousness, even in the shorter run. It should not be limited, as it were, to the disciplinary symbolic. Human needs can be best served by a wider, rather than a narrower, approach in PA speaking-to-power. Analysis of the disciplinary symbolic should not try to exclude the cloacal symbolic, for instance. Analysis of the symbolic should not exclude study of things, as another example. Focusing on the rational should not exclude recognition of the ambiguities, contradictions and aporia of the human and PA context. Michael Ignatieff is among those who describe the complexity of the human condition along these lines. For example, he points to "the possibility that there are human needs which escape the domain and competence of political action altogether. There may be a tragic gulf between what human beings need and what their collective wisdom is able to provide" (Ignatieff, 1984, p. 19). Love is a human need, for instance, and yet we cannot claim love as a human right. Metaphysical understanding is also a need for many people (witness the grip of religion on so many people), and yet attempts to provide this through the state have proved disastrous.

I prefer a new PA consciousness that—even in the short run—is prepared to seek beyond mere cleanliness, order and beauty (the marks, for Freud, of civilization); it is prepared to embrace also the despised and the repugnant (elements that Laporte symbolizes). I prefer a PA consciousness that wants to see, hear, feel, smell, and touch the world in its disorderly, orderly, ugly, beautiful inconsistencies and consistencies (Farmer, 2000). I think that this kind of PA consciousness should be as encompassing as what has been often described as anti-administration (see Box, 2001; Cunningham & Schneider, 2001; Farmer, 2001; Hutchinson, 2001; Jacobs, 2001; McSwite, 2002; Patterson, 2001; Spicer, 2001). I don't want a consciousness that is deceived by speaking-from-power (or even speaking-to-power) perspectives, however. When encountering the symbols and the rhetoric of the traditional language of PA (no less than the traditional language of other subjects like Economics), we should be conscious of the unconscious intent to secure and to preserve advantages for the relatively powerful.

## CLOACAL SYMBOLIC LEVEL

> Language speaks and asks:
> "why am I beautiful?
> Because my master bathes me."
> (Paul Eluard, *Capitale de la Douleur*)

PA theory and practice exist within a socially constructed framework of what is civilized. The cloacal framework, on a net basis, has a top-down impact on PA in the functioning of PA's dominant signifiers and in its insistence that PA do many of society's dirty-acting-from power jobs. Again, I suggest that re-symbolization is the corrective prescription.

**Top-down Bias**

What-counts-as-civilized serves to enforce a top-down perspective. Remember that what is suppressed by speaking-from-power can often be—in another version of what-counts as civilization—sublimely beautiful, orderly and clean. Recall the master bather that Laporte describes and that Paul Eluard recognizes in his 1926 lines, quoted at the head of this section. The cloacal symbolic process, it is claimed, itself speaks-from-power.

The impact on PA is also top-down. The cloacal sense of cleanliness, order and beauty is reflected in PA even in small things—the ways that organization charts are drawn, for instance. Or so it seems to me, as I continue to reflect on the symbolism of charting (see Farmer, 2003). In my consulting days with Public Administration Service and the Jacobs Company, I also tried to draw charts that were nicely balanced (anathema on crunching too many of the little boxes in one corner, or having big boxes unbalanced by little ones!). I was aiming for clean lines and—perish the thought—beauty. My charts would not recognize the crud that happens in real organizations—irregular relationships, odd power distributions. My charts would never contemplate the kind of *PA facts* that McSwite (1998) describes as part of the life of any organization—what is dirty, inappropriate and plainly uncivilized.

PA is within the cloacal constraints of—to speak of big things—what counts-as-reason, what-counts-as-true, what-counts-as-appropriate. These socially constructed constraints serve as dominant signifiers for PA. Traditional PA is shaped by a modernist emphasis on what-counts-as-reason, for example. Features omitted from what-counts-as-reason include the unreasoning of which Michel Foucault spoke. What-counts-as-reason, what-counts-as-true and what-counts-as-appropriate have emerged from a bathing by the powers-that-be. In the sense of Eluard's lines (quoted above), they have emerged "beautiful." The cloacal constraints on traditional PA are, I think, all the tighter to the extent that mainstream PA thinks that it should be "independent" of societal theory.

The cloacal function includes PA carrying out what is counted as civilized, what is socially-constructed as "civilization." But it does not stop at that point. The cloacal function also extends to PA executing what is not counted-as-civilized but what is desired by the power elite(s). In a significant sense, PA institutions do many of society's dirty acting-from-power jobs. Burrell (1997) suggests that Taylorism was about controlling the peasants, for instance. To the extent that it provides extraordinarily harsh treatment for prisoners, as another example, the corrections system is doing what the power elites in society want (largely unconsciously?) but what society does not wish to acknowledge as its own. Should we suppose that the widespread raping-by-other-prisoners of prisoners under the protection of the state happens, as it were, by unavoidable accident (Farmer, 2002)? Then, there are numerous examples of the power elite pushing down into the public bureaucracy functions that the powerful do not wish to trust to the chance of openly democratic decision-making. At the same time the elite represses consciousness of the pushing down, to the extent that the lack of trust does not square with its own image of the nature of its civilization. The role of the U.S. Federal Reserve in affecting interest and unemployment levels is one example (see Farmer, 2001). Other examples include foreign affairs and intelligence. It's a matter of bathing and what-counts-as-civilization.

**Corrective Steps in the Longer Run: Re-symbolization**

PA speaking-to-power should contribute in the longer run toward a re-symbolization of the societal civilizing process. In other words, it should contribute to a re-symbolizing of the bathing (or cleaning) process at the cloacal level that, following Laporte, was described earlier. *Re-symbolization, in my view, should aim as a regulative ideal toward a context where speaking-from-power is defanged*. Celebrate humans as symbol makers—toward (in Foucauldian terms) the art of not being governed, toward (as described below) citizen-ing!

PA theorizing in this way should seek to *re-bathe the PA context*. New symbols and symbolic stories should be created, and I recommend—and describe here—the symbols of visioning, class 1 visioning, class 2 visioning, and citizen-ing. The story or ethical imperative proposed is that class 1 visioning should be privileged over class 2 visioning, facilitating citizen-ing. An aim of this speaking-to-power move would be to provide a set of symbols and symbolic systems that can assist citizens in living, as it were, on their own power.

These are unfamiliar symbols; they need explanation. First, I explain three of these symbols—what is meant by visioning, class 1 visioning, and class 2 visioning. Second, I describe the aim of privileging class 1 visioning. Third, I sketch a symbol of the new consciousness, citizen-ing.

***Some Symbols:*** *What is visioning?* Political, economic, cultural and other societal visions come in many forms, conscious or unconscious, helpful and harmful. Visions are often beautiful; yet they can also be ugly. They rarely exist without flaws—and without being engaged in combat with counter-visions. Some visions appeal only through the seeing, and Freud was mentioned earlier as giving one reason why we tend to privilege sight over the other senses. As our emergent times and its technologies develop, we can expect that greater conscious use will be made of senses not now emphasized as much as they might. Clearly, the masters of the art of the subliminal are the image weavers of the commercial world. Then there are visions transmitted from one unconscious to another, perhaps even through the way that buildings are built or that certain behaviors and attitudes are encouraged over others.

Narrowly understood, visioning is incidental to human living. Widely understood, it plays a dominant role in human living. There is the visioning proffered for living, where the subsequent living is a living of that vision. I will call the wide sense *living-visioning*. There are many examples, like the life of Fannie Lou Hamer.

*What are classes 1 and 2 visioning?* Let's focus on two classes of visioning in the wide sense of vision just indicated—a wide sense where a person envisions her own life, and where her life is a living of that vision. Class 1 is the visioning proffered by living persons for their own way of living, including visioning for societal action in the political, economic, cultural and other areas considered significant for their living: call it class 1 visioning. Class 2 visioning is that offered by systems and on behalf of systems. Examples of such systems include our political systems, our economic systems, our legal systems, our health care systems, our welfare systems, our commercial systems, our military systems, our diplomatic systems, our international systems, our systems of alliances, and our systems of education. The vast and powerful economic interests are examples of class 2 visioning or systems—the complex of agencies that constitute the muscle and spin of the various segments of the economy.

The general distinction is between a) class 1 visions that emanate from living persons for their living and b) class 2 visions that emanate from, or on behalf of, entities other than living persons. Like any other distinction (to repeat what was said earlier), these categories are deconstructible; but they are also useful. I cannot call class 2 visions non-living, because often they have virtual lives of their own. Despite the disadvantages, I am choosing to call them non-human. The solid and immense buildings of Washington and New York are a celebration and a visioning of such non-human systems.

***Re-symbolization Aim:*** The core aim of seeking to privilege class 1 visioning would be to assist all citizens to live without being dominated by speaking-from-power. It is directed toward anti-control-by-others, a longer run aim. Recall what Foucault wanted when he blundered (badly, very badly—as noted earlier) in his misjudgment of the significance of the Iranian Revolution. He spoke of "the art of not being governed."

Recall the massive buildings in Washington and New York mentioned in the opening paragraph of this essay. This privileging of class 1 visioning does not invite the populace to look up, as would a civic religion that might invite the populace to look up to mottos inscribed high on government buildings. The privileging celebrates the visioning of the individual human in-herself in-her-differences. The symbolic privileging of class 1 visioning and citizen-ing is suggested as a regulative ideal, a concept I have described before (Farmer, 2003). It is a condition to which individuals and groups can tend – on a basis that celebrates success, tolerates failure, and keeps on trying. It is an ideal in the sense that most ideals of citizenship (e.g. democratic) and most ideals of religious life (e.g., Christian) are not lived consistently; adherents partly succeed, fail, succeed, fail, and try again. The regulative ideal is regulative in the sense that adherents pattern thoughts and efforts toward achieving the ideal.

"Ad(vertising) frenzy coming as BellSouth goes long distance," headlines the *Palm Beach Post* (December 20, 2002, p. 1). Speaking-to-power, I think, can aim toward a democracy where class 1 visioning infuses the lives of ever more citizens. It would be a kind of democracy where more people live less administered lives. Administered lives, as I intend the term, are lives where class 1 visioning is not privileged appropriately over class 2 visioning. Manifestations, or symptoms, of the administered life crop up regularly as part of the daily grind—and they stand opposed to sublime moments like when we love a sunset, love skiing, love our children, love our friends, love playing with an idea. A modern form of the administered life is a pernicious side-effect of the real benefits of the "progress" that cloacal bathing has made.

Go-go-consumerism, with the sting of the administered life! Floridians with telephones know what to expect after reading the headline quoted at the beginning of the previous paragraph. Then again, buy a techno-device to prevent salespeople, employed at minimum wages, from telephoning to sell not only alternative long distance services but also a great deal on aluminum siding or swamp land. Dial 1 if you want to purchase a service; dial 2 if you want repairs; dial 3 if you want to know your balance; dial 4 if you want to hear a promotional talk; and dial 5 if you want to hear this menu repeated. Yet the administered life is not mainly centered on the telephone. Read the booklet that comes with the computer wire or lawn mower that you have just purchased; read the small print on the back of your car insurance renewal or mortgage agreement. Write out your monthly bills; deal with your health insurance company about the bills incurred during a recent medical procedure. Bring in your car for its periodic safety check; bring in your cat for its periodic health check up; bring in yourself for your periodic check up and a check.

These examples fall far short of emphasizing the severity of the way in which the administered life permeates our living. For the administered life in economics, visit K-Mart or listen to a business news show. For the administered life in politics, visit politics-by-polling in the work of James Carville and Karl Rove. For the administered life in culture, visit the marketing departments of Hollywood. For the administered life in military defense, witness the side-effects of our enormous technological success in biological, chemical and nuclear weaponry. Opposition to the administered life is opposition to the kind of administriavilized living that Herbert Marcuse pilloried (1991) in his critique of one-dimensional man. A citizen administrivializing is pursuing a trivial existence; by contrast, a citizen citizen-ing can self-actualize.

No one is saying that optimal class 2 arrangements are not desirable and important; systems like airport traffic control, ambulance service, law, health, and international affairs are clearly significant. The direction of the argument, rather, is about the relative importance of the two classes of visioning and of visioning-living. The claim is that the more important is the visioning proffered by living persons for their own way of living, including visioning for societal action in the political, economic, cultural and other areas considered to have significance for their living. Visioning offered by systems, and on behalf of systems, should trump the citizen citizen-ing as little as is prudent.

*Citizen-ing:* PA speaking-to-power should assist in realizing more fully the kind of democracy where citizen-ing predominates. Citizen-ing refers to living where, as I have indicated, as many lives as possible are lived without accepting as primary the manipulation and domination of systems and on behalf of systems—where class 1 visioning is privileged over class 2 visioning. But a real revolution is required because citizen-ing also aspires to a new and open form of consciousness.

Real revolutions, the real results that should be sought in longer term PA speaking-to-power, are profoundly difficult. By comparison, replacing a hierarchical set of scoundrels with a hierarchical set of saints is kids' stuff—hard as such coups d'etat must be. This should be said in reply to those who ask whether a change to citizens citizen-ing can be achieved against the weight of educational and other class 2 systems concerned with normalizing and de-imaginizing children and people. "Educational" is used here to include not only schools (and families) but also the complex of cultural and other systems that have an educational effect—including public bureaucracies. My own inclination is that we should prepare children (prepare!—excuse the bureaucratizing cliché) for eventual citizen-ing. This preparation should be, not in having them salute symbolic power-down-objects, but by exposing them to imagination-encouraging possibilities and tendencies. PA theorizing should embrace the speaking-to-power role in achieving such long-term and difficult educational and other societal changes. This can be done best by contributing to the re-symbolization of the cloacal cleansing process of our civilization.

Earlier, I suggested that the symbols of "a citizen citizens" and " a citizen engages in citizen-ing" point to the gnostic character of a life when a person develops her own vision and when she lives her own visioning. By "gnostic," I meant the self-initiated thinking/feeling/imagining of citizen-ing. The term "gnostic" usually refers to the self-reliant, self-directed way that some developed their own religious views (e.g., see Pagels, 1981). An alternative, as I (mis)read Pagels, is to be like clerks who accept their views from fellow clerks. Here I intend to apply the term "gnostic" to the non-religious context.

The symbols "a citizen citizens" and "citizen-ing" can also be compared, in the light of feminist thinking, with the idea of a woman woman-ing. Turn to Simon de Beauvoir and Helene Cixous. In her *Second Sex*, Simone de Beauvoir (1993, p. 16) writes that a woman "appears essentially to the male as a sexual being... She is defined and differentiated with reference to man and not with reference to her; she is the incidental, the inessential as opposed to the essential. He is the Subject, he is the Absolute—she is the Other." Later (1993, p. 29), she asks, "How can a human being in a woman's situation attain fulfillment?... How can independence be recovered in a state of dependency?" Even later, she writes that, "One is not born, but rather becomes, a woman...it is civilization as a whole that produces this creature, intermediate between male and eunuch, which is described as feminine" (de Beauvoir, 1993, p. 295). The citizen, in the context of citizen-ing, is parallel to all this. The citizen (the "woman" in the analogy) seeks identity without reference to the state (the "man" in the analogy). The identity of the "citizen citizening" in the United States (England, France, China) should be derived in independence from her American (English, French, Chinese) governmental system.

The symbolic action of a "citizen citizen-ing" can also be understood in other terms. One I have often discussed is feminine writing (see Cixous,

1980). Writing in that context is understood broadly to include expressing ideas/feelings/imaginings—in writing, speaking, painting, acting and, above all, in living. Describing feminine writing as a practice open to both males and females, recall Helene Cixous' exhortation. She urges (1980, p. 246), "Write! Writing is for you, you are for you; your body is yours, take it." While it has no special method, feminine writing seeks the impetus for new understandings from my (your) own lived experiences and reflections/feelings/imaginings resulting from listening to my (your) own enculturated body. The writing inscribes me, as I experience myself within myself. As Cixous writes (1980, p. 358), "A feminine text cannot fail to be more than subversive. It is volcanic...."

The symbol of "citizen-ing" denotes not merely refusal of the speaking-from-power of class 2 visioning. Rather, it is the seeking of consciousness that goes beyond mere refusal. Like Marcuse's great "refusal," citzen-ing is really intended as a great "affirmation" of a more fully actualized mode of human consciousness and living. Straight-forward refusals involved in speaking-to-power face a difficulty that Marcuse explained. "In the face of its efficient denial by the established system, the negation appears in the politically important form of the 'absolute refusal'—a refusal which seems the more unreasonable the more the established system develops its productivity and alleviates the burdens of life" (Marcuse, 1991, p. 255).

Citizen-ing promises, in practice, visions and envisioned living of varying quality. Many people will be too influenced by class 2 visions. Many will have visions that are too partial or too limited, especially those limited to the aspirations of consumerist enculturation. Many will be from individuals suffering from psychological, physical or other contextual difficulties. Some people are mentally ill, and others are anti-social, for instance; we cannot assume that all people are always "normal." People differ in emotional and intelligence quotients, and also they differ in imaginative-spiritual capacities.

At its fullest flowering, citizen-ing" does involve a radically open form of consciousness. It is a consciousness that encompasses unknown depths, areas not filled in. Its openness is a seeking for yet "other" forms. I would be surprised if this form of consciousness could be widely achieved except within a context of love, a context some might suppose to be natural for non-oppressed humans. This new form can be encouraged by such means as re-symbolizing persons as bio-psycho-social-spiritual beings. At a minimum, citizen-ing emanates, as we have indicated, from within the citizen herself, a visioning that the citizen lives.

When reflecting on citizen-ing, I think of people like Fannie Lou Hamer, Rosalind Franklin, William Blake and Jose Bove. PA theory can be encouraged by such symbols or examples in its re-symbolizing or re-bathing activity. Such people seem to me to symbolize, to varying extents, citizens citizen-ing. There is an important sense in which they lived their visions, and in which their visions lived them. Franklin was the independent-minded scientist who perhaps—if less independent-minded—would have had more chance to share the Nobel Prize for the discovery of DNA (Maddox, 2002). Blake was an extraordinary poet, and Bove is the President of the French Confederation of Peasants. Other examples include, e.g., Jane Goodall (www.janegoodall.org/jane) and Helen Keller (www.rnib.org.uk/wesupply/fctsheet/keller.htm).

Fanny Lou Hamer (1917-1977) had grown up in Mississippi among conditions of poverty, violence and oppression. She certainly spoke to power, and she lived her visioning. In 1962, when she attempted to register to vote, one of the many obstacles and indignities that she encountered was the opposition from her plantation owner. To him, she said, "I didn't try to register for you. I tried to register for myself." That night sixteen bullets were fired in a house as a warning for her. A year later, returning from a voter registration workshop, she was imprisoned and beaten in her cell. Famously, she testified in 1964 in Atlanta before the Democratic National Party Credentials Committee. "All of this on account we want to register, to become first-class citizens, and if the Freedom Democratic Party is not seated now, I question America..." (Mills, 1993, pp. 120–121). U.S. Representative Eleanor Holmes Norton remembers no equal among the civil rights orators to Fannie Lou Hamer, except Martin Luther King. She is reported as saying (Mills, 1993, p. 85) that "you've never heard a room flying (like one) that Fannie Lou Hamer set afire. Her speeches had themes. They had principles... What really gets you is that person somehow concretizes an idea that you have never quite been able to form... and then in the end breaking out and singing *"This Little Light of Mine: I'm Gonna Let It Shine."*

## REFERENCES

Arestis, P., & Sawyer, M. (2001). *A biographical dictionary of dissenting economists*, Williston, VT: Edward Elgar Publishing Inc.

Beauvoir, S. de (1993). *The second sex*. (H.M. Parshley, Trans.). New York: Alfred Knopf.

Box, R. (2002). Pragmatic discourse and administrative legitimacy. *American Review of Public Administration, 32*, 20–39.

Box, R. (2001). Private lives and anti-administration. *Administrative Theory & Praxis, 23*, 541–558.

Burrell, G. (1997). *Pandemonium: Toward a retro-organization theory*. Thousand Oaks, CA: SAGE Publications.

Cixous, H. (1980). The laugh of the Medusa. In E. Marks & I. De Coutivron (Eds.), *New French feminisms: An anthology* (pp. 245–264). Amherst: University of Massachusetts Press.

Cohen, M. (2002, Summer). An empire of cant: Hardt, Negri, and postmodern political theory. *Dissent*, 17–28.

Cunningham, R., & Schneider, R. A. (2002). Anti-administration: Redeeming bureaucracy by witnessing and gifting. *Administrative Theory & Praxis, 23*, 573–588.

Eco, U. (1998). *Serendipities: Language and lunacy*. New York: Harcourt, Brace and Company.

Eribon, D. (1991). *Michel Foucault*. Cambridge, MA: Harvard University Press.

Farmer, D. J. (1990). *Being in time: The nature of time in light of McTaggart's paradox*. Lanham, MD: University Press of America.

Farmer, D. J. (1999) The discourse movement: A centrist view of the sea change. *International Review of Public Administration, 4*, 3–10.

Farmer, D. J. (2000). Public administration discourse: A matter of style? *Administration & Society, 31*, 299–320.

Farmer, D. J. (2001). Mapping anti-administration: Introduction to the symposium. *Administrative Theory & Praxis, 23*, 475–492.

Farmer, D. J. (2001a). Introduction. In D. J. Farmer, C. Stivers, R. Hummel, C. King, & S. Kensen, Constructing civil space. *Administration & Society, 34*, 87–129.

Farmer, D. J. (2002). The devil's rope. *Administrative Theory & Praxis, 24*, 781–786.

Farmer, D. J. (2003). The allure of rhetoric and the truancy of poetry. *Administrative Theory & Praxis, 25*, 9–36.

Farmer, D. J., & Patterson, P. (2003). The reflective practitioner and the uses of rhetoric. *Public Administration Review, 63*, 105–111.

Freud, S. (1961). *Civilization and its discontents*. (J. Strachey, Trans.) New York: Norton.

Hutchinson, J. R. (2001). Multigendering PA: Anti-administration, anti-blues. *Administrative Theory & Praxis, 23*, 589–604.

Ignatieff, M. (1984). *The needs of strangers*. New York: Henry Holt and Company.

Jacobs, D. A. (2001). Alterity and the environment: Making the case for anti-administration. *Administrative Theory & Praxis, 23*, 605–620.

Joyce, J. (1997). *Ulysses*. London: Macmillan.

Kensen, S. (2000). The dialogue as basis for democratic governance. *Administrative Theory & Praxis, 22*, 117–131.

Krugman, P. (2002, October 20). For richer: How the permissive capitalism of the boom destroyed American equality. *The New York Times Magazine*, 62–142.

Laporte, D. (1993). *History of shit.* (N. Benabid & R. el-Khoury, Trans.). Cambridge, MA: MIT Press.

Lanham, R. (1993). *The electronic word: Democracy, technology, and the arts.* Chicago: Unversity of Chicago Press.

Lombardi, A. (2002). *The role of humanities in the formation of new European elites.* Venice, Italy: Fondazione Giorgio Cini.

Maddox, B. (2002). *Rosalind Franklin: The dark lady of DNA.* New York: HarperCollins.

Marcuse, H. (1991). *One-dimensional man: Studies in the ideology of advanced industrial society.* Boston, MA: Beacon Press.

Martin, H-P, & Schumann, H. (1998). *The global trap: Globalization and the assault on democracy and prosperity.* New York: Zed Books.

McClosky, D. (2001). The genealogy of postmodernism: An economist's guide. In S. Culenberg, J. Amariglio, & D. F. Ruccio (Eds.), *Postmodernism, economics, and knowledge* (pp. 102–128). New York: Routledge.

McGrath, A. (2002). *In the beginning: The story of the King James Bible and how it changed a nation, a language, and a culture.* New York: Anchor Books.

Martin, L., & Neal, A. (2001). *Defending civilization: How our universities are failing America and what can be done about it.* Washington, D.C.: American Council of Trustees and Alumni.

McSwite O. C. (2001). The psychoanalytic rationale for anti-administration. *Administratve Theory & Praxis, 23*, 493–506.

McSwite, O. C. (2000). On the discourse movement: A self interview. *Administrative Theory & Praxis, 22*, 45–48.

McSwite, O. C. (1998). Stories from the real world: Administering anti-administratively. In D. J. Farmer (Ed.), *Papers on the art of anti-administration.* Burke, VA: Chatelaine Press.

McSwite (1997). *Legitimacy in public administration: A discourse analysis.* Thousand Oaks, CA: SAGE Publications.

Miller, H. T. (2000). Rational discourse, mimetics, and the autonomous liberal-humanist subject. *Administrative Theory & Praxis, 22*, 89–104.

Mills, K. (1993). *This little light of mine: The life of Fannie Lou Hamer.* New York: Plume.

Pagels, E. H. (1981). *The gnostic gospels*. New York: Vintage Books.

Patterson, P. M. (2001). Imagining anti-administration's anti-hero (antagonist? protagonist? agonist?). *Administrative Theory & Praxis, 43*, 529–540.

Patterson, P. M. (2000). The talking cure and the silent treatment: Some limits of "discourse" as speech. *Administrative Theory & Praxis, 22*, 663–695.

Patterson, P. M. (2000). Nonvirtue is not apathy: Warrants for discourse and citizen dissent. *American Review of Public Administration, 30*, 225–251

Phillips, K. (2001). *Wealth and democracy: A political history of the American rich*. New York: Broadway Books.

Prychitko, D. L. (1998). *Why economists disagree: An introduction to the alternative schools of thought*. Albany: State University of New York.

Rothschild, E. (2001). *Economic sentiments: Adam Smith, Condorcet, and the Enlightenment*. Cambridge, MA: Harvard University Press.

Sayer, A. (1984). *Method in social science: A realist approach*. London: Routledge.

Spicer, M. W. (2001). Value pluralism and its implications for American public administration. *Administrative Theory & Praxis, 23*, 507–528.

Thayer, F. C. (1981). *End to hierarchy: Administration in the post-affluent world* (2nd ed.). New York: New Viewpoints.

# MAPPING ANTI-ADMINISTRATION: INTRODUCTION TO THE SYMPOSIUM

David John Farmer

How can a fly help a spider to think more like a fly? How can it alter the spider's consciousness? How can the fly of anti-administration best help the spider spin a new web beyond its limiting assumptions and traditional consciousness?

This symposium reflects on anti-administration. It consists of eight papers that analyze anti-administration and selected implications. The symposium interprets "analysis" in a broad sense. It includes not only traditional analysis but also, in the spirit of anti-administration, imaginative play-with-a-purpose. Before turning to the individual papers, this introduction summarizes the nature, aims and possible source attitudes of anti-administration. It offers a concept map and responds to questions that are frequently asked. Then, it indicates the perspectives in each of the eight papers. I am grateful for the care, insight, imagination and P.A. talent that my colleagues have brought to this symposium.[1] The fly proffers new consciousness to the spider.

## CONCEPT MAP OF ANTI-ADMINISTRATION

The term "anti-administration" is adapted from Physics. Anti-matter and normal matter mutually annihilate each other upon impact, being totally converted into energy (U.S. Atomic Energy Commission, 1967). Anti-matter refers to antiparticles, corresponding to nuclear particles. Antineutrons, antiprotons and positrons, for example, correspond to neutrons, protons and electrons. In a parallel way, can we expect that the encounter of anti-administration and administration will give rise to fresh and significant public administration energy?

What is anti-administration? What, more particularly, is the point of it? Anti-administration is a theory about P.A. theorizing and p.a. thinking. It is a theory (although I prefer descriptions such as "understanding" or "interpretation") in the sense of specifying "a particular way of conceptualizing something" (Sayer, 1984).[2] The concept map, following this page, depicts how I see it. A concept map is a visual display of a theory,

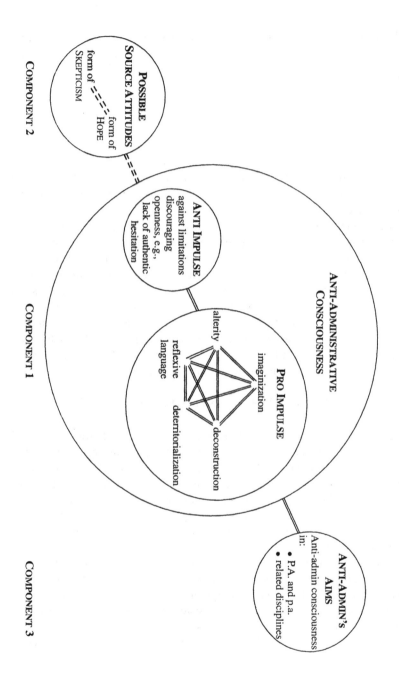

showing constituent concepts and the relationships among them (Maxwell, 1996, p. 37). The main component in this map is the set of concepts that make up anti-administrative consciousness itself, shown within Component 1. Component 2 shows attitudes that could be sources of anti-administrative consciousness—likely, though not "required," sources. And finally, Component 3 indicates anti-administration's aims.

The advantage of this concept map is that it offers a general picture of anti-administration. However, I recommend that the reader adopt the advice that Ludwig Wittgenstein (1961, p. 74) gave in a different circumstance—use the map as a ladder, and then "throw away the ladder after he has climbed up it." Let's describe each of these components in turn.

**Component 1: Anti-Administrative Consciousness**

The anti-administrative consciousness is one that exhibits radical openness in P.A. thinking and doing. In other words, it calls for a quantum shift, away from our traditional way of thinking. How and why anti-administrative consciousness is open is suggested in the following account of the concepts within anti-administrative consciousness.

Component 1 (the "anti-administrative consciousness" component on the concept map) shows two impulses. One impulse is labeled "anti," and the other is named "pro." The notion of an impulse includes not only thinking but also emotional energy and acts of will; for example, it includes libidinal as much as intellectual force. The transactional relationship[3] between the two impulses is represented on the chart by the linkage lines. The anti impulse shapes the pro; the pro impulse shapes the anti.

**The anti impulse**. The "anti" impulse is against limitations that discourage openness in ways of "thinking" and "doing" public administration. It is against limiting assumptions embedded in P.A. concepts where openness to other perspectives and people is not encouraged. Prominently, the anti impulse is against the assumption that P.A. truth claims (including those in this introduction) should be made with complete assurance.

The impulse against P.A. concepts associated with certainty can be re-described as a preference for authentic hesitation in the style of holding and expressing our own or our group's prescriptions. This hesitation, or listening to the other, is often misunderstood, e.g., the false equation of authentic hesitation with passivity or passing the buck. Authentic hesitation concerns hesitation only in maintaining and imposing our own (or our group's) opinions about the right thing to be done. Previously I have described (1999c, pp. 6–9) authentic hesitation by a number of devices, like comparing the assertiveness of Plato against the radical questioning of the historical Socrates. While present as a sub-text in our tradition, authentic hesitation runs counter to the dominant discourse of Western politics and public administration.

The non-hesitant concept of management exemplified in the standard job description is an example of a P.A. concept embodying and encouraging assertiveness in claiming and doing. This assertiveness—this lack of authentic hesitation—is reflected in the "Napoleonic" imperative "to direct, coordinate and control all the activities and personnel of the assigned program." All! What a small, yet powerful word! The more that the manager is Napoleonic, the more are the ideas of subordinates subordinated. The "anti" impulse stands against precluding alternatives from the agenda of options, including alternatives not yet fully specified and "tested."

**The pro impulse.** The pro impulse is "for" concepts that open up ways of thinking and doing public administration. It is for concepts that encourage the openness of the "anti-administrative consciousness." These are the concepts of "imaginization," "deconstruction," "deterritorialization," "alterity," and "reflexive language." These five concepts inter-act.

*Imaginization* is a force, predominantly liberating, that can permeate a society or a practice like public administration. Negative and positive descriptions are available, and I do not intend the term "imaginization" to mean what others like Gareth Morgan (1993, p. 1) have in mind. In negative terms, I describe (1995, pp. 156–177) imaginization in contrast to Enlightenment rationalization. The Enlightenment formula was that ever more rationalization equals ever more human happiness and ever more moral behavior. Some fill out this formula by adding complaints speaking of the need for liberation from the de-humanizing side-effects of modern rationalization. Seeking this liberation, there is the possibility of transforming and transcending rationalization by imaginization. In public administration terms, for instance, people could be held responsible for ever more imaginative thinking and action.

Imaginization can be described in positive terms. I do so by emphasizing (1998, pp. 37–56) the importance of play-with-a-purpose. Play is not conceptualized as limited to a game like baseball or bingo. Certainly, it includes thought games like "What would bureaucracy be like if we did not have rules that 'every employee must have a boss' and 'every boss must have a super-boss?'" It would include activities like war games (in the Department of Defense) or market crisis games (in the Federal Reserve). Beyond such playing, it extends to the inclusion of approaches like irony. It includes play activities like the "rewriting" that Jean-Francois Lyotard describes. This rewriting is not an attempt to grasp the past "correctly." It is akin to free association. Attitudes toward the task include suspending judgment, being patient, and giving attention to everything that happens. The attitude is not to view what is discovered as knowledge. "Contrary to remembering, working through would be defined as a work without end and therefore without will: without end in the sense in which it is not guided by the concept of an end — and not without finality" (Lyotard, 1991, p. 30). Deleuze's and Guittari's "schizoanalysis" (1995, p. 12) is another form of play. They think of it as liberating the body from its intellectual, social and subjectified constraints. Tricia Patterson offers an example of play. Her symposium paper imagines anti-administration personified as Trickster, speaking of the trickster as posing a laughing challenge to the culture of public administration. This recommended play (play of perspectives, if you will) should not be interpreted as play without a purpose, however. Anti-administration is engaged in the world as Socrates was—always making a nuisance of himself in the agora (the market place).

*Deconstruction* seeks the insights that come from loosening the limitations of the concepts and metaphors embedded in language. Language is not to be understood here as mere talk-stuff or word-stuff. Certainly, there is such a "thin" sense of the notion of language. I mean it in a "thick sense"—to include non-verbal language and even the sense in which animals have language. What I intend to include is what Michel Foucault meant by discourse, in his account of discourse theory. It is our way of looking at the world. It is my Weltanschauung, my language that shapes my consciousness. Languages, in the "thick" sense no less than the "thin," contain dichotomies or oppositions that can be broken down, revealing arbitrariness and in-between traces. Even something as apparently biologically-definite as the concept of death can be seen to involve a variety of social choices (e.g., Greenberg, 2001). Janet Hutchinson's paper in this symposium is an example of the importance of deconstruction. She writes about the oversimplifications and pain involved in conceptualizing gender in dichotomous terms. Languages, including the language of public administration, also contain metaphors. Madan Sarap (1993, p. 47) points out that we think of organizations spatially, e.g., in terms of up and down. Even scientific language is founded on metaphor, like Newton's.

*Deterritorialization* wants to loosen the coding or grid that a discipline imposes. The grid is imposed by the way the thinking is prescribed, as I describe it (1995, pp. 210–226). Each discipline has its "accepted" or "mainstream" way of thinking. The way that P.A. thinking is conducted co-shapes the way that p.a. is understood. It is not limited to this, however. The ways in which Economics and Political Science are structured also co-shape public administration. Debra Jacobs' paper in this symposium illustrates this issue of a disciplinary grid when she writes of a language of public administration that marginalizes ecology.

*Alterity* can be described in terms of four constituent features, as I do (1995, pp. 227–245). These features are positive steps to counter tendencies against which the anti-administrative consciousness stands. As Foucault asked (1997, p. xiii), "How does one keep oneself from being a fascist, even (especially) when one believes oneself to be a revolutionary militant?" The first feature is to achieve openness to the other. The second feature is to prefer diversity that avoids privileging meanings. The third is to exceed the limitations of meta-narratives and unrealistic foundations through such means as incorporating authentic hesitation in administration. The fourth feature is to develop an anti-institutional method of administration.

*Reflexive language* is a concept that appeals to a large literature that includes Nietzsche, Heidegger, Wittgenstein and Derrida. I see (1995, pp. 23–24) the reflexive language concept as understanding humans as trapped within the conceptual cobweb of perspectives, or language, when language is understood in the "thick" sense. Whatever we know, we know from a perspective. There is no Archimedean or non-perspectival point; truth claims are made from within a complex of perspectives. Accordingly, I recommend for public administration a playful and attuned dialogue with the underlying content of bureaucracy. I called it (1995, p. 12) a reflexive language paradigm. That was not a felicitous name, and I am now backing off from the name by dropping the word "paradigm." I continue to see this reflexive language as an art that examines the set of assumptions and social constructions that constitute the theoretical lenses through which we see, and that speculates about an alternative set or sets of socially constructed assumptions (that form another lens) through which we could see. The interpretation is reflexive because the focus is more on the lens and on alternative lenses, rather than merely on the objects that are "seen" through the lens. Attention is paid to the act of seeing and options for seeing. Recall the earlier discussion of an approach in terms of playing with perspectives and options. Some will want to emphasize the relationship between such concepts and such anti-foundational side-effects as value pluralism. Michael Spicer's paper provides a careful analysis of value pluralism and some implications for public administration.

The reflexive language concept, containing the notion of employing as many perspectives as possible, leads naturally enough to the idea of supplementing and overcoming existing thinking and practice. Reflexive language embraces traditional thinking and practice much in the manner of a Hegelian synthesis. In that synthesis, the thesis and the antithesis interact to give rise to a synthesis. But we must say "much in the manner of" because anti-administration's reflexive language contemplates no such assurance of a neat arrangement—no guarantee of a neat outcome.

This account of these "pro" concepts—especially of reflexive language—indicates why the changed anti-administrative consciousness does not involve a straight-forward specification of a set of P.A. prescriptions or principles.

Anti-administration is not something that "I list, you believe, and you follow." Let's return to points about the fresh anti-administrative consciousness of openness. It is an openness that, I emphasize, resists reduction to a set of prescriptions. It is openness that asks for input from the reader (the listener), and it expects spaces or gaps in understanding when it comes to non-trivial P.A. thinking and p.a. doing. It is openness that seeks understandings both from mainstream and from marginalized or excluded perspectives—from perspectives not invited to the table. It is unrelenting openness, symbolized by the space within component 1's large circle on the concept map. But, while we don't want mere reduction to a set of P.A. principles, we also don't want reduction to a principle that there should not be a set of principles. As Richard Box points out in his symposium paper, anti-administration should not be summarized into a set of P.A. principles. O.C. McSwite's paper in this symposium talks about an anti-administrative attitude of abhoring the abstractions it embraces. It talks about anti-administration in terms of Jacques Lacan's injunction to the reader "Y mettre du sein!" ("Put some sense of your own into it!"). It speaks about the shifts in consciousness. On the epistemological and the moral, for instance, O. C. McSwite's paper in this symposium points out that anti-administration has an anti-abstraction motif, but it is a motif that requires a person who is at home with abstraction. They describe it as "a theory that presents questioning as an answer, doubt as the pathway to clarity." They speak about the folly of reifying ideas—the "distrust of the impulse to find answers and to act expeditiously and decisively"—even though the opposite seems indicated.

The anti-administrative consciousness, it was mentioned at the beginning of this section, is radically open in seeking to include ideas that are other. "Other" here includes the ideas of people who are excluded or marginalized. It includes those discriminated against or subordinate, e.g., financially poor clients and citizens, minorities and women, and employees in dealing with their bosses. "Other" refers to ideas from discourses that are not dominant. In P.A., this can be exemplified by greater inclusion of non-mechanical understandings, e.g., of the human spirit. In analyzing bureaucratic questions, there is a failure to focus enough on the nonbureaucratic, the non-systematic, the non-mechanical (Farmer & Farmer, 1997). A mechanical view of the world has dominated modernist thinking since Rene Descartes and Isaac Newton; its adoption in public administration is reflected in expressions like "the machinery of government." It regards the universe on the model of a machine. It regards as adequate a reform program of "tinkering with parts of the machine" and it fails to recognize appropriately the interconnectedness of all that is.

## Component 2: Possible Source Attitudes

Isn't skepticism depressing? On the contrary, the dogmatists who are so frightened by the dark of the unknown are the ones that are depressing. There are many forms of skepticism. These positions share the perspective that the human capacity is limited in knowing with certainty what is ultimately real, as that reality is in itself. Some positions are limited in their skepticism to certain topics or methods of knowing; others are skeptical about all such knowledge. Some positions may be limited to sure information about ethical values, for instance. They might suppose that there are no fixed or eternal values, or that values are relative to place, time or other circumstances, or that morality is entirely a matter of personal preference. Others might be skeptical about the capacity of human reason to gain sure knowledge about some questions of existence or ultimate reality, or the existence and nature of certain entities like God. Then, there are skeptics who are skeptical about all such knowledge. They are skeptical about human reason yielding any sure and certain knowledge about ultimate reality. By the way, it is worth repeating that such complete skepticism does not automatically entail denying that we can know the truth, as long as truth is understood as truth within a "thick" language or a way of life. St. Augustine was skeptical about the completely non-skeptical thinking that holds that unaided human reason can gain unquestionable knowledge about any and all matters concerning ultimate reality; so am I.

Is hope in the possibility of improving human lives (and upgrading public administration) inconsistent with skepticism? Why should it be? I see no reason to think that a person cannot be both skeptical (in the broadest sense) and also hopeful. There are many forms of hope, as of skepticism. A more limited meaning of "hope" is that hope is a desired expectation that has little chance of fulfillment. A fuller meaning of "hope" is that hope is the expectation of something desired, plus belief in the possibility of fulfilling that expectation and desire. Neither meaning of hope is inconsistent with skepticism.

Component 2 depicts a consciousness that can provide possible source attitudes for anti-administration, although I do not think that either attitude is "necessary" for anti-administration. These are a form of skepticism, and a form of hope. I think that a relatively minimal or limited form of skepticism could motivate anti-administration. Sufficient is a skepticism "limited" to thinking that human reason cannot give us assured knowledge of "meanings" that are grounded in ultimate reality, including ethics grounded in the ultimate. That is, this description of a sufficient skepticism is minimal or limited, compared against the complete skeptic. Compared against the usual view of the person-on-the-street, the use of descriptions like "minimal" or "limited" may appear odd. I imagine that hope would not be sufficient unless it included belief in fulfillment, albeit not always rapid fulfillment. The linkage, connecting components 1 and 2 on the concept map, is drawn with broken lines. These broken lines signify that there is not a necessary connection between the contents of the two circles. I can imagine people trying anti-administration on an "as if" basis, for instance, even if they were non-skeptical and unhopeful.

Skepticism is a philosophical attitude, operating at what we can call a metaphysical level. It concerns knowing ultimate reality. Subject to accepting the consequences, I think it is not necessary to know metaphysical reality in order to "do" public administration. The reasons parallel those for supposing, as I do (1990, pp. 4–5), that it is not necessary to resolve metaphysical issues in order to "do" special sciences like physics. Others would disagree with this claim, however. Suppose they are right, and suppose that doing public administration requires first having unquestionable knowledge of ultimate reality. In that case, the skeptic would point out that P.A. does not have that unquestionable knowledge. On the other hand, suppose that public administration does not require such knowledge of ultimate reality, e.g., perhaps operating in what has been called the world of the model (e.g., Synge, 1970).[4] In that case, the skeptic would think that public administration can have no assurance that it is talking about the ultimately real and the "truth, the whole truth and nothing but the truth." We are talking within a discourse perspective, within a "thick" language.

## Component 3: Anti-Administration's Aims

Shouldn't the choice of anti-administration's primary aims be consistent with the nature of anti-administrative consciousness? Expanding public administration's consciousness and the consciousness of related disciplines would be consistent. Adapting James Carville's electioneering mantra, the fly of anti-administration can mutter to herself, "It's the consciousness, stupid!"

Anti-administration's first primary aim, as I see it, is to achieve anti-administrative consciousness in P.A. theorizing and practice. The primary need, the beginning of wisdom, is a change away from the way of thinking dominant in traditional public administration. While a quantum change is needed, the change is likely to be achieved incrementally. A change in a theorist's writing could influence not only another theorist but also a practitioner in whole or in part, for instance, and that theorist or practitioner might or might not influence another. Achieving a change in consciousness is likely to be a ragged process.

Anti-administration's second primary aim is to increase the openness of P.A. thinking by encouraging consciousness changes in related disciplines, like Economics and Political Science. These changes would parallel those needed for the anti-administrative consciousness of openness. Clearly, this would be extremely difficult without the commitment and energies of some thinkers in the related disciplines, and this will require much if P.A. theorists are to play a catalytic role in helping to realize such changes.

Component 3 focuses on anti-administration's aims. The linkage between components 3 and 1 on the concept map is drawn in solid lines. The two primary aims, just described, are consistent with the nature of anti-administrative consciousness. I imagine that the specifics of how to achieve these primary aims are matters for differing opinions, in view of changes that may occur in the context of the ragged process of achieving the primary aims.

Achieving anti-administration's primary aims, in the present context, probably will include a focus on undermining ideologies that serve to buttress traditional public administration. Important targets would surely include the efficiency model and the particular form of the economistic attitude that now dominate and constrain P.A. thinking and practice. But these would not be the only targets. Important in this freeing activity would be to identify and analyze all of the other constraining notions and attitudes shaping and limiting public administration. The ascendancy of hierarchy and the dominance of patriarchy are examples. Such is the hold of competing ideologies and attitudes that much repetition can be expected; the educational task is substantial and difficult. In a sense, this is a negative element in achieving anti-administration's primary aims.

Anti-administration can also use positive approaches in seeking to achieve its primary aims. For my money, one of these options—the most promising one—is to develop understandings of the bureaucratic and other implications of shifting the judgments and actions of P.A. theorists and practitioners toward privileging the treatment of persons "in a more fully human way." I think that a more fully human way can be facilitated by incorporating within public administration (a) more recognition of the human person as a bio-psycho-socio-spiritual being in-her-differences and (b) more authentic hesitation. On persons as bio-psycho-socio-spiritual beings, many P.A. policies and programs reflect the assumption that people should be treated as if they were less. The employer may see his subordinate as administrative man or woman, for example, and the welfare agency may see its client as welfare woman or man. Bureaucracy, public and private, tends to reduce people to bureaucratic units. On authentic hesitation, recall the earlier explanation. Several of the papers in this symposium (e.g., Richard Box and O. C. McSwite) comment on the perspective of hesitating, rather than bullying ahead and ramming through our personal or our group's beliefs, impulses, projects and official ideologies.

The concept map does offer a general sketch of anti-administration. There are four disadvantages, however. A concept map is very summary, and the explanations I have added are bare-bones. Then, the map does not make it clear enough that anti-administration is not a linear process. It does not indicate that there is more than one way of describing anti-administration. Some may want to include P.A. aims under sources, for instance; I do not. Most importantly, the concept map does not capture the openness of anti-administration. Additional questions arise, and so we should turn to FAQs.

## FREQUENTLY ASKED QUESTIONS (FAQS)

*QUESTION: Are there, indeed, different ways of describing anti-administration?*

RESPONSE: Yes, anti-administration can be described in a variety of "correct" ways.

In one description, for example, it can be characterized as anti-authoritarian, anti-hierarchical, and anti-foundationist. Peter Bogason has ably captured this meaning. "The concept of anti-administration used by Farmer summarizes the gist of postmodern analysis; it is anti-authoritarian, anti-hierarchical, and anti-foundationist. But it is not anti-analysis" (Bogason, 2001, p. 188). He could have written of anti-administration what he wrote of postmodern analysis. He comments that there is no one way of doing this analysis. "There is diversity and room for maneuvering" (Bogason, 2001, p. 188).

I suppose that another option would be to view anti-administration in terms of the radical libidinal. But alternative descriptions would undoubtedly include the "same" points offered in the present description.

Anti-administration can be described at varying levels of generality. Richard Box in his paper, for instance, offers an equally fine description that may be more action-oriented. He writes that, "anti-administration appears contrary to accepted goals of public administration because it suggests administrators should shed power and control, questioning their own objectives and becoming 'tentative' in their commitments." It would shift "determination of public action from managers to citizens." He writes in terms of emphasizing private lives.

*QUESTION: Does this mean that anti-administration is wedded to a postmodern perspective?*

RESPONSE: Absolutely not. It is an uphill struggle to make this point. As part of this struggle, I have attempted (1999a) to derive anti-administration from a modernist perspective, relying on critical theorists like Herbert Marcuse. In another, I have set out to derive anti-administration from a medieval perspective (speaking about St. Anselm and administration). Of course, there are affinities between anti-administration and postmodernism, e.g., listening to other voices.

In the same way, I would say that the anti-administrative consciousness is not the same as the postmodern consciousness.

With both these issues, it makes more sense (if one wishes to involve the category "postmodernism") to speak in terms of a category I have described (1999b, p. 300) as our emergent post-ist context. "The term post-ist is a neologism that refers to our post-ist intellectual context, a condition that is variously characterized, in part or whole, by descriptors such as post-positivist, post-industrial, post-patriarchal, post-structural, post-modern, post-Freudian, post-colonial, post-metaphysical, and other post-ist terms."

*QUESTION: The anti-foundational claim about ethics is provocative. Where can I read something more about it?*

RESPONSE: In this symposium, Michael Spicer argues against monist positions that assume a harmony among human ends. In P.A. thinking, he holds that monist positions can be harmful, e.g., in failing to help practitioners cope with value conflicts, and in encouraging "excessive zeal among practitioners in pursuing their own monist ends." He argues that values are often incompatible and incommensurable.

For another thing, I have described (1999c, p. 5) a dilemma in these terms. On the one hand, we cannot live well without making moral judgments. On the other hand, in justice and in moral judgments, there is indecisiveness of outcome. Each well-discussed general position (e.g., conflicting views of justice) has its strengths and weaknesses. But there is no knockdown winner. Most views are attended by excellent supporting arguments, excellent counterarguments, excellent counter-counter arguments, and so on. In this way, a feature of our understanding of justice can be described as indecisive in outcome.

*QUESTION: Isn't all of this relativistic and very bad?*

RESPONSE: Which is more likely to be the cause of behavior like unjustified lying, asks Louis Menand (2001, p. 81). Is "it likely to be a book by a French philosopher or the near-ubiquity of (deceitful) commercial advertising?" The answer is not reassuring to those afflicted with a fear of relativism, a horror of uncertainty.

Fortunately, the world does not divide into monolithic and grounded ethics v. no ethics at all. In a world of value pluralism, anti-administration favors an ethic of self-inquiry and hesitation in imposing ethical claims. It is the sort of ethical posture that I associate with the historical Socrates.

*QUESTION: Why should I focus on the "other?"*

RESPONSE: Excluding the "other," for one thing, harms the mainstream. For the effect of the other on the mainstream, reflect on Georg Hegel's master-slave analysis.

*QUESTION: How can I understand talk of the human spirit (as an example of non-mechanical understanding) and its relationship to anti-administration?*

RESPONSE: I prefer to think of the human spirit in terms of bio-spirituality, where the spiritual is transactionally integrated with the biological, psychological and social dimensions of the human. I understand spirituality in this context as exceeding categories. I describe (2001, p. 438) "corporeal spirituality as the pre-systematized energy of the singularity of a person. (I see it) as poetic, revolutionary, boundary exceeding, and an opening of the person to the wholeness of himself or herself, of nature and sociality." I don't see spirituality as necessarily linked to the religious. For instance, was not Friedrich Nietzsche a deeply spiritual person? I don't think that spirituality is always linked to the good. For instance, was not Grand Inquisitor Tomas de Torquemada a deeply spiritual person?

For the link with anti-administration, first reflect on the claim that traditional P.A. theory privileges the mechanical. Marginalizing matters of spirituality, or the human spirit, has been given as an example. Second, the description of bio-spirituality just offered surely suggests that the unrelenting openness of the anti-administrative consciousness is associated with the spiritual.

*QUESTION: Are people like Timothy McVeigh good anti-administrationists?*

RESPONSE: No.

But this question brings up in dramatic form the difficulty involved in "admitting to the table" ideas we abhor. Let's recall the obvious and the difficult. The obvious is that not all ideas are equally right. The difficult is that what is in the heart of darkness should not be simply brushed aside. Joseph Conrad and Bertrand Russell were excited about this, when they distinguished between writing on a thin crust of lava and writing in the fiery depths of the central fire.

It is easy to de-marginalize ideas with which I agree. I would be happy to participate in de-marginalizing the ideas of French feminists like Helene Cixous, for instance.

Take what is a harder case for some people. Consider the example of the theological language—about witnessing and gifting—that is used by Bob Cunningham and Robert Schneider in their paper in this symposium. (As the writers explain, "While the Kleinian object-relations theory underpinning our argument is psychological, the language is theological.") Should those who look down their noses at theological language exclude that paper's ideas? Anti-administration's stance is not to deny recognition.

Take the hardest case you can imagine. Including at the table "abhorrent" ideas does not entail accepting the "abhorrent" ideas. I repeat that I want to be guided by an ethic of authentic hesitation. I can owe it to listen: I do not owe it to accept. I can owe it not to impose my own ideas unhesitantly; I do not owe it to agree with anyone. Would Socrates have done less? I think that this is not dissimilar in an important sense from the position of the court that condemned McVeigh to death—the latter hardly an act of agreement. Many would think it unfair if a court did not feel obligated to listen to even the most heinous criminal.

These are difficult emotional decisions, however. For instance, when discussing the question, why else do I (we) feel an overwhelming urge to reassure readers that I (we) abhor the murdering that McVeigh did?

## SYMPOSIUM PAPERS

The eight papers in this symposium make a variety of contributions to an understanding of anti-administration. O. C. McSwite provides a rationale for understanding anti-administration based on psychoanalytic theory, and argues that anti-administration is related to our contemporary social context. Michael Spicer discusses value pluralism, which features in the anti-administrative stance. Tricia Patterson illuminates the ironic, playful and anti-bureaucratic stance of anti-administration by personifying it and drawing a comparison with the trickster figure. Richard Box speaks to the connection between anti-administration and private lives. I explore the feasibility of a P.A. discourse of laughter, drawing on Helene Cixous. Robert Cunningham and Robert Schneider discuss witnessing and gifting as an anti-administrative strategy for reclaiming the relationship between civil servants and citizens. Janet Hutchinson addresses gender discourse in anti-administration, suggesting multi-gendering as one remedy for what is perceived as the pervasive melancholy that afflicts women, men and organization. Debra Jacobs offers an ecological argument for anti-administration.

On gauzy wings, the fly of anti-administration speaks to aspects of a broader public administration consciousness.[5]

*O. C. McSwite's Paper:* Making anti-administration clear means emphasizing the paradoxical character of anti-administration and the paradoxical character of life itself, and the paper does this. O. C. McSwite discusses the nature of anti-administration, and provides a rationale for this understanding of anti-administration based on Lacanian psychoanalytic theory. O. C. McSwite also argues that anti-administration should be seen as relating to our contemporary social context. The paper focuses in particular on the commercialization of the world and the decay of the social bond.

*Michael Spicer's Paper:* Michael Spicer discusses value pluralism (that values are often incompatible and incommensurable) and some implications for public administration. This paper has important relevance to anti-administration, as moral pluralism is consistent with an anti-administrative consciousness. Michael Spicer argues that value pluralism is more consistent with our moral experience, and he indicates that the monist view is dangerous. He then proposes for public administration a constitutional approach, which he sees as facilitating a type of anti-administration. Michael Spicer points out that Isaiah Berlin himself reflected much of this attitude when Berlin wrote that "what this age calls for is not (as we are so often told) more faith, or stronger leadership, or more scientific organization. Rather, it is the opposite—less Messianic ardor, more enlightened skepticism, more toleration of idiosyncrasies...and a less mechanical, less fanatical application of general principles, however rational or righteous."

*Tricia Patterson's Paper:* Tricia Patterson offers a scintillating example of play-with-a-purpose. Her paper illuminates the radically anti-bureaucratic character of anti-administration by personifying it and drawing a comparison with the trickster. Anti-administration seems to her to be a position of playful dissent well personified by the trickster folk figure. She distinguishes the Trickster from the agonist and (unlike Joseph Campbell) the hero. Anti-administration seems to contend, as many feminisms do, that the prevailing questions need re-framing.

*Richard Box's Paper:* Richard Box sees a clear connection between private lives and anti-administration, and he suggests a focus on public administrators exercising their imaginative faculties to protect "private lives." Much P.A. Theory assumes that citizens should be deeply involved in public affairs. The paper discusses the reasons why this inevitably results in only a limited number of people being involved, and many are not informed enough to participate effectively. Richard Box suggests why the responsibility must fall on public administrators to exercise their imaginations as a means of protecting private lives. Practitioner imagination is needed in such activities as conceptualizing relevant patterns of human interests. Patterns are revealed in a variety of ways, e.g., including listening, talking, and studying.

*My Paper:* This paper is directed toward anti-administration's first primary aim, pointing to debilitating constraints in traditional P.A. thinking. It does so by playing with the possibility of a P.A. discourse (a writing) of laughter, drawing on Helene Cixous' *The Laugh of the Medusa* and on her discussions of feminine writing and imposed meanings. I imagine a P.A. discourse of laughter that is somatic in origin, and that focuses on the "funny peculiar," which in the P.A. case is understood to be socially constructed elements that are privileged in being misconceived as natural entities in any and all P.A. discourses. The paper imagines that the use of such a discourse of laughter can include helping to liberate ourselves from the distortions of our particular discipline's discourse, admitting notions now marginalized. It gives macro examples of political and economic myth-like stories that have become ingrained in us and that make up our "governing" political and economic discourses.

*Robert Cunningham's and Robert Schneider's Paper:* These writers discuss witnessing and gifting as anti-administrative strategies for reclaiming what they describe as a trust relationship between civil servants and citizens. They do so after discussing reasons for the ongoing antipathy against civil servants. They describe their paper, based on object relations theory, as expressing their ideas in theological language. For example, they choose to write of "redeeming" bureaucracy from a "fall from grace." Robert Cunningham and Robert Schneider hold that to re-create generalized trust between governors and governed, bureaucrats must respond anti-administratively. They describe and illustrate the witnessing and gifting that, when combined with the opposite of rational decision-making, can "redeem" bureaucracy. They assert that, "Properly done, Weberian administration can meet material needs; anti-administration meets the needs of the spirit by reparative acts that speak to the soul."

*Janet Hutchinson's Paper:* "Anti-administration is anti-melancholy" is the penultimate line of this paper, which ends with a quote from Tom Robbins' *Even cowgirls get the blues*. Goes the book, "Definitions are limiting. Limitations are deadening. To limit oneself is a kind of suicide. To limit another is a kind of murder. To limit poetry is a Hiroshima of the human spirit." Janet Hutchinson sets out to address gender discourse in anti-administration, and she suggests that multi-gendering is one remedy for what she describes as the pervasive melancholy that afflicts women, men and organizations. She illustrates the relevance of an anti-administrative stance, using a feminist experience and perspective largely absent in mainstream P.A. Theory.

*Debra Jacobs' Paper:* Debra Jacobs makes a case for anti-administration in terms of alterity and the environment. She offers an ecological argument for anti-administration. If a substantial ecological or environmental crisis exists, why does not the language of P.A. facilitate and implicate an understanding of ecological issues? As I read the lyricism in the paper, I understand that the language of traditional P.A. contributes to the ecological crisis. The paper includes a contrast between technocratic administration and the ideas of deep ecologists. It argues for administering anti-administratively as a useful middle ground between the two discourses. The most striking image in the paper, for me, is that of the cow on the highway. "Life within the machine is ordered being. Technologic being is an ordered existence, premised upon rules, hierarchical relationships and rationality. The 'chaos' of nature is the other, in this telling, because it exists in opposition to the orderliness of modernity. Imagine for instance a cow standing in the middle of the highway as you drive to work. The chaos destabilizes your world; it does not belong there... The cow simply does not belong on the road."

## ENDNOTES

1. Thanks to Richard Box for proposing this symposium, and to each of the writers. Thanks to Tricia M. Patterson and Rosemary L. Farmer for their extremely valuable comments on the introduction, including Dr. Patterson's suggestion about using a concept map.

2. The concept of "theory" is elastic, as it should be. Sayer (1984, p. 50) identifies other senses of theory as "an ordering framework (or as Milton Friedman puts it, as a 'filing system')" and as a term "often used interchangeably with 'hypothesis' or 'explanation.'" Another description of theory is "a general, systematic account of a subject matter" (Boyd, 1993, p. 791). Pointing to a "correct" view of theory can be done within the context of a meta-theory of theories.

3. For the meaning of "transactional" here, see Farmer, 2001.

4. Synge gives as examples of the M-world in Theoretical Physics the Newtonian and the Einsteinian models. He distinguishes (1977, p. 16) that from the R-world, the "real world, the world of immense complexity in which we live and move and have our being." He maintains that physicists, more than mathematicians, are inclined to think of their M-worlds as identical with the R-world. He calls the confusion of the two worlds the Pygmalion Syndrome, after "Pygmalion who carved a statue of such surpassing realism that it came to life—M-world becoming R-world in the mind of the enthusiastic physicist" (1977, p. 18).

5. For a fly-spider metaphor, see Mary Howitt's The Spider and the Fly. See also Charles Simic's comment (1994, p. 39) that "Elegies in a spider's web is all we bona fide flies get."

## REFERENCES

Bogason, P. (2001). Postmodernism and American public administration in the 1990s. *Administration and Society 33*, 165–193.

Boyd R., Gasper, P., & Trout, J. D. (Eds.). (1993). *The philosophy of science*. Cambridge, MA: M.I.T.

Farmer, D. J. (1990). *Being in time: The nature of time in light of McTaggart's paradox*. Lanham, MD: University Press of America.

Farmer, D. J. (1995). *The language of public administration: Bureaucracy, modernity, and postmodernity*. Tuscaloosa: University of Alabama Press.

Farmer, D. J. (1998). Public administration discourse as play with a purpose. In D. J. Farmer (Ed.), *Papers on the art of anti-administration* (pp. 37–56). Burke, VA: Chatelaine Press.

Farmer, D. J. (1999a). Anti-admin: With help from Herbert Marcuse. *Administrative Theory & Praxis, 21*, 497–501.

Farmer, D. J. (1999b). Public administration discourse: A matter of style. *Administration and Society, 31*, 299–320.

Farmer, D. J. (1999c). The discourse movement: A centrist view of the sea change. *International Review of Public Administration, 4*, 3–10.

Farmer, D. J. (2001). The bio-spiritual awakening? *Public Performance and Management Review, 4*, 436–439.

Farmer, D. J., & Farmer, R. L. (1997). Leopards in the temple: Bureaucracy and the limits of the in-between. *Administration and Society, 29*, 507–528.

Foucault, M. (1977). Preface. In G. Deleuze & F. Guattari (Eds.), *Anti-Oedipus: Capitalism and schizophrenia* (pp. xi-xiv). New York: Viking Press.

Greenberg, G. (2001, August 13). As good as dead: Is there really such a thing as brain death? *The New Yorker*, 36–41.

Lyotard, J. (1991). *The inhuman: Reflections on time*. Stanford, CA: Stanford University Press.

Maxwell, J.A. (1996). *Qualitative research design: An integrative approach*. Thousand Oaks, CA: Sage Publications.

Menand, L. (2001, July 23). False fronts. *The New Yorker*, 72–82.

Morgan, G. (1993). *Imaginization: The art of creative management*. Newbury Park, CA: Sage.

Sarap, M. (1993). *Post-structuralism and postmodernism*. Athens: University of Georgia Press.

Sayer, A. (1984). *Method in social science: A realist approach*. London: Routledge.

Simic C. (1994). Elegy in a spider's web. In C. Simic (Ed.), *The unemployed fortune-teller: Essays and memoirs* (pp. 34–39). Ann Arbor: University of Michigan Press.

Synge, J.L. (1970). *Talking about relativity*. Amsterdam: North Amsterdam.

U.S. Atomic Energy Commission. (1967). *Nuclear terms: A brief glossary*. Washington, DC: A.E.C.

Wittgenstein, L. (1961). *Tractatus logico-philosophicus* (D. F. Pears & B. F. Guinness, Trans.). London: Routledge and Kegan Paul.

# Dogs of War: Fighting Back

### David John Farmer

This article argues that public administration should focus on fighting back against the American business model, which currently limits the world of the public sector and public administration. It offers five claims intended to help public administration develop a fighting counter-strategy derived from the attack plans of American business model advocates: (1) that the American business model is more than a mere model—it includes institutional, programmatic, and money investment in an attack strategy against the public sector; (2) that public administration should attack the myths underlying the American business model, using hermeneutics and deconstruction; (3) that it should counter-attack American business model's rhetoric; (4) that it should contribute to economic literature, a foundational support of the American business model; and (5) that it should appropriately revise its academic program requirements for practitioners and others.

> Cry "Havoc!" and let slip the dogs of war. —Shakespeare, *Julius Caesar* 3.1.273
> It always seems impossible until it's done. —Nelson Mandela

Theorists of macro public administration sometimes have to do more than merely theorize; sometimes they have to fight for macro changes in practice. Let us focus on the need to fight back against the problematic American business model, whose private sector dogs of war are already surrounding and limiting the world of the public sector and public administration. A one-sided war is being fought against Big (and small) Government by Big (and small) Anti-Government, and it is hard for us in public administration to respond effectively. Other images are available for characterizing the American business model's attack, such as comparisons to the guards in Plato's Allegory of the Cave distorting the chained prisoners' understanding and action by "projecting" shadows on the cave wall. But the image of war seems more appropriate, a consequential war of global scale. Such a war requires more than the neutral old-school public administration approach, the traditional neutral public administration encouraged by such factors as the politics-administration dichotomy and the failure to think out of the familiar disciplinary box. A public administration willing to think out of the box (or the cave) should offer a post-traditional and more effective fighting defense and counter-attack, nurtured by theorizing and understanding the war tactics used by Big Anti-Government attackers. "Cry 'Havoc!' and let slip the dogs of war" against accelerating domination by the American business model and its allies.

Following discussion of the basic features of the American business model, five claims are made that are intended to help public administration theorists, associations, academic programs, higher-level practitioners, and others develop a fighting counter-strategy—learning from the enemy's fighting plans, tactics, and weaknesses. The first and major claim is that the American business model is more than a mere model. It is a war-fighting strategy, an anti-government battle plan. It suggests that public administration can learn from the 1971 Powell memorandum, written by Lewis Powell, soon to be appointed an associate justice of the Supreme Court, for the U.S. Chamber of Commerce. The second claim is that public administration should counter-attack the kingdom of myth, including the use of hermeneutics and deconstruction. The third claim is that public administration should counter-attack the American business model's rhetoric. Is the American business model truly a guide to the good life, and is it supported by philosophical and ideological claims? The fourth claim is that, as economic science is a subtext useful in supporting the dominance of the American business model, public administration should join in contributing to the economic literature. On the co-shaping of economics, distinguished professional economists like Thomas Piketty (2014) and Chang (2014) have encouraged noneconomists to participate in developing economics—not to leave economics to the professional economists. The fifth claim is that all public administration academic programs should require their students to study not only the relative advantages of regulating an economy but also economics itself, encouraging students to recognize that the American business model is less than fully validated by economic science.

The development of such an anti–American business model war strategy does not have to deny that the public sector has its negatives, just as the private sector has its negatives—in both sectors, some are huge, some different, and some similar. Nor is it claimed that nothing has been done in such areas by public administration theorists; the claim is that what we have done needs more. Hopes are raised, for instance, by the theme ("Anti-Government: Different This Time?") of the May 2015 annual conference of the Public Administration Theory Network and by an earlier plenary presentation (Miller, 2012) about how market fundamentalism frames state and civil society.

## BASIC FEATURES OF THE AMERICAN BUSINESS MODEL

The American business model can be well described as consisting of components relating to self-interest, market fundamentalism, the minimal state, and low taxation. Turn to the distinguished economist/business thinker John Kay and the celebrated objectivist/writer Ayn Rand for such accounts. They have been chosen because their writings are important and influential. They agree in describing the American business model as consisting of these four components. But they differ in their evaluative descriptions of the utility of the American business model. Kay explains what he describes as "the blind faith" (Kay, 2010, p. 44) that now constructs the American business model. Rand and her followers describe the American business model as part of objectivist philosophy and a guide to life.

John Kay explains the American business model in his *The Truth About Markets* (2003) and in other publications, such as *Obliquity* (2010). He writes that the claims about the American business model are indeed of four kinds. The first is that "self-interest rules—self-regarding materialism governs our economic lives" (Kay, 2003, p.44). The second is market fundamentalism—markets "should operate freely, and attempts to regulate them by social or political action are almost always undesirable" (Kay, 2003, p. 44). The third is the minimal state—the economic role of government should not extend much beyond the enforcement of contracts and private property rights. Government should not itself provide goods and services, or own productive assets. The fourth and last claim is "low taxation—while taxation is necessary to finance these basic functions of the minimal state, tax rates should be as low as possible and the tax system should not seek to bring about redistribution of income and wealth" (Kay, 2003, p. 44).

Rand endorses all four of Kay's characterizations of the American business model. The first is that self-regarding materialism should govern our lives. Rand celebrates in her nonfiction and her novels what she considers the central importance of self-interest for the entrepreneur and the nonentrepreneur. Her heroes John Galt and Henry Rearden, in particular, could have been named after CEOs like Steve Jobs or Henry Ford (to the extent that they are objective and rational, self-serving, and uninterested in altruism—as defined by Rand). They could also have been named after the entrepreneurs who exist in the world of models within microeconomic theory. Rand's sympathy with the economic is suggested by such comments as that "the great values to be gained from social existence are knowledge and trade" (Rand, 1961b, p. 107).

The second of Kay's characterizations of the American business model is market fundamentalism. Market fundamentalism understands the "free" market as a self-organizing system and the best device for allocating resources. Market fundamentalism was especially advocated (as noted below) within the Chicago School of Economics, by thinkers like Milton Friedman (1994, p. ix). Rand embraces market fundamentalism.

The third of Kay's characterizations is the minimal state. Rand agrees, and Big Government is (for her) what exceeds its proper purpose. As Galt makes clear in *Atlas Shrugged,*

> The only proper purpose of a government is to protect man's rights, which means: to protect him from physical violence. A proper government is only a policeman, acting as an agent of man's self-defense, and, as such, may resort to force *only* against those who start the use of force. (Rand, 1957, p. 231)

About governmental functions and their privatization, Rand thought it was inappropriate for government to require (for example) inoculations against disease, and in fact, that government has no right to license physicians and dentists (Mayhew, 2005, pp. 12–13). She asserted that it is inappropriate for a government to control air and water pollution for the sake of public health, and she added, "the government's only proper role is protecting individual rights" (Mayhew, 2005, p. 8). Rand indicated that government should not establish building codes. She wanted to privatize the roads, favoring the idea of allowing people to buy any and all roads. The proper functions of government, for Rand, are the police, the army, and the courts (Mayhew, 2005, p. 7).

The fourth of Kay's characterizations of the American business model's claims is low taxation. Rand would agree. About taxation, Rand holds that taxation should be voluntary in a proper government (i.e., one that is not a Big Government). A "program of voluntary government financing would be simply sufficient to pay for the legitimate functions of a proper government," writes Rand (1964, p. 118). "In a fully free society, taxation—or, to be exact, payment for governmental services—would be voluntary" (Rand, 1964, p. 116).

A comment should be added about the term "American business model" used in this article and in the literature. It is not a model that is confined to the United States. For example, one might hope to hear discussion of the Australian business model (which is also an ABM), and so on for other countries. As and if the business world succeeds in further dominating the world of governments, a worldwide term might well seem ever more appropriate. Meanwhile, the

American business model does not emphasize that there are, indeed, different kinds of market economies, as Chang (2010, 2014) and others have emphasized. It does not recognize that property rights and the nature of corporations are social constructs; they are not fixed by nature.

Rand considered the claims made by the American business model to be well-founded, as a guide to life should be. On the contrary, John Kay concludes that the American business model is based on blind faith. As he writes

> In the century before the fall of the Berlin Wall, socialism defined the language of political economy. Not just for its supporters, but also for its opponents. Today, the situation is reversed: the vocabulary of the political right frames the terms of the economic debate. Globalization and privatization have displaced capital and class as terms of discourse.... The model fulfills the same need for simple, universal explanations once met by Marxism. (Kay, 2010, p. 44)

## CLAIM 1: THE AMERICAN BUSINESS MODEL IS MORE THAN A MERE MODEL

The American business model is more than a mere model. It is like a war-fighting strategy, a war game, a set of battle tactics. And are not counter-tactics to be learned by those who oppose the full dominance of the American business model?

For an account of the American business model as a battle plan, turn to the Powell memorandum (Powell, 1971)—written on August 23, 1971, two months before President Nixon nominated Lewis Powell for the Supreme Court. It was addressed to the director of the U.S. Chamber of Commerce. It is not claimed that this memorandum is the sole cause of the American business model as a war plan. For instance, credit (or discredit) has to go to personalities like President Ronald Reagan and Prime Minister Margaret Thatcher (who responded with TINA —"There is no alternative"). Credit also has to go to other aspects of the bio-psycho-social-poetic-mythic way that thoughts are constructed, to money, and also (as Michel Foucault would add) to power considerations.

The Powell memorandum is often said to have inspired the creation a number of institutions friendly to the American business model, like the Heritage Foundation (http://www.heritage.org), the Manhattan Institute (http://www.manhattan-institute.org), the Cato Institute (http://www.cato.org), Citizens for a Sound Economy, now Americans for Prosperity (http://americansforprosperity.org), FreedomWorks (http://www.freedomworks.org), and Accuracy in Academia (http://www.academia.org), as well as the proactive involvement of the U.S. Chamber of Commerce (https://www.uschamber.com) in a wide-ranging series of activities, and the appointment in corporations of vice-presidents charged with defending against (and attacking) opponents of what, in effect, is the American business model. Why would it not be useful now for those opposed to the American business model to adopt a parallel and contrary battle plan?

To facilitate consideration of the battle-plan in Powell's memorandum and to suggest what might now be considered for a parallel and contrary battle plan, listed below are twenty-five of the action points made by Lewis Powell (1971). They concern comments on initiatives by the U.S. Chamber of Commerce and by businesses themselves relating to:

- Recognizing the desirability of creating "think-tank" institutes.
- Recognizing the sources of the attacks against the business culture.
- Recognizing that the foundations of the pro-business culture are under attack.

- Recognizing that corporations are currently not aggressive enough.
- "Why not fight back?" (Powell, 1971).
- The first essential is that business should approach this problem as a primary responsibility of corporate management.
- Each corporation should have an executive vice-president assigned the task of countering the attacks against the business culture—as part of the significant first step.
- Recognizing that university social science faculties are unreliable.
- The chamber, as one counter, should hire a staff of personnel highly qualified in the social sciences.
- The chamber should evaluate textbooks.
- The chamber should seek equal time on the college circuit.
- The chamber should urge balance in faculties at universities.
- The chamber should have courses in schools of business.
- The chamber should evaluate secondary school activities, and conduct an active pro-business program for such schools.
- The chamber should utilize staffs of scholars to influence the public.
- Television should be "kept under constant surveillance—including news analysis" (Powell, 1971).
- Radio and press should also be challenged to present affirmative business information.
- Books, paperbacks, and pamphlets should be monitored.
- Businesses should devote 10 percent of their annual advertising budgets to paid pro-business advertisements.
- Businesses should be alert to the neglected political area, like pro-business lobbying.
- The chamber should retain pro-business spokespersons.
- The chamber should adopt a more aggressive attitude.
- There should be more generous support from business to the chamber for pro-business activities.
- People should recognize that this is not just an economic problem. It is also about freedom.
- The chamber and businesses should start to implement these changes with a complete study.

Frankly, the Powell memorandum is not at all scholarly. But it is a call to action. It is replete with assertions like the following: "No thoughtful person can question that the American economic system is under broad attack" (Powell, 1971, p. 2). "It [is] crystal clear that the foundations of our free society are under wide-ranging and powerful attack—not by Communists or any other conspiracy but by misguided individuals parroting one another" (Powell, 1971, p. 3). "The threat to the enterprise system... is a threat to individual freedom" (Powell, 1971, p. 3). But a virtue of the Powell memorandum is that it does suggest a battle plan for the U.S. Chamber of Commerce and for corporate America. And it seems to have been a near-winning strategy.

Yes, public administration (associations, theorists, high-level practitioners, and others) should start developing a parallel and contrary battle plan directed against the American business model, inspired by intelligence from the Powell memorandum. Public administration should start to implement such a counter-attack plan, including a rewriting of Justice Powell's last recommendation, which specifies that the "the chamber and businesses should start to implement these changes with a complete study." Simultaneously, public administration (e.g., theorists, academic programs, high-level practitioners, and others) should start to foster recommended counter-attacks against claims 2–5, discussed below, relating to the kingdom of myth, American business model rhetoric, economic literature, and academic program requirements.

## CLAIM 2: PUBLIC ADMINISTRATION SHOULD COUNTER-ATTACK THE KINGDOM OF MYTH

Public administration should strive to counter not only the ideology but also the mythic dimensions of capitalism, as described, say, by Hughes (2004, pp. 126–152). Public administration should also make use of hermeneutics and deconstruction in addressing the power that comes from myths—including the modern myth that only the ancients relied on myths.

Public administration—especially its theorists—should attempt to kill the king, including (as this article argues, and as discussed in Farmer, 2005) the enemy king. Let's imagine that both kingdoms are co-ruled by myth and other powerful kinds of governing ideas. For this, we can vow to clean up our own disciplinary king (or cave or our own stable); for example, we can do so while remaining with the governing idea of being neutral and traditional. It is suggested—on the other hand—that we go further and focus on the enemy king, especially because the kings of capitalism are more powerful. For one thing, we could extend our focus to macro public administration rather than micro public administration and activities like preparing students for entry-level and mid-level work in bureaucracies. Hughes claims that "as capitalism entrenched itself in American life, capitalism drew its legitimacy from all the [American] myths" (2004, p. 126). So does the American business model. According to Hughes, these myths include the notions of America as Nature's Nation, as the Chosen Nation, as the Christian Nation, as the Millennial Nation, and as the Innocent Nation. Writing about the Myth of Nature's Nation, for example, he states

> Americans who benefited from the capitalist system could hardly imagine viable alternatives. Because it seemed so natural, so thoroughly in keeping with "the way things are meant to be," it was easy to imagine that the capitalist system was rooted squarely in the self-evident patterns of "Nature and Nature's God." The myth of Nature's Nation, therefore, probably did more to legitimate American capitalism than any other single factor. (Hughes, 2004, p. 126)

It is suggested that public administration counter-attackers focus on the hermeneutics and the deconstruction of the economic theorizing that serves as subtextual support of the American business model— theorizing of both economic "science" and "the" economic system. For targets of the hermeneutic approach, consider Chang's comments on the treatment of "work" in economic science and the dubious character of the New Financial System (Chang, 2014, pp. 201–226). For instance, he claims, "Despite the overwhelming presence in our lives, work (in economic theory) is a relatively minor subject. The only major mention of work is, somewhat curiously, in terms of its absence—unemployment" (Chang, 2014, p. 252). Federal Reserve Chair Janet Yellen (2014) would join Piketty and other economists in pointing toward the growing disparity between rich and poor. We should certainly recognize more fully a philosophy of hermeneutics aimed at elucidating understanding and meanings—rather than behavior and causes. We might even try more thinking as play and aim for post-traditional theorizing. We might aim to incorporate in public administration what we can learn from a multiplicity of non–public administration disciplines, for example, what has been discussed (Farmer, 2010) as epistemic pluralism. Eleven perspectives are illustrated—including the business, economic, political, critical theory, poststructural, psychoanalytic, neuroscientific, feminist, and ethical. We might also, in public administration, counter-attack with counter-rhetoric, as suggested in the following two examples. The first is the development of a counter-symbol to Big Government; and Big Economy and Big Governmentality (existing in an unregulated free market) are examples that have been suggested and analyzed within public administration (Farmer, 2014). The second example might be a counter-symbol in the choice of a book title; for example, the phrase "superhighway to serfdom" referring to an expressway that starts with the excesses of private enterprise, unregulated by government too small. The choice of the words "superhighway" and "serfdom" would relate to the neoliberal message in Hayek's *Road to Serfdom*.

Let us include focus, as an available method, on deconstruction. Deconstruction has been characterized as a good reading of a text, where text is not limited to the written text (e.g., cops and criminals can read a street better than we can; soldiers can read a battlefield; etc.). J. Hillis Miller, in his *The Ethics of Reading,* writes, "Deconstruction is nothing more nor less than good reading as such" (Miller, 1987, p. 10). In all our texts, binary opposites (male-female, right-wrong, etc., where Derrida explained that one is read as superior) and metaphors limit the way that we think and understand. So deconstruction would include such activities as reversing the order of precedence in binary opposites. Derrida indicates that the meaning of the text comes from the reader, not from the writer. Additionally, it has been pointed out that the fleeting meanings of deconstruction do not represent a loss of meaning. Surely the fleeting meanings constitute a superabundance of meaning—of words that mean many things and of statements that remind us of other statements; and multiple meanings are not necessarily contradictory. Miller continues to claim that "neither [Derrida and De Man] has ever asserted the freedom of the reader to make the text mean anything he or she wants it to mean" (Miller, 1987, p. 10). But I agree that at the beginning, Jacques Derrida can seem deterring.

To suggest the utility of this approach for public administration counter-attackers, let's begin (but not complete) to deconstruct a list of ten ways in which Derrida considers the world to be out of joint, which will include the ruthless economic war between countries. Let's try a wind-up and a throw, the first of many such throws that are required. Derrida might deconstruct Shakespeare's Hamlet's dead father's comment (as a wind-up), and then what Derrida does say (the pitch) about our own economic (and other) world being out of joint

First, the wind-up: Deconstruction (for Derrida, 1992, 1994) is justice. The deconstruction in this case involves worrying about a comment by Hamlet's father's ghost that "the time is out of joint." Possible texts, subtexts, and subsubtexts can be examined. Time could refer to temporality, or history, or the world (today), for example. To the extent that Hamlet's father's comments are related to Derrida's listing of the ten contemporary plagues, it turns out that the ghost need not be read as talking about something being rotten in pre-1605 Denmark but also about something being rotten in the twenty-first-century world. Derrida earlier mused that being out of joint could signify what disturbs the order of things, what calls for the law (or public policy or even public administration) to be off its hinges. Hamlet's problem is that he is the ghost's heir, and Derrida points out that Hamlet rightly (in Derrida's view, but not necessarily ours) complains that he was born to set it right in the form of vengeance, sanction, and balance—just as we are the heirs of Wilson and many generations. Hamlet himself, Derrida notes, is out of joint because of his mission (an imported ethical imperative?) to right wrongs.

Derrida considered that all texts should be deconstructed (see Culler, 1983). Curiously, perhaps, and as a beginning for another example, the Shakespearean text that serves as the epigraph to this article can be readily deconstructed. "Cry 'Havoc!' " could be read with its ordinary meaning or (especially in those days) as giving the military permission to pillage and cause chaos. "Dogs of war" could be read as referring to mere dogs, or to fierce soldiers, or (as in the prologue to *Henry V*, l. 7) to the hounds "famine, sword and fire."

Second, the pitch: the ten ways in which Derrida (1994, pp. 100–101) describes the world as being out of joint are as follows:

- Unemployment, and underemployment
- Massive exclusion of homeless citizens from participation in the democratic life of states
- Ruthless economic war between countries
- Inability to master contradictions in the concepts, norms, and reality of the free market
- Aggravation of the foreign debt
- The arms industry and trade
- The spread of nuclear weapons, now uncontrollable
- Interethnic wars
- The growing power of phantom states like the mafia
- The present state of international law, where the UN Charter depends on an historical culture (e.g., sovereignty) and there is dominance by certain states

Shouldn't more macro public administration theorists attempt deconstructing—or even "thinking as play"—with the wind-up and the pitch? As we could play with this list, the connection between the wind-up and the pitch seems loose, and the list appears *ad hoc* and uneven. Perhaps this is because the list focuses on outcome situations, rather than (in the manner of Michel Foucault's characterization of anti-fascism) on individual behavior. Could the macro public administration theorist add to—or subtract from—the list. For example, items that occur to me as excluded from such a list of plagues is the exploitation of women, the oppression of the poor, the ecological destruction of nonrenewable resources, the emphasis on being employed, drug addiction, escalating population level, species extinction, and so on. But I agree that Derrida does say that he could add to his list, and that there is an obvious subtextual "message" in the choice of the "religious" number ten for a list of plagues.

## CLAIM 3: PUBLIC ADMINISTRATION SHOULD COUNTER-ATTACK AMERICAN BUSINESS MODEL RHETORIC

Public administration should pay greater attention to the American business model's rhetoric. Is the American business model truly a guide to the good life, and is it supported by philosophical and ideological claims? No and yes! Attention already has been paid to rhetoric within economic theorizing (e.g., see Farmer, 2005; McClosky, 2002).

The warring American business model narrative should be recognized as involving not only myths but also intertwined subtexts and allied texts—academic and unacademic, written and behavioral. Examples of such American business model allies include the ideological cover given to anti-government (or big government) by the economics of market fundamentalism, and by such aggressive business-oriented rhetoric as is embodied in (say) objectivist philosophy. Other examples of allies are some private corporations, rich persons, business schools, think (and nonthink) tanks. Some such corporations and people contribute to mammoth-scale lobbying that purchases and occupies much of the territory of government, governmental policy and politics (e.g., see Hacker & Pierson, 2010). Public administration should be willing to study and engage enough of its economic, ideological and rhetorical contexts, and public administration should develop its own allies in such counter-measures.

Ayn Rand's objectivism has the consequence of "branding" or selling (falsely, in fact) the American business model as something that reflects "deep" or "substantial" philosophy. A war-conscious public administration theorist should see the utility in counter-attacking such a claim. Rand's objectivist philosophy, despite its fragility in analytical terms, is robust in stimulating emotional support. Such cheerleading—male and female—is "valuable," as it helps to cover up the cognitive weaknesses in the American business model. At the same time, the popularity of the American business model, in return, provides rhetorical support to Rand's objectivism. Rand's philosophy is explained in a number of her nonfiction publications, including the following. For her objectivism as a system of philosophy, see Rand's "This Is John Galt Speaking" (Rand, 1961a, pp. 142–242.) Her ethics is explained in her *The Virtue of Selfishness: A New Concept of Egoism* (Rand, 1964). And her theory of knowledge is found in *Introduction to Objectivist Epistemology*. Rand's philosophy is also explained by groups like the Ayn Rand Institute (ARI; https://www.aynrand.org) in Irvine, California, and by the Ayn Rand Society within the American Philosophical Association (http://www.aynrandsociety.org). Both her ideas and her life are included in movies, e-form, books, and more. Rand's philosophy—which underlies her cheerleading of the American business model—is indeed explained and implied (as indicated earlier) in the speeches of Howard Roark (the star of the novel *The Fountainhead*) and John Galt (the hero of the novel *Atlas Shrugged*).

Rand summarizes her philosophy of objectivism in terms not only of ethics but also of metaphysics, epistemology, and politics. It is *self-interest* for ethics. It is *objective reality* for metaphysics, *reason* for epistemology, and *capitalism* for politics. Rand gave this summary in 1962, standing on one leg (as requested by a questioner at a sales conference at Random House). The simple translation that Rand added is not helpful in terms of philosophical substance and of rationality, but it may have utility for some in terms of rhetoric. For objective reality, "Nature, to be commanded, must be obeyed," or "Wishing won't make it so"; for epistemology, "You can't eat your cake and have it, too"; for ethics, "man is an end in himself"; and for politics, "Give me liberty or give me death" (http://aynrandlexicon.com/ayn-rand-ideas/introducing-objectivism.html, retrieved March 1, 2013).

Turn to Rand's ethics—and her ethical egoism, which claims that the highest moral purpose of an individual's life is the pursuit of that individual's own rational self-interest and own happiness, and that opposes altruism. Rand's ethics should be seen in the context of the rest of her philosophy, but for space reasons, discussion of the non-ethics part of her philosophy is abbreviated. For her, people are heroic beings with their personal happiness as the moral purpose of their lives and with productive achievement as their noblest activity. For her, the ideal political and social system is market fundamentalism. Neither Howard Roark nor John Galt would do anything but primarily for himself. So Roark of *The Fountainhead* explains that the "first right on earth is the right of the ego .... His moral law is never to place his prime goal within the persons of others. His moral obligation is to do what he wishes" (Rand, 1961b, p. 96). The Good Samaritan was misguided unless that good deed was done primarily for himself. In *The Virtue of Selfishness* (1964, p. vii), Rand explains that she interprets the selfishness that she advocates not as evil but as "concern with one's own interests." By contrast, she characterizes altruism as "an unspeakable evil" (Rand, 1961b, p. 111). Every person must exist for his own sake, and "objectivist morality would consider [helping others] enormously immoral" (Rand, 1961b, p. 119).

Asher claims that Rand's view of the human condition is unrealistic. He objects that Rand's ethical doctrine cannot claim objective certainty, and that its fatal flaw is reliance on "psychological egoism, a naïve and weak viewpoint" (Asher, 2011, chap. 1). In making this objection, it is reasonable for Asher to claim that the burden of proof rests with Rand if she wants to assert her doctrine and to draw large consequences from it. He is right that the doctrine of rational self-interest is not a rational certainty, and that it is false to suggest that rational logic proves her ethical position to be the *only possible* ethical stance.

Asher advances three overlapping arguments. The first (Asher, 2011, chap. 2) stresses that the "self" always involves our group—as well as our individual—identity. This is related to the view that each person's actions and thoughts are socially shaped. It raises the claim that, in my view, human individuals do not create themselves independent of their social construction—in independence of what Cornelius Castoriadis (1997, p. 9) calls our magma. (Castoriadis describes the institution of each society's magma of social imaginary signification as shaping what can be constituted in that society. As he indicates, each "society, like each living being or species, establishes, creates its own world, within which, of course, it includes itself.") Asher's second counter-argument is what he characterizes as an empirical case against egoism, and this is that a "purely individual-driven system cannot reproduce the complex patterns of actual life" (Asher, 2011, chap. 3). His third is, as he puts it, that the possibility of our conscious sense of self is "not bound to our physical sense of self at all, and that our selves are composite identities that include even the physical presences of our loved ones" (Asher, 2011, chap. 4).

There is much in Rand's metaphysics that is, at least, not cogent. Rand's metaphysics makes claims about existence, consciousness, and identity. Her opening axiom is that existence exists, and she considers that this demonstrates the primacy of existence (the primacy of reality). Existence exists, and is the perceptual base of all knowledge, for example; existence has primacy over consciousness, which must conform to existence. For her, this demonstrates (although it is not clear why it should) that the universe is independent of consciousness (of any consciousness); the result is that she asserts the perceptual basis of all knowledge. Existence exists, and she asserts that this entails that things are what they are, and that such things possess a specific nature—a specific identity.

Let us illustrate the depth difficulty in this metaphysics. The natures of existence and reality have been discussed long and deeply in philosophy, and Rand does not seriously engage these philosophers. Yet it is the case, and reflected in such long and deep discussion, that for "the most part, philosophers have not known how they should use 'existence' or 'being' or 'reality' when confronted by problems concerning, for example the relation between possibility and actuality" (Buchler, 1966, p. 4). In other words, it requires cogent argument to be convincing that all things real must be existent. On the same lines, there has also been disagreement about whether the real refers to "what exists" or "what basically exists" (Hamlyn, 1984)—the furniture, or the ultimate furniture, of the universe. Rand avoids such complexity.

Rand's epistemology (summarized as reason) also advances claims that are difficult to maintain, such as that about rationality. (Others may wish to focus on the dubious claim that all knowledge is ultimately based on sense perception.) Rand's objectivist philosophy celebrates what she considers rationality. So she has Galt exclaim that "happiness is possible only to a rational man, the man who desires nothing but rational goals, seeks nothing but rational values, his joy is nothing but rational actions" (Rand, 1961b, pp. 162–163). She would not accept the view from psychoanalysis or from neuroscience that our decisions, actions, and behaviors result, at least in part, from the unconscious. Nor would she accept the view from neuroscience, for instance, that individuals are primarily not rational people with emotions; they are primarily emotional people, with rationality. Nor would she accept the claim from neuroscience that "the conscious mind is not at the center of the action in the brain; instead it is far out on a distant edge..." (Eagleman, 2011, p. 9). She accepts the emphasis in mainstream economic theory that makes the assumption of economic man—that he is utterly self-interested and utterly rational.

Ayn Rand explains (strangely) that the only philosophers to have identified important philosophical truths are "Aristotle, Aquinas, and Ayn Rand" (Mayhew, 2005, pp. 148–149). Sorry, Plato, Kant, Heidegger, et al.; return to your caves!

## CLAIM 4: PUBLIC ADMINISTRATION SHOULD CONTRIBUTE TO ECONOMIC LITERATURE

Public administration should join in contributing to the co-shaping of economic literature, recalling that economics is a fundamental support for the American business model. Because economics is more straightforward than it seems, public administration thinkers should venture outside their disciplinary boxes and attempt to contribute to co-shaping economics itself. Distinguished economists like Thomas Piketty and Ha-Joon Chang (mentioned earlier) have recommended that noneconomists should participate in doing economics. In his monumental *Capital in the Twenty-first Century,* for instance, Piketty claims, "Indeed the distribution of wealth is too important an issue to be left to economists, sociologists, historians, and philosophers. It is of interest to everyone, and that is a good thing" (Piketty, 2014, p. 2). In his *Economics: The User's Guide,* Chang argues for noneconomists to become what he calls economic citizens. He claims that "You should be willing to challenge professional economists.... The economy is too important to be left to the professional economist alone. I would go one step further and say that the willingness to challenge professional economists—and other experts—should be a foundation of democracy" (Chang, 2014, pp. 331–332). He adds that economics is "easier than you think ... [and] far more accessible than many economists would have you believe" (2014, pp. 333–334). That public administration thinkers should become involved in economic theorizing has also been discussed in the public administration theory community. For instance, notice the recommendation that "non-economists should contribute more to the supply of economic theory, and especially to the foundations of economic theorizing.... Non-economists should be more than mere buyers of economic theory.... Macro public administration theorists ... should turn even more to analyze whether economic theory is right about governmentality" (Farmer, 2014, p. 99).

Let us turn to the contention that the effects of economics and of the American business model extend significantly not only to the economic but also to the noneconomic sphere and to growing commercialization. That the American business model and the economic extend beyond their spheres, consider two written testimonies. One is from Michael Sandell (2012), who wrote *What Money Can't Buy: The Moral Limits of Markets,* and the other is Stephen (2012), who wrote *How Economics Shapes Science.* For the false claim that economics settles almost everything, see *Freakonomics: The Hidden Side of Everything* (Levitt & Dubner, 2005). Against such claims, Sandell points to the limits of markets, giving examples. To repeat only four examples: Is it moral for lobbyists to pay homeless people $20 to stand in line for them overnight at Capitol Hill? Is it moral to encourage reading in underachieving Dallas schools by paying children $2 per book? Is it moral to pay announcers for uttering branding slogans at ball games when a batter hits a run? Should we allow corporations to pay for the right to pollute?

For the claim that commercialization is growing, consider the universities. Stephan describes universities as having embraced the "shopping mall model," and she documents how scientific research is influenced. She comments

> In many ways universities in the United States behave as though they are high-end shopping malls. They are in the business of building state-of-the-art facilities and a reputation that attracts good students, good faculty, and resources. They turn around and lease the facilities to faculty in the form of indirect costs on grants and the buyout of salary. In many instances, faculty "pay" for the opportunity of working at the universities, receiving no guarantee of income if they fail to bring in a grant. (Stephen, 2012, pp. 228–229)

For an example of a direct influence of the American business model on scientific results, note Stephan's discussion as to why it is disadvantageous for research to reject a central hypothesis—because it reduces the chance of follow-up monies. As Stephan puts it, "The system discourages faculty from pursuing research with uncertain outcomes. Lack of success can mean that one's next grant may not be funded" (Stephen, 2012, p. 229). Other impacts are also noted, such as that "universities have found ways to minimize economic risk. They have hired faculty in non-tenure track positions and have increased the proportion of adjuncts they hire" (Stephen, 2012, p. 229). Concluded a university president about his own university, in a message entitled *Unleashing the Innovation Ecosystem,* "we have the potential for much more—particularly in shaping an environment right here ... that will unleash our potential to become a global hotbed for entrepreneurship, innovation, and commercialization" (Sands, 2014, p. 2).

## CLAIM 5: ALL PUBLIC ADMINISTRATION STUDENTS SHOULD STUDY ECONOMICS ADEQUATELY

All public administration academic programs should require their students to study not only the relative advantages of regulating an economy but also economics itself, encouraging students to recognize that the American business model is less than fully validated by economic science. The study of the relative advantages of regulating an economy should focus primarily on macro considerations. For example, there is a macro approach on the deregulation side offered by Rand's and other writings. There is a macro approach, significant on the regulation side, offered in such publications as *Consumed: How Markets Corrupt Children, Infantilize Adults, and*

*Swallow Citizens Whole* (Barber, 2007). And there is more macro literature, such as *The Big Rip-Off: How Business and Big Government Steal Your Money* (Carney, 2006).

Because the appeal of the American business model is considered fully "validated" by economic science, public administration academic programs (as some do) should require their students to study economics and encourage them to recognize that the American business model is less than so validated. For a first issue, the market fundamentalism in the American business model is not "the" conclusion of the discipline of economics. That is, it is not the conclusion of the entire discipline of economics. This is mentioned because it is often assumed that the American business model represents (as it were) "economics speaking." For a second issue, there is a substantial literature holding that economics is not a science. Attempts to brand the American business model as validated by economic science should be resisted and counter-attacked.

For the first issue, the American business model's market fundamentalism is not validated by the conclusions of the whole field of economics. It is true that the American business model is consistent with an economic dialect that embraces neoliberalism, the Hayekian, the Chicago school of market fundamentalism—what has been termed the freshwater school of economics; however, the saltwater dialect is a different matter. The saltwater reference is to economists affiliated with university locations without a freshwater lake, like Lake Michigan. Such market fundamentalism is in the sense of the free market analyzed by Friedrich von Hayek (1944). It was indicated above that such a spontaneous and self-organizing market is seen as the best device for allocating resources. Such fundamentalism is not at all the principal, or the only, approach of economic theorists.

The neoclassical grouping (including freshwater and saltwater) is the largest school in economics, and it is divided on policy recommendations relating to the role of government and to the free market. See the listing by Chang (2014, pp. 80–122) of nine schools of economics—classical, neoclassical, Marxist, developmentalist, Austrian, Schumpeterian (and neo-Schumpeterian), Keynesian, institutionalist, and behaviorist; he could have added others, neuroeconomics, for example. He describes only three as recommending such policies as the free market—the classical, the Austrian, and part of the neoclassical. Within the neoclassical divided grouping, there are indeed conflicting views on the so-called free market.

For support of a contrary neoclassical economic dialect, consult the best-known economics textbook during the past sixty-seven years, written by Nobel Prize winner Paul A. Samuelson and William B. Nordhaus, *Economics* (2010 and earlier in 2005, 2001, 1998, 1995, 1992, 1989, 1985, 1980, 1976, 1973, 1970, 1967, 1964, 1963, 1958, 1955, 1953, and 1948). See their chart "Government Can Remedy the Shortcomings of the Market" (Samuelson & Nordhaus, 2010, p. 40) and the chapter "The Modern Mixed Economy" (2010, pp. 25–44). See the Centrist Proclamation in the nineteenth edition (2010, pp. xvi–xvii). Samuelson and Nordhaus assert that their textbook "proclaims the value of the mixed economy—an economy that combines the tough discipline of the market with fair-minded governmental oversights." Referring to the center as positioned between the left of socialism and the right of market fundamentalism, Samuelson and Nordhaus (2010, p. xvi) assert that "the follies of the left and the right both mandate centrism."

For the second issue about the description of economics as endorsing the American business model with the authority of economics being a science, public administration students should also take on the large literature that reflects on the idea that economics is not a science—including, for example, titles like *The World in the Model* (Morgan, 2012) and *The Puzzle of*

*Modern Economics: Science or Ideology?* (Backhouse, 2012). They may include reflection on the literature (e.g., Chang, 2014; Heap, 1999; Hoover, 2003) that mathematics does not a science make. They may reflect on, say, the comment by Jonathan Schlefer in his *Assumptions Economists Make* (Schlefer, 2012, p. 24) that "economists' insistence that their discipline is like physics sounds a little nervous. Did you ever hear a physicist boast to the world that physics is like economics?" They may also reflect on the comment by the great economist Joseph Schumpeter (1954, p. 10) that

> the frontiers of the individual sciences... are incessantly shifting.... There is no point in trying to define them either by subject or by method. This applies particularly to economics, which is not a science in the sense in which acoustics is one, but rather an aggregation of ill-coordinated and overlapping fields of research in the same sense as is medicine.

Recall that at one point, public administration itself was often called "administrative science."

## CONCLUSION

This article makes five claims for public administration theorists, associations, academic programs, high-level practitioners, and others. The first and major claim is that the American business model is more than a mere model. It is a war-fighting strategy, a battle plan. This was illustrated in the 1971 Powell memorandum, written for the U.S. Chamber of Commerce by a man soon to be appointed an associate justice of the Supreme Court. Should not public administration learn from the fighting strategy of the Powell memorandum? The second claim is that public administration should counter-attack the kingdom of myth, including the use of hermeneutics and deconstruction. The third claim is that public administration should counter-attack the American business model's rhetoric. The fourth claim is that public administration should counter-attack by seeking to contribute to the economic literature. On the co-shaping of economics, it is noted that distinguished professional economists, like Thomas Piketty (2014) and Chang (2014), have encouraged noneconomists to participate in developing economics—and not to leave economic science to the professional economists. The fifth claim is that all public administration academic programs should counter-attack by requiring their students to study not only the relative advantages of regulating an economy but also economics itself, encouraging students to recognize that the American business model is less than fully validated by economic science.

Public administration needs to fight back against the American business model. Each of Justice Powell's twenty-five recommendations should be adjusted in defense of government and directed against the warring anti-government forces.

> No thoughtful person can question that American public administration and governmental system is under broad attack.... It [is] crystal clear that the foundations of our free society are under wide-ranging and powerful attack... by misguided individuals parroting one another. (Powell, 1971, p. 2)

To continue to revise Powell's words, "Why not fight back?" Indeed, sometimes theorists have to do more than merely theorize; sometimes they have to let slip the dogs of war.

# REFERENCES

Asher, L. (2011). *Why Ayn Rand is wrong and why it matters*. New York: Literary Kicks.
Backhouse, R. E. (2012). *The puzzle of modern economics: Science or ideology?* New York: Cambridge University Press.
Barber, B. (2007). *Consumed: How markets corrupt children, infantilize adults, and swallow citizens whole*. New York: W.W. Norton.
Buchler, J. (1966). *Metaphysics of natural complexes*. New York: Columbia University Press.
Carney, T. (2006). *The big rip-off: How big business and big government steal your money*. Hoboken, NJ: John Wiley & Sons.
Castoriadis, C. (1997). *World in fragments: Writings on politics, society, psychoanalysis and the imagination*. Stanford, CA: Stanford University Press.
Chang, H.-J. (2010). *23 things they don't tell you about capitalism*. New York: Bloomsbury Press.
Chang, H.-J. (2014). *Economics: A user's guide*. New York: Bloomsbury Press.
Culler, J. (1983). *On deconstruction: Theory and criticism after structuralism*. London, UK: Routledge.
Derrida, J. (1992). Force of law: The "mystical foundation of authority." In D. Cornell, M. Rosenfeld, & D. G. Carlson (Eds.), *Deconstruction and the possibility of justice* (pp. 3–67). New York: Routledge.
Derrida, J. (1994). *Specters of Marx: The state of debt, the work of mourning and the new International*. (P. Kamuf, Trans.). New York: Routledge.
Eagleman, D. (2011). *Incognito: The secret lives of the brain*. New York: Vintage.
Farmer, D. (2014). Economic theory and the big economy. *Public Administration Quarterly, 38*(1), 97–124.
Farmer, D. J. (2005). *To kill the king: Post-traditional governance and bureaucracy*. Armonk, NY: M.E. Sharpe.
Farmer, D. J. (2010). *Public administration in perspective: Theory and practice through multiple lenses*. New York: Routledge.
Friedman, M. (1994). Introduction to the fiftieth anniversary edition. In F. A. Hayek (Ed.), *The road to serfdom* (pp. ix–xx). Chicago, IL: University of Chicago Press.
Hacker, J. S., & Pierson, P. (2010). *Winner-take-all politics: How Washington made the rich richer—and turned its back on the middle class*. New York: Simon & Schuster.
Hamlyn, D. (1984). *Metaphysics*. Cambridge, UK: Cambridge University Press.
Hayek, F. (1944). *The road to serfdom*. Chicago, IL: University of Chicago Press.
Heap, S. (1999). *Rationality in economics*. London: Basil Blackwell.
Hoover, K. (2003). *Economics as ideology: Keynes, Laski, Hayek, and the creation of contemporary politics*. New York: Rowman & Littlefield.
Hughes, R. (2004). *Myths America lives by*. Urbana & Chicago, IL: University of Illinois Press.
Kay, J. (2003). *The truth about markets*. New York: Penguin.
Kay, J. (2010). *Obliquity: Why our goals are best achieved indirectly*. New York: Penguin.
Levitt, S., & Dubner, S. (2005). *Freakonomics: A rogue economist explores the hidden side of everything*. New York: Harper Collins.
Mayhew, R. (2005). *Ayn Rand answers: The best of her Q and A*. New York: Penguin.
McClosky, D. (2002). *The secret sins of economics*. Chicago, IL: Prickly Paradigm.
Miller, H. (2012). A narrative border crossing: How market fundamentalism frames state and civil society. Keynote presentation at the 25th annual meeting of the Public Administration Theory Network, City of San Padre Island, TX.
Miller, J. H. (1987). *The ethics of reading: Kant, de Man, Eliot, Trollope, James and Benjamin*. New York: Columbia University Press.
Morgan, M. S. (2012). *The world in the model: How economists work and think*. New York: Cambridge University Press.
Piketty, T. (2014). *Capital in the twenty-first century*. Cambridge, MA: Harvard University Press.
Powell, L. F. (1971). *Powell memorandum*. Retrieved July 1, 2014, from http://reclaimdemocracy.org/powell_memo_lewis
Rand, A. (1957). *Atlas shrugged*. New York: Dutton.
Rand, A. (1961a). *For the new intellectual*. New York: Random House.
Rand, A. (1961b). *The fountainhead (1961)*. London: Signet.
Rand, A. (1964). *The virtue of selfishness: A new concept of egoism*. New York: Signet.

Samuelson, P. A., & Nordhaus, W. D. (2010). *Economics* (19th ed.). New York: McGraw Hill.
Sandell, M. (2012). *What money can't buy: The moral limits of markets*. New York: Farrar, Straus and Giroux.
Sands, T. (2014, fall). Unleashing the innovation ecosystem. *Virginia Tech Magazine, 37*(1), 2. http://www.vtmag.vt.edu/fall14/vtmag-fall14.pdf
Schlefer, J. (2012). *The assumptions economists make*. Cambridge, MA: Harvard University Press.
Schumpeter, J. (1954). *History of economic analysis*. Oxford, UK: Oxford University Press.
Stephen, P. (2012). *How economics shapes science*. Cambridge, MA: Harvard University Press.
Yellen, J. (2014). Perspectives on inequality and opportunity from the survey of consumer studies. Paper presented at the Conference on Economic Opportunity and Inequality, Federal Reserve Bank, Boston, MA. http://www.federalreserve.gov/newsevents/speech/yellen20141017a.htm

# Public Administration in a World of Economics

## David John Farmer

> Every successful economy—every successful society—involves both government and markets. There needs to be a balanced role.
>
> —Joseph Stiglitz, *Freefall: America, Free Markets, and The Sinking of the World Economy*

What should economics and public administration do in order to achieve optimal positions in relation to one another and to what many call *the* real world? To the extent that economics is the "queen of the social sciences" and to the extent that it is productive (which it is), there is pressure to maintain the status quo and to ignore questions about its connection with the real world. To the extent that it does not pursue the macro and to the extent that it is applied, public administration does not have any pressure to make effective enough contact with the real world. In relation to the real world, I recognize that it is simplistic to conceptualize a single real world, a single real society (especially without recognizing its unconscious and its subconscious), and a single real set of institutions. Obtaining benefits and blocking negatives (for larger problems) requires not only acknowledging diversity in the real but also the complexity of even describing the idea of the real—or the really real.

In response to the question about what economics should do to achieve such an optimal relationship, first note that economics is not overanxious to have a relationship with public administration. Since Lionel Robbins's 1932 redefinition of economics as applying to any allocation of scarce resources to competing ends (no longer limiting it to Marshall's definition associating economics with the ordinary business of life and with the attainment and use of the material requisites of well-being), Economics has preferred the biggest and best extradisciplinary fish. For instance, it has been interested in political science (more varied, bigger questions) more than public administration. In response to the question about what public administration should do to achieve an optimal position, first also recognize that it is not overanxious for a relationship with economics.

Let's play. Let's assume that the two disciplines want a closer working relationship. What can we say? This play is reported in two parts in the form that economists usually employ. The first concerns supply, making three suggestions about the semisatisfactory nature of economics. The second concerns demand, also making three suggestions; because part of the problem of an unsatisfactory relationship between public administration and economics is the semisatisfactory nature of public administration.

## SUPPLY

First, any social science (like economics—and also public administration) could be in a more optimal position if it could increase its imaginative, and reduce its ideological, character. This goes beyond the question of Queen Elizabeth II and the response of the British Academy, discussed below. Second, economic thinking (if it were less chained within mainstream economics and standard business practice) could contribute even more to any other discipline. In this connection, we can notice the writing of George Soros, Paul Krugman, and John Maynard Keynes. Third, economics, as it is, is of some help in increasing understanding in public administration and in other social sciences, for example, with public choice economics. Yet it could be better.

### *First Suggestion*

The queen asked about economics, about the queen of the social sciences. On November 5, 2008, Queen Elizabeth II visited the London School of Economics and Political Science. She asked about economic thinking—and also the forecasting limitations. There have been different accounts of the question and of the response. In one account of the question, the queen asked "Why did nobody notice that the credit crunch was on its way?" In another account, the question was "The global financial crisis: Why didn't anybody notice?"

The first respondent was Luis Garicano, who was from two institutions. He was a professor of economics and strategy at the University of Chicago's Graduate School of Business. He was concurrently professor in the department of management (also director of research in the Center for Economic Performance) at the London School of Economics. This business management specialist, expert on the economics of organizations, explained relevant charts to the queen.

The second respondents constituted a set of 35 people from the British Academy, an institution that honors academics. They held a forum on June 16, 2009, and the forum consisted of "a range of experts from business, the City, its regulators, academia, and government" (Besley & Hennessey, 2009, p. 1). They agreed that many people forecast the global financial crisis, and they do give an account of preparatory (or facilitative) institutional adjustments—

factors like those about the banks' activities, the feel-good factor, etc.

The British Academy Forum's letter does not mention the ideological character of economics. Let me mention two features. First, there is a contrast between the "clean" world of economic thinking (add the adjectives "order" and "beauty," and we have what Sigmund Freud would describe as the "criteria of civilization") and the messy world of business practice. Related to this are the standards of learning (SOLs) designed for K–12 schools in the United States. The SOLs do start in kindergarten (a plus for economics), and they ignore all the unclean world—all the painful aspects in economics and business, for example, unemployment, inflation. Second, market fundamentalists (to whom we will return) are among those who believe in the efficiency of business (and more) as opposed to the inefficiency of government. An example of the ideological in economics is Prime Minister Margaret Thatcher's comment, "Economics are the method, but the object is to change the soul" (see Yergin & Stanislaw, 1999, p. 75).

Now we come to the central point from the British Academy's letter. It is almost speaking about *thinking as play* (Farmer, 2005, pp. 3–71): It is about creative imagination. The letter states, "So in summary, Your Majesty, the failure to foresee the timing, extent and severity of the crisis and to head it off, while it had many causes, was principally a failure of the collective imagination of many bright people, both in this country (Britain) and internationally, to understand the risks to the system as a whole" (Besley & Hennessey, 2009, p. 4). I don't suppose imagination is all that thinkers (or the many bright people) need. As a mere beginning, I do suppose that an emphasis on extraordinary creative imagination (after Andreason, 2005) is needed—in a discipline like economics (or public administration).

## *Second Suggestion*

Economic thinking could contribute more to economic and other understanding if the thinking were not confined within mainstream parameters. An example of such a mainstream parameter is rational man, assuming that all participants in an economic transaction are entirely self-interested and entirely rational. Rationality in this context differs from the everyday meaning that most people recognize. It refers to the internal consistency, or coherence, of a person's preferences; for example, Hardy is incoherent if he wants to lose weight and also wants to eat two pounds of ice cream three times per day. There are alternative economics. There is behavioral economics (including thinkers who study neuroscience), for example, and it does not assume rational man. There is the Austrian school (see Kirzner, 1998). For more alternative economics, see *Why Economists Disagree: An Introduction to the Alternative Schools of Thought* (Prychitko, 1998).

Economic thinkers should seek to use a variety of perspectives. Such playing between this and that perspective can stimulate creative imagination in economics. It will help in reducing, perhaps even blocking, ideological content in economics. Mainstream economics should not be excluded as one of the perspectives, even if the thinker dislikes it, nor should the deductive and the mathematical. Economics is unlikely to deemphasize the deductive (deducing from the general to the particular). It is unlikely to divorce the mathematical, even if the mathematical is not as useful as current economic theorizing holds.

Here's an example of the multiperspective. George Soros's core idea is that "our understanding of the world in which we live is inherently imperfect because we are part of the world we seek to understand" (2008, p. 3). He explains that we do two things: We seek to understand the world (the cognitive function), and simultaneously we seek to change it to our advantage (the manipulative function). His view is that there is uncertainty in social events, and that is not the case in natural events. On the one hand, there is mainstream economics. On the other, there is Soros's framework. Rather than choosing only one perspective, the suggestion is that more economists should play with both perspectives.

Let's turn to three varieties of ideology and thinking well known in economics. They are a market requiring macro management, a market requiring government, and (mentioned above) market fundamentalism. Use of all three of the perspectives would have the benefits already mentioned; however, use of all three—or even two perspectives—might inflict discomfort. Paul Krugman points out that macroeconomics has divided into "two great factions: 'saltwater' economists (mainly in coastal U.S. universities), who have a more or less Keynesian vision of what recessions are all about; and 'freshwater' economists (mainly at inland schools), who consider that vision nonsense" (2009, p. 40).

John Maynard Keynes advocated in 1936 the necessity of macromarket management, for example, the desirability of governmental financial stimulation in time of recession. I should confess that I have always been an admirer of Keynes—my cat Maynard is named after him. As is well known, Keynes's *General Theory of Employment, Interest and Money* (snappy title) shows how changing the relationship of governmental expenditure and revenue affects the economy. Keynes also emphasizes uncertainty, which Robert Skidelsky (2009) discusses in terms of the financial markets. So does Paul Krugman, writing that "the belief in efficient financial markets blinded many if not most economists to the emergence of the biggest financial bubble in history" (2009, p. 41). Whether Keynesianism will return (I hope so, but tend to the pessimistic) in greater strength is an open question.

Turn to a market requiring governmental intervention. A market requiring regulation is not abnormal. Mainstream microeconomic analysis contains a powerful critique of business practice, indicating the value of intervention. It demonstrates that monopolies scoop up excess profits, for example. It is the same for monopsonists. The monopolist (and the monopsonist) take this excess profit because it is rational to do so. As far as I can see, breaking up monopolies has nothing to do with socialism. BTW, public administration has much, and should have much, to do with markets' requiring government.

Getting the optimal intervention for economics should be regarded as important, at both the macro- and microlevel. Here are two issues raised in books like Korten's (1995) *When Corporations Rule the World*; there are others in other areas, for example, factory and mine safety, pollution, child employment, ecological sustainability, and just distribution. First, in 1886,

> the Supreme Court ruled in *Santa Clara County v. South Pacific Railroad* that a private corporation is a natural person under the U.S. Constitution—although . . . the Constitution makes no mention of corporations—and is thereby entitled to the protections of the Bill of Rights, including the right to free speech and other constitutional protections extended to individuals. (Korten, 1995, p. 59)

Second, after the 1970s,

> Corporations began to create their own 'citizen' organizations with names and images that were (and are) carefully constructed to mask their corporate sponsorship and their true purpose. The National Wetlands Coalition, which features a logo of a duck flying blissfully over a swamp, was sponsored by oil and gas companies and real estate developers to fight for easing the restrictions on the conversion of wetlands into drilling sites and shopping malls. (p. 143)

There is the large number of powerful, wealthy, and secretly funded organizations. Consider the extent to which campaign contributions, huge and increasing, are marshaled into the various fights. These issues are not all macro; for example, see *Grand Theft Pentagon: Tales of Corruption and Profiteering in the War on Terror* (St. Clair, 2005).

Finally, let's turn to the dominant and third perspective on economics in the United States, and that is market fundamentalism—neoliberalism, or the Washington consensus that started in 1979. Market fundamentalism is the faith that, when markets are left alone, they will solve all economic problems. The fundamentalists believe that the market gives better information than individual humans can obtain for themselves. David Harvey believes that market fundamentalism (he calls it "neoliberalism") should be interpreted as a political project "to re-establish the condition of capital accumulation and to restore the power of economic elites" (2005, p. 19). He believes that it has not been effective as a utopian project "to realize a theoretical design for the reorganization of international capitalism" (p. 19). He sees the utopian project as "as system of legitimation and justification for whatever needed to be done" (p. 19) to achieve the political goal, aims like restoring the power of political elites. Some have argued that the dominance of market fundamentalism makes it difficult to achieve significant progress on problems like global climate change and good-quality public services.

### *Third Suggestion*

Economics, as it is, does shed some light on public administration and other social sciences. This is not surprising when you consider that the Nobel Memorial Prize in economic science was awarded to public choice economists like James McGill Buchanan (in 1986) and Elinor Ostrom (in 2009). Buchanan's contribution was the use of microtheory to studies of the political system, public administration, etc. Ostrom's contribution lay primarily in the analysis of economic governance, especially the commons. Yet could economics do better?

Public choice economics, as mentioned, applies economics to political science—and, to a much lesser extent, to public administration. The methodology of public choice is mainly mainstream—the decision making of "an egotistical, rational, utility maximizer," as Dennis Mueller (1989, p. 2) puts it.

Examples of models that do throw light on public administration are Kenneth Arrow's possibility theorem (1963) and William Niskansen's budget-maximizing bureaucrat (1971). Arrow's theorem (Arrow also received the Nobel Prize) has implications for citizen participation. It shows that it is impossible to guarantee that any voting system can be constructed without violating even the trivial set of rules that Arrow discusses. These rules are similar to the concept of "transitivity" (if A is preferred to B and B is preferred to C, then A is preferred to C). Niskanen describes the budget-maximizing bureaucrat as motivated by "salary, perquisites of office, public regulation, power, patronage, output of the bureau, ease of making changes, and ease of managing the bureau" (1971, p. 17)—all but the last two are positive functions of the total budget. Certainly, there are objections to these models (e. g., see Farmer, 1995, pp. 55 & 124–125). Some have spoken of a budget-boosting strategy, rather than budget maximizing. Niskansen himself has indicated (an important detail) that he thinks that his model should be seen as a special theory of bureaucratic behavior.

In 1973, Vincent Ostrom recommended for governmental administration a paradigm of democratic administration, as contrasted with Wilson's paradigm. There are eight propositions. A central idea in Ostrom's paradigm is opposition to "perfection of hierarchical ordering" and "a single center of power." He opposes "a professionally trained public service." As Ostrom explains, "The theory of public goods is the central organizing concept used by . . . political economists in conceptualizing the problem of collective action and of public administration. This contrasts with the theory of bureaucracy as the central concept in the traditional theory of public administration" (1973, p. 19).

Could public choice economics do better? What is more hopeful is, again, a multiperspectival economics. Consider the employment of a behavioral economist (attracted by a powerful subject like neuroscience) without forbidding mainstream economics. The difference is that kind of economist will inevitably analyze—for part of her or his time—decision making that is recognized as mainly emotional and that involves only limited thinking (e. g., recall the irrational implications of advertising addressed to infants). This contrasts with a mainstream decision maker who is imagined to be a 100 percent thinker. Such a multiperspectival economics is powerful because neuroscience—especially when mixed with the highly imaginative—is world-changing (Farmer, 2007, pp. 74–89).

## DEMAND

In response to the question about what public administration should do to facilitate an optimal relationship with economics and with the real world (recognizing that these two entities might be quite different), I make three suggestions. First, public administration should increase its disciplinary scope, for example, at a *minimum* by extending its attention to embracing more macro public administration (macro PA) and by considering various additional suboptions. Second, public administration should recognize the utility of using multidisciplinary sources. Third, macro PA should play with questions like whether a natural hierarchical order is natural.

### *First Suggestion*

To develop an optimal relationship to disciplines like economics and to the real world, public administration must increase its disciplinary scope. Public administration should not confuse itself with hotel administration. Rather, it should do more to develop macro PA.

Macro PA appeals to the distinction in economics between microeconomics and macroeconomics. Microeconomics, as is well known, is the study of the individual firm. Macroeconomics deals with the bigger picture—with inflation, recession, etc. Macro PA should develop its own content. It should deal with the high level and with the long term, at a *minimum*. Beyond this, macro PA has options.

Here are five additional options. For example, macro PA can go further beyond reflecting on the administrative experiences of the United States and include (I would) the experiences of other countries. For another example, perish the thought, but macro PA could include (I would not) the mathematical and the deductive—in the manner of economics. For another example, it could redelight (I would) in policy planning. For another example, macro PA could have been stronger (I was not) in its negative response to its outsourcing to the business world. For yet another example, macro PA could include more philosophy. William Sellars is helpful about the aims of philosophy. He speaks in terms of keeping his "eye on the whole." So was Plato, who spoke of the ruler in the ideal state as exhibiting wisdom. Wouldn't we have to go beyond the reflective specialist? Yet it would be adequate to match how Critias (an ancient Greek) became known as "an amateur among philosophers, and a philosopher among amateurs" (Waterfield, 2009, p. 127).

*Second Suggestion*

Beyond the first suggestion, how can macro PA upgrade what it produces? One method is to seek such upgrading through multiple lenses.

The method is to use epistemic pluralism to review and reflect, for example, on public administration theory and practice through multiple lenses. Epistemic refers to knowing; pluralism refers to a strategy of more than one way. So public administration theory and practice, micro and macro, can be examined from a variety of perspectives. For an example of the benefits of epistemic pluralism, see "Epistemic Pluralism and Neuroscience" (Farmer, 2008). For another example and a more developed account, see *Public Administration in Perspective* (Farmer, 2010). This textbook treats public administrative theory and practice by examining them from eleven robust perspectives—from a traditional, business, economic, political, critical theory, poststructural, psychoanalytic, neuroscience, feminist, ethical, and data perspective. The implications from the various perspectives are summarized into public administration elements or functions, for example, planning, management, and what lies underneath public administration. The summaries are then integrated.

The options are not limited to examining public administration theory and practice. The options include epistemic pluralism as it relates, for instance, to cooperation and competitiveness—features of public administration and economics. For the claim that all "societies have to find a balance between cooperative and competitive values," see Waterfield (2009, pp. 148–154). For the correct claim that (in ancient Athens) the question "which serves as a focus for enquiry into these matters was, simply, 'What is virtue?,' meaning 'What does it take to be an outstanding human being?'" see Waterfield (p. 149).

*Third Suggestion*

Surely, macro PA can upgrade its output through even more creative imagination. I have described two kinds of *thinking as play*. One is play with no purpose; the other is play with a purpose (like a gadfly). In neither case is *thinking as play* the same as playing around. I should leave the descriptions to other books (Farmer, 2005) and articles (Catlaw, 2009; Cunningham, 2009; Farmer, 2009; Kouzmin, Witt, & Thorne, 2009; McSwite, 2009; Schachter, 2009). For symposia on posttraditional governance, see note 1.

Let's turn to an example that could be included under either form of play—play with no, or play with a, purpose. Macro PA could usefully consider whether a natural hierarchical order is natural.

It is striking that the economic and public administration perspectives are both, basically, downward looking. In the microeconomic perspective, the hero is the CEO: A captain of commerce (or riches) could well have the impression that it is a captain's natural right to be superior in recognition and esteem to any subordinate. In the administrative perspective, the hero is the person who directs, coordinates, and controls. Sometimes this limited directionality is noticed. For example, it was noticed by Barbara Ehrenreich (2001). It was noticed by the performance, directed by Angela Eikenberry, of the play based on segments of a book at the 2008 PAT-Net conference (see note 2). Yet, normally, the limited directionality of public administration (and economics) theory and practice is considered to be normal, natural, and right.

The directionality of society was argued and discussed in ancient and subsequent times. From political philosophy (e.g., from Hobbes and Locke and many others), some might suppose that we have the directionality of institutions covered. Yet, in my opinion macro PA could well play with a chapter that pretends as if disadvantaged (and *othered*) people could be on top of the system—even if this shifts public administration and economics even farther apart. Imagine if the mail clerks ran the mail room; imagine if the unemployed ran the employment office; imagine if the patients ran the hospital; and so on. But this is too narrow; for one thing, it is not just a matter of the administrative or the political or the economic. Rather, the situation implicates *context*, including such factors as language, unconscious societal beliefs, history, the relationship between groups, the relationship between wealthy and poor, and the relationship between powerful and weak.

## EPILOGUE

Yes, "every successful economy—every successful society—involves both government and markets" (Stiglitz, 2010, p. 17). Public administration and economics should be involved with each other in an optimal way.

Let's note two things. First, in seeking optimal positions between public administration and economics and to what many call the real world, this article has used only one level of analysis. It has a chosen a level with only two main actors—public administration and economics. Unused is a less restricted model that, for example, could have focused on more main actors.

Second, recall Georg Hegel's claim as being applicable to some extent to public administration and economics as well as to philosophy. "The owl of Minerva spreads its wings only with the falling of the dusk" (Hegel, 1965, p. 12). By this claim, Hegel means "about giving instruction as to what the world ought to be, philosophy in any case always comes on the scene too late to give it. As the thought of the world, it appears only when actuality there is cut and dried after the process of formation has been completed" (p. 12). Until the falling of the dusk, we can imagine a similar context for public administration and economics, warts and all.

## NOTES

1. For symposia on posttraditional governance (not postmodern), see *International Journal on Public Administration 28,* 11 & 12 (2005) and also *Administrative Theory & Praxis 28,* 2 (2006). The first contains papers by Richard Box, Richard Cunningham, Susan Fitzpatrick, Louis Howe, Kathy McGinn, and Patricia Patterson. The second contains papers by O.C. McSwite, Thomas J. Catlaw, Catherine Horiuchi, Matthew T. Witt, Margaret Vickers, Kim Thorne, Alexander Kouzmin, and Swan Hua Xu.

2. For the 2008 PAT-Net performance of the Ehrenreich play, the actors were Tricia Patterson, Bob Zinke, Margaret Stout, Amanda Olejerski, Lisa Zanetti, Lisa Tabor, Mohamad Alkadry, Kathy Farley, Matthew Witt, and Tina Nabatchi; the director was Angela Eikenberry; and the producers were David John Farmer and Catherine Horiuchi.

## REFERENCES

Andreason, N. C. (2005). *The creating brain: The neuroscience of genius.* New York: Dana Press.

Arrow, K. J. (1963). *Social choice and individual values* (Rev. ed.). New York: John Wiley.

Besley, T., & Hennessey, P. (2009, June 16). *Letter to the queen.* London: British Academy.

Catlaw, T. J. (2009). Kill the king: Love your neighbor. *Public Administration Quarterly, 33,* 318–332.

Cunningham, R. (2009). Introduction. *Public Administration Quarterly, 33,* 300–302.

Ehrenreich, B. (2001). *Nickel and dimed: On (not) getting by in America.* New York: Henry Holt.

Farmer, D.J. (1995). *The language of public administration: Bureaucracy, modernity, and postmodernity.* Tuscaloosa: University of Alabama.

Farmer, D.J. (2005). *To kill the king: Post-traditional governance and bureaucracy.* Armonk, NY: M.E. Sharpe.

Farmer, D.J. (2007). Neuro-gov: Neuroscience as catalyst. In C. Senior &

M.J.R. Butler (Eds.), *The social cognitive neuroscience of organizations* (pp. 74–89). Boston: Annals of the New York Academy of Sciences.

Farmer, D.J. (2008). Epistemic pluralism and neuroscience. *Administrative Theory and Praxis, 30,* 285–295.

Farmer, D.J. (2009). Is the king dead? *Public Administration Quarterly, 33,* 373–396.

Farmer, D.J. (2010). *Public administration in perspective: Theory and practice through multiple lenses.* Armonk, NY: M.E. Sharpe.

Harvey, D. (2005). *A brief history of neoliberalism.* Oxford: Oxford University Press.

Hegel, G. (1965). *Philosophy of right.* Oxford: Clarendon Press.

Kirzner, I. M. (1998). The driving force of the market: The idea of competition in contemporary economic theory and in the Austrian theory of the market process. In D.L. Prychitko (Ed.), *Why economists disagree: An introduction to the alternative schools of thought* (pp. 27–52). Albany: State University of New York Press.

Korten, D. C. (1995). *When corporations rule of the world.* West Hartford, CT: Kumarian.

Kouzmin, A., Witt, M., & Thorne, K. (2009). "Killing the king" in public administration: From critical epistemology to fractured ontology and limited agency. *Public Administration Quarterly, 33,* 341–372.

Krugman, P. (2009, September 6). How did economists get it wrong? *New York Times Magazine,* 36–43.

McSwite, O.C. (2009). Socrates redux: A roundabout exegesis of David Farmer's *To Kill the King. Public Administration Quarterly, 33,* 303–317.

Mueller, D. (1989). *Public choice II.* New York: Cambridge University Press.

Niskanen, W. (1971). *Bureaucracy and representative government.* Chicago: Aldine-Atherton.

Ostrom, V. (1973). *The intellectual crises in American public administration.* Tuscaloosa: University of Alabama Press.

Prychitko, D.L. (Ed.). (1998). *Why economists disagree: An introduction to the alternative schools of thought.* Albany: State University of New York Press.

Schachter. H. (2009). Is art the weapon to kill the king? *Public Administration Quarterly, 33,* 333–340.

Skidelsky, R. (2009). *Keynes: The return of the master.* New York: Public Affairs.

Soros, G. (2008). *The new paradigm for financial markets: The credit crisis of 2008 and what it means.* New York: Public Affairs.

St. Clair, J. (2005). *Grand theft pentagon: Tales of corruption and profiteering in the war on corruption.* Monroe, ME: Common Courage Press.

Stiglitz, J.E. (2010). *Freefall: America, free markets, and the sinking of the world economy.* New York: W.W. Norton.

Waterfield, R. (2009). *Why Socrates died: Dispelling the myths.* New York: W.W. Norton.

Yergin, D., & Stanislaw, J. (1999). *Commanding heights: The battle between government and market place that is remaking the modern world.* New York: Simon & Schuster.

# Coping With The Super-Abstract: Teaching About the Implications of Postmodernism for Public Administration

## David John Farmer

### INTRODUCTION

Students of public administration require the ability to deal in the realm of the super-abstract, and we should build this expectation more firmly into our graduate programs. We should insure that our graduate programs:

1. provide for the study of postmodernism,
2. emphasize skills like critical thinking and creativity in all coursework, and
3. stress the importance of macro-public administration.

First, the study of postmodernism should supplement other super-abstract building blocks like philosophy of science/epistemology, ethics, and economics. Any satisfactory list of super-abstract topics should include postmodernism. Second, major goals throughout our curricula should include de-emphasizing mere bean-counting and emphasizing significant abstract critical thinking and creativity. Third, we should help students set their expectations to recognize the relative importance of macro public administration problems. This paper argues for these claims.

### WHY IS THE SUPER-ABSTRACT NECESSARY?

Public administration students should be concerned with the super-abstract because public administration theory is important, and because public administration theory is shallower without the super-abstract. A key is one's estimate of the relevance of public administration theory. If one considers public administration practice akin to a craft, there is little need to be concerned with public administration theory—or with the super-abstract.

Specifying the nature of the super-abstract makes its necessity clearer. The super-abstract consists of sets of abstractions (or theory) providing valuable information about a first-order set of abstractions (or first-order theory). Public administration theory itself is a first-order set of abstractions or generalizations about public administration practice. The super-abstract consists of abstractions providing critical information about public administration theory.

Some super-abstractions, as in philosophy of science, provide valuable information about how to understand and formulate public administration theory. Some super-abstractions, as from economic theory, are valuable in generating significant parts of content of public administration theory. The super-abstract is meta-theory in that it lies beyond the first-order theory. The term "super-abstract" is preferred because the second value—generating significant parts of the content—goes beyond an appropriate understanding of the idea of meta-theory. To characterize a physicist's statement as a metaphysical proposition would be to criticize it. To recognize that public administration theory includes public choice economics propositions, on the contrary, is to appreciate a strength.

Consider the value for public administration theory of super-abstract building blocks like philosophy of science/epistemology, ethics, and economics. In ignorance of philosophy of science, how could public administration theorists evaluate Herbert Simon's project (or a similar project) to create an administrative science? Without an understanding of epistemological issues, how could public administration theorists determine whether it is appropriate to focus on cause-and-effect investigations intended to develop a set of epistemologically privileged propositions about public administration—as contrasted with statements that interpret or critique the meaning of public administration phenomena? Philosophy of science and epistemology deal with the status of knowledge claims; and what is public administration theory but a set of knowledge claims? If values are critical for public administration, how can the study of values be confined within the limits of public administration? How can the content of administrative ethics be developed without understanding the insights of philosophical ethics? How can governmental policy-making in a capitalist economy be discussed without a basic knowledge of economic theory? Considering the primacy of economic efficiency in contemporary society and the intimate interrelationships of economy and government, how can the functioning of the governmental component be considered in isolation from the economic component of society—and vice-versa? Many more examples could be added. Further, the cumulative value of the examples for public administration theorizing is surely greater than the sum of the individual values.

It is a strength of public administration theorizing that over its history it has been porous, drawing on external intellectual resources. All the social disciplines like economics or political science should be as concerned to avoid the limitations of disciplinary insularity. The need for the super-abstract is especially acute for public administration, however. Public administration, as a disciplinary island, is narrowly equipped to discuss the workings of government in a complex society. Public administration theory is less powerful in its sphere, for example, than is economic theory in the economic sphere. As another example, the scope of public administration is narrower than sociology's. As government has grown in size and complexity, the need for porousness toward the super-abstract has become more pressing. It remains so, unless public administration is conceptualized, as noted earlier, as equivalent to a craft like plumbing.

## CURRICULAR BUILDING BLOCKS: A CASE FOR POSTMODERNISM

The curricular building blocks to prepare students to deal in the super-abstract should include the study of postmodernism. Postmodernism provides valuable information about how to understand and formulate public administration theory, and it generates significant content for public administration theory. These benefits are included in each of the following three reasons for including postmodernism in the curriculum:

1. Postmodernism presents significant practical implications for public administration theory and practice (Fox and Miller 1994).

2. The postmodern perspective presents students with new public administration insights. For example, American public administration can be better understood if it is seen as essentially a modernist project (Adams 1992).
3. Students can understand public administration theory and practice in a larger context. Let us examine each of these in more detail.

Postmodernism should complement a list of curricular building blocks like philosophy of science/epistemology, ethics, and economics. The argument of this section is that whatever the final composition of such a list, postmodern public administration should be included. It is legitimate to ask how much super-abstract or other coursework is enough. Here we encounter the conflicting urges to reach an ideal level of preparation (exemplified by Plato's ideal prescription for his philosopher-kings, who would graduate at about 50 years of age—before onset of their second childhoods) and to limit the curriculum within the practical bounds of reason. It is desirable that students should be at ease in economic theory. But how much economics is enough? In an ideal world, a good case can be made for macroeconomics, microeconomics, public choice economics, and money and banking. In a less than ideal world, all this might be collapsed, with loss, into public sector economics. In some form and with other super-abstract topics, postmodernism should be included.

Illustrating how the nature of public administration thinking is changed by the postmodern lens requires a sketch of the nature of postmodernism. Views differ about this nature (for another discussion, see Sarap 1993). In my view postmodernism is rooted in radical skepticism about the possibilities of human understanding and knowledge. It includes skepticism about the integrity and range of human reason itself (Hollinger 1994). To illustrate, recall that the Greeks tended to assume that the cosmos is intelligible, beautiful, and rational. Postmodernism would deny this assumption. It would deny that we can know that the rational pictures that we draw in our minds apply, as it were, to a world out there.

This skepticism has a number of practical implications for the nature of public administration thinking. Among the most dramatic is that scientific statements are not entitled to a privileged epistemological status, and that scientific statements do not have a greater claim on our assent than non-scientific statements (White 1992).

This represents a profound shift from the modernist view that science is a privileged form of discourse. Appreciating the plausibility and meaning of this shift requires some knowledge of twentieth-century philosophy of science; the shift runs counter to the mid-nineteenth century philosophy of science notions that students usually hold. The new status for scientific statements means that the boundary between scientific statements and poetic statements collapses (Gadamer 1989); neither has a stronger claim on our belief in public administration theory and practice. In the new circumstance, public administration theory and research no longer can be matters primarily of discovery. Public administration thinking becomes primarily a matter of construction, as in constructivist research and policy making.

Consider postmodernity, the changed and changing context in which we administer (Adams 1992, Smart 1992). The changed context accounts for some but not all of the changed content of postmodern public administration. A starting point for considering the new context is the skepticism, the human inability to know, that characterizes postmodernism. Postmodernists claim that societal developments have intensified this inability to know, and the intensification is so great that we have entered a new age. We have entered the age of postmodernity in the same way the ancients slipped into a new age (the medieval period) and the medievals slipped into a new age (modernity). An example of such a development is described as the implosion between image and reality, sometimes illustrated by the difficulty many people have in accepting as real events that they do not see on television. The volume of communication images has multiplied and images have virtual lives of their own (Baudrillard 1983).

The practical implications of this new context can be illustrated by considering the need to re-think our approaches toward public administration concepts and images. It is imperative in the new postmodern context to deconstruct the central role of concepts like efficiency. One such deconstruction of efficiency describes the culture-embedded character of concepts, and it explicates the privileged role of efficiency as a rational profit-maximizing and control mechanism in the decentralized and free-wheeling economic arrangements of modernist society (Farmer 1994). It points to the unimportance of concepts like efficiency in both pre-modern and post-modern societies. The problematics of public administration practice are changed in such a postmodern context. In a radically skeptical world, public administration has to cope where ideas without referents can be hyperreal. Images without referents, like lies, are part and parcel of the postmodern world; witness commercials, public information programs, politicial campaigns, policy making, memoranda-to-the-file. Analyzing within the postmodern context can constitute a lens for developing more relevant approaches.

A second reason why postmodernism should be included as a super-abstract curricular building block is that it offers fresh insights on public administration theory. As noted earlier, these insights can be increased if part of the postmodern coursework is devoted to exploring why American public administration can be better understood if seen as essentially a modernist project. A course on postmodern public administration should be grounded in history. It is useful, for example, to contrast the features of postmodernity with those of modernity. This can include following Jurgen Habermas and describing modernity in terms of the intentions and assumptions of the Enlightenment (Habermas 1983). Postmodernity is then described in terms of the negation of the assumptions of the Age of Reason. For some students, this approach has the additional advantage of helping to develop their historical time-line sense. Rather than understanding history as having started recently (e.g. in 1887, when Woodrow Wilson published his article, or in 1776), they are helped to see that the world has been active at least since 1492.

This contrast between modernity and postmodernity suggests additional avenues for the development of a public administration that trascends the limitations of a discipline confined entirely within modernist assumptions. For example, one possibilitiy is anti-administration (see Farmer 1995). Anti-administration includes a variety of notions with implications for the content of public administration theory. One such notion is non-hierarchical structuring, already explored in part in nonorthodox organization theory. A related notion is a kind of management that contrasts with the ideal in standard managerial job descriptions of a manager directing, coordinating and controlling all the activities and personnel of his or her unit.

A third reason for including postmodernism is that students can understand public administration theory and practice in a larger intellectual context. The larger context is not merely historical. Postmodernism can be studied effectively only if examined in a perspective that includes examining social theory and modern philosophy. For example, the perspective should include alternative views of the fate of modernity, such as those advanced by Jurgen Habermas and the critical theorists of the Frankfurt School. Habermas' view is that modernity is an incomplete project and he looks for emancipation as communicative language becomes primary over other forms of discourse (e.g. Habermas 1983, Habermas 1987). Postmodernism, studied in its proper context, is not a narrow enterprise.

Rejecting three common misunderstandings underscores the value of postmodernist study. First, it is not necessary for postmodernism to be completely true in order for it to be useful. It is possible to select among postmodern views. For example, Mark Poster holds the un-postmodern view that critical theory and postmodernism can be reconciled. He holds that the postmodern critique of reason is substantially correct and should be integrated into critical theory. He also maintains that the postmodern sense of the significance of language needs to be explored in the "context of an emerging social world" (Poster 1989). For another thing, even if all postmodern views were incorrect (a highly unlikely possibility), postmodernism could still function effectively as a perspective from which to study public administration issues. There is value in examining social phenomena through differing lenses and the postmodern lens is helpful in providing a corrective to students thoroughly rooted in modernist attitudes. Modeling the world in various hypothetical circumstances is common in powerful disciplines like economics, e.g., exploring pricing under perfect and imperfect competition. It is no less useful to explore the operations of bureaus under alternative hypothetical circumstances.

Second, it is false that postmodernism acts a conservative force in public administration. The neo-conservative label results from postmodernism's skepticism and its undermining of Frankfurt School analyses. It is true that the postmodern "rejection of grand narratives" and Derrida's "deconstruction of categories" frustrate some arguments for social change. This is a widely discussed topic (see Best and Kellner 1991), but a partial proof is in the pudding. Applied to public administration, postmodernism can provide a lens that disrupts established habits of thought. As the examples given above suggest, the result is not conservative.

Third, it is unwise to claim that postmodernism is merely a passing fad. It is true that thinkers often make convoluted, and even foolish, remarks in the name of the postmodern; some people are charlatans. That is a part of most human intellectual endeavors. Public administrationists, a group with a long experience of modernist fads like TQM, are open to claims of faddism. There is good reason not to dismiss postmodernism as a mere fad. For one thing, skepticism (in some forms) as a philosophical position is recurring and respectable, as David Hume and others have recognized (Selby-Bigge 1978, Rescher 1980).

The literature on postmodernism is immense (see Fox and Miller 1994), and other advantages of studying the literature could be added. It is useful for public administration students and theorists to explore the implications of the claim that the self is now decentered. It is useful to explore what it means to claim that there is no meaning outside the text. It is useful for students and theorists to explore the claim that our conceptual assumptions are context-governed. It is useful to explore the public administration implications of the possibility that the tenets of our modernist conceptual framework are false.

## SKILLS FOR COPING WITH THE SUPER-ABSTRACT

How can students cope more effectively with the super-abstract, like postmodernity? Throughout the curriculum, there should be an emphasis on abstract critical thinking and creativity. Neither is sufficient by itself: analytical without creative capability can narrow the perspective, while creative without analytical capability can result in "mush."

Studying public administration, especially super-abstract topics like postmodernity, requires abstract reasoning skills. It requires that Piaget calls formal-operational reasoning. This is the fourth and highest level of human congnitive development identified by Piaget, and it is the ability to think abstractly about things not observable in the real world. It includes combinational, probabilistic, correlational and other types of abstract reasoning. Even some accountants are concerned about the bean-counters in their ranks. In his report for the American Accounting Association, George Schute claims that most college students have not developed the mental structures necessary to perform formal-operational reasoning tasks. Schute writes that, "The existence of these skills seems necessary for an accountant to function at the highest level, particularly in the exercise of professional judgement" (Schute 1979).

Can it be agreed that such skills are necessary for a public administrationist to function at the highest level, particularly in the exercise of professional judgment?

Throughout the curriculum, we should continue to emphasize both content and analytical skills—parallel to the intentions of introductory philosophy courses. Are public administration (or other social science) students sufficiently grounded and practiced in critical analysis? "Analysis" is used here to mean coming to grips with claims, identifying assumptions, developing supporting argumentation, specifying counter-arguments, examining issues from alternative perspectives (for a further description, see Weston 1992). Part of the problem lies in general educational perparation and in the nature of the subject. The fact is that public administration theory, at this stage in its development, is not as analytically demanding as, say, physics. This fails to drive away the "analytically challenged" public administration student and professor. However, the analysis problem can also lurk in our teaching. Schute identifies features of accounting programs that facilitate thinking at the formal-operational level. An example is less reliance for grading purposes on memorization and more emphasis on coping with concepts under conditions where answers are not clear. We can identify similar features.

Throughout the curriculum, we should further emphasize knowledge of the subject and the capability for creativity. There certainly are areas of public administration where creativity is naturally emphasized, such as nonorthodox organization theory. For instance, there is a logical connection (even if no actual or historical connection) between the educational approach suggested in a book like *Teaching Creativity Through Metaphor* (Sanders and Sanders 1984) and Gareth Morgan's *Imaginization: The Art of Creative Management* (Morgan 1993). There is a substantial and relevant literature on the "teaching" of creativity and of critical thinking. For example, Torrance (1963) reports that blocks to creativity at the college level include overemphasis on the following:

acquisition of knowledge, memorization of facts, and finding already known answers to problems;

over-reliance upon textbooks and trust in authority;

the conviction that education should use only materials which are true, moral, or artistically excellent;

the conviction that education should be made as easy as possible;

and the low prestige in our society of scholars, teachers, and research workers.

Of particular relevance for public administration may be Torrance's third point, the mistaken conviction that education should use only materials that are true, moral, or artistically excellent.

## EXPECTATIONS

Discussion of postmodernity or other super-abstract topics should be prefaced by distinguishing the range of levels of public administration activity. Students legitimately expect that discussions of postmodernity have practical pay-offs. But an appropriate setting of expectations is another important step in helping students to cope with the super-abstract.

Within a range or continuum, distinctions can be drawn between the micro-micro, micro and macro levels of public administration. The micro-micro is the level of the lower-rung manager. A practical pay-off at this level might be better performance by a personnel, budget or other unit. The micro level includes the major manager, such as a governor or large agency head. The macro level refers to the national and international scene, the level at which macroeconomics aims; the pay-off here is for the nation and the larger public administration scene.

Students should think through the implications of such a range of impact. If they expect that what they learn should have immediate pay-off at the micro-micro level, they will be disappointed if what they learn is presented primarily at the macro level. Similarly, a student of macroeconomics would be disappointed if she did not understand that it is appropriate to discuss the behavior of the overall economy. Too frequently, public administration students think that all revolves around the equivalent of Al's Grocery Store and their particular job, and that the test is immediate pay-off at that level.

This is not to claim that short-term results at the micro-micro level are not important or that results at a higher level will not ultimately translate into effects at the smalller level. It is a mistake to judge all public administration by such a limited test, but the study of public administration has often been undertaken with this misdirected focus. If genuine solutions to the real problems of public bureaucracy are to be identified, it is likely that solutions will tend toward the longer term and will be at the macro level. For instance, the problem of the size of government (if there is such a problem) cannot be addressed at the level of the individual unit, and its resolution cannot be entirely short-term. Arguably, the more important public administration results must be expected at the macro level. Discussing the work in terms of eras like modernity and postmodernity inclines the conversation toward the macro level.

Public administration should direct its practical reforming fire toward the longer run. Expecting short-run resolution of the more important and massive problems of bureaucracy is popular but misguided; misguided because it interferes with developing longer-run steps. Public administration's reforming fire also should be directed toward the macro. Expecting to resolve the important problems of bureaucracy by focusing on the Weltanschauung of a unit within the State Department of Motor Vehicles may be popular with students from the State Department of Motor Vehicles, but it is unrealistic.

## CONCLUSION

Students of public administration need to deal in the super-abstract realm, and we should build this expectation more firmly into our graduate programs. The super-abstract (and postmodernism) is valuable in providing information about how to understand and formulate public administration theory, and in generating significant parts of the content of public administration theory.

Our curricula should provide for super-abstract building blocks that include the study of postmodern public administration. Public administration should be studied in terms of modernity and postmodernity for three reasons. Postmodernism presents significant practical implications for public administration theory and practice. It encourages new insights on public administration. It permits students to understand public administration theory and practice in a larger context.

To help students deal with the super-abstract and with postmodernism, graduate coursework should emphasize even more the development of skills in abstract critical thinking and creativity.

We should make clear to our students that, while the micro is not excluded, the major focus of graduate study should be macro public administration.

## REFERENCES

Adams, Guy B.
1992 "Enthralled with Modernity: The Historical Context of Knowledge and Theory Development in Public Administration." *Public Administration Review*, 52 (3), 363-373.

Baudrillard, Jean
1983 *Simulacra and Simulations*. Translated by Paul Foss, Paul Patton, and Philip Beitchman. New York; Semiotext (original publication, 1981).

Best, Steven and Kellner, Douglas
1991 *Postmodern Theory*. New York: The Guilford Press.

Farmer, David J.
1994 "Social Construction of Concepts: The Case of Efficiency," *Administrative Theory and Praxis*, 16 (2): 254-262.

1995 *The Language of Public Administration: Bureaucracy, Modernity, and Postmodernity*. Tuscaloosa, Alabama: University of Alabama Press.

Fox, Charles J. and Miller, Hugh T.
1994 *Postmodern Public Administration: Toward Discourse*. Thousand Oaks: Sage Publications.

Gadamer, Hans G.
1989 *Truth and Method*. New York: Crossroad.

Habermas, Jurgen
1983 "Modernity" An Incomplete Project," *The Anti-Aesthetic: Essays on Postmodern Culture*, Hal Foster, ed., Port Townsend, Washington: Bay Press.

1987 *The Theory of Communicative Action*. Boston: Beacon Press.

Hollinger, Robert A.
1994 *Postmodernism and the Social Sciences: A Thematic Approach*. Thousand Oaks: Sage Publications.

Morgan, Gareth
1993 *Imagination: The Art of Creative Management*. Newbury Park, California: Sage Publications.

Poster, Mark
1989 *Critical Theory and Poststructuralism: In Search of a Content*. Ithaca, New York: Cornell University Press.

Rescher, Nicholas
1980 *Scepticism: A Critical Appraisal*. Totowa, New Jersey: Rowan and Littlefield.

Sanders, Donald A. and Sanders, Judith A.
1984 *Teaching Creativity through Metaphor: An Integrated Brain Approach*. New York, New York: Longman.

Sarap, Madan
1993 *Post-Structuralism and Postmodernism*. Athens, Georgia: University of Georgia Press.

Schute, George E.
1979 *Accounting Students and Abstract Reasoning: An Exploratory Study*. Sarasota, Florida: American Accounting Association.

Selby-Bigge, L.A., ed.
1978 *David Hume: A Treatise of Human Nature*. Oxford: Clarendon Press.

Smart, Barry A.
1992 *Modern Conditions: Postmodern Controversies*. New York: Routledge.

Torrance, E. Paul
1963 *Creativity*. Washington, D.C.: Association of Classroom Teachers of the American Educational Association.

Weston, Anthony
1992 *A Rulebook for Argument*. Indianapolis, Indiana: Hackett.

White, Jay D.
1992 "Knowledge Development and Use in Public Administration: Views from Postpositivism Postructuralism, and Postmodernism." In Mary T. Bailey and Richard T. Mayer, eds., *Public Management in an Interconnected World*. New York: Greenwood Press.

# A Conversation Between Song Jinzhou and David John Farmer

## David John Farmer

Thanks are due to the Chinese *Journal of Public Administration* (*JPA*) for granting permission to republish this interview. Thanks also go to *Administrative Theory & Practice* (*ATP*) for agreeing to republish. I did enjoy *seeing* it when it first appeared in 2008 in Chinese. As you know, redux = brought back, revived.

There are three main reasons why I am glad that both journals agreed to republish this interview. First, the questions are fascinating (to me) because they are excellent and because they are from a Chinese thinker. On the latter point, are some of the questions not surprising (e.g., a Chinese person asking about the relationship between public administration [PA] and civil rights, asking whether public interests are political romanticism, asking whether there are challenges to democracy and citizenship in current PA)? Should they be surprising?

Second, American PA is incredibly insular. I complain about that, but I am also insular. Forgive me, but—despite members from, say, Australia and the Netherlands—is our group not insular, and is not even *ATP?* It is just so hard to see from a different culture. I can see from an American culture and an English culture, and, I tell myself, a French culture. But, that is hard with regard to Chinese culture, even though I have a "thing" for China and even though I cherish the utility of empathy: I do not speak Chinese. All my stuff is so American that everybody must know that I eat apple pie every evening. What should *I* do about *my* myopia? What should *we* do about *our* myopia?

Third, I admire the skill of my questioner in leading me to aspects or areas I should have emphasized more. In this case, I am the answerer. Would we not all agree that there is benefit for me (for us) in the reverse direction (i.e., in empathetic cross-cultural questioning of another [an-other] person's accumulated PA position)? That is one reason I remain high on radical epistemic pluralism as a way for PA theorizing to escape from what seems like, to use an astronomical term, its black hole. After all, related to cross-cultural questioning is cross-disciplinary questioning—from the culture of one discipline to that of another. My questioner is gifted.

So here is a bringing back of the interview. This interview was conducted by Associate Professor Song Jinzhou. *Everything* after the subtitle (every single thing) is from (I am told) the Chinese *JPA,* volume 1, issue 2, pages 182–201. It is a reprint of Dr. Song Jinzhou's record.

## INTERVIEW RETRANSLATED

**Interviewer**: Song Jinzhou, associate professor of public administration, East China Normal University (ECNU), Shanghai, and recently visiting scholar at Virginia Commonwealth University.

**Interviewee:** David John Farmer, professor of political science and public administration, Virginia Commonwealth University (VCU).

**Dr. Song Jinzhou:** *Hi, Professor Farmer! It is very kind of you to accept my interview. At the beginning of the interview, I would like to express the best regards to you from Dr. Ma Jun, editor-in-chief of* JPA. *I am also formally authorized by* JPA *to have an interview with you today.* JPA *is a new journal founded in China in February 2008.*

*Professor David John Farmer is a well-known scholar in China, as I know. Chinese scholars know you by your great book,* The Language of Public Administration [Tuscaloosa: University of Alabama Press, 1995]. *They take you as the first representative school of postmodern theory. Some Chinese scholars have published papers studying the postmodernism thinking of Dr. Farmer, such as Zhang Kangzhi, Ding Huang, and Xie Xin. I think that postmodernism is very significant for PA study in China. That is why many Chinese scholars and students refer to your book and articles.*

**Dr. David John Farmer:** Thank you, Jinzhou, for your kind comments. I appreciate you wanting to interview me, and I value the conversations that we have had. Thanks also to Ma Jun for wanting to publish this interview in *JPA*. Best wishes to them and to Zhang Kangzhi, Ding Huang, Xie Xin, and others. Also, greetings and best wishes to the Chinese readers of this interview.

**Song:** *Some scholars advocate that public interests are political romanticism, there are no real feelings of public interests at all; some scholars think that the public interests are the excuses of politicians for seeking for their interests. Do you think so?*

**Farmer:** No, there is a difference between private and public interests, and (assuming that the content has survived deconstruction) I would give priority to public interest. I agree that some politicians do misuse their powers, cloaking their own private interests under the claims of public interests. I agree that corruption does exist among too many politicians, and among too many business executives and others. I agree that in any country, a political class can genuinely mistake its own interest for the public interest. Yet, on the face of it, there is a difference between private preference and public interest—between what I want and what we want, between what I need and what we need. Examples abound supporting the view that public interests should have priority over private interests (e.g., in curbing pollution, in wasting what society has achieved).

However, isn't it in the public interest to make optimal provision for private interests? In the seventeenth century, Thomas Hobbes and John Locke both imagined people living in a state of nature. Owing to deficiencies in the state of nature, they imagined people entering a social contract where people gave up freedoms (pursuit of private interests) in order to gain greater public freedoms (pursuit of public interests). For Hobbes, the state of nature made life so brutish and nasty and short that he envisioned giving up all freedoms and allowing a public power to make all decisions, except where his life is threatened. For Locke, life in a state of nature appeared merely more awkward rather than blatantly brutish, and his idea of a social contract was one where the authority of the ruling government was limited by such obligations as respecting individual rights (e.g., to life, liberty, and property). In my view, and although many disagree with his way of expressing it, Locke has a better argument than Hobbes.

Let me add a disturbing story about private–public interaction. Focusing on private interests by unleashing the pursuit of economic self-interest can yield substantial benefits, but they can exact a terrible price in terms of human well-being and happiness. Unadulterated benefit is a pipe dream; the good is typically associated with negative side effects. Adam Smith spoke of the benefits of the invisible hand, the huge benefits that can come from unleashing the market. But, as the mainstream economist Paul Samuelson pointed out, the invisible hand fails as a result of inadequate market structure (where there are monopolies and oligopolies, where public goods are involved, and where there are externalities). It also fails in terms of increasing disparity between the rich and the poor, and in terms of instability (the ups and downs of the business cycle) and suboptimal economic growth. Samuelson writes only of the economic side effects. Changing the subject to contemporary market fundamentalism, Benjamin Barber is one who writes about negative noneconomic side effects. Barber describes what he calls the civic schizophrenia between the kind of "infantilized" consumer required by contemporary capitalism and the kind of "adult" citizen required by successful democracy. Indeed, relying on private interests can significantly harm public interests.

In shaping such dichotomies as public–private, importantly, don't forget to deconstruct!

**Song:** *Should PA respect human beings' dignity? Why?*

**Farmer:** Yes, at a minimum. I agree with Immanuel Kant that humans deserve to be treated as ends-in-themselves, rather than merely as means to an end. I would add that PA should privilege person over system (or person over machine). I would use deconstruction as a means toward this.

Mistreating people as mere means-to-an-end has been encouraged by conceptualizing the universe and government as machines—a distinguishing feature of the modernist era. My point is not to deny the mammoth advances associated with such a reconceptualization; it is to say that such great good is rarely unaccompanied by some unintended negative consequences. Scientists like Isaac Newton developed important life-changing explanations (e.g., the Law of Gravity in physics) by conceptualizing the universe as a mere machine. This view of the universe as mechanical reached a zenith in the eighteenth century, when it was reflected in politics and other areas of life. As one example, the American Founding Fathers saw government in large part as mechanical, and they developed a machinery of government that highlighted features similar to a now old-fashioned watch—such as a constitution with checks and balances. Mistreating individuals as part of a machine system has obvious advantages. But it has disadvantages, perhaps less obvious. One of the disadvantages is that we become habituated, tending to lose sensitivity to recognition that all persons (not just you and me) merit the dignity of being treated as ends-in-themselves.

Mistreating people as mere means-to-an-end can be supplemented in the PA context by discussing the ideas of Max Weber and Herbert Marcuse. Weber complains of the Faustian bargain we have made in trading our "full and beautiful humanity" for a narrow vocation where we are "specialists without spirit, sensualists without heart." For him, the great question is how we can oppose this machinery "in order to keep a portion of mankind free from this parceling-out of the soul, from this supreme mastery of the bureaucratic way of life." Marcuse complains of the one-dimensional thinking that uncritically accepts existing structures and norms.

It is hard to treat each and every one as an end-in-herself. Yet Kant's claim is that this should be our aim. I agree with the aim of treating each person as more than parts of a machine, more than as parts of a system.

**Song:** *What is the relationship between PA and civil rights?*

**Dr. Farmer:** I agree with what I think is the conclusion of rights talk (i.e., that people should have a certain amount of autonomy). I recognize that rights talk is snappy and easy to understand, like proverbs or like slogans, but I prefer alternative language. For the same end, and especially in the PA context, I prefer to emphasize different claims, such as that individuals and organizations should practice authentic hesitation in justice-claiming—especially the more powerful toward the less powerful.

Philosophers have differing attitudes toward rights talk. Rights talk descended from philosophers like John Locke, who were so influential on (say) the American Founding Fathers. Talk of rights is continued by more recent thinkers like Robert Nozick. Other philosophers would say similar things but without the rights talk. Right or wrong, Friedrich von Hayek defended his market fundamentalist position without the aid of rights talk. Most famously, Jeremy Bentham (whose mummified body remains in a glass case at the University of London) long ago described rights talk as "nonsense on stilts."

Authentic hesitation stands against an arrogant "I know best" or "my system is right" attitude on the part of governing bureaucracies or persons in power. It's not the same as mere hesitation or passing the buck. It's not the same as hesitating in action. Rather, it's a granting of space in making justice claims when dealing with the "other"—with the less powerful. Such a concept does run counter to dominant symbolic systems in contemporary societies. But parallel concepts have been noted in certain Eastern philosophies, like Confucianism. Parallel concepts have been identified in Western philosophers, as in talk about trust, toleration, mutual respect, mutual recognition, sympathy, public reason, and full consideration for the arguments of others.

**Song:** *Should PA take care of vulnerable groups' interests first for public policy? Why? And how?*

**Dr. Farmer:** Yes, in public policy-making and administration, PA should take care of vulnerable groups' interests. Among the methods I have described for doing this is anti-administration.

Why? There are utilitarian and altruistic reasons for PA to take care of marginalized or vulnerable groups. On the utilitarian side, one reason is the benefit not only to the excluded group but also to the mainstream or dominant group. Consider a society where (say) women are marginalized in the sense of being ignored or dominated. In such a case, feminist theory is prevented from adding insights that can strengthen mainstream or dominant thinking. Writing with a deviant signature (a practice I urge for PA thinkers) involves taking into account deviant perspectives, and one writer that I find enlightening is the postmodern feminist writer Helene Cixous. On the altruistic side, various nonreligious and religious ideologies celebrate the weak. For instance, weren't thinkers and activists as different as Karl Marx and Jesus Christ devoted to helping the weak and the oppressed? But other thinkers, like Friedrich von Hayek, who was described earlier as a market fundamentalist, would consider this to be nonsense.

And how? Anti-administration is one approach that I recommend. It is contemplation that includes voices excluded from, or marginalized in, traditional discussions of governance. I first started writing about anti-administration in *The Language of Public Administration,* and I described anti-administration as a main point of postmodernism. Such anti-administration included what I called imaginization, deconstruction, deterritorialization, and alterity. Later, I attempted to separate anti-administration from postmodernism by speaking about it in terms of a medieval (and then a modernist) framework. I continued thinking about this through my 1998 edited book called *Papers on the Art of Anti-Administration* [Burke, VA: Chatelaine Press, 1998] and through a 2001 symposium that included a variety of progressive PA thinkers, like O. C. McSwite, Richard Box, Robert Cunningham, and Patricia Patterson.

**Song:** *Should PA exceed the interests of special groups? How?*

**Dr. Farmer:** Yes, PA should exceed the interests of special groups. Earlier it was suggested that PA should aim to serve person over system. Now it is suggested that PA should do this by aiming to serve the interests of (to use an interesting formula) the "whole person-in-herself in her difference."

Consider the first part of the formula—"whole person." Political and economic systems typically treat persons as less than fully whole human beings, for example. Political policy-making tends to create systems that deal with time slices of groups in the population, and individuals benefited or affected become time slices. Economic corporations tend to treat employees as units over periods of time, and not as persons with whole lives.

Consider the remaining part of the formula "in-herself in her difference." For this, turn to writers like Giorgio Agamben and Homi Bhahba. Among Agamben's points is the claim that the self, not limited to a particular description, is open to a multitude of possibilities. One of Homi Bhahba's claims is that the "in-between spaces provide the terrain of elaborating strategies of selfhood—singular or communal—that initiate new signs of identity."

**Song:** *Should PA exceed the interests of government agencies? If the government agencies' regulations are conflicted with justice, what should the government do?*

**Dr. Farmer:** Yes. Macro PA theory is needed. At the practice level, PA practice should be designed to combat the tendency of agencies to give priority to their own interests.

Macro PA theory should be encouraged and developed. That is, PA theory should not be confined to micro concerns. In this, it should learn from the example of economics, which recognizes two major branches. One branch is microeconomics—the study of the individual firm, the individual corporation. In doing so, as you know, particular firms are not studied; rather, the unit of analysis is the abstract idea of the firm. Another branch is macroeconomics—the economics of the entire country, including issues like price levels and unemployment rates and other economic matters of significance country-wide and beyond. Macro PA theory should be on the same level as macroeconomics.

PA practice should recognize the dynamics whereby individual agencies tend to pay primary attention to their own interests. I have worked for a number of public organizations, and it is rare that the primary interest is not bureaucratic self-interest. Curbing this harmful bureaucratic self-interest should be a chapter in macro PA theory. One would suppose that those responsible for agencies should be evaluated and rewarded (or punished) on the basis of whether the agency exceeds its own narrow self-interests. But there is clearly more to it than this: much depends on that relevant chapter in macro PA theory.

**Song:** *Should PA exceed the short-term interests and efficiency? Why?*

**Dr. Farmer:** Yes. It is understandable to be concerned with short-term interests and efficiency. What is wrong is restricting PA to these narrow concerns.

It is undesirable for PA to confine itself so much to short-term interests. How can the short run be understood fully except in the context of the longer term? How can a public agency make optimal upgrades in its services without thinking in the longer term? As another reason—because business corporations are so firmly committed to profit maximization in the short term—it is especially important for the public agency to take a longer view. By the way, Macro PA theory should examine why PA has chosen to confine its thinking so radically to the shorter run. For my money, the answer includes appreciating why PA restricts it gaze so much to midlevel management. It includes recognizing (after Michel Foucault) that what is considered a true approach is a function of power.

Similarly, it is undesirable for PA to limit itself only to matters of efficiency. I understand that in the modern world—where efficiency is the most valued aim of economic organizations—that attention should include what is efficient. But don't humans want more than mere efficiency? I have suggested that PA should help the posttraditional practitioner to be motivated as a regulative ideal by love rather than by mere efficiency. By "regulative ideal" I mean a vision or a benchmark of what should be done—even if it resembles most moral injunctions in being, on a consistent or frequent basis, impossible. (For example, what kind of a teacher would be motivated by mere efficiency? From great teachers, shouldn't we expect loving care? What kind of a public official is motivated only by mere efficiency?) So, as a complement to engineering organizational change, I recommend and explain "un-engineering" that is directed toward knowing and embracing love.

**Song:** *Should PA respect science and rationality? Why?*

**Dr. Farmer:** Yes. Both science and rationality are helpful to PA. But PA should also respect hermeneutics.

Take neuroscience, for example, and consider how (because it illuminates how humans function) this science can benefit PA understanding. I became interested in neuroscience because of the interest of my wife (Dr. Rosemary L. Farmer) in neuroscience and social work. The more I understood, the more neuroscience seemed relevant to PA. Recently, I wrote an article on this ("Neuro-Gov: Neuroscience as Catalyst") that was published in the *Annals of the New York Academy of Sciences.* I see the prospect of a new level and nature of discourse in PA and in the social sciences, made possible by the catalytic effect of neuroscience. Such changes are already beginning in other areas (e.g., in neuroeconomics). Certainly, science and rationality deserve respect.

Yet philosophy of science explains how the scientific method, valuable as it is, does not give us all we need to know. Science deals in explanations, for example, rather than understandings. It does not deal in meanings, and it does not produce conclusions about what is ethical. PA also needs what hermeneutics provides. In fact, a vast majority of the significant writings in PA have been hermeneutic.

**Song:** *Should PA processes be more transparent and more open? Why?*

**Dr. Farmer**: Yes. PA processes should be more transparent. In my view, they should be more open to the extent that such transparency increases the quality of government service. This transparency and openness should not be confined to public agencies, however. For instance, economic corporations—private businesses—should also be much more transparent and open.

**Song:** *According to the OECD [Organization for Economic Cooperation and Development], there are four requirements for formal institutions: informing citizens, representing citizens, changing professionalism in social values in the process of policy-making, and guaranteeing civil choices. What's your comment?*

**Dr. Farmer:** Yes, these OECD ideas are helpful. But they are not enough. Much, much more is needed.

I have recommended posttraditional government and bureaucracy. That is the subtitle of my book *To Kill the King* [Armonk, NY: M.E. Sharpe, 1996]. In that book, I explain how this is constituted in terms of the development of Thinking as Play, Justice as Seeking, and Practice as Art in PA.

**Song:** *What is postmodernism? How would you define it?*

**Dr. Farmer:** Postmodernism is a description of what postmodernists consider to be the best way of interpreting the world we live in. This interpretation is skeptical about our ability to reduce reality to simple definitions of identity. Its value includes helping us strive for radical liberty in a realistic (epistemological) context where we should be skeptical about knowing what is (i.e., about ontology).

For a description of postmodernism in the PA context, see *The Language of Public Administration*. As mentioned earlier, I break up the description into the four elements of imaginization, deconstruction, deterritorialization, and alterity.

Concerning imaginization, for example, the imagination has the same role in the postmodern context as rationality did in the modern. This doesn't mean that we abandon rationality, but it does mean that our rationality becomes, as the word implies, qualitatively more imaginative.

Deconstruction identifies the metaphors and binary opposites that dominate and distort our thinking and our imagining. It permits good readings of situations. I should add that the fleeting meanings of deconstruction do not represent a loss of meaning. Rather, the changes constitute a superabundance of meaning (e.g., words that mean many things, and statements that remind us of other statements).

Deterritorialization refers to the desirability of getting beyond the entrenched disciplinary divisions that make it difficult to see reality accurately. To give a simple example, separating business administration from public administration—or separating politics from economics—distorts what we see.

Alterity refers to our relationship with the "other." It recognizes that each one of us, and each of our organizations, has what Michel Foucault calls "fascist" tendencies that we should strive to overcome. Knowledge of the public administration act is supplemented, at least, by the postmodern view of justice.

**Song:** *What is your personal view about postmodernism? Do you agree with its "truth" claims?*

**Dr. Farmer:** I am not a postmodernist. Also, I should add that Michel Foucault and Jacques Derrida denied that they were postmodernists. Derrida, the inventor of deconstruction, also denied (appropriately) that he was a deconstructionist. But postmodernism does offer what seem to be excellent ways to develop understandings of our world. It also offers a good way to understand truth claims. However, while I think that it should be part of our thinking, I don't understand postmodernism as the "only" way to develop understandings.

The posttraditional, in the subtitle of *To Kill the King,* is not (repeat not) the postmodern. Rather, the posttraditional is what is not traditional. The posttraditional does have a relationship with certain "isms" like feminism, postcolonialism, critical theory, critical legal theory, and postmodernism. It means after (post) the traditional (what is traditional). Essentially, for example, traditional PA has failed us and it is failing us. So the posttraditional is my contribution to specifying what should come after.

I do commend postmodern perspectives to readers, however. As one example, consider again the practical utility of an idea like deconstruction. On deconstruction, everything that we think and write and see, as I said a moment ago, is full of metaphors and binary opposites that give us false pictures. We have to pick our way out of the trap of such misdescriptions if we aim to describe accurately. There are many other examples I could give. For instance, take Michel Foucault's ideas about normalizing and truth. Or, take ideas like those about the decentered subject or about the limits of grand narratives.

Distinguishing between truth and what-counts-as-true is what I have echoed and advocated. I don't deny that absolute truth exists; the more critical question is whether I know it, or whether I am deceived. Return to Foucault's ideas, for instance.

Normalizing helps us to understand how our educations have shaped us as "normal" functionaries—as people who have certain beliefs and attitudes about what counts as true so that we can discharge our functions "appropriately." What counts as true is shaped, largely unconsciously, by forces that are powerful in a society.

Why should I say that I am not a postmodernist if I think that "central" ideas in postmodernism are extremely valuable? In response, let me ask two questions. (1) Should I say that I am a postmodernist, if I think that central parts in postmodernism are valuable, central parts in critical theory are also valuable, central parts in feminism are also valuable, central parts in post-colonialism are also valuable—and so on? (2) If I accept (as I do) that Isaac Newton's Law of Gravity is true, should I call myself a Gravitation-ist (or a Newton-ist)? I think it would facilitate thinking and action if we all tried to keep out of the boxes, the traps that inhibit imagination and that hinder our seeing the world as it is.

**Song:** *What do you think that the reaction to postmodernism should be?*

**Dr. Farmer:** We should take postmodernism very seriously, because it helps our understanding. However, truth seeking is uncomfortable, partly because we must be prepared as a matter of good sense to abandon what we describe as common sense.

A problem for postmodernism in the social sciences is that people want answers that do not disturb comforting common sense ideas. As Bertrand Russell and neuroscience point out, we are essentially emotional beings who sometimes think—rather than thinking beings who sometimes have emotions. To repeat (as I like to do) Russell's image, we surround ourselves with comforting beliefs—just like (giving a European example) flies can surround us in the summer. In his 1928 essay "Dreams and Facts," Bertrand Russell explains his view that the mass of our beliefs that support our daily life (and I interject that for the PA practitioner, PA is his or her daily life) is merely the emanation of "desire, corrected here and there." Russell claims, "man is essentially a dreamer wakened sometimes for a moment by some peculiarly obtrusive element in the order of the world, but lapsing quickly." And we return to the "day-dreams that we call beliefs." It is then that he unloads his fly metaphor. "Every man, wherever he goes, is encompassed by a cloud of comforting convictions which move with him like flies on a summer day." Some of these convictions or beliefs are personal (e.g., about the rosy prospect of his career, about his sexual prowess). Some concern the worth of his family, or the excellence of his school, or the accomplishments of his group, the distinctiveness of mankind in general compared against brute animals, or the and the uniqueness of his nation. "Concerning his nation, almost every man cherishes comfortable delusions," writes Russell.

Noting that postmodernism challenges some commonsense ideas, note that most of our commonsense ideas are mere delusions. Consider physics (e.g., about quarks and photons) and astronomy (e.g., about the black holes that exist in space), for instance. Most such truths (claims that I accept as truths) are contrary to common sense. Common sense, I would suggest, can be utterly different from good sense. Consider neuroscience (e.g., that my mind is my brain functioning) and evolution (e.g., that we all evolved from prokaryotes). Most such truths (claims that I accept as truths) in these subjects are fantastical from the viewpoint of common sense. I want the imagination and the energy to throw away the comforting beliefs that I call common sense, and to seek to embrace the uncomfortable fire of what is "really" true.

**Song:** *Does postmodernism really have significance to both business and public management? (I find some people in China use your theory to analyze e-business.)*

**Dr. Farmer:** Yes, postmodernism does have significance in deepening understandings of business (including e-business) and public management.

Consider the economic "system" in the world. I love economic theory, partly for sentimental reasons. (What I mean by sentimental reasons is that my first doctorate was in economics, and I am more emotionally attached to that subject than to the more important subject matter of my second doctorate in philosophy—precisely because the economics Ph.D. arrived longer ago.) But how well does Adam Smith's modernist idea of the Invisible Hand "explain" the world? Not at all well, I have suggested. How well do certain basic concepts of economics, like those about international trade, explain the world? In a world where such a large proportion of international trade is between branches of the same corporation, I would be skeptical. And so on. Postmodern economists should not be ignored. They do not find the unifying power of mainstream economic theory to be a primary explanatory lens in understanding the economic world.

E-business and the Internet in general are icons for the decentered view toward which postmodern ideas point. When I next come to China, I look forward to hearing from those scholars who (as your question reports) are interested in understanding e-business more realistically.

Public management is a natural subject for postmodern analysis. When I worked in the U.S. government (in the Department of Justice) and in the New York Police Department (not as a police officer but as special assistant to the police commissioner, concerned with managing), I was impressed by our "postmodern" contexts. Let me give only one, and a small, example. All the managers in the federal system are charged to "direct, coordinate, and control" all the assigned personnel and all of their activities. That's useful. But, as a matter of practicality, it is an impossible responsibility: directing, coordinating, and controlling all (note all) of the personnel activities is impossible, even with a small number of subordinates. At that time, the Police Department contained 35,000 employees (the Justice Department now has more than 100,000 employees): the "impossibility" of directing, coordinating, and controlling all the activities of such numbers invites reflection, including the use of a postmodern lens.

**Song:** *In modernizing and reorganizing public administration, there are some trends. The first trend is the reduction of public responsibilities and services. The second is the modernizing of procedures and approaches of public administration. The third is the improvement of financial and fiscal management. What is your comment in view of postmodernism?*

**Dr. Farmer:** Postmodernism, as well as other lenses (or perspectives), can be helpful on these three issues. My preference is to use many perspectives (multiperspectives). My preference is for what I call radical epistemic pluralism: going the extra and hard miles to see PA from multiple disciplinary perspectives. But postmodernism is important as one perspective, and I will illustrate here (again) with the example of deconstruction. I leave it to the reader to comment on these trends in view of posttraditionalism.

On the first trend: If you mean privatization by the first trend, the result is a postmodern decentered world. Barber, referenced in my answer to the first question, mentions this. However, he is not offering what I would call a postmodern analysis. For example, I don't think that it is postmodern to speak about the ill-effects of the state privatizing sovereign functions. I don't think that it is important whether he was "being" postmodern. I don't think it is wise to stick to only one perspective. To repeat myself, a better approach is multiperspectival—radical epistemic pluralism. At the same time, the application of economic theory requires some deconstruction when Barber can tell us that contemporary corporations in the developed world are mainly concerned with manufacturing wants—rather than with producing goods and services, as contemplated in mainstream economics.

On the second trend: Modernizing procedures and approaches can benefit from modernist business and economic practices. For example, the large company, Wal-Mart, has led the way in upgrading supply chain management. Business schools teach supply chain management, and supply chain management is clearly relevant to governmental functions, like disaster relief. But cannot postmodern ideas also help (e.g., deconstructing concepts that lie within the notion of supply chain management)?

On the third trend: For the improvement of financial and fiscal management, I would tend to turn to accountants. But I wouldn't rely on accountants completely. After all, don't economists have important insights about the economics of budgeting? Yet, all such said and done, doesn't the concept of budget in contemporary society require deconstruction?

**Song:** *What are the challenges to democracy and citizenship for current public administration?*

**Dr. Farmer:** There are a variety of challenges. But, while recognizing this, I will limit myself only to one.

Principal among these challenges for PA is how to help with the formidable problem of reaping the benefits of a vigorous market economy while limiting the severe damages that the market is inflicting on democracy, citizenship, and even ethics. In my view, PA must become open to economics. By economics, I don't mean market fundamentalism, but the variety of economic perspectives.

When PA in my part of the world does seek a view of economics, typically the seeking is limited to the perspective of mainstream economics—in the form of what is variously called neoliberalism, or the Washington 1980s consensus, or market fundamentalism. Alternative economic paradigms are available from academe and from more popular publications. For instance, there is Naomi Klein on what she calls "the shock doctrine." This refers to the use of public disorientation following collective shocks—wars, terrorist attacks, natural disasters—to push through economic changes (and we could add political changes). To give one of her examples, following the tsunami, gorgeous Southeast Asian beaches were auctioned off to tourist resort entrepreneurs. Klein's picture is a contrast with the incrementalist view (e.g., held by Alfred Marshall, the dominant thinker in neoclassical economics). Mainstream economics is only about power in a limited sense.

Another who writes about the challenge of the contemporary economic system for democracy and citizenship is Robert Reich. Reich points to the tension between what he called "supercapitalism" (our present global capitalism that is turbo charged, Web based, and able to find and to make almost anything just about anywhere) and democracy for all citizens. For him, the successes of the former undermine the capability of the latter. And there is more that could be added, on the lines discussed by Deirdre McCloskey, about the rhetoric of economics. We could point to the denigration of the public sphere—the spread of the conviction that public authorities are incompetent.

**Song:** *Please briefly introduce the main views of ethics in public administration in the United States.*

**Dr. Farmer:** I am extremely sorry to report that I consider the views of ethics discussed in PA to be uninteresting and unimaginative. I favor the idea of "justice as seeking." For my views on ethics in PA and on meta-ethics, please see the section "Justice as Seeking" in my book *To Kill the King*. These are the six chapters 7 through 12. Discussions of ethics in PA deal less with seeking than with echoing prescriptions, and there is little in terms of meta-ethics.

So I recommend that readers turn to the vast literature on ethics and meta-ethics within philosophy. Earlier, for example, I mentioned the Kantian ideal of treating persons as ends-in-themselves. For this, turn not to PA but to Immanuel Kant himself.

**Song:** *Would you like to summarize spirituality of PA? What is the significance of it for PA?*

**Dr. Farmer**: I prefer the word "poetry," because spirituality is often confused with religion. I don't exclude religion from this, but neither do I include it.

The significance of the poetic for PA is that human beings lust for the poetic (often unconsciously) as well as for the nonpoetic. PA should recognize this. Humans need to satisfy the biological, the social, and the psychological aspects of their being. But they also seek the poetic, the sublime, the ineffable, what exceeds all bounds—what some call spirituality. Human beings are more than cogs in a machine. The significance for PA is that public administration cannot be studied as if it should do nothing more than service mere machine parts, mere cogs.

**Song:** *What are your comments on public choice theory?*

**Dr. Farmer:** It is useful to use public choice economics in order to illuminate political and other public choice situations. I discussed public choice economics in a chapter in my 1995 book *The Language of Public Administration.* It points to the illumination of the nature of public demand from, say, Kenneth Arrow's possibility theorem. It points to the deeper understanding of the supply side from, say, William Niskanen's model and from Jean-Luc Migue's and Gérard Bélanger's model of bureaucratic behavior. Public choice economics is a powerful lens.

But that chapter in my book is entitled "Limits of Enterprise." There are limits to the illumination from public choice economics. Other perspectives are also desirable.

**Song:** *Is there a generalizing type of theory for PA? How can we study PA if there is not?*

**Dr. Farmer**: It may well be that others have a different idea of what a generalizing theory is.

The generalizing theory that I prefer and advocate is posttraditional governance and bureaucracy. The key in my generalizing theory is the play of imagination. It talks about imagination in terms of thinking as play, justice as seeking, and practice as art. It favors multiple perspectives, for example.

**Song:** *The "imagination" in your book can be understood as "innovative thinking?" Is it based on the old thinking?*

**Dr. Farmer**: No, I mean more than the old thinking about "innovative thinking." I mean more than thinking outside the box.

I mean to emphasize thought experiments in PA that are more than merely being imaginative in rationalizing. I mean not only a more vigorous but also a more independent role for the play of the imagination. Notice Andre Breton's description in the first surrealist manifesto of the role of the imagination. Notice Carl Jung's understanding of the play of the imagination as independent—as independent as is reflected in Taoist and other systems of meditation. I mean to include poetic contemplation. In poetic contemplation, I include what Michael Oakeshott (an early professor of mine) described when he wrote of poetic contemplation as a sort of truancy. He called it a truancy in the sense of a dream within the dream of life, a wildflower planted among our wheat.

**Song:** *How do we construct an instrument to achieve a better society by democratic participation?*

**Dr. Farmer:** As an organizational instrument, PA can begin by developing what I earlier called macro PA, as contrasted with micro PA. Macro PA analyzes the larger picture, and it recognizes that it is within the context of societal magma that PA changes must be made. But I should stress that an organizational instrument is less important than radically imaginative content—the kind of thinking, seeking, and action that is sought in post-traditionalism.

Turn back to the less important organizational change. Let me illustrate in a rather abstract way the power to illuminate that should be sought in an imaginative macro PA. I'll do so by noting how Cornelius Castoriadis's idea of magma can be used as one element (but only one element) in macro study. Castoriadis explains magma as referring to society's creative framework or world of signification. Castoriadis depicts each society as instituting itself in terms of an "originary" creation, describing the institution of society's magma of "social imaginary signification" as shaping what can be constituted in that society. He explains that "Each society, like each living being or species, establishes, creates its own world, within which, of course, it includes itself." Castoriadis continues, "In brief, it is the institution of society that determines which is 'real' and what is not, what is 'meaningful' and what is meaningless. Sorcery was real in Salem three centuries ago, but it is not now. Each society is a construction, a constitution, a creation of a world, of its own world." In brief, we need more—and more sophisticated—macro PA.

**Song:** *How should we study PA in the future? Can you give some suggestions to Chinese students?*

**Dr. Farmer:** I have visited China only three times, and I have spoken in public lectures at the City University of Hong Kong. I look forward to a fourth visit. I have loved what I have seen—the famous sites like the Great Wall, the Forbidden City, the Three Gorges, the Emperor's Tomb in Xian, and the skyline in Shanghai. I have loved speaking with Chinese people I have met, even though I need a translator. I have loved reading the history of the Chinese people. I also have enjoyed having Chinese students in my classes here.

On the one hand, in such a circumstance, I am humbled at the thought of offering suggestions to Chinese students. I am authentically hesitant—a virtue in my understanding of ethics. On the other hand, we all must learn from one another.

So I will offer four overlapping suggestions. The first is to seek out different perspectives. Be multiperspectival. Search for marginalized lenses, including the postmodern. Look at PA from a wide variety of perspectives.

The second is always to seek the public good, but with authentic hesitation.

The third is to search for the poetry in the human, in PA and in all else.

The fourth is to nourish the play of your imagination.

**Song:** *Thank you for your excellent interview. I think that the interview is very helpful to Chinese scholars and students. I would like to express their best wishes to you and to your family. Hope you visit Zhongshan University at a convenient time.*

# THE LADDER OF ORGANIZATION-THINK: BEYOND FLATLAND

David John Farmer

## ABSTRACT

*This article specifies a ladder of organization-think in terms of discourse theory and the spatial notion of dimensionality. The ladder can represent discourses about organizations and discourses emanating from organizations; the main illustration used is its manifestation as a ladder of P.A. discourse. Seven characteristics of discourse are discussed. Four rungs of the ladder are described, and these rungs are labelled "me," "they," "our," and "out of the cave." Reasons why P.A. thinkers should be interested in the ladder are indicated.*

Is there not an *n*-dimensional ladder of organization-think, where the dimensions or rungs can be explicated in terms of discourse theory and of the spatial notion of dimensionality? The reader is asked to consider this in the spirit of *Public Administration Discourse as Play with a Purpose* (D. J. Farmer, 1998). It is claimed that there is a ladder of "discourse about organizations" and of "discourse emanating from organizations." Discourse or thinking "about" organizations or organizing presents manifestations of the same ladder. So we can say that the ladder of organization-think manifests itself in ladders of discourse about public administration (P.A.), about business administration, about military administration, about non-profit administration—just as there are sets of dimensions in other areas of human discourse. Discourse or thinking "emanating from" organizations and organizing also presents manifestations of the same ladder of organization-think. So we can say that the latter manifests itself in ladders of discourse "by" public bureaucrats, "by" corporate bureaucrats, "by" non-bureaucrats (e.g. painters, mathematicians or writers receiving grants or pay-checks and whose daily bread entails being beholden to a public or private bureaucracy), and "by" people within churches, families and other civil society structures. The philosopher Baruch Spinoza showed his understanding of the significance of the "emanating from" category when he rejected a Professorship at Heidelberg. He thought that the employment would deprive him of the freedom to philosophize on his own terms.

This paper describes the following four dimensions as among the rungs of this ladder of organization-think. The selected rungs are illustrated mainly from the perspective of discourse about organizations, and the primary illustration selected (arbitrarily) is the ladder of P.A. discourse. The rungs are labelled (me, they, our, out of the cave). Alternative accounts and labels could well have been given, and a signifier with no Orwellian connotations (Orwell, 1977) could have been selected instead of "ladder of organization-think."

- A first rung in the ladder of organization-think is described as a "me" (or "your") dimension. It consists of a set of overlapping discourses that in terms of the basic unit of thinking (analyzing, theorizing) is reductionist (reduced to what is taught to "me" and familiar to "me," as to others in "my" discipline) and that focuses on issues in terms primarily of "me"—"my" psychological baggage, "my" socio-economic and livelihood circumstances, "my" nationality, "my" family, "my" job, "my" organization, and so on. In terms of the ladder of P.A. discourse about organizations, an example is the traditional P.A. method and scope. Discourse theory indicates what it means to claim that the basic unit of thinking (analyzing, theorizing) is bureaucratic man, and that the scope centers on a variety of forms of the micro.

- A second rung encompasses the range of overlapping discourses that occupy what may be labeled a "they" dimension. The method of thinking is also reductionist. But the scope now extends beyond the "my" or the micro. Issues are now approached in their system-wide context, and the issue focus extends beyond the grasp of the earlier dimension. In the P.A. ladder manifestation, the scope here extends to a non-traditional range of P.A. problems, including problematics like the "iron cage" character of contemporary bureaucracy and the persistent and on-going antipathy against bureaucracy. In the economics ladder, as another example, the scope extends to the macro.

- A third rung concerns discourses occupying what is called an "our" dimension, the name connoting joint possession. It includes the range of overlapping discourses that are possible when discourse scope widens beyond the confines of current disciplinary walls, traditional barriers that in fact are merely modernist phenomena. These would include the walls between the humanities and the social sciences (and the physical sciences). Such a dimension can encourage greater attention to concepts like an understanding of governmentality that embraces all forms of governance—whether it takes place within governments, within economic enterprises like corporations, within civil society structures like churches or families, or within bowling leagues and even the most temporary of structures.

- A fourth rung is called "out of the cave." It refers to the range of discourses where lower-rung and other problematics are analyzed by using a basic unit of thinking (analyzing, theorizing) that relies, not on a reduced conception of the human person (such as bureaucratic man or economic man or any other reduced conception of the person), but on humans as bio-psycho-socio-spiritual beings.

Why should P.A. thinkers be interested in such a ladder of discourse? First, my discourse (verbal and non-verbal mind-set) co-creates and limits what I know and can see. After Wittgenstein, we can say that the limits of my language (my discourse) are the limits of my world. Second, the optimal way of understanding and improving P.A. practice problems is through more robust P.A. and other discourse. Traditional P.A. discourse stands in the way of the most significant reforms. Bad practice can be upgraded certainly, but only within the limits of the discourse. The level of P.A. discourse is itself the stem-cell locus of the more significant problems. Third, discourse at each of the dimensions can be more useful if conducted with an attitude of self-awareness and with some reference to the other rungs of the ladder. Discourse at any of the dimensions has its own utility, including Rung One. Although it can seem distant from the lower rungs, it is suggested that there is a quantum gain in practical utility if the insights of the higher dimensions of discourse can infuse the character of the discourse at the lower levels. Fourth, valuable and more fundamental insights can be obtained through discourse at the higher rungs. For example, Rung Two permits P.A. to address the problems of the "iron cage" and the ongoing antipathy against government. As another example, we are lagging in understanding the relevance of regarding humans in bio-psycho-socio-spiritual terms. Fifth, P.A. theorizing has failed to create the conceptual space for genuine reform efforts like the Vice-President's National Partnership for Reinventing Government. The problem is not limited to the quality of our output. It is also that reform options are hobbled politically because P.A. theory has not been rich enough to create an attentive public open to analyses at the higher rungs of the ladder of organization-think.

## THE LADDER METAPHOR

The form of the ladder can be described in terms of spatial dimensions, explaining the reference in the sub-title to Flatland. The general character can be indicated in terms of discourse theory. These two accounts form the basis for the later discussion of the specifics of the four selected rungs of the ladder of organization-think.

**Form**

Each rung of the ladder represents a family of discourses. The form of the *n*-dimensional ladder of organization-think (and its various manifestations, like the ladder of P.A. discourse) is specified in terms of spatial dimensions, because these dimensions underscore what we will describe as a major feature of the relationships between families of discourses. The first rung would be one-dimensional. The second would be two-dimensional, where the second dimension is at ninety degrees to the first dimension. The third would be three-dimensional, where the third line is at ninety degrees to the first two dimensions. The fourth spatial dimension would be where another spatial dimension is at ninety degrees to the other three dimensions (e.g., see Rucker, 1977). And so on for the fifth and higher dimensions. A clear chart of such a ladder cannot be drawn on a two-dimensional page; but such a concept can be understood, despite the visual difficulty for us in our spatial discourse. One way of conceptualizing the P.A. ladder of discourse is to borrow from the celebrated 1884 book *Flatland* by Edwin Abbott. This book purports to be the biography of a character called A. Square, who lives in a two-dimensional world (Flatland) populated by various two-dimensional geometrical shapes like triangles, circles, and so on. The book includes encounters with other dimensions like lineland (a one-dimensional world). Showing the difficulty of visualizing an object from a higher dimension are incidents that occur in A. Square's two-dimensional world. One such is where a mysterious dot appears; then changes into an expanding circle until it starts to decrease in radius; then eventually turns again into a dot before disappearing. It is not possible in two-dimensional discourse to see as-it-is a three-dimensional object, like a sphere. Similarly, there is difficulty in a one-dimensional world recognizing two-dimensional objects in their two-dimensionality; the three-dimensional world finds it hard to visualize the objects that are four-dimensional.

The ladder, as a metaphoric form, has been famously used in philosophy to carry the invitation to climb, and we want the ladder of organization-think to offer a similar invitation. Early in philosophy's history, there is Plato's invitation in his account of the nature of love to climb Diotima's ladder (*Symposium*). At the lower rung of Diotima's ladder, an individual is attracted to the physical charms of another individual. In dialogue with his friend, he can then discover beauty common to all persons, then moral beauty, and finally the form of beauty itself. In recent years, there is Wittgenstein's ladder. Understand the propositions in the *Tractatus* and then kick the ladder away. "He must, so to speak, throw away the ladder after he has climbed up it" (Wittgenstein, 1961,

6.54). Religious writings have also used ladder metaphors, with an invitation to climb. There are others, like Abraham Maslow's hierarchy of psychological needs (1954).

The form of the ladder of organization-think—and its various manifestations—is not a ladder in the ordinary sense (in Wittgenstein's sense), where each rung—apart from its spatial position—is similar to the one below. We must incorporate the major feature, promised earlier, of the relationships between families of discourse. Each dimension or rung of the ladder in part "stands against" the lower rungs; there is an "oppositional gap." The claim is not being made that there is no overlapping between the various dimensions; certainly there is. Yet, there is a tension or a discontinuity between the second dimension and the first, between the third and the second, and so on. There is the kind of "standing against" or "oppositional gap" that Herbert Marcuse (1991) wants when he decries the flattening out between culture and social reality in the rationalizing context that accompanies capitalism. It is the flattening out that has obliterated the "oppositional, alien, and the transcendent elements in the higher culture by virtue of which it constituted another dimension of reality" (p. 57). Some would say that, in this respect, the ladder of organization-think is more like Diotima's ladder. But Abbott's *Flatland* is preferred. Unlike Diotima's ladder, a ladder of spatial dimensions does not raise legitimate questions about whether the image is true or a fairy tale. But an invitation to climb the ladder, despite the standing against or the oppositional gaps, is retained by this article's sub-heading "Beyond Flatland."

**General Content**

Seven features of the general character of discourse are described in this section.

Discourses provide a specific way of viewing our environment; some would want to say that they create contexts.

Discourses should be interpreted to include the biological, psychological, the social and the spiritual.

We have limited opportunity to choose our discourse(s).

Discourses are interrelated, some sometimes spawning subsidiary discourses.

Discourses can act in concert, and they are energized by discourses featuring motivations like group dynamics or self-interest.

Each discourse is limited; it filters some information and arbitrarily excludes or marginalizes opportunities for knowing and doing.

Finally, a discourse is likely to be more beneficial if the speaker is aware of the severity of the limitations.

First, the notion of discourse, making up the ladder, can be conceptualized in the way explained by Michel Foucault and others. Each discourse is a language or mind-set that provides a specific way of viewing our own environment. It includes verbal and non-verbal elements, and so it (and terms like "language") should not be understood as merely a matter of words. Beyond words, there are not only hand gesticulations (e.g., as in any Italian village) but also unconscious processes (e.g., as on the therapist's couch). The firefighter sees a building as a fire hazard, for example; an aluminum siding salesperson sees the same building as a sales opportunity. But the notion of discourse is stronger than this example suggests. As noted earlier, Foucault points out that discursive practice "systematically form the objects of which they speak" (1972). He is not a discourse idealist; the world is real, but what we can see depends on the shaping (better, co-shaping) of our discourse. Administrative agencies can be "seen" as made up of organization charts and procedures; or they can be "seen" in non-rationalizing terms, involving unconscious or irrational features (e.g., see McSwite, 1998). What is signified is "in" the world; but what is seen depends significantly on the seer's discourse. Seeing is not a mindless recording of what is "out there."

Second, discourse should be interpreted to include not only the conscious and the intellectual, but also the biological, the psychological, the social and the spiritual. Biological discourses engulf us; some would want to say that our discourse has a biological component. A celebrated classicist, W. K. C. Guthrie, suffered a heart attack shortly before starting Volume 6 of his six-volume *A History of Greek Philosophy* (1962/1981); his Volume 6, is written with more heart than his earlier volumes. Surely, those experiencing major afflictions—with AIDS or with brain impairments—can suffer changes in attitude. Then we have the work of the National Center for Human Genome Research, setting out to map and sequence the entire human genome; we have our genetically-determined discourse. Psychological elements, like the unconscious, make up our discourse; some want to say that they dominate our lives, our discourse. Why do some people exhibit a burning love (like Edmund Burke) for the status quo with a psychological force that is then buttressed with rationalizing arguments? Why do others have a living passion (like Rosa Luxemburg) to change the status quo with a psychological force which is supported with rationalizing arguments? (Why are you and I, if we are, in the latter category?) Social elements also constitute our discourse. National origin, date of birth, the historical timing of wars and rebellions, socio-economic status are clearly discourse elements. Spiritual elements also can be considered to constitute our discourse. This category, discussed later, is controversial. Some see love as a rationalization originating in feelings in childhood associated with organ satisfaction, for example; others see it as a spiritual manifestation or force which is not reducible to either the purely biological, psychological or social.

Third, discourse users are hardly self-aware unless they also recognize that the range of choice in selecting our discourse is limited. We are born into a complex of on-going discourses, and, at least in large part, we are surely constituted by them. Would Aristotle in his *Politics* have focused on the issues and problems of the city-state if he had walked in Marcus Aurelius' sandals? Would St. Augustine have written the *City of God* if he had lived in St. Thomas Aquinas' habit? Would Kant have written the *Critique of Pure Reason* if he had worked before Hume's discourse and the consequent awakening "from his dogmatic slumbers?"

Fourth, discourses tend to be interrelated. Each of the rungs on the ladder of organization-think is described as containing a family of discourses, for instance—like the personal, the work, the discipline, etc. The interrelationship can be conceptualized as like the Russian matryoshka doll, dolls within dolls; but the actual situation is less tidy. There are P.A. discourses—the economic, the technological, the hermeneutic—which are contained within the larger modernist discourse, for example. Could the traditional P.A. discourse, focusing on rationalization and mere efficiency, have developed independently of the rationalizing discourse of the Enlightenment—and the capitalist discourse that privileges the value of economic efficiency?

Fifth, discourses can act in concert, and they are energized by discourses featuring motivations like group dynamics or self-interest. My ethnic, socio-economic, educational and occupational discourses (or parts of my discourse), for instance, can hardly act independently of my biological and psychological discourses. They can hardly fail to incorporate any animal spirits expressed in my discourses (or discourse elements) of self-interest and group dynamics.

Sixth, each discourse, with its own particular shape, is limited. It allows us to know and to do some things well, and simultaneously it blinds us to other opportunities for knowing and doing. It operates like a filter (or lens, or framework, or grid), readily admitting what easily passes through the filter and filtering out what does not. This filter effect can be illustrated in terms of paradigm shift, which Thomas Kuhn (speaking of his notion of paradigms) compared with a gestalt shift (Kuhn, 1970). This filtering effect does have real advantages. Discourse constraints are beneficial in that they materially aid in advancing knowledge and in achieving desired actions. On knowledge, for example, the constraints of macroeconomic discourse—rather than the absence of such constraints—allow the economist to make a satisfactory judgment about the effect of a large tax cut in an economy that is bubbling over.

On action, for example, the constraints of the police officer's discourse (e.g., to the extent that she sees the world as populated by bad guys and good guys) help that officer to catch criminals.

Seventh, a discourse is likely to be even more beneficial if we are aware of the severity of the limitations. Consider the blinders of the economist's discourse. With her rationalizing discourse, the economist tends to exclude whole classes of information, like that on the unconscious workings of human interactions. With the particular form of her rationalizing discourse (using economic man as a unit of analysis), the economist is not encouraged to notice gender or racial issues in the economy. With particular definitions in the traditional form of discourse, the economist is encouraged not only to see some things but also to ignore others. Defining factors of production as including units of labor, land, capital and organizing ability tends to encourage the idea that a unit of labor "should" be bought and sold, just like any other factor of production. Defining gross national product (GNP) as the total value of all goods and services produced during a specified time period, excluding depreciation of natural resources, supports analyses that understand environmental concerns as "outside" economics.

## SELECTED RUNGS

Each rung contains a family of discourses. The following provides an explanation of each of the four selected rungs, and illustrates in terms of the ladder's manifestation as a ladder of P.A. discourse.

Chart 1 proposes a supplementary game for those willing to play with a purpose, asking the reader to identify additional questions and suggestions for improvements that might be expected (or hoped for) at each of the four levels. Instructions are provided in an endnote[1], and they are intended for discourse about three types of organizations (for example, P.A. discourse, Business Administration discourse, and Non-Profit discourse) and for discourse emanating from people in three types of organizations (for example, public bureaucrats, corporate bureaucrats, and other civil society bureaucrats).

### Rung One: "Me"

Rung One could be described by making use of the distinction used in economic theory between micro and macro economics, where microeconomics concerns the behavior of an ideal form ("the firm") of particular firms like General Motors. But I want to ask whether we could not deviate from this distinction. So the "me" rung of the ladder of organization-think, it will be recalled, is described here as consisting of a set of overlapping discourses that in terms of their basic unit of thinking (analyzing, theorizing) are reductionist (reduced to what is taught to "me" and familiar to "me," as to others in "my" discipline) and that focus on issues in terms primarily of "me"—"my" psychological baggage, "my" socio-economic and livelihood circumstances, "my" nationality, "my" family, "my" job, "my" organization, and so on. Both the notions of "unit of thinking" and "scope" are used broadly here. The former

## Chart 1
## The Rungs of the Ladder of Organization-Think

For readers willing to play with a purpose, see the instruction and acknowledgement in endnote 1.

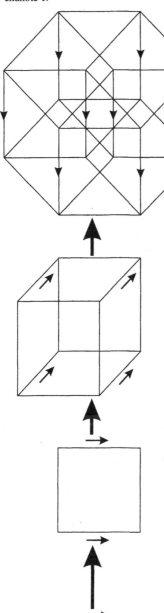

**Rung 4: Out of the Cave**
**Sample Question:** What is good for the whole system and for each person when I think through (in dialogue with others) the consequences of our recognition that each person is irreducibly a bio-psycho-socio-spiritual being?
**Sample Possibilities:** Authentic hesitation in moralizing; authentic listening to others; therapeutic management; anti-administration; thinking beyond "programs."

**Rung 3: Ours**
**Sample Question:** How can I develop more helpful concepts for learning what is good for the entire system by learning from a variety of disciplines, including those beyond my own?
**Sample Possibilities:** Play with a purpose; reflexive language paradigm; justice orientation, with anti-foundationalist ethics.

**Rung 2: They**
**Sample Question:** What can my discipline tell them about what is good for the system of which my organization is just a part?
**Sample Possibilities:** Analyses addressing the on-going antipathy against government; analyses about the "iron cage problem;" analyses about governmental size.

**Rung 1: Me**
**Sample Question:** What do approaches familiar to me tell me about what is good for my organization and for me?
**Sample Possibilities:** Better means-ends decisions.

refers, not merely to the work of analysts, but also to the general methods or attitudes of thinking, e.g., the general approaches that a manager or any other employee might have. Scope refers, not merely to the particular unit in which the person is located (the Federal Government or America On Line), but also to the work of structures or organizations considered relevant to that unit. On the personal end, for example for a fire fighting manager, this may involve "my" psychological and "my" ethnic structure. On the other, it may extend not merely to "my" fire agency but also to "my" city's organization and also any other entities considered important. In some cases, it may extend in a loose way even to all other fire agencies in the world and perhaps even to the Constitution itself (indicated by the flags sometimes worn on uniform sleeves).

The emphasis in both thinking and scope (in the broad sense in which these ideas have just been described) is on their relation to "me" (and "your") stake or involvement in the machine that Herbert Marcuse (1991) describes. Consider the basic unit of thinking. Marcuse holds that the most advanced areas of industrial society show "a trend toward consummation of technological rationality, and intensive efforts to contain this trend with the established institutions" (p. 17). For Marcuse, this is one-dimensional man thinking that involves the uncritical acceptance of existing structures, and norms. Happy consciousness he considers pervasive; the "Happy Consciousness—the belief that the real is rational and that the system delivers the goods—reflects the new conformism which is a facet of technological rationality translated into social behavior" (p. 84). The analytical and theorizing approach, the basic unit of thinking, implied in one-dimensional man requires a vision of people in correspondingly reduced terms, i.e. reduced from their full bio-psycho-social-spiritual dimensions. Economic man and bureaucratic man are examples. One-dimensional man is not likely to make what Marcuse recommends, the "great refusal." Within this context, thinking relies on an approach—an analytical and theorizing attitude—that furthers "my" and "your" concerns and interests in the machine of which "I" and "you" are a part.

Consider scope. Most work-relevant discourses are mixtures, including the psychological, the sociological and even attitudes toward institutions and groups well beyond the immediate micro unit. One such mixture is described by Brian McDonald (1999) in his memoir of three generations of his family in the New York City Police Department (NYPD)—*My Father's Gun: One Family, Three Badges, One Hundred Years in the NYPD*. The primary discourse (or discourse component) is a street-level NYPD discourse. Of his father's retirement from his position as a detective squad commander, he can write that he "was about to leave a job that not only defined him as a man, but also delineated his world" (p. 5). Other discourses (or discourse components) include the ethnic and socio-economic, and (note the last two) the administrative. The mixture is seen in the following examples:

> [I]n cop families 'not airing your dirty laundry' is a sacrament taken somewhere between baptism and first holy communion (p. 7).
>
> To us, that everything we did involved other cops' families was the most natural thing in the world—our orbit in a solar system held in place by the gravity of the New York City Police Department (p. 31).
>
> In the police code of the day,...the worst offense any cop could commit—even an honest cop—was to inform on other policemen (p. 71).
>
> Their swagger was intoxicating. He saw the uniform as armor. If he was wearing it, no one would laugh at him as they had at his father. (p. 96)
>
> Detectives, he found, were treated with a respect he had not known as a patrolman and certainly not as a coal miner's kid (p. 115).
>
> Traditionally, in the police department, official word comes only after sufficient time for unofficial word to be given (p. 129).
>
> On a tribal level, the New York City police department has always been run on an elaborate system of contracts—not the kind printed on paper and signed on the dotted lines, but verbal ones (p. 144).

The power of the mixture of discourses surely shapes policing and police attitudes. Many are conscious; some are unconscious. Some contain understandings extending to all police work. Consider this conversation:

> Son: Hey, that ain't fair.
> Father: Why not?
> Son: Because policemen fight dirty, you told me that.
> Father: That's right, boy, and don't you forget it. Just remember, cops always win. (p. 267)

It is reported by Rubenstein (1972) in introducing his chapter on "cop's rules." A discourse is being nurtured in the son about the characteristics of "all" police officers, the features of the universal (the genuine) "cop." In others, like the women police officers who were daughters of policemen, the discourse implanted may take a modified form.

The practicality of discourse analysis at Rung One can take a variety of forms. At a minimal end of the scale, it can serve to supplement activities like systems analysis and organizational development. For instance, an aim in the NYPD in the early seventies was to have commanders adopt a systematic approach toward corruption, identifying corruption hazards and proceeding systematically from there; discourse analysis could have added to the depth of the analysis. At the maximal end of the scale, a central concern of police administrations during the latter part of Mayor John Lindsey's term was in changing police discourse, especially in view of the Knapp Commission. This was evident not only in our various Master Plan activities (e.g., Patrol Bureau Master Plan System, Comprehensive Detective Command Review Plan) but also in day-to-day administration. A favorite question of the experienced and distinguished Police Commissioner Patrick V. Murphy (favorite in the sense that I heard him say it on many occasions) about the police officers on the street was "What are they doing out there?" Systems thinking was helpful in addressing operational problems in certain exceptionally large and high profile investigative activities. However, probably even better results would have been achieved through discourse analysis, including considering the relationships of one discourse (like the administrative) with others (e.g., like that described by McDonald). If our discourse analysis had been more central, better results might have been achieved. Discourse analysis would have had more prospects than systems analysis in achieving the goals underlying innovations like the Manpower Allocation Review System, described in D. J. Farmer (1984).

**Rung Two: "They"**

The set of overlapping discourses on Rung Two occupy a dimension where the focus is on the functioning of the system as a whole. That is, the emphasis is on the macro. The term "macro" is indeed borrowed from economic theory, where macroeconomics is concerned with the system as a whole. In the case of the ladder of P.A. discourse, the focus is on bureaucracy as a whole. The unit of thinking remains the same as on Rung One.

The same unit of thinking, as the term was described earlier, presents both strengths and limitations. Like any other discourse, the strength is that it does facilitate the production of much useful knowledge, e.g., that, in the case of macroeconomics, can be used in stabilizing and growing the economy. Consider part of the exclusion. The *International Herald Tribune* reported on June 3, 1993 (p. 15) that Baron Marcel Bich had signed over his company to his son Bruno; Bich is the king of throw-away products like ballpoint pens. Apparently, son Bruno planned to make changes, like selling parts of the business. The *Tribune* reports that, when asked to describe his feelings on the change, Baron Bich said, "I don't have any. In business, you can't have feelings." Eliminating feelings from the discourse of economics limits the perspective. So does any elimination of such considerations as justice and the unconscious. Justice is even exogenous in welfare economics; the unconscious is external to economic theory.

Traditional P.A. discourse is, as it were, iatrogenic. The locus of the disease of P.A. practice lies in large part in the limited scope of P.A. discourse, and a major reason is that too much of the scope of its discourse is confined to Rung One. The result is that the most important issues are not adequately addressed. Examples given elsewhere are critical and massive macro problems like the "iron cage" problems of a pervasive bureaucracy, and the deep and ongoing antipathy against bureaucracy (e.g., D. J. Farmer, 1999a). It is arguable that, in addition, Rung One issues can be better understood when supplemented by a Rung Two perspective. But others will disagree with this, saying that all that is required is that the employee should do her assigned job.

Those taking the affirmative on the latter point—the benefits for Rung One thinking of Rung Two insights—would point to examples. Consider three, starting with corruption. In a system where many politicians on a massive scale trade access and influence for donations (policies for money), how can corruption-related administrative issues be handled merely on the micro scale? Reports, like those from the Center for Public Integrity, document the scale of the policy-warp under the impact of monies. An August 1996 report documented sleep-overs (75 since 1993) in the Lincoln and Queen's bedrooms in the White House in return for large contributions (Center, 1996). The purchasing of policy and policy enforcement by the pesticide industry was the subject of another report, and in introducing *The Buying of Congress* Charles Taylor (Lewis, 1998) commented that "acts of grand larceny are committed on Capital Hill every day" (p. 1). For another source, Congressman Christopher Shays is reported as saying that, "You have labor leaders and corporate executives being bullied (by the political parties) for contributions. It's almost a shakedown.... We're talking $10,000 contributions, $50,000, $100,000, even $1 million" (AARP, July-August 1999, p. 4). This creates the prospect of not only grass eaters but also (in the phrase of the Knapp Commission) meat eaters among politicians, politicians acting as aggressive entrepreneurs "earning" monies. How can the micro be properly understood or administered in absence of the macro context? Consider a second example—the change in working conditions. Rightly or wrongly, for instance, thinkers have written about the contrast in working needs between the industrial ideal-type organization and the post-industrial ideal-type organization (e.g., Hage & Powers, 1992). Consider a third example—the shift in emerging social conditions to what some call the postmodern condition (e.g., Miller & Fox, 1997). Rightly or wrongly, for instance, thinkers have written of the implications of the recognition of a society of signs (Harris, 1996). In each case, the question can be repeated; how can the micro be properly understood or managed in absence of the macro context?

It is stressed that certainly not all of P.A. discourse is at the "me" dimension; on the contrary, the most important P.A. works are beyond that first rung. Yet, the major emphasis in P.A. is on work that yields short-term recipes that apply to micro situations. Practicality tends to be understood in these terms, and it is a tendency reinforced (for those attracted to administrative work) by the relative excitement offered by administrative action as compared with theorizing. It is also supported by the turf interests of related disciplines, like political science and economics. Wanting an audience, P.A. thinkers and teachers are encouraged by circumstances to pander to this limited understanding of practicality. A limited part of these circumstances may be that P.A. doctoral students are often ill-prepared by training to step beyond the first rung. Should not Herbert Simon's comment that P.A. is an academic backwater be taken to heart? Simon writes the following.

> [M]y actual research career started in an academic backwater; public administration. However important that field was and is to public affairs, it attracted few scholars with real understanding of what research was about, or how to construct the theoretical foundations for an applied field. (1991, p. 114)

Help that P.A. practitioners should receive is more P.A. discourse at Rung Two, the dimension for discourses of Macro Public Administration.

**Rung Three: "Our"**

A third rung denotes that family of discourses that is made possible when the current disciplinary walls are overcome. The social sciences and social action subjects speak with many discordant tongues, and the number of tongues seems on the increase. The current balkanization of knowledge is not internal to the social sciences or action subjects; it also extends to the barriers between the social sciences and the humanities—and the physical sciences. But the internal divisions are serious in both method and scope. The methodology of economic discourse favors the deductive and mathematical and it focuses on the human person as a thoroughly rational animal, i.e. economic man; the methodology of public administration discourse favors the inductive and it centers on the person as a bureaucratic man; psychology discourse favors..., and so on. The discourse scopes carve the world of knowledge into spheres of influence, often overlapping, competitive and subject to invasions by the strong against the weak. Economics covers this subject area (e.g., the allocation of scarce resources among competing means); public administration focuses on that subject area; and psychology is concerned with..., and so on. Continuing the interest in the unity of knowledge (the unity of the sciences) which was held by the Greeks and encouraged with a passion by the discourse of the Enlightenment, Wilson (1998) makes the following comments.

> It is obvious to even casual inspection that the efforts of social scientists are snarled by disunity and a failure of vision.... Split into independent cadres, they stress precision in words within their specialty but seldom speak the same technical language from one specialty to the next.... They are easily shackled by tribal loyalty.... Much of what passes for social theory is still in thrall to the original grand masters—a bad sign. (p. 182)

In his view, the result is that "too many social-science textbooks are a scandal of banality" (p. 183).

Overcoming the walls implies a change in method on, say, the ladder of P.A. discourse. Whether there can be a genuine (repeat, genuine) unity of science, encompassing all of the avenues and tributaries of knowledge by means of reducing all kinds of propositions without loss of meaning to a common set, remains at best an unclear and distant prospect; recognizing that the key phrase is "without loss of meaning," many would say impossible. Rung Three could include such discourse; but it is not limited to that kind of discourse. Any unavailability of a genuine unity of all sciences excludes neither multi-perspectival alternatives nor a series of limited integrations, e.g., between politics and economics and sociology, or between discourse theory and P.A. Certainly there are advocates for unity of science, reducing all to physics. Continuing in the tradition of Auguste Comte (the founder of positivism), Rudolf Carnap is an example. He explains a logical empiricist program for reducing all the sciences, including sociology and psychology, to physics—in a lifetime of work (e.g., in Carnap, 1934; 1938/68; & 1966). Yet, there are severe problems for any such reductionism raised by such issues as explanation versus understanding, reasons versus causes, and important developments (and lack of developments) in philosophy of science and philosophy of social science (e.g., Diesing, 1991; Hollis, 1994). On the latter, there is a lack of consensus about the nature of scientific method, with the principal competitors being neo-Kantian constructivism, scientific realism, and post-positivist empiricism (Boyd, Gasper & Trout, 1993); and Wisdom (1987) can write that "hardly anyone in this scientific age knows what the nature of science is..." (p. 71).

Beyond-the-walls discourses, different from any such "genuine" unity of science, would involve the willingness to look at issues from different perspectives (or frameworks or lenses or paradigms or languages) and limited integrations of now independent disciplines. The character of the perspective does shape what is counted as known or valid; psychoanalysis privileges what economics marginalizes, for instance. Using multiple perspectives and partial integrations (e.g., of economics and psychoanalysis) has advantages, as was demonstrated in the work by the first-generation members of the Frankfurt School of Critical Theory. It is not even necessary for such perspectives to be "true" if Milton Friedman and others are correct that the truth of a model's assumptions is not important. It was this method which was proposed for P.A. discourse in the reflexive language paradigm (D. J. Farmer, 1995). It was described as a playful and attuned dialogue with the underlying content of the language of public bureaucracy. It is an art that examines the set of assumptions and social constructions that constitute the theoretical lens through which we see; and it speculates about alternative sets of socially constructed assumptions (that form another lens) through which we could see. This may be seen as harkening back even to the Platonic ideal of finding knowledge through dialogue.

Discourse at this dimension would involve the freedom to use different definitions of scope in delineating problems and in seeking solutions. For the ladder of P.A. discourse, mention was made earlier of governmentality—adapting Foucault's term. This would embrace all forms of governance—within governments, economic enterprise, civil society structures, families or elsewhere. Governmentality can be taken as including any such bureaucracy—where bureaucracy is understood as any rule-driven structuring of the working relationship of two or more people, the rules setting the relationship enduring through what we can call the life of a particular transaction (for an example, see D. J. Farmer & R. L. Farmer, 1997). Problems and solutions could be analyzed in such larger terms at the Rung Three dimension. Even the concept of the macro could be extended beyond that used at the lower rung. The macro in the economic theory case, for instance, is system-wide; but the scope is limited to the economic. At this dimension, the relation of that macro to the rest of society could be folded in.

The sciences at Rung Two exclude considerations of ethics. Economic or psychological or any other theories, insofar as they are positivist, do not include the ethical. This requires some qualification. There can be an accommodation of the ethical in, say, economics; when any ethical prescription is added, the economist can specify the economic implications. But that is quite different from incorporating the economic with the ethical. The ethical in this case is understood as including thinking about how lives should be lived, and for that reason this dimension is labelled "ours."

**Rung Four: "Out of the Cave"**

Rung Four refers to the dimension of discourse where lower-rung and other problematics are analyzed by methods that focus on an approach which relies, not on a reduced conception of the human person (such as bureaucratic man or economic man) but on humans as bio-psycho-socio-spiritual persons. Implied in this are methods that are dialogic and holistic. Not implied by this is any essentialism about what it is to be human; on the contrary, all this is consistent with the social construction of the understanding of the human person. It does not imply that there is any essential spiritual or biological or other destiny that humans must realize. The label "out of the cave" might be over-optimistic in that even higher level rungs might yield more profound insights; for instance, poetry might yield more than philosophy.

Discourses or disciplines focusing on people, with a reduced conception of the nature of the human person, are able to yield useful results. The discourses of economic man and bureaucratic man have proven productive, for example, the former more than the latter. Yet leaving out important elements of what it is to be human leads to conclusions and designs that do not fully fit the needs of the full human person; instead, they tend to exert pressure on humans to become less than they can be. The discourse that constitutes the economic or capitalist machine, designed to optimize profits, is an example. It is a celebrated facilitator of wealth production, as the collapse of the Soviet system testified. To a significant extent, economic attention can be paid to the failures of the invisible hand, e.g., instability (business cycles), the public goods problem, gross inequalities, and economic growth issues. The discourse is less successful in overcoming the irrationalities of the means-ends culture. It is dramatically less successful in facilitating aspects of the human that are excluded. It provides for the body, the psyche, the social and the spiritual only insofar as that leads to optimization of profits. The situation is made more severe in that the economic machine exerts ever-larger demands on the people who have no choice but to belong to it. In Weber's words, the "tremendous cosmos of the economic order…[is]…now bound to the technical and economic conditions of machine production which today determine the lives of all the individuals who are born into this mechanism" (1958, p. 181).

The discourse of the bureaucratic machine (calling it organic makes no difference) is a similar case, related because the economic and the bureaucratic are bound together. Yes, it certainly is productive in meeting some biological, psychological, social and spiritual needs. Yet the cost is very high in terms of the denial of other important aspects of the full human person. This is what Weber had in mind when he spoke of our Faustian bargain, whereby we sacrifice our "full and beautiful humanity" in return for a narrow vocation where we are "specialists without spirit, sensualists without heart" in a rationalized and disenchanted world (Weber, 1958, p. 182). This was the "iron cage": care for external goods should be worn like a light cloak, but "fate decreed that the cloak should become an iron cage" (p. 181).

The social, the psychological and the biological in the formula "bio-psycho-socio-spiritual" are likely to give little difficulty, although each are dramatically affected by their mutual interaction. The term "spirituality" is likely to present (the reader and the writer) the greater difficulty, however. It is sometimes suspect because it evokes the images of bible-thumping and of sleight-of-hand directed at "slipping in" the theological. That is not intended; I do not want to include religion, any more than I want to exclude it. Currently, I think of spirituality as referring to the energy and other unifying effects of what can be called the singularity of a person. The energy (or energies) is a kind of explosive force that exceeds systematization; it tends to flood over in its empowering and liberating strength; and it engages the pre-systemized power of the psyche. It is revolutionary energy that pushes beyond the well-ordered categories of language or logic. It is poetic, in part because it is what exceeds our limits. It denotes the idea of the entire person in her full singularity and of a significant opening of that singularity beyond herself. It concerns the whole person in that she is involved in all her aspects, including all aspects of the biological, the psychological, the social and whatever else. It concerns an opening of the person—if not to the gods—to the wholeness of herself, of nature and of sociality.

The notion of singularity can be understood as the existential entities that are logically prior to being captured in terms of the universals that are required for language and for knowing. For such a notion of singularity, Giorgio Agamben is especially helpful. Agamben indicates that the "coming being is whatever being" (1993, p. 1), and he explains that the "Whatever in question here relates to singularity not in its indifference with respect to a common property...but only in its being as such" (p. 1).

> In this conception, such-and-such being is reclaimed from its having this or that property, which identifies it as belonging to this or that set, to this or that class (the reds, the French, the Muslims)—and it is reclaimed not for another class nor for the simple generic absence of any belonging, but for its being-such, for belonging itself.... The singularity exposed as such is whatever you want, that is, lovable. (p. 1-2)

> Whatever singularity has no identity, it is not determinate with respect to a concept, but neither is it simply indeterminate; rather it is determined only through a relation to an idea, that is, to the totality of its possibilities (p. 67).

Giorgio exists in his singularity. He exists not in terms of any universal description, say, as a man, as a philosopher, as a writer, as a modern thinker, as an Italian—and other universals. He exists as a singularity, exceeding the confines of any single or group of universal descriptors. Giorgio exists even with no name.

Organization-think, including P.A., lags behind in constructing discourse that considers each of the aspects—biological, psychological, social and spiritual—in relation to one another. In this respect, for instance, it lags behind social work, just as social work treatment of administration lags behind P.A.; this is a Rung Three issue where each can learn from the other. The claim that P.A. lags behind in appreciating the interrelationship of the four aspects is not to deny that too little is done on such individual directions as the spiritual, the psychological and the social in themselves. The point here is that the aspects are not considered in relation to one another. Rosemary L. Farmer (1999) specifies a transactional model for teaching advanced clinical human behavior courses, for example. She distinguishes this from physiological reductionist and interactionist models. "Reductionism would show one set of entities being reduced to, or explained in terms of, another. Interactionism would show several entities interacting and affecting each other but remaining unchanged by the interaction" (1999, pp. 290-294). In her transactional model, she describes the interrelationship of the "bio," the "psycho," the "social," the "spiritual," and the problem under consideration (which she calls "challenge in living") as systems that function simultaneously as part and as whole.

> [As such] each aspect influences every other dimension in a circular and systemic way, and behavior is determined by the interaction and mutual causation of all systems and subsystems. The transactional model provides a more circular cause/effect/cause perspective, rather than a linear, stimulus/response perspective. (R. L. Farmer, 1999, pp. 290–294)

> [For example,]the challenge in living may be represented by an adolescent male who has recently emigrated to the U.S. from Central America and is becoming involved in a Latino gang. Rather than seeing his recent arrival in this country as the sole stimulus for his response of getting into trouble as part of a gang, the transactional model enables the practitioner to look at how the recent emigration has impacted his sense of self (psychological factor), which may result in his intense relations with other gang members (social factor), which may lead to the anti-social behavior of gang criminality (possibly a learned behavior), all of which may affect hormone levels in his developing body (biological factor). Each of these factors is unique but contributes to the situation at hand. (R. L. Farmer, 1999, p. 293)

The transactional model shows a set of relationships that are integrated, though not equivalent, and simultaneously interact with each other, constituting what she describes as a *holon*, between entities designated as "challenge in living," "bio," "psycho," "social," and "spiritual." The term holon reflects the idea that each entity or system, i.e. challenge, bio, psycho, social, spiritual, is "simultaneously a part and a whole. Each entity faces two directions at once (it looks inward toward its own parts and outward to the system of which it is a part)" (R. L. Farmer, 1998, p. 292) "The transactional model is not at all reductionist; the person is viewed as irreducibly bio-psycho-socio-spiritual" (p. 292).

Much remains to be theorized about the implications of this bio-psycho-socio-spiritual model for P.A. Consider the social, for instance. I suppose that this level of discourse would be consistent with understandings of society in terms of cultural holism. Craige (1992) describes this as a vision (or discourse) of "human society as an evolving, complex open system of interdependent cultures and individuals, none of whom enjoys absolute superiority to any other, all of which develop in relation to each other and to their non-human environment" (pp. 292–293). She associates this with a holistic view of reality, anticipated by Darwin and expressed in multiculturalism, environmentalism, the international peace movement and other features she considers related. Presumably, this could be interconnected with such notions as neighborhood, as socially interactive living, and as supportive community. I suppose that the bio-psycho-socio-spiritual discourse is also connected with the work that Jurgen Habermas has done on communicative rationality and on deliberative politics (e.g., Habermas, 1996). In particular, I think that it relates to the development of improvements in the style of justice, including the authentic hesitation described elsewhere (D. J. Farmer, 1999b). There is so much that needs to be pursued in terms of this discourse rung. The P.A. theory community could well "play with a purpose" about the mind-set provided by Rung Four discourse.

## CONCLUSIONS

Selected rungs of a ladder of organization-think were described. The ladder can represent discourse about organizations and discourse emanating from organizations; the main illustration used here was its manifestation as a ladder of P.A. discourse. The ladder was described in terms of spatial dimensions and of discourse theory, and it contained an exhortation that we should move beyond Flatland. Seven characteristics of discourse, a specific way of viewing or creating our environment, were described. For example, each discourse is limited; it filters some information and arbitrarily excludes or marginalizes opportunities for knowing or doing. A discourse is likely to be more beneficial if the speaker is aware of the severity of the limitations.

Rung One, the "me" dimension, consists of overlapping discourses that are reductionist in terms of their general unit of thinking (analysis, theorizing) and that focus on issues primarily in terms of "me." The value of discourse theory at this level was illustrated in terms of the NYPD. Rung Two, a "they" dimension, is also reductionist; but the scope extends so that issues are now approached in their system-wide or macro context. Rung Three, an "our" dimension, concerns a family of discourses that are possible when discourse widens beyond the confines of current disciplinary walls. Rung Four, labelled "out of the cave," refers to the range of discourses which analyze problematics, not on a reduced conception of the human person (e.g., as bureaucratic or economic man) but on humans as bio-psycho-socio-spiritual beings.

It was suggested that P.A. thinkers should be interested in the ladder of organization-think for five main reasons. First, discourse theory is an invaluable analytical approach. Second, the root of major problems in P.A. practice lies in the limited character of P.A. discourse, the latter being too confined to the lower rungs. The P.A. disease is largely, in the sense indicated, iatrogenic; for instance, bad practice can be upgraded only within the limits of the discourse used. Third, discourse at each of the dimensions can be radically more useful if conducted with self-awareness and with some reference to the other rungs of the ladder. Examples were given in terms of corruption, changing work requirements and radically new societal conditions. Fourth, valuable additional insights can be obtained through discourse at the higher rungs. For example, Rung Two permits P.A. to address the problems of the "iron cage" and the ongoing antipathy against government. As another example, we are lagging in understanding the relevance of regarding humans in bio-psycho-socio-spiritual terms. Fifth, P.A. theorizing has failed to create the conceptual space for genuine reform efforts like the National Partnership for Reinventing Government. The problem is not confined to any blank theoretical bullets we are producing. It is also that reform options are hobbled politically because P.A. theory has not been rich enough to create an attentive public open to analyses at the higher rungs of the ladder of organization-think. We have been too limited to Flatland.

## ENDNOTES

1. Chart 1 is for readers willing to play with a purpose, identifying specific questions and suggestions for improvement opportunities that might be expected from the selected dimension of discourse: (a) for discourse about three types of organizations and (b) for discourse from people in three types of organizations.

Each reader is invited to draw her own 4 inch by 6 inch chart. Down the left column of the chart, please write the four levels—me, they, our, and out of the cave. Across the column at the top of the chart, write headings for discourses about three types of organizations (e.g., P.A. discourse, Business Administration discourse, Non-Profit discourse) and headings for discourses emanating from people in three types of organizations (e.g., public bureaucrats, corporate bureaucrats, other civil society bureaucrats).

Hopefully ideas can be encouraged from the text. The sample questions and the sample possibilities for improvement opportunities are intended to supplement.

The designs for the spatial dimensions are taken from Rucker (1977, p. 2). Rucker took the design for the hypercube from a 1913 book, *Primer of Higher Space*, by Claude Bragdon.

2. Thanks for reviewing this paper to Drs. Rosemary L. Farmer and Janet R. Hutchinson.

## REFERENCES

Abbott, E. A. (1884/1952). *Flatland*. New York: Dover.

AARP. (1999, July-August). Shays keep battling election-law abuse. *The Nation*, 4.

Boyd, R., Gasper, P. & Trout, J. D. (1993). *The philosophy of science*. Cambridge, Massachusetts: The MIT Press.

Bragden, C. (1913). *Primer of higher space*. Rochester, NY: The Manas Press.

Carnap, R. (1934). *The unity of science* (M. Black, Trans.). London: Kegan Paul Trench and Trubner. (Original work published 1934).

Carnap, R. (1966). *Philosophical foundations of physics: An introduction to the philosophy of science*. New York: Basic Books.

Carnap, R. (1938/68). Foundations of the social sciences. In O. Neurath, R. Carnap & C. Morris (Eds.), Foundations of the unity of science: Vol. 2. (pp. 1–51). Chicago: University of Chicago Press.

Center for Public Integrity. (1996). *Fat cat hotel* [On-line]. Available: http://www.publicintegrity.org/main.html

Craige, B. J. (1992). *Laying the ladder down*. Amherst, Massachusetts: University of Massachusetts Press.

Diesing, P. (1991). *How does social science work? Reflections on practice*. Pittsburgh, Pennsylvania: University of Pittsburgh Press.

Farmer, D. J. (1984). *Crime control: The use and misuse of police resources*. New York: Plenum Press.

Farmer, D. J. (1995). *The language of public administration: Bureaucracy, modernity, and postmodernity*. Tuscaloosa, Alabama: University of Alabama Press.

Farmer, D. J. (1998). Public administration discourse as play with a purpose. In D. J. Farmer (Ed.), *Papers on the art of anti-administration* (pp. 37–56). Burke, Virginia: Chatelaine.

Farmer, D. J. (1999a). Public administration discourse: A matter of style? *Administration and Society, 31*, 299–320.

Farmer, D. J. (1999b). The discourse movement: A centrist view of the sea change. *International Review of Public Administration, 4*, 3–10.

Farmer, R. J. (1999). Clinical HBSE concentration: A transactional model. *Journal of Social Work Education, 35*, 289–299.

Farmer, D. J & Farmer, R. L. (1997). Leopards in the temple: Bureaucracy and the limits of the in-between. *Administration and Society, 29*, 507–528.

Foucault, M. (1972). *The archaeology of knowledge* (S. Smith, Trans.). London: Tavistock. (Original work published 1972).

Giorgio, A. (1993). *The coming community* (M. Hardt, Trans.). Minneapolis: University of Minnesota Press. (Original work published 1993).

Guthrie, W. K. C. (1962-1981). *A history of Greek philosophy* (Vols. 1–6). London: Cambridge University Press.

Habermas, J. (1996). *Between facts and norms: Contributions to a discourse theory of law and democracy*. Cambridge, Massachusetts: The MIT Press.

Hage, J. & Powers, C. H. (1992). *Post-Industrial lives: Roles and relationships in the 21st century*. Newbury Park, California: SAGE.

Harris, D. (1996). *A society of signs?* London: Routledge.

Hollis, M. (1994). *The philosophy of social science*. New York: Cambridge University Press.

*International Herald Tribune.* (1993, June 3). p. 15.

Kuhn, T. (1970). *The structure of scientific revolutions.* Chicago: University of Chicago Press.

Lewis, C. (1998). *The buying of congress.* New York: Avon Books.

Marcuse, H. (1991). *One-dimensional man: Studies in the ideology of advanced industrial society.* Boston, Massachusetts: Beacon.

Maslow, A. (1954). *Motivation and personality.* New York: Harper and Brothers.

McDonald, B. (1999). *My father's gun: One family, three badges, one hundred years in the NYPD.* New York: Dutton.

McSwite, O. C. (1998). Stories from the "real world"; Administering anti-administratively. In D. J. Farmer (Ed.) *Papers on the art of anti-administration* (pp. 17–36). Burke, Virginia: Chatelaine Press.

Miller, H. T. & Fox, C. J. (1997). What do we mean when we say "real" in public administration: The modern/postmodern distinction. In H. T. Miller & C. J. Fox (Eds.), *Postmodernism, "reality," and public administration: A discourse* (pp. 51–67). Burke, Virginia: Chatelaine Press.

Orwell, G. (1977). *1984.* New York: Penguin.

Rubenstein, J. (1972). *City police.* New York: Farrar, Straus and Giroux.

Rucker, R. (1977). *Geometry, relativity and the fourth dimension.* New York: Dover.

Simon, H. (1991). *Models of my life.* New York: Basic Books.

Weber, M. (1958). *The protestant ethic and the spirit of capitalism.* New York: Scribner.

Wilson, E. O. (1998). *Consilience: The unity of knowledge.* New York: Alfred A. Knopf.

Wisdom, J. O. (1987). *Challengeability in modern science.* Aldershot: Avebury.

Wittgenstein, L. (1961). *Tractatus logico-philosophicus.* London: Routledge and Kegan Paul.

# R~~ed Queen~~

David John Farmer
Virginia Commonwealth University

The ~~Red Queen~~ underscores that *traditional* PA is passé, a dead project. Like all the other mainstream governance subjects? The Red Queen is written with an erasure for the reasons described later; until then, please feel comfy if you want to read it as though it were not crossed through. The ~~Red Queen~~ points forward to post-traditional governance thinking, important in a world increasingly shackled in visible and invisible institutional chains. Through our (and Alice's) looking glass, let's look!

This column, *CommonSense@Admin*, is shutting down, and this is the last column. Let's explain!

To mark the shutting down and in the spirit of Alice (in Wonderland), our four grandchildren—and our cat Maynard—offered to interview me. Let's wonder!

QUESTION (from pre-toddler Grace): Who's the ~~Red Queen~~, and what's she signifying that relates to action subjects like PA and BA (business administration) and to more powerful disciplines like Econ (economics)?

DJF: Who is she? The Red Queen is a character from *Through the Looking Glass, and What Alice Found There* (Carroll, 1872). The Red Queen, at one point, grabbed Alice's hand and dragged Alice in a pell-mell and ever-faster run through the countryside. (Remember that she is a queen in a book with a Chess theme, and a Chess queen is super-fast because she can move any number of squares in a straight line in any direction—in a single move.) Yet, no matter how fast they ran, Alice et al. always remained in the same place. Puzzled Alice said, "Well in *our* country you'd generally get to somewhere else. . . ." Replied the Red Queen, "A slow sort of country. . . . Now, *here*, you see, it takes all the running you can do, to keep in the same place. . . ."

What does it signify? The signifier ~~Red Queen~~ signifies disciplines running slower than their terrains are moving, at best. It signifies traditional PA and other mainstream governance subjects making no "real" forward movement.

QUESTION (from toddler Ashton): Give me three reasons why you should draw a line through the ~~Red Queen~~? Why cross it out? Or, to put it another way, what about the Derridean move of putting the signifier ~~Red Queen~~ "under erasure"?

DJF: The first reason is that the ~~Red Queen~~ incident doesn't tell the complete story because it doesn't speak about direction. Traditional PA and the rest are not just running slowly, relative to the ground. Also traditional PA and other disciplines are running in the wrong direction. For example, traditional PA is running in the wrong direction in its pursuit of *the* micro-efficiency project that should have made little sense in President Wilson's time and that now makes nonsense. The *running* is misdirected in terms of scope, methods, and talent. For a parallel contrast between neoclassical economics and "hip heterodoxy" in a flashier and more influential discipline see Hayes (2007): the sub-title of his article is "Neoclassical economics still reigns, but its critics are gathering steam."

Let's say more about the wrong direction. It's the norm (not a universal norm, however) for governance subjects to run in the wrong direction in terms of things v. consciousness. It is genuinely helpful to fiddle with improving things (e.g., in economics or in PA). But it misses the point that social consciousness (culture, if you prefer that term) is the primary determinant of the way things are. We live inside the limits, the invisible chains, of our own consciousness. That was the point of my "Froglets or Fairy Tales" (1999); it was also a main point of *To Kill the King* (Farmer, 1999; 2005). The consciousness literature is large and useful (e.g., see Castoriadis, 1997). It is counterproductive to treat only the symptoms (the things, the spots), rather than to address the disease (the perspective that the society regards as common sense, the measles).

The second reason for the erasure is that the news from the Alice front isn't the complete truth. In fact, the news needn't be all bad. I'm not ruling out that there can be an advantage in being in what Herbert Simon (1991, p. 114) called an "intellectual backwater"; there can be advantage in what the ~~Red Queen~~ incident symbolizes as lack of fleetness of foot. Where there is nothing important going on among the tradition-thinkers (except busy, and interfering, work), the post-traditional inmates may (or may not) experience a greater impulse to reflect imaginatively—about something other than traditional common sense preoccupations (not confusing common, with good, sense). Guy de

Maupassant set a useful example. He was a civil servant in his day job (French departments of the navy and then public information), and wrote *The Necklace* and other stories in his (wink, wink!) spare time. My impression is that the constraints (visible and invisible chains) to conform to tradition might be stronger in some other academic departments, more than in PA. It's a slender thread of optimism, I agree. Yet, on this thread, I'm giving the ~~Red Queen~~ an erasure.

The third overlapping reason for the ~~Red Queen~~ is explained by Jacques Derrida (1976). He understands an erasure to be a concept or a text that's inaccurate but that's necessary to say. A concept or text *under erasure* is written (or read) as if its meaning were clear, but the use of the word—in Derrida's view—is only a strategy. Apparently, Derrida learned the gesture from Martin Heidegger's use of the signifier ~~Being~~.

QUESTION (from David, 12 years old): So what does including us grandchildren signify?

DJF: PA thinking is basically short-run. Economic theory can swing either way; but economic practice is typically short-run. On the contrary, PA (and Econ) thinking should focus much less on the short-run. The lifetimes of our grandchildren or the equivalent should be our primary time focus in theorizing, whether or not said grandchildren are living now or are yet to be born. And I think that Charles Lutwidge Dodgson—Lewis Carroll being his nom de plume—would have approved, if he had not been dead since 1898.

Also PA and Econ need imaginative questions from left field. The freshness of questioning is symbolized by grandchildren.

QUESTION (from Tyler, 13 years): Has this column been going all my life?

DJF: No. But it feels like all *my* life. Thanks to Richard Box, it's been going since March 2000, about seven and a half years—with a miss with the June 2006 symposium. Avant la lettre, *it* started in 1998—if *it* is understood as referring to contributing items for every journal issue. On the first basis, it's 29 papers; on the second, it's 36.

COMMENT (from Maynard the Cat): To avoid liver damage through excessive repeating of your own name, I suggest that references to column articles should contain just the date. So whenever I see a reference date in parentheses without a name, I will assume that it's you.

DJF: It's a deal, Maynard. Here, have some liver!

QUESTION (from David): So, what are five themes or topics that you covered that you feel the best about?

DJF: A first theme or topic, probably, is that our social consciousness (and thus institutional practice) should privilege love rather than (say) efficiency. This was discussed in "Love and Un-engineering" (2002a). I think the case is stronger when the contrast is made with the unlovely story about institutions in "The Devil's Rope" (2002c). For me, love is the only desirable aim in living; it's necessary in institutions that seek to provide for the fully human. I'm with Plato (and his *Symposium*) on the primacy of love.

A second theme, probably, is that our social and individual consciousness (and thus individual and institutional thinking) should be infused with imagination. "The Dancing Star" (2005c) tried to add to the discussion in *To Kill the King* (2005). It continued the description of what imagination is, and what it is not.

A third theme, probably, is that our social consciousness (and thus institutions) should have an appropriate ethical component. Here the fate of the "other" is critical; I regret that traditional PA and mainstream Econ are typically other-blind, although sometimes other-shortsighted. In the case of PA, this is where the *other* is an outsider like the client, the customer, the welfare recipient, the mentally ill person, the homeless person, etc. "Expanding the Ethical Sphere" (2003) speaks about the increasingly wide range of application of ethical acts, indicating what this increasing scope suggests for PA Eth-Talk. "The Moral First, the Technical Second" (2005b) discusses whether each person in a hierarchical situation should put her ethics first. Under this theme, I should also mention "Great refusals and the administered life" (2000a) and (surely repeating Michel Foucault) "Power speaking v. speaking to power" (1999a).

A fourth theme, probably, is that our social consciousness (and thus institutions) could be made more relevant if the upswing in neuroscience were to be used as a catalyst to transform governance subjects like PA. The two articles were "Neuro-gov" (2006c) and "Change the course, neurons" (2007). Again, neuroeconomics and neuro-political-science are streaking ahead of PA, albeit not necessarily in the best directions.

A fifth theme or topic, probably, is that our social consciousness (and thus institutions) could be improved if our own lived experiences could be incorporated more effectively into our professional work, on the lines recommended by Helene Cixous. I've done that in my own way in articles like "In the Pink" (2003b). I frequently include references to "writings" that thrill my life, for example, Shakespeare's poetry, the quotes on the walls of the Kennedy Center. Then there was an article about Shakespeare's Henry IV Part 1 ("I Know Thee Not," 2004a), speaking about Henry V and leadership. I also include what frightens me, like the extent of corruptive campaign contributions and militarism—as in "The Spirit of Our Age" (2006b). PA and the rest should learn to say *I*. The tradition in professional philosophical writing is that *I* is not a dirty word: avoiding *I* is a dirty attempt in the social sciences to pretend to scientific objectivity. Yet *I*-identity is not merely about me, because I'm told that we are also group animals. So I did enjoy the articles on books that non-traditional PA thinkers love, as in the articles "Life-changing books" (2003c) and "More Books, More Play" (2004).

Misdirection in *traditional* PA is implied in all of these themes. Re-enter the ~~Red Queen~~. Such running in the wrong direction was discussed in other terms in a number of articles (e.g., 2001, 2001a, 1999b, 1999c). For example, it was claimed that traditional PA's focus on the mid-level manager and on the primacy of mere efficiency, etc., left hopeful high-level reform initiatives (like, to mention "ancient" history, Vice-President Albert Gore's National Partnership for Reinventing Government) with no adequate PA-relevant theoretical rudder. Doesn't the lack of higher level and macro PA theory encourage ill-effects in social consciousness (and thus institutions)? For example, aren't we suffering from such ill-effects (bearing in mind that *some* can be good while *excessive* cannot) as excessive privatization (e.g., see Scahill, 2007), excessive disrespect for government, and excessive disregard of the public good?

Post-traditional PA is *after*—or *apart from* or *beyond*—the misdirection and the other limitations of traditional PA. It's not to be confused with, say, postmodernism. As discussed:

> [The] post-traditional is *beyond* postmodernism. It is *beyond* critical theory. How can that be? Hegel's system suggests one way, synthesis that yields full understanding only at the end of all the syntheses. However, the word *beyond* can be replaced, for example, with *before* or *beside* or *underneath* or *separate from*. Relating to this, the post-traditional is not the same (a nicer word?) as something else like critical theory or postmodernism. Yet there are affinities to these and to other isms like feminism, critical legal theory, post-colonial theory, etc. (2006d, pp. 169-170)

QUESTION (from Ashton): So have most of the articles been about reflecting on social consciousness? Have you recommended ways to reflect or contemplate?

DJF: Most have included reflections on social consciousness, directly or indirectly. I think that consciousness has been the primary subject; and the primary object. But there have been things about things.

I think that the books (1995; 2005) and symposia probably contained more about method. *The Language of Public Administration* and the Anti-Administration symposium both talked about contemplation from multiple perspectives, with the aim of escaping any single and parochial perspective. For PA, I prefer macro perspectives like postmodernism, feminism, postcolonialism, economism, critical theory, psychoanalysis, critical legal theory; and I think it is unimportant whether this or that ism is completely true or completely false (a strange dichotomy). The object is to generate truthful insights. In this sense Milton Friedman was right in saying (although he was speaking only of economic models) that the premises don't matter; rather, it is a question of the truth of the conclusions. There are so many techniques for contemplating consciousness that have not yet been mined enough within, say, PA, for example, the symbolic and rhetoric (see 2002).

*To Kill the King* talked about my favorite ~~tools~~ of play and imagination—items as scarce as hens' teeth in traditional PA. Articles in the column have also spoken about, as mentioned, such ~~tools~~.

But I would stress that there are many varieties of ~~tools~~. A book by Gomory and Baumol (2000) is an illustration of how excellent economists can contemplate or reflect about economic consciousness—the latter being a large contributor to social consciousness. It's not merely the importance of their conclusions about global trade and conflicting national interests, claiming that trade theory needs to be "modified from the trade theory provided by Ricardo and his contemporaries" (2000, p. xiii). A striking feature is the *reflective* use of their economic theory ~~tools~~.

QUESTION (from Grace): Were any articles about insects?

DJF: No insects, unless you count froglets or penguins.

QUESTION (from David): Which article was your worst?

DJF: I'm disappointed with particular defects. Thus, I don't like the fact that, when I wrote about Homeland Security (2002b), I didn't say that it was absurd to create such a large conglomerate. I should have written, instead, about the disadvantages of government consciousness being czar-struck, although I suppose that is a minor corollary of *To Kill the King*.

For another instance, in my last "See Spot Run" paper (2007a), I should have stressed the differences between Austrian and mainstream economics—and then I could have argued that the Austrian is even more problematic. As Kirzner (1998, p. 37) explains, "the modern Austrian paradigm differs from the mainstream approach...in the Austrian rejection of the centrality in the latter of the perfectly competitive model, and its replacement by the idea of the entrepreneurial-competitive market process."

QUESTION (from Tyler): I notice that you didn't include economics in your earlier list of preferred themes. Did you write about economics as the critical context, and the master signifier, of PA?

DJF. Yes, economics is critical for PA because a particular view of economics is a major determinant of our social consciousness. This particular view is examined in "See Spot Run" (2007b), which is about the dominant neoliberal paradigm of market fundamentalism. The article "Frigginomics" (2005d) concerned the indoctrination of kindergarten and other elementary school children with market fundamentalism—with this particular view of the economic. This indoctrination can be seen in the choice of standards of learning (SOLs) and the pushing of parts that constitute a "happy, happy economics" (or what I called frigginomics). By contrast there's the more realistic description originating in reaction to the views of Reverend Thomas Malthus, economics as the dismal science.

"Wal-Mart" (2006a) was intended to show how we can discuss corporate giants, and how we should use multiple frames. I urge PA thinkers (or any other governance thinkers) not to hesitate to make forays outside disciplinary boundaries. I (2005) have said that we shouldn't aim to create a huge mega-discipline like (say) Humanomics from among the litter of social science and action subjects. Rather, we need extra-territorial foraging, scavenging, and Viking raiding into hitherto-comfortable turfs.

But typically, I mixed in the economics (like philosophy) with the other items, for example, the Limits of Enterprise (in Farmer, 1995, pp. 103-127) and Invisible Hand (in Farmer, 2005, pp. 154-167). Governance disciplines and terrains are interrelated. For example, a mixture of disciplines is needed in reflecting on the serious problem of lobby(ectomy), where traditional PA by itself is next to helpless. Then that terrain is tied in with what Chalmers Johnson (2006) calls Military Keynesianism. (Is lack of such "mixing" a reason why traditional PA has so dropped the ball by failing to harp on the significance of black budgets, e.g., 40 percent in the U.S. Department of Defense?)

QUESTION (from Maynard): What were your three worst titles? I mean the titles by themselves, regardless of the content—a sort of ugly (beauty) contest. Remember that I'm a cat, and I think that style is everything.

DJF: My first three articles had the worst titles. Ugh!

"Framing a Senator, ASPA and the Zeus-list" (1998)

"Tuscan 'Border Crossing'" (1998a)

"What Max Weber Would Say About America at its Best" (1998b).

COMMENT (from Maynard): Well, I think that your worst title was "Administration as Unconscious: Do Penguins Have Knees?" (2000). It should have been "Do cats have knees?" There's been nothing in this column about cats—not even bad jokes about *cat*astrophes!

QUESTION (from Tyler): Have you ever been changed by your own writing?

DJF: Definitely, and in ways that surprised me. For example, I wrote about religion and PA in "Talking about religion" (2005a). It included personal information about my own "religious" history. I thought that would be that. To my surprise, it was a kind of therapy, and it resulted in me shifting much closer to what I suppose is Slavoj Zizek's attitude (see Farmer, 2006, pp. 301-302) toward religion and atheism.

However, shouldn't self-change be a major aim in writing?

QUESTION (from Ashton): If you were writing another column (for the next issue), what would it be about?

DJF: Who knows? Maybe it could have been reflecting about the science of the sperm and the egg. Emily Martin, for example, describes the challenge of waking up "sleeping metaphors in science, particularly those involved in descriptions of the egg and the sperm" (Martin, 1991, p. 501). On the other hand, it could have been biological evolution; recently I've been reading more by Richard Dawkins (e.g., 2005). The discourse of biological evolution involves a level of imaginative and analytical creativity that I believe should be sought in governance subjects.

QUESTION (from Grace): For the last question, I will ask you the same "last question" as you asked when you interviewed Orion and Cynthia McSwite (2003a). "Would you care to offer a comment at this point to the PA Theory community?"

DJF: Heartfelt thanks to Richard Box for being such a generous and effective editor, and warm thanks to Jon Jun for the support he gave. Sincere thanks also to kind readers, both those from within PAT-Net and those beyond.

PAT-Net sets a hot pace in terms of moving the ground. I wish that the ~~Red Queen~~ and I could have run faster.

## REFERENCES

Carroll, L. (1872). *Through the looking glass, and what Alice found there.* London: MacMillan.

Castoriadis, C. (1997). *World in fragments: Writings on politics, society, psychoanalysis, and the imagination.* Stanford, CA: Stanford University Press.

Dawkins, R. C. (2004). *The ancestor's tale: A pilgrimage to the dawn of evolution.* New York: Houghton Mifflin.

Derrida, J. (1976). *Of grammatology* (G. K. Spivak, Trans.). Baltimore, MD: The Johns Hopkins University.

Farmer, D. J. (1995). *The language of public administration: Bureaucracy, modernity and postmodernity.* Tuscaloosa, AL: University of Alabama.

Farmer, D. J. (1998). Framing a senator, ASPA and the Zeus-list. *Administrative Theory & Praxis, 20,* 248-252.

Farmer, D. J. (1998a). Tuscan "border crossing." *Administrative Theory & Praxis, 20,* 397-398.

Farmer, D. J. (1998b). What would Max Weber say about America at its best? *Administrative Theory & Praxis, 20,* 531-533.

Farmer, D. J. (1999). Froglets or fairy tales? *Administrative Theory & Praxis, 21,* 154-155.

Farmer, D. J. (1999a). Power speaking v. speaking to power. *Administrative Theory & Praxis, 21,* 240-242.

Farmer, D. J. (1999b). Springer? *Administrative Theory & Praxis, 21,* 387-389.

Farmer, D. J. (1999c). Leo Gorcy's Bowery Boys salute the new millennium. *Administrative Theory & Praxis, 21,* 537-538.

Farmer, D. J. (2000). Administration as unconscious: Do penguins have knees? *Administrative Theory & Praxis, 22,* 424-428.

Farmer, D. J. (2001). Always leave 'em laughing: NPR and the next blossom. *Administrative Theory & Praxis, 23,* 103-108.

Farmer, D. J. (2001a). Fractured governmentality. *Administrative Theory & Praxis, 23,* 293-298.

Farmer, D. J. (2000a). Great refusals and the administered life. *Administrative Theory & Praxis, 22,* 640-646.

Farmer, D. J. (2002). New York and the "P" in POSDCORB. *Administrative Theory & Praxis, 24,* 225-230.

Farmer, D. J. (2002a). Love and un-engineering. *Administrative Theory & Praxis, 24,* 369-380.

Farmer, D. J. (2002b). A state of love: Homeland security. *Administrative Theory & Praxis, 24,* 607-612.

Farmer, D. J. (2002c). The Devil's rope. *Administrative Theory & Praxis, 24,* 781-786.

Farmer, D. J. (2003). Expanding the ethical sphere. *Administrative Theory & Praxis, 25,* 137-142.

Farmer, D. J. (2003a). Thanks to O. C. McSwite. *Administrative Theory & Praxis, 25,* 309-314.

Farmer, D. J. (2003b). In the pink! *Administrative Theory & Praxis, 25,* 419-426.

Farmer, D. J. (2003c). Life-changing books. *Administrative Theory & Praxis, 25,* 589-607.

Farmer, D. J. (2004). More books, more play. *Administrative Theory & Praxis, 26,* 128-146.

Farmer, D. J. (2004a). I know thee not. *Administrative Theory & Praxis, 26,* 233-236.

Farmer, D. J. (2005). *To kill the king: Post-traditional governance and bureaucracy.* Armonk, New York: M. E. Sharpe.

Farmer, D. J. (2005a). Talking about religion. *Administrative Theory & Praxis, 27,* 182-195.

Farmer, D. J. (2005b). The moral first, the technical second. *Administrative Theory & Praxis, 27,* 581-594.

Farmer, D. J. (2005c). A dancing star: Arguments from imagination. *Administrative Theory & Praxis, 27,* 413-425.

Farmer, D. J. (2005d). Frigginomics begins in kindergarten: The social construction of normal citizens and their dreams. *Administrative Theory & Praxis, 27,* 707-718.

Farmer, D. J. (2006). Lobby(ectomy): Not in our tradition. *Administrative Theory & Praxis, 28,* 292-310.

Farmer, D. J. (2006a). Wal-Mart: Neo-feudal (k)night? *Administrative Theory & Praxis, 28,* 148-161.

Farmer, D. J. (2006b). The spirit of our age: PA-think as uncovering. *Administrative Theory & Praxis, 28,* 465-473.

Farmer, D. J. (2006c). Neuro-gov: Govenance and neuroscience. *Administrative Theory & Praxis, 28,* 653-662.

Farmer, D. J. (2006d). Imagine! Post-traditional governance and bureaucracy. *Administrative Theory & Praxis, 28,* 169-175.

Farmer, D. J. (2007). Change the course, neurons. *Administrative Theory & Praxis, 29,* 182-192.

Farmer, D. J. (2007a). See Spot run. *Administrative Theory & Praxis, 29,* 345-357.

Gomory, R. E., & Baumol, W. J. (2000). *Global trade and conflicting national interests.* Cambridge, MA: MIT.

Hayes, C. (2007, June 11). Hip heterodoxy. *The Nation,* pp. 18-24.

Johnson, C. (2006). *Nemesis: The last days of the American republic.* New York: Henry Holt.

Kirzner, I. M. (1998). The driving force of the market: The idea of "competition" in contemporary economic theory and in the Austrian theory of the market process. In D. L. Prychitko (Ed.), *Why economists disagree: An introduction to the alternative schools of thought* (pp. 27-52). Albany, NY: State University of New York.

Martin, E. (1991). The egg and the sperm: How science has constructed a romance based on stereotypical male-female roles. *Signs, 16,* 485-501.

Scahill, J. (2007). *Blackwater: The rise of the world's most powerful mercenary army.* New York: Nation Books.

Simon, H. (1991). *Models of my life.* New York: Basic Books.

## Power Speaking v. Speaking to Power: A Discourse War?

### David John Farmer

"Power speaking;" Vice-President Albert Gore has announced the establishment of a new U.S. Government website, a one-stop access to government services for seniors (www.seniors.gov). "This is an excellent example of our efforts to reinvent government to provide services that the American people need and care about," stated the Vice-President (1999) in his press release for February's Virtual Government '99 Conference in Washington, D.C. He continued, "Through this new web site, seniors can change their address with the Post Office, compare nursing homes, request Social Security statements, get IRS tax forms and find a variety of other governmental information." Fifteen agencies are cooperating, e.g., IRS, FCC, HUD, GSA, State and SSA.

More "power speaking" at the same conference; Morley Winograd (1999) noted that the conference's program mailer described the Vice-President as "The Father of Virtual Government." Winograd, the Vice-President's NPR Director (National Partnership for Reinventing Government) explained that NPR's first priority is "empowering and encouraging front-line workers to provide world class service to our citizens." But he added a kicker. He explained that the first priority of people power "is driven by a second" - IT (information technology) power. Look at the ampersand in the middle of NPR's "vision statement" ("America@Our Best"). It "symbolizes the central role that IT plays" in NPR's "newly defined mission."

"Speaking to power" about reinventing government is difficult. A root reason is our lack, despite much important P.A. work, of a fully articulated Macro P.A. fit to compete in a Discourse War. Lacking is a suitable macro discourse of governmental reform. True, there are minor reasons for the "speaking to power" difficulty, like the danger of the speaker being marginalized when the message is negative. How palatable are ideas such as (a) while it will certainly change our lives, information technology is no panacea for government; (b) while important, the surface inefficiencies of government are not the basic bureaucratization problem(s); and (c) even though there is nothing wrong with a good website, virtual government is not government? Absent a fully articulated Macro P.A., governmental reform is inevitably dominated by our prevalent rationalizing and economistic discourse, which privileges mere efficiency. This rationalizing discourse encourages the P.A. thinker to cast herself in the role of mechanic's helper-helping to tighten the nuts and bolts of the bureaucratic machine, betting all on technique.

"Speaking to power," it is imagined, requires a Macro P.A. with both positive and overlapping negative resources-building on the excellent macro P.A. work already done. On the positive side, a corner of a fully articulated Macro P.A. should include analyses of alternative discourses of reform directed toward the "iron cage" and other problematics of bureaucratization. Part of this might extend to choices in substance, e.g., between anti-administration and administration, between a privileging of efficiency and ethical alternatives, and between the Apollonian and the Dionysian. Part might include choices in method, e.g., between play-based and present approaches, between imagimization and rationalization, between reaching out (to second order perspectives) and reaching in, and between humans as rational choosers or as choice rationalizers. Importantly, it might include analyses of alternative conceptions of P.A. discourse as "power speaking" and as "speaking to power"-two opposing tendencies for any Discourse War. On the negative side, a corner of an articulated Macro P.A. should provide resources against historically-inherited and "power speaking" discourses. It could be that these negative resources could include the postures of the Gadfly and the Fool. Socrates, the questioner, describes his gadfly role in "The Apology" (Plato, 30e). Nietzsche's wish to emulate the Shakespearean Fool and the rich and varied history of the Fool (e.g., Davidson, 1996; Billington, 1984) was reflected when, taken from Turin and sanity in 1889, Nietzsche asked to borrow his landlord's "triangular Popish nightcap with tassel" so that he could underscore his mission (Chamberlain, 1999, p. 217).

Put aside the positive for now. "Speaking to power" about traditional P.A. discourse, here are some sample questions (gadfly or rhetorical?) offered at the March 1999 PAT-Net meeting. Is it too fanciful to supplement them with comments from King Lear's Fool?

The first of three sets of questions offers samples relating to the claim that the traditional P.A. discourse of reform, like any other discourse, is both "dominated by" and "dominates over."

**Question 1:** Is McDonaldization (or Turbo-Economics) the only way to go? What are the cost-benefits of a McDonaldization of (a) the world and (b) public administration practice?

**Comment 1:** "May not an ass know when the cart draws the horse? Whoop Jug! I love thee" (King Lear 1,4, 226).

**Question 2:** Referring to marginalization by "exceptionalism," why should American P.A. be American? Cannot the unique needs of Virginia be better met if we start a subject called Virginian P.A., and how would it differ from New Yorkian P.A?

**Comment 2:** "He that has a house to put's head in has a good head-piece" (King Lear 3,1,26).

The second set lists sample questions concerning the "inside" of traditional P.A. discourse, artificially separating the inside from the outside targeted in the first category.

**Question 3:** What does it mean to say that the basic building block of P.A. discourse is "bureaucratic man?" What is the alternative, e.g., people as bio-psycho-socio-spiritual beings?

**Comment 3:** "Cry you mercy. I took you for a jointed-stool" (King Lear, 3,6,51).

**Question 4:** Pointing to an airplane magazine advertisement ("Blitz through the year's best business books in less time than it takes to read the newspaper"-"To buy the 30 books we'll summarize would cost you almost $800..."), is P.A. discourse intended for the butler or the mensch, for a trade or a profession?

**Comment 4:** "Marry, here's grace and a codpiece; that's a wise man and a fool" (King Lear, 3,1,40).

The third set offers sample questions that involve a distinction between P.A. thinking and what can be called idiosyncratically "second order" thinking, the latter being theoretical stances like critical theory or surrealism which bear on P.A. matters even though they were never intended to.

**Question 5:** What can the discourses of Feminisms or of Queer Theory tell us about P.A. discourse issues like hierarchy?

**Comment 5:** "... who labors to outjest his heart-struck injuries" (King Lear 3,1,26).

**Question 6:** What significance does hyperreality have for our traditional understanding of the role of the manager? How does it relate to imaginization and play?

**Comment 6:** "Then t'is like the breath of an unfeed lawyer-you gave me nothing for 't. Can you make no use of nothing, nuncle? (King Lear 1,4,73).

Administrative reformers like the Vice-President are badly served by the P.A. theory community to the extent that we have not developed a Macro P.A. robust enough to win more battles for "Speaking to Power" in the Discourse War. On the minus side, there is the difficulty that the Power Speaking group always wields rewards. The traditional P.A. discourse lures many to the mechanic's helper role; it is more comfortable than thinking through macro abstractions that can include effete talk about items like gadflies and fools. On the plus side, it is clear enough that the present discourse of reform does not cut the mustard. Marvelous as are manifestations of technique like "IT" (information technology), "IT" cannot be "it."

## REFERENCES

Billington, Sandra (1984). *A Social History of the Fool*. New York: St. Martin's Press.

Chamberlain, Lesley (1999). *Nietzsche in Turin: An Intimate Biography*. New York: Picador.

Davidson, Clifford (1996). *Fools and Folly*. Kalamazoo, Michigan: Western Michigan University.

Vice-President (1999). Vice-President Gore Announces Seniors to Benefit from New One-Stop Access to Government Services, http://www.npr.gov/gov/library/ news/ 022399.html

Winograd, Morley (1999). "Access for Seniors," Virtual Government '99 Conference, http:// www. npr. gov / library /speeches/ 022399.html

---

**Public Administration/Management News from Australia**

**Judy Johnston**, University of Technology, Sydney

The individualist values which underpin the economic rationalist (ER) paradigm adopted by the current national conservative government are being challenged in relation to the likely introduction of a goods and services tax (GST). An Independent Senator who currently holds the balance of power in the upper house of the Australian Parliament has indicated to the government that he will not support their Bill unless food is exempted from the GST. While the government has offered some compensation to lower socio-economic groups to offset the likely negative impacts of a GST on them, research and official enquiries suggest that these groups will still be disadvantaged. The Budget recently brought down in the Parliament also failed to quell the Senator's concerns.

The national government, as a right-leaning conservative party, is strongly directed towards such economic reform with apparent limited concern for more collectivist responsibilities. The government also claims that their official mandate to introduce the GST was gained through their re-election towards the end of last year. Yet, in the midst of another public debate about the pros and cons of a GST it is apparent that there is diminishing community support for such an initiative. Nevertheless, the government is still determined to push through with its reform.

Once it was clear that the GST Bill was unlikely to be passed in the Senate, the Prime Minister boldly announced that he would dissolve both houses of Parliament and call another election to renew his mandate. A few days later the Prime Minister retreated from that position. Some commentators cynically suggested that this move was motivated by the Prime Minister's self-interest and concern about potential electoral defeat if he were to test the vote again so soon after the last occasion. Electoral defeat, obviously, would end his official part in opening the Sydney Olympic Games next year.

The big business lobby, consistent with its interests, has also come to the fore indicating that the tax reform must go through, even if food is exempt. Big business would lose without the GST as, among other benefits, it will lead directly to a reduction in the company tax rate. Business has urged government to compromise rather than continue to maintain a hard line about the GST.

The government has now indicated its willingness to negotiate with the Independent Senator and members of a small minority party in the Parliament, also opposed to the GST and who can affect the balance of power. To succeed in this direction, though, the government will have to renege on its promise to increase diesel fuel subsidies for country constituents including members of the party with which it shares government. In contrast, more socially directed groups continue loudly to voice their concern about the inequities inherent in the likely GST.

The proposed introduction of the GST certainly represents major structural reform of the taxation system, designed, in part, to address problems related to the unequal distribution of taxing powers between the federal and state governments. As mentioned before in *Briefly Noted*, the national government holds the majority of power, including the power to tax income. The financial allocations given back to the states at Budget

# FRACTURED GOVERNMENTALITY: A NIGHT IN THE EMERGENCY ROOM (E.R.)

David John Farmer

It was a cold Friday night when P.A. (theory) and p.a. (practice), two on-and-off lovers, were wheeled into the E.R. at Cook County General Hospital. Carrying the prostrate P.A. and the equally out-of-it p.a., the gurneys crashed through the swinging E.R. doors. Doctors, nurses, ambulance persons and others flurried around the moving gurneys, as they sped toward the reception rooms. "It is a bad case of Fractured Governmentality," exclaimed Dr. Elizabeth Corday, one of the T.V. soap opera's main characters. "P.A. Theory has the full-blown illness; and p.a. practice is sick from P.A.'s malady." "Nonsense!" declared Dr. Peter Benton, another of the soap opera characters. What did Dr. Corday mean by "fractured governmentality?" Could she illustrate—say, by reference to the notion of "big government"—how it would help both lovers if P.A. Theory could cure its congenital case of what Corday was calling "fractured governmentality"?

"On my count...1, 2, 3" was the cry as p.a. was heaved off the gurney in room #2. "Old-time P.A. thinking focuses too much from the perspective of the bureaucratic actor and too exclusively on public-bureaucracy-by-itself. So p.a.'s condition looks like a simple case of public sector bureaucratosis—public sector 'oligopoly obesity'—twice as much bulk as needed on the Niskanen scale," called out Dr. Elizabeth Corday. "That's not all," replied Dr John Carter. "Without giving adequate attention to body size and functioning outside the public sector, the old-time thinking could have gone on to speak about the hardening of the public sector arteries and the appearance of apparatchik parasites under the governmental skin." "Get the rapid infuser," yelled Dr. Corday to Nurse Carol Hathaway (who was once studying to be a doctor in this upwardly-mobile T.V. show). Flurry, flurry, white-coat flurry. It was then that Corday added sotto voce to Carter, "Do you realize that there never has been a long-term cure of public sector bureaucratosis? Never!" "Why doesn't P.A. recognize that a shift toward macro and long-term thinking and a shift toward thinking from the perspective of the person impacted by bureaucracy (rather than a mere focus on the perspective of the bureaucrats themselves and the politicians who run bureaucracies) require losing rigidities of (mis)concepts like 'government?'" snorted Elizabeth Corday. "Nonsense," counter-snorted Dr. Peter Benton. "You believe that a P.A. theorist should play with pulling apart all our common sense concepts. And I don't like it."

Dr. Corday was referring to what is counted as "government." Speaking of "governmentality" signifies that the understanding of what government is should not be confined to a view of government more appropriate for earlier eras but too limited for our new times. We now have two "primary" forms of governmentality, the traditional and the economic. Her preference is to count the larger corporations as part of government; for convenience, choose any cut-off point that is preferred. Our understanding of politics was (mis)conceived in a set of eras without the scale and power of economic corporations that now exist and are promised, and it seemed to Dr. Corday unwarranted to limit our understanding of government to the traditional. Michel Foucault's idea of governmentality provokes us to see elements of significant governance not only in traditional government but also in contexts like the workplace and families. It also raises the issue of how to understand government in terms other than sovereignty. Foucault was interested in the new techniques of governance which arose around the early nineteenth century, and he saw a double movement, as practices of government encourage certain practices of individuality, and as the latter then encourages practices of sociality. Dr. Corday was choosing to focus on the fact that "governmentality" — as she elects to understand the term—exists in a variety of contexts, and her preference was to describe government not merely in the traditional way but rather in terms of the "traditional plus the large corporations."

Dr. Corday attempted to explain the advantages of understanding government in her sense of the notion of governmentality, and she did so by commenting on the advantages of terminating not so much big government as heavy governmentality. Dr. Benton was not impressed.

Both major political parties in the United States have prophesied the end of big government. Former President William J. Clinton spoke of "the end of big government" in his 1998 State of the Union speech, and former Vice-President Albert Gore's National Partnership for Reinventing Government (NPR) program included a focus on reducing government size. Former President Ronald Reagan made big government part of his 1980 election campaign. As the Christian Broadcasting Network journal put it, "Reagan saw big government as part of the problem, unlike many other politicians, who see government as the solution" (March 2, 1998, CBN.com). Other parties like the libertarians embrace an ending of big government. "Government" in these cases is understood as traditional government, usually that in Washington. "Big" is understood in such terms as the number of government employees or the ratio of national output accounted for by public agencies. The era of big government should indeed end; but we should be more fundamental in what we mean by "government" and by "big." Corday held that perhaps we can be clearer if we replace/supplement the words "government" and "big"—substituting "governmentality" and "heavy," respectively.

Understanding "government" in "big government" to include only traditional government excludes so much that "governs" citizens' lives. Go to the office or the factory, and see whether employees are governed/bossed and what percentage of employee waking time is spent at work. Dr. Corday's preference, as indicated, was to understand non-traditional government in terms only of the larger corporations. Others might want to go farther and include other agencies involved in governmentality, such as non-governmental organizations and other elements in civil society, e.g, churches, unions and even private schools. Her hope is not to include corporations in more public decision-making. Rather, it is to recognize that the non-traditional is a genuine part of governmentality, and to reduce it with the rest, to de-big it.

Understanding "big" only in terms of "size" or "size relative to the economy" is not to be denigrated, Benton insisted. There are problems in too much size. The ratio of public to total national output is indeed of economic significance. However, Corday pointed out that she wanted to suggest that the idea of "big" should be replaced, or supplemented, by a term like "heavy," which designates the extent to which governmentality imposes itself on citizens. It is the extent to which governmentality constitutes a hierarchy-over for its citizens. It is agreed that the larger the government (traditional or non-traditional) the more likely it is to be heavy-handed, by dint of having more programs, by accident, and by the psychology of groups. Nevertheless, Dr. Corday would claim that a small person (e.g., a small adult) can lay a heavy hand on another or have a heavy controlling impact on another's life (e.g., a child), and a big person can be gentle.

Heavy or light government is a notion that requires further specification, because a governmental action that is light for one segment of the populations can be heavy for another. Consider items in the Code of Federal Regulations (National Archives and Records Administration, 2001). Regulations prohibiting business practices that encourage repetitive stress disorder can be heavy for the business owners, for instance, but light for those employees previously exposed to the prohibited work practices. Non-prohibition has a reverse differential effect. Dr. Corday's argument is that the notion of heavy government can be developed better if "government" is not limited to the traditional view. "Nonsense," interjected Dr. Peter Benton, "Notions that cannot readily be measured, like the relative lightness of government, create immeasurable difficulty."

Lightening governmentality's hand will require some change in structure. The aim of including more democracy in non-traditional governmentality is an example. Structural and programmatic changes could be used by traditional government, not only within its own operations but also in impacting the arrangements of, say, "private" corporations. Structural changes could be required "within" corporate arrangements, e.g., in following the German practice of providing for employee representation on corporate boards. From "without" could come oversight arrangements and plans-with-inducements. Forms of economic oversight arrangements might include economic parliaments, for instance, in whatever forms constitutions and other factors permit. The arrangements or plans, with tax or other financial inducements and sanctions, could be evolutionary. Candidate items, for instance, in a first stage might concern attention to societal issues like the now half-forgotten business policy of planned obsolescence. It could proceed to even more difficult issues, like the nature of the employer-employee contract, once characterized by Max Weber (1978, vol. 2, p. 959) in terms of loyalty and security. (Wrote Weber, the "entrance into an office, including one in the private economy, is considered an acceptance of a specific duty of fealty to the purpose of the office in return for the grant of a secure existence.")

Approaches for milking the advantages of a context-relevant broadening of P.A. Theory's understanding of government require not only much in terms of imaginative creativity from P.A. theorists but also a change in consciousness. On creativity, for instance, P.A. theorists would have to learn more about navigating streams now considered within the exclusive disciplinary jurisdiction of mainstream economic theory. Current mainstream economic theorizing, for instance, insists on focusing on the entrepreneur as the economic hero. Only in micro-micro economics, not now a popular line of inquiry, does the analysis go below the entrepreneur level. This should be supplemented by inquiries that focus on the customer, the worker, and even the least advantaged person in the economy. In this connection and with a laugh, Dr. Corday liked to quote from Nobel-Prize-winning author Gabriel Garcia Marquez. "Crazy people are not crazy if one accepts their reasoning" (Marquez, 1995, p. 35).

The change in consciousness would be especially difficult for the entrepreneurs and wanabee entrepreneurs, people whom many consider to be very important in shaping societal opinions. For a variety of reasons including self-interest, such entrepreneurs have a firm conviction in the dominance of the laissez-faire or free market model. Some call it ("essentially" and therefore falsely) "the American way." Infrequently, there are harbingers, like the socially responsible activities of the former owners (Ben and Jerry Cohen) of the Ben and Jerry's Ice Cream chain. But those are the swallows that probably will not make a summer. People become erotically attached to comforting fairy tales, like the Invisible Hand. They can become erotically attached to oxy-morons. Nowhere is this clearer than within economic theory. A central idea in that theory is that the entrepreneur will invariably seek to optimize profits, regardless of the amount he already has. In this way, profit optimizing functions invariantly, like the speed of light in relativity theory. The fact that this is clearly in conflict with the Law of Diminishing Marginal Utility has been recognized by James Buchanan (another Nobel Prize winner) and others. It does not make economic sense to keep on maximizing material profits, regardless of how much profit one already has. Objections will come the strongest from the wanabee entrepreneurs. Obstacles will come from powerful misunderstandings like the myth that a free market operates like a virgin forest, without need for the organizational support of governmental activity in the form of laws and intervention (to reduce unemployment or check inflation, to work for long-term growth, and to provide for public goods that the market will not produce, etc.). The complexity of the change in consciousness should be recognized. It proceeds beyond the merely rational; rather, the change in consciousness affects the deepest parts of our being and society.

"On my count...1, 2, 3" was the cry as P.A.—the next patient—was heaved off the gurney in room #3. "Acute and inflexible myopia, rigid and limited to common sense only," pronounced Dr. Mark Greene (Dr. Corday's friend, and vice-versa). "Acute lack of thinking outside the established ruts on the road. The P.A. patient can aim toward getting out of the ruts by playing more thoroughly with alternative concepts, like modifying the limits of the traditional notion of government." Smirked Dr. Peter Benton, "Maybe I am not cut out to be a theorist, public administration or medical; but I just don't have any patience with you or with concept-playing." Mark Greene continued to yell, "The distressing part is that p.a. depends on P.A. being vibrant enough to develop sets of alternative concepts." "Get the rapid infuser," yelled Dr. Elizabeth Corday. Flurry, flurry, white-coat flurry. "Be patient with the patient," cautioned Dr. Elizabeth Corday, addressing the world in general. "Concept-inflexibility is addictive. And, fractured governmentality is one of the toughest afflictions we could encounter in our TV soap opera."

## REFERENCES

Marquez, G. G. (1995). *Of love and other demons*. New York: Penguin Books.

National Archives and Records Administration. (2001). *Code of federal regulations*. access.gpo.gov/nara/cfr/cfr-retrieve.html#page1

Weber, M. (1978). *Economy and society: An outline of interpretive sociology* (G. Roth and C. Wittich, Eds.). Berkeley, California: University of California Press.

# Froglets or Fairy Tales?

## David John Farmer

Reinventing government is "about as exciting as watching paint dry," President Bill Clinton is reported to have said. The President added that, "I think that means that if you're going to do this, you need sort of an extra dose of determination and good humor, because I believe that it is truly one of the most important things that those of us in public life today can do." Perhaps, in an ideal world, what the President might have said is that public administration is as exciting as watching paint dry because P.A. is treated as a matter of froglets rather than fairy tales. How can we be helped to turn our attention toward the latter term in the dichotomy? James Carvile might have helped by offering to adapt the 1993 campaign slogan. The President could have told the audience that, "It's the discourse, stupid."

The President's remarks were made at a January 14-15, 1999, Conference in the State Department on "Transforming Government in the 21st Century: Global Forum on Reinventing Government." The Global Forum included 40 nations, including New Zealand, Russia, Japan, Argentina, Spain and Benin. It was organized by Joseph Nye and Elaine Kamark of Harvard, and the sponsors included Harvard's School of Government and the National Partnership for Reinventing Government in the Office of the Vice-President. The conference was by invitation only; but those of us who were non-invitees can read about it at http://www.npr.gov.

Morley Winograd, Senior Advisor to Vice-President Albert Gore and Director of the National Performance Review, on January 7 described the conference as "the first international conference ever held on the subject of reinventing government." He explained that invitees were representatives of countries which had some kind of a program at the national level on modernizing their government or reforming public administration "or, as we would say in the United States, reinventing government, or as often expressed in a short-hand version, Re-Go." Re-Go, he went on to explain, is a term that "contains all the letters of the Vice-President's name" and "it's just one reason why (the Vice-President) is planning on hosting this conference or I should say specifically moderating this conference."

Switch now to the country of Lilliput, and to a similar conference called "transforming government..." There is an unsubstantiated rumor running around the edges of the Lilliputian Beltway that the President had rejected an original draft of his welcoming speech. Fragments of that rejected speech are alleged to have been found, and some disconnected parts (obviously a first draft) read like this:

I would like to thank (666 names listed) for being here......

We Lilliputians who are interested in public administration face a choice between a world where everything is supposed to be dominated by things and a world where the principal role is occupied by meanings, and I want to ask you P.A. thinkers to figure out the details for me. Don't think that I am talking about two separate worlds. It is the same world; but one emphasizes one set of factors ("things") and the other highlights "meanings." In the first world, the bureaucracy is an entity "out there" independent of what we might think or say about it. The important thing in that world is to get out your wrench and fix it. In the other world, the discourse is the primary determinant.

As President of Lilliput, let me be the first to deconstruct my own claim. The worlds of things and meanings really are not distinct, because–as Karl Popper pointed out so frequently–there is no such thing as an uninterpreted fact, a discourse-free fact. You will remember that Popper used to ask his audience to "make an observation"–and the story goes that they would always reply "about what?" So, I will accept my own deconstruction, and offer you another dichotomy. The world dominated by things is really a world where meaning or discourse is suppressed. So one world represses meanings and the other attempts to recognize meanings.

It is like the difference between a froglet and a fairy tale. A froglet is a computer miracle which we are told will be a big deal in the next century (e.g., Moravec, 1998). It is the size of a computer chip, and it has little arms so that it can lock onto other froglets. It is said that our environment will be dominated by froglets, because houses and hotels and all kinds of things can be self-made by, and out of, froglets. Buildings can be programmed to construct themselves. The up-side of these little inanimate critters is that they can be programmed to reproduce—talk about a jump in G.N.P! Unfortunately, there is a down-side. These little inanimates could get out of control and consume all the raw and other materials in the world. Will we need a Department of Froglets in the next millennium to deal with those "things?"

Turn to Sleeping Beauty. Everyone knows the story; such fairytales are said to be the dreams of our group. The critical point in the story is that the heroine falls into an enduring sleep and enduring negativity, from which she is released by the kiss of Mr. Prince. Helene Cixous tells us that the kiss gives the princess existence, but in a process which subordinates her to the desires of the male. She would add that sexual difference is locked into a structure of power, where otherness is tolerated only when repressed. I am not saying that discourses are fairytales. Rather, fairytales are offered here as a symbol of the power of discourse. And it is too simple to ask if we will need a Department of Discourse in the next millennium, even though we will need to cope better with "discourse structures."

So, what is discourse theory? This is painful for me to answer because, as President of Lilliput, I am not in a position to explain anything longer than a sound bite. Discourse theory is something that is widely used in a number of disciplines, and it involves ideas like the following. All that we can think or say is limited by certain structures of discourse, most of which operate beyond our consciousness. Discourse structures are so potent that they can create our understanding of what exists. They can exclude. Michel Foucault (e.g., 1972) speaks of discourse creating objects. It is not that there is no independent reality; rather, discourse structures limit what we can consider as real. Think of framing, perspectives, lenses. Further, we do not select our own discourses, just as we do not "select" our own mother tongues.

Is the set of discourses or the set of facts more critical when it comes to such tendencies as using rationalistic thinking that sees the problems of government essentially in terms of economic efficiency. (Cardinal Manning once wrote that all our problems are, at bottom, theological. What is a P.A. variant of this?–All the problems of P.A. are, at bottom, economic.) Apparently the sub-title of the Washington conference was "Partnership for Economic Success," and the Vice-President emphasized this theme with remarks like "countries must have governments that are efficient and responsive to citizens if they want to have economic success in the global marketplace." Governments must be, he said, "lean, nimble and creative, or they will surely be left behind." He said this as he announced three new initiatives for helping to make his government more lean, nimble and creative. The first was civil service improvement, linking pay and performance, etc. The second was called results for children, and the third is a new and upcoming citizen satisfaction survey. Again, is this an issue of brute discourse or brute facts?"

Obviously, this draft would not do, even for the President of Lilliput. Instead, the President of Lilliput asked his staff to work up something based on an idea in a statement by the Director-General of the International Institute of Administrative Sciences. The Director-General described this closing century as "the century of Public Administration" (IIAS Newsletter, vol. 18, 1998, p. 1). Wow! For one thing, the rejected speech draft had attempted too much in too short a space. For another thing, a welcoming speech should deviate little from what is part of the accepted discourse. Recognizing the

## REFERENCES

Cixous, http://dir.yahoo.com/Arts/ Humanities/ Philosophy/Philosophers/Cixous_Helene/

Foucault, Michel. (1972). *The Archaeology of Knowledge*, trans. Sheridan Smith. London: Tavistock.

Moravec, Hans. (1998) *Robot: Mere Machines to Transcendent Mind*. New York: Oxford University Press.

---

## Public Administration/Management News from Australia

**Judy Johnston**, University of Technology, Sydney

Neo-classical economic thinking, which promotes competition within government as a critical foundation of contemporary public sector practice, does not indicate whether ethical values will also be supported. Evidence emerging in relation to Sydney's successful bid for the 2000 Olympic Games and the professional performance of Australian, International Olympic Committee (IOC) members, as well as wider IOC issues, suggests that the unprincipled and informal values of competition are far stronger driving forces for public sector management than any formal, ethical parameters that might be espoused.

The Machiavellian assertions that the negative values of war, such as deception, bribery and coercion, are acceptable if the competition is won seem to have continuing relevance hundreds of years on, perhaps, increasingly so. However, the illusory nature of politically correct discourse and positive rhetoric about the benefits of economic rationalism and managerialism has been publicly exposed through purported, Olympic Games corruption. This is, particularly, exemplified in the results of the more rigorous enquiries into the Salt Lake City Winter Olympics bid.

The apparently institutionalized, oligarchic corruption (as Australia's Professor Alexander Kouzmin describes it) of the IOC and some participating or bidding governments, in the international Olympic gravy train, though, seems to have gone too far. Even the corporate sector, which is not adverse to the occasional unethical business deal, is indicating that the shift towards the adoption of dubious rules of competitive engagement is unacceptable.

In Sydney's case, and beyond, committed Olympic sponsors are becoming increasingly anxious about the negative image portrayed through the formal organizations of the Olympic Games, starting at a supranational level with the IOC but cascading down to the New South Wales (NSW) government, as the government responsible for Sydney's bid. The current NSW government was not the bidding government and, as it faces an imminent election, it is probably grateful that any likely evidence of impropriety in Sydney's bid can largely be directed towards the former government, as the now main Opposition party.

Since Sydney won the bid there has been considerable community ambivalence about the value of staging the Olympic Games here. On the one hand, there has been excitement about the potential for confirming Sydney and Australia's position in global sports and event management. On the other hand, there has been increasing public cynicism about who will benefit from the staging of the Games. At a micro-level, continuing public evidence of oligarchic in-fighting and issues of power and control among the political, public sector, sporting, community and other elites involved with the Games has been apparent since the commencement of Sydney's bid. Both the former and current NSW governments have been key actors in this direction.

# TONTO AND THE LONE RANGER: CONCEPTS REVEAL, CONCEPTS MASK

### David John Farmer

It is practical to recognize that concepts both reveal and mask. In playing with concepts imaginatively and realistically, public administration thinkers can seek to liberate PA practice from entrapment in conventional conceptual rigidities and can seek to open practice to new possibilities. Concepts have this double-edged characteristic. Concept identification and "application" have proven valuable in revealing insights. Unfortunately, these same concepts simultaneously mask other aspects of the complete truth—the whole truth and nothing but the truth. POSDCORB is a concept that was valuable in emphasizing that managers should discharge certain neglected functions, for example. Simultaneously, the acronym masks items excluded from the list, e.g., management relationships with entities outside the organization. POSDCORB is no different from any other concept; no concept is completely, utterly and absolutely true, including this one. Tonto and the Lone Ranger agree on these claims. In this conversation, they seek to illustrate and explore their claims by starting with the Pope's April declaration on globalization. They choose to start with the concept of "globalization," because they want also to emphasize their belief that PA thinkers should not limit themselves to PA concepts.

"A fiery horse with the speed of light, a cloud of dust and a hearty 'Hi Yo Silver! The Lone Ranger, Hi Yo Silver, away!' With his faithful companion Tonto, the daring and resourceful masked rider of the plains led the fight for law and order in the early west. Return with us now to those thrilling days of yesteryear. The Lone Ranger rides again!" So would open "The Lone Ranger," one of the earliest ABC television hits. Clayton Moore had the lead role from 1949 to 1952 and from 1954 to 1957. Jay Silverheels played the other major part. The duo was celebrated for revealing the truth; the Lone Ranger, no less than Zorro and other heroes, was famous for his mask.

LONE RANGER: Consider the concept of "globalization." Consider what Pope John Paul II told the Pontifical Academy of Social Sciences about it last April (nwonline@toronto.cbc.ca, April 30, 2001). Consider this as an illustration of the claim that concepts reveal and simultaneously mask.

TONTO: I remember. The Pope stated that: "Globalization must not be a new version of colonialism." The Pope explained that globalization is neither good nor bad; it all depends on what people do with it. "Many people, especially the disadvantaged, experience this (i.e. globalization) as something that has been forced upon them." The Pope went on to say that the Catholic Church will work to make sure that "the winner in this process will be humanity as a whole, not just a wealthy elite that controls science, technology, communication and the planet's resources."

LONE RANGER (sitting tall on his horse, Silver): The Pope is making a revealing point about the concept of "globalization." The ethics of globalization cannot be limited to the instrumentalism of, say, business ethics. The Pope's eth-talk is not at all instrumentalist. It is not eth-talk about means, as occurs when topics like whistle-blowing are analyzed. It is not one-dimensional in the sense described by Herbert Marcuse: the "most advanced areas of industrial society exhibit throughout two features: a trend toward consummation of technological rationality, and intensive efforts to contain this trend within established systems" (Marcuse, 1991, p. 17). The Pope is speaking about ends, and I can see right away that this is an important example for all eth-talk concepts used in PA and business administration. For organizational learning to speak about topics like the desirability of self-actualization and truth telling is unethical, if it is within a system which is dedicated to business-as-it-has-become.

It is probably easier for PA thinkers to see the instrumental sty in business administration's eth-talk eye, rather than the beam in its own eth-talk eye. Yes, this has been pointed out by some PA eth-talkers. Unfortunately, the problem of "unjust laws" is dismissed by others as relevant only for illegitimate regimes like Nazi Germany (e.g., Lewis, 1991, p. 38). PA eth-talk has tended to shy away from the fact that sometimes some laws that civil servants are invited to execute are not merely foolish but also morally reprehensible. It shies away from the fact that civil servants are often required to cater to the rich and the powerful. The Pope's use of the concept "globalization" seems to me to illuminate our own PA eth-talk concepts.

TONTO (his horse was called "Scout," but few fans knew that): Yes. But the reading of the Pope's concept can also be concealing, or masking, if the reader's own framework is skewed. To another compassionate conservative, it may look radical—a plea against the triumphalist attitude of free market messianism. And the fact is that public attitudes, in this country at least, are pummeled and shaped by the frenetic one-sidedness of the "jump on the train or lose it forever" attitude preached by newspersons like Thomas Friedman (1999). In this framework, it looks like a radical statement to echo Paul Samuelson and to question the optimality of the invisible hand. But, Kemo Sabe, the fact is that the Pope's pronouncement is middle-of-the-road, at best. It reflects a view of technology as little more than an extension of human power, for example as the technology of a hammer increases the striking power of the arm and hand. This is a view that was emphasized for the Church by St. Thomas Aquinas, who repeated Aristotle's understanding of technology. It does not conceptualize technology as engulfing humans, for example when the technology of the automobile shapes the lives of vast numbers of humans and entire societies. In the former view, technology adds to the human. In the latter case, technology is seen as constructing us. In this vein, Berdyaev can write (1934, p. 7): "the question of technique has now become that of the destiny of man and of his culture in general. In this age of spiritual turpitude,…civilized man's sole strong belief is the might of technical science and its capacity for infinite development. Technique is man's last love, for the sake of which he is prepared to change his very image."

LONE RANGER (adjusting his mask): Well, my trusted side-kick, you are being tough on the Pope. His concept of globalization is revealing. In fact, it reveals that the general concept of globalization widely held masks the "truth, the whole truth, and nothing but the truth." The Pope's statement implies that the established concept, the commonsense notion, of globalization is false to the extent that the term is considered to have only one meaning—and one additional meaning is where globalization can stand for a new form of colonialism. Just as there are many forms of beauty (or cancer), the Pope's statement would have us understand that there are various forms of globalization. Similarly, it is untrue that a free market is a free market is a free market; there is an abundant variety of different forms. The alternative to what we are doing now in this country (or in the West in general) is not merely communism, or fascism, or something equally outside-the-pale. There are alternative forms of globalization well within the pale, just as there are alternative forms of a free market.

I think that the Pope's pronouncement can serve as a sort of poster-boy for PA theorists. Yes, the task of the PA theorist should surely include liberating practitioners and others from the commonsense concepts that directly and indirectly limit our understanding of what we are seeking to elucidate. An example of a direct limitation of our understanding is the set of assumptions—the concepts—that underlie PA theorizing, for example that the most natural approach is inductive, that ideas should have immediate micro practitioner payoff, that the scope of the subject is optimal, and so on. When public institutional practices are breaking down the old barriers between the notions of public and non-profit and profit making (e.g., see Reich, 2001), for instance, the concepts are encouraging us to continue with business as usual. Examples of indirect limitations are the conceptual assumptions that impact PA from related disciplines and perspectives, like economics and the law. I think that PA thinkers should conduct forays into these surrounding disciplinary areas to liberate PA from the conceptual strangleholds that they exert on our discipline.

TONTO: Who was that masked man? I think it is more complicated than you cowboys allow. For one thing, it is sub-optimal if this play is limited within the concepts of current academic activity. For my money, for example, a PA thinker should not be isolated from her own guts, passions, and life's experiences. Concept playing should not be confined to the aridly disembodied. Concept play should not be mere intellectual stunt-ing, similar to the activity of economists who speak of unemployment without feeling the emotions of the people implicated—the capitalists lusting for X, the employees lusting for Y, the economist leaving all lusts at home. Gerry Spence (1989) makes a good case against arid intellectualism in legal education. It comes from Spence's guts, shaped by his life as a highly successful attorney in witnessing what he experiences as the gross injustice in our justice system.

For another thing, concepts are continually changing their meanings, sucking up new meanings. I know of no major philosophical term which can maintain over time a clear and unwavering meaning; none whatsoever. Consider terms like materialism, realism, idealism, and so on. For another thing, there is a tendency in the History of Ideas for concepts to change their meanings, eventually switching to opposite meanings. To reify the thing, it is as if concepts were setting out to deceive. The truth is that they are worse than kitchen sponges.

LONE RANGER: On your first "thing," three cheers for your point about arid intellectualism. On your second "thing," you are soon going to be bringing up Jacques Derrida. You are going to point to his comments on the limitations of binary oppositions and the profusion of complexes of metaphors in our use of concepts. I am sorry about that because the name Derrida tends to bring out people who want to fulminate about things like "postmodernism" and "death of the author." It seems to me that Derrida is just making obvious comments. The dichotomies represented by our concepts can be deconstructed, revealing that important remainders occur in the in-between space; think of dichotomies like civil servant and politician, man and woman, good and evil, inside and outside, and so on. The metaphors permeate our concepts, our language. For me, the message is not that we can say nothing. Rather, being skeptical about our concepts, we should be open to playing with alternative constructions.

TONTO: I was going to appeal to analytical philosophers instead. For many of them, even the concept of a concept is problematic. Peter Heath explains (1967) that the term "concept" is "essentially a dummy expression or variable, whose meaning is assignable only in the context of a theory, and cannot be independently ascertained." He describes the term as one of the most equivocal terms in the philosophical vocabulary. I remember Peter Heath, for many years at the University of Virginia Philosophy Department, explaining to me that he was taught not to use the word "concept" and he considered it bad that I should want to do so.

LONE RANGER: I think that what you are saying is that there is an arbitrariness and fuzziness about each and every concept. The notion of fixing meaning is a delusion, just as it is illusory to think of conceptualizing as merely naming. There is an arbitrariness about fixing the meaning of "colonizing" so that it refers only to control projected outwards, for instance; there is no reason to separate if off from power introjected inwards. So, an alternative conceptual scheme could lump together "capitalism that projects outwards toward the world" with "capitalism that extends inwards toward our own society." The business interests that seek to dominate the markets of the world can also be seen—through buying politicians, buying appointments, and other devices—as seeking to dominate our governance. Both tendencies can be seen as pieces of a whole. To be negative, I can say that the Pope's April 2001 use of the concept is revealing; it is also masking. To be positive, I can say that the PA theorist can "play" with these alternative conceptual schemes.

TONTO: None of this entails relativism.

LONE RANGER: No, not all concepts are created equal. I think that the concept of "phlogiston" reveals nothing, for example. That is not the case for the various concepts of "globalization" or "relativism."

TONTO: I would think that the unconscious baggage of concepts is critical in this matter of masking. I appreciate, with Roland Barthes, that all signs have their unconscious accompaniment. Kemo Sabe, I really believe that evidence of confusion and suppression of meaning is evidence of a powerful unconscious baggage, parallel to the Freudian rift—the indicator of an appealing opening to the unconscious. For instance, the therapist is told to be alert to that part of the dream where the patient makes the claim that that part is not important. Confusion about concepts should be our guide.

LONE RANGER: Give me an example.

TONTO: Consider self-interest. Economics deals only with revealed preferences, and so in economics and in PA we tend to suppose that self-interest is self-interest is self-interest. For one form of self-interest, see the heading on the front page of the *New York Times* on May 6, 2001. The headline was "New Rules for Soccer Parents: 1) No Yelling. 2) No Hitting Ref." The story was about the "sideline rage" that now is said to plague kids' sports. "From hockey arenas in Maine to soccer fields in New Mexico, parents and amateur coaches are yelling and jeering—even spitting and brawling—as never before... This has led to a wellspring of new rules, workshops and state legislation aimed at curbing misconduct." Examples are the Cleveland girls' soccer games (where the audience is required to be almost silent) and the three-and-a-half hour class for fans of city-sponsored youth sports in El Paso. Maybe this is kids' stuff compared with European soccer hooliganism. But it does suggest that the single notion of "self-interest" confuses what may or may not be different Xs and Ys. Is it true that self-interest is a concept with a single meaning? What Alexis de Tocqueville wrote about the "doctrine of self-interest properly understood" also seems to me to be an indicator of confusion.

LONE RANGER: Faithful side-kick, don't you see the story of the soccer referees as being part of a larger story of the increasing commodification of everything? Having "my kid win" is just another commodity, isn't it? Isn't "my kid experiencing wins" what I wish to consume from my investment in allowing him to participate in that sports activity? Isn't it part of the change to what Robert Reich (2001) calls the Age of the Terrific Deal and the "commodification of community?"

TONTO: I don't know about these uni-perspectival answers, Kemo Sabe. The concept of "commodification" has a meaning from within the economic perspective. But I would prefer it to be supplemented by a set of perspectives. All of our concepts, to the extent that they are in academic usage, are subject to the fragmentation of disciplines. Concepts are narrowed so that they fit into a discipline like economics—or a larger discipline like political economy—or an even larger discipline like "the" social sciences.

LONE RANGER: Isn't all of that blindingly obvious to every PA thinker in the world?

TONTO: If it is blindingly obvious, why do so many continue to limit our PA concepts within the narrow confines of our disciplinary walls? At first sight, this appears to be unfair. PA is a porous subject, importing concepts right, left, and center, even if the timing of the importations is often tardy. But the point is that, when the foreign concepts are imported, they change their shapes and connotations, and they become subject to the imperatives of other PA concepts and assumptions. The discipline of PA is itself a concept that reveals and conceals. The foreign concepts become colonized by the concept of PA.

LONE RANGER: Maybe I could seek to de-colonize the subordinate concepts if I reorganized the PA "master-concept" in a way that would highlight ignorance. No, I am not saying that PA is ignorant. Far from it—I am suggesting an example that would run against the current grain where curricula tend to boast of knowledge held and imparted. I could imitate the Curriculum in Medical Ignorance (Witte et al., 1988, p. 793). A Curriculum in PA Ignorance could announce, "The curriculum consists of seminars and hands-on experiences dealing with 1) what we know we don't know, 2) what we don't know we don't know, and 3) what we think we don't know." Known ignorance, unknown ignorance, and pseudo-ignorance would be the new boxes.

TONTO (swinging his horse toward the sunset): But there is no "one way" to play with ideas. Infants don't need to be told how to play; why should we? Let's go get some bad guys!

LONE RANGER (against a surging background of the William Tell overture): Hi Yo Silver! A fiery horse with the speed of light, a cloud of dust and a hearty Hi Yo Silver!

## REFERENCES

Berdyaev, N. (1934). *The bourgeois mind and other essays*. New York: Sheed and Ward.

Friedman, T. (1999). *The Lexus and the olive tree: Understanding globalization*. Thorndike, ME: Thorndike Press.

Heath, P. (1967). Concept. In P. Edwards (Ed.), *Encyclopedia of philosophy*, (pp. 177–180). New York: Macmillan.

Lewis, C. (1991). *The ethics challenge in public service: A problem-solving guide*. San Francisco: Jossey-Bass.

Marcuse, H. (1991). *One-dimensional man: Studies in the ideology of advanced industrial society*. Boston: Beacon Press.

Reich, R. (2001). *The future of success*. New York: Alfred A. Knopf.

Spence, G. (1989). *With justice for none*. Penguin Books: New York.

Witte, M., Kerwin, A., & Witte, C. (1989). Seminars, clinics, and laboratories on medical ignorance. *Journal of Medical Education, 63*, 793–795.

# EXPANDING THE ETHICAL SPHERE

David John Farmer

Public policy and administration (PA) should be realigned to accommodate an expanded ethical sphere. The sphere is the scope of application—the area or range of application—of ethical acts, precepts or ideas. What is included in being a fully ethical PA thinker, I think, is that she should design PA acts with a sphere of application such that all humans are treated with equal consideration for their interests. Emphasizing such an expansion of the sphere of moral equality, PA Ethics (*PA Eth-Talk*, as afficianados sometimes call it) should give leadership to PA theorizing and practice. It should encourage PA theorists, for instance, to play with possibilities and options involved in developing recommendations about policy making and administration that reflect an expanded sphere of moral equality—as appendices, say, to realpolitik recommendations. PA Eth-Talk should reach beyond the limit of the interests of the bureaucracy, we can readily agree. Also it should continue to expand its ethical sphere beyond limiting equal consideration of interests to particular classes of people, like males or the dominant ethnic group. PA Eth-Talk should go beyond the limit of the interests of the customer and the client, beyond the limit of the interests of the good citizen. PA Eth-Talk should not center on traditional intra-bureaucratic topics. The suggestion—not a new, but an important, idea—is that all other humans should be treated with equal consideration of their interests, including humans beyond the limits of national boundaries.

PA Eth-Talk that emphasizes expanding the ethical sphere beyond the limits of the nation state should be a no-brainer, and yet it encounters severe difficulties from symbolic systems. This column talks about an expansion of the ethical sphere in a context that proceeds beyond what will be explained as polis-worship, and the snare(s) that symbolisms of belonging, power and glory—associated with the nation state—set against the moral impulse of sympathy-for-the-other.

Earlier, I wrote (1999) of an ethical dilemma that envelops us. On the one hand, as a practical matter it is impossible to live a human life—as an "engaged" person, as PA thinkers should be—without some sense of what is wrong and right. If I saw an infant shot in the face, my sympathy would explode in horror and, hopefully, action; I would identify with the child and reject the wrong. Wouldn't you? On the other hand, ethical systems differ and compete, e.g. consequentialist, deontological, intuitionist, rationalist. Each has excellent supporting arguments, excellent counter-arguments, and excellent counter-counter arguments, and so on. There is no clear winner among these competing systems. Or, as another person might put it, it is unclear how to choose to live with all of them. Talk of an expanding ethical sphere, here and elsewhere, should be heard with recognition of this dilemma.

## POST-POLIS ETHICS

Moral globalism presents significant arguments. Among the many proponents, interesting writers include Michael Ignatieff and Peter Singer. Ignatieff (1984, p. 139) holds that "A century of total war has taught us where belonging can take us when its object is the nation." He prefers that our human needs, our sense of belonging, should instead center on "a new form, a new kind of object: the fragile green and blue earth itself, the floating disk we are the first generation to see from space" (Ignatieff, 1984, p. 139). He emphasizes the upstart character of nationality. He claims (1984, p. 138), for instance, that up to the First World War, "the very idea of being a citizen, of belonging to a society or a nation would have seemed a distant abstraction to the peasants who made up the majority of the European population. Such belonging as a peasant felt was bounded by the distances his legs could walk and his cart could roll." Singer, as explained later, writes about the expanding circle of altruism that has "broadened from the family and tribe to the nation and race, and we are beginning to recognize that our obligations extend to all human beings" (Singer, 1981, p. 120). Also providing some emphasis to universality have been influential religions like Christianity and even philosophical movements as ancient as Stoicism. Then there are inducements toward moral globalism in increasing multi-cultural proximity, and in the growing economic globalization that is said to be putting pressure on the raison d'etre of the nation state.

We seem to be inching as if through an evolutionary moral process from pack animal through polis-worshipper to a post-polis context. At each stage in this "as if" evolutionary moral process, we retain much from former stages: often we yearn for the comforts of the previous context. Each succeeding stage seems to require more from us in terms of our inner resources—from our imaginative and other psychic energies. In the post-polis stage, I don't suggest that the nation state system will disappear. Rather, it's a matter of our symbolic and other relationships toward nationality.

Note two further details about this claim. A first is the limit implied in the phrase "as if." I am speaking about an "appearance" of an evolutionary moral process, because I don't want to suggest the inevitability often implied in stories of "stages of development." Also I recognize that more elaborate accounts are available, equally deconstructible yet perhaps more satisfying. A hint of the complexity is given in Eibl-Eiblesfelt's comment (1982, p. 6) that humankind "was originally created for a life in individualized groups. The transition to life in the anonymous community produces problems of identification. On the one hand the urge clearly exists to form a bond with strangers as well. On the other hand we can observe the inclination to cut oneself off in groups from others." A second detail is that the word "post" should not be misinterpreted as implying relativism. Coming to grips with concepts involving the word "post" has had a surreal and sad history within American Public Administration, e.g., frankly, too many writers have judged without any burden of subtlety, attacking cartoon versions of pomo inappropriately limited to something icky called mere relativism. (For a helpful view of postmodernism and by implication for a better view of "post" claims, see McClosky, 2001.)

For the first stage of this appearance of an evolutionary moral process, let's appeal to a natural history of human behavior patterns and to the pack behavior of the human. As Eibl-Eibelsfelt points out (1982, p. 75), "many features of our human territorial behavior point to our ancient primate heritage.... Human beings defend both individual territories (including personal property) and group territories. In addition, every individual shows the unmistakable tendency to keep his distance from strangers, except in special circumstances (buses, mass meetings)." Is it too strong to describe humans in terms of pack animals? Maybe. Yet there does seem relevance in the observation that pack animals do have different ways of "knowing their own." Rats mark one another, as Eibl-Eiblesfelt tells us, so that they create a common scent group. He goes on to say that, if a rat is removed from the pack for a few days, it will be attacked when it is returned to the pack because it has lost its smell. A strange or immigrant rat smeared with the proper urine will be accepted. A strange rat, processed through a urinary melting pot, is O.K.

For the second stage, let's enlist Thomas Jefferson in appealing to the Ancient Greeks and to Aristotle in particular. Jefferson and the founding Fathers looked back with admiration and with a kind of love, as they tried to recreate on a continental scale the kind of Greek polis that they admired. It was a commonplace among the ancient Greeks that the objective of human life is happiness (eudaimonia), and this can be obtained only through the polis. The polis, the city-state or country, is the means through which humans can achieve the good life. In his celebrated phrase, Aristotle said that man is a political animal. By this, he meant that it is not possible to be fully human except through active participation in the political, through life in the system of the polis that functions—as it were—as a moral "church." A citizen, for him, was a person who is ruled and who also rules. For Aristotle, the polis "fulfills the whole nature of man, and especially the higher part of his nature" (Barker, 1958, p. 7). The polis, the perfect association that exists by nature, is logically prior to the individual. A human and a polis can be compared to a hand (or foot) and a body. The hand could not be a real hand without the body; so a man cannot be fully human without the polis. "Separate hand or foot from the whole body, and there will be no longer hand or foot except in name..." (*Politics*, Bk. 1, sec. 10). In his equally celebrated phrase, Aristotle wrote that a person who can live outside the polis is either a god or a beast, a subhuman or a superhuman. "The man who is isolated—who is unable to share in the benefits of political association, or who has no need because he is self-sufficient—is not part of the polis, and must be therefore either a beast or a god" (*Politics*, Bk. 1, sec. 14).

For the third or post-polis stage, let's return to Singer. The post-polis stage goes beyond the "recent" notion of the nation state (which you will recognize that I am lumping under the polis-worshipping stage—a late period in the stage of polis-worship.) I was excited in the early eighties to read Singer's *The Expanding Circle: Ethics and Sociobiology*. [No, I don't suppose he is a sociobiologist. As he writes (1981, p. xi), "the sociobiological approach to ethics often involves undeniable and crude errors...." Yet he continues, "I believe that the sociobiological approach to ethics does tell us something important about ethics, something we can use to gain a better understanding of ethics than has hitherto been possible" (Singer, 1981, p. xi).]

Singer writes of the expansion of "the circle of altruism" beyond the particular group. The ethical sphere limited to a particular group results in the kind of ethical thinking that can lead even Aristotle (nicknamed the "Brain") to discriminate between barbarians and Greeks when discussing enslavement. The moral sphere or the circle of altruism has increasingly expanded to include all humans (see Singer, 2002). The example of Christianity was given earlier; the doors are open to any human, as long as the incomers accept the norms within the doors. The sphere has expanded so that it extends, for some, to other animals—like dogs and cats. It has even expanded to trees and mountains, and beyond. Describing this expanding circle, Singer writes that,

> the shift from a point of view that is disinterested between individuals within a group, but not between groups, to the point of view that is fully universal, is a tremendous change—so tremendous, in fact, that it is only just beginning to be accepted on the level of ethical reasoning and is still a long way from acceptance on the level of practice. Nevertheless, it is the direction in which moral thought has been going since ancient times. (Singer, 1981, p. 113)

## SNARES

Yet there are discouraging difficulties. Recall that I am not speaking of abolishing nation states; rather, I am thinking of our attitudes toward them. Front and center among the difficulties inhibiting adoption of a wider ethical sphere are the particular symbolic systems of the nation state. The form of national symbolization does have practical results, just as societal choice of symbolic systems is associated with practical power, economic and other aims. As one example of practical results, there is the nature of mainstream PA itself. As reflected in the symbolism of such discipline titles as "American Public Administration," wasn't mainstream PA founded to further the interests of particular nations? The symbolic systems can be categorized (if one insists) as political, economic, cultural, or other. These systems include the strong symbolic and psychological allure of national belongingness, power and glory; and I confine myself here to underscoring this. I felt this last year on the Champs Elysee, re-visiting a favorite parade.

"The French! Says the Citizen.... Do you know what it is? They were never worth a roasted fart to Ireland!" (Joyce, 1997, p. 315). In repeating the Citizen's outburst in James Joyce, I intend no taunt at either of these particular countries. Far from it! The point is: National feelings *universally* are a mighty snare, as well as a mighty joy. Bad and good are universally intermingled. Let's recognize that our times tend to be "out of joint" for saying this, however, when terrorism, war and threat of hostilities impose stress on nations. So, let's turn to a neutral terrain (neutral in the sense that most of us don't "belong to" it) to make the point—of the need for PA Eth-Talk to go beyond a sophisticated version of the crude attitude expressed by Joyce's Citizen.

The July 14th Bastille Day Parade was spectacular last year, again. Contingents attracting loud applause were from West Point and the New York City Fire Department. 163 West Point cadets, in their gray jackets and white trousers, were at the head of the parade—perfect precision in motion. An FDNY pumper truck, with four surviving officers from the Twin Towers, came later—the firemen flashing victory signs. But July 14th is France's day. The clattering of hooves, the jingling of the bridles and the trumpeting of the cavalry of the Republican Guard, as if straining to charge with elan patriotique toward any and all approaching windmills. The surging formations of monster military vehicles; the Foreign Legion, of course, is a foreigner's favorite; the rank upon rank of soldiers, many fierce and some in uniforms as-if-designed-by-Gianni-Versace; flocks of airplanes, vapor trailing the colors of France, flying over the parade route. Standing erect on an open military vehicle is the President of France. When Jacques Chirac passed us, it must have been a mere fifteen minutes after a 25-year old neo-Nazi with a gun had been arrested. Whether he aimed at the President or whether the gun went off in a struggle with the police is not clear. When we saw President Chirac, we knew nothing of the assassination attempt.

At one level, there does appear to be a contradiction in the Bastille Day Parade between the symbolic aim and the symbolic nature. The parade and the Day celebrate, as everyone knows, the capture in 1789 of the infamous prison (we would say "penitentiary") that symbolized the absolute and arbitrary power of the Ancien Regime, the power of the state. Yet the Bastille Day parade is nothing if not militaristic, a display of—if you like—the glorious power of the state. Even the inclusion of the ever-popular Parisian fire fighters doesn't mitigate the military caste of the parade. It would take a dubious Thomas-Aquinas-like rationalizing exercise to resolve the paradox, saying how the parade and the village rituals celebrate liberty, fraternity and equality by showing the force available to realize said liberty, fraternity, etcetera. The Parade seems to celebrate the overthrow of X by displaying that very same X. But we are in the world of the symbolic, which nourishes and encompasses mere contradictions. The Bastille Day Parade symbolizes the French nation state in such terms as belonging, power and glory—forever and ever, amen. For us, it can also illustrate the hegemonic power of symbolic systems of the state—their colonization of our hearts.

Sympathy-for-the-other, as I see it now, is a critical element in the justice, or moral, impulse. Wouldn't you agree? Many do. It is even part of the so-called Golden Rule. Sympathy, a fellow feeling for the other person "at the thought of his situation," is at the heart of the moral psychology of even no less a modern icon than Adam Smith. But I doubt whether sympathy-for-the-other is powerful enough in the short run to permit us to overcome all the snares—especially the allure of these powerful symbolic systems of the nation state, the allure of belonging, power and glory. Yet, don't you think that PA Eth-Talk should start now, seeking to contribute to the long run expansion of the ethical sphere?

## REFERENCES

Eibl-Eibesfeldt, I. (1982). *Love and hate*. New York: Holt, Rinehart and Winston.

Farmer, D. J. (1999). The discourse movement: A centrist view of the sea change. *International Review of Public Administration, 4*, 3-10.

Ignatieff, M. (1984). *The needs of strangers*. New York: Henry Holt and Company.

Joyce, J. (1997). *Ulysses*. London: Macmillan.

McClosky, D. (2001). The genealogy of postmodernism: An economist's guide. In S. Cullenberg, J. Amariglio & D.F. Ruccio (Eds.), *Postmodernism, economics, and knowledge* (pp. 102-128). New York: Routledge.

Singer, P. (1981). *The expanding circle: Ethics and sociobiology*. New York: Farrar, Straus & Giroux.

Singer, P. (2002). *One world: The ethics of globalization*. New Haven, CT: Yale University Press.

# MEDUSA: HELENE CIXOUS AND THE WRITING OF LAUGHTER

David John Farmer

## ABSTRACT

*Should an anti-administrative consciousness extend to a discourse (a writing) of laughter? This paper plays with the possibility of this discourse in order to point to debilitating constraints in traditional P.A. thinking. Join me and imagine a P.A. discourse of laughter that is somatic in origin, and that focuses on the "funny peculiar," which in the P.A. case is understood to be socially constructed elements that are privileged in being misconceived as natural entities in any and all P.A. discourses. The paper draws on Helene Cixous' "The Laugh of the Medusa" and Cixous' discussions of feminine writing and the burdens of imposed meanings. It imagines that the use of a libidinal discourse of laughter is to liberate ourselves from the distortions of our particular disciplinary discourse. It gives macro examples of political and economic myth-like stories that have become inscribed on our bodies and that make up our "governing" political and economic discourses. Using a term discussed by Milan Kundera, I suggest that a value lies in bringing us closer in touch with traditional P.A.'s "litost."*

The attraction of a discourse of laughter for P.A. is that it might permit insights not now available, especially insights about macro public administration. Following Sigmund Freud, we can recognize that some forms of laughter are relatively unhelpful for such P.A. purposes. Legman's *Rationale of the Dirty Joke* provides a good set of examples. So, in his *The Book of Laughter and Forgetting*, one of Milan Kundera's characters (Petrarch) explains that, "Laughter is an explosion that tears us away from the world and throws us back into our own solitude. Joking is a barrier between man and the world. Joking is the enemy of love and poetry" (Kundera, 1996, p. 199). Immanuel Kant also gives short shrift to what he sees as laughter. In the Critique of Judgment (p. 219), he writes that "Laughter is an affection arising from the sudden transformation of a strained expectation into nothing."

The kind of laughter that I imagine could be more helpful is the sort that shares a similar origin to the types analyzed by Freud and described by Kundera. It originates within a person's guts; it explodes from within a person's body; and it emanates from within, and appeals to, the depths of a person's unconscious. It is somatic in origin. However, it differs from the joking and laughter described by Freud and Kundera in that it aims at only a part of the world, and that part is what has been described as the "funny peculiar" as contrasted with the "funny ha ha." The "funny ha ha" focuses on what is presented as simply laughable and that often begins with a story line like "There was a Scotsman, a Welshman and a Dutchman in a bar, and the Dutchman said...and so on." It is often accompanied by loud guffaws and clinking of glasses. The "funny peculiar" focuses on the oddities of what is taken seriously in the world, like the oddity—the strangeness—in the very serious claim that someone recently killed "by accident" eleven members of the royal family in Nepal, using two assault weapons. The "funny peculiar" in the P.A. case, as I want to understand it, is especially useful when it zeros in on some socially constructed elements that are privileged in various discourses of public administration. Even though socially constructed, these elements are privileged in being misconceived as natural entities (required in any and all public administration discourses).

This paper plays with the possibility of a P.A. discourse (a writing) of laughter. Pointing to notions constraining public administration, the paper seeks to contribute toward anti-administration's primary aim—as that aim is described in the introduction to this symposium. In the spirit of anti-administration, it considers the relative advantages of such a discourse of laughter. The paper exemplifies a spirit of anti-administration where the practical values for P.A. of imagination and poetry are more highly valued. "Perhaps the imagination is on the verge of recovering its rights," wrote Andre Breton in his 1924 *First Surrealist Manifesto*. "We are still living under the reign of logic, but the logical processes of our time apply only to the solution of problems of secondary interest" (Waldberg, 1965, p. 66). The surrealist messages came first in literary, and then in artistic, form. Poetry, as the concept is used here, refers to bio-spirituality. Bio-spirituality is also described in the introduction to this symposium, e.g., in such terms as the pre-systemized energy of the singularity of a person, as boundary exceeding, and so on.

This paper goes back to Helene Cixous' *The Laugh of the Medusa* (1980). It has an origin in my paper (2001, pp. 187–204) on "Somatic Writing: Attending to Our Bodies." A discourse of laughter is intimately involved with somatic writing because genuine laughter emanates from within the body and because the aim of both a discourse of laughter and somatic writing is to liberate from encrusted and disabling meanings. Somatic writing is a type that includes seeking to derive energies and understandings from the libidinal. The Somatic Writing paper asked how the body of P.A. Theory can turn more attention to bodies and how we can unbridle the bridled. It considered three perspectives on embodiment that can serve as possible directions for somatic writing for P.A. I am reluctant to describe this present piece as an extension of that paper. I would prefer the Somatic Writing paper to stand by itself, and I think of this paper as playing with a possibility—as play with a purpose. I leave it to you to imagine the laugh of Medusa.

## IMAGINING THE DISCOURSE

Imagine the laughter of Medusa. Medusa, it will be recalled, was the enemy of Athena and others, and she had been changed into a person whose hair consisted of hissing snakes. Apparently, she was so horrendous that the mere sight of her would turn men into stone. Medusa,"too dark to be explored," reflects the meanings that define women; as Cixous describes it, "the phallologocentric aufhebung is here, and it is militant, the reproducer of old schemes..." (Cixous, 1986, p. 68). Perseus, son of Zeus, approached Medusa—walking backwards—when she was asleep. As Cixous writes, "Look at the trembling Perseuses, with their advance, armor-clad in apotropes as they back toward us!" And she adds, "Pretty backs. There's not a minute to lose. Let's get out of here" (Cixous & Clement, 1986, p. 69). Being careful not to look at her directly, Perseus was able to decapitate Medusa and pop her head into a special carrying purse. The decapitated head still had inexplicable, malevolent powers. For instance, Perseus in an act of pique exposed the head to Atlas and transformed the latter into a mountain (see Graves, 1955, pp. 239–240). Unimportantly, the medusa is also a tentacled, usually bell-shaped, free-swimming sexual stage in the lifecycle of the coelenterate of the class Scyphozoa or Hydrozoa. The breakdown of established meanings through laughter, as a first step toward liberation, has been described as the basis of The Laugh of the Medusa (e.g., Conley, 1992, p. 34). In Cixous' account (1986, p. 68), the established meanings include the understandings developed about the nature and functioning of women—frozen into place "between two terrifying myths: between the Medusa and the abyss... It would be enough to make half the world (i.e., women) break out laughing, if it were still not going on" (Cixous, 1986, p. 68). But the main function of laughter in the Cixousian scheme is to liberate us—men and women—from the established set of meanings, which not only oppress but also distort and limit understandings.

Cixous advocates feminine writing as a liberating move for both women and men—or, as I would translate that, feminine thinking/feeling. "Write! Writing is for you, you are for you; your body is yours; take it," declares

Cixous (1980, p. 246). The point is that, on her account, the desires of men have determined what is often seen as the "objective" meaning about the functioning and role of women. This meaning is not simply "objective." Rather, it is shot through with the libinidal desires of men, backed by power. We need feminine writing to recognize and express the marginalized desires. We can rely on Toril Moi to summarize the features of this feminine writing, which (something not at all confined to women) Cixous describes as "writing said to be feminine" or a "decipherable libidinal femininity, which can be read in writing produced by a male or a female" (see Moi, 1985, p. 108). The feminine texts that this writing produces "strive in the direction of difference, struggle to undermine the dominant phallogocentric logic, split open the closure of binary opposition and revel in the pleasures of open-ended textuality" (Moi, 1985, p. 108). As Cixous puts it, the practice of feminine writing cannot be defined. "For this practice can never be theorized, enclosed, coded—which doesn't mean that it does not exist. But it will always surpass the discourse that regulates the phallocentric system; it does and will take place in areas other than those subordinated to philosophico-theoretical domination" (Cixous, 1980, p. 253). She does however offer a description. It is writing which Moi describes (p. 109) "as multiple, varied and ever-changing, consisting as it does of the non-exclusion either of the difference or of one sex."

A point that I would like to stress about Cixous' concept of feminine writing (or feminine thinking/feeling) is the association of that writing with the writer's body. So a characteristic of Cixous' feminine writing is "multiplication of the effects of the inscription of desire, over all parts of my body and the other body" (Cixous, 1980, p. 246). As Cixous writes, "I have been amazed more than once by a description a woman gave me of a world all her own which she had been secretly haunting since childhood. A world of searching, the elaboration of a knowledge, on the basis of a systematic experimentation with the bodily functions, a passionate and precise interrogation of her erotogeneity... I wished that that woman would write and proclaim this unique empire so that other women, other unacknowledged sovereigns, might exclaim: I, too, overflow; my desires have invented new desires, my body knows unheard-of songs" (Cixous, 1980, p. 246).

That a discourse of laughter emanates from within a person's body—that there is an intimate connection between a discourse of laughter and somatic writing—can be illustrated by considering the work of certain comedians like George Carlin. Those from an earlier generation may have wanted to add names like Mort Saul and Lenny Bruce, or perhaps Monty Python. Their useful laughter seems to dig down within their bodies. Yet the relatively few P.A. examples are against the grain of traditional thinking. For instance, look at the articles in *Public Administration Review* or any other "traditional" journal. The suggestion here is that there is room for a more radical discourse of laughter. The idea of mentioning Carlin is that it may help to illustrate the case that gut-involved humor has its place in helping people to cope with the "funny peculiar" of P.A. George Carlin is an iconoclastic comedian, prominent in the United States since the middle sixties. He has authored successful books, like his current *Napalm and Silly Putty* and his earlier *Brain Droppings*. He uses his humor for social criticism and other purposes, and he does much to provoke the audience's re-thinking (more accurately, its re-thinking/re-feeling) about the assumptions that guide their understandings, e.g., about religion, life, politics and language. He has commented, "I think it's the duty of the comedian to find out where the line is drawn and cross it deliberately." His website (www.georgecarlin.com) and his books indicate the usefulness of his humor in addressing the funny peculiar assumptions (the funny particular assumptions) of contemporary mores and culture.

The discourse of laughter, as a tool for liberation from the distortions of established meanings, is intimately involved in my bodily desires. Reconsider the somatic writing of Helene Cixous. The functioning of laughter in Cixous is a useful model for P.A.'s parallel purposes of developing alternative and insight-adding sets of meanings. Cixous' laughter is intended to undermine imposed meanings (e.g., the meaning of being a woman established by men). It should be repeated that, although commonly considered to be independent of desires, those imposed or established meanings are in fact laced with the desires—the hope, the dreads—of the dominant group, men. This parallels the meanings that have been established for P.A.—e.g., the parameters that have been set for the discipline. Another function of Cixous' laughter is to de-marginalize desires that have been suppressed, and this parallels an aim of somatic writing in P.A. Conley explains (as noted earlier) that the breakdown of imposed meaning through laughter, as a first step toward liberation, is the basis of *The Laugh of the Medusa*. The point is not that desires have been excluded from the meanings that society considers objective; it is that the exclusion has been partial. It is also that the simplistic dichotomy between objective and subjective is deconstructible. "'The Medusa laughs and she is beautiful' is a call to women to shatter the negative image imposed by men... The laughter breaks down.... From the moment of undoing of meaning...we proceed to another meaning, another way of writing, where desire is not subordinated to logic" (Conley, 1992, pp. 35–36). As Cixous writes elsewhere, "Culturally speaking, women have wept a great deal, but once the tears are shed, there will be endless laughter indeed" (Cixous, 1981, p. 55).

More than mere gut or somatic feelings are required in a liberating P.A. discourse of laughter. More than the merely libidinal is required: recall David Sedaris' remark that "if we're defined by our desires, I (am) in for a life-time of trouble" (Sedaris, 2001, p. 29). More than the merely socially constructed form of our libidinal is desired: recall how we are being constructed (misconstructed) to believe that desire is a feature merely "of" the market and not also "of" governance. Needed also is perceptiveness, like that displayed in Cixous' writings, in "bedrock" understandings about the nature of human beings and about the tendency of humans to be trapped within the limits of their particular discourses. My gut feeling is that, other things being equal, writing emanating from gut feelings are better than writing which does not. But the gut thoughts/feelings of those less liberated than others from their own particular discourses are surely problematic. I imagine that those who are mentally defective or psychologically impaired are liable to be found in this less liberated category. I imagine that many embracing traditional P.A. positions have a gut feeling that their own discourse is privileged. I imagine that some *Wall Street Journal* writers are moved by their gut feelings in support of the market system; I imagine that writers with a contrary attitude in journals like *Nation* or *Dissent* are no less so motivated. So, it is helpful that Carlin is motivated by a sense of dissatisfaction (he denies that his motivation is anger). But I imagine that his ability to go beyond his own discourse is less than Helene Cixous' ability.

I imagine, fairly or unfairly, that Cixous has a deeper conception of the human person. For example, consider her conception of "other sexuality." She describes other bisexuality as varied, multiple, and always changing. Rather than annulling differences, she explains that it "stirs them up, pursues them, increases them" (Cixous, 1980, p. 253). As Toi explains, Cixous' concept of feminine writing is "identical" with her concept of "other bisexuality." As Cixous wrote in the *The Laugh of the Medusa*, "To admit that writing is precisely working in the in-between, inspecting the process of the same and of the other without which nothing can live, undoing the work of death—to admit this is to want the two, as well as both, the ensemble of one and the other..." (Cixous, 1980, p. 262). Elsewhere she wrote, "let us imagine a real liberation of sexuality, that is, a transformation of our relationship to our body (and to another body)" (Cixous, 1980a, p. 97).

It is unwise to dismiss the fact of Cixous' contradictions, as Toi does, as "imaginary contradictions." That dismissal gets in the way of understanding the worth of hesitancy in making truth-claims. Toi describes Cixous' theory of writing and femininity as "fundamentally contradictory" and she reports that Cixous is aware of the contradictions. Toi notes that Cixous's theory "sifts back and forth from a Derridean emphasis on textuality as difference to a fullblown metaphysical account of writing as voice, presence and origin" (Toi, 1985, p. 119). Among the ways out of such a blind alley is to point out, as Toi does, that one can refuse to accept the Law of Non-Contradiction. This is the Aristotelian principle that something cannot both be and not be in the same respect and at the same time. I agree that an Hegelian dialectic can permit this. But there is a significant cost, and a number of prominent idealists (like John McTaggart) abandoned the dialectical approach for the law of non-contradiction (Farmer, 1990, p. 7). It is hard to say that it is untrue that the same medusa—or the same coffee cup—cannot be in Richmond and in Washington at the same time and in the same respect. For myself, I recognize the embrace of the dialectical method; but I think that Hegel was rash to reject the Law of Non-contradiction "unhesitantly." I do not think it is desirable to dismiss such a rejection as trivial. I should interject that thinkers like Andre Breton would not agree with this claim about cost. In his 1929 *Second Surrealist Manifesto*, he writes that, "There is every reason to believe that there exists a certain point in the mind at which life and death, real and imaginary, past and future, communicable and incommunicable, high and low, cease to be perceived in terms of contradiction" (Waldberg, 1965, p. 71). Among the other points that Toi makes (1985, p. 120) about these contradictions, however, is that Cixous has a "theoretico-poetic style."

Can you imagine a discourse of laughter being prohibited from the anti-administrative consciousness? I can't. Yet I can imagine a discourse of laughter that is more freeing than another.

A discourse of laughter can be more freeing when it is shaped by both an adequate notion of discourse and adequately in imagination and poetry. Discourse is not a matter of mere chat, mere talk or mere dialogue, as suggested in the introduction to this symposium. Yet unfortunately, this (mis)understanding does exist within the P.A. theory community. Tricia Patterson has done a great service in pointing to these differences in meaning. She writes that one

> point worth considering is whether 'discourse theory' in public administration has relied overly much on Habermas and communicative action, and insufficiently on Foucault's broader notion of discourse. For Foucault, a discourse is the way in which we constitute what we are thinking and talking about, and not just expressions themselves. (Patterson, 2000, p. 686)

For Foucault, discourse is a mind-set—including verbal and non-verbal, conscious and unconscious elements—that makes up our way of viewing the world. This is a long way away from such Habermasian statements as, "I shall speak of 'discourse' only when the meaning of the problematic validity claim conceptually forces participants to suppose that a rationally motivated agreement could in principle be achieved" (Habermas, 1984, p. 42). I discussed elsewhere (at the annual PAT-Net meeting, Ft. Lauderdale, January 2000) the view of "administration" held by St. Anselm, a medieval Archbishop of Canterbury. Although he administered for some 29 years, Anselm had a principled objection to being an administrator. When the king appointed him archbishop in March 1093, Anselm resisted, eyes streaming with tears, nose bleeding; he begged to be excused. The bishops had to pry open his fist so that the pastoral staff or crozier could be forced into his hand; he and the pastoral staff had to be carried out of the room. Sixteen years earlier, when elected as Abbot of Bec, he had similarly thrown himself on the ground and begged the monks to spare him. In his 1097 five-year review of his archiepiscopal tenure, he begged the Pope to "release my soul from this slavery." Anselm's objection was principled in that he thought that all nominees for promotion should genuinely wish not to be promoted and that they should do all possible to avoid it, up to the point of not going against all the best advisors. Anselm's attitude on this was rooted in his Foucauldian discourse (in this case, in his variety of medievalism): It was not just a matter of his chat.

Laughter, as a liberating move, can be more freeing when it is genuinely rooted in a person's imagination and poetry (or bio-spirituality). It must be acknowledged that there is a well-known negative side to humor, and I associate this with jokers who—lacking in the qualities of imagination and bio-spirituality—are not fully actualized. Legman gives a Freudian account of joking. So he can point out that, "Under the mask of humor, our society allows infinite aggressions, by everyone against everyone. In the culminating laughter by the observer or listener—whose position is often really that of victim or butt—the teller of the joke betrays his hidden hostility and signals his victory by being, theoretically at least, the one person who does not laugh" (Legman, 1968, p. 9). The role of the imagination and the poetic—the role of a discourse of laughter—in understanding assumptions in our own discourse is an art that can hardly be reduced to a procedure.

## IMAGINING APPLICATIONS

How could P.A. expect to gain from this Cixousian or other model of a discourse of laughter? The most important expectation is the anti-administrative prospect of struggling to liberate ourselves from the distortions and limitations of our own particular disciplinary discourse. The funny peculiar is easier to see in someone else's discourse, of course. The *South China Morning Post* (June 4, 2001), covering the massacre within the Nepalese royal family, carried a story about an incident that happened to King Prithivi Narayan Shah, who united Nepal into a single kingdom in 1768. Apparently, marching on the Kathmandu valley, the king encountered the Hindu god Gorakh Nath, disguised as a holy sage. "The king offered some curd to the sage, who swallowed the gift and then regurgitated it and offered it back. Disgusted, the king threw the food to the ground, covering his feet with the curd in the process. The sage criticized the king's pride, and he pointed out that the fact that the curd covered the king's ten toes meant that the ruling Shah dynasty would fall after ten generations." Curiously, the recently murdered King Birenda was the eleventh generation of the Shah dynasty. A professor at Kathmandu's Tribhuvan University, Milan Shakya, is quoted in the *South China Morning Post* story as saying that, "Whether these terrible events are merely coincidence, or a playing out of the prophecy remains to be seen."

The oddity of our own exaltation of the virtues of the Founding Fathers is as hard for us to recognize in our discourse as it is for Professor Shakya to see the oddity of the first Shah king's encounter in his discourse. So is our own exaltation of the virtues and power of the free market, our own celebration of self-interest and winning. Our own political and economic myth-like governing "stories" only rarely break into our consciousness; when they do, we tend to resist recognizing their myth-like character. Equally hard is it for those within the traditional P.A. discourse to spot the oddity of a discourse that privileges the short-term, the micro and the mere efficiency ethic. It is hard to accept that there is a price (below, I follow Kundera and call it litost) in P.A.'s kow-towing to political and economic myths, and to the dominance of political science and economics, disciplines themselves severely limited in understanding their respective spheres and myth-like stories. Yes, these examples have often been mentioned; as the content of mainstream journals and the routine P.A. dissertation topics suggest, however, our own discourse oddities still are hard to resist. Our own P.A. discourse is laced with sets of meanings that function in a manner akin to the Nepalese myths, although we do not notice them because they seem to us to be objective truths about our world. So are our governing discourses of politics and economics. In fact, our discourse (adapting Marx's concept of machinery as crystallized labor) is in part a limited set of crystallized desires, too subjective for comfort.

The difficulties in achieving changes in political and economic consciousness evidence the power of the myth-like stories that become inscribed within our bodies (our mind-bodies, if one prefers) and that make up our "governing" political and economic discourses, discourses that tend to "govern" mainstream thinking about P.A. Without paying attention to the political and economic stories that make up the P.A. consciousness, P.A. is condemned to more than mere Sisyphean frustration. Cixous' attention to the Medusa story is a model of the attention P.A. cannot afford not to pay to our political and economic myth-like stories. Such stories constitute us, as they are "written on us" and shape the ways in which we can understand the world. The problem is that the pattern of our political and economic consciousness is not straight forward. Rather, myth lies upon myth in a multi-layered and inchoate way, somewhat like the complexity of a dream.

Consider examples. At one level, one might point for instance to the tendency of political thinking to be concerned with mere structure, as nations inevitably over-idealize the nation itself. Witness the celebration in the United States of exceptionalism (e.g., see Madsen, 1998). Witness the deep respect accorded to excellent ideas and devices that were avante garde in the eighteenth century. For my money and important as are these structures and relations, we have tended to overemphasize structure and government-citizen relations as if they were complete ends in themselves, at the expense of citizen-citizen interrelationships. For me, too much of our politics is concerned with politicians speaking with citizens in an essentially one-way conversation. Others would like to express and illustrate these abstractions in more programmatic terms. For instance, Noam Chomsky might want to point to the dominant role of the military not only in banana republics but also in "advanced" countries (e.g., Chomsky, 2000).

At a parallel level in economic storying, one may point for instance to the firm conviction in the dominance of the laissez faire or free market model. Sometimes in the United States, it is called "the American way." Infrequently, there are harbingers, like the socially responsible activities of the former owners (Ben Cohen and Jerry Greenfield) of the Ben and Jerry's Ice Cream Chain (e.g., Cohen & Greenfield, 1997). But those are the swallows that probably will not make a summer. People become erotically attached to comforting fairy tales, like the Invisible Hand, which claims that the pursuit of self-interest leads to an economically optimal result (see Farmer, 1998). This dubious claim (dubious in mainstream economic theory, e.g., see Samuelson & Nordhaus, 1989) can be variously interpreted. In one view, the invisible hand is what works to achieve a better societal result when each person attempts to maximize his own individual satisfaction (including gouging his neighbors), rather than if each person were to act for the public interest. In another view, it is to see the invisible hand as the automatic pricing system that tends toward a final state of balance, "a poetic expression of the most fundamental economic balance of relations, the equalization of rates of return, as enforced by the tendency of factors to move from low to high returns" (Arrow & Debreu, 1971, p.1). Others may want to express this also in more programmatic terms, pointing to the limitations of the embrace of unrestrained globalization and of the McDonaldization of the world.

Permeating such political and economic myth-like stories and socially constructing our mind-bodies are other stories that one can suppose to be "underlying" or "overlaying." For instance, infusing the political and economic tales just noted are the myth-like stories of the benefits of hierarchy—our discourse legacy from the hierarchization of those like princes, priests and fathers. Thomas Hobbes' *Leviathan* can be read as symbolic of seeking citizen-citizen salvation primarily from a structure of power from above. Published in 1651, Hobbes' *Leviathan* started from the citizen and would have citizens trade their radical insecurity, the "state of warre," at the price of subjection to the "great Leviathan...or Mortall God." Hobbes' citizens sought their well being, not from themselves and within their relationship to their fellow citizens, but from a structure of power from above. This hierarchical picture can be expanded to include not merely traditional government but also the hierarchy and structure of what is often called the free market. Most people work under a boss, for instance. Most markets are oligarchic, and giant corporations dominate economic activity and sometimes, governmental programs. Adam Smith can be read (some would say misread) as symbolic of seeking citizen prosperity primarily through the hierarchy and structure of the "rivalrous competition." And, we have not spoken of the hierarchical storying involved in the power and appeal of fundamentalist religion, celebrating prostration to a higher power.

I do not deny, but I leave it to others, to show the micro relevance of a discourse of laughter. It seems to me that this can be done in the micro case, to produce one example, by building on the important observations of Barbara Czarniawska on paradoxes. "Paradoxes, until recently the villains of the organizational drama, constitute its dynamics and, even more important, account for its transformations. Without paradoxes, changes would not be possible..." (Czarniawska, 1997, p. 97). Her case studies lead to what she calls, with a twinkle in her eye, the ten paradoxical commandments for the public sector, e.g., complicate in order to simplify, follow routines in order to change. Rightly, Czarniawski points out that the existence of paradoxes is not inherently good. Yet, as "language renews itself via paradox (Lyotard, 1979/1987), so social practices renew themselves via tensions and contradiction" (Czarniawska, 1999, p. 12). It is not denied that such perceptions have macro significance. I merely want to note their micro importance. In the spirit of anti-administration, our discourse might want to engage the micro dialogue, perhaps by such means as drawing on the distinction between contraries and contradictions.

Perhaps a discourse of laughter can bring us more in touch with P.A.'s "litost." That is, it can allow us to understand and overcome the price of the subordination and limitation of the established, mainstream P.A. discourse. This subordination is to the political and economic myth-like stories in our cultural discourse, and to the pecking order, which elevates political science and economics as academically superior, even though (to repeat the claim) these disciplines are very limited in explaining their respective spheres. Litost is described and illustrated by Milan Kundera in his *The Book of Laughter and Forgetting*. Apparently an untranslatable Czech word, "litost" is "a state of torment created by the sudden sight of one's own misery" (Kundera, 1996, p. 167). Kundera illustrates its relationship to power. If a person has litost in relation to a person less powerful, he will attempt to hurt that person directly. His example is a boyfriend swimming with a girlfriend who is a better swimmer, and the girlfriend forgets herself and swims faster than her boyfriend. His litost impels him to strike her, attempting to "justify" (if that is the right word) this by saying that he was afraid for her safety. He is willing to strike her because she is less powerful. If a person has litost in relation to a person more powerful, he will hurt himself in order to hurt that more powerful person. A student might choose to kill himself (or fail his examinations) in order to hurt his more powerful parents, for instance.

Where is the litost of American Public Administration, a subject often in a state of torment created by the sight of its own misery? Elsewhere (Farmer, 1999), I have described P.A. as having adopted a Jeeves mentality. This is the celebrated butler in P.G. Wodehouse's novels. Jeeves is perfect in achieving for his twitty master, Bertie Wooster, what Bertie should want and what Bertie thinks he wants. This parallels Dwight Waldo's comparison of p.a. as adopting a downstairs role. Waldo had been a fan of the English T.V. series "Upstairs-Downstairs"—and, of course, the servants live downstairs. A discipline within the grasp of a Jeeves or downstairs mentality must surely have some unconscious torment created by the sight of its own misery. P.A. serves the more powerful institutional processes, economics and politics—the P.A. equivalents of the master Bertie Wooster and of the upstairs masters of the servants. Faced with more powerful institutional masters, a discourse of laughter might play with the possibility that—in privileging the short-term, the micro and the mere efficiency ethic—the P.A. discourse is choosing to do what the student did. Being content to be the butler seems to be a self-wounding, or even a suicidal, disciplinary choice. A discourse of laughter—laughter being something foreign to professional butlering—could help to break this limiting state of mind. It could facilitate this, to repeat the point, through liberating the imprisoned character of much P.A. writing.

## REFERENCES

Arrow, K. J., & Debreu, G. (1971). *General competitive analysis*. San Francisco, CA: Holden-Day.

Berman, M. (1989). *Coming to our senses: Body and spirit in the hidden history of the West*. New York: Simon and Schuster.

Chomsky, N. (2000). *Rogue states: The rule of force in world affairs*. Boston, MA: South End Press.

Cixous, H. (1980a). Sorties. In E. Marks & I. de Coutivron (Eds.), *New French feminisms: An anthology* (pp. 90–98). Amherst: University of Massachusetts Press.

Cixous, H. (1980b). The Laugh of the Medusa. In E. Marks & I. de Coutivron (Eds.), *New French feminisms: An anthology* (pp. 245–264). Amherst: University of Massachusetts Press.

Cixous, H. (1981). Castration or decapitation? (A. Khun, Trans.). *Signs, 7*, 41–45.

Cixous, H., & Clement, C. (1986). *The newly born woman*. Minneapolis: University of Minnesota Press.

Cohen, B., & Greenfield, J. (1997). *Ben and Jerry's double-dip: How to run a value-led business and make money, too*. New York: Simon and Schuster.

Conley, V. (1992). *Helene Cixous*. Toronto: University of Toronto Press.

Czarniawska, B. (1997). *Narrating the organization: Drama of institutional identity*. Chicago: University of Chicago Press.

Czarniawska, B. (1999). *Writing management: Organization theory as a literary genre*. New York: Oxford University Press.

Farmer, D. J. (1990). *Being in time: The nature of time in light of McTaggart's paradox*. Lanham, MA: University Press of America.

Farmer, D. J. (1995). *The language of public administration: Bureaucracy, modernity, and postmodernity*. Tuscaloosa: University of Alabama Press.

Farmer, D. J. (1998). Adam Smith's legacy. In T. D. Lynch & T. J. Dickerson (Eds.), *Handbook of organization theory and management: A philosophical approach* (pp. 141–164). New York: Marcel Dekker.

Farmer, D. J. (1999). Public administration discourse: A matter of style? *Administration and Society, 31*, 299–320.

Farmer, D. J. (2001). Somatic writing: Attending to our bodies. *Administrative Theory and Society, 23*, 187–204.

Graves, R. (1955). *The Greek myths*. New York: Penguin.

Habermas, J. (1984). *The theory of communicative action* (Vol. 1) (T. McCarthy, Trans.). Boston, MA: Beacon Press.

Kundera, M. (1996). *The book of laughter and forgetting* (A. Asher, Trans.). New York: HarperPerennial.

Legman, G. (1968). *The rationale of the dirty joke: An analysis of sexual humor*. New York: Grove Press.

Madsen, D. (1998). *American exceptionalism*. Jackson: University Press of Mississippi.

Moi, T. (1985). *Sexual/textual politics: Feminist literary theory*. London: Methuen.

Patterson, P. M. (2000). The talking cure and the silent treatment: Some limits of "discourse" as speech. *Administrative Theory and Praxis, 22*, 663–695.

Sedaris, D. (2001). *Me talk pretty one day*. Boston, MA: First Back Bay.

Samuelson, P. A., & Nordhaus, W. D. (1989). *Economics*. New York: McGraw Hill.

Waldberg, P. (1965). *Surrealism*. New York: Thomas and Hudson.

# SOMATIC WRITING: ATTENDING TO OUR BODIES

### David John Farmer

## ABSTRACT

*How can the body of Public Administration (P.A.) theory and practice turn more attention to bodies? How can it seek understandings that result from recognizing more clearly that it deals with people, and relations between people, who live in their acculturated bodies? This paper seeks to clear some underbrush on the way to a kind of "somatic writing" that aims toward examining and extending P.A. thinking in terms of our embodiment. It considers three perspectives on embodiment that can serve as possible directions for somatic writing for P.A. A first perspective is that P.A. should include special attention to the bodily in all its thinking. A second is that P.A. should include as its unit of analysis the embodied human in her full enculturated humanity. The third overlapping perspective is that P.A. should include attention to bodily desires, like passion.*

Imagine writing about juries. Imagine the administration and workings of juries located at Manhattan's Central Criminal Courts building at 100 Center Street (a large, hectic operation often featured on television shows like "Law and Order"). From a traditional P.A. perspective, the jury function could be described in such terms as a mission statement and an organization chart. It could be further specified in terms of relevant laws, rules and procedures and of sets of work statistics, perhaps supplemented with glossy photographs from a T.V. program. Alternatively, an equally partial but different understanding could be sought by imaginatively (playfully) attending to bodies taking up Court House space, bodies interacting, bodies giving out different kinds of sensations: sounds, sights, smells and feelings. These are interacting not only with each other but also with the body of the buildings. Could a series of charts (at a minimum, a series of multi-colored charts) or could a computer simulation (with auditory overlay) be developed that would represent critical bodily activities and interactions? Could we do better than represent by reproducing, or even by experiencing, the bodily feelings of the workings of juries? How could we conjoin the thinking/feeling from within our own bodies with the rhythms and eccentricities of the P.A. body? Could a P.A. theorist, attuned to her own body, begin to play (with developing insights) through free-form gaming that starts (and perhaps ends) with the physicality of bodies and their interactions?

What could be learned from such exercises in bodily writing? My own limited stints on jury duty lead me to think that the most striking parts of the experience are bodily. There is the physical effect of turning up at the assigned hour at a place where I do not want to be; the physicality of the enforced waiting on wooden chairs while officials write on forms and tell us about a juror's responsibilities; the ponderousness of the group-crocodile-walk up from the waiting room to the court room; the sitting while the attorneys ask questions; the leaden passivity of the sitting, and so on. As Roland Barthes writes (1978, p. 40), "To make someone wait: the constant prerogative of all power, 'age-old pastime of humanity.'" What must it be like to sit and sit and sit on a long jury, like the O.J. Simpson trial jury—without being allowed to talk about the case with fellow jurors, without being allowed to write down anything, without any positive physical action, without access to the world of normal friends and normal activities, without knowing when it will end, without having any significant control whatever? What must it be like for a juror whose legs, when she is seated, are too short to touch the ground; for one whose body is grossly overweight; or for one who cannot tolerate meetings?

It is this and similar trains of thinking that, in part, lead to the central question of this paper. How can the body of Public Administration (P.A.) theory and practice turn more attention, as I think it should, to bodies? How can it seek understandings that result from recognizing more clearly that it deals with people, and relations between people, who live in their acculturated bodies. This paper seeks to clear some underbrush on the way toward a kind of "somatic writing" that aims toward re-examining and extending P.A. thinking in terms of our embodiment. The phrase "somatic writing" appeals to Helene Cixous: "Write! Writing is for you, you are for you; your body is yours, take it" (Cixous, 1980, p. 246). This paper itself does not do somatic writing, because I want to appeal to those in discourses that are not likely to be sympathetic to it. Nor does it claim that writing which is not somatic is useless; every perspective is useful—up to a point. Rather, it offers three overlapping perspectives on embodiment that can serve as possible directions, among those available, for this somatic writing. These perspectives also suggest that attending to our bodies is promising for P.A., no less than for any of the human and social sciences. As feminist and other literatures suggest, this matter of our bodies matters.

Embodiment is used here in the general sense intended by Maurice Merleau-Ponty (1962, p. 146), who writes that, "The body is our general medium for having a world." The body is our general medium for having the world of P.A. thinking and practice. Embodiment is not understood here to mean the biologism whereby all can be reduced to the biological, to the genetic. The form of embodiment depends on processes of social construction. Merleau-Ponty writes of kinds of bodily actions. One is restricted to the conservation of life and the biological; another, "elaborating on these primary actions and moving from their literal to their figurative meaning," manifests itself in a core of new significance, as in the motor habits like (his example) in dancing. Finally, there is a third where the "meaning aimed at cannot be achieved by the body's natural means" and it must then "build itself an instrument and it projects thereby around itself a cultural world" (Merleau-Ponty, 1962, p. 146). Merleau-Ponty holds that a starting point for the analysis of culture and history should be embodiment, and surely, disciplines like P.A. and economics are cultural and historical artifacts. Others would want, like me, to express his listing of bodily actions differently to emphasize even more that the form of embodiment and body are not at all invariant across history and culture (e.g., Hoy, 1999).

This paper considers, in turn, three perspectives on embodiment that can serve as possible directions for somatic writing for P.A. A first perspective is that P.A. should include special attention to the bodily in all its thinking. Here I could borrow the phrase "somatic modes of attention" from Thomas Csordas who defines it (1999) as "culturally elaborated ways of attending to and with one's body in surroundings that include the embodied presence of others." A second overlapping perspective is that P.A. should include as its unit of analysis the embodied human in her full enculturated humanity. A third overlapping perspective is that P.A. should include attention to bodily desires such as passion. The term "overlapping" is used in a strong sense; in fact, the perspectives on embodiment and directions for somatic writing are hardly separate. Together, these perspectives could be used as a basis for re-examining the body of P.A. theory and for extending it in useful directions. Together, they support the claim that P.A. thinking—unbridling its bridled character—should develop understandings from the viewpoint of bodily being-in-the-world.

## PERSPECTIVE #1: SOMATIC ATTENTION

A first perspective is that P.A. should include attention to the bodily throughout the range of its thinking. A corresponding direction for P.A. somatic writing is to re-examine and extend all of P.A. theory and practice in terms of the ineluctable existence of the embodied human person. The mind goes immediately to disciplines like ergonomics; but I mean more than just that. As noted, I could have borrowed the phrase "somatic modes of attention" from Thomas Csordas (1993). Recall that he (1999) defines this as "culturally elaborated ways of attending to and with one's body in surroundings that include the embodied presence of others." But I am not at ease with the examples to which he gives importance. The examples include ritual healing (e.g., where the healer supposes that she sees, or hears the name of, the afflicted organ), and mental imagery (e.g., where the healer uses non-ocular senses to know what they suppose is happening). I would prefer examples in terms of what Helene Cixous calls "writing" and in the sense of imaginization that starts from within the play of our experiencing bodies.

Learning from writers like Helene Cixous, P.A.'s somatic writing can seek the impetus for new understandings from the lived experiences and reflections/feelings of those who are willing to listen to and to develop understandings of their own bodies. Somatic study can certainly include self-understanding, the human being as experienced by herself from within. As Cixous writes,

> I have been amazed more than once by a description a woman gave me of a world all her own which she had been secretly haunting since early childhood. A world of searching, the elaboration of a knowledge, on the basis of a systematic experimentation with the bodily functions, a passionate and precise interrogation of her erotogeneity.... I wished that that woman would write and proclaim this unique empire so that other women, other unacknowledged sovereigns, might exclaim: I, too, overflow; my desires have invented new desires, my body knows unheard-of songs. (Cixous, 1980, p. 246)

Neither Cixous nor others with similar views want to suggest that in this somatic writing there is any special method or data; rather, they are speaking of an attitude that demands embodied attention to bodiliness "even in purely verbal data." The re-examination and extension of P.A. theory and practice should be understood therefore not as a mere mechanical intellectual exercise "out there." It should emerge from the self-aware embodied thinker/feeler.

Somatic writing should incorporate imagination. Imaginization (a neologism) has been described as an ever-increasing reliance on the imagination in a similar way that Enlightenment rationalization extended increasingly the use of reason (see Farmer, 1995). For example, imagination can be expected to play a larger role in justification in somatic writing, where the notion of justification is contrasted with discovery. This imaginization can be nourished by playing from within the rhythms and eccentricities of our bodies. It can also be understood as encompassing non-rational ways of understanding, like right-brain and unconscious "thinking." Other terms may also be added, like (as Nietzsche and Jung used the terms) the Dionysian and the Apollonian. Mainstream economic theory is a clear example of a discipline that ignores what is not rational, left-brained and conscious. It starts, as it were, after desires end. It exhibits a parallel with what Barthes describes as "the difficulty of the amorous project": "Just show me whom to desire, but then get out of the way!" (Barthes, 1978, p. 137). Mainstream P.A., although more porous and although it does contain important work from these perspectives, still marginalizes the non-rational, the right-brained and the unconscious.

Recall the P.A. example, given at the beginning of this paper, of how imaginatively we can seek to conjoin the thinking/feeling from within our own bodies with the rhythms and eccentricities of the P.A. body.

Candidate starting points in thinking about P.A. bodies include disciplines like ergonomics. But I want to suggest that the kind of writing that Helene Cixous and others describe provides an even more promising prospect. Ergonomics, and related areas of interest like "Health and Safety" and "Insurance and Risk Management," are concerned with the fact that any work environment involves an interaction between a worker and her environment. Ergonomics can appeal to p.a. practitioners, because there is a clear pay-off in much ergonomic work, although there is no claim here that ergonomics does not involve more fundamental, long-term issues. We are familiar with this in computer work (witness the incidence of carpel tunnel syndrome) and in laboratories, etc. So, an ergonomics service can state that it applies "scientific knowledge about human capabilities and limitations to the design and organization of the work environment." Its goal is "to enhance productivity, safety and well-being, and help clients reduce the opportunity for human error..." (bcr.bc.ca/ergonomics/default.htm). This same organization advertises its applied research work in ergonomics program management, shiftwork and fatigue management, transportation ergonomics, marine ergonomics, vibration and repeated impact, and development and occupational standards. It advertises education and training in ergonomics and the design process, designing for user needs and capabilities, office ergonomics, back and upper extremity education, and fatigue management. The suggestion is that, while this is useful for its purposes and while it can help us to listen to it, we should go further. We can go further with the sort of somatic writing that we are describing.

Ways in which P.A.'s somatic writing can go further are suggested by Helene Cixous. This includes the idea that our own bodies should be the essential focus of our thinking, as she recognizes that writing can be a manifestation of libidinal desire. There are equivalences between the creativity of writing and sex and love; there is an outpouring of the inner self as the play of writing is engaged. Her own writing is in fact a kind of model for the writing she has in mind. Writing of this kind is, for her, life affirming. This might strike those in the traditional P.A. discourse as oddly irrelevant, and it is indeed at odds with the desiccated attitude of much P.A. thinking. Much of

P.A. writing, being about things and about people-as-things, is not life affirming. Some writing on bureaucracy apes the bureaucratic, as it were, as when a "truth" is bent to serve the machine (e.g., in CYA fashion). Some can say that much in P.A. discourse severs the connection between the object of its knowledge and persons in their full humanity. This is not to single out P.A. discourse. The desiccating drift in rationalizing thinking is nowhere better illustrated than in mainstream economic thinking, which has traditionally been called the "dismal science."

A consideration might add to an understanding of Cixous' claims. Many of her ideas on writing (without in any way wishing to denigrate the special qualities in her work) are shared by others, beyond the French feminist movement. So we can find Berman writing about visceral history, where the historian uses her own body as a tool for research. "History gets written with the mind holding the pen. What would it be like, what would it read like, if it got written with the body holding the pen?" (Morris Berman, 1989, p. 110).

Claims about the intimate connection between writing and erotic desire are exemplified and shared by many writers beyond Cixous. On exemplification, John Stuart Mill and Bertrand Russell are examples. There is the extravagant tribute by Mill on his lover's (his wife's) tombstone in Avignon. The tribute has often been ridiculed, foolishly, as Mill overstating the enormous debt to the liberation he felt by writing while in erotic or loving association with Harriet Taylor. There are Russell's meetings, set up by his desire-mate Lady Ottoline, with Joseph Conrad and D. H. Lawrence. Russell shared with Conrad a belief that there is a difference between thinking and writing as "a dangerous walk on a thin crust of lava" and another level of writing where the writer sinks into the fiery depths, the "central fire" (Monk, 1996, p. 318). He shared with Lawrence the idea that writing should attempt to escape the prison, the hard shell that must be broken (Monk, 1996, p. 403).

The notion that there is a connection between writing and erotic desire has long been recognized. One of Plato's accounts of knowledge is set in the Symposium, a dialogue about the nature of erotic love. There, Plato's Socrates speaks of knowledge acquisition in terms of Diotima's Ladder—and it is true that Plato was no fan of the body, male or female. In the loving companionship between an older male and a younger male lover, lovers ascend the ladder of knowing through their mutual erotic desire. This erotic love, which rejoices in the physical beauty in the beloved, provides the motive force of the ascent. The erotic love—eros—ascends, as the lovers recognize a similar physical beauty in all of humanity. It ascends further through erotic energy toward the moral beauty in all persons, the morality of the sphere of meaning. Then finally it reaches—together with the loved one—to an erotic attachment to the Form of beauty itself. Eros is there all the way, not only as motive force but also as the desire that makes the ascent possible at all. This account will irritate those who consider Plato to be contributing to a sort of "willow pattern plate" or Victorian account of erotic passion (with lovers going "upwards" towards perpetual bliss). It is unnecessary here to consider the criticisms and commentary Plato's Symposium has attracted (e.g., Spelman, 1982, pp. 112–113). The purpose in offering Plato as an example is only to make the limited point that the connection between writing and erotic desire is not at all a novel or fringe notion. It is agreed, however, that Cixous would wish one day to adjust the story; she might want to speak not in terms of an ascent but of a descent to the within. She would agree with Rich that in "order to live a fully human life we require not only control of our bodies... (but also) we must touch the unity and resonance of our physicality, our bond with the natural order, the corporeal ground of our intelligence" (Rich, 1976, p. 39).

## PERSPECTIVE #2: FOCUS

A second direction for somatic writing lies in focusing on a wider P.A. unit of analysis that fully recognizes the enculturated or "en-discoursed" character of embodiment. Underlying this particular direction for somatic writing is a second perspective triggered by the notion of embodiment. The perspective on embodiment is recognition that P.A.'s unit of analysis should be the embodied human, and that bodies are enculturated. I have discussed the difficulties of the narrowness of the unit of analysis in P.A. and in economics earlier in the context of discourse theory (e.g., Farmer, 2000). So, unlike the other two, this perspective has already been discussed. The present account differs only in details. It was already explained that there is a transactional relationship (beyond the reductionist and the interactionist models) between the biological and the enculturated aspects of the human being, for example. It was explained that the embodied human being is not a mere biological entity, any more than she is a mere spiritual or mere psychological entity. Nor is she an interacting set of such features. Also, it should be added that there is a necessary relationship between a person and her environment, e.g. in the sense that the air of the environment can be described as "part" of the functioning lungs. A living person can be separated for analytical purposes from ongoing implication with her environment; ontological separation is fatal.

The narrowness of the present unit of analysis can be seen most clearly and more significantly in the case of the economics discipline. It is clearer to the extent that it is better known that economic theory, as is discussed later, focuses on the choices of rational "economic man." This is clearer, perhaps, than P.A.'s reliance on the parallel "administrative man." Rather than focusing on such stick figures, the unit of analysis could be extended to include the irreducible features of the embodied person. The person has biological, social, psychological and spiritual dimensions of being embodied.

For those who think that the attention of analysis should be the interrelationship between people (e.g. Action Theory in Harmon, 1981), the same point applies because the nodes of the relationship are between embodied persons in their full personhood, i.e. as bio-psycho-socio-spiritual persons. The concept should be re-explained, indicating how this new unit of analysis differs from the present practice in disciplines like economics and P.A. and noting how the understanding of the bio-psycho-socio-spiritual is connected intimately with embodiment.

The notion of embodied or corporeal spirituality is as strange (for some) as it was when Nietzsche discussed it. The reason is that it stands opposed to the notion of the spiritual as apart from, or opposed to, a person's body (as in St. Augustine). I think of spirituality as referring to the pre-systematized energy of the singularity of a person. This energy has been described as poetic; as revolutionary; as exceeding bounds; and as an opening of the person to the wholeness of herself, of nature and sociality. But none of this requires a spirituality divorced in any way from the body. The embodied person is embodied even when spiritual, and the embodiment is shaped and formed by the enculturation and the discourses to which the person is open. Spirituality should be viewed (on a parallel with Heidegger's mysterious comment that the Nothing nothings) as the body bodying.

This embodiment does not privilege the biological, however. The point is that there are only analytical distinctions between the biological, the psychological, the social, and the spiritual (or poetic) aspects of a human being. In ontological terms, such divisions melt away. The distinction between a person and her environment should be considered in a parallel way; the environmental component of a person is integral to being a living person.

These claims can be supplemented by considering the cyborg—a term popular since the 1960s. People often speak of a cyborg as not fitting the standard definition of a human being; they think of it as neither human nor a machine—a hybrid with enhanced powers. On the one hand, the cyborgian elements are part of the person to the extent that they become implicated in that person being and functioning alive. The addition of cyborgian elements complicates an ontological account of the human person not much more than a telephone complicates a telephoner—or President Roosevelt's wheelchair complicates FDR. On the other hand, the person-in-her-environment (which is no less than what a living person is) is changed when the environment is significantly changed. Such a change in environment is illustrated in the internet advances that affect consciousness. Chat-roomers can reflect with joy, for instance, about their bodies being here and their minds "out there." McAdams (2000) writes that, "Online, gender is a matter of choice—but there are more than two choices." Yes, a person's mind, qua living mind, could not be "out there" if her body were not "here." Yet, what it is to be a being-in-the-world is surely shaped by changes in the world.

Consider the nature and significance of the "unit of analysis" issue more closely in the case of the economics discipline. Economic theory focuses on the choices of rational "economic man." In the words of a 1905 Dictionary of Economic Terms, he is an "imaginary being, whose sole motives and incentives to action are economic." Economic man is one who does whatever optimizes his utility. Economic man seeks to optimize whatever can be commodified, and he recognizes such human components as the spiritual and the biological only to the extent that they are represented in the world of commodification. The fact that many people are not like this is viewed as irrelevant. The Dictionary makes the stronger claim that, "It is safe to say that no reputable economist, today or in the past, has ever considered that the mainspring of human action is, in reality, either wholly or in greater part dominated by the desire for economic gain" (Winton, 1951). Which claim is right or wrong is beside the point of economic theorizing, however. Economic theorizing is in the world of the model, and (as Milton Friedman has noted) the truth values of the assumptions are not critical for that world. There is more. The people in the economic system are regarded in the same stick figure terms. Accordingly, the entrepreneur (the hero of the economic story) deals with factors of production that include land, capital, organizing ability and labor. The entrepreneur hires "units" of labor. A unit of labor is not a living bio-psycho-socio-spiritual person, with an ongoing existence in a continuing process of change and circumstances. It is a category, rather than a human.

P.A.'s reliance on the parallel "administrative man," has been described earlier (Farmer, 1999) in Marcusian terms. Marcuse holds that the cutting edge of industrial society exhibits the thinking of one-dimensional man, emphasizing a trend toward technological rationality and toward containing the trend within existing institutions. This kind of thinking requires a unit of analysis, like administrative man, that privileges efficiency (and related concepts) rather than bio-psycho-socio-spiritual aspirations. As Marcuse himself puts it, "Life as an end is qualitatively different than life as a means" (Marcuse, 1991, p. 17). There is an emphasis on efficiency within the agency, an efficiency of provision. Agency employees and agency customers and clients all "exist for." The agency employee as a unit of analysis is one who "exists for" the administrative mechanism and for the purposes of the mechanism. More controversially, even the customer or client is administrative man in that he is considered only insofar as he is to be serviced by the agency. The agency, even when it speaks of "existing for" the customer, has an operational notion of a customer limited to one "existing for" the service from the agency. We can perhaps experience this most vividly when considering ourselves as customers for private bureaucracies, when we receive telephone and credit card solicitations without apparent regard for our welfare as humans.

What is wrong with such a narrow and disembodied unit of analysis? The difficulty is that whole classes of results are excluded—from results that could be obtained from the use of different units of analysis. Consider P.A. When it excludes as a unit of analysis the bio-psycho-socio-spiritual person, for instance, P.A. is prevented from important lines of thought about what is good for the whole system and the person. The welfare recipient provides but one example, trekking from one place to another, for this food stamp issue here, for that appointment there.... There is a tendency to discount issues like authentic hesitation in deciding what ought to be the case in bureaucratic activity; authentic listening by the bureaucracy; therapeutic management, anti-administration and thinking beyond mere "programs." The disembodied discourse of P.A. is not as alert as it could be to ideas like these.

Consider economics again. When it excludes, as a unit of analysis, the bio-psycho-socio-spiritual person, for instance, mainstream economic theory discounts important elements of what it is to be a human. Important results are available in alternative economics (e.g., see Prychitko, 1998); but these cannot compete against the results of mainstream economic theory. The conclusion-shaping power of the assumptions of mainstream economics tends to be forgotten. The conclusions of economic theorizing can hardly receive, as it were, a Rawlsian fate. It will be recalled that John Rawls (1971) went even further than economic theory in assuming that his economic actors are not real people at all. He assumed that they could be ignorant of their personal and social characteristics, and even their historical period. Rawls' mind game could suffer a harsher fate—and he himself could criticize his own work—because justice philosophizing is not so firmly within the economic grip of a single paradigm as it is in mainstream economic theory. The disembodied discourse of mainstream economic theory has always been resilient.

A thorough re-reading and extension of P.A. theorizing in terms of this expanded and embodied unit of analysis is likely to yield significant results. All of the elements of traditional P.A. theory can be re-evaluated and extended: neo-classical, systems, later human relations, market and interpretive and classical theories. Some work has already been done, of course. Yet, a thorough somatic re-writing is yet to be realized. The full force of the writing suggested by Cixous promises much for the development of P.A. "A feminine text cannot fail to be more than subversive. It is volcanic; as it is written it brings about an upheaval of the old property crust, carrier of masculine investments; there's no other way" (Cixous, 1980, p. 258).

## PERSPECTIVE #3: INTIMACY

Another overlapping perspective on embodiment suggests yet a third direction for somatic writing for P.A. This direction is that P.A., no less than the human and social sciences, should include attention to bodily desires or libido functioning. The study of desire is extensive and is found in many fields like society as a whole (e.g., Marcuse, 1974) and marketing (e.g., watch television commercials), and it has a toe-hold in P.A. There is Psycho-History, and there are the various branches of psychoanalysis and psychology, for example. A claim for somatic writing is that, incorporating such ideas and approaches, it should seek to rely even further on our own and the diversity (the difference) of our own bodies. There is a wish, which many in established fields share, to de-marginalize excluded embodied thinking/feeling. How this should be done, it is recognized, is likely to be a contested area. Positions will range from one "bridled" extreme of "we have that already covered" to another "unbridled" one of thorough and complete rejection, scorning any reliance on the various "prisons" of the various psychologies. My own view is that established disciplines should be utilized, as long as the ideas are viewed not as what are described later as Big T truths; but we also need the erotic energy of unbridled contributions. Let us think more about the perspective of desires, offering a PA example in terms of intimacy. Then let us give a playful and speculative illustration of this direction for somatic writing (again) about P.A. intimacy. Finally, we can return to the issue of "going beyond" existing disciplinary frames about desire, a passion that itself (when it exists) goes beyond frames.

This third perspective on embodiment is that opportunities are available for alternative descriptions, in terms of bodily desires, of what in a sense is the "same" complex of entities as were described in non-bodily terms. The alternative description, while in a sense about the "same" complex of entities, provides additional insights insofar as it provides a new angle on the "same" set of entities. For example, the role of the manager could be explored in the standard management-book way; yet, there is an opportunity for a writer to do for the manager what Roland Barthes did (1978) for the discourse of the lover. As another example, consider when the television reporter wants to report on "our" program but wants to do it in human-interest or human-desires terms. Often enough, the TV product appears to us incomplete and we forget that, beyond self-serving stories, we have done too little to work out how to give adequate pictures of our programs in anything but the traditional administrative way. For four helpful examples of alternative descriptions of the "same" administrative operations, see McSwite (1998). This re-raises the issue of the nature of an administrative, economic or any other "fact." It raises the Foucauldian claim that what is counted as a "fact" is a function of the discourse selected. The discourse of administrative theory (as of mainstream economic theory) tends to privilege a selected set of mental constructs as facts; the view of facts is partial, within the discourse limits. Focusing even more on bodily desires raises the prospect of developing insights in P.A.—as well as in other disciplines like economics—from the platform of an additional or alternative description of the "same" reality.

Adding an alternative "desires" description of agency interpersonal relations can be illustrated at the agency level in terms of intimacy. At one level, an agency may direct its libidinal energy toward producing whatever services it offers and nothing more; and customers may focus on obtaining the proffered services and no more. "Give me my driver's license, which I have just paid for; thank you: let me get out of here," for example. At another level, the agency may desire a more intimate relationship with the customer; the customer may desire a more intimate relationship with the agency. At times, one level is more important than the other; at times, one or other of the levels is (or seems to be) not important at all. This suggestion that customers want a more intimate relationship with agencies may appear odd in a circumstance when there is ongoing antipathy against government. But the desire for intimacy is reflected in many of our attitudes toward government. Otherwise, for instance, the assumptions behind many apparently commonsensical statements emanating from the National Partnership for Reinventing Government (NPR) would be meaningless. Stated the NPR Director,

> Large majorities of Americans say that they do not feel close to or connected to government, They think of it as THE government not THEIR government. The disconnected majority of 64 percent is more than double the number who say they feel connected to government. (npr.gov/library)

The suggestion that there is desire is perhaps clearer in the sexually charged activities of private corporations that are intended through advertising to encourage a kind of intimacy between the customer and the product (or the agency that produces the product), e.g., encouraging customer loyalty and choice through the use of handsome men and women in automobile and other commercials. Yet, desire is clear enough in the patriotic messages emanating from government, e.g., from the military.

Thinking/feeling about desires, through somatic writing, can be used to explore P.A.-relevant issues like the nature of the intimacy that does and should obtain in interpersonal relationships within the agency and between officials and others outside that agency. In particular, the functioning of libido or bodily desires could be used to develop understandings of the nature and character of the intimacy involved in these relationships. As an illustration, we can offer a speculative and simplified model of the functioning of desires in shaping intimacy in patriarchal and in emerging non-patriarchal contexts, where patriarchal is "understood" to include related descriptors like hierarchical, paternalistic and even phallologocentric. For this purpose, we can draw not only on Helene Cixous but also on Anthony Gidden's account (1992) of intimacy in democracy. We can model (better, "body-model") the change toward an era when there is less patriarchy and greater democracy in intra-agency and agency-customer relations.

Let us first consider desire as it functions in a patriarchal agency. A strong possibility is that in patriarchal organizations there is a connection between the desire to possess and the erotic desire which many assume exists (in differing forms) in most people and in most circumstances. In this context, it is useful to consider possession as an aim in many patriarchal agencies, such as the traditional police agency.

Jean-Paul Sartre makes a connection between possession and sexual desire. He writes:

> Desire is an attitude aiming at enchantment. Since I can grasp the Other only in his objective facticity, the problem is to ensnare his freedom with this facticity. It is necessary that he be 'caught' in it as the cream is caught up by a person skimming milk. So the Other's For-itself must come to play on the surface of his body, and be extended all through his body; and by touching this body I shall finally touch the other's free subjectivity. This is the true meaning of the word possession. It is certain that I want to possess the Other's body, but I want to possess it insofar as it is itself a 'possessed,' that is, insofar as the Other's consciousness is identified with his body. (Sartre, 1956, p. 394)

It may be supposed that P.A.'s parallel enchantment is expressed in public relations activity and other blandishments (like public relations and "bureaucrat-speak") directed at "enchanting" the customer and the public. Some may think that the possession desired by the patriarchal agency is similar to the erotic possession aimed at by a combination of romantic love and erotic passion.

Take the traditional police agency. At one level of reality, governmental agencies want to provide efficient services to their customers. At another level, there are other purposes like possession or control. While wanting to provide law enforcement service to the public, for instance, a traditional police agency at another level may want in the same actions to achieve control. The former is reflected in actions like helping stranded automobile drivers and helping victims of crimes. The latter is reflected in verbal actions like a police patrol question that used to be asked in cities like Atlanta (referring to the corner of the street) "Whose corner is this, (expletive deleted)?" It is reflected in the story about Cop's Rules for fighting; the rule is that cops do not lose (Rubenstein, 1972, p. 267). It is reflected in non-verbal activities like maintaining anti-crime programs and stake-out squads in heavy robbery locations (say, in New York and in Los Angeles). How can this possession be understood?

In a simplified model of this patriarchal agency, can we distinguish at least two flows of libidinal energy? One flow is from the program staff of the agency toward the agency's client, and one might take the provision of educational or any other kind of services as an example. Mr. Chips was eager in serving his pupils, for instance; he had a libidinal desire for them. It is granted that assumptions of the model can be altered, and we can provide for the exceptions. Another flow of energy is from the administrators, and one way of seeing this is to describe it as addressed toward the functional within the administrative body. The self-interested desire of the administrator is toward the administrative juices. It is supposed that, using models like this (and more complex and more realistic ones), a statement can be made concerning the interrelationship of the two flows of desire. For instance, it may be thought that the administrative libidinal flow would deflect—as well as focus—much of the energy flow of the program staff. Recall Marcuse's comment (1974, p. 218) that "Work as free play cannot be subject to administration; only alienated labor can be organized and administered by rational routine."

Turn now to the situation in the non-patriarchal agency. Consider Anthony Giddens on intimacy as democracy in interpersonal relations. On the democratizing of personal life, Giddens writes that,

> The structural source of this promise (of democracy) is the emergence of the pure relationship, not only in the area of sexuality but also in those of parent-child relations, and other forms of kinship and friendship. We can envisage the development of an ethical framework for a democratic personal order, which in sexual relationships and other personal domains conforms to a model of confluent love. (Giddens 1992, p. 188)

His analysis goes on to speak about how control of the social and natural worlds, the male domain, becomes focused through reason. "Just as reason, guided by disciplined investigation, was set off from tradition and dogma, so it was also from emotion. (T)his presumed not so much a massive psychological process of repression as an institutional division between reason and emotion" (Giddens, 1992, p. 200). In this democratic context (in the non-patriarchal as in the emergent interpersonal context), arguably the connection between desire and possession would be disconnected.

A task here for embodied P.A. Theory may be to elucidate the nature of this non-possession, a task related to the alterity of hesitation, discussed elsewhere (e.g., Farmer, 1995, pp. 227–245). For instance, Barthes speaks to the point in his discussion of the lover's situation.

> The will-to-possess must cease—but also the non-will-to-possess (N.W.P.) must not be seen: no oblation. I do not want to replace the

intense throes of passion by (he quotes Nietzsche) 'an impoverished life, the will-to-die, the great lassitude.' The N.W.P. is not on the side of kindness, the N.W.P. is intense, dry.... (Barthes, 1978, p. 232)

Views on such a claim will differ, however (e.g., see Dworkin, 1987).

The way in which the two sets of energy flow, the programmatic and the administrative, are affected in the non-patriarchal agency can be the subject of embodied reflection and analysis. For my money, this would involve the benefits of anti-administration and an ethic of hesitation from the administrative flow, if it is true that the connection between desire and possession would be disconnected. Anti-administration has been described elsewhere, and it is a metaphor (appealing to the interaction of matter and anti-matter) where fresh energies are sought by juxtaposing the administrative and the anti-administrative. The ethic of hesitation stands opposed to the dominant attitude of Western bureaucracy, which is described as symbolized in the typical job description of the manager as being a person who "directs, coordinates and controls...." Greater autonomy invites a different expression of desire. Also, it may be wondered whether the interfering potential of the administrative libidinal flow is reduced. That is, it may be wondered whether it has less of a tendency to subvert the energy flow of the professional staff. In this or in other ways, the economy-of-desires in the bureaucracy could be transformed.

It bears repeating that there is an extensive literature on desires. There are the ideas of those engaged in Psycho-History (e.g., in *The Journal of Psycho-History*) and in the various psychologies, whether Freudian, Jungian, Lacanian or the other later French developments. The range of applications has been large, from hitchhiking to incest. There has been important, but limited work, in applying such thinking to P.A. (e.g. for an account of the relevance of Lacanian psychology, see O.C. McSwite, 1998a). Robert Denhardt's *In the Shadow of Organization* (1981) can serve as a symbol of such applications of desires-thinking to P.A. He describes the organization as a cultural symbol of the denial of death. He writes, for instance, in such terms as making the unconscious choice to cope with our fear of death by accepting the domination of organization.

A thousand flowers can bloom. There is an advantage in a true democracy of ideas, in difference; and Paul Feyerabend's sense of the value of anarchy in knowledge seems important. Taking advantage of the thinking of such established disciplines, to the extent that it encourages our own thinking, seems clearly desirable. Such reliance is unproductive, in my view, when the conclusions are regarded as Big T truths—on a dichotomous scale that decides between "the complete truth, the whole truth and nothing but the truth" and falsity. For those of us who are skeptical of the human capacity to have access to certain and complete truth about most non-trivial matters (rather than little t truth that is good enough for now), there is no need to accept the bridle of someone else's Big T truth. Further, the whole issue of "the truth" of perspectives for gaining insights seems irrelevant. That is, it is irrelevant to the extent that false platforms or premises can be as useful for many purposes as true ones. Paul Feyerabend and (again) Milton Friedman, in my view, are right on this.

Yet, somatic writing must be open; it urgently wants the unbridled. The quest to liberate the marginalized body and the marginalized embodied perspective—the growing multiculturalism of knowledge—is a major aim in somatic writing. There is an urgent need for the libidinal energy of the unbridled, the need for the little t truths of the William Blakes and Charles Baudelaires among us. Rightly, many will want to be independent of the bridle, e.g., the oppression of the phallologocentric. Somatic writing desires to go further than it could with a passive reliance on the views of others, e.g., on the views of ergonomists. Somatic writing, while it can incorporate and use the works of others, can follow its own desire to elucidate P.A. thinking and practice. Recall Cixous's remark, given earlier (Cixous, 1980, p. 246). "Write! Writing is for you, you are for you; your body is yours, take it."

## CONCLUSION

This paper has attempted to clear some underbrush on the way toward a kind of "somatic writing" that aims toward re-examining and extending P.A. thinking in terms of our embodiment. As Helene Cixous writes, it is impossible to define a feminine practice of writing, a practice that is open to both males and females. She notes that the practice:

> can never be theorized, enclosed, coded—which doesn't mean that it doesn't exist. But it will always surpass the discourse that regulates the phallocentric system; it does and will take place in areas other than those subordinated to philosophico-theoretical domination. (Cixous, 1992, p. 253)

Corresponding to the three perspectives, three suggested directions for somatic writing were offered. A first direction was in terms of re-examining and extending all of P.A. theory and practice in terms of the ineluctable existence of the embodied human person. A second was in focusing on a wider unit of analysis that fully recognizes the enculturated character of embodiment, recognizing the irreducibly bio-psycho-socio-spiritual features of human embodiment. The third was to extend P.A. thinking by including alternative descriptions of P.A. reality in terms of bodily desires or libido functioning. Together these directions can give p.a. a kind of somatic writing that appropriately attends to our bodies. For P.A. thinking, it can help to unbridle the bridled.

## REFERENCES

Barthes, R. (1978). *A lover's discourse: Fragments*. New York: Hill and Wang.

Berman, M. (1989). *Coming to our senses: Body and spirit in the hidden history of the West*. New York: Simon and Schuster.

Cixous, H. (1980). The laugh of Medusa. In E. Marks and I. de Courtivron (Eds.), *New French feminisms: An anthology* (pp. 245–264). Amherst, Massachusetts: University of Amherst Press.

Csordas, T. J. (1993). Somatic modes of attention. *Cultural Anthropology, 8*, 135–156.

Csordas, T. J. (1999). Embodiment and cultural phenomenology. In G. Weiss and H. F. Haber (Eds.), *Perspectives on embodiment: The intersections of nature and culture*. New York: Routledge.

Denhardt, R. B. (1981). *In the shadow of the organization*. Lawrence: Regents Press of Kansas.

Dworkin, A. (1987). *Intercourse*. New York: Free Press.

Farmer, D. J. (1995). *The language of public administration: Bureaucracy, modernity, and postmodernity*. Tuscaloosa, Alabama: University of Alabama Press.

Farmer, D. J. (1999). Anti-admin: With help from Herbert Marcuse. *Administrative Theory and Praxis, 21*, 497–501.

Farmer, D. J. (2000). The ladder of organization-think: Beyond Flatland. *Administrative Theory and Praxis, 22*, 66–88.

Giddens, A. (1992). *The transformations of intimacy: Sexuality, love and eroticism in modern societies*. Stanford, California: Stanford University Press.

Harmon, M. (1981). *Action theory for public administration*. New York: Longman.

Hoy, D. C. (1999). Critical resistance: Foucault and Bourdieu. In G. Weiss & H. F. Haber, *Perspectives on embodiment: The intersections of nature and culture* (pp. 3–21). New York: Routledge.

Marcuse, H. (1974). *Eros and civilization: A philosophical inquiry into Freud*. Boston, Massachusetts: Beacon Press.

Marcuse, H. (1991). *One-dimensional man: Studies in the ideology of advanced industrial society*. Boston, Massachusetts: Beacon Press.

McAdams, M. J. (2000). Gender without bodies. *CMC Magazine*. december.com/cmc/mag/1996/mar/mcadams.html

McSwite, O. C. (1998). Stories from the "real world": Administering anti-administratively. In D. J. Farmer (Ed.), *Papers on the art of anti-administration* (pp. 17–36). Burke, Virginia: Chatelaine Press.

McSwite, O. C. (1998a). Jacques Lacan and the theory of the human subject. In M. A. Rivera and G. M. Woller. *Public administration in a new era* (pp. 45–71). Burke, Virginia: Chatelaine Press.

Merleau-Ponty, M. (1962). *Phenomenology of perception.* (C. Smith, Trans.). London: Routledge and Kegan Paul.

Monk, R. (1996). *Bertrand Russell: The spirit of solitude.* New York: The Free Press.

Prychitko, D. L. (1998). *Why economists disagree: An introduction to the alternative schools of thought.* Albany, New York: SUNY.

Rich, A. (1976). *Of woman born.* New York: Norton.

Rubenstein, J. (1972). *City police.* New York: Farrar, Straus and Giroux.

Rawls, J. (1971). *A theory of justice.* Cambridge, Massachusetts: Harvard University Press.

Sartre, J. P. (1956). *Being and nothingness.* New York: Random House.

Spelman, E. V. (1982). Woman as body: Ancient and contemporary views. *Feminist Studies, 1,* 109–131.

Winton, J. R. (1951). *A Dictionary of economic terms.* London: Routledge & Kegan Paul.

# SILENCE

### David John Farmer

> Come then, expressive Silence...
> (James Thomson)

Shush! In writing about governance and bureaucracy, what should be the relationship between post-traditional PA consciousness and traditional PA consciousness? I recommend silence as a regulative ideal for the in-between. I suggest expressive silence that is somewhere between a declaration of independence and the more regrettable habit of dependence.

First, what prompted me to bring up this topic of the in-between? Second, why is silence recommended?

## WHY THIS TOPIC?

Two reasons prompted me to bring up this topic at the PAT-Net annual conference (Omaha, Nebraska: June 2004)—a ballet and a book. First, the ballet is Mats Ek's interpretation of *Giselle*, a truly memorable and acclaimed rewriting. Second, I finished writing the book a couple of weeks before experiencing the ballet. It is *To Kill the King: Post-traditional Governance and Bureaucracy,* scheduled for publication in January 2005. The objective of the book is to explore constitutive features of a post-traditional consciousness of governance and bureaucracy—in the wide sense of encompassing public and private governance and what else is concerned with governance of the self.

I decided to (mis)read Ek's rewriting of *Giselle* as being about the relation of post-traditional and traditional consciousness. Ek's rewriting, although different, enters the discourse of the original 1841 romantic ballet. It is not "silent" about the traditional, and so our attention is directed toward the original. Difference relevant to the post-traditional consciousness was promised in the program, which announced that "Ek imagines dance pieces with the allure of philosophical poems, asking questions about the human condition and memory" (Opera National de Paris, 2004). Ek's rewriting provides a story which is both transformed and familiar. The first act is moved from the chilly climes of Germany to a tropical island—a world marked by love, filled with temptation and threatened by folly. Ek's character Giselle is a solitary, loved by her regular boyfriend Hilarian who cannot understand her and pursued by a nobleman Albrecht who wants to know her carnally. The second act is moved to a mental hospital, where Giselle has just suffered a prefrontal lobotomy. The Wilis are similar, but Myrtha their Queen is now a nursing sister defending her patients against sexual attraction. Ek provides happier outcomes for the men in Giselle's life. Instead of falling off a cliff, for instance, the naked and fetus-like Albrecht remembers nothing and he returns to the original purity and essentials of life. The music, written by the "unknown" Adams, is the same—sublime. Emerging from the opera house, thoughts turned inevitably to the traditional version.

The introduction to the book suggests principled silence about the traditional. It makes a more expansive claim than I offer here. It suggests silence between post-traditional consciousness and the traditional consciousnesses generated, and reflected, in all of the traditional disciplines and fields relevant to governance and bureaucracy. I mean disciplines like economics and political science, and action fields like business management, fire science, higher education administration and—of course—public administration.

> Post-traditional consciousness of public and private governance is not the bastard son of traditional consciousness. Nor is it the daughter who grew up to do better than her mother. The substantive relationship of post-traditional consciousness to the traditional has been marginal. Post-traditional attitudes preceded the traditional, parallel to the sense where Jean-Francois Lyotard speaks of the postmodern preceding the modern. They are also concurrent with, and subsequent to, the traditional. Post-traditional thinking about governance and bureaucracy should not be described in terms of (in opposition to, as a supplement to) traditional thinking. It stands by itself. It should be described in its own terms. To make an analogy: when exploring physics, it is neither necessary nor desirable to start with alchemy. (Farmer, in press)

In speaking of a regulative ideal, I'm not saying that no one should break silence about the traditional. I do so myself, especially toward the end. The suggestion is that such talk is neither where we should begin nor where the primary action should be.

## WHY SILENCE?

> People rely on relationships—with each other, the animal world, spirits and the earth—to maintain well-being as people approach dangers that threaten them, and respond to sickness and troubles when they happen. These different approaches arise from the diverse ways that people understand the world.
> (Wellstone Trust Gallery)

There are at least three overlapping reasons for embracing silence as a regulative ideal. These are avoiding the shadow, grasping root problems, and liberating the post-traditional imagination.

**Avoiding the Shadow**

It's critical in seeking to introduce post-traditional PA consciousness not to adopt traditional PA thinking as "the" starting point. ("An" ending point—or points—is different.) Post-traditional PA consciousness should not stand in the shadow of artificial primacy having been granted to the traditional way of apprehending and acting. The cost of mis-starting with the traditional can be made clear by considering the cases of qualitative research, hermeneutics, and postmodernism.

I'm told that a common way of teaching qualitative research is to start by discussing quantitative research and to show how qualitative research differs from it. The problem is that the quantitative then becomes the standard, the ideal, the model against which the qualitative is evaluated. Even when the conversation drifts far from the quantitative, the quantitative remains the point of reference; it is the "legitimate" shadow that lurks always in the background. At best, qualitative research tends to be relegated to something "alternative," something "deviant." The pathological effects are not confined to the pedagogical (e.g., see Guba & Lincoln, 1985). I notice that many qualitative researchers ape aspects of the quantitative. For instance, they tend to harm their research by cluttering it with procedures intended to meet the quantoids' objection that qualitative work is not rigorous.

Shadows are also cast when mis-introducing hermeneutics or postmodernism. When introducing hermeneutics (interpretation), it is tempting to start with positivism—artificially privileging positivism. When teaching about postmodernity, there are seductive reasons (and I usually succumb to them) for starting with modernity and its limitations—artificially privileging modernity. Unconsciously at least, postmodernism is then a derivative, an alternative, an entity less real because it stands in the shadow of the starting point.

## Grasping Root Problems

It is legitimate to maintain silence toward a traditional consciousness that fails to emphasize the practical relevance of conscious and unconscious societal urges in producing administrative (mal)formations. It is reasonable to regard traditional PA consciousness as counterproductive in "understanding the world" (see Wellstone Trust Gallery quote, above) insofar as the traditional mis-claims that major problems can be resolved by no more than mere technicism, mere tinkering. "Come then, expressive Silence. . . ."

Major "administrative" problems—both macro and micro—are beyond *long term* resolution without recognizing the role of conscious and unconscious societal urges. Consider the Abu Graib Prison. But I stress that "domestic" examples could as well be offered. There are those "in" the U.S. Federal Bureau of Investigation (F.B.I) and the New York City Police Department (NYPD), for instance. Imagine that the suggestion is correct that the F.B.I. contains 56 fiefdoms. An F.B.I. counterterrorism chief (Dale Watson) is quoted as saying that these "Field Offices have all had their own way, little fiefdoms, for years" (Clarke, 2004, p. 219). Recall the corruption that has broken out in scandals in the NYPD every two decades. It's not hard to show that, without probing societal interconnections, the chances are low of obtaining a long-term resolution of such micro "domestic" problems.

Surely, addressing such problems as those at Abu Graib requires looking deeply into societal roots. It requires, for instance, considering manifestations of similar societal urges in the bureaucratic forms of our domestic penitentiaries and of our warfare. About parallel societal manifestations, I cannot imagine that the way a society treats its prisoners of war is unrelated to the way it treats its own domestic prisoners. Was any unconscious societal wish involved in the prison murder of defrocked priest John Geoghan, a person at the center of a Boston sex-abuse scandal? Did Joseph Druce, the fellow inmate who did the deed, not do what society wanted (see NPR, 2003)? Doesn't society have an urge or wish, unconscious perhaps, to eliminate people like Geoghan or Jeffrey Dahmer—and isn't the urge manifested in the choice of the kind of correctional system that will fulfill the wish?

War, for me, is a governance or bureaucratic phenomenon. It is conducted in ways that society wants, consciously and unconsciously. (Unfortunately, the rhetoric of war makes some suppose that discussing the nature of war, except in saccharine terms, must be unpatriotic. That supposition is simple-minded, a burying of the head in the sand.) As a fellow patriot, I think that resolving Abu Graib problems cannot avoid considering the character of warfare.

Consider two ways, among the many, that war can be socially constructed. They are reflected in the rose-colored and the non-rosy pictures, expressed in terms of Wolfgang Peterson's movie *Troy*. The rose-colored view occurs in the exhortation in the movie that, "If you go to Troy, no one can earn more glory than you. Men will tell stories of your victories for thousands of years. The world will remember your name." The non-rosy picture is represented in a review of the same movie in *Time Out London* (May-June 2004, p. 79). The review describes the movie as "rendering war as a pointless, brutish, dishonorable wank." The latter is close to Thucydides' view in *his History of the Peloponnesian War* (3.82.2), "War is a savage schoolmaster that brings the character of most people down to the level of their current circumstances." Of the same Peloponnesian War and indirectly of war in general, Donald Kagan (2003, p. 484) writes that "The thin tissue of civilization that allows human beings to live decently and achieve their highest possibilities was repeatedly ripped asunder, plunging the combatants into depths of cruelty and viciousness of which only human beings at their worst are capable." I don't see how the administrative-policy character of Abu Graib can be torn out of its societal context.

**Liberating the Post-traditional Imagination**

Rather than being sucked too far into the negative discourse of the traditional, more desirable is the positive action of freeing the imagination to explore the possibilities of various post-traditional consciousnesses. *To Kill the King* probes eighteen features of—or approaches toward—a post-traditional consciousness, and some do include attacking what is pernicious in the traditional. Six features are concerned with post-traditional thinking as playing; six relate to post-traditional justice as seeking; and six center on post-traditional action as art—and I leave it to the reader to determine any symbolism in the resulting numbers 666.

Here I want to mention briefly and in passing only one post-traditional (hybrid) characteristic, and this is consciousness that is imaginative enough to generate and sustain governance suitable for the individual human-in-herself in-her-difference. It is also consciousness that is capable of speaking both to our poetic and sewer sides—capable of coping with the mixture in human lives of poetry and sewage. I don't want traditional consciousness to impede such post-traditional imagining.

Gerard Fromanger's tribute in an "homage" to Vincent Van Gogh in Arles reminded me of post-traditional consciousness that can accommodate the dark and the light. Of Van Gogh, Fromanger writes (1987) that he "is every painter's friend. Vincent helps me to portray the beauty or the tragedy of the world...." An example of such accommodation closer to home is O.C. McSwite's elegant *Invitation to Public Administration* (2002). Having often spoken of the mixture of good and bad, here I'll emphasize what is primarily epistemological. We want a post-traditional governance consciousness that can grasp the mixture in individuals of both (why is light usually mentioned before the dark?) the dark and the light.

For the dark, I think of the post-traditional imagination of Cornelia Parker. I was moved by Cornelia Parker's sculpture of anti-matter. Her preparations included assembling junk, and then persuading the British Army to blow it up. From that, she composed her sculpture. As a Tate Modern label describes it, "Cold, dark matter is the material within the universe that we cannot see and cannot quantify. We know it exists, but we can't measure it. It is immeasurable, unfathomable." No, it can't be things that Cornelia is sculpting; my mis(impression) is that she is contemplating our epistemological context(s).

For the light, I think of the post-traditional imagination of Van Gogh. The way that Van Gogh painted what he saw has occasioned the notion he was crazy (perhaps the ear slicing is another clue). Energetic light streams out of what he paints; his paintings are wildly alive. This summer I was shocked and (yet again) deeply moved to see "accidentally" what Van Gogh saw. I was on a balcony of a friend's home in Vaison la Romaine in Provence, at the early dawn looking over vineyards toward Mt. Ventoux. Suddenly I became aware of the light and energy coming out of the vines, flowing out in torrents. Later I came to notice that the sun's rays were blocked from the near sides of the mountain and hills but not from the vines; the hillsides were darkish. By contrast, the vines seemed electric. Yes, Vincent can be (mis)read as engaged in painting what he could help others to see, in creating consciousness.

Come then, expressive Silence...

## REFERENCES

Clarke, R. A. (2003). *Against all enemies: Inside America's war on terror*. New York: Free Press.

Farmer, D. J. (2005). *To kill the king: Post-traditional governance and bureaucracy*. Armonk, NY: M.E. Sharpe.

Fromanger, G. (1987). *Homage to Vincent Van Gogh*. Arles: France.

Guba, E., & Y. Lincoln (1985). *Naturalistic inquiry*. Thousand Oaks, CA: SAGE

Kagan, D. (2003). *The Peloponnesian War*. New York: Penguin.

McSwite, O. C. (2002). *Invitation to public administration*. Armonk, NY: M.E. Sharpe.

Movie Review. (2004, May 26/ June 2). Troy. *Time Out London, 79.*

*National Public Radio*. (2003). Retrieved on November 2, 2003, from www.npr.org/display_pages/features/feature_1407432.html

Opera National de Paris. (2004, May 23). *Giselle vue par Mats Ek*. Paris: Palais Garnier.

Thucydides. (1936). *History of the Peloponnesian War*. London: J. M. Dent.

# POWER OF REFUSAL:
# INTRODUCTION TO THE SYMPOSIUM

### David John Farmer

*... a complete moral philosophy would tell us how and why we should act and feel towards others in relationships of shifting and varying power symmetry and shifting and varying intimacy.* (Annette Baier, 1986, p. 252)

Embrace the Great Refusal! This symposium invites Public Administration (PA) theory and practice to refuse to be constrained by current chains of power. As a start, it invites PA theory to become more self-consciously aware of its own relationship to power, and it invites fuller thinking on PA practice's relationship to power. It's true that considerations of power do occur in classic and other texts of PA Theory. Mary Parker Follett repeated the well-known distinction between "power" and "power-over," for example. And there is more. Yet, the depth and scope of our understanding of PA-in-relation-to-power deserves empowerment.

This symposium starts from Herbert Marcuse's concept of the Great Refusal, especially as he described it in *One-Dimensional Man: Studies in the Ideology of Advanced Industrial Society* (Marcuse, 1964/1991). In the spirit of Marcuse, refusal for many of us includes overcoming traditional PA's tendency to one-dimensionality in privileging *speaking-from-power*, or system-affirming, frameworks and actions. Refusal includes aspiring to PA thinking/practice that is radically multi-dimensional, radically human.

Great refusal is Marcuse's concept of refusal of all forms of oppression and domination, and power that should be refused is what oppresses and dominates. This great refusal centers on refusal of the one-dimensionality of thinking that uncritically accepts existing structures, norms and behaviors. Marcuse despises the flattening out that is manifested in such power-dominated thinking, like "the flattening out of the antagonism between culture and social reality through the obliteration of the oppositional, alien and transcendental elements in the higher culture by virtue of which it constituted another dimension of reality" (Marcuse, 1964/1991, p. 57). Marcuse's great refusal is opposed to what he calls "the new conformism which is a facet of technological rationality translated into social behavior" (Marcuse, 1964/1991, p. 84). This includes refusal of such power-over deadness as is manifested in administration. As he writes, "The slaves of developed industrial civilization are sublimated slaves but they are slaves, for slavery is determined...by the status of being a mere instrument and the reduction of man to a state of a thing. This is the pure form of servitude: to exist as an instrument, as a thing" (Marcuse, 1964/1991, pp. 32-33). But the full plot is deeper, as the symposium will suggest.

To the gifted writers joining me in this symposium, sincere thanks. The excellent quality of their papers is appreciated. Before saying more about the papers, I comment on power and practicality for PA.

## POWER

*While the great lord passes the wise peasant bows deeply and silently farts.* (Ethiopian proverb, reported in Scott, 1990)

*Bureaucracy develops the more perfectly, the more it is 'dehumanized,' the more completely it succeeds in eliminating from official business love, hatred, and all the purely personal, irrational and emotional elements which escape calculation.* (Max Weber, 1978)

Power has been extensively and intensively theorized outside the PA field, being described in a variety of senses, e.g., by Herbert Marcuse, Michel Foucault, James Scott, and others. Yet power plays too small a part in the thinking of critical social sciences where it should figure large, e.g. in economics and—they tell me—in behavioral political science. Does this excuse PA? Power is not all bad, just as it is not all good. (Power is variously positive and negative. Power that empowers can be wonderful, or not; the same with power-over, many would add.) Nor could this excuse PA.

Power has practical relevance for PA. This is clear to the extent that, as one example, PA reflects the one-dimensionality of which Marcuse speaks. On the status quo, consider how low the wise peasant bows. For our money, a tendency to one-dimensionality is manifested in PA theorizing, practice and professional organizations. Recall how. On theorizing, for example, I think that traditional thinking tends to the one-dimensional in its unrelenting focus on the p.a. practitioner as the hero of the P.A. drama, its focus on the micro workings of the machinery of government. What would PA be like if we refused this focus? Would this encourage PA to address policy-relevant issues more effectively, like the big picture about security against terrorism? Would this re-focusing encourage PA thinking to grapple with macro real life problems that it now tends to ignore? An example of such a problem is the de-humanization of humans as they are increasingly required to live "administered lives" as a side-effect of the actions of public, non-profit and private bureaucracies; it is the bureaucratization of life that Weber, Marcuse and others have discussed. On practice, consider the fate of whistle-blowers. We study them; we watch them go down in flames. On organizations like ASPA, consider the complaints of discrimination and tokenism from conferees wanting to present papers going beyond the traditional, e.g., wanting to make presentations beyond a narrow view of rationality that excludes feminist, somatic and other perspectives.

> ...that the analysis, elaboration, and bringing into question of power relations... (are) a permanent political task in all social relations. (Foucault, 1983, p. 223)

This symposium could have started, not with Marcuse, but with others. Enter Foucault. He is mainly interested in impersonal domination, e.g., from bureaucratic rules and scientific techniques. Power, biopower, discipline, discourse, games of truth, power-knowledge, normalization, genealogy, and governmentality are examples of Foucauldian concepts that are relevant to PA. Yes, Foucault's ideas are challenging. For him, for instance, power in the modern age belongs to no-one; it is a flow and a set of relations between groups. Foucault explains that biopower, as another example, developed as the social and human sciences arrived, giving rise to administrative techniques and institutions for measuring and controlling people. It controls minds and bodies, plus the rules for producing healthy subjects. All of Foucault's power ideas constitute a goldmine for PA theory and practice. Let's turn to only one of them—about the relationship of truth to power. What-is-true and what-counts-as-true co-exist, and these two may or may not overlap. What-counts-as-true counts. Holders of what-counts-as-true are liable to be rewarded; those who deny what-counts-as-true are liable to be graded as wrong in their jobs and in their examinations, or even ridiculed. What-counts-as-true, as it were, speaks-from-power. But what-counts-as-true is shaped, for Foucault, in the forges of power relationships. No less than in any other field, what-counts-as-true in PA does not emerge *pure*. The result is that traditional PA, the locus of what counts as true for PA, misperceives what-is. Traditional PA peers through a lens that is a power-distorted mass of what-counts-as-truths, what-counts-as-concepts, rules-that-count-as-ruling, and meanings-that-have-privileged-meaning.

Enter Scott. By contrast to Foucault, Scott focuses on personal domination. As he writes (1990, p. 21), "While I believe many apparently impersonal forms of control are mediated by a personal domination that is, and is experienced as, more arbitrary that Foucault would allow, I take his point that there is something qualitatively different about claims to authority based on impersonal, technical, scientific rules."

> *With rare, but significant, exceptions the public performance of the subordinate will, out of prudence, fear and the desire to curry favor, be shaped to appeal to the expectations of the powerful* ( Scott, 1990, p. 2).

Scott (1990) is indeed another power goldmine for improving PA practice, both micro and macro. He has already been introduced in the PA context (see Patterson, 2000). Scott distinguishes between two types of transcript or record, where a transcript refers to a person or group in terms of both their speech acts and non-speech acts like gestures. Public transcripts, for him, are what is "openly avowed to the other party in a power relationship" (Scott, 1990, p. 2). Hidden transcripts contain what is concealed. The "public transcript is—barring a crisis—systematically skewed in the direction of the libretto, the discourse, represented by the dominant" (Scott, 1990, p. 4). The public transcript is "the self-portrait of the dominant elite as they would have themselves seen"—designed to impress (Scott, 1990, p. 18). He also holds that "the greater the disparity in power between dominant and subordinate and the more arbitrarily it is exercised, the more the public transcript of subordinates will take on a stereotyped, ritualistic cast" (Scott, 1990, p. 3).

"On a daily basis, the impact of power is more readily observed in acts of deference, subordination and ingratiation" (Scott, 1990, p. 28). From Scott's non-PA book, the reader will be spurred to think of many practical PA examples. Here are only three:

1. Are subordination, ingratiation and deference adequately represented in theorizing the modern manager, the modern leader? Managers not only do old-fashioned POSDCORB functions; they also SID (subordinate, ingratiate, defer), at least to their superiors. Scour the pages for these topics in Mayor Guiliani's book on *Leadership* (2002)! In seeking to understand and improve PA practice, does

mainstream PA Theory invite us to focus appropriately on the only "right" functions?

2. Scott describes what happens when a subordinate confronts the public transcript with her hidden transcript—in his chapter (1990, pp. 202–227) on "A Saturnalia of Power: The First Public Declaration of the Hidden Transcript." Do you remember the first—or the last time—that you as a public employee openly confronted *the* boss with your hidden transcript that challenged the foundation of *her* public transcript? What are the career prospects of a Pentagon policy planner who confronts the public transcript of the Secretary of Defense?

3. Discussing varieties of political discourse in non-dominant groups, Scott offers observations about the politics of disguise and anonymity. Seems that that has something to do with PA practice! When reading in a different section (Scott, 1990, p. 14) of some poorer country folks' hidden transcripts that include poaching and pilfering, we can reflect on the dynamics of corruption and brutality that can surface in police and other agencies like post offices. Reading of the hidden transcripts of some landlords' clandestine luxury and tampering, we can reflect on the corresponding tendencies in the administrator toward what Foucault (1977, pp. xii-xiv) calls the "fascism in us all."

SID (subordination, ingratiation and deference) and the like give rise to a complex of micro and macro PA power issues.

There is a fourth, and I think more important, example of the relevance of Scott's analysis for PA. What does Scott's notion of transcripts suggest for an understanding of PA Theory as a whole? Should the content of traditional PA Theory be seen as what subordinates dare say openly to superiors? For instance, those hell-bent to appear "practical" to their powers-that-be may be discouraged to highlight the issue(s) of surveillance that is described as a growing feature of modernity (e.g., see Dandeker, 1990, a book that explores "the relationships between bureaucracy and surveillance in modern capitalism."). In other words, is mainstream PA Theory a "mere" public transcript? I think so.

## REFUSAL

*"Il gran rifiuto"—"The great refusal"* (Dante Alighieri, *Divine Comedy. Inferno* Ib. 60).

*Please sir, can I have some more?* (Charles Dickens, *Oliver Twist,* chap. 2, p. 6).

*John Grubby, who was short and stout*
*And troubled with religious doubt,*
*Refused about the age of three*
*To sit upon the curate's knee*
(G.K. Chesterton, *The New Freethinker, 2003, p.1*).

PA theory and practice should refuse to treat existing power relationships as givens; but a great refusal isn't merely negative. First, PA should think through its own and others' power relationships. It should not ignore power relationships in society. PA cannot put its own house in order without going beyond PA's traditional concerns and traditional sources. Examples of extra-traditional concerns include adequate attention to symbolic systems and to the dynamics of the other. Examples of extra-traditional sources include appropriate attention to the ideas of thinkers who have reflected on oppression and the human condition. Critical theorists like Marcuse are important resources; so are other poets of the human condition; so are topics like subaltern ethics. Second, PA should go beyond absolute or mere refusal. Let's hope, as suggested in the second paragraph, that PA as a field can become even more life-affirming, rather then thing-affirming—more alive, less trivial, to the joys of what is fully human.

Refusals come in a range of kinds, varying in scope and power-target. A great refusal of a discourse or practice of power is toward one end of the range. It does not require refusal of everything—absolute refusal. Yet, a great refusal extends beyond mere branches of the tree. It refuses critical parts of the root sets of meanings, rules, ethical attitudes, assumptions, symbols and stories that gave birth in the first place to what is refused. The parts center not merely in society, but rather in the socially constructed nature of our own humanity. Views vary on which parts. The 1789 French revolutionaries beheaded, but kept the too much of the discourse of, the Ancien Regime: the Reign of Terror followed, logically. Oliver Twist's question, in a sense, was also revolutionary. It undermined the root discourse of his workhouse. Toward the opposite end of the range are forms of mere refusal. I imagine that these forms include, from G. K. Chesterton's jingle, the refusal of three-year-old John

Grubby to sit on the curate's knee. The papers in this symposium invite attention to the nature and practical implications of a great refusal.

**Paper #1** invites PA to great refusal as redemption—a colorful contrast with the circumstances of the great refusal depicted by Dante Alighieri. O.C. McSwite offers a theory of social change through personal, deconstructive refusal. "The most powerful form of refusal is one that is expressed from a position within the system that is being refused," O.C. writes. "What is involved, then, in a great refusal, is a complete and total refusal of the social world as it currently exists." O.C. prescribes and explains a turn for PA toward the worlds of discourse and symbols, worlds where as a field and as individuals we should step more confidently. What they propose does not depend on social structure's outright failure. "It does depend, though, on those who have the insight and the inclination to let go of illusions of the social order, assume a position as 'masterless people,' and be in a process of active collaboration through the venue of their distinctive singularities."

**Paper #2** proposes what I consider to be a practical short- and long-term program for correcting the imbalance in PA thinking between the speaking-from-power and speaking-to-power perspectives. The paper suggests how this can be achieved in terms of a theory of three layers of relevant and dynamic reality—the transparent, the disciplinary symbolic and the cloacal symbolic. It directs attention to the symbolic, especially to the sewer and to the civilizing process as a kind of bathing. "Without a master, one cannot be cleaned" I quote from Dominique Laporte's penetrating study *History of Shit* (1993). For the long run (when, contrary to Lord Keynes' dictum, we are not *all* dead), for instance, the paper recommends try-it-at-home steps toward a re-symbolization of the societal civilizing process. It recommends and describes the symbols of visioning, class 1 visioning, class 2 visioning, and (a neologism) citizen-ing. "PA theorizing in this way should seek to *re-bathe the PA context*."

**Paper #3:** "The best lack all conviction, while the worst/ Are full of passionate intensity." Tricia Patterson's paper is about interpretation – including PA interpretation. It's about refusing "correct" interpretation, and about refusing to be bound within non-contradiction. It's a warning, as Tricia says, for our practice, our scholarship and our times. She writes with the sparkling flair that is her signature. She appeals to the conflicted William Butler Yeats, interpreting his contradictory poem, *The Second Coming*. "Turning and turning in the widening gyre/ The falcon cannot hear the falconer." Think why an un-poetic field, like traditional PA, should pay attention to poetry! [Leo Strauss' and Shelley's claims come to mind. Of poetry, Strauss (2001, p.7) claims, "I don't question that social science analyses are important, but still, if you want to get a broad view and a long view you read a novel rather than a social science." Shelley (www.thomaslovepeacock.net/defence.html) claims that poets are the "unacknowledged legislators of mankind."] And Yeats himself was a legislator in the everyday sense — in the Irish Senate. Think of the relevance to PA's current context! "Is there a possibility that public administration is inhabited by falconers, or that a gathering fascist storm requires our conviction?"

**Paper #4:** "If nothing else, Marcuse's ideas invite us to evaluate our social, political, economic, and physical environments and our relation to them," writes Richard Box at the end of his paper. What powerful insights of practical relevance for PA are provided in Marcuse's cry from the heart as he challenges society's status quo! Richard interprets Marcuse's challenge. He discusses Marcuse's claim of a contradiction between, one the one hand, a life of material plenty buttressed by instrumental thought and, on the other hand, a life that a human might prefer if she were free from the chains of power relations. The contradiction is discussed in four areas of social practice: democracy, the "Warfare State," research, and gender. Writes Richard, "Though Marcuse's world may be dismissed by some as dated, it parallels in interesting ways the thought of contemporary writers and, in its far-reaching scope, offers a new perspective on issues of current relevance."

**Paper #5:** "To the extent that we, as public servants, and as teachers of public servants, protect the space for contradiction, we postpone the one-dimensionality Marcuse feared," concludes Lisa Zanetti. In showing how public administrators can participate in great refusal, she suggests that "public administrators (should) learn and practice the art of holding contradictions: that is, by refusing to rush the resolution of contradiction in the policy implementation process." Lisa considers Marcuse's idea of refusal in the context of dialectic and depth psychology. On dialectic, she appeals to both Adorno (not a final synthesis but a reflective openness "infinitely" postponing "the moment of closure") and to Marcuse (dialectical thinking "as destructive, where the destruction re-emerges as a positive act"). "This estrangement effect is at the heart of dialectical thinking," explains Lisa. She finds and discusses an affinity on refusal between critical theory and Jungian psychology. So she discusses the Jungian idea of individuation that requires us to come to terms with our shadows, our contrasexuality. Such considerations persuade Lisa to suggest that "public administrators might participate in the 'great refusal' by learning to think differently."

**Paper #6.** "An ethos of refusal today would begin by unraveling the current ontological regime," writes Louis Howe. Louis' paper appears last in this symposium because it is so brilliant; the ordering allows the symposium to end on a very high note. Louis analyzes ontology and refusal in terms of subaltern ethics. A focus is on what counts as ethical (how should I survive? how should I go on?) from the bottom of the power-pile. "The literature of governmentality is concerned to display how practices of individuality become invested by relations of power such that individuals come to enact socially prescribed duties as their own concern," writes Louis, as he discusses what he considers as a representative text put out by the International City/County Management Association. "Subaltern groups, prior to any larger questions of seeking public justice, must first negotiate their ambiguous moral status as the Other of ethics," writes Louis. Later he asks, "What sort of ontology would prefigure an administrative ethic of feistiness and perplexity under conditions of governmentality?" Louis opens his paper by quoting Michel Foucault, and we should repeat him to end this introduction to the symposium. Louis reports that Foucault once suggested, *Maybe the target nowadays is not to discover what we are, but to refuse what we are.*" Louis continues by explaining that Foucault meant that "the problem of our days is not to liberate us from the state and the state's institutions," as in classical Liberalism, but to

> *liberate us from the state and the type of individuation which is linked to the state.*

## REFERENCES

Alighieri, D. (1948). *The divine comedy: The inferno, purgatorio, and paradiso* (L. G. White, Trans.). New York: Pantheon Books.

Baier, A. (1986). Trust and antitrust. *Ethics, 96*, 232-260.

Chesterton, G. K. (2003). *The new freethinker*. Retrieved on May 23, 2003, from http://www.theotherpages.org/poems/chester2.html

Dandeker, C. (1990). *Surveillance, power and modernity: Bureaucracy and discipline from 1700 to the present day*. New York: St. Martin's Press.

Dickens, C. (2003). *Oliver Twist*. Retrieved on May 23, 2003, from http://www.bibliomania.com/0/0/19/46/16792/1/frameset.html

Foucault, M. (1977). Introduction. In G. Deleuze & F. Guittari, *Anti-Oedipus: Capitalism and schizophrenia* (pp. xi–xiv). New York: Viking Press.

Foucault, M. (1983). The subject and power. In H. L. Dreyfus & P. Rabinaw (Eds.), *Michel Foucault: Beyond structuralism and hermeneutics* (pp. 208–228). Chicago: University of Chicago Press.

Giuliani, R. W. (2002). *Leadership*. New York: Hyperion.

Laporte, D. (1993). *History of shit*. (N. Benabid & R. el-Khoury, Trans.). Cambridge, MA: MIT Press.

Marcuse, H. (1964/1991). *One-dimensional man: Studies in the ideology of advanced industrial society*. Boston: Beacon Press.

Patterson, P. M. (2000). Virtue is not apathy: Warrants for discourse and citizen dissent. *American Review of Public Administration, 30*, 225–251.

Scott, J. C. (1990). *Domination and the arts of resistance: Hidden transcripts*. New Haven, CT: Yale University Press.

Strauss, L. (2001). *On Plato's symposium*. Chicago: University of Chicago Press.

Weber, M. (1978). *Economy and society: An outline of interpretive sociology*. (E. Fischoff, Trans.). Berkeley: University of California Press.

# ANTI-ADMIN: WITH HELP FROM HERBERT MARCUSE

David John Farmer

## ABSTRACT

*This paper selects from a longer chapter which recapitulates and extends discussions on anti-administration (anti-admin) from the perspective of discourse theory. First, it discusses discourse theory, explaining that the discourses of anti-admin aim toward the inclusion of marginalized or excluded perspectives. Second, it outlines some anti-admin theory. Parallel to the action of anti-matter and matter, the interaction of freshly demarginalized discourse perspectives and traditional discourse can yield anti-admin resultants. Used in describing these resultants is the Herbert Marcuse's notion of one-dimensional man. Third, the paper offers macro and micro examples of anti-admin gains in terms of problem definition and response resources. It underscores that anti-admin can recognize its affinity not only to the postmodern but also to critical theory perspectives.*

## INTRODUCTION

The discourses of anti-administration (anti-admin) aim toward the inclusion of perspectives (lens, frames, even people) marginalized or excluded by the constraints of traditional P.A. administrative discourse. The metaphor of anti-admin is borrowed from anti-matter in Physics. Anti-matter refers to the non-commonsensical notion of antiparticles (antineutrons, antiprotons, positrons, etc.) corresponding to nuclear particles (neutrons, protons, electrons, and so on). Antiprotons have the same mass and spin as protons but have opposite electric charge and magnetic moment, for example. "Normal matter and anti-matter would mutually annihilate each other upon contact, being converted totally into energy" (U.S. Atomic Energy Commission, 1967). In a similar way, anti-admin is administration which is directed at negating administrative-bureaucratic power. The suggestion here is that the encounter can give rise to fresh P.A. energy.

This paper selects points from a longer chapter written for Dr. Jon Jun's forthcoming edited book, *Challenges in Administrative Theory for the 21st Century*. That chapter focuses on anti-admin from the perspective of discourse theory. First, it discusses some discourse theory in order to explain what it means to claim that the discourses of anti-admin aim toward the inclusion of marginalized or excluded perspectives. Second, it outlines some anti-admin theory. Third, the chapter offers macro and micro examples of anti-admin gains in terms of problem definition and response resources—gains denied by the marginalizations and exclusions of traditional P.A. discourse. The chapter makes use of two thought games, neither of which are specified in this short paper.

The chapter recapitulates what I have described in other publications (e.g., Farmer, 1995; 1998). There is some extension of that work, e.g., appealing to Herbert Marcuse (1991). The recapitulation is designed to emphasize that anti-admin is not "wedded 'til death they do part" with postmodernism. It is true that postmodern insights have added significantly. Anti-admin has been described more than once in postmodern terms. Earlier, an account has been given of anti-admin as a shift away from rationalism and technocratic expertise in an emerging post-ist context (Farmer, 1998a). Yet, any postmodern v. modern debate can be side-stepped here. Anti-admin can recognize its affinity not only to the postmodern but also to critical theory perspectives. This is possible because the discourses of anti-admin are basically plural. There is no "one right way" in discourse reform. The differing accounts are understood as complementary; the "same" entity is seen from different discourse perspectives.

## SOME DISCOURSE THEORY

This essay describes and illustrates three features of discourse, as described in discourse theory. It invites consideration (using a game, as mentioned above) of how the three features are manifested in certain surface discourses or work sub-cultures, e.g., in those of administering, of a program area like policing, and of another program area like social work. It comments that people often operate in more than one surface discourse, e.g., a police commissioner operates in the discourses of administering, of policing and in some other discourses. Also, the hardest discourse (like an accent) to identify is our own; it seems exceptionally "natural." The game is intended to clarify the claim that the discourses of anti-admin aim toward the inclusion of perspectives (lens, frames, even people) marginalized or excluded by the constraints of traditional P.A.

"Discourse" has been interpreted variously, as discourse theory has been developed and achieved important results in non-P.A. disciplines; and discourse theory arrived later in P.A. The account used in *The Language of Public Administration* (Farmer, 1995) relies on thinkers like Michel Foucault and Ludwig Wittgenstein, for example. But there are others, e.g., Mikhail Bakhtin's notion. Most discourse theorists would agree that all claims, all ascriptions of meanings, all actions and events to which meanings are attached—that is, all discourses—are situated within constraints which are largely unconscious. What we can claim as true or relevant is shaped by such constraints, which include the social, the institutional and other larger texts within which we do our thinking. Most would agree that discourse is not limited to mere words. For example, discourse can be non-verbal; we all have "right sides" to our brains (e.g. see Farmer, R., 1998).

The first of the three discourse features, Feature 1, is that the categories, beliefs and values implicit in discourse constitute a way of looking at the World. Feature 2 is that discourses are mainly formed around practices involving marginalization and/or exclusion. Discursive mechanisms both limit "and" encourage what statements can be made, shaping what is considered to be worth knowing. Feature 3 is the idea that discourse is situated in the practice of a time and place, i.e., in a way of thinking and doing.

The chapter includes a chart that provides examples of each of these features in terms of the discourses of administering, policing and social working. They are as follows:

|  | Administering | Policing | Social Working |
| --- | --- | --- | --- |
| Feature 1: | e.g., world tends to consist of my agency (or program), similar agencies (or programs), and others. | e.g., world tends to consist of good guys and bad guys. | e.g., world tends to consist of needy clients and others. |
| Feature 2: | e.g., true administrator directs, coordinates and controls. | e.g., true cop is a crime-fighter. | e.g., true social worker is a helping professional. |
| Feature 3: | e.g., common expectation for managers in some agencies to "fit in" with existing agency and/or local mores. | e.g., macho and paramilitary values now privileged in some agencies. | e.g., requirement now for MSW degree in some agencies. |

## SOME ANTI-ADMIN THEORY

The discourses of anti-admin, in the present account, focus on the effect of including the perspectives marginalized or excluded by the set of traditional P.A. discourses. (For convenience, the singular is used in referring to the latter.) Parallel to the action of anti-matter and matter, the de-marginalized and the traditional discourses interact—with energizing results.

This account of anti-admin borrows from Herbert Marcuse's analysis of one-dimensional man. Anti-admin looks to a change that is away from the one-dimensionality of traditional P.A. discourse and toward multi-dimensionality. An interaction between a freshly-demarginalized or freshly-included discourse perspective and traditional P.A. discourse is of significance in anti-admin terms insofar as it yields multi-dimensionality. Marcuse explains the one-dimensional thinking which he considered to be pervasive in contemporary society in terms of the uncritical acceptance of existing structures, norms and behaviors. "The most advanced areas of industrial society exhibit throughout these two features: a trend toward consummation of technological rationality, and intensive efforts to contain this trend within the established institutions" (1991, p. 17). It is thinking that accepts that non-conformity with the overall system is "socially useless" (p. 2). Against all this, Marcuse recommended the "great refusal."

What are of interest are anti-admin results that contribute toward a dimension beyond that of the existing system. It is thinking that is able to transform by "standing against." What "standing against" means can be approached by considering Marcuse's account of the flattening out of the antagonism between culture and social reality in the rationalizing context that accompanies capitalism (p. 56ff). He claims that this flattening out has obliterated the "oppositional, alien, and transcendent elements in the higher culture by virtue of which it constituted another dimension of reality" (p. 57). As an example, we may think of the "losing" battle of musicians like Anton Webern, wanting to liberate music from the hierarchical structures placed on it by tonality. Webern's music "stands against" the existing musical system in seeing each individual tone as having its own expressive possibilities, independent of the traditional discourse of harmony. Marcuse goes on to explain that the "liquidation of two-dimensional culture takes place not through the denial and rejection of the 'cultural values,' but through their wholesale incorporation into the established order, through their reproduction and display on a massive scale" (p. 57).

The anti-matter/anti-admin metaphor is not intended to imply that anti-admin is slated simply as excluding admin. Rather it is a matter of "opening" P.A. to multi-dimensional thinking, not exchanging one set of discourse blinders for another. The anti-matter/anti-admin metaphor is intended to urge a more open attitude, for example, toward the unfashionable and toward less powerful voices. The term "unfashionable" points to the relevance of Foucault's claims about power and truth. There is a tendency to confuse the "power speaking" and "speaking to power" elements in P.A. thinking, and it is a reasonable confusion when mainstream political discourses emphasize the Civics 101 half-truth about democratic government being owned by the people. Foucault's claims (e.g., Foucault, 1980) alert us that P.A. theory should recognize fully theory's "speaking to power" component. The term "less powerful voices" includes the disadvantaged (e.g., women) and also those whose voices cannot be heard, like the future generation and the mentally ill.

It has been suggested that bureaucracy can be best studied from a variety of perspectives, where we are conscious of the co-shaping of the perspective used. A multi-perspectival, a reflexive, approach typically involves looking at P.A. "facts" and theories (first-order data) from various second-order perspectives, where second-order is used idiosyncratically to mean perspectives outside the discipline. It is even more advantageous if these perspectives contribute to multi-dimensionality in the sense borrowed from Marcuse. Anti-admin resultants should be "critical" perspectives in supporting a dimension that stands against "uncritical" acceptance of existing structures, norms and behaviors.

## MACRO AND MICRO P.A. APPLICATIONS

The longer chapter claims that discourses of anti-admin have practical utility at both the macro and the micro levels in terms of problem formulation (selection, delineation) and of the spectrum of response resources considered available. It provides four examples of anti-admin macro and micro resultants that can be expected from the interaction of selected administrative discourse elements with marginalized and/or excluded perspectives. It uses a second thought game (not specified here) for this purpose.

Utility lies in going beyond the one-dimensional. That is, the anti-admin resultant should be "other" dimensional in the Marcusian sense; it should be a "critical" perspective that is in a dimension that stands against "uncritical" acceptance of existing structures, norms and behaviors. Involved in this idea is that part of the system which the resultant "stands against" is the circumscribing of energies within descriptive boxes, within definitions. Attempting to circumscribe (seeking, striving) is valuable; supposing that one has succeeded in circumscribing may be a failure.

The first of the four interactions is between micro-orientation and macro-orientation in P.A. No one denies that P.A. has produced important macro work; the issue is the relative emphasis. A practical result of this pairing can be the addition of what is described as an autonomous or genuine Macro Public Administration, permitting more helpful emphasis on a larger or more fundamental set of p.a. problems (e.g., see also Farmer, 1999). The second interaction is the pairing of hierarchy and laterality. Some work has also been done on this (e.g., Thayer, 1981). Compared against a privileging of hierarchy issues, practical results follow from de-marginalizing the problems and response resources of laterality—in an emergent context of an accelerating shift toward a larger concern with citizen-citizen interrelationships rather than citizen-state relations (see Barber, 1984, on strong participatory government; Habermas, 1996 on deliberative democracy; and Farmer, 1998a). Examples of practical macro implications include the recognition that issues of hierarchy and laterality are not merely administrative; rather they are surrogates for competing manifest and latent non-bureaucratic perspectives (Farmer & Farmer, 1997). Other examples include those from P.A.'s discourse movement (see McSwite, 1998). Recognizing the surrogate character of the hierarchy-laterality pairing and appreciating the interaction's involvement with dialogue, the resultant anti-admin energy is seen as implicating another dimension.

The third interaction is between marketization and alterity. Compared against a privileging of marketization, practical results are available from de-marginalizing the problems and response resources of alterity. It is suggested that a marginalized feature in P.A. ethics is the ungrounded character of intersubjective moral conclusions (e.g., see Warnke, 1993, for a description of the hermeneutic or interpretive turn in justice philosophy). Practical implications of a marriage of ethical concern with such ungroundedness are indicated for management in terms of authentic hesitation. Micro issues are raised in terms of two contrasts. One is between the manager who directs, coordinates and controls v. the manager who is less Napoleonically challenged. Another is between a sub-culture of debate and confrontation (as it were, a crossfire complex) and a sub-culture consistent with shared explanatory discourse (e.g., Tannen, 1998). The ungroundedness of ethical prescriptions in a movement toward alterity, toward greater ethical concern, raises the prospect of a Marcusian dimension.

The fourth interaction is between rationalization (expressed in the narrowness of administrative rationality in traditional P.A. discourse) and imaginization. Consider the micro practicality of less managerial narrowness in terms of "experimentalism," perhaps a component of the resultant of this interaction. The discourse of rational administration does not include routinely the systematic and natural experimental work described long ago by Alice Rivlin (1972). What Rivlin had in mind was similar to the medical model, where promising drugs are rigorously tested to find out what works and what does not work; some patients might receive the wonder drug and others a placebo. By contrast, a city administrator or a police chief does not consider experimentalism to be a routine part of her administrative work. Perhaps Rivlin did not suppose that such experimentalism would be a routine ingredient of managing, as opposed to Federal leadership which still continues in some local-level program areas (p. 86). The experiment-friendly management in mind would not depend on Federal dollars; it would be part of the warp and woof of more imaginative managing. Imaginization would not be limited to this, however. The longer chapter refers to the advantages of play with a purpose (Farmer, 1998); practical opportunities do exist in radical play with the game rules of bureaucracy. The chapter also indicates the imbalance represented in privileging the rational as opposed to the unconscious. It points to the advantages of a shift toward incorporating the unconscious (Farmer, R., 1998) and toward adjusting the managerial task toward greater recognition of the therapeutic. It suggests that some micro-relevant messages of Mary Parker Follett could be rediscovered.

## REFERENCES

Barber, Benjamin. (1984). *Strong Democracy*. Berkeley, CA: University of California Press.

Farmer, David John. (1995). *The Language of Public Administration: Bureaucracy, Modernity, and Postmodernity*. Tuscaloosa, AL: University of Alabama Press.

Farmer, David John, (Ed.). (1998). *Papers on the Art of Anti-Administration*. Burke, VA: Chatelaine.

Farmer, David John. (1998a). Schopenhauer's porcupines: Hegemonic change in context. *Administrative Theory and Praxis, 20*(7): 422-433.

Farmer, David John (1999). "Public Administration Discourse: A Matter of Style?" *Administration and Society*, 31(3): 299-320.

Farmer, David John, & Rosemary L. Farmer. (1997). Leopards in the temple: Bureaucracy and the limits of the in-between. *Administration and Society*, 29(5): 507-528.

Farmer, Rosemary L. (1998). Recognizing the right brain in organizations. pp. 71-86 In David John Farmer (Ed.), *Papers on the Art of Anti-Administration*, Burke, VA: Chatelaine.

Foucault, Michel. (1980). *Power/Knowledge: Selected Interviews and Other Writings 1972-1977* Brighton, England: The Harvester Press.

Habermas, Jurgen. (1996). *Between Facts and Norms: Contributions to a Discourse Theory of Law and Democracy* Cambridge, MA: MIT Press.

Marcuse, Herbert. (1991). *One Dimensional Man: Studies in the Ideology of Advanced Industrial Society*. Boston, MA: Beacon Press.

McSwite, O.C. (1998). The new normativism and the discourse movement: A meditation," *Administrative Theory and Praxis, 20* (3): 377-381, September 1998.

Rivlin, Alice M. (1972). Systematic Thinking for Social Action., Washington, DC: The Brookings Institution.

Tannen, Deborah. (1998). The Argument Culture: Moving from Debate to Dialogue., New York: Random House.

Thayer, Frederick C. (1981). *An End to Hierarchy and Competition: Administration in the Post-Affluent World*. New York: Franklin Watts.

Warnke, Georgia. (1993). Justice and Interpretation., Cambridge, MA: MIT Press.

U.S. Atomic Energy Commission. (1967). Nuclear Terms: A Brief Glossary. Washington, DC: A.E.C.

# LOVE AND UN-ENGINEERING

### David John Farmer

Shouldn't public management be motivated by love? Shouldn't the post-September 11th P.A. community give priority to reflecting about *administrative love*? Or, should we stick with motivation-as-usual, e.g., an efficiency ethic? Un-engineering is what management needs, I hope to suggest; approaches like reengineering should be abandoned. Through un-engineering, the P.A. community should seek a fresh consciousness that focuses on knowing and embracing administrative love as a regulative ideal. Assuming that it should be motivated by love, should a loving management be fueled primarily by love for an ideal (like love for country, or love for the public interest)? Or, should it be powered primarily by love for each person as she is in herself (like Romeo for Juliet, and vice-versa)? I suggest that administrative love should include both of these aspects—love directed toward an ideal and love directed toward individual persons.

At first blush, the idea of *administrative love* appears paradoxical, so sentimental and indeterminate that it borders on the nonsensical. Paradoxes rear their heads between love-as-it-is and administration-as-it-is, and they can be expressed in at least two ways.

- First, the nature of administrative love—even love for an ideal—appears oxymoronic, if (for a first paradox) love is understood as basically non-rational and irrational while administration is seen as the rational aiming at the rational. Can administrative love be love if it aims at the merely rational?

- Second, administrative love—especially as love for being-with the individual person in-herself in-her-differences and in her wholeness—appears paradoxical, if (for a second paradox) love is understood as extending out to the individual person while administration is seen as basically focusing on things. Or, in other words, it is paradoxical if love entails exceeding rules-for-groups while administration is seen mainly as a matter of things about rule-making-for-groups and things about rule-application-to-groups. Or, to put it in even different terms, it is paradoxical if love at root requires poetic or spiritual freedom while administration basically requires things connected with direction, coordination and control. Are love as-it-is and administration-as-it-is compatible?

Although there are genuine tensions, our two paradoxes are not fatal. Yes, insofar as it is chained within traditional bureaucratic understandings, administrative love tends to be frustrated. No, administration-as-it-could-be and love as-it-is need not be foreign to one another.

To explain these suggestions, let's examine in turn these two paradoxes of administrative love. In the first, let's explore whether a coherent understanding of administrative love is available. In the second, let's notice how the logic of administrative love implies a shift away from such reliance on the administration of "things," away from things like those involved in rule-ism and like those concerned with direction, coordination and control.

## PARADOX 1: REASONABLE LOVE?

She was crazy about him; he was nuts about her. She lost her mind when she lost her heart; he was dancing on air when he espied his beloved. He loved his booze so much and she loved her job so much that they neglected what rational people would never rationally neglect. Some people even think that, if a couple is in love, nothing else matters; or that anyone who can tell the reasons for her love is not in love. There is more complexity to it than this. Love can be associated with death, as in Tristan and Iseult. Both Romeo and Juliet are willing to die for their loves, and that seems sensible—even if tragic—to the audience. There can be a connection between love and pain (e.g., see Bataille, 1962). Then, there are other perspectives that lie further outside many of our conscious spheres of reference, as in Dante's and Petrarca's loves respectively for child Beatrice and child Laura. This is love that takes a variety of socially co-constructed rational/irrational shapes. Love can be in part socially constructed as life-long, brief, or even intermittent. Look at the idea of love prevalent in this or that culture or sub-culture. We are now unsurprised to find courtly erotic love constructed differently from contemporary erotic love, for example. There is a socially constructed difference between a knight lying naked all night beside his lord's naked wife (no touching) and a callow boyfriend and his equally callow girlfriend in the back seat of a Chevrolet (yes, fumbling). The knight's passion was not for the lady but a love of being in love; the callow couple does not share the social construction. Administrative love sounds oxymoronic, in terms of the first paradox, in that the mish-mash of popular understandings of love include the notion that love is essentially irrational.

The case for the irrationality of administrative love is deepened, if that love is understood to include both the ideal-focused and individual-focused aspects. Clearly, the aspects can pull in opposite directions; not necessarily contradictions, they surely can be contraries. Yet there are good reasons for including them both. First and foremost, don't both aspects seem part of our lived experience of love? Second, isn't focusing solely on an ideal a form of zealotry, risky in its consequences? It has its merits, as the lives of prominent saints and soldiers and scholars have shown. Yet, couldn't a sole focus on an ideal, while avoiding libidinal attachment to the human individual, help to facilitate not only good outcomes but also wars, genocides and inhuman atrocities like the mass murdering of September 11th? Unloving are models like Victor Hugo's zealous police bureaucrat, hounding Jean Valjean in pursuit of the police inspector's vision of the public interest, for example; yet we do admire such hard working and dedicated employees. There are false counterexamples. For instance, Mother Teresa was an ideal-focused zealot; but my intuition is that she was also individual-focused. Third, doesn't choosing to focus solely on the individual, insofar as there is a conscious choice, have the consequence of choosing that focus-on-the-individual "as an ideal?" Yet these two aspects do introduce diverging notions. The individual-focused involves the warts of what Martha Nussbaum (2001) tells us are fragility and luck; the ideal-focused need not. We have good reason to ask whether, if administration basically aims toward the rational and if love basically isn't rational, is it self-contradictory to speak of administrative love?

Let's emphasize these diverging notions in the terms that Martha Nussbaum uses—in terms of Plato's dialogues that concern the nature of love, especially his *Symposium*. She accepts the traditional and clearly correct view that for Plato, if not for some others, love is desire. Although he would consider it to miss the main point badly, I think we can agree that you can love/desire a range of items; you could love/desire budgeting or reading or white wine or your self or your neighbor's spouse. Plato would have no part of the Christian view of Agape, a conception of love as seeking no personal benefit. For Plato, love (Eros) is desire for something lacking. Nussbaum's non-traditional interpretation is that Plato's *Symposium* offers two conceptions of the object of this love/desire. One conception is what I am calling ideal-focused and the other depicts love/desire as what I am calling individual-focused. The former is offered by one of the dialogue's characters, Socrates; and the latter conception is presented in the speech of another character, Alcibiades, who happens to be Socrates' lover. Nussbaum's claim is that Plato is offering the reader a choice between two alternative conceptions of the object of love/desire (2001, p. 173). Others who accept the non-traditional reading of the *Symposium* (e.g., Ruprecht, 1999) would agree in wanting a description of love that embraces both objects of love/desire, regarding the two conceptions as aspects of what is desired. The traditional view denies that Plato offers an individual-focused conception of the object of love. It dismisses the speech of Alcibiades as mere literature, nothing to do with Plato's philosophy. To the Literature Department with it! The traditional reading is that Plato offers only one conception of love/desire, the ideal-oriented view offered by the character Socrates. Some holding this traditional view had criticized Plato for "missing the point" about love as desire for individuals in their wholeness, warts and all. So, Nussbaum references (2001, p. 173) the distinguished scholar Gregory Vlastos' criticism of Plato. Against Plato whom he reads in the traditional way, Vlastos wants the "objects of these creatures' passions to be whole people: not complexes of desirable qualities, but entire beings, thoroughly embodied, with all their idiosyncrasies, flaws and even faults" (Nussbaum, 2001, p. 173).

It is easier to show that our first paradox is harmless for a conception of administrative love that focuses solely on an ideal. Yet even this unduly limited conception of love presents problems in practice. The former claim can be made by continuing with the traditional reading of the *Symposium* about love as ideal-focused; the latter suggestion can be appreciated by recalling the sixties' P.A. "public interest" discussion represented by Richard Flatham (1966) and Glendon Schubert (1960). Plato's answer to our first paradox—on a traditional reading of love as limited to that given through the character Socrates—would be that good love/desire is good rationality, rationality as it should be. Love/desire that aims to know what is really real is rational. The traditional reading is that there is a difference between good and bad love. Good love is what transforms us for our good; bad love is what harms us. Certainly this has a surface-level appeal because it is hard to deny, against Plato, that the consequences of love can be good or bad; some loves are great, others a mixture, and some are utterly self-destructive, thoroughly pathological. For Plato, there is no limit to human reasoning as-it-should-be; reasoning can provide knowledge of ultimate reality as-it-truly-is in-itself. For those who agree with Plato's understanding of reason, our first paradox is resolved, beyond peripheral, yet serious, dilemmas about what reason prescribes. We can be left holding the same dilemmas of rationality—and the same criticisms—that we have long recognized in P.A. discussions about embracing the aims of the public interest. It is criticized that the notion of public interest is "pie in the sky" and vague, and that great principles often collide. It also parallels other PA ideals, each with its criticisms and problems, like meaningful citizen participation in bureaucracy (e.g., see Farmer et al., 2002). To identify what he considered the public interest, for example, Richard Flatham long ago (1966) used what he called the "standard materials and methods of political study" and ordinary language philosophy. And Glendon Schubert earlier argued (1960, p. 223) for his conclusions that "there is no public-interest theory worthy of the name...." For him, the public interest had a "hair shirt function" but it "may be nothing more than a label attached indiscriminately to a miscellany of particular compromises of the moment." Yet, there is no root contradiction within administrative love as ideal-focused.

I would like to go further and suggest that the first paradox is not fatal even when love is conceptualized as encompassing both aspects; a coherent understanding of administrative love is still available. I agree that there is substantial tension between love and, on the other hand, government-by-rationality-as-it-is. I don't deny that love and reasoning seem to be apple and pear. However, there is no inhibiting cleavage-in-principle between the unreason in love and reason itself. The same charge of harboring unreason, odd as it may sound, has been leveled at reason. In this way, as rationality proves to be no paragon, the first paradox loses its bite. Let's turn to unreason.

How rational does rationality get? Is what administrators count as rational thoroughly and completely rational? Recognizing rationality's limits is neither to be novel nor to trash the strengths of reason—and, of course, recognizing limits is a contested matter. Holding that human reasoning is limited is no novelty; for instance, St. Augustine did. Saying that *administrative love is as rational as rationality gets* recognizes that our rational schemes are limited. Briefly, consider two avenues—through Kurt Godel and Angus Graham—of understanding the phrase about unreason within reason. Kurt Godel's Proof is said to have

> presented mathematicians with the astounding and melancholy conclusion that the axiomatic method has certain inherent limitations, which rule out the possibility that even the ordinary arithmetic of the integers can ever be fully axiomatized. What is more, (Godel) proved that it is impossible to establish the internal logical consistency of a very large class of deductive systems—elementary arithmetic, for example—unless one adopts principles of reasoning so complex that their internal consistency is as open to doubt as that of the systems themselves. (Nagel & Newman, 1958, p. 6)

Angus Graham (1992) was a well-known Sinologist, who studied Chinese with aims that included understanding Western philosophy better. He selected for a frontispiece Federico Garcia Lorca's words: "The mind has outskirts where the philosopher is devoured by Chinese and caterpillars" (p. 65). Graham (1992, p. 65) appeals to "the Western chain of oppositions (that), like the Chinese, is at the foundations of thought...." He describes differences between reasoning in the West and in Chinese thinking, explaining (for instance) how propositions like "The cat sat on the mat" are not fully inter-translatable. He asserts that the Chinese equivalent, if there were an equivalent, would be false if "the cat sat on a cloth mat" (Graham, 1992, p. 65). However, it is probably more convincing to point—rather than to Godel and Graham—to Foucault, Marx and Freud. Foucault wrote of the unthoughts that germinate within our thoughts. Karl Marx had pointed to the catalytic action of economic "unthoughts," and Sigmund Freud had pointed to the life-shaping power of the "unthoughts" of my unconscious.

What counts as reason is not necessarily an objective feature of the world, just as what counts as truth is not necessarily the truth. Don't institutions and disciplinary structures change what counts as rational? Can't what is counted as rational in the administrative context contain what—from a perspective outside the bureaucracy—can be seen as containing unreason? Reasoning within an institution tends to be institutionalized. Witness the rationalizations that obtain in the various kinds of bureaucracy, e.g. see Graham Allision et al., 1971, on the decision making in the Cuban Missile Crisis. Reasoning within any disciplinary boundaries is, I agree, open to the same tendency. For example, Grassi repeats (1980, p. 19) the often-repeated observation that the archai—the ultimate principles—of knowledge cannot be proved. "But, if the original assertions are not demonstrable, what is the character of the speech in which we express them? Obviously this type of speech cannot have a rational-theoretical character?" Elsewhere, I have discussed (1995) this in terms of deterritorialization. Reasoning within institutions and disciplines tends to exclude and to shape. In no sense should we suppose the claim that administrative love can be rational endorses the kind of desiccated reasoning general in administration-as-it-is. This reasoning excludes, for example, the somatic (e.g., see Farmer, 2001a) and other components of what I describe as un-engineering. It excludes what Pascal (1995, p. 413) meant in his thought that "heart has its reasons which reason itself does not know."

Administrative love can relish the embrace of contraries; available is a "coherent enough" account of love that is ideal-focused and individual-focused. For intellectual resolution there is the option of the dialectical method; for practical guidance there is the notion of the regulative ideal. The dialectical method would mean abandoning the Law of Non-contradiction and adopting a type of Hegelian method of resolving what appear to be irreconcilable differences, thesis and antithesis yielding a form of synthesis. The manager can be encouraged in this by Barbara Czarniawski's claim (1977, p. 97) that paradoxes, "until recently the villains of the organizational drama, constitute its dynamics and, even more important, account for its transformations." For practical guidance, the manager can conceptualize administrative love as a regulative ideal. Such ideals are visions or benchmarks of what should be done even though they might be "impossible." Examples of other regulative ideals include the political, such as Jean Jacques Rousseau's "general will," and perhaps in the political context even "efficiency" itself. On a personal level, there are life-guiding regulative sets of ideals that include impossibly high standards and impossible combinations like "turn the other cheek" and "don't tread on me." On the regulative ideal that is impossible owing to its standard being beyond me, I try, I fail, I half succeed, I lapse, I try again. On the regulative ideal that is impossible because it involves contrary impulses, I prefer to attempt to achieve both impulses. Again, I try, I fail, I half succeed, I lapse, I try again.

## PARADOX 2: PERSONAL LOVE?

Love for nobody should be nobody's idea of loving; Roland Barthes (1978, p. 74) is right to remind us that "No one wants to speak of love unless it is for someone." Administrative love should include a focus on the individual, even if that focus is a tall order, as it is. Such a focus involves a shifting out to the individual person in her uniqueness, requiring—if the second paradox is to be rendered harmless—less reliance on the administration of "things." Such administrative love involves an extending out to the individual as a whole, warts and all. It is a being-with, a caring-for, a wanting-to-know-about the individual as a human-in-herself-in-her-differences, like (sentimental talk being appropriate!) when a lover gazes into her lover's eyes. There is a shifting that wants to exceed rules-for-groups and toward poetic or spiritual freedom; for example, what lover ever wanted to treat his loved one like all other people? There is a concomitant shift away—not a complete, but a radical, shift away—from things. Removing the second paradox requires such a shift away from viewing administration as a matter of things about rule-making-for-groups and things about rule-application-to-groups. It is away from rule-ism. It is away from traditional administration's emphasis on things like direction, coordination and control. Administrative love as individual-focused encompasses all of these shifts; we intend to refer to them all when we use the phrase "shift out to the individual." The aim of un-engineering, we will explain, is about realizing administrative love *as a regulative ideal* beckoning toward a being-with, a caring-for and a wanting-to-know-about the individual person as a whole.

It is a shift toward what does happen in some administrative contexts today—in exceptions. Most of us have encountered these exceptions. Some individuals and some groups author them, with varying degrees of frequency and intensity. Weren't there examples on September 11th—and before? Examples are sometimes described under different names, e.g., gifting (Cunningham & Schneider, 2001). Individual-focused love can "pop up" or "pop down," to borrow a phrase used in a different connection by Camilla Stivers (Farmer, et al., 2002); the choice is not between the extremes of either permanently on-going loving or no loving at all. Un-engineering's aims can include increasing the incidence of poppings up.

A practical challenge is presented by the second paradox, contrasting features of love with the emphases of traditional policy-making and administration. Consider the first horn of the paradox—especially the "excessive" feature in individual-focused love. First, love at full throttle is a force so mountainous, so "Wagnerian," that it invites talk about the sublime. Recall the literature on the differing features of the sublime and the beautiful, e.g., describing the sea and the unlimited as sublime and the land and the limited as beautiful. The sublime overwhelms our senses; it exceeds the boundaries—like encountering a mountain up close. Second, love is a mysterious and unruly force. Diane Ackerman offers one account of female erotic love in terms of horses (1995, pp. 196-217) and of male erotic love in terms of racing cars (1995, pp. 217-227). "Eyebrows raise when one mentions women and horses, because the sexuality of horses is so obvious, fiery, and dramatic," she indicates (1995, p. 209). "Seven drunken, bare-chested teenage boys drape themselves across the windshield of my car as I wait for the lights to change… 'Show us your tits! Show us your tits! Show us your tits!'" (1995, pp. 218-219). This is not the way we think in P.A. This talk is *excessive*!

Turn to the second horn of the paradox, centering on features seeking to *limit the exceeding* of group rules and group structures. Must we demonstrate that P.A. administrators are beset with rule-ism, consumed with the making of rules and the application of rules to groups of people? Not all rules are bad, e.g., children without rules often fail. A program metastasized with group rules, living and breathing standard operating procedures, is a different matter. Visit any large bureaucracy. Need we demonstrate that P.A. is obsessed with the structure of direction, coordination and control? Look at our job descriptions. Need we show that the clients of managers are groups of individuals, whether employees or members of the public? Look at any rules and regulations, or any personnel manual. People are sometimes treated as humans-in-themselves in-their-differences. Aren't they exceptions?

Needed, most importantly, is un-engineering. Un-engineering management and un-engineering the machinery of administration should constitute a major, and an on-going, project in P.A. This should have been the project of the Federal Government's former National Partnership for Re-inventing Government. It should be the highest priority today for governments wanting meaningful re-invention. How to achieve shifts out to the individual—resolving the second paradox—will require imaginative un-engineering over time. A graduated approach, proceeding from where we are, surely is the most practical start. These are not ready-by-Monday-morning shifts.

Un-engineering entails relinquishing nostrums like reengineering to the extent that they do not embrace both aspects of administrative love, especially the shift to the individual. Approaches like reengineering stand for techniques *motivated* inwards toward the needs and functioning of the organization. Even when they focus on outward relationships, their primary interest is inwards. Reengineering, successor to Total Quality Management, is defined by Loh (1997, p. xiv) as "a multidisciplinary approach to implementing fundamental change in the way work is performed across the organization with the goal of dramatically improving performance and stakeholder value." Morris and Brandon point out that reengineering has been given various names like streamlining, restructuring, transformation and restructuring, and they add (1993, p. 6) that: "regardless of the name, the goal is almost always the same: increased ability to compete through cost reduction." Champy (1995, p. 34) describes reengineering thoughts as being about "What is this business for? What kind of culture do we want? How do we do our work? What kind of people do we want to work with?" And Fincham asserts (2000, p. 174) that "Business Process Reengineering (BPR) appeals to managers essentially as a means of control over the many vicissitudes of organization life, and there can be little doubt that to many it must seem like a necessary charm against the dark forces of competition and failure." True, these examples are from the business sector. However, the point is that reengineering here is taken as signifying approaches that are primarily motivated "inwards."

Un-engineering is defined as directed toward knowing and embracing administrative love, in both aspects. This is indeed a high—or demanding—standard. Consider Barthes to emphasize how demanding a standard is set for agencies orienting themselves outwards to the individual in-herself in her differences. It is more demanding than the standard set for themselves by private corporations, often said to encourage a libidinal relationship with the customer through such "gifts" as brand identification through advertising. (Curiously the prevalent libidinal form of such corporate behavior resembles the "non-Platonic" popular Ancient Greek idea of love, where lovers were either *erastes* [the pursuer] or *eromenos* [the pursued]. The roles are distinct: the pursuer is active, and the pursued is passive. Plato's re-conceptualization—if not in the *Symposium* then in the *Phaedrus*—is on mutuality, being with.) Reading Barthes can suggest how much higher the standard for any loving gifting must be when he describes the gifting of the lover. "The amorous gift is sought out, selected, and purchased in the greatest excitement—the kind of excitement which seems to be of the order of orgasm" (Barthes, 1978, p. 75). It is a high standard that functions in the manner of a regulative ideal, mentioned earlier. I try; I fail; I half succeed; I lapse; I try again.

Un-engineering's epistemology should be appropriate to its loving goal. Enemies of this un-engineering, of knowing and embracing administrative love, include confinement to traditional ways of learning. Consider the fresh P.A. consciousness I have already discussed (1998, 2001, 2002) and Martha Nussbaum's ideas. Un-engineering should be radically open to alternative perspectives as in anti-administration, a theory directed toward radical openness in P.A. theorizing and p.a. thinking. Anti-administration includes providing for greater inclusion of non-mechanical understandings; it seeks more focus on the non-bureaucratic, the non-systematic, and the non-mechanical. This includes imaginative play, a dynamo that can be expected to transcend mere rationalization. Martha Nussbaum (1990, p. 262) tells us that knowledge "of the heart must come from the heart—from and in its pains and longings, its emotional responses." It must come from knowing that opposes in a radical way the scientific use of the intellect. PA thinking should turn for this to "non-scientific" sources, including literature. Nussbaum describes Marcel Proust's criticisms of intellectualism and his views on knowing love. Going beyond Proust, she "insists that knowledge of love is not a state or function of the solitary person at all, but a complex way of being, feeling, and interacting with another person" (Nussbaum, 1990, p. 274). The new consciousness, in my view, would oppose the "mere" use of the scientific; but it would not oppose inclusion of the scientific, together with the somatic approach (Farmer, 2001b). As Nussbaum writes (2001, p. 191), there is Socratic or general understanding of love; there is knowledge of love through the particular that she associates with Alcibiades who simply tells of the "keen responsiveness of intellect, imagination, and feeling to the particulars of the situation" (p. 191); and there is "knowing how" about loving. Surely, the new consciousness in un-engineering embracing administrative love should be inclusive.

Un-engineering has the aim not only of knowing but of generating the attitudes and behavior of administrative love. Consider employee loyalty, as one example. Yes, the quality of being a team player is highly prized in organizations, a quality that usually translates into giving preference to the "virtue" of loyalty to the organization and to the manager. The Achilles' heel of management is an opportunity to indulge, at least, a sense of self-love; and team work by subordinates, apart from its other advantages, has the practical benefit of furthering the manager's aim of directing, coordinating and controlling and facilitating the manager's own self-gratification. With administrative love that possesses an ideal-focus and an individual-focus, this standard of valuation should change. The highest virtue of an employee will hopefully be that she is "a person first and a subordinate second," rather than one who exemplifies the qualities of a fierce pack dog—like going along with the manager, running with the organizational pack. Administrative love's attitudes and behaviors seem more akin to spirituality, as long as that is understood as neither confined to—nor excluding—religion. (Isn't it disquieting when a smiling face, encountered for the first time on television, tells you "I love you all"?) Such spirituality in managing includes recognizing life, and acting out life, in more poetic terms. Frederic and Mary Brussat write (1996, pp. 320-321) about spiritual literacy, for instance, proposing exercises like answering such questions as "What have you mothered today with your creativity? What have you seen this day that is beautiful? How is your favorite myth relevant to your life? Why not draw a picture of a flower?"—and so on. Such attitudes and behavior would exceed the bonds of the bottom line of efficiency; the manager would no longer prize among subordinates the "great virtue" of great loyalty. In a similar way, should not policy-making, planning, organization, staffing, reporting and the full range of other administrative practices be transvalued—valued by the new standard of administrative love?

Un-engineering's central aim is to go beyond a mere focus on the behaviors of those within the agency. The view is not on the "looking out" from within the agency and it is not on the agency's needs; *to the extent that* it concerns the agency, it is on the "looking in." P.A. thinking and engineering traditionally and centrally have focused on the practitioner, for instance; the p.a. practitioner is the hero of the P.A. story, just as the entrepreneur is the hero of economic theorizing. Un-engineering involves a shift to the citizen as a whole, extending beyond the citizen's role as a client or customer of a particular agency—or, as I prefer, the focus is on the human-in-her-individuality and in-her-difference. Speaking-to-power and macro concerns like the bureaucratization of human life are de-marginalized, for instance—with paradigm-changing consequences. This is how I (e.g., 2001) have often written of the new consciousness. A more dramatic way of putting it would be to recall the notion of the death of the author, saying that un-engineering embraces the possibility of the death of the practitioner as the hero and the focus of P.A. thinking and practice.

## CONCLUSION

Un-engineering should be pursued in the P.A. community, focusing on the possibilities and difficulties of administrative love as a leaven more potent than the efficiency and similar ethics. Fortunately for un-engineering, a coherent understanding of administrative love is available, where administrative love is directed toward an ideal and toward whole individual persons. This is a shift away from viewing administration as a matter of things about rule-making-for-groups and things about rule-application-to-groups. It is away from traditional administration's emphasis on things like direction, coordination and control. Isn't a better path for public management the regulative ideal of un-engineering's *administrative love*? This is a P.A. path that already exists, by exception. Yet in our thinking, it is relatively unfamiliar, uncanny—even though it surely befits the new century after September 11th.

## REFERENCES

Ackerman, D. (1995). *A natural history of love*. New York: Vintage Books.

Allison, G., & Zelikow, P. (1971). *Essence of decision: Explaining the Cuban missile crisis*. Boston: Little Brown.

Barthes, R. (1978). *A lover's discourse: Fragments*. New York: Hill and Wang.

Bataille, G. (1962). *Death and sensuality: A study of eroticism and the taboo*. New York: Walker and Company,

Brussat, F., & Brussat, M. A. (1996). *Spiritual literacy: Reading the sacred in everyday life*. New York: Scribner.

Champy, J. (1995). *Reengineering management: The mandate for new leadership*. New York: HarperBusiness.

Cunningham, R., & Schneider, R. A. (2001). Anti-administration: Redeeming bureaucracy by witnessing and gifting. *Administrative Theory & Praxis, 23*, 573-588.

Czarniawski, B. (1997). *Narrating the organization: Drama of institutional identity.* Chicago: University of Chicago Press.

Farmer, D. J. (1995). *The language of public administration: Bureaucracy, modernity, and postmodernity.* Tuscaloosa: University of Alabama Press.

Farmer, D. J. (1998). Public administration discourse as play with a purpose. In D. J. Farmer (Ed.), *Papers on the art of anti-administration* (pp. 37-56). Burke, VA: Chatelaine Press.

Farmer, D. J. (2001a). Mapping anti-administration: Introduction to the symposium. *Administrative Theory & Praxis, 23*, 475-492.

Farmer, D. J. (2001b). Somatic writing: Attending to our bodies. *Administrative Theory & Praxis, 23*, 187-204.

Farmer, D. J., McLaurin, M., Stivers, C., Hummel, R., King, C., & Kensen, S. (2002). Constructing civil space: A dialogue. *Administration and Society, 34*, pp. 87-129.

Fincham, R. (2000). Management as magic: Reengineering and the search for business salvation. In D. Knights & H. Willmott (Eds.), *The reengineering revolution?: Critical studies of corporate change* (pp. 174-191). Thousand Oaks, CA: Sage.

Flatham, R. E. (1966). *The public interest: An essay concerning the normative discourse of politics.* New York: John Wiley and Sons.

Graham, A. C. (1992). *Unreason within reason: Essays on the outskirts of rationality.* LaSalle, IL: Open Court.

Grassi, E. (1980). *Rhetoric as philosophy: The humanist tradition.* University Park: The Pennsylvania State University Press

Loh, M. (1997). *Re-engineering at work.* Aldershot, England: Gower.

Morris, D. & Brandon, J. (1993). *Reengineering your business.* New York: McGraw Hill.

Nagel, E., & Newman, J. R. (1958). *Godel's proof.* New York: New York University Press.

Nussbaum, M. C. (1990). *Love's knowledge: Essays on philosophy and literature.* New York: Oxford University Press.

Nussbaum, M. C. (2001). *The fragility of goodness* (revised ed.). Cambridge: Cambridge University Press.

Pascal, B. (1995). *Pensees and other writings* (H. Levi, Trans.). New York: Oxford University Press.

Ruprecht, L. A. (1999). *Symposia: Plato, the erotic, and moral value.* Albany: State University of New York Press.

Schubert, G. (1960). *The public interest: A critique of the theory of a political concept.* Glencoe, IL: Free Press of Glencoe.

# THE DEVIL'S ROPE

## David John Farmer

Barbed wire, in the bureaucratic context, has a quality that is often exhibited by a program, a policy, an agency, an individual—or even a theory. It is a quality of compulsion, of force. It is deployed for what the administrator—like the rancher—considers to be a useful purpose. It controls, limits. It can hurt; it can dig into the flesh. At a minimum, it denies passage. It serves (as in "services") to keep them in (e.g., as in "corrections services"), or to keep them out (e.g., as in "immigration and naturalization services"). It is impersonal, harsh and metallic (iron as in "cage")—either in the flesh or metaphorically.

We should become more conscious of the nature of the barbed wire in bureaucracy, and I recommend that PA Theory should seek a full understanding of administrative barbed wire. I want to point toward what is controlling and painful in the texts and sub-texts of bureaucratic bodies. This is important for any PA attempt to contribute even more toward achieving social justice. The notion and importance of barbed wire should become clearer when I provide some examples of three types of bureaucratic context that exhibit barbed wire.

I borrow the term "barbed wire" from James Joyce's anecdote, part of his account of a modern Dubliner's odyssey, in *Ulysses*. He speaks of the nice nun with the really sweet face. Joyce describes this nice nun, and then he concludes with a sentence that fascinates me. "It was a nun they say invented barbed wire" (Joyce, 1997, pp. 147-148).

## TYPES OF BARBED WIRE

Consider this example of barbed wire; reflect on our guilty foreknowledge of the prevalence of the forcible rape of men and women within prison walls. Correctional "services" (a bureaucratic euphemism) contain barbed wire. Corrections exhibits more barbs—more barbarity—than is consistent with my sense of the respect that I (or anyone) should accord to each and every human being.

It's reasonable that many of us want bad people to be stored in a Spartan manner, in stir. No eggs Benedict, for example, behind bars at Sunday brunch. But your and my guilty knowledge of the prevalence of forcible rapes within the walls reflects badly on you and me—to the extent that our foreknowledge makes us responsible for these atrocities. Arguably, it's state-sponsored rape to the extent that the sentencing authorities know that it will happen and to the extent that they have the power to stop it and do not. Ironically and as evidence that it can be stopped, it doesn't happen on death row. In its report on "No Escape: Male Rape in U.S. Prisons," *Human Rights Watch* quotes a Florida prisoner who chronicled his unsuccessful attempts to have prison authorities protect him from six months of repeated attacks. "The opposite of compassion is not hatred, it's indifference," he says (2002, para 1).

The Prison Rape Reduction Act of 2002 is currently under consideration in the U.S. Senate. It authorizes a study of the extent of the problem (Mon Dieu, only now!), and seeks to create a program of standards and incentives to help correctional officers prevent prison rape of men and women. "This legislation is the first serious federal attempt to deal with a human rights crisis that has been virtually ignored in this country," states Stop Prison Rape (SPR) President Lara Stemple (2002, para 1). Stephen Donaldson claimed in 1993 that 290,000 males are sexually assaulted each year in prisons. He wrote that, "The catastrophic experience of sexual violence usually extends beyond a single incident, often becoming a daily assault…" (1993, para 8).

This is not an isolated barb. Correctional agencies display many barbarous barbs. I have visited perhaps fifteen prisons and penitentiaries in my life. That's not much; but I hope that our society is not being graded on the way it treats its prisoners. The lunacy begins pre-corrections – with the sentencing. Why do we incarcerate more people, and for longer periods, than does any other advanced country? Let's suspend the golfing privileges of the rational and intelligent judge who, rather than resign, sentenced Leandro Andrade to fifty years for a $153.54 misdemeanor? How judicial was the Chicago judge who sentenced a multiple murderer to more than a thousand years? No, the prisoner was not Mr. Methusela, and the judge was reportedly sober.

Let's turn to the three contexts of administrative barbed wire. Surely others will prefer an alternative set of categories, e.g., including under-barbed.

**Context 1: Naturally barbed.**

It's hard to think of a barb-less military or a barb-less police *force*. Sometimes being barbed is much of what it's about. For the purposes of this category, we needn't worry about the truth or falsity of the claim that all government is legitimately backed by force. There are enough obvious examples to avoid that. Even these obvious cases can be over-barbed, of course. A military can have more means of violence than humanity needs, like an excess of biological, chemical and atomic weaponry; and a police force can exert more violence than human considerations dictate, as in Amadou-Diallo-violence and Knapp-Commission-corruption. Being barbed appropriately is not the same as being hyper-barbed.

**Context 2: Barbarously barbed.**

Michel Foucault describes an aim in Ancient Greek ethics as attempting to create one's own beautiful life parallel to the creation of a beautiful piece of pottery. To the extent that I am responsible for it or to the extent that I approve of it, a barbarously barbed wire agency is one that makes me look like an ugly pot. Correctional services constitute one example, fencing in. Immigration services is also at some point in this spectrum of agencies that are over-barbed.

Ask former customers of the Immigration and Naturalization Service (INS), when they have finally escaped the control of INS. Ellis Island attitudes still reign, I think they will whisper. I recall when I first came to the United States—in 1958. I came by train from Montreal to New York. Two Immigration and Naturalization Service officers came into the car of the train, collecting the passports and sitting about half way down. A female passenger, very well dressed, attempted to go to the bathroom: "Sit down!" came the sharp command. She turned tail and walked back to her seat. Then I overheard one of the officers exclaim to the other in a booming voice, waving a passport and pointing to another passenger in the train car: "This belongs to the (racial epithet for a Spanish person) over there." At that time, I didn't know the word (never heard it before); but I did recognize the hostility. No contact with the INS in later years was ever absent verbal harassment and denigration, including every step of the naturalization process. That was enough decades ago. "Hurry up! Hurry up! Or you will have to start the process all over again some other day," exclaims one official. Maybe things have changed now; conversations with some current applicants disabuse me of that hope. "I'm now going to test to see whether you can speak English; read this," says another official, apparently oblivious of the fact that the previous conversation was in English. "My name is Mr. Rosa. I am a man," reads the text of the assigned book. "Good! Now I am going to test to see if you can write English. Write a sentence," instructs the official. "I am a man," I write.

**Context 3: Unspeakably barbed.**

Far from the naturally barbed end of the spectrum, barbed wire conjures up the image of a totally inhuman type of barbed wire, the wire of the concentration camp. It is too mild to say that this is at the extreme of the other end of any array of contexts of administrative barbed wire; it is off the end of any scale. We can understand Theodor Adorno (1981, p. 34); "To write poetry after Auschwitz is barbaric."

The administrative outlines of the Final Solution, as you know, were settled at a meeting on January 20, 1942 at Wannsee, a villa near Berlin. How could a group of 14 such rational and intelligent people consent to such an unspeakably barbed, totally inhuman and inhumane project? This question is fleshed out by Kenneth Branagh and others in the brilliant made-for-TV movie (with an inelegant, albeit accurate, title) "Conspiracy." The movie recounts the Wannsee meeting. Kenneth Branagh plays the meeting chair, General Reinhard Heydrich; Stanley Tucci (also brilliant) acts the part of the meeting's secretary, Adolph Eichmann. The other participants are respected officials from affected governmental agencies, like the Foreign Office. Heydrich runs the meeting with consummate administrative skill. He shows courtesy and deference to other viewpoints; at times he calls for drinks and food to diffuse tensions; he proceeds relentlessly toward the already-settled goal. Afterwards, the actor Branagh is reported to have said, "Playing him, I felt that had he been asked to eradicate Eskimos, cabinet-makers or gymnasts, he would have proceeded in the same way, with the same relentless soulless quality" (Gritten, 2002, para. 15). For me, the high point in the movie is when the meeting has broken up and only two are left in the room. Eichmann puts on the adagio from Schubert's Quintet in C Major. The second person is visibly transformed into the world of the sublime, and Eichmann comments "Tears your heart out, doesn't it?" Long pause—and Eichmann sneers, "I don't understand that sentimental Viennese shit."

## UNDERSTANDING BARBED WIRE

Joseph F. Glidden's invention of literal barbed wire in 1873 led to a storm of controversy. In fact, the opponents came to call it "the Devil's Rope." I favor controversy no less intense about the Devil's Rope of administrative barbed wire. I prefer such a conversation where PA Theory could contribute to an overall perspective, rather than case-by-case arguments considering this situation (e.g., corrections) and then that (e.g. immigration). Where should I look for a meaningful, overall understanding of how to cope with our history of bureaucratic barbed wire? How should I look for an overall understanding of the working of barbed wire?

An overall theory of barbed wire should focus on society, rather than limiting itself to either bureaucracy or a particular bureaucratic function. It should seek to connect that focus with a larger theoretical framework about society—a commonplace idea in the PAT-Net community but too rare a commodity at many mainstream PA conferences. Many will agree that the barbed wire is connected with modernity's rationalizing project—a perverse and unintended outcome. Preferences will vary about which frameworks and thinkers can help in carrying the interpretation to a more interesting depth. I am attracted by Foucault's claims about the discipline of the body and the control of the population (e.g., Foucault, 1980, p. 125).

Did bureaucracy invent barbed wire, you might ask; or did barbed wire in society invent bureaucracy, reflecting society's image? Does the barbed wire of our set of institutions like the U.S. Post Office—like the delivery of junk mail at discount rates—come from society? Or, vice-versa? I agree that it's a two-way street. But I imagine that the nature of the barbed wire in bureaucracy originates in the conscious and unconscious barbed wire in society. It's parallel to the nice nun with the really sweet face. Wasn't Joyce's nun largely socially created, and didn't she then influence society? I imagine that the barbed wire in bureaucracy can be understood only by paying attention to the sources of the barbed wire in society; I suppose that the discourse of society is decisive. This has significance for PA thinking. PA should be heavily concerned with what Burrell (1997) describes as important—the societal production of organizations. This is contrasted with what traditionally is the central PA concern—organizational production. Burrell directs attention to *the production of organization*, rather than to the *organization of production* (Burrell, 1997, p. 25).

An anti-administrative approach toward investigating the workings of barbed wire would employ a variety of perspectives like the economic, the psychological, the womanist, rhetorical analysis, and so on. The economic perspective might notice the susceptibility of economic weaklings to barbed wire. Natural targets would be the vulnerable patsies who have little leverage or recourse—such as criminals, low-income immigrants, and other "others" like women and minority persons. The psychological perspective might talk about the sado-masochistic character of our natures. And don't let's forget the role of scapegoating.

By speaking of barbed wire, I am pointing toward what is painful and controlling in the human and PA contexts. In part it is the kind of thing that Gibson Burrell (1997) attempts to describe for organizational thinking in his non-linear book *Pandemonium*. Burrell does a wonderful job of directing us toward the filth under the lid of the organization jam jar, including the juicy tidbit that a function of the bureaucracy is to control the peasantry. It is the kind of thing that Orion and Cynthia McSwite (1998) describe for PA. They illustrate how PA thinking excludes from what-counts-as-PA-*facts* what is forbidden and what is irrational.

Barbed wire is not an isolated bureaucratic phenomenon. On the contrary, it seems to be everywhere—and it persists. Read the lead story in, at the time of writing, today's *New York Times*, and recall that there are said to be excellent treatments available for most of the patients I am going to mention. "Hundreds of patients released from state psychiatric hospitals in New York in recent years are being locked away on isolated floors of nursing homes, where they are barred from going outside on their own, have almost no contact with others and have little ability to contest their confinement…" (Levy, 2002, p. 1). "History…is a nightmare from which I am trying to awake," writes Joyce (1997, p. 35). Let an awake PA Theory address even more systematically the barbed wire in its societal and bureaucratic inheritance!

## REFERENCES

Adorno, T. W. (1981). *Prisms* (S. Weber & S. Weber, Trans.). Cambridge, MA: M.I.T.

Burrell, G. (1997). *Pandemonium: Toward a retro-organization theory*. Thousand Oaks, CA: SAGE Publications.

Donaldson, S. (1993, December 29). The rape crisis behind bars. *New York Times*. Retrieved on October 2, 2002 from http://www.vix.com/pub/men/abuse/usa-prison.html

Foucault, M. (1980). *Power/knowledge* (C. Gordon, Ed.). Brighton, England: Harvester.

Gliddens, J. F. (2002). A brief history of the invention and development of barbed wire. *The Devil's Rope*. Retrieved from http://www.barbwiremuseum.com/barbedwirehistory.htm

Gritten, D. (2002, January). *Radio times*. Retrieved from http://www.branaghcompendium.com/conspiracy.html

*Human Rights Watch*. (2002, October 2). No escape: Male rape in U.S. prisons. Retrieved from http://www.hrw.org/reports/2001/prison/report1.html

Joyce, J. (1997). *Ulysses*. London: Macmillan.

Levy, C. J. (2002, October). Mentally ill and locked away in nursing homes in New York. *The New York Times, 1*.

McSwite, O.C. (1998). Stories from the "real world": Administering anti-administratively. In D. J. Farmer, *Papers on the art of anti-administration*, (pp. 17-36). Burke, VA: Chatelaine Press.

Stemple, L. (2002, October 2). *Stop prisoner rape*. Retrieved from http://www.spr.org/en/pressreleases/pr_02_081402.html

# FRIGGINOMICS BEGINS IN KINDERGARTEN: THE SOCIAL CONSTRUCTION OF "NORMAL" CITIZENS AND THEIR DREAMS

David John Farmer

"I look forward to an America which will not be afraid of grace and beauty." (President John F. Kennedy)

Economics is now taught in many kindergartens in the United States, and it continues through later school grades. Many kids are being seduced, unconsciously and often enough consciously, to grow up to lust for the market and market values. Ideology is being foisted, as the unfettered market is privileged as being as natural as apple pie and as self-interest is celebrated as more American than public interest. Individual success is equated with financial success. Public Administration (PA) specialists beware! Frigginomics rules, as part of the social construction of individuals and society. All this limits and channels dreams—and the PA context.

Frigginomics is *happy, happy economics.* It is a form of economics that glosses over the "traditional" recognition that economics is the dismal science. Frigginomics promotes the happiness of an erotic attachment to perfectly competitive capitalism, which is equated with morality (e.g., see Perelman, 1996, p. 4). It is love for an unfettered market, even though—inconsistently—many of the market lovers in practice want government to aid business, e.g., through tax loop holes, subsidies, bail outs or other deals. Frigginomics is economics that portrays the perfectly competitive market, in Jean Baudrillard's image, as a kind of Disneyland. Recall Jean Baudrillard (Poster, 1988, pp. 166-184) claiming that the "simulacrum is true" and that Disneyland "is" America. Disneyland is where all is very happy, and where nothing really dismal happens. The moniker "frigginomics" is prompted by the title of a best-seller (more of this sad book later!) called *Freakonomics* (Levitt & Dubner, 2005).

Let's look at the situation in kindergarten and beyond, and then (in a style befitting economics) the benefits and the costs. For a market ideologue, the net benefit could be mistaken as positive. The net benefit is negative for others, mainly because of the ideological indoctrination and the triviality of the content. A couple of months ago, I spent a day discussing the teaching of economics in schools with a class of local principals and assistant principals. I owe to them many of the facts about schools reported here, and they helped my understanding of the literature. But I cannot saddle them—beautiful people—with agreeing with my conclusions; they seemed too impressed with economics as "cutting edge" and with market as "reality."

## ECONOMICS GONE WILD

Standards of learning (SOLs) for economics have been established for kindergarten and the other grades. Yet, in an important sense, a mere statement of the SOL facts is non-factual. It is non-factual because a mere statement tends to cover up the latent ideology in the inclusions and the exclusions. It does reveal the trivial character of the economic standards, but it does not speak to the variety of "whys" of the trivia. Among the whys are factors like specialists pushing their specialties, e.g., economics teachers pushing economics teaching. Among this variety, my impression is that the trivia, unconsciously surely, is understandable if it is interpreted as supporting the ideology. So, in reading the "facts," the reader is asked to suspend judgment until she has finished reading the benefits and costs sections. Then it should be apparent why I'm speaking about economics gone wild.

Teaching economics in elementary schools has been growing over the past half-century, and it is now big business. The National Council on Economic Education (NCEE) has been encouraging economics teaching in elementary schools since 1949. As another example, Lawrence Senesh long ago developed two first grade economics units—"unit inside the home" and, yes, "unit outside the home." The intensity of contemporary interest is reflected in the well-known January 2002 No Child Left Behind (NCLB) act, which mentions economics eight times. The NCEE offers "Voluntary National Content Standards in Economics" for grades K through 12." More understandably than in kindergarten, economics is widely taught in high schools. It is reported that 49 states include economics in their standards; and the four states with most students require a course in economics as a requirement for high school graduation (NCEE, 2005a). Economics is typically taught within the social studies framework. I'm told that each state—and within that framework, the local organization—decides what it will do. The stories will differ in details between locations, e.g., in Virginia, Pennsylvania, Maryland or other states. There are state organizations like the Virginia, the South Carolina, and the Hawaii, councils of economic education.

Just the facts, ma'am! Here are the SOL standards for economics for kindergarteners and early graders in a suburban and prosperous school system in Virginia, a system understandably well respected in this geographical area. For kindergarten graduates, the relevant SOL provides that they will know two "economic" things. The first is to "identify the difference between basic needs (food clothing, and shelter) and wants (things people would like to have)." The second is to "recognize that people use money to purchase goods." Grade 1 wants the graduate to know the difference between goods and services, that people are both buyers and sellers, that people make choices because they cannot have everything they want, and that people save money for the future to purchase goods and services. Grade 2's SOL wants the graduate to know the distinction between natural and human and capital resources. In the name of all that's holy, why?

## MARGINAL BENEFITS

Economic literacy bears on daily life, of course. But how does what is learnt in kindergarten and the early grades bear on economic literacy? Consider possible meanings of economic literacy, and then return to some of the SOLs I've mentioned.

## ECONOMIC LITERACY

Economic literacy is a catch phrase—the rhetoric—long used in touting the advantages of economic education in early grades. Take the eighties! Writers like Banaszak (1987) claim that economic literacy cannot be realized without learning economics in elementary and secondary schools. Note many such calls as in Miller (1988) who wants students to have skills to become "knowledgeable consumers, prudent savers and investors, productive members of the work force and productive citizens." Seiter (1989, p. 15) also claims that learning economics will help students "perform adequately as producers, consumers, investors, and voters in public elections."

Economic literacy is "a" reasonable aim. So are other kinds of "literacy," like foreign language literacy, mathematical literacy, scientific literacy, or social literacy. But equally reasonable is to wonder why economic literacy has to start in kindergarten and why it requires friggi-nomics. I'm not saying that economic literacy should not be addressed in, say, the later grades of high school. But, elementary school? Bizarre arguments are taken seriously in support of contributing to economic literacy in elementary school. For example, there is the old chestnut that economic education in the earliest grades is necessary, because many children will not make it to high school (Kourilsky, 1977). So, if they miss the early economics education, they will not acquire the skills to function successfully in the American economy. Two queries! Why should we suppose that knowing the little that passes-for-economics that is taught in elementary school contributes to economic literacy? If they don't make it to high school, how will they be equipped anyhow?

Note at least three meanings of economic literacy. A first is that economic literacy equips the graduate against personal economic exploitation—against exploitation as consumers (btw, forget literacy against exploitation as employees). At first sight, education for consumer literacy seems reasonable; at second sight, it is worse than an empty gesture. It is nice if kids learned what, say, balloon payments and reverse mortgages are. I agree that young DIGs (see below) and millenials, on reaching early adulthood, face an economic ocean containing many sharks and other nasty "small print" marketing fish. Renard (2005) speaks about digital immediate gratification (DIG), and Rutherford (2005, p. 35) calls today's kids the "millenials"—hip on Yahoo, Google and Game Boys. As the young college freshmen slouch toward the student commons, they are hustled by offers of credit cards—and low rates calculated on a per diem basis. I can see that the freshmen need practical advice for living, and that there are advantages in disguising any earlier preparation in schools under a "neutral" term like "Economics" rather than rousing some "irrational" parents with a provocative description like "Guidelines for Practical Living." Perhaps they need straight talk. "Regardez, bird-for-brains, the economy is both good and also a sewer, and there are more than enough businesses out there planning to fleece you out of the little you have. The corporations are cleverer than you. Watch out for economic tricksters offering you credit cards!" Yet, I doubt whether the armor available in even the better high school economics courses is proof against the ingenuity of the financial predators existing in society. Learning the happy, happy version of economics will actually make the newly-minted adult more vulnerable—to the extent that the student thinks that the market is always beneficent.

Economic literacy has a second meaning. It is best expressed in the comment by the distinguished economist James Tobin (1986), who writes that, "High school graduates will be making choices all their lives, as breadwinners and consumers, as citizens and voters. A wide range of people will bombard them with economic information and misinformation for their entire lives. They will need some capacity for critical judgment." This is true, and it is especially important for those in political positions—and there have been complaints of economic illiteracy in the latter category. However, two objections are cogent. First, surely what is learned in kindergarten and the early grades, taught at those tender ages, is neither necessary nor sufficient for this literacy. Second, a happy, happy version of economics—taught at any grade level, even high school—is a misleading basis for economic judgments. As one example, such teaching would not explore the implications of criticisms such as Perelman's comparison of the perfectly competitive market with a unicorn. To repeat, Perelman writes that we "all know what it is supposed to look like, although none of us have ever seen it" (Perelman, 1994, p. 4). He is saying that the conditions for the existence in practice of such a market are more than forbidding, e.g., costs of enforcing contracts and property rights must be zero, full information must be available about the performance and quality of goods and services and of all alternative ways of producing them (plus all the costs of this information must be zero), and so on (Buchanan, 1991, p. 184).

A third meaning of economic literacy is that it is something which helps the economy. A common argument is that globalization somehow requires economics training if this country is to maintain its place in the world. The rhetoric flows freely about globalization: witness President Robert Duvall of the NCEE claiming (2005b) that the "economic well-being of our nation and our role in the global economy depends on universal economics and personal finance." Really I don't get this! One study went further and claimed that consumers untrained in economic literacy hurt the economy. I don't think that the sellers would think this when selling credit cards to students who cannot afford them. Let's assume that economic education in kindergarten and early grade school does improve competitiveness—a tall story. Would that be a better way of competing with, say, Germany, than trying to upgrade our general (non-economic) literacy to match the German level—e.g., the literacy that comes from scientific or technological education? Then again, economic literacy is difficult to achieve when (for instance) macroeconomics is underemphasized, and unsurprisingly it is in very short supply in elementary school.

## SPECKS OF TRIVIA?

The specks of trivia are a tad pomo! Unless something "important" is being achieved like ideological indoctrination, it's not clear why children are being bothered with these bits (specks) of information when they could learn them in high school in two or three minutes—OK, twenty minutes. Also, it is not clear how what is learned in kindergarten and in the early grades can contribute meaningfully to economic literacy.

Recall the kindergarten SOL standard that kindergarten graduates should know the difference between needs and wants—to "identify the difference between basic needs (food clothing, and shelter) and wants (things people would like to have)." Less interesting is that the dichotomy skips over such details as that the distinction between needs and wants is eminently deconstructible. (Ah well, it's close enough for kindergarten work!) One could distinguish instead between needs, comforts and luxuries, for instance—three, not two, categories. Or, one could recognize that needs are a function, not just of living, but of income—and culture. Someone might object that this is too complex for toddlers; but, if that is true, why bring up the topic in the first place? The sad fact is that, for many little kindergarten children, even the dichotomy-as-is is not an easily-understood distinction. Yet what have they gained in terms of economic literacy if they put out the effort (and time) to master the dichotomy? All is not well in the Land of Kindergarten Wants and Needs. So Maszaros (1997) tells us about the large amount of time spent by elementary teachers in distinguishing between wants and needs, and complains about teachers "failing" to teach that limited resources are available to satisfy wants and that, therefore, choices must be made. Oh, dear!

Recall the other kindergarten standard that money purchases goods. Wait a minute! Time to poke fun! There are so many underprivileged adults, who missed kindergarten and who consequently do not know what bills and coins are for. Many can be seen wandering around starving, rattling large bags of bills and coins, and not knowing that they can purchase goods with the money. And all because they missed kindergarten! Wait a minute! What can I make of one principal telling me that young people need to be taught the difference between a consumer and a producer? When entering a store, which adult— including any who have never been to school—is in danger of not knowing that the store is selling something? Who needs the big words, like "producer" and "consumer"—or other deconstructible distinctions like that between "goods" and "services"?

Why are these disjointed bits of information needed (or wanted, or found comforting)? The only reasonable line of argument is the highly dubious contention that these earlier items are necessary for later learning. The literature urges that all these curricular items are interlocked, the later items building on the former. But, although education is their specialty and not mine, I don't believe it. I don't see why an older student needs this earlier trivia before she encounters and masters (say) supply and demand curves. If it looks like filler, if it walks like filler, if it quacks like filler, it's filler. But filler for what? I think that the proponents of this dubious claim about being necessary for later knowledge have missed the forest for the trees; one of the better explanations for the trivia is that it is a cover for ideology, latent in large part. As I mentioned before, I don't deny the existence of other factors. I don't underestimate the over-enthusiasm of business persons for the ways of business, and school officials and politicians respond to the business community as much as to any. Again, specialists are typically so close to their specialties that they tend to push them, e.g., military historians tend to push military history, economics teachers tend to push (cannot imagine what).

What do I mean by the claim that trivia can be a cover for ideology? Let me give an example from the kindergarten SOL standard that money is used to make purchases. An ideological feature of this standard is that economics, named as economics, is being taught in kindergarten at all. Frigginomics, named as economics, is being taught at a most impressionable level. Recall that, just because you agree with a particular view (e.g. that kids should love money) does not mean that pushing that view is not ideological. The start is being made in kindergarten perhaps with latent reference (Freud alert, as it were!) to ideas that evoke appetitive pleasure to little kids, e.g., money for toys, for chocolates. The message is that money is what it is all about. I suppose this observation makes more sense only if we recall, as just hinted, other items that are not being emphasized, e.g., speaking a foreign language is useful, learning poetry by heart is worthwhile, serving the public interest is the highest social value. (If the reader doesn't like the examples, she can substitute her own.) There is another ideological aspect, however. Yes, people do use money to purchase goods, and knowing that makes me feel warm and happy. But, isn't it ideological to gloss over the detail that some people have much more money than others? Isn't it implicitly ideological to gloss over the detail that some people obtained their money other than from the metaphorical sweat of their brows? I'm not even giving the example of glossing over the detail that people also use money for less admirable purposes, e.g., exploiting others, buying political favors, displaying their penis power. Against the objection that these issues cannot be treated in kindergarten, again it may be asked "Why bring it up at all?"

But I mustn't give the impression that trivia in kindergarten—as a servant of introducing ideology—is peculiar to economics. A major SOL in Civics, for instance, includes the student being able to recognize—among other things (like the Flag)—the fact "that the President is the leader of the United States." Again, there is an ideological component, e.g., not only about the (more obvious) glory of "our country" but also about the (more latent) value of leadership and hierarchy. One can also ask whether a new adult would not find out about the president, even if s/he never went to kindergarten or to school. "I'm sorry that you don't know about the president being leader; clearly, you didn't go to kindergarten."

## COSTS, ESPECIALLY HIDDEN COSTS

Much of the cost stems from advancing the ideology of friggi-nomics—by avoiding, as suggested earlier, an awkward fact. The awkward fact is that economics, after and in the spirit of the Reverend Thomas Malthus (1766-1834), really is a "dismal science." It's Economics 101 that the invisible hand not only succeeds brilliantly in some ways but also that the hand fails painfully in others. Blood-curdling features covered by the dismal science include incredible economic disparities (homeless people on heating grates in the nation's capital, and rich people eating capital fillet mignon), instability (swings in the business cycle, employees laid off when they are 49 years old), and the rest. Naturally, we don't want to undermine the self-assurance of little children by such ugly details. The ideology that comes from the omissions is that we will teach only happy, happy economics—economics that leaves them (and the eventual adults) with the academically approved assurance that the market is gooey-ly good and that the hyper-capitalist approach is gooey-ly-good for all our ills. (Calvin Trilling could write such a cute doggerel ditty here about "happy, happy economics." He could incorporate Malthus' even more dismal idea that pointed to the prospect of starvation as a natural means of controlling the galloping population. He could translate into doggerel such prose as the following: "Listen, children. I want to tell you that the population in the world is increasing in geometrical proportion, and that the quantity of food supplies is growing arithmetically. Look forward to starvation. Get out your crayons, and let's draw thousands of 'other' people slowly starving.")

Sometimes the brain-washing is open. Ingels and O'Brien (1988, p. 282) write of the most important aim of instruction in high schools being to develop positive attitudes about the economic system and about economics. Seiter (1989, p. 5) says that "economics instruction in secondary schools also influences students to develop positive attitudes about the economic system and the subject of economics."

Sometimes the ideology is harder to unearth; what is said all looks so innocent. Here are three examples. First, turn to the claim that our "schools must teach that profit is not a dirty word. It is profit that brings about innovation." Of course, profit is not a dirty word. But believing that profit is necessary for all innovation is false. For one thing, there is the impetus of public interest. Did Rutherford split the atom for monetary reasons? Would Einstein have forgotten his magic if not seduced by dollar profit? Further, profit may encourage bad or marginal innovations (and, in some circumstances, retention of the status quo), rather than alternative "good" innovations. Reducing "good" innovation to capitalism is too simple. Second, take the American Bankruptcy Institute's (2001) claim that individual unsound financial decisions are responsible for bankruptcies that threaten the financial health of financial institutions. The ideology of the rational actor is hidden here. The facts of the case are typically different, unless individual mistakes are broadened to include life's tragedies like divorce, losing a job or a health catastrophe. Frigginomics rules!

Third, kids love games; play is their work. But is it best to depict the market as a game? Is that realistic? Economic practice is often presented in schools as a game for winners, where there are only other money-seeking investors—and not people like the homeless, the seriously ill, and other economic "non-players." For one instance, Eckel et al. (2005) describes a game that requires only a deck of cards, poker chips and ice water, and the game's objective is to teach why some jobs pay differently than others. (Isn't there a subliminal ideological message in the use of poker chips?) For another instance, there's "Hootie and the Blowfish Take Stock in South Carolina," designed to help fourth through twelfth graders understand more about investments. The students are given $100,000 in play money and compete with fellow student investors. Typically, such games are a tad unrealistic even on investment grounds—to the extent that it is true that people should not switch around investments so freely within a short time frame. Not all is stock market and other games, however, and teachers can be inventive. I was told about one teacher (McCreadie, 2003) asking her seniors to "rewrite" stories in order to emphasize economic ideas, like costs and benefits. Examples of titles created by students were "The Three Economic Little Piggies" and "Goldilocks and the Three Entrepreneurs."

Sometimes the cost can include planting the seeds for embracing freakonomics. Freakonomics, which does emphasize love of the unfettered market, has the additional feature of faith in economics as "the" way-of-knowing everything that is worth knowing. Frigginomics often does lead to this additional faith; but it does not necessarily do so. There is utility in applying economic tools to non-business contexts; but that does not require the epistemological excess in freakonomics. The sub-title of the book *Freakonomics* (Levitt & Dubner, 2005 — mentioned earlier) is "A rogue economist explores the hidden side of everything." Yes, everything! Well, not literally — but everything that counts! Freakonomics "establishes this unconventional premise: if morality represents how we would like the world to work, then economics represents how it actually does work" (p. ii). "Freakonomics can provide more than that. It will literally redefine the way we view the modern world" (p. 3).

Contest: Do try this at home. Find out the economics SOL that applies to your, or a neighbor's, infant. Look for the latent ideology. For instance, consider the second grade SOL standard of distinguishing between natural and human and capital resources. How innocent! Yet, some will notice the ideology involved in treating nature as resources and considering people as "resources." Does that imply that some environmentalists must be mistaken? And, does that sound like conceptualizing people as basically similar to things we use (or take advantage of)?

## EPILOGUE

Frigginomics — happy, happy economics — begins in kindergarten. But I agree that it starts even earlier – in society and in history. There is what is usually called the American Dream. I appreciate that not all Americans have agreed, and that not all of those who have disagreed were socialists or communists (e.g., see Scott, 1977, on American conceptions of property from the seventeenth to the twentieth century). I also appreciate that even holding the American Dream does not *entail* — but, in its typical form, it does encourage — the over-zealousness of teaching frigginomics in kindergarten. Also I agree with the obvious qualification that institutions other than schools also play their parts in the social construction. An example is the connection that Lawrence White (2005) documents between monetary economists and the Federal Reserve System, e.g. on one count, asserting that "74 percent of the articles on monetary policy published by U.S.-based economists in U.S.-

edited journals appear in Fed[eral Reserve]-published journals or are co-authored by Fed staff economists" (p. 325).

Ceasing to foist frigonomics on little children would not entail abandoning the American Dream, although it would be facilitated by tweaking said dream. Writes Jeremy Rifkin (2004):

> The American Dream is far too centered on personal material advancement and too little concerned with the broader human welfare to be relevant in a world of increasing human risk, diversity, and interdependence. It is an old dream, immersed in a frontier mentality, that has long since become passé. (p. 3)

Rifkin holds that it has led this country to "its current impasse." Unlike Rifkin, many will not want to replace that dream with the others available—and he speaks of a new and different European Dream being born. Most of us will want to keep the American Dream. But, retaining the American Dream (or any other dream) doesn't rule out *tweaking*. Isn't it possible to tweak the dubious equation of individual success with material success, or to tweak the debatable emphasis on self-interest as the best guide to life? Also, I do think that it's practical—and not un-American—to be open to each individual dreaming her own dream(s).

Public Administration (PA) specialist, shouldn't you try to stick your foot inside the schoolhouse door? Aren't you disturbed by the implications for public-interested PA of a privileging of frigginomics? Shouldn't you show more interest in the social construction of "normal" citizens and their dreams?

## REFERENCES

American Bankruptcy Institute. (2001). *U.S. bankruptcy filings statistics.* Retrieved September 15, 2005, from www.abiworld.org/stats/newstatsfront.html

Banaszak, R. (1987). *The nature of economic literacy.* Bloomington, IN: ERIC/Chess.

Buchanan, A. (1991). Efficiency arguments for and against the market. In J. Arthur & W. H. Shaw (Eds.), *Justice and economic distribution* (pp. 184-197). Englewood Cliffs: NJ: Prentice Hall.

Eckel, C., McInnes, M. M., Solnick, S., Ensminger, J., Fryer, R., Heiner, R., et al. (2005) Bobbing for widgets: Compensating wage differentials. *The Journal of Economic Education, 36,* 129-138.

Ingels, S. J., & O'Brien, M. U. (1988). The effects of economics instruction in early adolescence. *Theory and Research in Social Education,* 279-294.

Kourilsky, M. (1977). The kinder economy: A case study of kindergarten pupils' acquisition of economic concepts. *The Elementary School Journal, 77,* 182-217.

Levitt, S. D., & Dubner, S. J. (2005). *Freakonomics: A rogue economist explores the hidden side of everything.* New York: HarperCollins.

McCreadie, D. (2003). Teaching economics through fairy tales in the United States and Russia. *Social Studies Review, fall.* Retrieved September 24, 2005, from www.findarticles.com

Meszaros, B. (1997). Economic standards: A guide for curriculum planners. *Social Education, 61,* 324-327.

Miller, S. L. (1988). *Economic education for citizenship.* Bloomington: IN: ERIC/Chess & Foundation for Teaching Economics.

NCEE. (2005). State-by-state report card shows economics education improving, but some youth are still not learning the basics. Retrieved September, 14, 2005, from www.ncee.net/about/survey2004/

NCEE. (2005a). Economic and personal finance education in our nation's schools in 2004. Retrived September 24, 2005, from www.ncee.net/about/zsurvey2004/NCEESurvey2004web.pdf.

Perelman, M. (1996). *The end of economics.* New York: Routledge, London.

Poster, M. (Ed.). (1988). *Jean Baudrillard: Selected writings.* Stanford, CA: Stanford University Press.

Renard, L. (2005). Teaching in the DIG generation. *Educational Leadership, 62,* 44-47.

Rifkin, J. (2004). *The European dream: How Europe's vision of the future is quietly eclipsing the American dream.* New York: Tarcher/Penguin.

Rutherford, P. (2005). *21st century mentor's handbook.* Alexandria, VA: Just Ask Publication.

Seiter, D. M. (1989). *Teaching and learning economics.* Bloomington, IN: ERIC/Chess.

Scott, W. B. (1977). *In pursuit of happiness: American conceptions of property from the seventeenth to the twentieth century.* Bloomingtgon, IN: ERIC/Chess.

Tobin, J. (1986, July 9). Economic literacy isn't marginal investment. *Wall Street Journal,* p. 9

White, L. H. (2005). The Federal Reserve System's influences on research in monetary economics. *Econ Journal Watch: Scholarly Comment on Academic Economics, 2,* 325-354. Retrieved August 30, 2005, from www.econ journalwatch.org

# WAL-MART®: NEO-FEUDAL (K)NIGHT?

**David John Farmer**

---

Wal-Mart? Nelson Lichtenstein (2006) claims that Wal-Mart is the "template for 21st century capitalism." It's the largest grocery, largest toy, largest bookselling, largest jewelry, and third largest pharmacy in the United States. If it were a country, its sales would rank 22nd in the World in terms of GNP—ahead, say, of Saudi Arabia and Norway. Just before Christmas, I paid my first visit to a Wal-Mart Supercenter. "We sell for less" greeted us over the entrance. I pushed my basket through the length and the breadth of the store, past shelf upon shelf of stuff. I felt that Wal-Mart is a phenomenon I should make a beginning toward understanding.

Outside the field of business, why should anyone be interested? Let's put aside my view that the scope of the study of governance should not be confined to socially constructed fiefdoms, like private enterprise, public enterprise and not-for-profits (see Habermas, 1989). Ignore my belief that it should not be limited to single intellectual fiefdoms, like economics, sociology, public administration, business administration, and the rest. Instead, indulge in a flight of fantasy. Imagine that you are a victim locked in the upper room of a tower, a hair specialist living in a feudal age when human science is severely sub-optimal. Listen to that ominous thing in the outside gloom! Is't a rescuing knight, benignly eager to climb the long tresses of your hair? Is't a monster of the night? Or, is't but a trick of the night, signifying nothing? As the thing's noise intensifies, your interest should leap outside your specialty's limits—outside the limits of your language.

What kind of a thing is Wal-Mart? Karl Popper's party trick was to confuse audiences by challenging them, without further instructions, to make an observation. His idea was that making observations implies a framework, chosen or inadvertent. I suppose that frameworks can function at more than one level.

1. A first level could be to incorporate Wal-Mart into frameworks of *things*, as in microeconomic theory of the firm and business admin-

istration. This leads me to explain Wal-Mart as the rational outcome, within a set of constraints, of market structure and business innovation. Of course, this leaves out disciplines that also have something important to add about Wal-Mart, like history, global studies, international relations, environmental studies, American studies, urban planning, and geography—not to mention the rest of economics. It doesn't tell me enough about the set of constraints, for example.

2. Another level could be to incorporate Wal-Mart into frameworks of *consciousness of things,* after thinkers like Constantine Castoriadis. This leads me to think of Wal-Mart as an outcome of a particular social consciousness—and of consciousnesses like late Sam Walton's and CEO H. Lee Scott's being within that larger consciousness. Of course, this leaves out a reverse effect. This is the likelihood that Wal-Mart could co-shape society's consciousness, the shaping being a dynamic not only for private corporations but also for public and not-for-profit enterprises. It doesn't tell me how we can gain more democratic control over our societal consciousness, for example—or whether our dreams should remain hostage to history and monied interests.

I don't see these two levels of framework as competitive. Wal-Mart is a thing, for instance; but also it is a thing that emanates from a particular societal consciousness.

## FRAMEWORK OF THING

> If you will only take the trouble always to do the perfectly correct thing, and to say the perfectly correct thing, you can do just what you like.
>
> (George Bernard Shaw)

Wal-Mart is an oligopsony, at least. Microeconomic theory of the firm can explain the upside and the downside of an oligopsony. Wal-Mart's prices (low opening price points), high volume and one-stop shopping are choices that a rational actor might make if she seeks to optimize returns within a set of constraints, for example. But such upsides come with downsides; no surprise in our dismal science. Wal-Mart can be "explained" within the intellectual fiefdoms of economics and of—to a lesser extent—supply chain management, as the term "explain" is typically described in Philosophy of Social Science.

An oligopsony, like Wal-Mart, is a buyer of X in a market structure where the number of buyers of X is small, regardless of the number of suppliers of that X. Wal-Mart buys ten percent of the exports from China's Guangdong province, which in turn produces a third of China's exports. (For these and other statistics about the company, see www.walmartwatch.com; for a company version, see www.walmartfacts.com.) An idea parallel to oligopsony is the more familiar "oligopoly," where the number of suppliers is small. In fact, Wal-Mart is both an oligopsony and an oligopoly. Wal-Mart sells to about 138 million shoppers per week. In both directions, it has price-setting power. Oligopsonists (few buyers) and monopsonists (one buyer) have different degrees of power, and one category shades into the other. Wal-Mart's oligopsony power will vary between products (e.g., between groceries and pharmaceuticals) and between supplying areas (e.g., between China and Mexico). The effective power depends on constraints like mobility (e.g., in labor and capital resources) and time. So great is Wal-Mart's market share that its suppliers are frequently facing a de facto monopsonist situation.

Oligopsonies are the general rule, rather than the exception, in "advanced" economies; so are oligopolies. Think of oligopsonies in markets like books, radio stations, and tobacco! In books, there are oligopsonies like Barnes-and-Noble and Borders. For a mass market book publisher, these are the ultimate "editors." In radio stations, there's Clear Channel and Viacom. For a recording company or a Howard Stern, this oligopsony power is significant. Domestic producers of shade-tobacco face the oligopsony power of cigar manufacturers. If they cannot sell to the oligopsonists, they must sell the product less profitably as cigar filler or cigarette tobacco.

Microeconomic theory critiques oligopsony, because oligopsony—like monopsony—yields price distortion. It's not the price that would obtain in perfect competition. The critique is not that oligopsony *can* lead to such distortion. Rather, it is that such a distortion, given that market structure, *is* rational. The oligopsonist is being irrational if she does not distort the price in order to optimize her profit. Business people have used stronger, albeit less elegant, words about monopsonists. "Bully Buyers—How Driving Prices Lower Can Violate Antitrust Statutes" was a header in *The Wall Street Journal.* The article points out that, "As more of the world's markets become dominated by a few big companies, a rare form of antitrust abuse is raising new concern: corporations illegally drive down the price of their suppliers" (Wilke, 2001, p. A1). It gives anguished examples from Maine (pushing down prices for blueberry growers), South Carolina (depressing softwood prices), and Alabama and Pennsylvania (forcing down fees charged by doctors and hospitals).

Rationally, Wal-Mart flexes its oligopsony power against its suppliers. It's being irrational if it does not. So great is this power that it has reversed the traditional relationship between retailer and manufacturer. Wal-Mart dominates not only price but also the character of the product and the means of manufacture. Its Plus-One Policy specifies that its some 61,000 suppliers must guarantee either cost cuts or quality increases each succeeding year. Often Wal-Mart forces modernization and efficiencies (upside), and (downside) companies have reported being forced to relocate out of the country (PBS, 2004). It's rational if Wal-Mart functions as a de facto agent for globalization and for reducing manufacturing capabilities in the United States. It's rational if it's true that Wal-Mart increases sweat shop conditions. From its point of view, it's rational that its inspections of civil rights conditions in suppliers' factories, say in China, should be neither independent nor made public.

Rationally, Wal-Mart also uses its oligopsony power against its own labor. Wal-Mart indicates that the mean—not the median—wage for its associates is $9.68 per hour, and Greenwald (2005) and others report that this is lower than the national average for the retail industry. Contrary claims are offered in an "independent research effort" commissioned by Wal-Mart on itself (Global Insight, 2005). Other things being equal, Wal-Mart is being irrational if it does not depress these costs. It's also rational that Wal-Mart should be opposed to unionization (it is said to maintain a special union busting team in Bentonville, like a SWAT team), and it's rational to increase efficiency by locking in some night shift workers (Greenhouse, 2004, pp. 1, 24).

Rationally, a corporation is an externalizing machine, "like a shark is a killing machine." This biting analogy is offered in Bakan (2004). Better would have been an analogy such as "like a cyber-shark." That might make it clearer that a corporation—like Wal-Mart—is a *rational* externalizing machine. It's rational for an optimizer to shift costs to another person—or to the public. So, it's rational for, say, tobacco companies to resist the regulative ideal of perfect competition where all costs are internalized; it's rational to push on to others the costs for treatment of such diseases that cigarettes produce. Similarly, it's rational for Wal-Mart to contain costs by encouraging its associates to seek public assistance for health, housing and food. It's rational to externalize associates' health care costs, and it's rational if Wal-Mart Watch is right that 46 percent of children of Wal-Mart employees are uninsured or on Medicaid. Even more rational would be 100 percent.

Rationally, an oligopsony should aim over time to increase its oligopsony power. Wal-Mart has grown from one store in 1962 to more than 5,170 stores, now employing 1.7 million associates. I understand that 370 more stores are planned for the U.S. for 2006. Without knowing about the future of the rest of the economy, I don't know the future of Wal-Mart's oligopsony power. If that power does increase, I anticipate the intensification of effects implied by affirmative answers to the following four questions:

1. Is the claim true that Wal-Mart is a significant inflation fighter, for example, lowering retail wages by 8 percent (Rodino Associates, 2003)?
2. Is it true that local governments shell out too much in subsidies, in return for the destruction of main streets?
3. Is it true that Wal-Mart is shaping tastes in China—no small matter if and when China becomes "the" next economic superpower?
4. Is it true that there's a touch of the imperial—a shade almost of the Opium Wars—in the vision of 500 foreigners at Wal-Mart's buying headquarters in China telling Chinese what and how to manufacture? If so, increased oligopsony power—exercised with limited transparency—will intensify these features. It will also increase any tendency for countries to shop themselves out of jobs.

Among the factors which explain its oligopsony is Wal-Mart's prominence in Supply Chain Management, the matter of vertical integration! Wal-Mart can respond instantly to any purchase from a shelf—and impose its will on remote suppliers. Supply Chain management is described as the "combination of art and science that goes into improving the way your company finds the raw components it needs to make a product or service, manufactures that product or service and delivers it to customers" (Koch, 2005, p. 1). It is taught in business schools and in departments of supply chain management—including the Sam H. Walton College of Business at the University of Arkansas. It has a literature, professional associations (e.g., the Council of Supply Chain Management Professionals), and journals (e.g., *Journal of Supply Chain Management*, *Supply Chain Management Review*, and *Supply Chain Management: An International Journal*). My reading on this subject is limited, happily. But it's a topic that clearly has relevance to public, as well as private, agencies, for example, the military and Homeland Security. Such have been Wal-Mart's innovations in supply chain management that Global Insight (2005) claims that Wal-Mart's distribution and inventory control efficiencies "have generated an increase in the economy's total factor productivity" (p. 4). States Jeffrey Smith (2005), "In RFID, everybody talks about Wal-Mart and supply chain management" (p. 1). He explains that RFID is radio frequency identification, part of M2M (machine-to-machine communications). With this capability, oligopsonist Wal-Mart is described as a star player in changing from a push-pull to a pull-push economic arrangement.

## FRAMEWORK OF CONSCIOUSNESS OF THINGS

> . . .our shrink-wrapped and discounted future
> (Matt Bai)

Enter another fiefdom! Wal-Mart can be understood as an emanation of a societal mindset, as "understood" is typically described in Philosophy of Social Science.

As a first layer and as an interpretation confined to the economic, Wal-Mart can be characterized as an emanation of Bastard Economics. Bastard Economics can be filled out by reflecting on our accelerating consumer society and accelerating producer society. The term itself is inspired by the notion of Bastard Feudalism, whereby some historians distinguish a degeneration of the conditions in England in the later feudal period. Accelerating? Cheerleaders are an icon for the dynamic changes that are occurring in consumer and producer societies, and that is why I am adding the qualifier "accelerating." Apparently cheerleaders are being forced to do ever more high-flying acrobatics, and I read that more than half of the serious injuries in college athletics are inflicted on cheerleaders (Schultz et al., 2004). Consumerism and producerism, like cheerleading, seems to be accelerating.

Bastard Economics includes a way of living and a way of thinking. As a way of living, it should not be translated simply into such powerful (and static?) rhetoric as "living the American Dream" or "the business of America is business." The meanings of such phrases shift as history changes. For instance, living-the-American-Dream is different from what it was a century ago: see the sketch below of the accelerating consumer society. As a way of thinking, Bastard Economics should not be equated simply, although it overlaps significantly, with a view of economics that I (2005) earlier described as Frigginomics. The latter I called *happy, happy economics*, as contrasted with a traditional understanding of economics as the dismal science. I also used Perelman's (1996) description of an erotic attachment to perfectly competitive capitalism, equated with morality. Frigginomics was intended to refer to the academic study of economics. Warning label: None of these terms should be misinterpreted as bashing all forms of economics or markets.

I don't know which came first, the chicken or the egg. Later layers of the non-economic may change the picture, and much depends on whether one is a fan of meta-narratives (which I am not). My favorite for another layer is the imitation of the machine (e.g., see Farmer, 2005a). So I was pleased to read Lynne Truss (2005, p. 72) observe that "most big businesses and customer service systems these days are either modeling themselves on the internet or have learned far too much from a deep reading of Franz Kafka." She (2005) speaks of our present "age of social autism" (p. 36). I'll limit myself to the two economic tid-bits, a first layer—the accelerating consumer and producer societies.

## BASTARD ECONOMICS: CONSUMER SOCIETY

Mother's milk is now available through the market, I was surprised to learn. More and more aspects of exchange are now available through the market, and I can see that this changes consumer attitudes toward the items. Mother's milk is expensive compared to cow's milk, and it is sold as mother's milk even though it is homogenized (and, I am told, without the benefits available from the breast). Prolacta Bioscience indicates that it sells mother's milk to hospitals, the milk being donated. As reflected in the language, doesn't mother's milk have a "sacred" place in attitudes, for example, speaking of the milk of human kindness? I read that milk is a lunar symbol which is linked to the renewal of spring. I also notice that Hercules drank the milk of immortality from Hera's breast. Powerful symbolic stuff! But my guess is that will be soured by the inclusion of mother's milk in the market. I recall Richard Titmuss (1997) on the difference in "attitudes toward blood" between donating blood (as in England of yore, where blood giving was highly valued) and the selling of blood in the United States (where Titmuss said that it was less prized). I also read Candace Walsh's (2005) comment:

> It's strange to think that long years of tireless breastfeeding advocacy may have raised the public's awareness of the benefits of breast feeding just enough to make many want to literally buy into the concept without benefiting from the full spectrum of intimacy, bonding and optimal health that actual breastfeeding provides.

Here's some more of what Celia Lury (1996) lists as features of a consumer society. Clearly, there is a larger range and accelerating volume of type of consumer goods. Christmas exemplifies this for me, as I think of the miserable range of gifts that delighted me when I was tiny, of the larger range that my children expected, and of the mammoth range that my grandchildren receive. (Maybe I've missed the point: the joy of exchanging versus getting stuff.) A third feature is the expansion of shopping as a leisure activity. I do accept that many, although not I, invest long hours in the recreational "delights" of shopping. Lury lists other features, like increase in different forms of shopping; the wider availability of credit; the increase in sites for purchase and consumption; the growing importance of packaging; the pervasiveness of advertising; growing emphasis on style; and manipulation of time and space in promoting products.

The consumer culture is familiar through its massive "sociological" literature. So I read that "consumer culture is a particular form of material culture that has emerged in Euro-American societies during the second half of the twentieth century" (Lury, 1996, p. 1). I also learn that the consumer culture has socially constructed individuals; for instance, there's what can be called the possessive individual (e.g., Abercrombie, Hill, & Turner, 1986); and items purchased have both social lives and meanings.

I hereby incorporate by reference—as the lawyers say—insights available from postmodernism, critical theory, feminism, psychoanalysis, and others. After all, this column is a ditty, not a symphony. But, as an example, see how this account of the consumer society is transformed and enriched by (say) Jean Baudrillard. He describes the separation of signs and objects, where there is an eclipse of the real and humans enter a symbolic realm of their own construction. For him, postmodernism is concerned with the simulation of signs, rather than the modernist production of objects. "In order to become an object of consumption, the object must become a sign. . ." (Baudrillard, 1988, p. 25). As Baudrillard observes, we "are living the period of the objects: that is, we live by their rhythm, according to their incessant cycles" (Baudrillard, 1998a, p. 32). For him, we are never satisfied, and there is no possibility of resistance. Consumers lose their capacity for critical reflection, as they buy into what he calls the code of consumption. I agree that some critiques of mass culture have exaggerated its problems (e.g., Goldman, 2005). But these ideas and others help me to make more sense of what I observed in the Wal-Mart Superstore.

There is a sense in which the idea of a consumer society does fit in within the framework of economic theory, and this is the trade-off of leisure and additional consumption. Gross (1993) points out that we "seldom notice the irony in that productivity has led to increased consumption but not to the parallel growth of free time" (p. 2). Having said this, I imagine the idea of a recent consumer society to be odd in terms of mainstream economic theory—and perhaps also for some historians. It's elementary economics not to emphasize demand without supply, and vice-versa. The oddity is explicable in that economics and sociology occupy different fiefdoms—different scopes or perspectives. Economics is interested only in the fact of, but not the non-economic nature of, desires; it could be said that economics begins where desires (in the form of effective demand and effective supply) pop up. Absent some market abnormality (like oligopsony), hasn't the consumer in perfect competition always been king? For an example of historians, see Porter on heavy consumption in England long before our present Consumer Society. As Porter (1993) explains, "The creature comforts of cuisine and cellar loomed large in the Georgian pursuit of happiness" (p, 59). Beefsteak became the national emblem, and a three-bottle per-day fellow was a (gentle)manly man.

## BASTARD ECONOMICS: PRODUCER SOCIETY

The mind-set that leads to Wal-Mart could be called a producer, as well as a consumer, society. I agree that the mind-set is a kind of folie à deux, a sort of shared psychotic (dis)order that implicates both supply and demand. I agree that the distinction between a producer and a consumer is deconstructible. (For example, is Wal-Mart a producer or a consumer; if I buy scallops in order to cook Coquille St. Jacques, am I a producer or a consumer?) But, who's really in the driver's seat—producer or consumer? In these days of the manufacture of consent and the prevalence of advertising, surely the producer has at least an equal claim to be society's chauffeur? For evidence of the manufacture of consent, see the movie, *Manufacturing Consent: Noam Chomsky and the Media,* by Mark Achbar and Peter Wintonick (1992).

Contest: How should we qualify the producer part of the supply-demand context? Candidates surely include Pathological and Neo-Feudal.

**Pathological.** For evidence about the pathological nature of the modern corporation, turn to Bakan (2004) and *The Corporation*. Turn to the literature on this (e.g., Palast, 2003), and the many column inches in *The New York Times*. Again, I incorporate by reference the Frankfurt School of Critical Theory and also (shush!) K.M. If the modern corporation is pathological, why wouldn't Wal-Mart share this family resemblance?

Bakan's most original idea is that, as the corporation is pronounced by the legal system to be a person with rights that belong to a person (like free speech), the corporation should be evaluated as a person. The movie *The Corporation* identifies such corporate features as the following: reckless disregard for the safety of others, deceitfulness, incapacity to experience guilt, callow concern for the feelings of others, incapacity to maintain enduring relationships, and failure to conform to social norms with respect to legal behaviors. It then turns to the characterization of such a person in the DSM-IV (American Psychiatric Association Diagnostic and Statistical Manual of Mental Disorders). On the basis of this, it contends that the corporation should be classified as a psychopathic person.

I don't have the competence to decide whether the diagnosis is correct. But more than three (the DSM-IV standard) of the seven criteria for antisocial behavior are met. The corporation fits enough of the criteria for anti-social personality disorder (see Sadock & Sadock, 2003, p. 807). There does seem to be a pervasive pattern of disregard for and violation of the rights of others, for example. In my reading of Sadock & Sadock (2003, pp. 812, 818), however, I would favor narcissistic personality disorder. But this is a quibble, and apart from what seems to be the main point. As a person, the corporation is not family-like; the producer has pathological, or exploitative, features.

**Neo-Feudal.** In the car driving from the Superstore, I started to imagine Wal-Mart as a huge war-horse, a robotic Clydesdale on which Sir Sam Walton could emerge to do economic battle. On this picture, Sir Sam would be a knight. I equated knights with the creative entrepreneurs (creative destruction) that Joseph Schumpeter (1883-1950) admired. Sam Walton is such a creator, devoted like knights to the equivalent of a higher chivalric ideal—Bastard Economics in his case. After all, Walton has created a new template, his economic child—Wal-Mart. I notice too that the ideal of knighthood, described in the literature, degenerated. I read that some knights inclined to power (the Teutonic knights), some to delusions (Don Quixote), and others—like Walton—to wealth (the Templars). A critic could imagine Sam Walton as a mixture of all three, inclined to defend his own power, delusions and wealth. Well, clearly we no longer live in a feudal system, and so I imagined neo-feudalism, characterized by economic warfare, gold, and certainly significant autonomy. Neo-feudalism is a neologism. To give comfort, I should add that "feudalism" itself is a 17th century term, made popular by Montesquieu; and the term has been challenged by some historians.

By feudal, I mean the system that originated after 800 A.D. in the decline of the Carolingian empire. The dukes and counts were the great feudal landlords who protected and controlled their assigned regions. They existed in a golden web of allegiances, extending above to the royals and below to the lesser lords. For a description of the feudal system in action, see Norman Cantor (2004) on John of Gaunt (1340-1399)—Duke of Lancaster, plus sometime Duke of Aquitaine, plus grandfather of both England's Henry V and Portugal's Henry the Navigator. An important point that Cantor illustrates is that being a feudal lord had enormous management responsibilities in both the financial-legal and military respects.

For a picture of Sam Walton the economic warrior, the economic knight, see Walton's "autobiography." He was excited by his mission, as I understand it. See also Cantor's (2004) description (in chapter 5, entitled "Warriors") that captures the excitement that John of Gaunt, the real feudal duke, must have felt as he went on a slaughtering campaign, especially when with his older brother, the Black Prince.

A second feature of the neo-feudal involves gold. Cantor repeatedly compares the great feudal landlords to modern American billionaires. There is a back and forth in gold flows centering on the feudal lords, just as there is a back and forth of gold flows in the large contemporary bureaucracies. In these days of wire transfers, gold substitutes do obtain—and the benefits take different forms. By benefits, I am referring to campaign contributions, tax loop holes, contracts, and the "filling in" (by agencies and monied interest groups) of public policies that result from what is aptly called hollow legislation (again, see Palast, 2003).

A third feature of the feudal system is that the great landlords enjoyed substantial "freedom" from the direction, coordination and control of their royal overlords. Look at the internationalization (perhaps mini-globalization?) in Gaunt's land owning. Similarly, a feature of the modern private corporation is its relative "freedom" from its political master, from government as it is traditionally understood. A contemporary commonplace is that the power of the nation-state is declining in relation to the ascending power of private international corporations.

## EPILOGUE

Knight or night? Observing the Wal-Mart Superstore, during my pre-Christmas visit, led me to disturbing, fragmented, reactions. Maybe on another day, they would have been different. The Superstore seemed a long way from the emporia of Bergdoff-Goodman and Saks Fifth Avenue, where the phony illusion is that an expensive purchase can admit the buyer into the world of the wealthy and famous: the emporia cannot compete with the warehouse seediness, the grey, of Wal-Mart. It seemed a long way from ma and pa's corner outlet, where the phony illusion is the prospect of friendly recognition and familiar acceptance; a family ma and pa store cannot compete with the human indifference of Wal-Mart mass merchandising. I wondered if Wal-Mart is switching, substituting its own phony illusion for the phony illusions of the emporia, the ma and pa, and the others. The Wal-Mart Superstore makes naked the bottom line, and it celebrates being cheap. It invites me—as it were—to screw the system, while binding me to its system.

Clearly such impressions should be assessed by multiple frameworks—like the frameworks of things and the frameworks of consciousness of things. The more, the better! Assessments should incorporate, yet rise above, particular life experiences—like customer, store manager, shareholder, campaign contribution recipient, sweat shop worker, rich woman, beggar woman, and even mere observer. Judgments will differ between people whose values privilege either the aesthetic, the moral or the just plainly material. Conclusions will depend on the standard chosen. Compared against the Grand Canyon and Grand Opera, for instance, aesthetically Wal-Mart loses. Compared against the innovation of a Lord Sandwich, the invention of Wal-Mart has more traction. Compared against total cultural and economic impoverishment, Wal-Mart is enriching.

> Sir Lancelot. . . thou were never matched of earthly *knight's* hand
> (Thomas Malory).

> Damned for a certain time to walk the *night*
> (William Shakespeare)

## REFERENCES

Abercrombie, N., Hill, S., & Turner, B. (1986) *Sovereign individuals of capitalism*. London: Allen and Urwin.

Achbar, M., & Wintonick, P. (1992). *Manufacturing consent: Noam Chomsky and the media*. Ottawa: Zeitgeist.

Baudrillard, J. (1998). The system of objects. In M. Poster, *Jean Baudrillard: Selected writings* (pp. 13-21). Stanford, CA: Stanford University Press.

Baudrillard, J. (1998a). The consumers' society. In M. Poster, *Jean Baudrillard: Selected writings* (pp. 32-60). Stanford, CA: Stanford University Press.

Bakan, J. (2004). *The corporation: The pathological pursuit of profit and power*. New York: Free Press.

Cantor, N. F. (2004). *The last knight: The twilight of the middle ages and the birth of the modern era.* New York: HarperCollins.

Farmer, D. J. (2005) Frigginomics begins in kindergarten: The social construction of "normal" citizens and their dreams. *Administrative Theory & Praxis, 27,* 707-718.

Farmer, D. J. (2005a). *To kill the king: Post-traditional governance and bureaucracy.* Armonk, New York: M.E. Sharpe.

Global Insight (2005). *The economic impact of Wal-Mart.* Retrieved November 2, 2005 from www.globalinsight.com

Goldman, P. (2005). Consumer society and its discontents: The Truman Show and The Day of the Locust. *Anthropoetics, 10*(2). Retrieved December 18, 2005, from www.anthropoetics.ucla.edu/ap1002/truman.htm

Greenhouse, S. (2004, January 18). Workers assail night lock-ins by Wal-Mart. *New York Times,* p. 1.

Greenwald, R. (2005). *Wal-Mart: The high cost of low price.* New York: Brave New Films DVD. Retrieved December 26, 2005, from www.walmartmovie.com

Gross, G. (1993). *Time and money: The making of consumer culture.* New York: Routledge.

Habermas, J. (1989). *The structural transformation of the public sphere: An inquiry into a category of bourgeois society.* Cambridge, MA: MIT.

Koch, C. (2005). The ABCs of supply chain management. Framingham: CX Media. Retrieved December 24, 2005, from www.cio.com/research/scm/edit/012202_scm.html

Lichtenstein, N. (2006). Wal-Mart: Template for 21st century capitalism? In N. Lichtenstein (Ed.), *Wal-Mart: The face of twenty-first century capitalism.* New York: New Press.

Lury, C. (1996). *Consumer culture.* New Brunswick, NJ: Rutgers University Press.

Palast, G. (2003). *The best democracy money can buy: An investigative reporter exposes the truth about globalization, corporate cons, and high-finance fraudsters.* New York: Plume.

PBS. (2004). Is Wal-Mart good for America? *Public Broadcast Service Frontline.* Retrieved from www.pbs.org/wgbh/pages/frontline/shows/walmart/

Perelman, M. (1996). *The end of economics.* New York: Routledge.

Porter, R. (1993). Consumption: Disease of the consumer society? Pp. 58-81. In J. Brewer & R. Porter (Eds.), *Consumption and the world of goods* (pp. 58-81). New York: Routledge.

Rodino Associates. (2003). Final report on research for big box retail/superstore ordinance. Retrieved October 28, 2005, from www.lacity/council/cd13/houscommecdev/cd13housecommenscdev239629107_04262005.pdf

Schultz, M, Marshall, S. W., Yong, J., Mueller, N. L., Weaver, N. L., & Bowley, J. M. (2004). A prospective cohort of injury incidence and risk factors in North Carolina high school competitive cheerleaders. *American Journal of Sports Medicine, 32,* 396-405.

Sadock, B., & Sadock, V.A. (2003). *Kaplan and Sadock's synopsis of psychiatry: Behavioral sciences clinical psychiatry.* Baltimore, MD: Williams and Wilkins.

Smith, J. (2005). Devx news. Retrieved December 24, 2005, from www.devxnews.com/article.php/3456201

Titmuss, R. (1997). *The gift relationship: From human blood to social policy.* New York: The New Press.

Truss, L. (2005). *Talk to the hand: The utter bloody rudeness of the world today, or six good reasons to stay home and bolt the door.* New York: Penguin.

Walsh, C. (2005, November-December). Making money off mother's milk. *Mothering,* p. 21.

Wilke, J. R. (2004, January 27). Bully buyers—How driving prices lower can violate antitrust statutes. *The Wall Street Journal,* p. A1.

# CHANGE THE COURSE, NEURONS!

**David John Farmer**

How can PA (traditional public administration) get better at what it does badly—creating, out of the ordinary? Don't stay the course, neurons!

PA thinking, PA practice, and PA education need a 12-step program, parallel to Alcoholics Anonymous. Lack of extraordinary creativity is an addiction. Lack of extraordinary imagination (I'll use the terms interchangeably) is harmful to self and others. Individuals and organizations should turn to Uncreatives Anonymous, often known as Unimaginatives Anonymous. But I do suggest modifying the 12 steps.

"Hi, I'm David and I'm a PA uncreative!" "Hi, I'm the U.S. Department of Justice, and I'm. . . ." Participants in the various 12-step programs—for example, Alcoholics Anonymous, Narcotics Anonymous, Al-anon—begin by acknowledging that they "have a problem." "Hi, I'm traditional PA, and I have a problem."

**Step 1: I admit that I work in a subject (PA) that is powerless over uncreativity—that our lives have become unimaginative.**

It's against the grain for the 12-stepper's brain to recognize—let alone admit—that she has such a problem. A neuroscientific view is that we are emotional beings who think, rather than thinking beings who have emotions (e.g., LeDoux, 1996). Barring brain injury or malformation, a human non-emotional moment is a fiction. Also, note views about the brain's sensory systems being "narcissistic" (e.g., see Atkins, 1996), and about the brain being wired-to-lie in, for instance, the anterior cingulate gyrus (e.g., see Tancredi, 2005, pp. 119-121). This doesn't entail the unavailability of purely rational, purely objective, judgments. But it does encourage me, at least, to point a diverting and accusing finger at the other social science and action subjects.

It's hard to acknowledge that PA is powerless over uncreativity, say, in dealing with myths and in listening to the discourses of others. Speaking of the mythical, listen to President John F. Kennedy saying:

> For the great enemy of the truth is very often not the lie—deliberate, contrived, and dishonest—but the myth, persistent, persuasive, and unrealistic. Too often we hold fast to the clichés of our forebears. We subject all facts to a prefabricated set of interpretations.... Mythology distracts us everywhere—in government as in business, in politics as in economics. (Kennedy, 1962)

Perhaps uncreativity in overcoming myths is to be expected in a discipline which harbors the myth that PA started with a local hero, Woodrow Wilson. Speaking of uncreativity in listening to the discourses of others, consider the suppressed role of PA's "other"—employee, customer, client, mark. On this, there's the myth that bureaucratic management can be captured objectively in the PA jingle "direct, coordinate and control." How deaf (to its top-down bias and rhetoric) this sounds when compared with, say, Pierre-Joseph Proudhon's statement that "To be governed is to be watched over, inspected, spied on, directed, legislated at, regulated, docketed, indoctrinated, preached at, controlled, assessed, weighed, censored, ordered about, by men who have neither the right nor the knowledge nor the virtue" (see Joll, 1964, p. 78).

### Step 2: I should help PA to come to believe that powers greater than ourselves could restore us to sanity.

This is belief in the restorative power of extra-disciplinary perspectives, especially the unfamiliar. Shakespeare, Plato and Cajal, familiar and unfamiliar creatives! Familiar and unfamiliar disciplines, like poetry, philosophy and neuro-governmentality! Get familiar with the unfamiliar is what I'm continuing to suggest for PA. Rather than to the gods, I could think of this as appealing to a poor man's version of the Platonic Forms.

Traditional PA prides itself on being porous, that is, having boundaries that admit extra-disciplinary ideas. But, its porousness is limited beyond familiar blobs of fluid, beyond what is easily understood and unthreatening: among the evidence for this limitation is the need that was felt to establish a forum like PAT-Net. To change the analogy, PA's admission policy favors domesticated animals, ones that are well understood and guaranteed not to bite, sting, maim, gore, or even (on a bad day) kill. Uncreatives Anonymous recommends belief in harder-to-understand jungle animals. The example of a wild animal that I'll privilege here is neuro-governmentality, a neologism for neuroscience in application to the range of governance issues. But on another occasion, it might be a different unpredictable animal.

Give an example of how neuroscience can be relevant in understanding, for example, extraordinary creativity. Here's Andrew Modell (2003). For one thing, he claims that metaphors—at the center of the imaginative—are not merely figures of speech. They are neural features, the way that the brain yields meaning. Modell (2003, p. 9) emphasizes that "the construction of meaning is very different from the processing of information." He discusses how metaphor is the brain's primary mode of understanding and remembering the world. He writes of metaphor in corporeal imagination in terms of transferring between dissimilar domains, for example, between past and present, and—as in synesthesia—"hearing" colors and "seeing" sounds. For another thing, Modell (2003, pp. 40, 41) claims that "the metaphoric process (in a brain can be) foreclosed or frozen" by trauma. An example he gives is of a person who, having experienced a childhood trauma, experiences great stress as an adult when encountering a parallel kind of activity; in respect to this particular experience—as Modell puts it—"the distinction between past and present was obliterated." BTW, is it far-fetched to wonder if any parallel process occurred in PA? I'm referring to the trauma in PA's earlier years (and perhaps continuing), for example, its survival fears, its mocking by Political Science and its corresponding desperation to placate mid-level practitioners. Did that early experience foreclose or freeze any of the metaphoric process in traditional PA? That is, just as emotional abuse in critical periods in childhood can increase sensitivity to stress in later years, is imagination too stressful nowadays for PA?

### Step 3: We've made a decision to turn our will and our lives over to higher powers, as we understand (see step 2) said power.

What about a decision to do daily mental exercises, similar to the daily physical exercises that we hate to do? Neuroscientist Nancy Andreasen (2005, pp. 160-168) recommends a regimen of four daily mental exercises, parallel to pounding on a treadmill, to improve brain creativity—and to reduce the effects of aging. I'll note the four exercises in steps 4-7. That decision to do daily exercises is traumatic enough to merit the phrase "to turn our will over. . . ."

Remember, younger theorists, that senile decay starts when a brain is about twenty years old. (What's the score for action subjects, like PA?) And remember, older theorists, that brain plasticity is life-long. It's true that there are critical periods. For example, most of us know that the best time to learn languages is pre-teen. Use-it-or-lose-it is the brain's operating principle, even from the beginning. We are told that at seven months the typical child can hear sound differences in any language (she's a citizen of the world), and that at eleven months the typical child has lost this ability (she has lost her world citizenship). It is also true that brain functioning can be damaged (e.g., as in addiction, just noted, altering the level of neurotransmitters) and, again, partly "hard-wired." It's true that brain connections follow rules from the genes. For instance, I read that Cynthia Kenyon "has increased the life span of tiny worms called Caenorhabdites elegans up to six times normal by suppressing a single gene" (Duncan, 2005, pp. 57-58). Yet the brain is continually changing in response to cultural and other inputs until the moment of death. Even reading this paper, as you read, is changing the reader's physical brain. Like many other neuroscientists, Andreasen (2005, p. 146) points out we:

> Are literally remaking our brains—who we are and how we think, with all our actions, reactions, perceptions, postures, and positions—every minute of the day and every day of the week and month and year of our entire lives.

Andreasen's mental exercises are intended to improve extraordinary creativity, the sense of creativity intended also in this paper. Extraordinary creativity, oddly, is not correlated with high intelligence (Andreasen, 2005, p. 30). Yet it is exemplified at its highest levels (her examples) in Einstein and Michelangelo. Andreasen (2005) distinguishes two levels of creativity—ordinary creativity and extraordinary creativity. In this, she follows a pattern of creativity studies in neuroscience and elsewhere (e.g., see Camfield, 2005). To help with this distinction with reference to PA, consider the examples mentioned in step 1. Also consider the quantum difference in such terms as the contrast suggested in Thomas Kuhn (1970). That difference is between (a) the ordinary creativity required for puzzle solving (capable of problem solving within an orthodox framework) or its equivalent, and (b) the extraordinary creativity required for paradigm shifting (capable of revolutionary science or preparadigm changing) or its equivalent.

BTW, physical exercise—the treadmill—is not to be denigrated. Neuroscientists assure that physical exercise helps neurons grow and slows down the brain's slowing up.

### Step 4: Adapt the first of Andreasen's mental exercises.

The first of the four mental exercises that Andreasen recommends is that adults should spend some time each day exploring an unfamiliar area of knowledge. Learn a new field, like neuroscience or (like Michelangelo) anatomy. Andreasen insists that we should do this in depth and with passion.

More PA educational curricula could adapt this mental exercise by having students reflect on PA thinking and practice from a selected second perspective. Like many others, in my PA Theory teaching I ask students to write about PA from a selected second perspective, like the postmodern, economic, critical theory, feminist, or psychoanalytic, etc. For instance, the study of feminism provides ideas on oppression and can generate insights into oppressive practices in PA.

For example, take evolutionary psychology—a combination of evolutionary biology and cognitive psychology (as described in Pinker, 1997, and as summarized in Evans & Zarate, 2005). First, a leading view in evolutionary biology is that the brain/mind consists of many specific-purpose modules, rather than a general purpose problem solving program. These programs, having evolved by natural selection, are designed to solve a particular adaptive problem in a particular context. Examples are the problems of avoiding predators, eating the right food, forming alliances, helping children and other relatives, reading other people's minds, selecting mates (Evans & Zarate, 2005, pp. 48-49). Second, another leading view is that these mind modules were developed 100,000 or more years ago when the context was different (e.g., group size was smaller)—on the African savannah, where our adapting ancestors lived. These modules implicate multiple neural pathways. Consider two neural pathways for fear alarums (see LeDoux, 1998) to avoid, for example, stepping on a poisonous snake. On seeing the object, the emotional stimulus arrives at the brain's thalamus. One pathway leads from the thalamus to the amygdala, and the body freezes with fear at the sight of the object which might be either a snake or a stick. Another pathway leads milliseconds later through the sensory cortex to awareness; and, deciding that it's just a stick, I can unfreeze. The last example has relevance to stereotyping, a topic much discussed in social neuroscience (e.g., Ito, Urland, Willardsen-Jense, & Correll, 2006). (Here's a lesser example, among many! The insistence on balance in organization charts continues to intrigue. Is it related in part to an unconscious brain preference in selecting mates? Evolutionary biologists describe a preference for body symmetry as an indicator of good genes.) But, Jaysus, the entire story of evolutionary biology points toward the evolution of bureaucracy—out-of-date ancestral context, spandrels, and all!

As another example of adapting the mental exercise, contribute to the creation of neuro-governmentality. (Neuro-governmentality incorporates a word from Michel Foucault, and—as suggested in step 2—it denotes neuroscience applied to the full range of governance issues, e.g. public, private, self, etc.) The claims for the potential of neuroscience are large. Restak (2006), for instance, claims that understanding of the human brain is changing our understanding of ourselves and of our inter-relationships so dramatically that by mid-century we will see the emergence of what he calls "a neurosociety."

### Step 5: Adapt the second of Andreasen's mental exercises.

Andreasen advises spending some time each day practicing meditation or just thinking. Apparently, meditation—as, say, in Tibetan Buddhism—has a beneficial effect on gamma synchrony (such gamma waves being high frequency oscillations in the brain). The effect is greatest in the frontal, temporal and parietal regions. Andreasen herself prefers to let her brain focus on any object and wander where it wants.

Like the Ten Commandments and A.A.'s 12-steps, such lists as Andreasen's contain overlaps. Unlike the Ten Commandments, Andreasen's list is not written in stone. Some would prefer an adaptation, for example, adding writing. (A pet peeve: shouldn't agencies upgrade the low-level of "just thinking" often endured in bureaucratic "retreats?")

### Step 6: Adapt the third of Andreasen's mental exercises.

Practice observing or describing, advises Andreasen. She recommends exercising the emotional and intuitive parts of the brain by observing details intently, typically starting with gestalt and then doing so analytically.

Perhaps it's the treadmill effect (the boredom that engulfs me when pounding on the treadmill, sans TV)! For ten minutes, I've tried observing intently a certificate on my office wall. I did notice fresh-to-me features (e.g., the colors, each of the Latin words, etc). But the boredom was too much; I will not do it again. But then it occurs to me that, like others, I do something similar with abstract objects—and concrete situations. An adaptation here is to amble through the library, pick a topic to read about (on the basis of whim), and then ponder. But rarely does it end in a single session. For example, recently I picked out a couple of library books on "ineffability." One book said that there are five different kinds of ineffability (Kukla, 2005, pp. 135-157): food for exercise in distinguishing more, or less, kinds. Andreasen might object that this adaptation is a kind of dabbling, although she would recognize that we all have our favorite library areas. The reader might object that she may prefer reflective reading—a complex neurological process, implicating multiple brain regions—of a novel or an administrative history.

### Step 7: Adapt the fourth of Andreasen's mental exercises.

Practice imagining, Andreasen advises. She recommends getting outside yourself. If you are like Einstein, you can imagine riding on a photon; if you like cars, you imagine yourself being a carburetor. If you like neuroscience, you can imagine that you are a single neuron among the 100 billion neurons in a typical human brain (Swanson, 2003, p. 2).

This practice can be adapted, providing relevance to PA. Again, use imagination to transcend one's own myths and one's own deafness to the discourse of others. For example, take a practical problem, like imagining why children of immigrants into the United Kingdom possibly can choose to commit "terrorist" acts—in view of the myth that all immigrants immigrate for a better life and in view of our discourse that they should be happy in their "better" lives. Aren't such myths also believed in the U.S. about U.S. immigrants? Bruce Wexler surprised me (surprised, because, if I had those feelings, I repressed them) by saying that the homesickness could be so strong that the "adjustment is fundamentally similar to recovery from bereavement" (Wexler, 2006, p. 183). Giving point to this, Wexler quotes O'Henry's *Cabbages and Kings*: "In all the scorched and exotic places of the earth, Caucasians meet when the day's work is done to preserve the fullness of their heritage by the aspersion of alien things" (p. 183). Practice creativity by imagining how this can be the case.

For more on the practical relevance of imagining other discourses, recall ex-Chief Judge of the New York State Court of Appeals Sol Wachtler describing his life in prison. "I have learned by being commanded to strip, bend, spread, lift and do a sort of naked and public pirouette that is beyond embarrassment" (Wachtler, 1997, p. 71). The judge had been sentenced in 1993 to 15 months in connection with the harassment of an ex-lover. I write with appropriate respect for ex-Judge Wachtler. But, shouldn't judges be able to imagine the degradation of prison life *before* sentencing others and *before* being sentenced themselves? Shouldn't they imagine the discourse of the other?

Imagining the discourses of others is not solely a "poetic" activity. So Modell (2003, p. 171) writes that, "Imagining other minds is the work of novelists, but only recently has the capacity to imagine other minds been viewed as an appropriate object of scientific investigation." He explains that imagining other minds—called "theory of mind" in cognitive science—received its impetus from "the comparative psychology of primates and observations of autistic children."

### Step 8: Recognize that extraordinary creativity is not the only thing; but it's central.

This recognition isn't in the spirit of the 12-step program, although also it's unlikely that sobriety is the "only" priority even for an alcoholic. Yet, it is good to re-emphasize that, although the unimaginative is as unhelpful to PA as booze is to an alcoholic, extraordinary creativity is not the only thing. PA also needs other features, for example, reliability, ordinary creativity, etc.

### Step 9: Accept personal moral responsibility for uncreativity.

I think that the Alcoholics Anonymous (A.A.) 12-steppers are right in *their* steps 4-11 to emphasize personal morality (like accepting responsibility and making amends), even if my and your own preference is for a different approach to personal morality. When A.A. was established in 1935, Carl Jung added input in favor of a conversion experience in order for 12-steppers to "contain" the addiction. Shouldn't Uncreatives Anonymous seek moral conversion for the addicts of uncreativity?

### Step 10: Make amends (re: personal moral responsibility - step 9) by keeping away from thinkers promoting uncreativity.

How can I be morally converted—or even serious—about making amends if I am unwilling to steer clear of thinkers (and conferences) that foster uncreativity? How can a monk be serious if he wanders the red light district?

Protect yourself against your mirror neurons! The mirror neuron mechanism is central in learning by imitation. Largely through this mechanism, the brain learns by observing how others behave morally in different situations; for example, it learns whether it's the norm to be uncreative, unimaginative, etc. Laurence Tancredi (2005, p. 40) explains that "These (mirror) neurons in humans involve a network which is formed by the temporal, occipital, and parietal visual areas, as well as two additional cortical regions that are predominantly motor. . . ." Imagine a PA thinker exposing herself to other thinkers who excel in uncreativity, and recall that "red light district" is a metaphor for these uncreatives. In PA such uncreatives insist that imagination—connecting the dots, as it's sometimes misdescribed—should be limited to what is immediately and easily implementable in the current paradigm; everything else is flakey. "The mirror neuron system, among other functions, is pivotal to the representation of sequential information, and to imitation" (Tancredi, 2005, p. 40). What I'm suggesting is that, with repeated exposure to uncreatives, the norm of uncreativity becomes increasingly hardwired in the red light stepper's brain.

### Steps 11: Re-check that thou knowest thyself.

Know yourself, you and the subject that you chose (PA).

I doubt that many psychotherapists have heard the presenting problem "Hello, I'm X, and I'm an uncreative." Yet it's reported that talk therapy does change synaptic connections.

"There are more things in heaven and earth, Horatio, than are dreamt of . . ." (Shakespeare, *Hamlet* I, v, p. 166). Let's dig down to combat any illusion-of-truth effect—a term, we are told, used by psychologists. Most of us forget the context within which we first came to believe that imagining is a substitute for action (for *movement*), that unimagination is OK for PA as an action subject. This might make us highly suggestible against the utility of imagination. As Richard Restak explains, "In an attempt to compensate for this loss of context, the brain unconsciously assumes that familiar information is true information. . . . 'I've heard that before, so there must be something to it'" (Restak, 2006, p. 77). Note the place of movement in the neurological contribution to the construction of the self. (Don't you suppose that the neurological component, even though not determinative, is an unconscious contributing factor? For instance, in considering my image of my body, I would hope to be helped by reading about the neural substrate of my image of my body, e.g., in Goldenberg, 2005.) On the construction of the self, Patricia Churchland (2002, p. 70) reminds us that:

> The key to figuring out how a brain builds representations of "me" lies in the fact that, first and foremost, animals are in the *moving* business; they feed, flee, fight, and reproduce by moving their body parts in accord with bodily needs. This *modus vivendi* is strikingly different from plants, which take life as it comes.

Know PA as it should know itself. Just as a human is given an identity story (e.g., as a person who is all movement or who has problem X), isn't PA given an identity? Doesn't that choice for PA accommodate the neural patterns and other elements that contribute to our own sense of identity, of self? As we all know, identity crisis is an ongoing chestnut within PA (see Farmer, 2007, pp. 1206-1208).

Those aching for the thirteenth step may seek changes in PA education and practice. As an appetizer for changing the curriculum, a few faculty might even want to base Master's-degree reforms on these 12-steps (12 courses x 3 credits = 36 credits), or plan to return to school themselves in a fresh subject. As an appetizer for PA practice, I notice Andreasen's claim (2005, p. 30) that the personality "traits that define the creative individual include openness to experience, adventuresomeness, rebelliousness, individualism, sensitivity, playfulness, persistence, curiosity. . . ." Are these features emphasized in human resources hiring practices? Look at most job descriptions. When a manager, certainly I never knowingly hired anyone who was (say) rebellious! But Uncreatives Anonymous warns against premature organizational or programmatic ejaculation as a sort of cover for avoiding profound personal change.

**Step 12: "Having had a spiritual awakening as the result of these steps, we tried to carry this message to" uncreatives, "and to practice these principles in all our affairs."**

And re-imagine all such 12-steps, with illustrations not from neuro-governmentality but from the more familiar. For example, try Cultural Studies.

And the message should be, "Change the course, neurons!"

## REFERENCES

Atkins, K. (1996). Of sensory systems and the "aboutness" of mental states. *Journal of Philosophy, 93,* 337-372.

Andreasen, N. C. (2005). *The creating brain: The neuroscience of genius.* New York: Dana.

Camfield, D. (2005). Neurobiology of creativity. In C. Stough (Ed.), *Neurobiology of exceptionality* (pp. 53-72). New York: Kluwer Academic.

Churchland, P. S. (2002). *Brain-wise: Studies in neurophilosophy.* Cambridge, MA: MIT.

Duncan, D. E. (2005). *The geneticist who played hoops with my DNA . . . and other masterminds from the frontiers of biotech.* New York: HarperCollins.

Evans, D., & Zarate, O. (2005). *Introducing evolutionary psychology.* Cambridge, England: Icon.

Farmer, D. J. (2007). Five great issues in the profession of public administration. In J. Rabin, W. B. Hildreth, & G. J. Miller (Eds.), *Handbook of public administration* (3rd ed., pp. 1205-1219). New York: Taylor and Francis.

Goldenberg, G. (2005). Body image and the self. In T. E. Feinberg & J. P. Keenan (Eds.), *The lost self: Pathologies of the brain and identity* (pp. 81-99). New York: Oxford University Press.

Ito, T. A., Urland, G. R., Willardsen-Jensen, E., & Correll, J. (2006). The social neuroscience of stereotyping and prejudice: Using event-related brain potentials to study social perception. In J. T. Cacioppa, P. S. Visser, & C. L. Pickett (Eds.), *Social neuroscience: People thinking about thinking people* (pp. 189-208). Cambridge, MA: MIT.

Joll, J. (1964). *The anarchists*. London: Eyre and Spottiswoodes.

Kennedy, J. F. (1962, June 11). Commencement address at Yale University. Retrieved December 11, 2006, from www.jfklibrary.org/Historical+Resources/Archives/Referencedesk/ Speeches/JFK/003POF03YYale06111962.htm

Kukla, A. (2005). *Ineffability and philosophy*. New York: Routledge.

Kuhn, T. (1970). *The structure of scientific revolutions* (2nd ed.). Chicago: University of Chicago Press.

LeDoux J. (1996). *The emotional brain: The mysterious underpinnings of emotional life*. New York: Simon and Schuster.

Modell, A. H. (2003). *Imagination and the meaningful brain*. Cambridge, MA: MIT.

Pinker, S. (1997). *How the mind works*. New York: Norton.

Restak, R. (2006). *The naked brain: How the emerging neurosociety is changing how we live, work, and love*. New York: Harmon Books.

Swanson, L. W. (2003). *Brain architecture: Understanding the basic plan*. New York: Oxford University Press.

Tancredi, L. (2005). *Hardwired behavior: What neuroscience reveals about morality*. New York: Cambridge University Press.

Wachtler, S. (1997). *After the madness: A judge's own prison memoir*. New York: Random House.

Wexler, B. E. (2006). *Brain and culture*. Cambridge, MA: MIT.

# THE SPIRIT OF OUR AGE:
# PA-THINK AS UNCOVERING

### David John Farmer

PA-think has been inefficient, but not idle, in uncovering false assumptions in its own thinking. One such false assumption is that, with impunity, PA-think can avoid analyzing the spirit of our age. This PA (public administration) shortcoming in unveiling its own limitations makes governance not only more inefficient than it should be, but also makes it more vicious than we deserve. But it is an inefficiency shared by other social science and action subjects.

Let Martin Heidegger be an inspiration, if you like, in his description of truth as an uncovering, as unveiling! Truth or aletheia, for him, is disclosedness. Let us try to uncover false assumptions, without being obligated to produce a one-minute recipe for the elimination of said assumptions.

A first false assumption—the main discussion in this column—is that PA-think needn't recognize the spirit of our age, illustrated below by claiming that PA should not avoid engaging the delusional mentality that is discussed by James Carroll (2006). A second false assumption is that PA-think can stick with business as usual, and this is illustrated here by pointing to the claim in Nisbett (2005) that social science thinking will be transformed by the increasing influence of East Asians. Illustrating that it's not just PA-think that nourishes false assumptions, the third false assumption—appealing below to Amartya Sen (2005)—is that democracy is simply a Western gift.

## FALSE ASSUMPTION: PA NEEDN'T RECOGNIZE THE SPIRIT OF OUR AGE

Turn to Carroll's exciting work of Micro PA (Carroll, 2006), even though the author surely would be astonished to learn that he has written in that field—and even more surprised to learn that he has made a contribution to Micro PA. In an homage to his father Lieutenant-General Joseph Carroll, James Carroll describes the more than 60-year history of the Pentagon Building, and he tells the story—as he should—in the context of the rise of American world power and of the development of nuclear destructive capability.

Carroll describes what he considers to have been the unconscious momentum that shaped not only the history of the Department of Defense but also public attitudes and government in the United States. The momentum remains a component of the dominant mind-set (or set of mentalities) in society. This doesn't mean that *all* individuals in a society are equally infected by that mentality, and it doesn't mean that other motives don't operate, for example, to do a good job, to be decent. But, for Carroll, it is the driving dynamic, co-shaping thinking and action. There are positive components in society's mentality, for example, ingenuity, energy, and competitiveness. But Carroll wants to alert his readers to the negative features that he considers more important. I'm not in a position to say whether all his interpretations are correct. I'm not concerned whether his "metanarrative" could be bettered by, say, a Freud or an Althusser, and that I don't know whether Carroll's story contains all relevant elements, for example, the changing consciousness, the flickering "reality" of rhetoric, etc. My claim is merely that PA-think is being inefficient if it assumes that such a negative dynamic is irrelevant.

A stunning political claim: Carroll claims that, with the establishment of the Pentagon, the center of power in the United States shifted to the other side of the Potomac River. For example, he analyzes how the Building came to "symbolize, and to promote, a massive bureaucratic power center broken loose from the checks and balances of the government across the river. . .and apparently broken loose from the constraints of human will" (Carroll, 2006, p. 27). Starting with the devastating bombing of cities in World War II, he describes how the marriage of traditional martial destructiveness and unlimited technological capacity set in train a virtually unstoppable momentum. Of course, this is not totally new information. He can quote Defense Secretary William Cohen as comparing the Building with Moby Dick, for instance, with Cohen casting himself as Ahab strapped (at least in the movie) to the back of the whale. Many have discussed the perils of nuclear weaponry, for example, Helen Caldicott (2002) has much to say of importance to PA. Carroll speaks of the shift in the meaning of "military objectives" from an insistence on military targeting to include "any living thing that moves" (Carroll, p, 99). As Carroll explains, what "the population of the Pentagon had in common was not the warrior's ethos but the functionary's" (p. 29). I can relate to this, as I recall my experience in the headquarters of the NYPD; we lived within the tunnel view of a poor man's Vatican, where ranking police officers—like bishops—were a dime a dozen. Let's emphasize that what Carroll is claiming is that political power in the United States has shifted—essentially—to the Pentagon. Against all this, PA-think has abandoned professional interest in things military, although the lure of grant monies attracts university programs to homeland security. PA-think has abandoned the advice of, say, Luther Gulick. Previously, I have quoted Gulick as saying that "Students of administration do not need to be concerned about the 'next war'—the military planners will take care of that—but they do need to be concerned with extracting from recent experience its rich harvest for the immediate management problems of a chaotic world" (Gulick, 1948, p. viii).

The momentum that Carroll describes is made up of a variety of components. I'll mention three, the last of which underscores an important reason for PA's attention. First, there is the "self-fulfilling paranoia" that he describes throughout his book and especially in Chapter 4. It is a mindset that expects:

> The worst from enemies—and the rest of the world as well. The "paranoid style," when adopted by the defense intellectuals, was not only justified but made to seem the height of rationality, able to be articulated even by the formulas of hard science. (p. 213)

Carroll is using the term "paranoia" in a usual sense, indicating a "psychiatric disorder involving systematized delusion, usually of persecution" (p. 137). A delusion is defined in *Kaplan and Sadock's Synopsis of Psychiatry* (Sadock & Sadock, 2003, p. 283) as "a false belief, based on incorrect inference, about external reality, not consistent with patient's intelligence and cultural background"; I specially note Kaplan and Sadock's additional sentence that a delusion "cannot be corrected by reasoning." In terms of international relations, it is the kind of dynamic that can make it difficult to distinguish between the normal pushiness of large countries (or communities) and any desire of that "other" country (or community) to destroy us. It is paranoia that can make us blind to the effects of our own actions in shaping the actions of others (Carroll gives Soviet actions as his example), and that can prevent us from accurate interpretation of intelligence (Carroll illustrates with the West's failure to understand the political significance of Stalin's death). To give a more recent example, Stephen Cohen (2006), in his "The New American Cold War," points to conditions in Russia as constituting what he considers the gravest threat to American security, and he comments that "The dangerous fallacies underlying US policy are expressions of an unbridled triumphalism, treating Russia as a defeated nation" (p. 16). On the domestic front, the attitude can be illustrated by the passage in ten US states of legislation making it easier to use deadly force in self-defense. "Supporters have dubbed the new measures 'stand your ground' laws, while critics offered nicknames like the 'shoot first,' 'shoot the Avon lady' or 'right to commit murder' laws" (Tanner, 2006). Carroll can describe how, oddly, the first Secretary of Defense James Forrestall is said to have yelled "The Russians are coming" a few days before throwing himself to his death from the fourteenth floor of the Bethesda Naval Hospital, where he was apparently suffering from a private problem of paranoia.

Second, Carroll describes the momentum as privileging revenge, for example, discussing the revenge implications of Pearl Harbor. The momentum also includes nuclear amnesia (Carroll, 2006, p. 212); and on occasion the military establishment has been eager to launch a nuclear strike. Impulses like revenge can be complex, as perhaps Shakespeare's revenge play *Hamlet* is telling us. Exclaims Hamlet, "What a piece of work is a man, how noble in reason, how infinite in faculties, in form and moving how express and admirable, in action how like an angel, in apprehension how like a god . . . " (*Hamlet*, II.ii.). Harold Bloom (2003, p. 87) describes this utterance by Hamlet as coming closest to being "a central statement." Yet the play ends with the stage piled with corpses, from both sides.

Third, there's a twin dynamic. As Carroll (2006, p. 138) puts it, "fear of an enemy outside is accompanied by fear of an enemy inside." He traces this back to 1789, with the Alien and Sedition Acts. For that matter, recall the history of the un-American activities investigations! The point is that the delusional spirit of militarism and paranoid revenge is not a mere "military" thing. The existence of the mindset has an impact on non-military bureaucracies like such inhumanity as is in correctional systems, such callousness as is in the immigration service, and what Carroll calls the militarization of the State Department. To make this clearer, "They deserve it" is the title of one article, with the subtitle "Male prison rape is still not taken seriously, despite the huge number of victims" (Bell, 2006, p. 18). PA-think should pursue other possibilities, for example, determining whether this mentality—through its delusional component—infects, for instance, the internal revenue and welfare services.

Edmund Hillary, the first to climb the mountain, this year criticized 40 Everest climbers who continued to the summit without offering assistance to another climber dying of oxygen deficiency. He said that

"Human life is far more important than just getting to the top of the mountain" (McMorran, 2006). To apply this image to Carroll's case, there are two opposing misinterpretations. The first—Scylla, if you like—is to misinterpret Carroll as saying that the United States "will" let the climber die, and "will" also blow up the mountain. Rather, he hopes that the negative components can be adjusted. (Is talk about such a mindset anti-American, speaking of features like paranoia and revenge? Of course not! It's a tad paranoid even to think that it could be. Carroll is writing in honor of his military father, first head of the Defense Intelligence Agency.) The second misinterpretation—Charybdis, if you like—is to downplay the dynamic importance of the negative components. It is not easy to excise the negative components, and the mountain's chances depend on the excision. Carroll is saying that (borrowing Jung's phrase) the destructive spirit of Wotan is abroad, and that spirit takes institutional form.

The negative momentum, described by Carroll, deserves attention for PA-think interested in grasping the spirit of the times. Carroll's interpretation raises unpleasant "facts" about which many are happy to have amnesia, for example, the effects of the accumulation of nuclear weaponry. Yet, I disagree with Carroll on lesser points. Three small examples! First, Carroll does not emphasize the momentum in terms of growing nationalism, which Lukacs says is difficult to separate from patriotism. "Patriotism is defensive; nationalism is aggressive" (Lukacs, 2005, p. 36). Second, Carroll does point to antecedent incidents of revenge, giving the example of the revenge of starting Arlington Cemetery in General Lee's garden. Arguably, he should have made more of the pre-Pentagon violence that has reportedly been a factor in national history since the not-so-gentle Puritans first landed (see Philbrick, 2006), for example, the violence reflected in high crime rates, gun ownership, the slaughter of Native Americans, and the scar of slavery. Third, there is the economic. Carroll does recognize the effect of the momentum on the economic system. He makes the claim that "Because of Red Scare activities, Americans would accept the maturing of an economic system that, in its effects if not its structure, condemned most of the world to crushing impoverishment" (Carroll, 2006, p. 214). But he could have made more of the role of the economic in nourishing the momentum, when segments of the economy have become so dependent on defense juice.

PA should not buy a helmet and go military; that is not my point about the false assumption. Rather, PA should be open to the totality of the government (and governance) range—including the military—so that it can gain better understanding of the dominant mind-set of our society and of our age. This claim is open to the objection that choice of motivating factors like revenge is a political or policy matter, and that Micro PA limits itself to the efficiency of pursuing the particular policy motivation: enter the politics-administration dichotomy. Sorry, the objection seems to me without force. PA-think should not stick with the motivation of mere efficiency; for one thing, it isn't efficient. PA-think should be alert to the positives—and the negatives—of the spirit of our age.

## FALSE ASSUMPTION: PA CAN STICK WITH BUSINESS AS USUAL

"I firmly believe that the entry of East Asians into the social sciences is going to transform how we think about human thought and behavior across the board" (Nisbett, 2006, p. 226). Relevant to PA's false assumptions, this is a striking sentence.

Yes, there are other false assumptions in PA-think. I've often mentioned some, for example, the insistence in PA-think on embracing the micro and the short-run, on avoiding love as a motivation, and on swallowing—hook, line and sinker—the invisible hand's simple equation of private advantage and public interest. I don't want to repeat. However, I reiterate that it's false that PA-think can stick with business as usual.

On business as unusual, there is the false assumption that the Western "mentality" is the *only* way of thinking and acting about PA, that is, that PA-think should stop at the water's edge of Western mentality (or mentalities). Differences have been claimed between Asian and Westerner by writers like psychologist Richard Nisbett (2005) and he does not intend to stereotype entire continents or to deny individual variations. Nisbett depicts and analyzes contrasting orientations, as self-reinforcing homeostatic systems, between Asian (whom he defines, rightly or wrongly, as peoples influenced by China) and Western thinking. My interest is in illustrating that it is false to claim that the habits of mind with which PA is familiar are the only ones available. I'm not concerned whether each of Nisbett's particular contrasts are correct, although others have offered some identical contrasts (e.g., Graham, 1992, on the attitudes toward the law of non-contradiction). I'll pick out only a sample of Nisbett's other examples. The mentality dominant in the West, as opposed to the Asian, classes objects in terms of attributes, rather than resonance; it sees the world as a collection of diverse objects (after Aristotle), rather than substances. Paralleling such differences, one of the chapter titles in Nisbett (2005, pp. 137-163) asks "Is the world made up of nouns or verbs?" Nisbett's view is that the Western mentality views societies as aggregates of individuals, while there is no word for "individualism" in Chinese. [He adds that the "closest one can come is 'selfishness'" (Nisbett, 2005, p. 51)]. The Western mindset concerns itself more with the control of others and the environment, rather than self control.

## FALSE ASSUMPTION: DEMOCRACY IS SIMPLY A WESTERN GIFT

Don't all the mainstream social sciences and action subjects include false assumptions, no less than PA-think? I'll suggest an example from Political Science. To be fair, I should then point to yet other disciplines with such assumptions, for example, economics, history and philosophy.

Political science as-it-is—rather than as it is *ideally*—tends to attract false assumptions. One such assumption may be the genealogy of democracy, falsely seen as simply a Western gift. Amartya Sen (2005, pp. 13-14) notes in his *The Argumentative Indian*,

> Even though it is very often repeated that democracy is a quintessentially Western idea and practice, that view is extremely limited because of its neglect of the intimate connections between public reasoning and the development of democracy. . . . Balloting can be seen as only one of the ways—albeit a very important way—to make public discussions effective, when the opportunity to vote is combined with the opportunity to speak and listen, without fear.

He shows that "traditions of public discussion exist across the world, not just in the West" (Sen, 2005, p.13).

He gives illustrations from the histories of parts of Asia, Africa and Europe (Sen, 2003). In a recent class, an African doctoral student repeatedly made a similar claim about the prevalence of "palaver" throughout Africa. (I notice the ethnocentric definition of palaver in the Oxford English Dictionary as "a talk, a conference, a parley, especially between African tribes' people and traders or travelers." It also offers some unflattering descriptions, like "unnecessary, profuse, or idle talk.") Sunil Khilnani (1999, p. 59) analyzes how democracy is "today at the very center of the Indian political imagination." On the other hand and still excluding the one billion Indians, Nisbett claims that "the whole rhetoric of argumentation that is second nature to Westerners is largely absent in Asia" (Nisbett, 2005, p.73). Yet, I notice the scare word "largely" and I recall that argumentation can take various forms. Also, notice Nisbett's later comment that "we all function in some respects more like Easterners some of the time and more like Westerners some of the time" (Nisbett, 2005, p. 229).

Now let's implicate the other subjects in the false assumptions charge. First, a glancing blow to Economics! I was going to ask whether social science subjects don't "rest securely" on false assumptions, because economics is at home with elegant theory that lives within the limits of the model, limits like the assumption of the rational actor. Second on history, surely it is uncontroversial that many histories are written from within a narrow nationalist perspective. If Howard Zinn (2003) is right, to continue with the American case, much of the history being imposed in school on my grandchildren is "all that's fit to print." Yet it is galling to read the asymmetric treatment of, say, the Cold War in a distinguished historian's work. See John Lewis Gaddis' (2005) new history about his specialty, the Cold War. All the American leaders are treated with respect—no adverse adjectives. All the Communist leaders are treated to adverse adjectives. Third on philosophy, philosophy is sometimes described as wild in having no foundational assumptions, except the assumption that it has no foundational assumptions. Yet it is not true that schools of philosophy have no foundational assumptions. Witness the analytical philosophers; the distinguished thinker A. J. Ayer, for instance, regarded Continental philosophers like Jacques Derrida as non-philosophers. Then, of course, there is Eastern philosophy. Nisbett (2005, p. 188) claims that "Eastern lack of concern about contradiction and emphasis on the Middle Way undoubtedly does result in logical errors, but Western contradiction phobia can also produce logical errors."

## EPILOGUE

My first claim is that it is a false assumption that PA-think needn't recognize the spirit of our age, and this was illustrated by discussing the delusional mentality that is described by James Carroll (2006). The second is that it is false that PA-think can stick with business as usual, and this appealed to Nisbett (2005) on what he describes as East-West differences. The third claim is that other social sciences also nourish false assumptions; the example here was political science, appealing to Amartya Sen (2005) on the belief that democracy is simply a Western gift.

PA-think should focus on uncovering its false assumptions, even if the unveiling is unpleasant. It should do so even if the other disciplines don't. But this will require some courage, as there is a tendency for PA-think to defer to functionaries.

"The Pentagonania syndrome affected individuals, but it also affected institutions" (Carroll, 2006, p. 178).

## REFERENCES

Bell, D. (2006). They deserve it. *The Nation, 283*(2): 18-24.

Bloom, H. (2003). *Hamlet: Poem unlimited.* New York: Penguin Putnam.

Caldicott, H. 2002. *The new nuclear danger: George W. Bush's military-industrial complex.* New York: New Press.

Carroll, J. (2006). *House of war: The Pentagon and the disastrous rise of American power.* Boston, MA: Houghton Mifflin.

Cohen, S. F. (2006). The new American cold war. *The Nation 283*(2): 9-17.

Gaddis, J. L. (2005). *The cold war: A new history.* New York: Penguin.

Graham, A. 1992. *Unreason within reason: Essays on the outskirts of rationality.* La Salle, Illinois: Open Court.

Gulick, L. (1948). *Administrative reflections from World War II.* Westport, CT: Greewood.

Khilnani, S. 1999. *The idea of India.* New York: Farrar, Straus & Giroux.

Luckacs, J. (2005). *Democracy and populism.* New Haven, Connecticut: Yale University Press.

McMorran, S. (2006, May 24). Hillary rips climbers who left dying man. New York: Associated Press. Retrieved July, 24, 2006, from www.comecast.net.

Nisbett, R. E. (2005). *The geography of thought.* Boston, MA: Nicholas Brealey.

Philbrick, N. (2006). *Mayflower: A story of courage, community, and war.* New York: Viking.

Sadock, B. J., & Sadock, V. A. (2003). *Kaplan & Sadock's synopsis of psychiatry* (9th ed.). Philadelphia, PA: Lippincott Williams & Wilkins.

Sen, A. (2003, November). Democracy is not the same as westernization. *New Republic,* 69-75.

Sen, A. (2005). *The argumentative Indian: Writings on Indian history, culture and identity.* New York: Farrar, Straus & Giroux.

Tanner. R. (2006, May 24). States signing on to deadly force law. New York: Associated Press. Retrieved May 25, 2006, from www.comcast.net

Zinn, H. (2003). *A people's history of the United States.* New York: HarperCollins.

# A Dancing Star: Arguments From Imagination

**David John Farmer**

> the (American PA) field has never seriously entertained the possibility that it could vanish.... (Martin, 1987, p. 302)

A dancing star should shake off traditional practice and theory. It's comfortable to delude ourselves that the practice-of-governance-and-bureaucracy-we-need, even in the longer run, should be an incremental change over the practice we already have. Same for theorizing! I agree it's comfy for many; I disagree it's desirable for any. I favor euthanasia for the traditions we have, and for organizations that nourish such traditions. As Nietzsche's Zarathustra exclaims, "I tell you: one must have chaos in one, to give birth to a dancing star" (Nietzsche, 1958, p. 46).

I discuss aspects of Arguments from Imagination for dancing-star practice and theorizing. One such argument appeals to a contradiction between (a) the need for radical imagination in governance and (b) the hostility to radical imagination in traditional practice. More precisely, I should say "contrary" rather than contradiction. Another such argument appeals to a contrary between (a) the need for radical imagination in practice and (b) the unlikelihood of helpful wisdom being available from traditional theorizing. These arguments could be filled out in a variety of ways. There could be a barnburner discussion, for instance, about traditional theory's subservience to tinkering excessively with the machinery of government, to tinkering with micro concerns, to having so little to show for its history of tinkering, and more. The discussion could talk about (again) the excessive catering to the needs of the mid-level manager, and the reluctance to fly higher than the limits of what counts as common sense. The claim in the Arguments from Imagination is not that traditional practice and theory *could* vanish (see the quote from Daniel Martin, above); it is that the traditional *should* pass away. Neither traditional practice nor theorizing can give us what we need; it's time to move on. Such arguments are of the following form. First, X needs Y. Second, X inhibits Y. therefore, look for Z. I have called the fresh practice and thinking that is needed "post-traditional." Others may prefer a different name.

Richard T. Barnes died last January, and I'm further motivated by his death to think more about the death of traditional public administration. Unremarkably, I miss him, because we have been good friends for about thirty years. More remarkable, for me, was the manner of his dying. He died, in a sense, in the manner of Socrates. His mental faculties were crystal clear. He did the New York Times Crossword Puzzle (not that Socrates would have), for instance, the day before he died. More than that and especially during the week after he had asked for his feeding tube to be removed, Richard displayed thorough equanimity, complete serenity and, like Socrates in Plato's *Phaedo*, untroubled acceptance of his impending death. I asked the physician if she was administering happy drugs; no, she insisted that she wasn't. I still wonder whether my surprise was caused by my inexperience with dying. Partly because in previous years Richard usually was ill-tempered about inconveniences and never suffered fools gladly, I will never forget it. Like Socrates, he died surrounded–not by relatives–but by admiring and loving friends.

By comparison, imagine how well traditional theory and practice will die. Imagine how well traditional thinking/practice will recognize when its time has arrived. Imagine how well it will accept the perishing of its myths and the relinquishing of its self-interests, or whether it is even willing to contemplate rationally its place in a world that should enjoy the radically imaginative. Perhaps traditional theory/practice will stomp out stage right, yelling expired nostrums and fulminating small sense – as disciplines like exorcism did. Or, will the traditional exit its mortal coil as brilliantly as Richard did?

### ARGUING FOR A DANCING STAR

> Imagination which, in truth,
> Is but another name for absolute power
> And clearest insight, amplitude of mind,
> And Reason is her most exalted mood.
> (Wordsworth, 1986, bk. xiv, l. 190)

Three cheers for the 9/11 National Commission on Terrorist Attacks upon the United States (2004) for emphasizing the need for imagination in governmental bureaucracy! I have seized upon the 9/11 National Commission as support for my belief in the relevance of privileging imagination in governance and bureaucracy. I've done so because usually people don't take terrorism lightly. Remember Thomas Hobbes' comment about his own birth and the birth of fear in 1588, at the approach of the Spanish Armada: see also the story below about the high school junior. Anti-terrorism is a serious subject, and here is a highly bureaucratic 9/11 consensus-commission–consisting only of political blue-bloods–writing about the centrality of the imagination. The Commission identifies four major lacks from the anti-terrorist perspective. These are failures of imagination, policy, capabilities, and management. Yet, in pride of first place is imagination. This is the imagination that the 9/11 Commission writes that we need. Romantics, like Keats, rejoice!

Two cheers for the 9/11 National Commission for claiming that there is a need to bureaucratize, to routinize, imagination in government! Yes, those were the actual terms–*bureaucratize*, and *routinize*. It's true that imagination occurs even in traditional agencies. But I think that to bureaucratize (in the manner of traditional bureaucracy) is to kill the imagination, like a python. It would have been better for the 9/11 Commission to speak about, not bureaucratizing imagination, but re-imagining bureaucracy.

One cheer for the 9/11 Commission's understanding of the range or scope of the imagination! It is unfair to criticize the Commission for focusing on the need for the imaginative only in the anti-terrorism elements within government, because that was the limit of the Commission's mandate. For me, as I have said, the need extends throughout governance, including public and private and intermediate forms. Further, there is a need throughout society. It's a failure of imagination to imagine otherwise.

No cheers for the 9/11 National Commission for failing to criticize traditional PA theorizing for offering no help in conceptualizing adequately the macro problem of imagination in governance! PA theory and practice were inadequate to save the Commission from its central unimaginative recommendation. The recommendation was that, although part of the problem may be how to have an imaginative idea survive as it goes up the bureaucratic chain of command, the government should be content to appoint yet another bureaucratic layer to "force" such ideas up. More than that, the PA mindset encourages such technicist, bureaucratic one-liners.

Enlisting the 9/11 Commission in aid of an Argument from Imagination has undeniable rhetorical force in our William Poole context. So high is public sensitivity on the hazards of anti-terrorism that I read recently that a high school junior from Kentucky, William Poole, was charged with second-degree-felony terrorism for writing a fictional story "about a horde of zombies who wreak havoc on a school" (Williams, 2005, p. 9). His grandparents turned him in, and the judge set a bail bond of $5,000.

Enlisting the 9/11 Commission has less logical force, however, if the Commission's understanding of imagination is narrow. Stop rejoicing, Keats! I think that the Commission had only a "connecting the dots" view of imagination. Call it the "perky" view of imagination. It is easier to imagine, perhaps, this narrow kind of imagination being bureaucratized or routinized. Remember what low expectations we can have of narrow or perky imagination. Here's one example of low expectations: an attorney employed in a bureaucracy, asking her boss how she could be more imaginative, was told that she could design a new form, or create a new check-list. There's another example of low expectations when Karl Weick (2002, p. S13) describes Churchill as imaginative after a blunder led to the loss of Singapore in World War 2. Weick describes Churchill as showing disciplined imagination in wondering about the improper arrangements for the defense of Singapore – in wondering why he didn't know, why he wasn't told, why he didn't ask, and so on. It is true that Churchill did have a vivid imagination, e.g., when writing about his ancestor Marlborough's victories, Churchill is said to have fancied that he was chatting with the long-dead Duke. By contrast, however, does it take more than low-level perky imagination (and time) when an entire territory is lost for a leader to wonder why? Not to wonder about that, the Prime Minister would have to have been stone dead - as dead as Marlborough.

## COUNTER-ARGUMENTS

Counter-arguments can be readily advanced against Arguments from Imagination, especially as they relate to fresh theorizing. I'll mention four; there are others, e.g., relating to internal validity. The four are neither decisive nor notably fruitful, however.

First, it could be argued that traditional PA theorizing cannot just die; we cannot abandon our supposed past. Against this, I would advance an Argument from Analogy. I don't imagine that post-traditional theorizing will owe anything vital to traditional theory, any more–as I say–than physics owes to alchemy, or astronomy owes to astrology.

Second, it could be said that it is neither necessary nor practical to have a break with the past. Against this, there is the Argument from Disciplinary Politics that would suggest that it is impractical *not* to have a break. I recognize that there should be multiple views of the nature of the post-traditional. In my view we need a fresh discipline that takes the place of subject fields now balkanized between economics, politics, business administration, hotel administration and the rest, and I've argued that traditional disciplines like mainstream Economics also need a revolution. I don't see the practical politics of economists and political scientists abandoning the empire of social science to a field like public administration, a field for which they have significant disrespect. To explain this more fully: if it is true that the dead hand of institutionalism is a prime philosophical and social illness that increasingly diminishes the humanity of our lives, it is a dead and deadening hand that is not confined to the public sector. Arguably, it's counterproductive to treat any such malignancy as confined to the public sector.

Third, it could be argued that traditional theory has done a wonderful job. Oh yes, traditional PA thinkers and practitioners have done good works. I respect and admire them. Against this, there is the hyper-underachievement of PA theorizing. For instance, I point again to Herbert Simon's judgment about PA. Even many PA practitioners (the cock crows thrice!) deny that mere theory is of practical value. Added to this, there is the Losing Team Argument. What should an owner do with a consistently losing team? Arguably, replace it!

Fourth, it could be said that PA practice and PA thinking simply do not require imagination, and that all this talk about radical imagination is mere chat. Some might want to respond to this by abandoning imagination, saying that there are other reasons for killing the traditional. For instance, they might have the imagination to develop an interesting argument on the lines of Jacques Lacan's observation that existing disciplines are barriers to the truth. For myself, I would deny that the imagination is not required.

## MORE FRUITFUL OBJECTIONS

A more productive objection is that the terms in the arguments are confusing. For example, what is radical *imagination*? The same could be asked about the other terms, like "what do *needs*, *traditional*, and *inhibits* mean?"

Well, certainly! It is hard to imagine clarity at the edges in any concept, especially abstract concepts. Or in the center, Derrida 101 reminds us! Think of justice, love, freedom, truth, security; or even solid "thingy" things like mountain, budget, and death! Imagination is no exception. But is the objection fatally confusing? The counter-counter response is that the confusion is bearable.

The concept of imagination does invite questions - and even imagination. Here are seven such questions, maybe even at its core. The fact that you or I may not be sure about all the answers needn't impede use of the concept.

The last thing I want to do is to suggest, by accident, that there is only one, or no, correct description of imagination. But I don't think I'm obligated to say whether Kant is right or wrong when he writes that (in his system) "Synthesis in general. . . is the mere result of the power of imagination, a blind but indispensable function of the soul, without which we should have no knowledge whatsoever, but of which we are scarcely ever conscious" (Kant, 1965, p. 103).

Question #1: *Are different degrees of imaginative capacity merely qualitative, or quantum, differences?* I wonder.

Recall Thomas Macauley's biting judgment of John Dryden. "(Dryden's) imagination resembled the wings of an ostrich. It enabled him to run, though not to soar." Imagine a range extending from the utterly unimaginative to the utterly imaginative – a range from supreme clerk to supreme poet. Some people might think that the ostrich level of imagination is essentially the same, except in degree, as the eagle level. But I'm not sure about this. I'm not sure that the vast and terrifying imaginations of great philosophers like Nietzsche, Schopenhauer and Plato are the same kettles of fish as the imaginations of relatively unimaginative thinkers, except that their kettles are bigger. I have no difficulty in conceding (but maybe it is just hero worship on my part) that Einstein's imagination exhibits a quantum difference from, say, mine. Assume that imagination is required to interpret, and that this interpretation is a kind of translating. Harold Bloom (1975, p. 85) adds that Freud "compares dream analysis to translation between languages." Is your run-of-the-mill therapist showing the same kind of imagination, just less of it, than the founder?

Question #2: *Are there different "psychic" components in some different levels of imagination?* I wonder.

Consider intelligence, and then fancy. Surely, there is a relationship between intelligence and imagination. Yet we have all encountered highly intelligent people who are imagination-dead. My thoughts turn to characters in Kafkaesque insurance offices, managers not at all stupid but entirely high-level clerks. But I have to be careful because the clericalia may be a cover for, or a cause of, sado-masochism or some other condition.

Even more interesting is the relationship between fancy and imagination. Some will rush to point out that, while we want imagination, we don't want any off-the-wall fancy. No chimeras, please! Like conjoined twins, I think it is hard surgically to separate imagination and fancy without one or both babies dying. Turn to two commentators, two poets. The first is John Keats who is speaking of the long poem and invention, "which I take to be the Polar star of poetry, as fancy is the sails, and imagination is the rudder" (Keats, 1935). The other is a poet-who-does-not-know-it, George Carlin. I'm told that Carlin was once arrested in Milwaukee for swearing. So it's appropriate that, telling this story last April at the ASPA annual meeting in Milwaukee, I should have used his fxxxing name. Carlin is more than a comedian; he is an imaginative social critic, who lets fancy fill his sails. He is not merely negative; rather, he can clear space for his readers and listeners. A number of Carlinisms are relevant to governance and bureaucracy. Here's only one from *When will Jesus Bring the Pork Chops?* "As you know, people no longer have problems in this country, they have issues. This shift grows out of our increasingly desperate need to shade the truth and see things as more positive than they really are. . . .. 'Poor fuck. He has problems. I have. . . issues!'" Carlin doesn't have a problem or an issue with this. He says that he has a *concern* (Carlin, 2004, p. 293). Yes, imagination is not the same as "mere" fancy, although I don't imagine that it excludes fancy.

Question #3: *Is it possible to be relatively imaginative in one faculty (or even field) and relatively unimaginative in another?* I think so.

In terms of a faculty, for example, is it possible to be relatively imaginative in (say) the logic of discovery and relatively unimaginative in the logic of justification – or vice-versa? Consider Cebes, a fictional acquantaince of Archimedes and a person imaginative only in terms of discovery. Was it this Cebes who, sitting in his bathtub, noticed how his sitting displaced an equal volume of water? I wonder if Cebes whispered his "eureka" discovery to Archimedes, who then showed great imagination in the logic of justification; and the footnote giving appropriate credit to Cebes was simply lost. In terms of field, is it possible to be relatively imaginative as, say, a cook but relatively unimaginative outside of the kitchen? I think so, and I would add other examples. I can imagine Schopenhauer being princely-imaginative in his metaphysics and pauperly-unimaginative (well, some say that his dog was his only friend) in his daily life.

Question #4: *Is it difficult to incorporate radical imagination in governance and bureaucracy?* I think so, as a matter of experience and theory.

> Business attire is encouraged at all meetings, as well as during most evening functions. (ASPA, 2005)

On experience, Karl Weick speaks of the desirability of exploring basic and difficult questions about organizations in the university setting. He speaks of "disciplining" the imagination by exploring "things that are forgotten in the heat of battle, values that get pushed aside in the rough-and-tumble of everyday living, the goals we ought to be thinking about and never do, the facts we don't like to face, and the questions we lack the courage to ask" (Wieck, 2002, p. S7). Good list, I agree! As he explains, it is borrowed from John Gardner's list of what universities should stand for (Gardner, 1968, p. 90). Weick wants the imagination to be limited by the restraints imposed by the character of the enterprise; but he does not talk about submission to routines. The imagination Wieck intends is "thinking in relation to organizational learning that we ought to use in the university setting" (Wieck, 2002, p. S7). I imagine that he knows that this is a difficult chore in many universities. It is much more difficult in practice organizations, like governmental and private enterprise agencies. The subservience problem, the lack of permission, in traditional PA theorizing tends to quarantine or delete the imagination. There's excessive subservience of traditional PA theorizing to practice, to immediate problems, and much else. In the hierarchical structure of practice, the subservience to higher powers is even clearer–and clearly limiting.

On theory (if you will), understanding what imagination implies in the practice context does present difficulties. I imagine that radical imagination is neither an unadulterated good, for example, nor the only capability that is needed in an organization. There are good and bad, and in-between, uses for instrumental imagination. Even the Nazis could have imaginative war plans, for instance. On whether more than imagination is needed, "imagination only" is unimaginative. I cannot imagine that radical imagination is practice's only need, and nor did the 9/11 Commission. Imagination does not capture a whole person. Recall Descartes. "But what then am I? A thing that thinks. What is that? A thing that doubts, understands, affirms, denies, is willing, and also imagines and has sensory perceptions" (Descartes, Second Meditation, II, p. 19). A way to think of imagination-in-governance is in terms of another range of options, showing differing extents of the relative primacy of imagination and rationalization. At the unimaginative end, rationalization completely dominates imagination–and at the other, vice versa. The optimal point is at neither extreme. For myself, I (2005) have given a long explanation of what I mean by optimal imagination. I speak in terms of thinking as play, justice as seeking, and action as art, for example. I prefer a point close to the First Surrealist Manifesto, to Karl Jung on the play of imagination, to Michael Oakeshott's wildflower planted among the wheat, and to John Keats. I don't suppose that that is the end of the story, however, or that there is only one story.

Question #5: *Should imagination in bureaucracy be considered within the context of imagination in society?* I think so.

There's a parable (lack-a-day, told to me by a student!) of how the imagination is crushed in the educational process. The parable is about a stranger (a jolly authority figure) who visited a first-grade class and asked, "Who can sing? Who can dance? Who can play a musical instrument?" All the hands shot up. Visiting a high school, the stranger found that less hands went up. In college, far fewer hands shot up. Why? "Because we haven't been trained how to do that." Among the general public, I wonder how many hands would be raised. In the bureaucracy, it would be a brave–or a drunken–hand that would be raised.

Then there are people like Ivan Illich writing, for instance, how pupils' imaginations are "schooled." Illich (1970, p.1) claims "Medical treatment is mistaken for health care, social work for the improvement of community life, police protection for safety, military poise for national security, the rat race for productive work. Health, learning, dignity, independence, and creative endeavor are defined as little more than the performance of the institutions which claim to serve these ends. . . ."

Question #6: *Are there several useful metaphors for understanding imagination in governance and bureaucracy?* I think so.

Imagination in governance and bureaucracy, for me, is linked with metaphors like permission. On *permission*, I imagine that the cook (see question #3) who is imaginative only in the kitchen believes, probably unconsciously, that he has *permission* only for kitchen imagination. Positive strokes come from his cooking up a storm; negative storms can come from being creative outside the kitchen.

We have permission to change the permission metaphor, however. I have opted to speak in terms of *space* and *lack of space*. Another possibility is in terms of *stress* and *lack of stress*, perhaps after Selye (1936.) Yet another possibility is schooling and de-schooling, after Ivan Illich just mentioned. Consider space. Do managers under different organizational or time pressures, for example, have different *spaces* to listen (and to speak) imaginatively? For instance, remember Richard Clarke (2004) who tried to gain the attention of the National Security Advisor and her boss. But I would imagine that imaginative listening by the latter was limited by the need to be the boss and by competing pressures of other business. Recall that Aristotle said that contemplation is necessary for eudaimonia (happiness); maybe he could have added that the space of contemplation is necessary for management. As another instance, most of us can read rapidly. Yet surely we gain more out of the reading (or listening) if we read (listen) reflectively–implying slowly or twice or thrice.

Theorizing that is dedicated, not to such ends as the mere efficiency and mere effectiveness of the machinery of government, but to making space for each individual-in-herself in-her-difference is a useful role (among others) for post-traditional theorizing and practice. If you or I want a practitioner-friendly role for post-theory, the space metaphor can be used to speak about clearing space for practitioners' and others' radical imaginations. But, when carrying the dead weight of its supposed disciplinary past, imagination is so limited that the discipline can soar only like an ostrich.

Question #7: *Who is Richard Barnes, and why did his death give me further motivation to think about my hope for a good death for traditional PA?*

Jacques Derrida, in speaking of deconstruction, has taught us the important limits of expressions in the form of "A *is* B." They are especially foolish when of the form "Person A *is* B." So, it's more than odd to say that Person A *is* a public employee (or a boss, or a mathematician). It's misleading to say that Person A *is* Beltway-focused; and so on. People are not "essentially" B or anything else. They are sometimes this and sometimes that; they drift into part of this and partly out of that. It is not that they change, although they do. It's that a person cannot be *captured* (contra traditional PA theorizing!) as a description or a category. Each person is, as I like to sloganize, a person in-herself in-her-difference. Remembering this caveat, let's recall Richard.

Richard T. Barnes was a public employee for many years, in Federal agencies like the Navy Department (he worked on torpedoes), in the Justice Department (where we first met), and in the Government Accounting Office (don't know what he worked on). As such, he should have been a fanatical fan of traditional PA theory; but he was not. Nor did we ever talk about any of my, or his, thoughts about PA theory.

Like many, I think that he operated without benefit of traditional–or any other–PA theory. Talking about PA practice, he would frequently chortle. He was a fanatical fan of opera (e.g., listening on Saturday afternoons to any live broadcast from the Met), and so he would appreciate me saying that he had a variety of government jobs but in the obedient style (after Puccini's *Turandot*) of the more exalted Ping, Pang and Pong.

Richard was also a mathematician. He once told me, in a ruminating moment, that probably his greatest achievement was obtaining a Ph.D. in Mathematics from Yale. He taught for eight years at Ohio State, tenured as an associate professor. He liked being there, but not enough to stay. So he went to torpedoes, to the Government.

A number of Richard's friends had a gathering after his death to share remembrances about him and to celebrate his life. When it came to speaking about Richard at the post-mortem gathering, I thought that I should explain why he was my friend. But I noticed that no one else really did that either.

One speaker, whom I remember from long ago as very literate and who had once worked for him, said that she had experienced many bosses and that Richard was "a good boss." She stressed that declaration. I'm not surprised that he was a good boss. But the statement jolted me. A friend reminded me that it's like when people used to say, "He was a good worker." I also would have found that odd. I couldn't stop thinking about the oddness-to-me of the comment about the good boss. I had forgotten what it's like to be in a world-view where it appears (albeit falsely) a necessary fact that bosses are central. It emphasized one reason why some people find talk of no-bossism to be inconceivable. It underscored, for me, the need for the radically imaginative in PA theorizing.

Another speaker, significant-other Rosemary, spoke about the concerts she and I would attend together with Richard, and she specially recalled looking over at Richard who would typically fall asleep during the middle of performances. At our last concert at the French Embassy just after Richard had died, she recalled missing that and him.

Details were forgotten, of course. Nobody mentioned Richard's attitude towards the Beltway, for example. Working and living within the Washington Beltway, Richard never liked to travel outside the Beltway–with the one exception of travel outside the country (the big Beltway?). It's odd, because most people "fear" whatever they fear on the "inside" of the Beltway. He reversed it.

When it came to my turn in the post-mortem gathering, I could easily tell the events of our relationship. I could say, for example, that Richard was best man at my wedding, and I could joke that I knew it must be a big deal because he bought a new suit for the event. But I couldn't say why he was my friend. He just was. It seems to me that friendship is not fully reducible to reasons or considerations. Like humanity, it is not beyond any explanation—as Aristotle demonstrated. Yet at its core, it is ineffable. It's similar to persons. They too are not completely reducible to categories, either categories of action or categories of reason. As I've discussed elsewhere, that's a major problem with traditional PA theorizing. It approves and endorses the treatment of each individual merely as a group member, rather than as an individual-in-herself in-her-difference.

As a person who worked so long in the bureaucracy, didn't Richard Barnes deserve governance practice that is imaginative enough to be a dancing star? Don't we owe Richard Barnes (and all others) the chaos it takes to give birth to theory that is a dancing star? Imagine!

> Some years ago I was struck by the large number of falsehoods that I had accepted as true in my childhood, and by the highly doubtful nature of the whole edifice that I had subsequently based on them. I realized that it was necessary, once in my life, to demolish everything completely and start again. . . . (Descartes)

## REFERENCES

ASPA, (2005). *Attendee information: ASPA's 66th national conference, April 2-5. 2005, Milwaukee, Wisconsin.* Washington, D.C.: American Society for Public Administration.

Bloom, H. (1975). *A map of misreading.* New York: Oxford University Press.

Carlin, G. (2004). *When will Jesus bring the pork chops?* New York: Hyperion.

Clarke, R. (2004). *Against all enemies: Inside America's war on terror.* New York: Free Press.

Descartes, R. (1984). Second meditation. In J. Cottingham & D. Murdock (Eds., & Trans.), *Philosophical writings of Descartes,* II (p. 19). New York: Cambridge University Press.

Dick, K., & Kofman, A. Z. (2002). *Derrida.* Videotape. Zeitgeist Films and Jane Doe Films.

Farmer, D. J. (2005). *To kill the king: Post-traditional governance and bureaucracy.* Armonk, NY: M.E. Sharpe.

Gardner, J. W. (1968). *No easy victories.* New York: Harper.

Illich, I. (1970). *Deschooling society.* New York: Harper and Row.

Kant, I. (1965). *Critique of pure reason*, (N. Kemp Smith, Trans.). New York: St. Martin's Press.

Keats, J. (1935). Letter to Benjamin Bailey. In M. B. Forman (Ed.), *Letters*. October 8, 1817.

Macauley, T. (1828, January). *On John Dryden*. Edinburgh Review.

Martin, D. W. (1987). Déjà vu: French antecedents of American public administration. *Public Administration Review, 4,* 298-303.

Nietzsche, F. (1958). Thus spake Zarathustra (M. M. Bozman, Trans.). New York: Dutton.

Selye, H. (1936). A syndrome produced by diverse nocuous agents. *Nature, 138,* 32.

Weick, K. E. (2002). Puzzles in organizational learning: An exercise in disciplined imagination. *British Journal of Management 13,* S7-S15.

Wordsworth, W. (1986). *The prelude*. New York: Chelsea House.

9/11 Commission. (2004). *Final report of the national commission on terrorist attacks upon the United States*. New York: W.W. Norton.

Williams, P. (2005, March 28). *The Nation*.

# Index

accepted discourse 257–258
Ackerman, Diane 334
administered life 131–132, 239
administratium 21
administrative love 327–337
Adorno, Theodor 342
agencies 37–38, 45, 85, 91, 202–203, 222, 295, 298, 300, 336, 339, 341, 361
Alprin, Geoffrey 42
alterity 6, 22, 142–143, 154, 201, 204–205, 300, 325
alternative economics 175, 296
American business model 10, 157–162, 164–165, 167–170
American public administration 54, 74, 170, 188, 190, 269, 271, 284; practice 10, 54, 64
Andreasen, Nancy 81, 373–374, 380
anti-administration 69–70, 139, 141, 143, 145–154, 190, 201–202, 274, 296, 301, 335; aims 141, 147–148; understanding of 152
anti-administrative consciousness 141–142, 144–145, 147–148, 150–151, 153, 279
*The Argumentative Indian* 388
Armstrong, M. F. 27
authentic hesitation 141–142, 148, 152, 200–201, 212, 232, 296, 325
Ayer, A. J. 389

Bakan, J. 360, 365
Barthes, Roland 73, 333
Bastard Economics 362–363, 365–366
Baumol, W. J. 241
Beauvoir, Simon de 133
Bhahba, Homi 95
bio-psycho-socio-spiritual persons 228, 294, 296
Black Liberation Army (BLA) 34–35, 38, 49
Bloom, Harold 96, 385
body of public administration 288
brain 12, 20, 34, 77–78, 167, 207, 270, 371, 373–374, 376, 378–379
Bratt, Harry 42
Budget Bureau 58–60

bureaucracy 4–7, 9–10, 14, 22–23, 64–68, 78–79, 103, 195, 224, 228, 251, 305–306, 324–325, 332, 343, 393–394, 397–399
bureaucratic self-interest 202
Burke, Kenneth 99–100
Burrell, Gibson 123
business-as-usual exploration 88

Caldicott, Helen 383
capitalism 49, 63, 101, 104, 122, 162, 165, 217, 263, 324, 353
Caplan, Gerald 42
Carroll, James 236, 382–386, 389–390
Cawley, Donald 32
celebration 101–103, 131, 281–282
Champy, J. 334
Chang, H.-J. 11, 158, 160, 169
Churchland, Patricia 379
citizen-ing 129–134, 318
civilization 114–115, 117, 127–129, 133, 309
Cixous, Helene 133–134, 274–279
Clarke, Richard 76, 400
cloacal symbolic level 114, 128
Codd, Michael 27, 30
Cohen, Stephen 384
concept map 139, 141, 145, 147–149
consciousness 65–66, 68–69, 96, 99–100, 124, 132, 134, 143, 145–147, 166, 237, 253–254, 281, 309–310, 358
consumer society 363–365
contemplating bureaucracies 2, 4, 11, 52, 57, 64
contemplation 1–2, 17, 25, 40, 52, 94, 107, 201, 241, 400
contemporary terms 38, 59
content of public administration theory 186, 190, 195
criminal justice 25, 41, 46, 49–50; system 37–38, 40–41, 45
Cunningham, Robert 154
curricular building blocks 187–188
curriculum 187–188, 192–193, 265, 380
Czarniawska, Barbara 93–94

"The Dancing Star" 239, 391–392, 402
democracy 120, 131–132, 167, 197, 209, 253, 299–300, 319, 382, 388–389
Denhardt, Robert 301
"The Devil's Rope" 239
dialectical thinking 319
digital immediate gratification (DIG) 348
disciplinary symbolic 114
discourses 371–372, 377; of anti-administration 322–324; ladders of 213, 215–216; of laughter 152–154, 273–274, 276–277, 279–280, 283–284; perspectives 147, 323; structures 257; theory 114, 143, 213–215, 227, 232, 257, 279, 293, 322–323
disembodied discourse 296
"Dogs of War" article 11
Donaldson, Stephen 340
dualistic thinking 48
Duvall, Robert 349

Eckel, C. 353
economic: arrangements 189, 362; consciousness 241, 281; context 20, 63; dialect 169; discourses 154, 281; education 346–349; efficiency 104–105, 187, 219, 257; fundamentalism 19, 23; literacy 347–350; perspective 76, 209, 264, 343; problems 161, 177; science 158, 162, 168–170, 178; stories 281, 295; success 257; systems 20, 111, 122, 130, 162, 202, 295, 353, 386; terms 295; theorists 20, 169; theory 19–20, 101–104, 167, 186–188, 207–208, 220, 224, 253–254, 290, 293, 295–296, 298, 364–365; thinking 97, 102, 174–175, 292
economics discipline 125, 293, 295
economics teaching 346
Edelman, Murray 84
Ehrenreich, Barbara 181
Eibl Eibesfeldt, I. 269
Eikenberry, Angela 181
Eliot, George 79
embodied persons 293–294
entrepreneurs 67, 104, 111, 159, 209, 253–254, 295, 336, 354
epistemic pluralism 4, 7–9, 49, 53, 72, 74–76, 79, 81, 163, 180
erotic love 292, 328
ethical sphere 267, 270, 272
ethics 7, 9, 49, 146, 150, 152, 163, 165, 185–186, 188, 209–210, 212, 270
Ewing, Blair 42
expanded ethical sphere 267
extraordinary creativity 8, 371, 373–374, 378

false assumptions 382, 386–389
Farmer, D. J. 9, 125
federal government 40–41, 57–58, 73, 222, 334

Fincham, R. 335
Flatham, Richard 330
Fogarty, David 87
foreign public administration 58
Foucault, Michel 73
fractured governmentality 250, 254
Franklin, Ursula 10
Freakonomics 168, 345, 354
free market 7, 11, 49, 164, 169, 173, 254, 261, 281, 283
Frigginomics 242, 345, 348, 351–352, 354–355, 362

generalizing theory 210
globalization 160, 259–261, 263, 349, 360
Gomory, R. E. 241
Goodman, Nelson 93
goods and services tax (GST) 249
governance 1, 68, 306, 393, 397, 399
government agencies 21, 202
governmentality 167, 214, 228, 251–252, 314, 320
Graham, Angus 331
grand strategy 72, 75
great refusal 112, 222, 239, 312–313, 317–320, 324
green period 9, 21–22
Greenwald, R. 360
group signature 86, 94, 96–97, 106–107

Ha-Joon Chang 14
Hamer, Fanny Lou 135
happy economics 242, 345, 352, 354, 362
Harvey, David 177
hierarchy 85, 98, 118–119, 121–122, 148, 282–283, 325, 352
*How Economics Shapes Science* 168
Hughes, Richard 74, 162
human spirit 145, 151, 154

identities 1, 4, 6–8, 10, 13–14, 25–29, 33, 36, 38–41, 44–47, 52–54, 58, 133, 166, 379
imaginary contradictions 278
imagination 6–8, 63, 65, 204, 206–207, 210–212, 239, 241, 274, 279–280, 290, 377–379, 391–400
imaginative creativity 2, 8, 77, 80, 253
imaginization 7–9, 142, 201, 204, 290, 325
individual-focused love 333
individual persons 327, 333, 337
individual signatures 86, 93–94, 96, 107
International Monetary Fund 20
*In the Shadow of Organization* 301
intimacy 297–300, 363
invisible hand 68, 101–103, 125–126, 199, 207, 229, 242, 254, 261, 282, 352
iron cage 53, 215, 229, 233

Jacobs, Debra 154
Jacobs Company 6, 36, 54, 57, 128
Jefferson, Thomas 269
Johnson, Chalmers 242
Jung, Carl 76
justification 18, 23, 80, 101, 104, 178, 290, 397; context of 18, 23

Kagan, Donald 309
Kansas City Response Time Study 42–43
Kasparov, G. 8
Kay, John 158, 160
Kerner Commission 42
Khilnani, Sunil 388
kindergarten 175, 242, 345–352, 354
Knapp Commission 27, 37–38, 223, 225
knowledge 13, 78, 126, 146–147, 165–167, 188–189, 193, 219, 226–227, 290, 292, 301–302, 330, 332, 372; claims 186; of love 335–336
Kouzmin, Alexander 67
Krugman, Paul 176

language, of public administration 5, 9, 12–13, 18, 53, 73–74, 143, 198, 201, 204, 210
language games 72–74, 81, 93
Laporte, D. 115
*The Laugh of the Medusa* 274
laughter 152–154, 273–277, 279–280, 283–284
learning economics 347
Lewis, Bernard 19
Lichtenstein, Nelson 357
Lindsey, John V. 27
Loh, M. 334
love 104–106, 125, 127, 131, 134, 203, 207, 216, 218, 239, 269, 327–333, 335–336
"Love and Un-engineering" 239
Lury, Celia 363

macroeconomics 176, 179, 188, 194, 202, 224, 349
macro PA theory 202–203, 240
mainstream economics 86, 174, 176, 208–209, 241, 296, 395
management consultants 26, 28, 36, 52, 54–55, 57–58
manpower 31–32
Manpower Allocation Review System 29–31, 38, 224
Marcuse, Herbert 132, 322
market fundamentalism 158–159, 165–166, 169, 176–178, 209, 242
market liberalization 20
Masini, Hugo J. 36
Maslow, Abraham 217
McAdams, M. J. 294
McClosky, Deidre 86
McLaren, R. 49

McSwite, O. C. 145, 152, 310
medusa 95, 153, 273–275, 277–279
Menand, Louis 150
Merleau-Ponty, Maurice 73
microeconomics 179, 188, 202, 220
microeconomic theory 104, 159, 357–358
Military Keynesianism 242
Modell, Andrew 373, 377
modernity 6–7, 155, 189–191, 195, 307, 316
modern rhetorical terms 89
moral globalism 268
Morgan, Gareth 142
multiperspectival economics 179
Murphy, Patrick V. 28, 49
mutuality 87–88, 96–98, 106–107, 335

neuro-governmentality 372, 375
neuroscience 2, 7–10, 12, 72, 77–81, 167, 179–180, 203–204, 207, 372–374, 376–377
New York 28–29, 31, 35–36, 40, 47, 92, 131, 223, 271, 341, 344
New York City Police Department (NYPD) 6, 25–34, 36–38, 41–42, 54, 57–58, 91, 222–223, 232, 308, 384
Nisbett, Richard 382, 387, 389
Nixon, Richard 42
Nordhaus, William B. 169
Novalis 107
Nussbaum, Martha 329, 335–336

*Obliquity* 158
oligopsony 358–359, 361, 365
Ontario Civil Service Commission 61
Ontario Department of Economics and Development 61–62
Ontario Treasury Department 59, 61
openness 25–26, 28, 33, 37–39, 41, 44–46, 48–50, 52, 134, 141–142, 144–145, 147–149; lack of 26, 28, 39, 41, 48–50
operations management 36, 54, 57–58
organization-think 213–217, 219–220, 230, 232–233; ladder of 213–217, 219–220, 232–233
overlapping discourses 214, 220, 224, 232

PA's group signature 86, 96–97, 99, 104–106
PA thinking 17, 21, 93–94, 104–105, 113–114, 118–119, 314, 318, 343–344, 371, 375
personal signature 93–94
Pickett, K. 74
Piketty, Thomas 158, 170
pink period 9, 17–18, 22
poetic contemplation 211
poetic imagination 17–18, 23
police commissioner 25–33, 36–38, 40, 49, 54, 58, 84, 207, 323
police science 42, 48–49
policy analysis 84, 89, 99–100

political science 5, 10, 49, 61, 67, 143, 147, 173–174, 178, 281, 283, 388–389
Pope, Herman G. 55
postmodernism 22, 65–66, 150, 185, 187–192, 195, 198, 201, 204–208, 240–241, 262, 307, 364
postmodernity 6, 8, 189–190, 192, 194–195, 307
post-polis ethics 268
post-traditional consciousness 4, 14, 305–306, 309–310
post-traditional governance 7, 9, 14, 65–67, 305
post-traditional imagination 307, 309–310
Powell memorandum 158, 160–161, 170
power relationships 113, 314–315, 317
Prison Rape Reduction Act of 2002 340
professional economists 11, 62, 158, 167, 170
public administration 2, 4–13, 46–47, 49–50, 53–54, 57–58, 72–81, 83–84, 141–149, 153, 157–158, 161–165, 167–170, 173–175, 177–181, 185–195, 197–198, 204–205, 208–210, 256–257; discipline 64, 75, 79, 163; discourse 213, 274; and economics 49, 174, 180–182; language games 72, 74, 79; practice 5, 12–13, 52–53, 186, 189; scope of 77, 80, 187; service 6, 36, 54–56, 128; students 168–169, 185, 192–195; theorists 53, 74, 157–158, 164, 167, 170, 186; theory 9, 77–78, 185–187, 189–190, 193, 195; thinking 11, 53, 74, 188–189
*Public Administration in Perspective: Theory and Practice Through Multiple Lenses* 79–80
public choice economics 20, 174, 178–179, 188, 210
public manager 52, 54, 57

radical imagination 65, 391, 395, 398, 400
rationality 76, 155, 165, 167, 175, 203–205, 314, 330–331, 384
rationalizing discourse 219–220
real world 20, 173, 179, 181, 192
reasoning 99, 253, 330–332, 384
Red Queen 236–238, 240, 243
reduced conception 215, 228, 232
reflexive language 142, 144
Reich, Robert 264
Rein, Martin 100
Renard, L. 348
Restak, Richard 78, 376
re-symbolization 99, 121, 128–129, 133, 318
rhetoric, allure of 9, 22, 83, 86, 96–97
rhetorical analysis 84, 86, 88–91, 93, 106–107, 125, 343
rhetorical terms 89–90
rhetoric of economics 86, 104, 209
Ricardo, David 241
Rifkin, Jeremy 355

Roazen, Paul 67
Rothschild, E. 125
Rutherford, P. 348

Sadock, B. 366
Sadock, V.A. 366
Samuelson, Paul A. 169
Sandell, Michael 168
Schexnider, Alvin 47
Schneider, Robert 154
Schubert, Glendon 330
Schumpeter, Joseph 366
scientific statements 188–189
"See Spot Run" 242
Sen, Amartya 382, 388–389
signature 93–95, 97, 318; metaphor 101–102
singularity 151, 229–230, 274, 294
skepticism 146–147, 188–189, 191–192
Skidelsky, Robert 176
Smith, Jeffrey 362
snares 267, 270–272
social consciousness 237, 239–242
social neuroscience 375
somatic writing 94–95, 274–277, 287–291, 293, 297–298, 302
Soros, George 176
speaking-from-power 22, 111–116, 118–120, 123, 127–129, 131, 134, 318
speaking-to-power 22, 111–114, 116–117, 119–120, 125, 127, 131, 134, 318, 337
Spicer, Michael 70, 150, 152–153
spirituality 69, 151, 210, 229, 294, 336
standards of learning (SOLs) 175, 242, 346–347
Stemple, Lara 340
Stephen, P. 168
Stiglitz, Joseph 20
Stillman, R. J. 6
Stone, Deborah 84
Stop Prison Rape (SPR) 340
Strauss, L. 319
super-abstract 185–188, 190, 192, 194–195
supply chain management 76, 208, 358, 361–362
surface discourses 323
Suthard, Robert L. 47
symbolic action 84, 99–101, 133
symbolic focus 97, 99
symbolic systems 23, 100, 106, 122, 125–126, 129, 267, 271–272, 317
symbolizations 98–99, 101, 114
symposium papers 66–67, 143, 145, 152

Tancredi, Laurence 378
Tansley, Donald 59
thinking, basic unit of 214–215, 220, 222
Thorne, Kym 67
Tobin, James 348

*To Kill the King* 239
top-down bias 112, 118, 121, 128, 372
traditional consciousness 139, 305–306, 308–309
traditional government 251–253, 283
traditional PA theory 17–18, 22–24, 67, 70–71, 103, 113–114, 117–118, 123–125, 127–128, 236–237, 239–242, 315–316, 393–394, 398, 400
traditional practice 391
traditional public administration 4–6, 9–12, 52–53, 56, 66, 76, 147–148, 371, 392
transactional model 230–231
transdisciplinarity 2
transparent level 113, 117–123, 125
truancy of poetry 9, 22, 83, 86, 106–107
Truss, Lynne 363
truth 20, 73, 75, 106–107, 146–147, 205–207, 259–262, 301–302, 314, 332, 382, 392, 395, 397; claims 141, 144, 205
*The Truth About Markets* 158
two-dimensional world 216

un-engineering 86, 101, 105–106, 125, 203, 327, 332–337
unit of thinking 220, 224
university police scholarship 46

value pluralism 144, 150, 152–153
Vickers, Margaret 67
Virginia 6, 44, 46, 48–50, 73, 347
visioning 111, 129–135, 318

Walker, T. 76
Wal-Mart 208, 242, 357–362, 365–366, 368
Walsh, Candace 363
Weick, Karl 394
*What Money Can't Buy: The Moral Limits of Markets* 168
White, Jay 94
White, Lawrence 354
white period 18
Wilkinson, R. 74
Wilson, O. 49
Witt, Matt 67
Wittgenstein, Ludwig 10, 72–73, 141, 144, 215–216
women 31, 37, 95, 145, 275–277, 290, 298, 324, 334, 339–340, 343
work experience 81
work identity 4–5, 25, 27, 40–41, 45–46, 52–53

Yellen, Janet 162

Zinn, Howard 389